W9-CEZ-372

STRATEGIC ASIA 2003–04

ABOUT NBR

The National Bureau of Asian Research, an independent, nonpartisan institution, is committed to promoting effective and far-sighted policy in the United States, throughout Asia, and in Russia. NBR identifies and analyzes problems of critical importance in this region and provides unmatched expertise to educate, inform, and promote dialogue for business, the U.S. government, and academe. NBR enlists the very best specialists and encourages the development of new generations of specialists to focus on issues of practical interest to decision makers. NBR does not take policy positions, but rather sponsors studies by the world's leading specialists to promote the development of effective and far-sighted policy. Underlying and guiding all NBR programs are the universal values of freedom, justice, security, and prosperity.

NBR's research agenda is developed and guided by a bipartisan Board of Advisors composed of individuals drawn from academia, business, and government, including 32 U.S. Senators and 48 Representatives. Its operations are overseen by a distinguished national Board of Directors. NBR was founded in 1989 with a major grant from the Henry M. Jackson Foundation.

STRATEGIC ASIA 2003–04

FRAGILITY AND CRISIS

Edited by
Richard J. Ellings and Aaron L. Friedberg
with Michael Wills

With contributions from
Zachary Abuza, Michael H. Armacost, Victor D. Cha,
Thomas J. Christensen, Kathleen A. Collins, Nicholas Eberstadt,
Joseph P. Ferguson, Ellen L. Frost, Bates Gill, John H. Gill, Michael A. Glosny,
John B. Haseman, Dwight H. Perkins, Gilbert Rozman, Robert A. Scalapino,
Sheldon W. Simon, Robert G. Sutter, and William C. Wohlforth

The National Bureau of Asian Research
Seattle, Washington

THE NATIONAL BUREAU OF ASIAN RESEARCH

Published in the United States of America by
The National Bureau of Asian Research, Seattle, Washington
http://www.nbr.org

Preparation of this publication was supported in part by the U.S. Department of Energy under Grant No. DE-FG03-03SF22724. The views expressed in these papers are those of the authors, and do not necessarily reflect the views of the Department of Energy.

NBR makes no warranties or representations regarding the accuracy of any map in this volume. Depicted boundaries are meant as guidelines only and do not represent the view of NBR, the volume contributors, or NBR's funders.

Publisher's Cataloging-in-Publication Data
Strategic Asia 2003-04 : fragility and crisis / edited by Richard J. Ellings and Aaron L. Friedberg with Michael Wills ; with contributions from Zachary M. Abuza ... [et al.].
    p. cm.
  Includes bibliographical references and index.
  ISBN 0-9713938-3-4

    1. Asia--Politics and government--1945- 2. Asia--Strategic aspects.
3. National security--Asia. 4. Asia--Economic conditions--1945- 5. United States--Relations--Asia. 6. Asia--Relations--United States. I. Ellings, Richard J. II. Friedberg, Aaron L., 1956- III. Wills, Michael, 1970- IV. Abuza, Zachary.

DS35.2.S77 2003   327.1'095
                                        QBI03-200617

Design and publishing services by The National Bureau of Asian Research
Cover design by Todd Duren at Firefly Graphics

Printed in Canada

The paper used in this publication meets the minimum requirements of American National Standard for Information Sciences—Permanence of Paper for Printed Library Materials, ANSI Z39.48-1992.

CONTENTS

Strategic Asia: Regional Studies

Northeast Asia: The Geopolitics of the Korean Nuclear Crisis   251
Gilbert Rozman

    Four parties seeking to shape U.S.-DPRK relations / How far
    does multilateralism go?

Southeast Asia: Whither Security Regionalism?   269
Sheldon W. Simon

    ASEAN: has expansion led to the Peter Principle? / The ARF: is the
    tail wagging the dog? / Other forms of regional security cooperation /
    Southeast Asia and a rising China: an economic embrace and political
    caution / The increasing role of other extra-regional powers

Central Asia: Defying "Great Game" Expectations   291
Kathleen A. Collins and William C. Wohlforth

    The great powers' interests in Central Asia / Great power actions
    in Central Asia / The Central Asian states' responses

Strategic Asia: Special Studies

Terrorism: The War on Terrorism in Southeast Asia   321
Zachary Abuza

    Al Qaeda comes to Southeast Asia / Developing the network / Origins
    of Jemaah Islamiyah / Organizational structure / The fall of Suharto
    and the jihad in the Malukus / Jemaah Islamiyah becomes a terrorist
    organization / The current state of Jemaah Islamiyah / Fighting the war
    on terror: regional responses / The limits of regional cooperation

Proliferation: The Growing Challenge of Proliferation in Asia   365
Bates Gill

    Supply-side and demand-side drivers / Proliferation channels in
    Asia / (In)efficacy of global, regional, and national responses / Future
    proliferation challenges for Strategic Asia

Economic Integration: Implications of   399
Regional Economic Integration
Ellen L. Frost

    Current trends and recent initiatives / Asian goals / Prospects for
    success / Strategic implications / Implications for the United States:
    is integration compatible with U.S. interests?

PREFACE

Strategic Asia 2003–04: Fragility and Crisis is the third in a series of annual volumes from NBR's Strategic Asia Program. Like its predecessors, it is an integrated set of entirely original studies aiming to provide the most authoritative information and analysis possible on strategic issues affecting U.S. interests in Asia. A companion website makes the Strategic Asia books and their accompanying executive summaries available online, together with the groundbreaking Strategic Asia database. The database contains an unprecedented wealth of essential data, ranging from demographic, trade, and financial statistics to political information and measures of nations' economic performance and military capabilities. Consequently, there is now a single place to go for strategic analysis and data on the Asia Pacific.

The National Bureau of Asian Research (NBR) developed the Strategic Asia program to fulfill three goals: 1) to provide a comprehensive understanding of the strategic environment in Asia; 2) to look forward five years, and in some cases beyond, to contemplate the region's future; and 3) to establish a record of data and assessment that will assist in understanding Asia's changing strategic landscape and the implications for regional stability. In essence, the aim of the Strategic Asia Program is to help policymakers, strategists, and scholars comprehend this critical region.

The first volume in the series, *Strategic Asia 2001–02: Power and Purpose*, provided a baseline assessment of the balance of power in Asia. It also assessed the perceptions and strategies of the largest and most significant Asian powers—China, Japan, Korea, Russia, and India—and analyzed emerging patterns of interaction among them. Each of the studies in *Power and Purpose* looked forward to determine where the underlying trajectories and strategies of the major Asian powers might lead them and the region. The second volume, *Strategic Asia 2002–03: Asian Aftershocks*, examined how the September 11, 2001 terrorist attacks on the United States and their aftermath changed the distribution of power in Asia, spurred America's unprecedented involvement in Central and Southeast Asia, caused key states to alter their perceptions and policies, and set in motion new patterns of strategic interaction. *Asian Aftershocks* also considered the extent to which radical Islam is likely to be a significant political force in the region.

Readers will note major improvements in this third volume, including changes in how the book is structured. In comparison with the ones that preceded it, *Strategic Asia 2003–04: Fragility and Crisis* has twice the number of chapters, a special section that examines subregional dynamics, and five—rather than one—special studies that address cross-cutting issues in the region. The book identifies several sources of fragility in the strategic environment in Asia, including structural weaknesses in the political and economic systems of key countries and underlying problems in regional economic and security institutions and frameworks. With an expanded range of studies, *Fragility and Crisis* assesses the impact of a number of dramatic developments and crises—the U.S.-led war in Iraq, the unfolding nuclear crisis on the Korean Peninsula, terrorist attacks in Southeast Asia, and economic shocks such as the SARS outbreak. *Fragility and Crisis* considers the short- and long-term implications of these developments for regional stability and for U.S. interests in Asia, and pinpoints fault-lines around which future challenges may arise.

Research Directors and Advisors

The Strategic Asia Program was led this year by Program Director Richard Ellings (The National Bureau of Asian Research) and Research Director Aaron Friedberg (Princeton University, now with Vice President Dick Cheney's staff). Former Chairman of the Joint Chiefs of Staff General (Ret.) John Shalikashvili serves as the program's Senior Advisor. The various studies that make up the volume are written by some of the nation's leading specialists in Asian affairs and international relations.

The Strategic Asia Program is advised by an executive committee that helps guide the program's development. Members of the committee include: Thomas Christensen, Princeton University; Nicholas Eberstadt, American Enterprise Institute; Herbert Ellison, University of Washington; Donald Emmerson, Stanford University; Francine Frankel, University of Pennsylvania; James Fuller, Pacific Northwest National Laboratory; Mark Hamilton, University of Alaska; Kenneth Pyle, University of Washington; Richard

Samuels, Massachusetts Institute of Technology; Robert Scalapino, University of California-Berkeley; Sheldon Simon, Arizona State University; Michael Swaine, Carnegie Endowment for International Peace; Enders Wimbush, Booz Allen Hamilton; and William Wohlforth, Dartmouth College. (Aaron Friedberg, Office of the Vice President, Michael Green, National Security Council, and Ashley Tellis, Department of State, are currently on leave of absence from the program while on government service.)

The studies in this year's volume were reviewed variously by many members of the executive committee as well as by an independent group of specialists, including: Judith Bannister, consultant; Ralph Cossa, Pacific Forum/CSIS; Martha Crenshaw, Wesleyan University; Richard Cronin, Congressional Research Service; Scott Davis, Department of Energy; Charles Downs, consultant; Karl Jackson, Johns Hopkins University; Neil Joeck, Lawrence Livermore National Laboratory; Nicholas Lardy, Institute for International Economics; Chae-Jin Lee, Claremont McKenna College; Edward Lincoln, Council on Foreign Relations; Deepa Ollapally, University of Pennsylvania; William Overholt, RAND Center for Asia Pacific Policy; Bruce Parrott, Johns Hopkins University; T. J. Pempel, University of California-Berkeley; James Pryzstup, National Defense University; Gary Samore, International Institute for Strategic Studies; and Robert Scher, Department of State.

Geographical Coverage

The Strategic Asia Program considers as "Asia" the entire eastern half of the Eurasian landmass and the arc of offshore islands in the western Pacific. This vast expanse can be pictured as an area centered on China and consisting of four distinct sub-regions arrayed clockwise around it: Northeast Asia (including the Russian Far East, the Korean Peninsula, and Japan), Southeast Asia (including both its mainland and maritime components), South Asia (including India and Pakistan, and bordered to the west by Afghanistan), and Central Asia (Kazakhstan, Kyrgyzstan, Tajikistan, Turkmenistan, Uzbekistan, and southern Russia). Strategic Asia is thus defined as including the following countries and territories:

Afghanistan	Cambodia	Japan
Australia	China	Kazakhstan
Bangladesh	East Timor	Kyrgyzstan
Bhutan	Hong Kong	Laos
Brunei	India	Macao
Burma (Myanmar)	Indonesia	Malaysia

Mongolia	Philippines	Tajikistan
Nepal	Russia	Thailand
New Zealand	Singapore	Turkmenistan
North Korea	South Korea	Uzbekistan
Pakistan	Sri Lanka	Vietnam
Papua New Guinea	Taiwan	

The program also collects data on the United States and Canada because of their strategic relevance to the region.

Organization of the Report

Strategic Asia 2003–04: Fragility and Crisis differs in structure from the first two Strategic Asia books. It continues to provide assessments of key countries and regions, but features expanded coverage of sub-regional relations and a range of special, topical studies. *Fragility and Crisis* begins with an introduction that explores important themes in this year's report and draws attention to key findings from the various studies. The introduction is followed by *country studies* that analyzes the forces shaping the evolving strategies of nine key states: the United States, China, Japan, South Korea, North Korea, Russia, India, Pakistan, and Indonesia. The *regional studies* section of the report contains three chapters examining patterns of interaction among key clusters of states in Northeast, Southeast, and Central Asia. These are followed by an increased number of *special studies* examining issues that cut across (and tie together) various regions, including terrorism, nuclear proliferation, economic developments, and demographic trends. *Fragility and Crisis* concludes with a statistical appendix of data drawn from the Strategic Asia database.

Executive Summary

In addition to their presentation in this volume, key findings from *Strategic Asia 2003–04: Fragility and Crisis* are available in a separate executive summary. This concise summary, organized along the same lines as the full report, including relevant tables and figures, captures key dynamics in the region and highlights their implications for policymakers and corporate decision makers. The executive summary is available on the Strategic Asia website and in printed form from The National Bureau of Asian Research.

Strategic Asia Website and Database – http://strategicasia.nbr.org

The Strategic Asia website represents a technological breakthrough and extraordinary resource for scholars, other professional researchers, students, and anyone interested in data on Asia. It is designed for the non-specialist

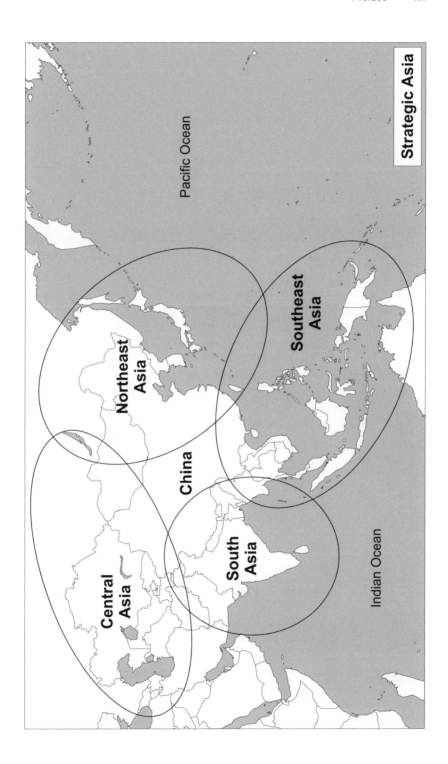

Strategic Asia

and specialist alike with technology that enables users to obtain and manipulate a broad range of data and view and download reports. It is updated and developed throughout the year. The freely accessible database allows users to download or dynamically link to data sets. The online database currently contains about 100 "indicators" (such as GDP, population, or defense expenditures) for each country and territory in the region for each year since 1990. The indicators are divided into 12 thematic areas:

- National economy
- Foreign trade, aid, and investment
- Monetary indicators
- Fiscal indicators
- Population
- Energy and environment
- Information infrastructure
- Conventional military forces
- Nuclear, biological, and chemical forces
- Force projection
- Politics
- International relations

The Strategic Asia database leverages Extensible Markup Language (XML) and was built in .NET, Microsoft's next generation XML platform. XML is the emerging *lingua franca* for sharing data among diverse applications on diverse platforms. Leading applications such as Microsoft Office XP and Microsoft SQL Server support XML, as does the latest version of the statistical analysis tool SPSS.

Presenting data in an XML format allows users—individuals, organizations, businesses, and other websites—to dynamically link to all or part of the Strategic Asia Program's data set. For example, a user can embed a data set from the Strategic Asia website in an Excel spreadsheet on his/her local computer and thus always have access to the most current data. The user also has access to metadata—information about data. Click on any data point and see the original source and the date that particular piece of information was last updated. As XML becomes a universal standard for dynamic data integration, NBR will be able to seamlessly incorporate data from primary sources and channel it quickly to end users.

Attribution

Readers of Strategic Asia reports and visitors to the Strategic Asia website may use data, charts, graphs, and quotes from these sources without requesting permission from The National Bureau of Asian Research on the condition that they cite NBR *and* the appropriate primary source in any published work. No report, chapter, separate study, or extensive text, or any other substantial part of the Strategic Asia Program's products, may be reproduced without the written permission of The National Bureau of Asian Research. To request permission please write to the Managing Editor at The National Bureau of Asian Research, 4518 University Way NE, Suite 300, Seattle, WA 98105, or at nbr@nbr.org.

Acknowledgements

General Shalikashvili has served as Senior Advisor to Strategic Asia since the program commenced. He has been an inspirational part of our team, providing founding Research Director Aaron Friedberg, others associated with the program, and me with invaluable counsel. In June 2003, Aaron left his posts at Princeton University and NBR to assume his current position as Deputy National Security Advisor to Vice President Dick Cheney. While a loss for the program, the country is benefiting greatly from Aaron's extraordinary acumen and judgment.

NBR organizes meetings between Strategic Asia personnel and policy and business leaders throughout the year. Several of us briefed Condoleezza Rice and Michael Green in the White House last fall. Shortly afterward, Trisha Dedik, Scott Davis, and Toby Dalton of the National Nuclear Security Administration at the Department of Energy hosted an interagency discussion with Strategic Asia authors on strategic and proliferation issues; and their advice has been appreciated throughout the year. At various points we met with Senator Chuck Hagel, Congressman Jim Leach (and his Asia Pacific Subcommittee staff director Jamie McCormick), Congressman Norm Dicks (and his key aide George Behan), Bob Zoellick, Linton Brooks, Andrew Marshall, Richard Haass, Marin Strmecki, Daniel Schmidt, Dianne Sehler, James Schlesinger, Carla and Rod Hills, Rudy de Leon, Bob Bauerlein, and Stanley Roth, among others. We owe all—those named and many unnamed—an enormous debt for sharing their valuable time with us.

We would like to aim a spotlight at Strategic Asia's prestigious partners and sponsors. Supporters of the program this year include the Lynde and Harry Bradley Foundation, the Department of Energy, the Boeing Company, the GE Foundation, and the Microsoft Corporation. The Henry M. Jackson Foundation's core support to NBR also contributes to the success of Strategic Asia. None of our efforts would have been possible without the commitment of these sponsors. Special thanks, as always, go to Brigitte Allen, who coordinates our relations with these and all of NBR's supporters, and who this year celebrates her new U.S. citizenship.

This year's research planning meeting was hosted by the Near East and South Asia (NESA) Center at National Defense University led by Alina Romanowski and Roger Harrison. With the snow blowing in across the Anacostia, the research team spent a day in lively discussion in a superb venue. The generous professionalism of the NESA staff ensured that our research efforts got off to a good start. Special thanks are owed to Jack Gill and Elizabeth Hopkins for facilitating this event.

The success of the Strategic Asia program as a whole, not to mention the book, depends on the efforts of many NBR staff. On a day-to-day basis no one is more important to the program than Michael Wills. Other than the database (which he co-established two years ago), he manages every step of the program, working with NBR colleagues, the authors, advisors, reviewers, government officials, senior congressional staff, Aaron, and me. He serves as chief copyeditor, manages the research and editing process, and coordinates policy meetings. The high quality of the program may be based on collaborating with the best people in Asian studies, but no less so on Michael's capacity to manage this ambitious collaboration and the contributions of other outstanding members of NBR's team. In regards to the latter, Jody Ferguson co-authored the North Korea chapter; Erica Johnson assisted once again with much of the copyediting, as did Gael Tarleton. Erica and Gael also put together the Executive Summary that accompanies this volume. (And General Shalikashvili provided valuable guidance in shaping the new format of this year's summary.) Julie Bennion was responsible for book production and locating the image that graces the cover, which was created by graphic artist Todd Duren of Firefly Productions.

Karolos Karnikis and Erick Thompson have been tremendously busy this year making major improvements to the Strategic Asia website and database. In addition to enhancing the performance of these online resources, Karolos and Erick coordinated an innovative project with a team of computer science students from Seattle University. This successful endeavor has led to the development of a prototype data source synchronization tool that will greatly facilitate data collection. Karolos also directed the work of this year's Strategic Asia research and database team—Jonathan Acuff, Neil Beck, Allison Clark, Peter Mattis, and Rajeev Majumdar. These dedicated and hardworking assistants have developed the database, provided research assistance to the authors, and, together with Mahin Karim, helped enromously with copyediting and proofreading this book.

Acknowledgements are due to those behind the scenes at NBR whose work makes all of our programs possible—Kailani Chin-Hidano, together with Rian Jensen, Jay Juntti, Nikita Kovrigin, Julia Rindlaub, and Tracy Timmons-Gray. There is nothing fragile or crisis-prone about this extraordinary team. Nor is there, to say the least, about the dean of Asian studies, Bob Scalapino. I was privileged to be his student at the University of California, where I enjoyed my last, extraordinary class from him 30 years ago. It is no less an honor to learn from Bob today.

Richard J. Ellings
August 2003

STRATEGIC ASIA

INTRODUCTION

FRAGILITY AND CRISIS

Richard J. Ellings and Robert A. Scalapino

ABSTRACT

Asia is in better shape than during the Cold War, but it remains fragile and prone to crisis—and this condition will hold for the foreseeable future. Security risks in Asia stem from unprecedented, rapid change in the balance of power, legacies of past wars, rising nationalism, strategic competition, radical Islamist terrorism, the nature of the North Korean regime, uncertainty about China's future, and other causes. Providing some stability to the region is the domestic focus of the major powers on economic reform and development, and their increasing embrace of globalization. Most important to the region's stability, however, and out of its own interests, the United States continues to: 1) serve as the flexible, off-shore balancer through this period of upheaval; 2) protect freedom of the seas from the Indian Ocean through the Strait of Malacca to the Pacific; 3) open its economy to encourage trade and investment in the region; 4) otherwise encourage globalization and democratization; and 5) provide leadership in building and supporting effective institutions, organizing coalitions, and acting unilaterally when necessary, to deal with threats to regional security. The United States will continue to need to adjust its policies, alliance relationships, and deployments appropriate to the changes in Asia ahead.

Richard Ellings is President of The National Bureau of Asian Research and Director of the Strategic Asia Program. Robert Scalapino is Robson Research Professor of Government Emeritus at the University of California, Berkeley. The authors wish to thank Aaron Friedberg for his leadership and counsel.

Introduction

The strengths of the United States in post-September 11 Asia are established and substantial: alliances, forward lines of defense, diplomatic ties, investments, markets, suppliers of goods, and extensive cultural links. But the risks in the region are equally significant. Moreover, the dangers add up to more than the simple sum of the "hot spots" frequently attracting the attention of reporters and pundits, such as North Korea, Taiwan, and Kashmir. Indeed, at first glance the potential for trouble seems perilous. The future of many of the 37 governments in "Strategic Asia" is problematic. Several are communist, many are authoritarian, some are experimenting with democracy but have weak institutions and scant experience with the rule of law. Only a few are firmly established democracies. Ethnic, religious, and ideological conflicts threaten to destabilize societies in Central, South, and Southeast Asia. Historical legacies of wars past cause distrust, even enmity, between powerful countries, while epochal changes in the balance of power, highlighted by the collapse of the Soviet Union and the meteoric rise of China, are shaking Asia to its core. Not surprisingly in this period of upheaval, major states meticulously monitor each other's defense, foreign, and economic policies, often adjusting their own accordingly. Recent nuclear proliferation and terrorist attacks exemplify the strategic connections in the region and are emblematic of the far-reaching changes and vulnerabilities there. Without a great deal of imagination, one can foresee frightening events igniting a sub-regional or perhaps Asia-wide conflagration. At the very least, the future of the region over the next quarter of a century or longer, in comparison with that of Europe or the Americas, is highly uncertain. Once again the locus of world power, "Strategic Asia" also remains in fundamental ways fragile and prone to crisis.

Prior volumes in the *Strategic Asia* series and other studies have carefully documented Asia's preeminent economic, diplomatic, and security importance to the United States, together with the growing recognition of this fact in U.S. policy.[1] The risks to American interests in the region have also received attention. There are exceptional studies in the following pages and studies elsewhere of a wide range of important issues and threats.[2] Less work has been done that integrates approaches for the purposes of assessing the broader strategic environment and considering together the critical factors that challenge U.S. policymakers to prioritize issues.

In attempting to lay the groundwork for such an analysis, we argue that the first step must be to disaggregate the risks in Asia by examining them separately at the national, international, and transnational levels of analysis. The next step is to understand the net effect among these risks. Upon doing this, the regional dangers outlined above appear to be somewhat less daunting. Indeed, the argument here is that trends both in the region and in U.S. policy, elucidated by the studies contained in this volume, suggest that the enormous challenges can be managed, but that the road ahead will be full of bumps and potholes. Asia is fragile, and crises will develop. The inherent instability of Asia is a fact.

There are several bases for an optimistic "net assessment." As one of the authors put it at the three-quarter mark of the twentieth century, a much more dire time, "To acknowledge a strong element of crisis in contemporary political and economic affairs is not to assert that all is darkness."[3] Today, in contrast with the period when that conclusion was drawn, the most powerful states in the region are acting cautiously, even constructively, in domestic and international affairs as their priorities are, and seem likely to remain for some time, economic reform and growth. Overall growth for 2003 in Asia is estimated at 3.5–4 percent, with further gains anticipated in 2004. Arms competition in most of Asia is moderate, and major power aggression, with the possible exception of China against Taiwan, seems doubtful over the next five years and probably well beyond. With its superior military might, the United States remains an effective off-shore balancer even through this period of fundamental power realignment. The world's leading country is also sticking largely to its traditional agendas of free trade and democracy by leaving the doors to its economy open (giving stability to Asian economies), by urging governments to respect human rights, and by encouraging the forces of globalization that in turn exert strong pressures on states to reform politically as well as economically.

As a consequence, the United States, together with its allies and friends, is providing an insecure, politically immature region with a degree of stability and a model of civil society. In the process, it is helping to constrain nationalism, repression, historical rivalries, various forms of dangerous collusion, proliferation of weapons of mass destruction (WMD), and transnational threats such as terrorism and financial contagion.

Domestic Sources of Fragility and Resilience

China

In the first *Strategic Asia* volume, Aaron Friedberg pointed out that one country increasingly links the various sub-regions of Asia.[4] China, still Asia's most populous country by far, is located at the crossroads of Asia's heartland, making the country important to much of what transpires around its borders. In times of major change in China, effects radiate through the entire region—and the contemporary period happens to be one of those times. China is experiencing simultaneously wrenching industrialization, urbanization, unprecedented integration with the world, and the transformation of its economy from one of command socialism to some, as yet not fully determined, form of capitalism. Further, in concert with economic change—indeed, as a product of it—the country inevitably faces an ever-growing need to modernize its political system.

Because of these factors, coupled with its likely return to great influence, most scenarios for region-wide stability place their emphasis on China. These scenarios are often based on China's failures or successes in handling the transformations noted above, by its relationship to problems on its periphery, by its relative growth and dissatisfaction or satisfaction with the world around it, or by a combination of internal and external factors. Taiwan is frequently proffered as the most likely issue over which the United States and China might go to war. On the other hand, with both economic and strategic interests in mind, Washington, like Beijing, wants a bilateral relationship that is on balance positive. As recent U.S. policy indicates, the Bush administration views China as the outside power with the most influence over North Korea's nuclear ambitions. Japanese defense strategy is driven primarily by considerations related to China. India measures itself in some ways by Chinese successes and failures, and devises its strategic military forces in part with China in mind. Thus, more than other powers in the region, China figures in any broad assessment of the future of Asian security, and it links the sub-regions of Asia strategically.

In many respects, China is representative of some broader trends of advancing political openness in authoritarian societies, and of hope and anxiety in the economic realm. The fourth generation leaders now in power are individuals with a technocratic background combined with lengthy Communist Party service at the municipal and provincial levels. President Hu Jintao and Premier Wen Jiabao appear to be working smoothly together, and in broader terms, collective leadership seems to be operating effectively. Some observers, however, believe that ex-President Jiang Zemin, still Chairman of the Central Military Commission and having numerous past allies in high positions, remains a force with which to reckon.

In any case, the new leadership, lacking charisma, must depend upon performance. Hu has promised clean and open government, catering to the people's needs. The government has recovered from the bungled efforts to conceal the SARS outbreak. Meanwhile, the effectiveness of its ideology continues to decline, with nationalism to some extent taking its place as a means of appealing for unity and political support. The broad shift from hard authoritarianism to authoritarian pluralism continues, with Chinese society increasingly evincing class and regional differences. Moreover, at the grass roots, public dissatisfaction is openly voiced on occasion, with farmers angry over high taxes and corruption and workers dismissed from faltering state-owned enterprises publicly protesting. Intellectuals are speaking out, criticizing policy flaws and demanding a government based on law. Yet the line between the permissible and the unacceptable remains blurred, and various individuals continue to be subject to sanctions.

On the economic front, advances are continuing despite the SARS threat. Aided by extensive government investment and rapidly expanding trade, overall GDP rose 8.2 percent in the first half of 2003 according to official statistics, and seems destined to retain or increase that growth for the year. China is now the world's top recipient of foreign direct investment. FDI reached over $30 billion for the same period, a gain of 34 percent, with the likelihood that the figure for the full year would surpass the $52 billion that arrived in 2002. Meanwhile, foreign trade also surged forward, reaching $376 billion in the first half of 2003, a 39 percent increase. China's trade surplus for that period, moreover, was $4.5 billion.

On the negative side, the service sector was strongly affected by SARS, and urban unemployment reached 4.5 percent. Adding the massive numbers of rural under- and unemployed workers reveals a serious long-term problem. Parts of interior China are growing slowly or are in recession. The economic boom is centered in coastal regions and key interior cities. In addition, the banking-financial sector remains in serious difficulties despite various reform efforts. More than $500 billion in unredeemable loans remain on the books, and the newly formed China Banking Regulatory Commission is seeking effective means of remedying the situation.

Thus far, China has resisted demands from foreign governments to revalue its currency. However, calls at home for such reforms as creating fair market rules, protecting private property, reducing government regulations, and taking sterner measures against corruption are growing louder, with some indication that the present government will respond.

To stay on course for development, and due to the regime's optimism regarding Taiwan, plus national interest considerations, the Chinese leadership has decided to cooperate with the United States on a range of security issues, from North Korea to the war on terrorism. Indeed, as pointed out by Thomas Christensen and Michael Glosny in this volume (pages 53–79), U.S.-China relations have never been better.

In sum, China is in the midst of another revolution, far less violent than the original communist victory, and more promising in terms of the citizens' livelihood and rights. It is a revolution that faces myriad difficulties and the outcome is far from clear. On balance, though, China is the rising power of East Asia, and that is being reflected in its overall development and growing regional and international activities.

Japan

Contemporary Japan presents a sharp contrast with its big neighbor. Japanese democracy continues to operate with a full range of political rights for the citizenry, but under a one-and-a-half party system that has frustrated those who seek basic reforms. The Liberal Democratic Party (LDP), either singly or as the leader of a coalition, has dominated the national political stage for decades, yet its current leader, Koizumi Junichiro, has been stymied in his reform efforts by a combination of entrenched bureaucrats and rural-based LDP conservatives. Koizumi came to office with strong public support, presenting a new, attractive personal image and a pledge to conduct in-depth changes in Japan's faltering economic order. His popularity has recently declined in the absence of significant reform, and with an economy still fragile, but there are no obvious competitors. In mid-2003, however, the two largest opposition parties, the Democratic Party of Japan under Naoto Kan and the Liberal Party, agreed to merge. Thus, some effort to challenge the LDP is being made, although the new union still holds a decided minority of Diet seats and lags in public opinion polls.

A general election may well be held shortly, but there are few indications that major changes will take place. The Japanese electorate appear to be disillusioned with all parties, and with politics in general. Hence, the tendency to vote for independents has increased except in the staunchly conservative rural districts, whose voters are greatly over-represented in Japan's electoral system.

Despite the lengthy recession and the lack of popular politicians, Japan is far from seething with revolt. This nation still has the second largest economy in the world, and the average Japanese is living well, with class or regional differences relatively modest. Rather than a rise in leftist radicalism, the most pervasive political trend at present is a rise of nationalism, reflected in Japan's quest to be accepted as a major nation and the moves to strengthen its military power and role. Recently, new laws have been passed enabling Japan's military forces to go to Iraq and equipping them with a much wider range of sophisticated weapons. The threat of a resurgent Japanese militarism seems greatly exaggerated, but despite its domestic problems, Japan wants to be accorded greater respect with full sovereign rights. It maintains a double-hedge strategy to maximize its maneuverability, but with a difference this year. As noted by Michael Armacost in this volume (pages 81–107), Japan has recently aligned its policies more closely with its ally, the United States, most notably with regard to Iraq and North Korea.[5]

Meanwhile, Japan has dragged its feet on reforming its economy.[6] Nevertheless, after more than 13 years of recession, it is showing modest signs of recovery, with mid-year figures marking the sixth straight quarter of expansion. Using April–June figures, GDP was growing at an annualized basis of 2.3 percent. The improvement of overseas economies, especially that of the United States, was helpful since Japanese exports remain a key factor in the economic picture.

Deflation continues to be a problem, as does unemployment, which has dipped slightly but remains at 5.3 percent. Banking reform, moreover, is an urgency not yet fulfilled. In the longer run however, with Japanese society aging rapidly and its population declining, key issues will be whether this nation, historically reclusive, will accept expanded immigration and have much chance for growth. The Japanese economy will also remain dependent upon external factors, chief among them the U.S. economy.

In sum, Japan represents an advanced society with an open if somewhat inhibiting political system and an economic order that once served as a model for many developing Asian states, but now is in need of significant adjustments. At this point, Japan stands at a crossroads, with opportunities and challenges interwoven. The need is for a leadership capable of effecting the necessary changes and a citizenry prepared to support them.

South Korea

The Republic of Korea, one of East Asia's success stories, also faces challenges both on the domestic and regional fronts. When Roh Moo Hyun took office as president in February 2003, defeating a conservative opponent, he benefited from having been distant from recent political activities, thereby possessing a fresh and clean image. Roh had long been a liberal reformer, close to labor and progressive circles. With the public weary of scandal, he began his tenure with the support of some 75 percent of the citizenry according to public opinion polls. Toward mid-year, however, with doubts about Roh's ability to fashion a coherent program, tense relations with the conservative media, and a dip in the economy, his approval rating had dropped precipitously.

The country is debating its fundamental strategy toward the North and for its security.[7] Many Koreans, especially younger ones, are arguing that the United States rather than North Korea is the real problem, and that China is the possible answer to national reconciliation. Victor Cha's judgment, what he terms "a close call," is that the South will retain its cooperation and alliance with the United States.

Roh heads a government that holds only a minority of seats in the National Assembly. He and his party hope to take control of that body in the April 2004 parliamentary elections, so that he does not remain in lame duck status for another three years. He will need help, however, both with respect to the domestic economy and in relations with other nations, especially North Korea.

South Korean democracy is still evolving. Roh is only the fourth president to be chosen in a competitive election. While major political progress has been made, problems remain, among them extensive regionalism and recurrent scandals in the business sector, some involving collusion between large *chaebol* and government officials. The latter problem was highlighted by the suicide of Chung Mong Hun, a top executive of Hyundai, in mid-2003. Hyundai has been charged with secretly paying $400 million to the North to facilitate the summit meeting between Kim Dae Jung and Kim Jong Il in 2000. Chung, a key figure in promoting South Korean operations in the North, including the Mount Kumgang tourism project, had just inaugurated the Kaesong industrial park in June 2003. This project is intended to draw South Korean business to a special zone, utilizing cheap North Korean labor to conduct manufacturing activities in such fields as textiles.

Meanwhile, the ROK economy presents a mixed picture at this point. Having grown by 6.1 percent in 2002, GDP expanded by 3.7 percent in the first quarter of 2003, but further contraction followed. Predictions regarding this year have been lowered to 3–4 percent, and some experts have estimated an even sharper decline. Foreign direct investment has dropped and domestic consumer spending is down, with a sizeable household debt having accumulated from extensive spending during 2002 when interest rates were low. Labor unrest has been another problem, but recently the Roh government took a stern position with respect to railway workers. The government is also committed to further liberalization, pledging to remove South Korea's extensive remaining barriers to foreign goods and services. In addition, a supplementary budget has been enacted to stimulate the economy at a time when many overseas markets are sluggish. Thus, while the South Korean economy continues to benefit from earlier reform measures, including the reduction of bank and corporate debts, the current international scene together with the domestic picture raise concerns. The Roh government's promise to double per capita income to $20,000 by the end of this decade will require a combination of effective economic policies at home and a supportive international environment. On balance, however, the future of South Korea remains promising.

North Korea

In strident contrast, the Democratic People's Republic of Korea (DPRK) remains a failing society while the political-military elite are protected by a hard authoritarian and highly traditional order. Reluctantly, the regime has begun to alter its isolationist stance while still seeking to keep its people largely ignorant of the modern world. Hard facts—political or economic—are scarce with respect to the DPRK, but the political system clearly rests on a close alliance between Kim Jong Il and the military, with a "military first" policy cementing those ties. Pyongyang remains the center for top leaders, and enjoys better conditions than most of the outlying areas.

Despite the hardships of recent years, there are no visible signs of political instability. The number of refugees has increased in the past year, almost all of them fleeing economic hardship, but there is no mass exodus. Further, few high level defections have taken place in the recent past.

At the same time, key figures including Kim Jong Il have been forced to recognize the need for economic changes if collapse is to be avoided. Kim himself on numerous occasions in recent years, especially when in China or Russia, has indicated a strong interest in the economic reforms underway in those nations. In July 2002, a major move was made in the North, with prices and wages being increased tenfold or more so as to accord with black market and private sellers' prices. An attempt was made, moreover, to tie wages to worker productivity. However, the venture proved a failure, and rampant inflation resulted. It has been estimated that due to energy shortages and bad policies, key factories, with the exception of military plants, are operating at only 25–30 percent capacity. Moreover, despite some gains in agricultural production, North Korea remains heavily dependent upon food from external sources, with China being a key provider. Another effort at change took place in early 2003, when the government asserted that local markets could sell manufactured goods as well as food, with prices being set increasingly by the marketplace. Fundamental reforms, however, will depend both upon the willingness of the leadership to accept political risks and the creation of a new technocratic class apart from the military.

With exports lagging behind those in the early 1990s, before the collapse of the Soviet Union and the East European communist states, the North appears to be highly dependent upon military sales, with evidence also of substantial drug dealings. Not surprisingly, therefore, economic and technical assistance is likely to rank high in the negotiations that lie ahead.

Taiwan

Taiwan made the political journey from authoritarian politics to democracy in a remarkably short period of time, with Chen Shui-bian, currently in the third year of his presidency, a symbol of the new order. Chen was the first opposition leader to be elected over the candidate of the long dominant Kuomintang (KMT). Chen's tenure has not been without difficulties. The Democratic Progressive Party in coalition with its ally, the Taiwan

Solidarity Union, has only 101 seats in the 225-seat legislature, compared to 112 for the opposition KMT and People First Party. With the next presidential election looming in the spring of 2004, moreover, the two opposition leaders, Lien Chan and James Soong (Soong Chu-yu), have agreed to an amalgamation that may make Chen's reelection bid more difficult. Perhaps with the election in mind, Chen has strengthened his nationalist messages, referring to Taiwan on several occasions as a sovereign state and advocating a referendum prior to the election. While he has asserted that the referendum would determine the future of Taiwan's fourth nuclear power plant, and that no referendum on independence would be held unless China resorted to force against Taiwan, the move was not appreciated in Beijing.

Chen's future, however, may hinge more on economic than on political matters. Taiwan suffered negative growth in 2001, and grew 3.5 percent in 2002, with an official forecast of 3.5 percent again in 2003 despite the setback due to SARS. This forecast is based upon hopes for strong export growth and gains in private investment. Domestic consumption has remained flat. In an effort to stimulate the Taiwanese economy, Chen appointed a bipartisan presidential economic advisory team in late May headed by a vice-chairman of the KMT. Meanwhile, the Taiwanese business community continues to pour investment into mainland China together with expanded trade. Fears that the Taiwanese manufacturing sector will be hollowed out as a result of China's cheap labor are frequently expressed, but there is little alternative except to pursue the field of higher technology as well as the service sector, and move toward greater openness. Foreign investment remains limited, and unemployment has lessened slightly but remains substantial, running about 4.5 percent. Thus, Taiwan faces important economic challenges that can best be met through greater cooperation across political lines and continuing reforms.

As in other cases, however, international trends, especially relations with China, will remain important. Notable among these is the scale of Taiwanese investment in China. Several hundred thousand Taiwanese now reside on the mainland, concentrated in Shanghai. This phenomenon is regarded by the mainland as indicative that time is on its side, with current trends marking the beginnings of the full integration of the mainland and Taiwanese economies and a basis for eventual political integration.

Hong Kong

Hong Kong's situation is far graver than that of Taiwan on both the political and economic fronts. In mid-2003, Chief Executive Tung Chee-hua faced major street protests over the government's proposed internal security bill. Opponents labeled the measure a threat to democracy. Two key officials under fire resigned, and Tung, after engaging in talks with the dissidents, promised to make some revisions in the bill. Beijing was put in a very awkward position—how to support Tung without appearing to intervene too greatly. Tung remains in office with Beijing's support but, despite his pledge to be responsive to the community, the indications are that his approval rating among Hong Kong citizens is low at this point.

A key problem is the weak economy. A combination of mainland competitiveness for investment and production, together with the impact of the SARS epidemic, has created serious problems. Unemployment topped 8 percent in mid-2003. Consumer spending spiraled down, as did tourism. The end of the SARS threat should allow improvements, but the IMF forecast is that GDP growth in 2003 will be 2.2 percent. Full recovery may be protracted, with Hong Kong, like others, facing the problem of how to deal with the challenges mounted by China's economic competitiveness.

Southeast Asia

The 10 nations of Southeast Asia, with their large population and strategic location, are a vital part of the political, economic, and security issues confronting the Asia Pacific today. The rising problem of terrorism in this area is one example of the region's connections with the broader world. Its growing economic interaction and changing politics are testimonies to the impact of globalization here.

On the political front, leadership remains critically important, with considerable variations. Indonesia, the largest Southeast Asian nation, is led by President Megawati Sukarnoputri, regarded by many as a reasonable and moderate but not strong leader. It is very likely that she will run for reelection in the 2004 elections. Thus far, the military has refrained from seeking to regain political power, preferring to protect its autonomy. At this point, Indonesia has moved from military authoritarian rule to civilian governance with relative openness, but possessing the type of fragility that weak authority at the center and rising regional autonomy produces. Thus, the nation continues to struggle against separatism and terrorist attacks by Muslim extremists, despite the fact that the majority of Indonesian Muslims are moderate. Sterner measures are now being taken against terrorism after a protracted period of relative indulgence.

Thailand presents a somewhat different political picture. Under a strong leader, Prime Minister Thaksin Shinawatra, who is aided by a popular monarch in the background and moderate ethnic-religious divisions except in the southernmost part of the country, Thailand has maintained a high level of political cohesion in recent times. However, Thaksin has struck hard at so-called underground mafias including drug czars, and more recently against Muslim extremists, with a sizeable number of deaths resulting. Meanwhile, Thaksin has maintained his popularity with a combination of strong nationalist appeals and progressive reform efforts.

The Philippines, in contrast to Thailand, remains burdened with problems of separatism, continuing military involvement in politics, and indecisive leadership. President Gloria Macapagal-Arroyo, while intelligent and personable, has not been a strong leader. Moreover, she announced in December 2002 that she would not run for reelection in 2004. The recent mini-mutiny on the part of some 300 soldiers was easily put down, but their complaints of rampant corruption in top military ranks and poor pay and equipment received a sympathetic response in many quarters, and the president was forced to appoint several commissions to recommend actions. Meanwhile, talks with the rebellious Moro Islamic Liberation Front (MILF) reopened in mid-2003, but fundamental resolution of the key issues will prove difficult. And if President Arroyo holds to her decision to step down, there are no obvious candidates at this point to take her place.

Malaysia also faces a change of leaders, but with the new order already determined. After 23 years in power, Prime Minister Mahathir Mohamad is stepping down, and has selected Abdullah Ahmad Badawi as his successor, a man known as a moderate and conciliator. While Mahathir has been abrasive on many occasions and exhibited a strong anti-Western tendency, he has built the United Malays National Organization (UMNO) into a dominant party despite significant racial-religious divisions in the country, and has pursued policies that have underwritten the Malaysian economy. Malaysia's political future, however, remains uncertain.

Singapore represents the prototype of a strong leader-one party system despite being encased in democratic institutions. Prime Minister Goh Chok Tong, with elder statesman Lee Kuan Yew in the background and Lee's son destined to succeed Goh, leads a party—the People's Action Party—that took 82 of the 84 parliamentary seats in the 2001 elections, and need fear no major competition in the period ahead. Hence, the government has survived a serious economic downturn with minimal damage.

Burma presents an authoritarian order of a traditional type, namely, a military junta that continues to suppress opposition from such individuals as Aung San Suu Kyi and her National League for Democracy. Once again, after a brief period of greater rights for Suu Kyi, a crackdown took place, resulting in her return to detention. Defying international criticism, including that of other ASEAN members, the junta insists that the priority must be upon "law and order," not freedom.

Vietnam is another authoritarian state, governed by an aging group of communists who have been willing to compromise with market economics but not with any group or individual challenging their rule. In contrast, Cambodia while governed by another strong man, Hun Sen, held elections in 2003 that were reasonably open and fair. Hun Sen's Cambodian People's Party obtained some 47 percent of the vote, although it will have to create another coalition to obtain approval for a new government by a two-thirds majority of the National Assembly, as required by the constitution. King Norodom Sihanouk, ailing but widely revered, may once again play an important role in this respect. But the opposition parties have pledged sharp resistance. Meanwhile, Laos, East Asia's poorest country, continues to operate under communist rule, with the Lao People's Revolutionary Party totally dominating the legislature and permitting no opposition. Strife with the ethnic Hmong was recently highlighted when two foreign journalists traveling with Hmong bands were arrested.

Southeast Asian states are divided today into three broad political categories: hard authoritarian systems—Vietnam, Laos, and Burma; non-competitive, one-party dominant systems—Singapore; and politically open societies, albeit, with varying degrees of restraint—Indonesia, Thailand, the Philippines, Malaysia, and Cambodia. Military dominance of politics has greatly lessened in recent times, and the public expression of griev-ances expanded. At this point, however, the citizenry tends to accord lead-ership greater importance than institutions, and stability vies with freedom as the primary goal.

On the economic front, Southeast Asia also presents a varied picture, but with growth for the region near the 4–4.5 percent mark, a generally encouraging sign. Indonesia, beset with extensive unemployment and sta-bility problems, is growing at 3.5–4.0 percent. Economic growth is cur-rently strong in Thailand, running around 6 percent, aided by rising con-sumer spending and expanding exports. The Thaksin government is engag-ing in various supportive efforts including a $2.4 billion fund to assist troubled sectors of the economy. Malaysia is showing a 4–4.5 percent growth, abetted by strong consumer spending, financial reform, and im-provements in corporate governance. The Philippines is also among those currently achieving a 4–4.5 percent GDP gain, with advances in control-ling the government's fiscal expansion. Foreign investors, however, remain troubled by a combination of factors including corruption and terrorism. Cambodia, despite numerous economic problems, reports a GDP growth of 5 percent, but with growing foreign debt and declining private invest-ment. The country needs at least 7 percent growth to tackle widespread poverty. Laos is in a similar situation. Vietnam, however, is advancing at a 6 percent GDP rate, buoyed by rising foreign investment and industrial growth. This is taking place despite widespread corruption at every level.

As one overseas Vietnamese entrepreneur explained it, "To do business in Vietnam, you must have a clever head and dirty hands."

Southeast Asia's most advanced economy and once its leader in growth, Singapore, is slumping, with an estimated GDP increase of 0–1 percent in 2003, and record unemployment. Domestic demand and external trade have both been seriously affected by international conditions, ranging from China's rising competition to economic decline in the United States, Japan, and Europe. The average Singaporean continues to live comparatively well, but adjustments to current and future global conditions are urgent.

South Asia

Meanwhile, South Asia, a region largely dominated by India, continues to strive for growth in the midst of domestic strife and dark international clouds. As in Southeast Asia, various South Asian leaders, especially women, have inherited power as members of a political family, with husbands or fathers preceding them.

India's democracy remains remarkably strong, a testimony to the unity with which several generations of Indian leaders, widely ranging in political views, have supported the system learned under British tutelage. The division of authority between the center and the states that marks the Indian system has also been of major benefit. Elsewhere in South Asia, politics is more precarious, with competitive politics surviving in Sri Lanka, Bangladesh, and Nepal, but facing multiple threats. Pakistan also maintains a semblance of openness under military governance, but the political future remains highly uncertain. Indeed, to the amazement of many, the United States' destruction of the Taliban regime in Afghanistan and Saddam Hussein's in Iraq has not produced revolution in Pakistan, at least as of August 2003. General Pervez Musharraf has managed to outmaneuver the radicals while keeping a lid on the conflict with India.

In the economic realm also, South Asia exhibits vast differences. India, having largely abandoned an earlier proclivity for Laskian socialism, is now nurturing the private sector, and its key industrial companies operate with greater efficiency and transparency than do those of China, according to some experts.[8] Its GDP growth rate at some 6 percent is still below that of China, but India is a growing force on the international economic front, increasingly attractive to foreign investors. As Jack Gill reminds us in this volume (pages 181–207), however, the country remains the major concentration of poverty in the world, with 400 million people earning less than a dollar a day.

Elsewhere in South Asia, domestic instability and weak economic policies have combined to place multiple obstacles in front of economic advances. Nevertheless, the Pakistani economy has gained ground recently, with GDP growth currently in the vicinity of 5 percent, aided by a significant U.S. aid package. In the smaller countries of the sub-continent, growth is presently ranging between 3–5 percent, supported in some cases with external assistance. Growth, however, is not reaching the levels necessary if the massive poverty of the region is to be alleviated. And without greater benefits to the masses, political stability will always be threatened.

The United States currently enjoys its best relations ever with both India and Pakistan, but this situation may be "transitory" due to tough issues ahead.[9] It is a tricky game to support two countries that are at each other's throats, not to mention the separate complexities in U.S.-Indian and U.S.-Pakistani relations.

Russia

A brief comment is warranted on domestic trends with respect to Russia, a power whose status and policies still influence the Asia Pacific region. Russia presently enjoys relative political stability under a popular leader, Vladimir Putin. However, struggles between the Kremlin and the economic oligarchs continue and political violence, particularly assassination, is always a distinct possibility. After a series of economic blows, Russia's economy is on a strong upward climb, with 30 percent growth since 1998 and predictions of a 6 percent GDP increase for 2003. An ample number of problems remain, among them the economic dominance of a dozen corporate giants; a major gap between Russia's powerful rich and 40 million poor; and weak foreign investment. The need for further reforms is great, but recent gains have been significant. With oil and gas pipelines developed in the years ahead, moreover, the Russian Far East will increasingly become a vital part of Northeast Asia. Russia seems to be gradually returning to major power status, with an increasing focus upon Asia as well as the West. Its strategy, according to William Wohlforth (see pages 165–79), is one of soft balancing among the major powers.

To sum up this portion of our review, domestic trends in key countries do not suggest a wholly negative picture. There is expanding openness in several authoritarian states. With the exception of North Korea, the regional powers—China, Japan, South Korea, India, and Russia—are inwardly focused on mostly positive economic goals. (As is always the case when drawing sweeping generalizations about contemporary Asia, North Korea stands in a class by itself.) Beyond Pakistan, parts of Central Asia, Indonesia, and, again, North Korea, prospects for domestic stability over the near and medium term are reasonably good, although predictions must be cautious. An ideology agitating for revolution and aggression, such as that of

Table 1. Great Power Rankings in Asia: Relative Standing[a]

	Defense expenditures		Merchandise trade		GDP ($ constant)		Composite ranking	
	1976	2001	1975	2001	1975	2001	1975/76	2001
China	2	2	3	1	4	2	3	1
India	4	4	9	11	3	4	4	5
Japan	3	3	1	2	1	1	1	2
Russia	1	1	2	9	2	6	1	4
South Korea	7	5	6	3	5	3	5	3

Sources: Defense expenditures from IISS, *The Military Balance*, London: International Institute of Strategic Studies, various editions; Merchandise trade data from IMF, *International Financial Statistics*, 2002 CD-ROM; GDP data from World Bank, *World Development Indicators*, 2002 CD-ROM. Note: a) Table shows relative standing among countries in Strategic Asia. The country with the highest value is ranked "1." In 2001, 37 countries are identifed in Strategic Asia; prior to the break-up of the Soviet Union, fewer countries comprised the region (e.g., the Central Asian states are included in the 2001 rankings, but not in the 1975 rankings). In most categories some data are missing for one or more countries (e.g., six countries had yet to report 2001 GDP data to the World Bank).

radical Islam, has not achieved dominance in any states of Asia, and the only country of strategic importance threatened by that possibility in the near term is Pakistan. In addition, economic growth, while not as robust as in the era prior to 1997, appears to be advancing and is rather impressive in view of the weak American, Japanese, and European economies. Based upon this survey of Asian countries, especially when contrasted with a few decades ago, trends are generally positive.

International Sources of Fragility and Resilience

Let there be no doubt, however—Asia is fragile, and it is so first and foremost because of the scale and rate of change in its core structure, that is, in its balance of power. The old structure, buttressed by Japan on one side of Northeast Asia and the Soviet Union on the other, weakened in the 1980s and then collapsed in the early 1990s with the demise of Soviet power. The void in Eurasia was not immediately filled, as Russia staggered and a multitude of experimental spin-off states emerged out of the ashes of the Soviet empire. Poorly developed states, together with great power inattention, provided terrorists an environment to build political support and bases in Central and South Asia.[10] Meanwhile, Japan, still with the biggest Asian economy by a good margin, experienced over a decade of economic stagnation, and Southeast Asia, suffering from the financial crisis of 1997–98 and extension of ASEAN membership to Burma, Vietnam, Cambodia, and Laos, deteriorated as an economic force and coherent international actor. In contrast, during this same period China grew from an economic, mili-

Table 2. Ranking of Average GDP Growth in Asia[a]

	1972–76	1997–2001
China	11	3
India	19	10
Japan	10	26
Russia	8	21
South Korea	2	16

Sources: World Bank, *World Development Indicators*, 2002 CD-ROM. Note: a) Table shows relative standing among countries in Strategic Asia (as defined in Table 1).

tary, and diplomatic backwater to arguably the leading nation in Asia, a nation with the intention of being a truly great power in every way. (See Table 1 for a comparison of rankings between 1975/76 and 2001.) South Asia demonstrated nuclear weapons capability, and India maintained moderate economic growth. The impact of all this ferment on the balance of power was dramatic. Asia was fundamentally altered, albeit with an element of ambiguity, with Japan weakening, China rising rapidly, and an ambitious India setting out on a new economic path, one with stronger internationalist dimensions.

Driven by political collapse and economic reform, the transformation in Asia is unprecedented in its scale and rapidity in peacetime. An indication of the changing fortunes of key actors is provided in Table 2, a comparison of rankings of recent GDP growth among Asian countries with rankings from a quarter of a century ago.

As Robert Gilpin has argued so convincingly, the single greatest challenge in international relations is for nations to adjust peacefully to changes in relative power among states.[11] Given the extraordinary scale and rapidity of change in Asia, and with the outcome not clear, one is struck by the success of the region thus far in avoiding war, let alone the reckless jockeying for power that one would reasonably expect in this unsettled environment. No Asian power, for example, has yet built a military capable of major regional aggression, nor a navy with the power and legitimacy to protect Asia's sea lines of communication (SLOCs). China, Russia, and India do not possess fleets anywhere near capable of patrolling the SLOCs, and Japan, which could develop one soonest, has neither the will nor external acceptance. Should they develop sub-regional capabilities, one has difficulty imagining these powers working together felicitously to divide the job. Asia's powers have longstanding disagreements over ocean sovereignty and boundaries, and the deep distrust that marks their relations would surely manifest itself in efforts to carve up area responsibilities. Other times of change and ambiguity have not been as benign; witness the emergence of Germany and Japan in the late nineteenth through mid-twentieth centuries.

Even if the region possessed an inherently stable balance in the ingredients of power, however, the rivalries and bitter feelings left over from colonization and warfare would be sufficient to cause, at a minimum, serious strains. While resentment and nationalism are difficult variables on which to base predictions, there is no doubt that they persist in Asia. China is a dissatisfied power, having endured the humiliation of defeat and colonization in the nineteenth through twentieth centuries. Chinese officials and writers regularly express their nation's victimization. They voice their dissatisfaction with the United States' preponderant position in the region, which they view as damaging to their national interests. Reflecting these sentiments and its commitment to assert control over Taiwan, China has been raising defense expenditures faster than its rate of GDP growth—by more than twice the rate of GDP growth last year, for example. It is reasonable to assume that if Chinese power continues to expand, China will eventually seek to resume in some form its historic, dominant position in Asia, replacing U.S.-led security arrangements with those of its own design.

Asian memories of aggression and occupation haunt the region. Chinese and Korean attitudes about the Japanese, although revealing admiration for economic achievements, are rooted in Japan's invasions and occupations from the late nineteenth century through World War II. Unsatisfied with Japanese apologies, China and the two Koreas frequently raise this history in their dealings with Japan. How Japanese textbooks handle World War II is one of the more highly publicized problems, but few opportunities are lost in dredging up old grudges. When drums filled with mustard gas from Japanese war stocks in northern China badly injured workers who mistakenly opened them in August 2003, the Chinese government felt obliged to protest. The incident, although not disrupting overall bilateral relations, was just one development that tainted the atmosphere during a week when the two countries were to celebrate the 25th anniversary of their friendship treaty. China highlighted the week by unveiling a new memorial to commemorate those massacred in the Japanese invasion of 1937. Japan finished off the week with senior ministers and 55 members of parliament paying respects to dead Japanese soldiers, some of whom China sees as war criminals, at the Yasukuni Shrine. Indeed, polls indicate that anti-Japanese feelings are the norm in China and Korea, even among the younger generations with no direct memories of last century's conflicts.[12]

Negative feelings are also directed at the United States. Significant Chinese email traffic cheered the terrorists following September 11, seeing America as deserving the attacks for its arrogance. This was not the first outburst. The United States was widely denounced by the Chinese for scuttling their nation's bid for the 2000 Olympics, bombing the Chinese embassy in Belgrade in 1999, and for the collision between the Chinese fighter and the EP-3 "spy" plane in 2001. Rather than a general antipathy towards Americans as a people, however, Chinese have seemed more upset with the U.S. government and U.S. policy.

The consensus among specialists is that nationalism is not only alive and well, it is rising in Asia: in Japan, which is wearying of verbal attacks on its history and worried about military buildups in North Korea and China; in South Korea, which is trying to find its own path to national reconciliation and to accommodate growing Chinese power; and in China, which, still stinging from its weakness and subjugation over the past century and a half, fully senses its rise and seeming destiny to return to greatness. The same could be said about India, which is emerging as the clear winner, at least in terms of political and economic development, over Pakistan. Any prognosis into Asia's future must take into account the phenomenon and associated dangers of rising nationalism.

Intra-Regional Dynamics

Intra-regional dynamics, driven by particular rivalries and competitions, provide another window on the strategic environment in Asia. Here we are looking at strategic interdependencies. In Northeast Asia, ambitions and threat calculations of various actors are feeding off of one another, resulting in significant, albeit not race-level, arms competition.[13] China, according to the most recent Department of Defense report to Congress on the country's military power, is deploying 75 new missiles per year that can target Taiwan, developing weapons to counter U.S. forces that might come to the defense of Taiwan, and "exploring coercive strategies designed to bring Taipei to terms quickly."[14] A combination of Chinese military development and North Korea's nuclear and missile programs has moved Japan to deploy reconnaissance satellites, accelerate anti-ballistic missile research and development, take other measures, and give more serious consideration to the nuclear option. Little noticed in the West, China and India propel each other's longer range nuclear force development, and India and Pakistan remain locked in a robust nuclear and conventional arms competition. In another type of interdependent relationship, China continues to buy major arms from Russia. For four years running Chinese procurement of advanced weapons systems from Russia has exceeded $2 billion annually, twice the average rate of the 1990s. Money and keeping factories open seem to be the prime incentives for Russia; military modernization and power seem to be those of China.[15]

As Bates Gill documents in his chapter on proliferation (pages 365–97), Russia, China, Pakistan, and North Korea are the principal players in the proliferation of nuclear technology, materials, and delivery systems in Asia. The forces driving proliferation in the region are multiple, but one case, the North Korean nuclear weapons program, is worth special attention here because of its crisis nature.[16] The very existence of the DPRK appears to depend upon its potential to wreak havoc on its neighbors 1) for defense, as this odious regime is loved by no one, 2) for offense, as the regime's major claim to legitimacy is the reunification of Korea, and 3) for international extortion, as the country has insufficient means to sustain itself. This is important to understand because of the resulting pressures South Korea and Japan are under to consider "weaponizing" in response, and because all parties need to know the grave difficulties in any negotiations ahead. At the same time, there is widely shared interest in Northeast Asia in heading off a nuclear arms race before it begins. Thus, the United States was successful in convincing China to convene trilateral talks with North Korean officials, and more recently, North Korea finally accepted a multilateral framework for dialogue involving the six concerned nations.

The ultimate hope for these negotiations lies in the willingness of all parties to reach an agreement involving pledges to the North of security and subsequent economic assistance in exchange for fully verifiable abandonment of its nuclear arms programs. Negotiations are likely to be difficult and protracted. It is hard to imagine North Korea either giving up weapons it has been developing for 30 years and upon which it relies so heavily, or, because of its secretive nature, allowing full verification of any nuclear agreement. Therefore, the world may have to live with one of three outcomes short of war or regime change.[17] The first is an agreement that accomplishes only part of the goal but keeps the lid on the crisis, leaving the North Koreans in possession of some nuclear arms but seemingly with their known programs capped for some limited period of time. The second would be continuation of the status quo—nuclear cold war behind a thin façade—in which the DPRK covertly possesses and continues to develop nuclear weapons but does not test or openly deploy them, and Japan and South Korea, while perhaps not acknowledging these weapons publicly, prepare conventional defenses for them. The third possibility would be nuclear breakout in the region, in which the DPRK tests and openly deploys nuclear arms, with Japan and South Korea having to decide whether they take the nuclear path themselves, fully "nuclearizing" the region. Because of the continuing proliferation threat, in each of these outcomes all of the surrounding states, working together or separately, would need to discourage North Korean trade in nuclear and related items.

International Institutions as a Source of Stability

While the United Nations currently plays minor roles in Asia, an important source of regional stability is the multilateral trade and investment regime governed by the World Trade Organization (WTO), International Monetary Fund (IMF), and the World Bank. Stability is derived from the basic economic functions these institutions imperfectly, but helpfully, fulfill: providing the basic rules for commerce and reductions in tariff levels and other barriers; providing a legitimate process for trade disputes to be resolved; providing short-term liquidity; and providing long-term development loans. By encouraging trade and thus efficiency in the global economy, and by helping alleviate some of the worst effects of economic downturns, the WTO and international financial institutions (IFIs) encourage economic growth worldwide and help stabilize societies wracked by economic problems.

That said, IFIs' reputations were not burnished during the Asian financial crisis. Popular opinion ran against the IMF for the sacrifices it was perceived to inflict and reforms it demanded; governments in the hardest hit countries fell. Indonesia, perhaps the most deeply wounded by the crisis, underwent a political revolution as a consequence and shows residual effects of the crisis six years later. Yet, there were some vigorous recoveries, particularly by South Korea, which received $58 billion in short-term support and paid it back in full in 2001, three years eight months early. In retrospect, many of the reforms advocated by the IMF were badly needed—in some cases are still needed. The experience did much to sensitize the IMF and world leaders to the challenges associated with the rapid international movement of capital. Indeed, the crisis provides a case study of both the modern global economy and the stabilizing function IFIs need to play.

Asia has various regional organizations, most of which have had limited or unrealized value. It is a sign of the changing and ambiguous distribution of power that different states are competing by proposing new ways of organizing economic and security relations in the region.

Two studies in this volume evaluate these institutions, one by Sheldon Simon on ASEAN and the ASEAN Regional Forum (ARF) (see pages 269–89), and the other by Ellen Frost on the economic experiments underway (pages 399–433). ASEAN faces numerous challenges: separatist movements in Indonesia and the Philippines, arms smuggling, piracy, illegal migration, drug trafficking, terrorism and Muslim radicals, the gradual projection of Chinese forces in the South China Sea, and the general accretion of Chinese influence in the region. ASEAN has weakened since the countries of Southeast Asia were hit by the 1997–98 financial crisis and the organization expanded its membership to include very different types of states. Indonesia's continued domestic disarray has further undercut ASEAN. Indonesia is by far the largest country in the region, and its leadership is needed to give ASEAN direction and influence. As Sheldon Simon points out, ASEAN's norms of non-use of force, peaceful resolution of disputes among members, and non-interference in the internal affairs of members need revisiting as they sharply limit the organization's options.

The ARF, an initiative by ASEAN to provide its members more clout with great powers on issues of interest to ASEAN, remains a proto-institution. It consists of dialogues and does not maintain a permanent secretariat. Due to its weakness and need for consensus, it has been unwilling to take on core security issues. Interestingly, other forms of regional security cooperation are underway to fill the void, principally led by the United States but also among small groups of like-minded states in the region. For example, there is intelligence sharing among Malaysia, Singapore, and the Philippines, and bilateral cooperation on piracy and terrorism in the Strait of Malacca and the interdiction of militants fleeing the Philippines. The point here is that security cooperation is taking place in the region, but the trend seems to be less within the ASEAN framework.

International economic cooperation, in contrast, is a complicated growth industry that reflects the rise of China and the concerns and insecurities of Japan, Southeast Asia, and India. Recent free trade and other initiatives from the region—especially from China but also from others—exclude the United States. Were these initiatives to succeed, according to Ellen Frost, they would produce modest economic benefits for Asian countries, but just as importantly they would strengthen China's ties in the region. It is the hope of Southeast Asians that deeper economic ties with China would enhance prospects for amicable relations with their giant neighbor. As history teaches us, however, economic ties may or may not be conducive or even relevant to peaceful relations when other issues are at stake.

To sum up, Northeast Asian powers are translating their fears, ambitions, nationalism, and strategic competitions into military modernization and buildups, hedging strategies, and diplomatic and economic initiatives. Global and regional institutions are helpful but play minor, supporting roles. When viewed from the perspective of the international activity of Asian governments, whether alone or acting together, the region is fragile and prone to crisis. Rapid changes in the distribution of power and longstanding rivalries promote uneasiness. If this were the whole story, there would be a solid basis for pessimism—but, in fact, the situation is more complex.

Transnational Sources of Fragility and Resilience

Transnational actors are non-state actors—people, companies, unofficial flows of information and money, most trade in goods and services, diseases, and so on. Globalization, the transnational process in which free market economic exchange affects societies, creates and distributes wealth, spurs nations to develop rule of law, spreads ideas at the speed of light, and integrates the world economy. Political-terrorist movements that are not directed by governments, such as Al Qaeda-led, radical Islamist groups, are another form of transnational activity. Whereas globalization is arguably the major transnational force for human progress today, terrorism is the chief transnational threat.

Terrorism and terrorist links span the width of Asia's enormous geography. As argued earlier, the void left in the wake of the collapse of the Soviet Union—through Central Asia and Afghanistan in particular—together with toleration by the United States and other governments, allowed radical Islamists, loosely under Osama Bin Laden's direction, to strike deals with the Taliban, build training camps in a variety of countries, and nurture a worldwide network. Zachary Abuza documents this network in Southeast Asia in chilling detail (see pages 321–63).

Al Qaeda found Southeast Asia attractive for several reasons. Among these were the growth of Islamic social, economic, and political grievances and the existence of "countries of convenience" for terrorist attacks, money laundering, and training. The terrorist network in the region started with the development of groups like the still powerful Jemaah Islamiyah in Indonesia, which is likely responsible for the bombings in Bali in October 2002 and Jakarta in August 2003.

Since September 11, the United States and then one government after another have comprehended the dimensions of the threat. The Philippines was the first country to work closely with the United States, which has been forthcoming with troops, training, supplies, intelligence, and money to support the government's war against the Muslim insurgent group Abu Sayyaf. According to sources closely following events, China has been more forthcoming with intelligence on Central Asian terrorists than most anticipated. Following the bombings in Bali, Indonesia began to take the problem more seriously, but outsiders still felt the need 10 months later to urge the country to do more following the J. W. Marriott Hotel attack.[18]

Governments in Asia have thus reacted differently to the terrorist threat, and further cooperation is required to disrupt the illicit flow of people, money, materials, and weapons across boundaries. Because of the geography of the region, reducing it to zero is unlikely. But the trend has clearly been positive, as governments have increasingly seen common interest in making terrorism a priority and cooperating to deal with it.

What makes terrorism so dangerous today, of course, is the potential lethality of the weapons used. The ultimate fear is that terrorists will acquire a nuclear weapon and detonate it in a major city, but the possibilities short of this nightmare could be devastating enough, as illustrated in New York and Washington, DC, by three passenger jets commandeered as manned missiles. Another deep concern is the assumption of power by radical Islamists in a major country like Pakistan or Indonesia. It follows that the war on terrorism, while ebbing and flowing in the future, will unfortunately be a long-term feature of Asian—and global—affairs.

Two other negative aspects viewed through the "transnational" lens are the spread of disease and environmental "spillover." The SARS outbreak, which experts believe will return, is the most recent case of disease disrupting a number of nations' economies and politics. As Nicholas Eberstadt points out in this volume (pages 453–84), HIV/AIDS is a devastating problem in China, parts of Southeast Asia, India, and Russia. Like diseases, environmental problems in one country can damage others. Indonesian fires became a major issue in Southeast Asia as smoke threatened the quality of life and health of citizens—and threatened the tourist industries—of neighboring countries. Acid rain, oil spills, and global warming are other examples. While these phenomena cause problems between states and for people and economies, they do not seem at this juncture to threaten the stability of any sub-region of Asia. The scenario that most observers are keeping an eye on is the failure of a government—and so a change of leadership—in the event of uncontrolled transmission of a disease such as SARS.

Far more pervasive a factor and instrumental in shaping the politics, welfare, and potential stability of Asian countries are the forces of globalization. In a quarter of a century, from the moment Deng Xiaopeng and his colleagues in China began experimenting with economic reforms and opening the country to the world's products, technologies, ideas, and investment, until today, sustained economic growth has transformed that country. Most Chinese today are far better off, more educated, and freer. The lessons come from the United States, Japan, and the tigers of Asia, and, frankly, from hundreds of years of history. The greatest powers on earth have been trading powers, and the great periods of economic growth and development of civilizations have come when trade flourished. The plight of North Korea amply demonstrates the results of self-imposed isolation.

The decision to unleash the forces of globalization is a political one. Society must be organized to facilitate international economic exchange. Investment and trade then generate jobs and rising standards of living, which in turn require many things that affect society. Workers need education and mobility; contracts must be enforceable; businesses need fair taxation and judicial systems; and investors need companies to be transparent before they purchase them. Rule of law becomes a broader issue as people become more educated, travel abroad, and desire modern justice and governmental institutions. And so the process can go, transforming a society and its citizens' expectations far beyond the economic realm.

In Asia, to the surprise of many observers, democracy came quite suddenly to South Korea and Taiwan, societies steeped in Confucian traditions. No less vulnerable to the tide were the Philippines and Indonesia. Democracy always looks different in practice from one country to another due to cultural and historical idiosyncrasies, and it does not develop in one single step, but the attractiveness of popular government, as exemplified by these four examples, seems no less compelling in Asia than in Europe or America.

The downsides to globalization are the downsides of capitalism—the business cycle, including panics, and dislocations of workers in ailing industries and companies. Not every boat rises with the tide. Losers tend to be older workers who are less apt to retrain or move for new jobs. Governments devise mechanisms and policies to ameliorate these problems, but never completely. A cautionary note should be added here as well. There is nothing irreversible in history, including open borders.

But to the extent history is a guide, a lesson is that democracies tend not to fight each other. Hence, the expectation ought to be that as democracy spreads across Asia the region will become inherently more stable. In this way, globalization is an enormously important phenomenon working positively in Asia over the long term, as the region has seemingly committed itself for the foreseeable future to market economies and robust trade. It is a long-term proposition that serves as a justification for a sustained U.S. strategy of engagement in Asia.

Conclusion

This assessment began by listing the pervasive dangers and sources of instability in Asia. These evolving threats to Asian, and in many instances American, interests have been sufficiently understood in Washington to put American lives and treasure on the line for half a century. For all its changes since World War II, the region has remained fragile and prone to crisis— and America has known it.

This was certainly the case during the Cold War. In 1975, when *Asia and the Road Ahead* was published, the Soviet Union cast a long shadow from Central Asia through Mongolia to the Korean Peninsula and down to Vietnam. It had amassed a million soldiers on the Chinese border. Communism was achieving victory in Indochina and there were setbacks in Africa. China was still led by Mao Zedong and had yet to open to the world and break out of a series of policies that were disastrous for the Chinese people. Sensing a diminution in the threat from the Soviet Union and in America's international resolve that year, China was seeking a more equidistant position between the superpowers. The United States seemed in jeopardy of leaving not only Vietnam but much of the rest of Asia and other crucial parts of the world as well. Yet, through turmoil at home as well as abroad, it sustained its alliances and the essential elements of its internationalism.

Today, by contrast, Asia is free of the Soviet threat, and most Asians are far more prosperous and educated than at any time in their history. Major Asian nations are focusing on economic development as participants in the global economy. America's commitment to a stable military balance in the region, unlike its failure to fulfill that role in Europe and Asia in the 1930s, moderates the international behavior of these states.[19] U.S. forces, headquartered at the Pacific Command in Hawaii, also protect Asia's oceans, the lifeline of regional trade. Current and potential threats remain, of course: principally North Korea, which could drive nuclear proliferation and destabilize all of Northeast Asia; terrorism; and possibly China, whose future politics and ambition are uncertain.

Should the United States keep its commitment to a stable balance, freedom of the seas, expanding trade, and supporting democracy, globalization should continue to accelerate international progress, and in so doing restrain nationalism. The caveat here is that parts of Asia still resist global norms and ways. And should the United States remain willing to provide leadership to international institutions, organize coalitions when threats arise, and act unilaterally when it must, there is a reasonable chance that rogue states, WMD proliferation, terrorism, and other problems can be managed.

An important question for the future of the region, then, pertains to the world's sole superpower, which lies across the Pacific Ocean. Will it remain committed in Asia through the 2004 presidential elections, through the difficult times ahead in Iraq and Afghanistan, and through today's economic problems and budget deficits and beyond? The analysis here suggests that the costs of America's withdrawal from Asia—greatly heightened risks of engaging the nation in arms races and war—should give pause to any national security decision maker in Washington who might contemplate such a course. And the historical record underscores this notion. America has remained engaged in Asia through more challenging circumstances, and seems likely to stay engaged there for some time to come.

Endnotes

[1] Richard J. Ellings and Aaron L. Friedberg, eds., *Strategic Asia 2001–02: Power and Purpose*, Seattle: The National Bureau of Asian Research, 2001; Richard J. Ellings and Aaron L. Friedberg, eds., *Strategic Asia 2002–03: Asian Aftershocks*, Seattle: The National Bureau of Asian Research, 2002.

[2] For example, see Charles E. Morrison, ed., *Asia-Pacific Security Outlook, 2003*, Tokyo: Japan Center for International Exchange, 2003.

[3] Robert Scalapino, *Asia and the Road Ahead: Issues for Major Powers*, Berkeley, Calif.: University of California Press, 1975, p. 2.

[4] Aaron Friedberg, "Introduction," in Ellings and Friedberg, eds., *Strategic Asia 2001–02: Power and Purpose*, p. 4–6. Also, see map of Strategic Asia on p. xiii of the current volume.

[5] For a discussion of the double hedge strategy, see Eric Heginbotham and Richard J. Samuels, "Japan," in Ellings and Friedberg, eds., *Strategic Asia 2002–03: Asian Aftershocks*, pp. 95–130.

[6] See the chapter by Dwight Perkins in this volume (pages 435–51).

[7] See the chapter on South Korea in this volume (pages 109–29).

[8] Yasheng Huang and Tarun Khanna, "Can India Overtake China?" *Foreign Policy*, July/August 2003, p. 74–81.

[9] See Jack Gill's analyses of India and Pakistan in this volume (pages 181–207 and 209–27).

[10] Rather than serving as the locus of an intense "great game," Central Asian states received unsystematic attention from the big powers. See Kathleen Collins and William Wohlforth's argument in this volume (pages 291–317).

[11] Robert Gilpin, *War and Change in World Politics*, Cambridge: Cambridge University Press, 1981, p. 230.

[12] See results from the August 26–September 2, 2002 *Asahi Shimbun*–Chinese Academy of Social Sciences and the Japan Research Center (China) polls in James J. Pryzstup, "Congratulations, Concern, Competition, and Cooperation," *Comparative Connections*, vol. 4, no. 4 (January 2003), <www.csis.org/pacfor/cc>; the October 25–November 18, 2000 *Tong-a Ilbo–Asahi Shimbun* "Joint Public Opinion Poll" in *Tong-a Ilbo*, December 4, 2000, translated as "Multi-National Citizens' Poll on Current State Surrounding Korean Peninsula," FBIS, December 4, 2000; the 1997 "Japan in Chinese Youth's Eyes Poll" in Li Heng, "Japan's Diplomatic Failure Towards China: Poll," *People's Daily Online*, December 10, 2002.

[13] See Gilbert Rozman's analysis of strategic interactions in Northeast Asia in this volume (pages 251–67).

[14] *Annual Report on the Military Power of the People's Republic of China* (Report to Congress Pursuant to the FY2000 National Defense Authorization Act), Department of Defense, July 28, 2003, p. 6.

[15] See William Wohlforth's analysis of Russia in this volume (pages 165–79).

[16] See the chapter on North Korea by Nicholas Eberstadt and Joseph Ferguson in this volume (pages 131–63). For background, see Nicholas Eberstadt and Richard J. Ellings, eds., *Korea's Future and the Great Powers*, Seattle: University of Washington Press, 2001.

[17] Compare with the three scenarios drawn by Nicholas Eberstadt and Joseph Ferguson in the chapter on North Korea.

[18] Jeremy Wagstaff, David Lague, and John McBeth, "Time to Get Tough," *Far Eastern Economic Review*, August 14, 2003, pp. 12–16.

[19] See Robert Sutter's analysis of the United States in Asia in this volume (pages 33–51).

STRATEGIC ASIA

COUNTRY STUDIES

United States – Key Indicators and Forecasts

Economy and Trade	2002[a]	2003[b]	2004[b]
GDP ($tr) / (PPP GDP)	10.4 (PPP GDP in 2002 = $10.1 tr)		
GDP growth (%)	2.4	2.2	3.6
Inflation (%)	1.6	2.3	2.3
Budget balance (% of GDP)	-3.6	-4.6	-3.8
Major export destinations (2001)	Canada (22%), Mexico (14%), Japan (8%)		

Population and Energy	2002[a]	2005[b]	2010[b]
Population (m)	287.7	295.7	309.2
Population growth (%)	0.9	0.9	0.9
Oil production (m bbl/d)	9.1	9.0	9.2
Oil consumption (m bbl/d)	19.7	20.5	23.0

Politics	
President	George W. Bush (Rep., since Jan 2001)
Dominant party	Republican Party (since Jan 1995)
Next election	November 2004 (legislative and presidential)

Military	
Armed forces (2002)	1,414,000
Defense expenditure (2001)	$322.4 bn (3.2% of GDP)
Conventional capabilities	Unrivalled conventional military capabilities
	Continued integration of forces, improvement
	in rapid deployment of ground forces
Weapons of mass destruction	Large nuclear arsenal (being reduced)
	Ongoing disposal of CBW stockpiles

Source: The National Bureau of Asian Research, compiled from International Monetary Fund, *World Economic Outlook*; Central Intelligence Agency, *World Factbook*; U.S. Census Bureau, *International Data Base*; Energy Information Administration, *Country Analysis Brief—United States*; International Institute of Strategic Studies, *The Military Balance*. Notes: a) Date for 2002 may be estimates; b) Data for 2003, 2004, 2005, and 2010 are projections. Additional data on the United States are available in the Strategic Asia Database at <http://strategicasia.nbr.org>.

U.S. LEADERSHIP: PREVAILING STRENGTHS AMID CHALLENGES

Robert G. Sutter

ABSTRACT

Emphasis on China and Asia in the national security strategy of the George W. Bush administration gave way to a more reactive and less coherent U.S. approach driven by developments, particularly in Iraq, the war on terrorism, and Korea. U.S. policy can be diverted or challenged in many areas, foreshadowing a somewhat weaker U.S. policy stance in Asia. Given overall U.S. strengths in Asia, however, U.S. officials probably will continue to manage relatively effectively. The Bush administration has improved relations with the major Asian powers. The United States remains the partner of choice for most Asian governments. If the ongoing North Korean crisis were to combine with other possible significant complications for U.S. policy (e.g., failure in Iraq; U.S. economic downturn; decay in Pakistan, Afghanistan; India-Pakistan, China-Taiwan conflict; major terrorist attack on the United States) it would more seriously disrupt U.S. leadership and stability in Asia.

Robert Sutter is a Visiting Professor in the School of Foreign Service at Georgetown University. The author benefited greatly from comments of other authors, reviews by Richard Ellings, William Overholt, and Michael Wills, and research assistance by Neil Beck, Allison Clark, Rajeev Majumdar, and Peter Mattis.

Introduction

The George W. Bush administration initially emphasized China and Asia's central position in U.S. national security strategy, but by the second half of the president's term this focus gave way to a more reactive and less coherent U.S. approach to the region. The war on terrorism and a redirection of strategic interests to Southwest Asia became the new focal points of U.S. national security policy. In Asia, the administration was forced to react to North Korean provocations and crises in U.S. relations with both North and South Korea. U.S. defense, intelligence, and other officials remained wary of potential adverse trends in Asia, notably rising Chinese military power and assertiveness. U.S. forces were deployed to the western Pacific to improve the U.S. ability to deal with contingencies possibly involving China, as well as more immediate threats posed by North Korea.[1]

The large-scale deployment of U.S. forces and resources to the Persian Gulf in the U.S.-led war against Iraq in 2003 showed that U.S. strategic focus would be in the Persian Gulf and Southwest Asia for the remainder of President Bush's term. This added to U.S. leaders' preoccupation with homeland security, the global war on terrorism, and instability in frontline anti-terrorism states, Afghanistan and Pakistan, all of which shifted U.S. emphasis away from China and much of the East Asian periphery.[2] Chinese leader Jiang Zemin and newly appointed President and Communist Party leader Hu Jintao worked hard to reach common ground and avoid confrontation with the United States, easing U.S. leaders' concerns, at least for the time being. Southeast Asia emerged as a new front in the war on terrorism, but its importance remained secondary in U.S. policy priorities.[3]

North Korea took provocative actions in late 2002 and 2003, breaking declared non-proliferation commitments and reactivating nuclear facilities frozen under the 1994 U.S.-North Korea Agreed Framework accord. This posed a major challenge for U.S. policy that was not well anticipated by the U.S. government. The administration's reaction was complicated by deep internal divisions over how to handle North Korea and by strong differences in U.S. and South Korean policy toward North Korea and broader alliance relations.[4] Tensions in U.S.-South Korean alliance relations and anti-American sentiment in South Korea rose markedly and were important factors in the election of South Korea's new president in December 2002.[5] Subsequent U.S. and South Korean efforts to ease tensions, bridge differences, and solidify relations remained awkward in 2003, adding to the arguments of those claiming that the alliance was in crisis and poised for a major change in the next few years.[6]

U.S. administration differences with South Korea, China, Japan, and other concerned powers over how to deal with North Korea focused for months on tactics dealing with the form of negotiation. At least for the time being, all agreed to pursue a diplomatic solution. The Bush administration in 2003 made some progress in forging a broader international consensus in the face of North Korea's provocations, notably seeing China play a more active role in trying to restrain the North. Nonetheless, differences among the powers and within the United States remained strong. Whatever delicate consensus was achieved could be shattered in the event the United States were provoked by North Korean proliferation activities, or for other reasons, to resort to military initiatives or other forceful action to deal with North Korea's nuclear program. U.S.-led efforts to monitor and intercept illegal North Korean trade and to seek political and perhaps other international sanctions against the North Korean regime elicited signs of strong reservations and opposition from both China and South Korea in mid-2003.

Asian elite and public opinion joined the worldwide complaints against U.S. unilateral actions and dominance in international affairs at the time of the U.S.-led attack on Iraq and repeated U.S. policy declarations supporting preemptive actions against adversaries.[7] In practice, however, the Bush administration sought to deal with issues in most of Asia through consultation and engagement. Despite continued strong negative reactions throughout the region critical of U.S. foreign policy, most Asian governments reacted pragmatically and with restraint to the U.S. military assault on Iraq and other sensitive issues in U.S. foreign policy.[8] China muffled past opposition to U.S. "hegemonism," contributing to the most significant improvement in U.S.-China relations in over a decade.[9]

The U.S. administration's overall record in Asia and the outlook for U.S. policy over the next few years are matters of debate among specialists. Many criticize the Bush administration for mishandling the Korean crises, for issuing unilateralist policy declarations adding to tension in the region, and for a lack of attention to economic, environmental, and multilateral measures seen as important to long-range Asian stability and smooth U.S.-Asian relations.[10] They sometimes predict dire consequences, most immediately involving dangerous nuclear proliferation, war on the Korean Peninsula, rupture of the U.S. alliance with South Korea, and confrontation with China. Some add that the administration's tendency to "pre-empt" threats by attacking first could set a bad precedent for such Asian hot spots as the Taiwan Strait and Kashmir.[11]

While such criticisms have merit, they need to be balanced by appropriate attention to the many favorable trends in Asia for U.S. policy and interests, which foreshadow a positive overall assessment of continued U.S. leadership in the region. At a time of U.S. preoccupation with other priorities, the Bush administration has adjusted in generally pragmatic ways to unexpected challenges, notably on the Korean Peninsula. The U.S. ability to manage the crises with both North and South Korea without undue negative consequences, and to sustain U.S. leadership and other regional interests, seems good for the next few years. In particular, there are several important underlying strengths in the U.S. leadership position in Asia, and the Bush administration has succeeded in improving U.S. relations with each of the great powers in Asia. For at least the next few years the United States will remain by far the dominant power in Asia. Its realigned military forces backed by broad U.S. military and economic power and influence will be well positioned to deal with regional contingencies. Regional powers likely will remain domestically focused, mutually suspicious, and reluctant to confront the United States for some time. Of course, U.S. policy directions will be influenced by other developments, notably the situation in Iraq and nearby countries, the Korean crises, the broader war on terrorism, and U.S. economic conditions. Such preoccupations and diversions mean that significant U.S. policy initiatives or revival of the earlier Bush administration interest in focusing on China seem unlikely under prevailing circumstances.

Underlying U.S. Strengths in Post-Cold War Asia

Several key strengths in prevailing U.S.-Asian relations support the Bush administration's ability to manage Asian crises and to sustain U.S. leadership in promoting stability, development, and U.S. values in Asia. Government leaders on both sides of the Pacific continue to place a high value on the U.S. security commitment and military presence in Asia. There were few murmurings in the United States to withdraw from Asia after the Cold War, and U.S. resolve to remain actively involved in regional security has been strengthened since the September 11, 2001 terrorist attacks. The strong U.S. military presence is generally welcomed by Asian government leaders, and even Chinese leaders have notably modified their past criticism of the U.S. security role.[12] Debate over the size and deployment of U.S. forces in South Korea has become a key element in the crises facing U.S. policy on the Korean Peninsula. Nevertheless, Seoul and Washington appear determined to manage the debate without jeopardizing strong mutual interests supported by a continued U.S. military presence in the South.[13] U.S. officials took pains to reassure South Korea and others in Asia that the proposed realignment of U.S. forces on the peninsula, and the broader U.S. realignment of forces abroad, would enhance rather than reduce the U.S. ability to deter and defeat foes. These assurances had more weight following the impressive U.S. military victories in Afghanistan and Iraq.[14]

The Bush administration has a less activist international economic policy than the Clinton administration, but the United States maintains open markets despite aberrations in 2002 such as moves to protect U.S. farmers and steel manufacturers. Washington seeks greater economic opportunity and openness, and regional leaders continue to view the United States as their preferred economic partner. The administration's economic policy leaders, especially the special trade representative, pursue broad free trade initiatives in the World Trade Organization as well as specific free trade arrangements with individual Southeast Asian nations. This is welcomed by Asian governments that view the U.S. economy as vitally important to Asian economic well-being, especially after the Asian financial crisis and Japan's persisting stagnation. Though China is a new engine of regional growth, U.S. economic prospects remain much more important for Asian development. The United States in recent years has absorbed an increasing share (about 40 percent, according to U.S. government figures) of exports from China, which is emerging as the export-manufacturing base for investors from a wide range of advanced Asian Pacific economies. The U.S. market continues to absorb one-third of the exports of Japan—by far the largest exporter in Asia. The economies of South Korea, Taiwan, and ASEAN rely on the U.S. market to receive around 20 percent of their exports. Meanwhile, U.S. foreign direct investment has grown notably in China, but the level there is only about one-third of the level of U.S. investment in Australia, Hong Kong, or Singapore, and less than one-fifth of U.S. investment in Japan.[15]

Strong U.S. domestic pressure in the post-Cold War period pushed democracy, human rights, and other American values in international affairs. In Asia there was resistance from authoritarian governments seeking to preserve their ruling prerogatives and Asian democracies fearing regional instability. The Bush administration has placed a strong rhetorical emphasis on American values, but its policy implementation has been more pragmatic, especially as it sought allies and supporters in the global war on terrorism and other endeavors. This adjustment generally is welcomed in Asia and has worked to ease U.S. differences with authoritarian governments in the region.[16]

The United States is preeminent in Strategic Asia. U.S. power appeared to belie predictions in earlier decades of an inevitable U.S. decline, as the United States became more powerful and influential in Asia and the Pacific than at any time since the defeat of Japan in World War II. There was concern over possible U.S. "over-reach"—stretching military and economic commitments beyond capabilities, but existing commitments in the wake of the toppling of Saddam Hussein seemed manageable and allowed for planned realignment and downsizing of U.S. forces in Asia and elsewhere. While some in the region might wish to challenge or confront the United

States, most are loath to do so given the dangers they would face in opposition to the world's dominant power, with a leadership seemingly prepared to use that power against its enemies.[17]

The asymmetry of power between the United States and Asian states will not change soon. Realigned U.S. military forces in Asia, backed by the unsurpassed military capabilities demonstrated in recent conflicts in Europe and Asia, seem well positioned to deal with regional contingencies. The overall importance of the U.S. economy to Asian economic well-being has risen in the post-Cold War period in the eyes of Asian governments seeking international outreach and economic development as a foundation for their development. The major regional powers, including a stagnating Japan and a rising China, are domestically preoccupied and are likely to remain so for some time to come.[18] Focused on internal issues, they seek support from the United States and other powers, and do not seek difficulties in their foreign relations. In theory, there is a danger that the Asian powers may align against the United States and its interests in significant ways. The Asian nations, including leading regional powers Japan and China, are actively maneuvering and hedging, seeking new and more multifaceted arrangements to secure their interests in the uncertain regional environment. They sometimes cooperate together in broader arrangements like ASEAN+3 (the 10 ASEAN states plus China, Japan, and South Korea) that promote U.S.-backed goals of regional cooperation. Although some Americans are wary of regional arrangements that exclude the United States, in practice, the Asian nations remain deeply suspicious of one another, indicating that cooperation seriously detrimental to U.S. interests remains unlikely.[19]

U.S. policymakers also have done a better job in managing the domestic pressures that often push U.S. policy in directions that are detrimental to a sound and balanced approach to Asia. President Bill Clinton's engagement policy toward China in his second term was much more coherent than the policy in his first term, which appeared to be driven by competing U.S. domestic interests. President Bush's policy is better suited to mainstream U.S. opinion regarding China and has the added advantage of avoiding the need for significant concessions toward China on sensitive issues like Taiwan.[20] President Bush's attention to Japan reduced Japanese concerns caused by the Clinton administration's emphasis on China and its tough public criticism of Japan's economic policies.[21]

The Bush administration's tough stance toward North Korea remains a major weakness, which poses obvious and serious difficulties for U.S. influence in Asia. The difficulty of meshing a tough stance to North Korea while supporting the South's asymmetrical engagement efforts with Pyongyang has not been fully addressed. U.S. policy drifted, with leaders in Washington and much of the rest of the world focused on other more immediate problems. North Korean brinksmanship in 2002 and 2003 brought the issue to a head, forcing the United States to act. The possibility of unilateral, forceful U.S. actions, including a military attack on North Korea, remains. However, the danger that Bush administration hard-liners would push policy to an extreme is mitigated to some degree by strong countervailing opinion in the administration and more broadly in the Congress, the media, and among U.S. experts and opinion leaders, warning of dire consequences of excessive U.S. pressure on the North Korean regime.[22]

U.S. Relations with the Asian Powers

The Bush administration's success in improving U.S. relations with all the great powers in Asia adds to the strength of American leadership in the region and reinforces Washington's ability to deal with crises on the Korean Peninsula and other regional difficulties.[23]

The administration came to power with plans to markedly enhance the political and military partnership with Japan. The government of Prime Minister Koizumi Junichiro was a responsive partner, though constraints imposed by economic stagnation and political differences in Japan have limited cooperation to some degree. Highlights of U.S.-Japan relations included Japan's strong backing in the war on terrorism, including an unprecedented Indian Ocean naval deployment in support of allied operations in the war in Afghanistan, and Prime Minister Koizumi's outspoken support for the U.S.-led attack on Iraq. Koizumi may have diverged from U.S. interests by meeting Kim Jong Il in September 2002, but he found common ground with the Bush administration in its subsequent efforts to deal with North Korea's provocative nuclear weapons development. The potential negative side effects of Japan's more active military role (e.g. heightened regional angst, greater military preparations by China, South Korea) received little public attention from U.S. policymakers.[24] It remained unclear in 2003 how much influence President Bush's repeated gestures of appreciation for Prime Minister Koizumi and other signs of strong U.S. government support for Japan were having on pervasive Japanese concerns about Japan's declining standing in Asian and world affairs.

Compared with traditional allies, the Indian government was more understanding and generally more supportive of U.S. policy regarding sensitive issues in missile defense, arms control, the United Nations, and the war in Iraq. It welcomed the Bush administration's plans for a greater Indian role in Asian security and world affairs, and the steadily expanding U.S. military relationship with India. The terrorist attacks of September 11, 2001 proved to be a catalyst in improving U.S.-Indian relations, although the United States and India differed over definitions of terrorists as they applied to Kashmir and militants supported by Pakistan—the core issue that could precipitate an India-Pakistan war.[25]

The improvement of U.S. relations with Russia seen in the first Bush-Putin summit in the months before the terrorist attacks on America was markedly enhanced by cooperation after September 11, 2001. Russian support was essential in facilitating U.S.-led military operations in Central Asia against the Taliban regime in Afghanistan. Russia saw its interests served by fostering closer economic and strategic cooperation with the United States and the West, and by playing down past differences over U.S. missile defense programs and NATO enlargement. Maneuvering in the United Nations in the months prior to the war in Iraq saw Russia join with France and others in standing against U.S. military actions to topple Saddam Hussein without renewed UN approval. It was unclear if this reversal in bilateral cooperation was prompted by Russian concerns involving economic and other key interests in Iraq (and broader concerns regarding anticipated hostile reaction in the region and among the sizeable Russian Muslim population), or if it was part of a broader Russian decision to reverse course and seek to join with other world powers to resist and weaken the United States. After the U.S.-led coalition succeeded militarily in Iraq and senior Bush administration officials made significant gestures to ease tensions with Moscow, Russia appeared prepared to resume a more cooperative stance toward the United States.[26]

The breakthrough in U.S. relations with China by far was the most important success for Bush administration policy in Asia. The rapid rise of China's power and influence, especially around China's periphery in Asia, initially received negative attention in the United States and prompted a steady stream of media, congressional, and other commentary warning of PRC efforts to push the United States out of Asia. In contrast, actual Chinese behavior in the region and in improving relations with the Bush administration seemed to underscore strong awareness by Chinese leaders of the difficulties involved in direct competition with the United States.[27]

The power and policies of the Bush administration indeed did change the Asian situation in important and sometimes negative respects for Chinese interests, especially after the September 11 terrorist attacks. Chinese leaders nonetheless reacted with restraint and moderation—helping to set the stage for a significant upswing in bilateral relations. American specialists hold different views about what factors were most important in causing the favorable turn in China-U.S. relations in 2001–03, but tend to agree that the improvement in U.S.-Chinese relations reinforced Beijing's moderate policies toward the United States, Asia, and world affairs.[28]

Looking to the future, some predict a major breakthrough in U.S.-China cooperation in Asia,[29] but others take fuller account of the many deeply rooted differences that Chinese and U.S. leaders will continue to grapple with in the years ahead. Although the United States and China have more common ground in Asia, they differ over Taiwan, how to secure stability in Korea, and ultimately which power will be paramount in Asia. The Chinese military build-up focused on Taiwan—and U.S. forces that might assist Taiwan in a conflict—presents a fundamental long-term problem for U.S.-China relations, which is little affected by Chinese leaders hinting at possible pull-back of some missiles focused on Taiwan. China remains the sole power building an array of more modern military forces to attack Americans. U.S. forces respond with enhanced preparations. Below the surface of amity also lies a wide range of contentious security, political, economic and other issues that make the U.S. bilateral relationship with China by far the most contentious and complicated U.S. relationship in Asia.[30]

Challenges and Preoccupations

U.S. security policy in Asia remains reactive in key areas, notably Korea, and the degree of U.S. attention to (and influence in) the region depends on developments in Iraq, the broader war on terrorism, and the crises in Korea. Positive breakthroughs in these areas could enhance the U.S. position in Asia; major setbacks in one or more of them could substantially weaken the ability of the United States to pursue the broad objectives of promoting security and stability, economic openness and development, and U.S. values in Asia. Though many of the negative contingencies noted below may not occur or result in substantial adverse trends for U.S. policy, concern over these possibilities is sure to preoccupy U.S. leaders over the next few years.

There are so many areas where U.S. policy could be diverted or negatively affected that it seems prudent to forecast an overall U.S. policy stance in Asia for the next few years that will be somewhat weaker than in the past two years. The existing strengths of U.S. leadership in Asia should allow U.S. officials to manage potential adverse developments and preoccupations relatively effectively, barring convergence of several major crises. However, U.S. policy also appears not to be in a position to pursue major strategic initiatives. U.S. leaders most likely will be preoccupied with a wide range of serious challenges and will endeavor to preserve U.S. interests in Asia by pursuing existing policies and limiting damage from negative developments.

Immediately after the relatively smooth U.S.-led military campaign in Iraq, the U.S. government appeared to be in a stronger position to manage post-war Iraq and avoid major complications for U.S. policy in the Middle East. However, the situation remained complicated and delicate, involving major controversies over post-war Iraq, relations with Iran and Syria, and the Middle East peace process. If U.S. policy is perceived to be failing because of protracted instability in Iraq, successful terrorist attacks against U.S. targets in the region or elsewhere, or major splits among world powers over policies in post-war Iraq, this would adversely affect overall U.S. leadership in Asia.[31] Such circumstances would almost certainly place U.S. policy on the defensive.

The large-scale deployment of military forces and other government resources to the U.S.-led war and occupation in Iraq seem to ensure that America's strategic emphasis will focus on Southwest Asia for the rest of the U.S. presidential term and probably longer. Stabilizing Iraq and avoiding negative trends in the Persian Gulf and the Middle East represent large tasks for U.S. leaders. Building and maintaining international coalitions to help with peacekeeping, reconstruction, and establishing good government in Iraq require U.S. officials to engage in attentive diplomacy and other persuasive efforts in the face of widespread international antipathy to the U.S. decision to launch the war against Iraq without the full endorsement of the UN Security Council.[32]

Popular and elite opinion in much of the world opposed the U.S. war and demonstrated broader concerns over U.S. dominance and "hegemony" in world affairs. France, Germany, Russia, and governments in the Middle East and much of the Muslim world strongly criticized the U.S. decision to attack Iraq. In much of Asia, however, the governments stood at odds with their publics and non-government elites and reacted more pragmatically in dealing with the United States over the Iraq war and broader concerns flowing from U.S. international dominance. Prime Minister Koizumi was outspoken in support of Japan's U.S. ally, quick to lend military support within the confines of Japan's existing constraints on deployments abroad, and prominent in providing post-war economic assistance. South Korea's new president pushed a reluctant parliament to approve the deployment of non-combat troops to Iraq, repeatedly stressing the importance for South Korea of preserving a close alliance relationship with the United States in the face of North Korea's provocations. Chinese leaders showed little interest in being associated closely with international resistance to U.S. leadership in Iraq, and endeavored to persuade U.S. officials, without any resort to pressure or confrontation, of the utility of the United Nations playing a leading role in post-war Iraq. Similarly, India's government remained restrained in criticizing the U.S. attack on Iraq, even though there was political pressure in the country for a much tougher anti-U.S. stance.[33]

Among the broader security concerns preoccupying U.S. leaders is how to manage the wide-ranging military deployments throughout Southwest Asia that have expanded markedly as a result of the wars in Afghanistan and Iraq. These deployments remain sensitive and often controversial in host countries. Balancing the utility of such commitments with potential adverse consequences for host governments and broader U.S. interests in regional stability requires constant attention and willingness to adjust the U.S. posture when required by circumstances.[34] Further complications arise from the broader U.S. drive to carry out a global realignment of U.S. forces stationed abroad in order to deal with twenty-first century threats.

Other contingencies that could seriously weaken U.S. policy in Asia include possible setbacks in the war on terrorism and broader U.S. economic trends. Setbacks in the war on terrorism could involve large-scale terrorist attacks, possibly involving weapons of mass destruction (WMD), against U.S. or allied targets, and regime failure in such front-line states as Afghanistan or Pakistan, where political conditions and governance remain unstable and weak. Pakistan's recent role as a major proliferator of WMD equipment and technology to North Korea and others is a serious added complication for U.S. policy. A major—possibly nuclear—war between India and Pakistan precipitated by disputes over Kashmir or other issues would be disastrous. World economic trends remain uncertain in 2003, with the U.S. economy among those grappling with slow recovery and large-scale government budget and trade deficits. If past practice is any guide, major setbacks in the pace and scope of the U.S. recovery are likely to prompt heavy partisan attack, as candidates seeking to unseat President Bush in the 2004 election target the costs to the United States of the administration's wide-ranging military deployments abroad.[35]

In Korea, the Bush administration had some success in the immediate aftermath of the war in Iraq in limiting the damage from the crises in U.S. relations with North Korea and in U.S. relations with South Korea, but few predict a quick solution to either set of problems. The crises place U.S. policy on the peninsula in a reactive stance—responding to unanticipated events and endeavoring to buy time, limiting the damage to U.S. interests, and holding out the possibility of resolution in accord with U.S. interests.

North Korea's breaking of nuclear safeguards, and other provocative actions in 2002 and 2003, forced the Bush administration to retreat from its initial hard line. Washington settled on an approach that sought to involve other powers and international organizations in dealing with the North Korea problem, while maintaining that the United States would not be "blackmailed" by North Korean threats. For months, the Bush administration refused to agree to North Korean demands for direct U.S.-North Korean talks until North Korea provided nuclear safeguards. This resulted in a "no war/no negotiation" standoff that was roundly criticized in the United States and abroad. Critics in both U.S. political parties and overseas commentators saw major inconsistencies in the U.S. government's stance toward North Korea and Iraq, and warned that delaying talks risked North Korea developing nuclear weapons, possibly for export to terrorists for use against the United States. South Korea, Russia, and China were prominent among international powers pressing for a more flexible U.S. stance.[36]

With the help of China and possibly others, a compromise was reached and three-party (North Korea-United States-China) talks began in April 2003. They featured a North Korean delegate telling a U.S. counterpart that the North already had nuclear weapons, demonstrating that coming to terms over safeguards regarding North Korea's overt and covert nuclear programs would be even more difficult than the protracted negotiations that led to the 1994 Agreed Framework accord. The Bush administration in 2003 made some progress in forging a broader international consensus in the face of Pyongyang provocations, notably seeing China play a more active role in trying to restrain the North and seek a diplomatic solution. Nonetheless, this delicate consensus probably would shatter in the event the United States resorts to military initiatives or other forceful action to deal with the crisis. U.S.-led efforts to monitor and intercept illegal North Korean trade[37] and to seek international sanctions against the North Korean regime elicited strong reservations and opposition from both China and South Korea in mid-2003.[38]

Washington reacted to the crisis in U.S.-South Korea relations with diplomacy to build bridges to the new South Korean government along with the fastest paced U.S. negotiations with an Asian ally to realign U.S. forces in 30 years. The U.S. push to reach an accord in 2003 on deploying large numbers of U.S. troops and dependents south of Seoul, and possibly to reduce the size of U.S. forces in Korea, raised angst in the new South Korean government. Seoul responded with efforts to reassure Americans and others of South Korea's determination to strengthen alliance relations. President Roh Moo Hyun not only pressed reluctant legislators to support South Korean troop deployments to Iraq but also contradicted his own criticism of U.S. policy during the December 2002 election campaign by offering paeans of support for the United States during extensive interviews with U.S. media and other prominent Americans in 2003. Such steps facilitated closer U.S.-South Korea official contact, and the U.S.-South Korean summit of May 2003 passed without incident. However, they had only a small effect in the uphill struggle to resolve U.S.-South Korea tensions, generated by deep differences and strong South Korean resentment over the asymmetrical nature of the alliance relationship. In addition, the United States and South Korea differ over how to deal with North Korea, and evince divergent approaches to China, Japan, and regional security trends.[39]

Southeast Asia remained a second front in the U.S.-led war on terrorism. The U.S. government sought the support of the region's governments— many with large Muslim populations—for the wars in Afghanistan and Iraq, and for greater cooperation in confronting pockets of extremism that make Southeast Asia vulnerable to terrorism. U.S. summits with several Southeast Asian leaders after the September 2001 attacks achieved mixed results. Strong actions against terrorist groups by Singapore and Malaysia were welcomed by Washington, which criticized Indonesia's less resolute actions, at least until the Bali bombings of October 2002 underlined the danger terrorists posed to Indonesia and energized its government to act against them.

The small U.S. military deployment against the Abu Sayyaf militants in the southern Philippines in 2002 had the strong support of President Gloria Macapagal-Arroyo, though broader political support in the Philippines was weaker. Plans for a larger U.S. military deployment that were leaked in 2003 challenged deeply rooted Philippine sensitivities about U.S. combat activities in the country and were deemed unconstitutional; the deployments were subsequently cancelled. The Arroyo government appeared interested in enlisting U.S. support for military efforts against the much larger Moro Islamic Liberation Front (MILF) insurgency, since the group had some contacts with international terrorist groups. The United States provided the Philippines with expanded aid and training, but was reluctant to be drawn into broader counter-insurgency in the country. President Arroyo was among the few Southeast Asian leaders to support the U.S.-led attack on Iraq, which for a time was widely criticized in the region. The short duration of the war and the relatively small number of casualties helped to ameliorate the negative impact of the Iraq war on U.S. relations with the region, though popular and elite opinion remained sharply critical of U.S. "unilateralism" in international affairs.[40]

Progress in implementing U.S.-ASEAN declarations to cooperate against terrorism and to heighten vigilance against security dangers in the region saw numerous arrests and actions curbing the freedom of extremist groups. The Bali bombings—the worst terrorist atrocity in Southeast Asia— increased regional cooperation with the United States against terrorism. The U.S. effort to improve cooperation with Indonesia's military remained hampered by legal restrictions backed by concerns in the U.S. Congress and elsewhere that Indonesia's military had not done enough to improve its human rights practices and to bring to justice military personnel who engaged in gross violations of human rights.[41] Meanwhile, the Bush administration tried to build more constructive relations with ASEAN on more conventional political and economic issues. Most important was the U.S. Enterprise for ASEAN Initiative announced in late 2002 that planned a series of U.S. free trade agreements with those in ASEAN willing to meet U.S. free trade conditions.[42]

The death of scores of Australian tourists in the Bali bombings also solidified the Australian government's strong resolve in support of the broad U.S. objectives in the war on terrorism. Prime Minister John Howard articulated his own version of a doctrine of preemption against terrorist threats to Australia, causing some concern in neighboring Indonesia and Malaysia and opposition at home. His government remained steadfast in supporting the U.S.-led attack on Iraq, despite large-scale anti-war demonstrations in Australia.[43] Critics in Australia and abroad saw Howard's pro-U.S. leanings coming at the expense of Australia's need to collaborate more closely with its Asian neighbors, some of whom, notably Malaysian Prime Minister Mahathir Mohamad, exclude Australia from regional fora like ASEAN+3 on grounds of its "pro-West" leanings.

Conclusion

The crisis with North Korea presents the most immediate problem for U.S. policy in Asia. The most likely outcome is a protracted process involving diplomacy, negotiations, and possible sanctions and military moves to seek safeguards regarding North Korea's nuclear program. Recent U.S. policy regarding North Korea buys time and keeps South Korea and other powers in an ostensibly common front, but it may not resolve North Korea's nuclear weapons development, or deep U.S. differences with South Korea, China, and others at home and abroad on how to deal with the North. Negotiations and other aspects of the U.S. and international efforts to deal with North Korea over the next months (and possibly years) may bring episodes of improvement in U.S. relations with concerned powers balanced with episodes of crisis. The process is likely to be prolonged because of the mix of Pyongyang's rigidity and frequent brinksmanship, Washington's refusal to be blackmailed, and seemingly insufficient U.S. power/influence to coerce the North. In this context, U.S. alliance management (notably, relations with South Korea) and great power diplomacy (notably, relations with China) over this issue will be complicated and probably difficult. The Bush administration's ability to manage U.S. domestic criticism may also be challenged, especially at times of tension with North Korea. Overall, the process promises to preoccupy Washington and weaken U.S. leadership in Asian affairs.

Less likely is a more assertive U.S. policy involving U.S. pressure or perhaps military attack. This could come in response to a North Korean nuclear test or transfer of nuclear material to terrorists. Such an assertive U.S. stance in the face of North Korea's military power and the strong opposition of key powers—especially South Korea and China—makes a war on the Korean Peninsula more probable. Also less likely is Washington offering major concessions to Pyongyang without a clear path to the North's denuclearization in order to ease the crisis. Concessions would smooth U.S. relations with South Korea, China, and others in Asia, but would face strong opposition from conservatives in Congress and elsewhere.

Other potential flashpoints in Asia include the Taiwan Strait. At least for the duration of the Bush administration, Chinese leaders seem sufficiently constrained by U.S. power. They also seem satisfied with recent trends in cross-Strait relations—especially burgeoning mainland-Taiwan economic relations. These circumstances appear likely to prompt Chinese leaders to avoid aggressive actions. There probably will be little let up in the Chinese military build-up opposite Taiwan as PRC leaders have set a long-term course to achieve military dominance over Taiwan.[44] Taiwan's leaders chafe under Chinese policy, and seek to take initiatives in cross-Strait or international relations, sometimes at the risk of disrupting the prevailing modus vivendi in cross-Strait ties. However, the Bush administration in the recent past has come down hard on Taiwanese leaders who risk such disruption, and the fear of alienating U.S. support probably will be sufficient to curb possible Taiwan actions that might provoke a harsh response from China.[45]

Southeast Asia is an area of serious concern in the war on terrorism but appears to hold few major problems for U.S. policy, though managing sometimes difficult U.S. security ties with countries like Indonesia and the Philippines represents a complication in the broader U.S. war on terror. As noted earlier, such major failures for U.S. policy in Central and South Asia as government collapse in Afghanistan or Pakistan, or a war between India and Pakistan, remain distinct possibilities; there appears to be too much at stake for U.S. leaders not to give a high priority to diplomatic and other efforts to prevent such negative outcomes.

In this context, the longer-term U.S. strategic concern with the rise of China and the possible threat it poses for U.S. interests in Asia—a view widely prevalent at the early stages of the Bush administration—will receive less attention in the next few years. Washington's earlier focus on post-Cold War changing power relations in Asia, centered on the rise of China, Japan's relative decline, and other factors, was interrupted by the war on terrorism, the military campaigns against Afghanistan and Iraq, and the ascendancy of U.S. power and military involvement in southwest Asia. China and the other Asian powers remain preoccupied and unwilling to confront U.S. power; this situation seems likely to keep them from seriously challenging U.S. leadership in Asia for the next few years. Moreover, dealing with the North Korean nuclear challenge poses an added preoccupation that at least over the short term reduces the likelihood that China or other Asian powers will adopt more assertive and potentially disruptive policies. They presumably would be loath to worsen an already delicate situation in ways that would adversely affect their interests in development and security. It is possible over the longer term, later in this decade, that recently installed Chinese leaders may decide on a more assertive and less accommodating posture toward the United States in Asia, notably over Taiwan. This presumably would raise the priority of the Chinese strategic threat in U.S. policy considerations.

In sum, the Korean crises involving both North and South Korea seem unlikely to be resolved soon or satisfactorily. The process for dealing with the Korean crises will preoccupy U.S. policy and on balance will probably weaken U.S. leadership in the region. Nevertheless, the crises appear likely to remain manageable, particularly given the continued broad strengths in U.S. power and influence in Asia. Those strengths will continue to support U.S. regional leadership, notably in the war on terrorism, and regional stability and development compatible with U.S. interests.

If protracted Korean crises were to combine with other significant complications for U.S. policy, it would be more difficult for the U.S. government to manage the crises smoothly and it would increase the likelihood of disruption of U.S. interests in Northeast Asia. Those complications include the factors noted above—failure of U.S. policy toward Iraq, a major U.S. economic downturn, failure of governance in Pakistan or Afghanistan, an India-Pakistan war, a military confrontation in the Taiwan Strait, and/or a major terrorist attack on the United States.

Endnotes

[1] Aaron Friedberg, "United States," in Richard Ellings and Aaron Friedberg with Michael Wills, eds., *Strategic Asia 2002–03: Asian Aftershocks*, Seattle: The National Bureau of Asian Research, 2002, p. 20; Jonathan Pollack, "Learning by Doing: The Bush Administration in East Asia," in Robert Hathaway and Wilson Lee, *George W. Bush and Asia*, Washington, DC: Woodrow Wilson Center for Scholars, 2003, p. 58; "U.S. commander wants Guam military buildup," Kyodo, August 25, 2002; "U.S. attack submarines moving to Guam," Reuters, October 1, 2002; James McIntyre, "U.S. command seeks buildup in Pacific," CNN, February 1, 2003.

[2] Greg Jaffe, "Pentagon prepares to scatter soldiers to remote corners," *Wall Street Journal*, May 27, 2003, p. 1.

[3] Michael Swaine, "Reverse Course? The Fragile Turnaround in U.S.-China Relations," *Carnegie Endowment for International Peace Policy Brief*, no. 22, February 2003, pp. 1–3; Catharin Dalpino, "The Bush Administration and Southeast Asia," in Hathaway and Lee, *George W. Bush and Asia*, p. 107. See the chapters on Terrorism and on Southeast Asia in this volume.

[4] See the chapters on South Korea, North Korea and Northeast Asia herein.

[5] See the Korea chapter in last year's Strategic Asia volume, Nicholas Eberstadt, "Korea," in Ellings and Friedberg, *Strategic Asia 2002–03: Asian Aftershocks*, pp. 131–82.

[6] See the South Korea chapter in this volume. See also Ralph Cossa, "Diplomacy Fails with Iraq; Is North Korea Next?" and Donald Gross, "Tensions Escalate in Korea as the U.S. Targets Iraq," *Comparative Connections*, April 2003, <www.csis.org/pacfor>; Larry Niksch, "Korea-U.S. Relations: Issues for Congress," *Congressional Research Service Issue Brief*, no. IB98045, May 5, 2003.

[7] *What the World Thinks in 2002*, Pew Research Center, December 2002, <http://people-press.org/reports>; Raymond Copson, "Iraq War: Background and Issues Overview," *Congressional Research Service Report*, no. RL31715, updated April 22, 2003.

[8] See quarterly reviews of Asian government reactions in *Comparative Connections*. See also the specific country chapters in this volume.

[9] See the China chapter in this volume.

[10] Some contrast the Bush administration's emphasis on national security issues with the Clinton administration's emphasis on international economic initiatives. Robert Hathaway, "Introduction," in Hathaway and Lee, *George W. Bush and Asia*, p. 7.

[11] Most of the contributors in an authoritative Woodrow Wilson International Center assessment of the Bush administration's policy toward Asia were sharply critical. See Hathaway and Lee, *George W. Bush and Asia*. For a more favorable assessment of U.S. policy in Asia see Satu A. Limaye, "Almost Quiet on the Asia-Pacific Front" in *Asia-Pacific Responses to U.S. Security Policies*, Honolulu: Asia Pacific Center for Security Studies, 2003.

[12] Michael Swaine, "Reverse Course? The Fragile Turnaround in U.S.-China Relations," pp. 1–3; Bonnie Glaser, "China and U.S. Disagree, but with Smiles," *Comparative Connections*, April 2003; Robert Sutter, "Grading Bush's China Policy," *Pacnet Newsletter*, no. 10, March 8, 2002.

[13] Ralph Cossa, "Bush-Roh: Closing the Gap," *Pacnet Newsletter*, no. 20, May 20, 2003.

[14] Jaffe, "Pentagon prepares to scatter soldiers to remote corners," *Wall Street Journal*; Paul Wolfowitz, "Sustaining the U.S. Commitment in Asia," *Pacnet Newsletter*, no. 22A, June 5, 2003; and Ralph Cossa, "Force Restructuring Anxiety," *Pacnet Newsletter*, no. 22, June 3, 2003.

[15] Figures from U.S. Department of Commerce, 2002. Chinese government figures show Chinese exports to the United States as much less than seen in U.S. government figures.

[16] The United States did not seek to bring China's human rights conditions be-

fore the UN Human Rights Commission in 2003. George Gedda, "U.S. won't propose resolution on China," Associated Press, April 11, 2003.

[17] "The acceptability of American power," *Economist*, June 29, 2002.

[18] See the China and Japan chapters in this volume.

[19] Benjamin Self, "China and Japan: a Façade of Friendship," *Washington Quarterly*, vol. 26, no. 1 (Winter 2002–2003), pp. 77–88; Robert Sutter, *The United States and East Asia*, Lanham, Md.: Rowman and Littlefield, 2003, pp. 199–200, 222–23.

[20] Hugo Restall, "Tough love for China," *Wall Street Journal*, October 21, 2002.

[21] Richard Cronin, "Japan-U.S. Relations: Issue for Congress," *Congressional Research Service Issue Brief, no. IB97004*, updated April 25, 2003.

[22] Ralph Cossa, "Diplomacy Fails with Iraq, is North Korea Next?" *Comparative Connections*, April 2003.

[23] See the Japan, China, Russia, and India chapters of this volume.

[24] See the Japan chapter in this volume and Brad Glosserman, "U.S.-Japan Relations: How High is Up?" *Comparative Connections*, April 2003; John Miller, "The Glacier Moves: Japan's Response to U.S. Security Policies," in *Asia-Pacific Responses to U.S. Security Policies*, Honolulu: Asia Pacific Center for Security Studies, 2003.

[25] See the India chapter in this volume and Mohan Malik, "High Hopes: India's Response to U.S. Security Policies," in *Asia-Pacific Responses to U.S. Security Policies*, Honolulu: Asia Pacific Center for Security Studies, 2003.

[26] See the Russia chapter in this volume and Joseph Ferguson, "U.S.-Russian Partnership: a Casualty of War?" *Comparative Connections*, April 2003; Rajan Menon, "Why Russia says 'nyet' to the U.S.," *Chicago Tribune*, March 12, 2003. See also William Wohlforth, "Russia" in Ellings and Friedberg, *Strategic Asia 2002–03: Asian Aftershocks*, pp. 183–222.

[27] See the China chapter in this volume; and Andrew Nathan and Bruce Gilley, *China's New Rulers: The Secret Files*, New York: New York Review Book, 2002, pp. 207–09. See also Thomas Christensen, "China" in Ellings and Friedberg, *Strategic Asia 2002–03: Asian Aftershocks*, pp. 51–94.

[28] Michael Swaine, "Reverse Course? The Fragile Turnaround in U.S.-China Relations"; Michael Yahuda, "China's Win-Win Globalization," *YaleGlobal online*, February 19, 2003, <www.yaleglobal.yale.edu>.

[29] Joseph Kahn, "Hands across the Pacific," *New York Times*, November 11, 2002.

[30] See the China chapter in this volume and Kerry Dumbaugh, "China-U.S. Relations," *Congressional Research Service Issue Brief*, no. IB98018, updated March 14, 2002.

[31] Copson, "Iraq War: Background and Issues Overview," *Congressional Research Service Report*.

[32] Thomas Donnelly, "Lessons of a three week war," *Weekly Standard*, April 22, 2003; Thomas Donnelly, "Brave New World: an Enduring Pax Americana," *AEI National Security Outlook*, April 2003.

[33] See the respective chapters in this volume. See also *Asia-Pacific Responses to U.S. Security Policies*.

[34] "Unintended Consequences of an Expanded U.S. Military Presence in the Muslim World," *Schlesinger Working Group Scope Paper*, Washington, DC:

Georgetown University – Institute for the Study of Diplomacy, March 18, 2003.

[35] For a review of post-Iraq war issues for the United States, see Copson, *Iraq War: Background and Issues Overview*.

[36] See the chapter on Northeast Asia in this volume; Gross, "Tensions Escalate in Korea as the U.S. Targets Iraq," *Comparative Connections*, April 2003; and Ralph Cossa, "Trials, Tribulations, Trends and Tirades" *Comparative Connections*, January 2003.

[37] Guy Dinmore, "U.S. plans to confront North Korea on the high seas," *Financial Times*, June 5, 2003.

[38] Gross, "Tension Escalate in Korea as the U.S. Targets Iraq," *Comparative Connections*; David Sanger, "North Korea and U.S. plan talks in Beijing next week," *New York Times*, April 16, 2003; Ralph Cossa, "U.S.-DPRK: Who Blinked and Why?" *Pacnet Newsletter*, no. 18, April 21, 2003.

[39] Victor Cha, "The Coming Change in the U.S.-Korea Alliance," *The National Interest*, April 9, 2003; Seongho Sheen, "Grudging Partner: South Korea's Response to U.S. Security Policies," in *Asia-Pacific Responses to U.S. Security Policies*; "The president counsels patience," *Far Eastern Economic Review*, May 22, 2003.

[40] See the Southeast Asia and Terrorism chapters in this volume. Anthony Smith, "Indonesia's Response to U.S. Security Policies" and Satu A. Limaye, "Almost Quiet on the Asia-Pacific Front;" Catharin Dalpino, "The Bush Administration and Southeast Asia," pp. 107–111; Richard Baker, "U.S. Southeast Asia Relations in the Shadow of Iraq," *Comparative Connection*, April 2003.

[41] Peter Brookes, "The Anti-Terrorist Coalition in the Pacific," *Heritage Lectures*, December 12, 2002.

[42] Trish Saywell and Murray Hiebert, "Engaging the U.S. with trade," *Far Eastern Economic Review*, May 22, 2003; "U.S. eyes free trade deals with Five nations," *Washington Times*, May 9, 2003.

[43] "Howard: Why Iraq must be disarmed," CNN, March 13, 2003.

[44] U.S. Department of Defense, "Annual Report on the Military Power of the People's Republic of China, 2002," <www.defenselink.mil/news/Jul2002/p07122002_p133-02.html>.

[45] David Brown, "Chen Adopts a More Cautious Approach," *Comparative Connections*, April 2003.

China – Key Indicators and Forecasts

Economy and Trade	2002^a	2003^b	2004^b
GDP ($tr) / (PPP GDP)	1.2 (PPP GDP in 2002 = $5.7 tr)		
GDP growth (%)	8.0	7.5	7.5
Inflation (%)	-0.8	0.2	1.5
Budget balance (% of GDP)	1.9	1.4	1.1
Major export destinations (2001)	U.S. (20%), Hong Kong (17%), Japan (17%)		

Population and Energy	2002^a	2005^b	2010^b
Population (m)	1,279.2	1,302.2	1,342.8
Population growth (%)	0.6	0.6	0.7
Oil production (m bbl/d)	3.4	3.5	3.6
Oil consumption (m bbl/d)	5.3	5.1	6.2

Politics	
President	Hu Jintao (CPP, since Mar 2003)
Dominant party	Chinese Communist Party (since Oct 1949)
Next party congress	2007

Military	
Armed forces (2002)	2,270,000
Defense expenditure (2001)	$46.1 bn (est.) (4.0% of GDP)
Conventional capabilities	World's largest military with poor equipment
	Ongoing modernization efforts, continued
	naval, fighter, and cruise missile build-ups
Weapons of mass destruction	Moderate nuclear arsenal (passive posture)
	Some proliferation activities will continue

Source: The National Bureau of Asian Research, compiled from International Monetary Fund, *World Economic Outlook*; Central Intelligence Agency, *World Factbook*; U.S. Census Bureau, *International Data Base*; Energy Information Administration, *Country Analysis Brief—China*; International Institute of Strategic Studies, *The Military Balance*. Notes: a) Data for 2002 may be estimates; b) Data for 2003, 2004, 2005, and 2010 are projections. Additional data on China are available in the Strategic Asia Database at <http://strategicasia.nbr.org>.

SOURCES OF STABILITY IN U.S.-CHINA SECURITY RELATIONS

Thomas J. Christensen and Michael A. Glosny

ABSTRACT

Since the period before the Tiananmen massacre, U.S.-PRC relations have never been as good as they are today. For a combination of international and domestic reasons, the two countries have decided to cooperate on a range of security issues, including North Korea and the war on terror. One important reason for the current cooperation is that Beijing and Washington both have managed the Taiwan issue more deftly than in the past. In particular, Washington's assurance that it does not support Taiwanese independence has allowed an increasingly sophisticated CCP foreign policy elite to be more tolerant of U.S. security policies in other areas, such as Central Asia, Southwest Asia, Southeast Asia, and North Korea. Beijing is also less likely to destabilize bilateral relations through threats, bluster, or coercion against Taiwan, the United States, or its regional allies. This chapter analyzes the reasons for this cooperation and questions whether it might disappear if certain conditions were to change in the next several years.

Thomas Christensen is Professor of Politics and International Affairs at Princeton University. Michael Glosny is a doctoral candidate in political science at the Massachusetts Institute of Technology. They are grateful to Richard Ellings, Aaron Friedberg, James Przystup, Michael Swaine, Michael Wills, an anonymous reviewer, and the other authors in this volume, for helpful comments.

Introduction

Since the period prior to the Tiananmen massacre of June 4, 1989, U.S.-PRC relations have never been as good as they are today. This is particularly remarkable given the Bush administration's early tough approach to China, the EP-3 crisis of April 2001, and the continued build-up of the Chinese military. In addition, many aspects of the U.S. global war on terror had the potential of aggravating concerns about U.S. encirclement in the People's Republic of China (PRC). Despite these potentially destabilizing trends, U.S.-PRC relations have improved dramatically since September 11, 2001. For a combination of international and domestic reasons, the two have decided to cooperate actively on a variety of important issues.

One important reason that Washington and Beijing have been able to maintain a spirit of cooperation is that both have managed the Taiwan issue more deftly than in the past. Beijing is more confident than it has been in previous years in its ability to prevent Taiwanese independence and to encourage Taiwanese accommodation of the mainland without the use of force. This confidence has precluded much of Beijing's provocative bluster toward Taiwan in the period 1995–2000. There are several reasons for this increased confidence, including economic trends across the Strait and the steady build-up of the PRC's coercive power. However, one centrally important reason for the higher comfort levels in Beijing has been the successful and nuanced deterrence strategy that the Bush administration has developed toward cross-Strait relations, particularly since the spring of 2002. Washington has done more than simply threaten to intervene if the PRC opens fire on Taiwan or to transfer advanced weapons to the island; it has also reassured Beijing directly that the United States does not support Taiwanese independence and will not use U.S. military superiority to help bring about such an outcome. Precisely because the United States is focused on the global war on terror, Beijing remains confident, at least for the time being, that Washington will be reluctant to provoke conflict with the mainland over the Taiwan issue. U.S. distraction elsewhere and the need for PRC cooperation in the region signal to security analysts in Beijing that the Bush administration's assurances on Taiwan are not just empty diplomatic gestures. When Beijing is confident that the United States does not plan to encourage permanent Taiwanese separation from the mainland, Chinese Communist Party (CCP) elites are much more tolerant of and cooperative with U.S. security policies in other areas, such as Central Asia, Southwest Asia, Southeast Asia, and North Korea.

Domestic political factors in the PRC have also contributed to improved U.S.-PRC relations. The most prominent of these is the ongoing political transition to a younger generation of leaders who seem less myopic and more aware of the counterproductive nature of bluster and belligerence in cross-Strait relations and in the PRC's relations with the United States and regional actors. The 16th Party Congress in November 2002 and the National People's Congress (NPC) in March 2003 heralded the new leadership of Party General Secretary and President Hu Jintao. In November, Hu became General Secretary of the CCP, while loyalists of former president Jiang Zemin like Zeng Qinghong, gained prominent positions on the Standing Committee of the Politburo. In March, Hu Jintao became president of the PRC; Jiang Zemin maintained his powerful position as chairman of the State Central Military Commission (CMC); and, as long anticipated, Li Zhaoxing replaced Tang Jiaxuan as foreign minister.[1]

Although these high profile meetings are important, the generational transition process among advisors and top officials has been under way for a long time and was hardly completed at the NPC. For example, Jiang continues to wield considerable power on security policy from his chairmanship on the State CMC and on general Party matters through his well-placed protégés. That said, particularly since the NPC and the active campaign against SARS that followed it in the spring of 2003, Hu Jintao seems to have consolidated his institutional leadership much faster than many expected, especially in the arena of foreign affairs and security affairs, where he seemed weakest.[2] Although Hu is something of an enigma, there is cautious optimism in the PRC that once he consolidates his power he will push for somewhat greater transparency and accountability in PRC politics, as well as more flexible thinking in foreign affairs.[3]

Rumors of internal Party struggles are always intriguing, but too much focus on leadership changes can steal attention from more fundamental realities in PRC domestic politics that must be of concern to leaders in both the Jiang and the Hu camps. The CCP as a whole remains worried about social and economic stability at home. The need to produce new jobs for the unemployed and underemployed during China's massive economic restructuring means that PRC leaders need to avoid unnecessary conflict with key economic partners like Japan, the United States, and Taiwan. The concern for domestic stability is, of course, a double-edged sword for PRC security policy. Trouble in the economy or in politics can make the CCP more insular, but challenges to its legitimacy at home can make the Party even more sensitive to appearing weak in protecting the PRC's national pride on the world stage. If one adds to this the potential for rivalry between leadership groups during the transition, one could imagine a destabilizing competition among factions within the CCP to appear the most resolute and nationalist in handling issues such as Taiwan, should trouble arise in cross-Strait relations.[4]

The potential for tension in cross-Strait relations always exists, however, especially in the run-up to the Taiwanese presidential elections scheduled for March 2004, most mainland analysts believe that the situation will be relatively stable until after the election. One major reason for this has been the moderation of the Bush administration toward cross-Strait relations, particularly its many public and private statements of "non-support" for Taiwanese independence. Analysts in Beijing believe that there is a limit to how provocative Taipei can become toward the mainland if it does not sense a degree of support, if not encouragement, from Washington. Moreover, for various reasons, Washington's current position seems sturdy. The Bush administration will continue to have clear realpolitik incentives to limit friction with the PRC during the ongoing war on terror and the crisis over North Korea. Moreover, the domestic political environment will likely allow the President to maintain such a policy, even during a presidential election year in the United States. Popular, conservative, and hawkish George W. Bush has been relatively insulated from the normal criticisms a president might receive for offering anything less than unconditional support for Taiwan's security.

These international and domestic factors in combination suggest that neither the United States nor the PRC are looking to create tension, and both are behaving with general moderation on the one issue that could most easily lead to conflict between the two: Taiwan. This chapter will outline the reasons for near-term optimism (the next two to three years) regarding U.S.-PRC relations. We will first explore Beijing's strategic goals and why cooperation with the United States is necessary to achieve them. We will then outline the ways in which Beijing and Washington have established a generally cooperative, non-antagonistic working relationship in the war on terror, non-proliferation, and in addressing the problem of North Korean nuclear weapons development. Special attention will be paid to events relating to Taiwan that occurred since the publication of the last edition of *Strategic Asia*. Next we will discuss the early stages of new thinking by CCP leaders and why these changes *might* take deeper root. We will conclude by discussing the international and domestic factors that in the longer term might derail the current warming of bilateral relations.

The Strategic Goals of the Chinese Communist Party

The CCP's strategic goals have not changed much since the first edition of *Strategic Asia* was published in 2001. In order to understand fully the meaning of recent events in the relationship, or to make informed predictions about the future, it is necessary to review briefly the main strategic goals of the CCP:

1) Regime security—protecting the CCP from overthrow, crippling internal divisions, and infiltration by foreign or domestic opponents.
2) Preserving territorial integrity—preventing the breakup of a large, diverse, and ethnically complex nation, including the prevention of Taiwan's permanent legal separation from the mainland, preventing Tibetan independence, and quelling Muslim uprisings in Xinjiang.[5]
3) Gaining international prestige, power, and respect by increasing China's "comprehensive national power" (*zonghe guoli*), which involves not only military but economic and political power.[6]

In general, the CCP hopes to concentrate internally on its economic development and modernization, while undergoing a smooth political transition. Economic growth does more than just stabilize Chinese society and provide a degree of regime legitimacy, it is also very important for the PRC's international security strategy. Beijing has successfully used growing economic interdependence with Taiwan and other Asian neighbors, especially South Korea and the ASEAN states, to support its diplomatic strategy. This economic integration, along with the PRC's growing involvement in bilateral and multilateral agreements, have increased its prestige and power in East Asia, Southeast Asia, and Central Asia.[7] The PRC's continued success in this endeavor, especially over the past few years, means that Beijing is more confident in the face of what might otherwise seem like a full-scale encirclement campaign by the United States in Central Asia, South Asia, and along China's East Asian maritime periphery since September 11, 2001. The recognition that regional actors are unlikely to align casually with the United States against Chinese interests takes much of the edge off Beijing's concerns about what might otherwise appear to be a tense, zero-sum competition in the region with an economically and militarily superior power.

Given this general sense of confidence, some of the CCP's strategic writers have emphasized that the next two decades provide China a "strategic opportunity" (*zhanlüe jiyu*) that Beijing needs to "grasp" by avoiding unnecessary conflict and concentrating on economic and military modernization.[8] One recent article in an influential journal goes further still, including in the "strategic opportunity" the goal of political liberalization and democratization as a way to improve the PRC's prestige and its strategic position in relation to Taiwan, the United States, and regional nations.[9]

Beijing's economic modernization and strategic goals require a stable if not friendly relationship with the United States, and would be very difficult to accomplish in the face of a hostile one. The CCP's regime security rests on its ability to keep people employed and the economy growing. With China's integration with the world economy, economic downturns or sanctions resulting from a rupture in the relationship could threaten PRC growth, and, thereby, CCP regime security. Unnecessarily hostile relations with the United States can also make it more difficult for Beijing to maintain China's territorial integrity, because Washington might alter its position of non-support for Taiwanese independence. In terms of gaining power and prestige in the region, the PRC will have an easier time if it is seen as cooperative toward the United States and as a respected actor in Washington. Asia specialists often warn U.S. foreign policy elites that they should not force regional actors to make the devil's choice between China and the United States in their strategic orientation. The same advice applies to CCP foreign policy elites, and they seem increasingly aware of this.

However, Beijing elites also view military modernization and a stronger regional military posture as helpful for achieving all three security goals above. Continued military modernization can improve the CCP's nationalist credentials at home, deter Taiwan's formal independence, potentially coerce Taiwan into surrendering to Beijing's minimal if not maximal demands, and increase the PRC's regional power and prestige. So, while the PRC has focused on maintaining fast-paced economic growth, in the past few years it has also increased the official defense budget and expenditures on important extra-budgetary items, such as arms imports from Russia, at a rate considerably higher than the GNP growth rate.[10]

As discussed in detail in last year's *Strategic Asia* volume, the PRC's strategic focus in its military modernization is largely on developing more credible ways to coerce Taiwan and to develop asymmetric strategies that would delay, dissuade, or reverse any U.S. attempts to assist the island militarily. For example, the People's Liberation Army (PLA) has emphasized development of a more potent submarine force—by relying on imported Russian submarines, torpedoes, and advanced propulsion system technology and accelerating domestic production of submarines and weapons systems. The PLA is also exploiting a combination of Russian and indigenous knowledge to improve its ballistic and cruise missile capabilities.[11] Protecting Taiwan from the threat of coercion is much more difficult than protecting it from invasion and domination, so we should expect Washington and Taipei to react in ways that will almost guarantee a security competition of sorts between the United States and the PRC and across the Taiwan Strait. The key question is whether the tensions that normally accompany such a competition will be calmed or exacerbated by the general political atmosphere in U.S.-China relations and cross-Strait relations. For reasons discussed below, we believe that for the next few years the tensions surrounding this security competition should be manageable and seem less likely to spiral out of control than they did just a few years ago.

Improved Atmospherics, Cooperation in the War on Terror, and Tepid PRC Opposition to the War in Iraq

Since September 11, 2001, and especially since the spring of 2002, U.S.-PRC relations have been quite stable and, one might say, almost warm. The top leaders of each country have met face-to-face four times and have exchanged several phone calls; several other visits, exchanges, and phone calls involving high-level officials on both sides have also taken place. The rhetoric of "strategic competitor," "threat," and "enemy," has been traded in, at least on the American side, for terms like "candid, constructive and cooperative," "side by side," and "great friend."[12] The most notable and vivid example of this new relationship was then-President Jiang Zemin's October 2002 trip to President Bush's ranch in Crawford, Texas, a place reserved for friends. While one should be careful not to read too much into atmospherics and summit-related rhetoric, there has been a noticeable warming in the terms in which both sides speak of each other. Moreover, beyond the rhetoric and the diplomatic flourishes there has been real mutual understanding and concrete cooperation between the two sides on important issues.

As discussed in last year's edition of *Strategic Asia*, for a range of reasons related to its strategic objectives, Beijing chose not to oppose U.S. efforts in the global war on terror and, in fact, actively assisted Washington's effort by urging Pakistan to support the war in Afghanistan, tracking finances of terror groups, providing intelligence on groups in Central Asia and Southeast Asia, and granting financial and humanitarian support to post-Taliban Afghanistan.[13] The United States reciprocated this cooperative behavior in August 2002 by branding the East Turkestan Independence Movement (ETIM), which militantly opposes Beijing's rule over Xinjiang, as a "terrorist organization" and freezing its assets in the United States. This policy suggested a true partnership in the global war on terror and helped reduce mistrust of the United States in China over the Taiwan issue. By publicly condemning ETIM, the Bush administration reduced the credibility in Beijing of the theory that the United States was trying to contain and split China by supporting several independence groups around the country, most notably in Taiwan.[14]

The PRC also did not actively oppose the U.S. war in Iraq. Beijing was usually mentioned at the end of the list of opponents, if at all. In the summer of 2002, several interlocutors suggested not only that the PRC would not veto a UN resolution for war, but would want to support it to help build goodwill with the United States.[15] The PRC supported UN Security Council Resolution 1441 and demanded Iraqi compliance with this and other

UN demands for Iraqi disarmament. Overt Russian and French opposition to the use of force before the war allowed the PRC to backslide into opposition at the eleventh hour. But as late as January 2003, one was struck by the matter-of-fact way that the upcoming war was discussed in Beijing, the tacit acceptance of the war there, and how Beijing analysts listed Iraq as one of the areas of new-found cooperation between the United States and the PRC in this era of "great power cooperation."[16] This was a far cry from the NATO operation in Kosovo in 1999, where the PRC vigorously opposed military action in the United Nations and provided active support for the Yugoslav government during the war.

Taiwan: Reasons for Near-Term Optimism

The Taiwan issue is critically important for CCP regime stability, and is often the most important issue in U.S.-PRC relations. Stability in U.S.-PRC relations on the Taiwan issue reduces the chance for near-term crisis and conflict. It also improves the overall relationship by removing a sense of mistrust, making the CCP less likely to view other bilateral issues through the lens of zero-sum competition, and, therefore, less likely to overreact to minor irritants. General stability in U.S.-PRC relations on Taiwan also means that the PRC is less likely to respond to adjustments in U.S. security policy toward Taiwan by threatening U.S. national security interests elsewhere (e.g. by proliferating Chinese weapons to U.S. adversaries in other parts of the world) or by taking advantage of temporary U.S. strategic distractions in other military theaters to put coercive pressure on Taiwan.

As detailed in last year's edition of *Strategic Asia*, PRC analysts are relatively confident that various trends in cross-Strait relations continue to be favorable to the mainland's quest for long-term unification and unfavorable to the forces favoring Taiwan's independence. These factors include Taiwan's increasing economic dependence on the mainland, measured in tens of billions of dollars in cross-Strait trade, with a huge imbalance in Taiwan's favor, and as much as $100 billion in Taiwanese accumulated investment on the mainland. In addition, an increasing number of Taiwanese citizens (numbered in the hundreds of thousands) reside on the mainland. The steady growth of PLA coercive military options against Taiwan and the PRC's growing diplomatic weight in the region also guarantee that few regional actors, if any, would be eager to line up on Taiwan's side in a conflict.[17] Finally, there is also hope in Beijing that the pan-Blue alliance between the Kuomintang's Lien Chan and the People's First Party's James Soong will hold together and produce a new president in 2004 who is more accommodating to the mainland than President Chen Shui-bian from the traditionally pro-independence Democratic Progressive Party (DPP).[18]

A successful U.S. deterrence strategy is also a major factor for stability. Such a strategy requires both credible threats of intervention and assistance to Taiwan if the PRC were to attack the island, and credible assurances that the United States is not using its military superiority and its defense relationship with Taiwan to encourage future Taiwanese independence. By combining toughness with conditionality, the United States neither invites nor provokes a PRC attack on Taiwan and helps to stabilize cross-Strait relations.[19] The threat of U.S. intervention seems highly credible given President Bush's April 2001 pledge to "do whatever it takes" to assist in Taiwan's defense, an unprecedented arms sales package offered to Taiwan in the same month, and the reputation for resolve that the administration gained by overthrowing the Taliban in Afghanistan and Saddam Hussein's government in Iraq.[20] Given events since September 11, 2001, recent U.S. assurances to Beijing on the Taiwan issue also seem credible, at least for the time being. While the United States is focused on the global war on terror, Iraq, North Korea, and future terrorist threats, Beijing believes that Washington will continue to seek stability and the status quo across the Taiwan Strait so that it can focus on important threats to U.S. national security. When combined with political assurances that the United States does not support moves towards Taiwanese independence, the PRC's confidence over long-term trends in cross-Strait relations reduces sensitivity in Beijing to regional aspects of the U.S. global war on terror, including U.S. deployments in Central Asia, Pakistan, and the Philippines, and the increased military activity of Japan as part of the U.S.-Japan alliance.

The most important example of U.S. support for the status quo was the Bush administration's stern response to President Chen Shui-bian's August 3, 2002 statement referring to "one country on each side" of the Taiwan Strait (*yi bian yi guo*). The United States responded by sending the U.S. representative in Taipei, Douglas Paal, to express concern to the Taiwanese government. Moreover, press reports claim that prominent Republicans inside and outside the administration "read the riot act" to the Mainland Affairs Council (MAC) Chairwoman Tsai Ying-wen when she came to Washington to explain the remark. Moreover, the President and top-ranking administration officials stated repeatedly that the United States does not support Taiwanese independence.[21] The PRC press claims that, in private meetings between President Bush and President Jiang, Bush went further, stating that he "opposes" Taiwanese independence.[22] Statements of non-support for or opposition to Taiwanese independence are important because most strategic analysts in Beijing do not believe that Taipei's political leaders will risk taking provocative diplomatic moves without U.S. support. All things being equal, if the United States opposes provocative diplomatic moves in Taipei, this reduces fears on the mainland of Taiwanese independence and, thereby, reduces the likelihood of war across the Strait and across the Pacific.[23]

A parallel, constructive trend exists in mainland thinking about how to deal with Taiwan's democracy. There is a growing realization among CCP leaders that strong reactions and threats against President Chen and the DPP have been counterproductive in the past. This realization has led to patience in Beijing and has further reduced the likelihood that some statement or action by President Chen in this election season will spark a new crisis in the Taiwan Strait in the short term.[24]

Focus on war elsewhere has helped stabilize the cross-Strait situation, but may also have prevented a potential chance for improvements in cross-Strait relations. Before the war in Iraq, Chen Shui-bian's ruling DPP had planned to use the publication of an "assessment" (*pinggu*) of cross-Strait relations to improve the prospects of setting up direct trade, transportation, and communications links across the Strait (the "three links") and improve its domestic image as managers of cross-straits relations.[25] In March, the MAC suggested that the ongoing Iraq and North Korean crises made it an inappropriate time to release the assessment.[26] This was most likely the case because the war would have stolen public attention away from the assessment, thereby undercutting the domestic political advantages of its publication. By the time the Iraq war ended, the SARS crisis had scarred Beijing's image in Taiwan further and provided the DPP some political cover to shelve any accommodating proposals toward the mainland.

Non-Proliferation: Promise of Future Cooperation

According to Chinese press reports, the PRC's proliferation practices were a major topic of conversation when then-Vice President Hu Jintao met with Vice President Dick Cheney in Washington in April 2002.[27] These conversations apparently made a difference in Beijing. During Deputy Secretary of State Richard Armitage's August 2002 visit to Beijing, the PRC took initial steps to address U.S. concerns by announcing domestic "PRC Regulations on the Export of Missiles and Related Materials and Technologies."[28] On the eve of the Crawford summit in October 2002, the PRC announced several more export control measures.[29]

These moves demonstrate a growing understanding in the PRC that after September 11, non-proliferation is even more important to Washington and that Beijing needs to make strides in this area in order to improve U.S.-PRC relations. In addition to these export control measures, the manner in which the proliferation issue is discussed in Beijing reflects a growing desire to cooperate with the United States and minimize problems. In the past, the PRC often linked its proliferation of sensitive materials and weapons to U.S. arms sales to Taiwan. The rather emphatic, recent statements of Chinese security analysts and the creation of domestic laws, not just international understandings, to curb proliferation suggest that the PRC might be de-linking PRC proliferation from U.S. arms sales to Taiwan.[30]

Chinese experts report privately and hopefully that top CCP leaders moved seriously and aggressively on this issue since the spring of 2002, and that President Hu Jintao has taken it on as an issue of personal concern on which he would like to demonstrate his skill as a foreign policy leader in the national security arena.[31] However, in non-proliferation, the ultimate proof is in the amount and type of goods and technologies flowing out of China. As Bates Gill reports in his chapter on proliferation in this volume, it is still too soon to tell whether concrete PRC actions to restrict proliferation will follow the recent promulgation of new export controls. For a range of reasons that are beyond the scope of this study, one should not expect full U.S. satisfaction with PRC proliferation behavior in the near future. In fact, in May 2003 the United States imposed significant sanctions on Norinco, a major PRC trading company, for selling weapons related technologies to Iran.[32] However, this episode has not led to much acrimony.[33] As James Lilley, former ambassador to China, argues, it is because the relationship is currently so solid that when such problems arise they can be kept under control.[34] Improved implementation of non-proliferation agreements could help to achieve the PRC's strategic goals by improving relations with the United States and improving its reputation in the region and the world as a responsible power. Post-September 11, Beijing's backsliding on this issue could do severe damage to U.S.-PRC relations. Fortunately, many CCP elites seem to fully grasp this reality.

North Korea: From Passivity to U.S.-PRC Cooperation

In early 2003, the North Korean nuclear crisis, not Taiwan, appeared to be the issue over which PRC-U.S. relations might sour. In October 2002, the Bush administration presented convincing evidence of North Korean efforts to enrich uranium in violation of bilateral agreements with the United States and South Korea and multilateral agreements under the Nuclear Non-Proliferation Treaty (NPT). The North responded with further violations of the terms of its Agreed Framework with the United States and its NPT commitments by re-starting activities at the Yongbyon nuclear facility, where the DPRK has thousands of fuel rods and the ability to reprocess them relatively quickly (in a matter of months) into several bombs worth of weapons-grade plutonium. For its part, the PRC initially responded by issuing statements that it preferred not to see a nuclear North Korea, holding discussions with low-ranking North Korean officials, and offering to host talks on the matter in Beijing if other states would organize them. While these were all arguably constructive steps, they were not very energetic and they were accompanied by criticisms of the United States for failing to accept the North's demands for bilateral talks. Washington became angry and frustrated that the PRC—the regional actor with the most influence over North Korea—was not actively doing much to help resolve the nuclear crisis peacefully and multilaterally, as Washington wished.[35]

Before Beijing decided to put pressure on North Korea and work for a negotiated solution, two things needed to happen. First, Beijing needed to believe that if it did not take strong measures, something even worse than a nuclear North Korea might come to pass: e.g. a war on the peninsula started by a U.S. preemptive strike on Yongbyon, which could produce the collapse of the North Korean regime. Moreover, there needed to be some sense of urgency about the prospect of conflict. Second, the PRC needed to undergo the formal stage of state power transition in the NPC of mid-March 2003 so that officials in the Foreign Ministry and elsewhere felt secure enough in their jobs to advance bolder and more aggressive policy initiatives. By April, both of these developments had occurred.

Although a nuclear North Korea would present serious security problems for the PRC, preventing such an outcome is not Beijing's most important goal. Beijing has been even more concerned about the potential for precipitous collapse of the DPRK regime, which could bring hundreds of thousands of refugees flowing into China, could potentially put U.S. troops on China's border, and could require large sums of capital from regional actors to help with the construction of a unified and stable Korea. Much of that capital might be diverted from investment in China. The worst outcome for Beijing would be if such a collapse were brought about by war. In the diplomatic lead-up to the war in Iraq, U.S. use of force against North Korea seemed unlikely and, therefore, so did the threat of war in the near-term. Until late February or early March, U.S. leaders continually emphasized the differences between the North Korean and Iraqi crises and how the former could be solved through diplomacy. Solving the North Korea problem in any way other than peaceful negotiation seemed almost unfathomable to Beijing elites. Therefore, there was not much urgency in the crisis from Beijing's perspective.

If press reports are accurate, sometime beginning in late February or March, Washington began changing its diplomatic position on North Korea and began hinting privately at a future U.S. strike. Washington also insisted that diplomacy could not occur bilaterally with North Korea. About the time that the war in Iraq began, Washington apparently began putting additional pressure on North Korea and on regional allies and non-allies, such as the PRC and Russia, by hinting that the United States might decide to destroy North Korean plutonium reprocessing facilities in Yongbyon if a peaceful, diplomatic solution were not possible. In its diplomacy, the Bush administration apparently began placing more emphasis on the danger that North Korea might pass on weapons-grade material or actual weapons to terrorists or rogue states, and less emphasis on the danger of a direct North Korean nuclear strike on the United States or Japan, a scenario that seemed less plausible and therefore less dangerous to Asian leaders. By changing tactics, Washington apparently made the threat of a U.S. attack on Yongbyon seem more credible in Beijing and elsewhere. Washington's new approach successfully mobilized Seoul, Tokyo, and Beijing to become more active in seeking a multilateral diplomatic solution.[36]

There was no substitute for military victory in Iraq in this process. The U.S. military success in the Iraq war clearly impressed CCP analysts that conflict in North Korea was no longer beyond the realm of imagination. It is still far too soon to judge all the lessons that the Chinese military have culled from the Iraq war. Initial indicators suggest that they were impressed with U.S. mobility, command and control, and the accuracy and destructiveness of conventional firepower, but still see certain key vulnerabilities in the U.S. military, especially its reliance on satellites for intelligence gathering and targeting purposes.[37] But what was likely just as important as the details of the spectacular battlefield success of U.S. military forces in Iraq was the general U.S. willingness to invade Iraq without UN backing and to risk significant casualties in that process. After U.S. forces entered Baghdad, leading Chinese scholar Shi Yinhong stated: "Now there is some recognition of a possible time sequence in the U.S. approach to North Korea, and that has created a sense of urgency in China."[38]

There was also a domestic component to the timing of PRC cooperation with the United States on North Korea. Before the formal power transition at the NPC, CCP leaders, particularly those in state organs like the Foreign Ministry, were still cautious about hurting their chances for promotion by championing bold and unprecedented policy initiatives on sensitive topics like North Korea. Only after the NPC, when various Foreign Ministry and military leaders, including Foreign Minister Li Zhaoxing, were promoted to their current positions, did CCP elites feel secure enough to take novel actions to help solve the crisis peacefully. The conclusion of both the Iraq war and the NPC therefore freed CCP elites to address the North Korean problem in more creative ways.

In late March and April, the caution that had characterized PRC policy before the NPC was jettisoned. Beijing successfully pressured and cajoled

Pyongyang to accept a joint meeting on the crisis with both U.S. and PRC representatives present. According to press reports, to achieve this outcome Beijing began adopting various measures, from briefly cutting off oil to the North (under the pretense of technical difficulties), to offering to host a multilateral (or at least trilateral) meeting on the issue, to placing conditions on when and why the PRC would honor its 1961 defense commitment to the North.[39] Although the United States did not initially get its full wish list in the form of a truly multilateral forum involving all of the regional actors, the trilateral setting with an active PRC and the apparent acquiescence of both Seoul and Tokyo to this formula was arguably much closer to the original U.S. position than to the North Korean one.

The North Koreans reportedly used the April meetings with the United States and the PRC in Beijing to admit to having nuclear weapons, and to threaten the creation of more if their proposal for a road map was not met. Because of the ambiguity in the DPRK statements, press reports differed over whether North Korean representatives stated that plutonium fuel rod reprocessing was near completion or whether preparations for such reprocessing were now complete. Some news reports suggested that Pyongyang even went so far as to threaten the export of weapons or weapons-grade material from Yongbyon if the United States did not negotiate with Pyongyang on the latter's terms.[40]

Despite the North Korean revelations and threats, both Beijing and Washington considered the conference to be productive.[41] From Beijing's perspective, open dialogue between North Korea and the United States, with the potential for future discussions in Beijing, was an improvement. In addition, Beijing happily found itself in a prestigious leading role in regional security management. For its part, Washington achieved more than just a face-saving way to establish contact with the North. Beijing's presence and participation meant that any startling statements or obstreperous behavior by Pyongyang would be directed, at least in part, at the hosts in Beijing as well. In fact, from discussing this issue with knowledgeable people in Washington, Beijing clearly was upset about North Korean behavior. Thus, if tensions are to escalate in the future because of Pyongyang's truculence, a tougher U.S. position toward North Korea should do less damage to U.S.-PRC relations than it otherwise would. For example, Beijing will be much less likely to assist the North in a crisis or military conflict.[42] Finally, any recognition of these realities in Pyongyang might encourage the DPRK to be more cooperative on nuclear issues, thereby preventing the need for tougher measures.

Whether or not any comprehensive settlement of the North Korean crisis is possible is too hard to judge at the time of writing (July 2003). Public reports of North Korea's statements about the possible nuclear tests (a "physical demonstration" of the weapons' existence), the advanced status of its reprocessing of spent fuel, etc., suggest that the North is still adopting a hard stance and that there are no easy solutions to this crisis. There is no doubt, though, that there has been something of a turnaround in PRC foreign policy. Although the PRC cannot be expected to try to help the United States to fully strangle the DPRK economy, it might participate in significant targeted sanctions, in the searching of North Korean land, sea, and air transport and, in particular, in limiting and monitoring more closely the use of Chinese airspace by DPRK planes. How far China would be willing to help in pressuring the current regime in Pyongyang is an open question. But recent changes in PRC foreign policy on the North Korean issue suggest that the United States should be alert and open-minded about the possibility of further significant cooperation from the PRC on the North Korea issue. For example, the PRC has apparently helped isolate North Korea in international diplomatic forums and is reported to have intercepted and detained DPRK ships.[43]

Although the North Korean crisis has provided a major opportunity for U.S.-PRC cooperation, it still could become a major source of conflict if frictions form between Beijing and Washington over the proper issues to raise in negotiations or if negotiations fail. Beijing seems eager to prove itself helpful on this issue, but we should recognize that it has its own long-term interests on the peninsula. Traditionally, Beijing has wanted to sustain North Korea as a buffer state. That goal is still evident in CCP strategic thinking. But it is being eclipsed perhaps by a broader, longer-term goal: to compete with Tokyo and Washington for positive relations with Seoul in anticipation of eventual unification of the peninsula under Seoul's leadership. Given these goals, there is a growing sense in some circles in the CCP that regime change in North Korea would not be the worst outcome from the PRC's perspective, as long as it is not carried out by the United States along the lines of the war in Iraq. Since Seoul, like Beijing, is nervous about the prospect of a U.S. military attack on North Korea, Beijing might be astutely positioning itself diplomatically by distancing itself from North Korea but also opposing military options by the United States. Whether differences over how to handle North Korea create major fissures in the relationship between Beijing and Washington or Seoul and Washington will be determined in large part by how accommodating Pyongyang is to the demands of the international community, and how tough and how isolated the United States will prove in leveling sanctions against North Korea.

Addressing SARS: New Thinking after the NPC?

Since the March 2003 NPC, the PRC adopted an about-face not only on North Korea policy but also on the crisis related to Severe Acute Respiratory Syndrome (SARS). This epidemic, though most basically a health problem, has huge implications for China's domestic stability and foreign relations. The CCP's cover-up of the spread of the disease in the weeks leading up to the March NPC did severe damage to the prospects for containing the disease at home and abroad.[44] Although some have speculated that SARS might constitute the PRC's Chernobyl, it is far too soon to draw such a sweeping conclusion.[45] In fact, by mid-summer the disease seemed to be under control, at least temporarily. However, Beijing's initial response to the disease—to lie about bad news during a leadership transition—undercut much of the goodwill it had accumulated in the region, particularly in Southeast Asia, through economic policy and diplomacy since the 1997—98 Asian financial crisis, when Beijing refused to devalue its currency and provided some financial aid to its neighbors.[46] Without intentional deception by the CCP, it is doubtful that even a quickly spreading disease would have caused such damage to the PRC's reputation. The negative fallout is also exacerbated by the economic impact on the region, particularly in key industries such as air travel and tourism.[47]

If CCP policy was passive and secretive before the NPC, there has been a more proactive and transparent process since then, especially in Beijing. What is more important is that the CCP basically admitted that its previous statements about SARS had been false and that greater transparency was needed to fight the disease, albeit only after the NPC was over and after the lies were revealed to the foreign press by a PLA doctor.[48] Despite the less than principled way it came about, the CCP's acknowledgment of its cover-up could have positive implications for long-term reform in China, a point made in some of the frank criticisms one hears about the regime from CCP elites themselves.[49] Although there was a backlash against the press in May and June, some in China remain hopeful that the SARS crisis will prove an important watershed in creating a freer marketplace of ideas in China. The prevarications and cover-ups occurred before Hu Jintao became president and the more effective and transparent measures were raised after the transition at the NPC. However fortuitous its origins, this chronology might provide a political opportunity for Hu's leadership group to distinguish itself from Jiang's by promoting more accountability and transparency in government.

Since the maintenance of domestic stability is the core security challenge facing the CCP, and economic growth is the single best guarantor of domestic stability, crises like SARS in the future could provide real challenges to PRC security. Some leading economic analysts place China's second quarter GNP growth from zero to negative two percent, with increased unemployment accompanying the drop, while others claim a more modest impact.[50] Whatever the actual damage, CCP elites have long argued that the maintenance of growth rates near 8 percent are necessary to ensure social and political stability in the PRC. Given these high targets, crises such as SARS could prove politically destabilizing in the future.

At the time of this writing, the SARS crisis seems under control, so this may prove a short-lived shock to the PRC economy. But if the disease were to return in the fall and winter and more severe economic damage is done, SARS could have an impact on everything from PRC relations with Taiwan to relations with Southeast Asia and the United States. Moreover, a return of SARS is only one of several possible shocks to the Chinese economy. As discussed in detail in previous editions of *Strategic Asia* and in Dwight Perkins's contribution to this volume, the Chinese banking system is burdened with a very high ratio of non-performing loans in the decrepit state-owned sector, and the PRC government has been running large deficits to create new jobs during a period of regional and global recession. World Trade Organization regulations call for greater competition in banking and in other previously protected sectors of the Chinese economy, including agriculture and state-owned industry. If domestic reformers in the PRC choose to comply with these regulations, this could cause rapid growth of unemployment, particularly in the state-owned sector of the economy, and thereby fuel domestic and social instability. A crisis created by such factors or by a natural or a man-made disaster might make Beijing more likely to turn inward and more eager to avoid international conflicts.[51] On the other hand, given the importance of nationalism to the CCP's legitimacy in a post-communist era, under such conditions, Beijing could also become hypersensitive to perceived or real slights to its nationalist reputation from Taiwan or elsewhere.

At least in the short term, SARS has done considerable damage to cross-Strait relations. The SARS epidemic provided the DPP the opportunity to adopt a political posture with which it was more comfortable than it was with the aforementioned "assessment." Because of SARS, the DPP could more reasonably push for limiting rather than increasing economic and social contacts with the mainland on the grounds of national security and health interests, and could criticize the pan-Blue opposition parties for recklessly endangering the public by pushing for faster integration with the mainland.[52] In the spring of 2003, President Chen has repeatedly used the SARS crisis and Taiwan's lack of membership in the World Health Organization (WHO) to assert Taiwan's sovereign national identity and China's perfidy. By labeling the SARS epidemic as a national security crisis for Taiwan, by viewing control of travel between Taiwan and the mainland as the "front-line" in the war against SARS, and by adopting policies encouraging Taiwanese businesses to return their base of operations from the mainland to Taiwan, Chen seems to be taking the opportunity to move firmly back to his traditional pro-independence roots.

For its part, the PRC's continued insistence on keeping Taiwan out of the WHO (even as an observer) during the health crisis has only aggravated the situation.[53] Since the SARS crisis began, President Chen has suggested that he would like to hold an unprecedented nationwide referendum on the question of Taiwan's accession to the WHO and the controversy over the construction of a fourth nuclear power plant. The creation of any "national" referendum, even on a purely domestic issue like the power plant, is controversial on the mainland because it suggests that Taiwan is a complete nation-state. What makes this issue even more explosive is that President Chen has supported, in principle, a national referendum on Taiwan's future political status. A referendum law could create some of the legal and institutional groundwork for a referendum on independence some time in the future.[54] For this reason, a "national" referendum on any issue in Taiwan will be much more controversial on the mainland than might be evident on the surface. The Bush administration's expression of "serious concern" (guanqie) to Chen's government over the issue might have helped take the edge off this problem in Beijing and reassured the PRC.[55]

Despite the challenges that the SARS crisis created for the improvement of cross-Strait relations, if the epidemic proves short-lived and does not return later in the year, the damage should be limited. Moreover, the Taiwanese government has suffered criticism at home for its handling of SARS cases on the island. This could easily offset any damage done to the pan-Blue opposition by their association with the mainland. The DPP still trails the pan-Blue ticket in the polls by a significant margin, despite SARS. So, President Chen faces significant obstacles to re-election in March 2004.[56]

Beijing's initial handling of the SARS crisis and the recent handling of the WHO issue suggests that new thinking in China has yet to take very deep root at the top. That said, there are some clear signs of increased debate and policy flexibility in Beijing. One is struck, for example, by a series of articles by well-placed Chinese analysts emphasizing the positive nature of U.S.-PRC relations, expressing calm over the state of cross-Strait relations, entertaining new approaches to pressure North Korea and to limit PRC weapons proliferation, and addressing issues like political reform, domestic transparency, and government accountability.[57] In perhaps the most striking and fascinating recent article, Liu Jianfei of the Central Party School discusses how the best way for the PRC to guarantee its national security would be to democratize over the next two decades. Liu argues that "anti-China" forces in the United States would have much less policy traction if China were a democracy. He also argues that the mainland would be much more attractive to broad swathes of the Taiwanese public as a partner for unification if it were a democracy. Moreover, "independence" forces would be less likely to use the democracy gap across the Taiwan Strait to gain local and international support for their cause.[58] Of course, it would be an exaggeration to call this piece representative of CCP thinking on these matters, but the fact that Liu, a professor in the Party School's Strategic Studies Institute, is willing and able to publish such an article exemplifies some positive trends in China's intellectual environment in the past several years. However, it is still too soon to tell whether these trends will continue, and whether the recent pro-democracy protests in Hong Kong may lead to a backlash against such writings on the mainland.[59]

What might we look for to see if new thinking is taking deeper root in China in ways that might positively influence U.S.-China relations over the longer term? First, we would look for more assessments of the durability of Sino-American cooperation beyond the immediate phases of the war on terror and the North Korean crisis. Leading Chinese analysts still seem concerned that the spirit of cooperation might be tactical and tied to Washington's need for assistance and fewer distractions during the war on terror, the attempt to stabilize and rebuild Iraq, and the Korea crisis.[60] Second, we should expect the PRC to resist the traditional temptation to bandwagon with great powers in the UN and elsewhere that are opposing U.S. policy on issues like Iraq. Third, we should expect a China that addresses issues like SARS frankly and effectively in an instinctive manner, not only after international news sources and individual Chinese citizens push for greater transparency. Fourth, we should expect a PRC that adopts more creative and confident policies toward Taiwan, avoiding the ham-fisted tactics of isolating Taiwan diplomatically in arenas like the WHO during a health crisis. Fifth, we should expect a ferment at the highest levels of the kind of creative thinking demonstrated by scholars like Liu Jianfei regarding democracy as a road to Chinese power, prestige, and security. Liu is correct that the vast divide in political systems is the most destabilizing long-term factor in U.S.-China relations.

The Challenges Ahead

Current U.S.-PRC relations are quite positive, and the importance of this cannot be overstated. If recent news reports are accurate, the United States is currently involved in a process of restructuring its alliances and overseas military deployments with potentially dramatic implications for East Asia.[61] The deployment of more long-range naval and air firepower in Guam, improvement of security relations with India, encouragement of a more active Japan, and the creation of new or expanding security cooperation on access rights for U.S. forces in Southeast Asia might suggest to some observers in Beijing that the United States is encircling China with these allies, bases, and access arrangements. Especially after the initial U.S. responses in the region to the September 11 attacks, concerns about this in Beijing could increase fears that the United States is preparing to confront the PRC over Taiwan in the future, regardless of whether Beijing's or Taipei's behavior precipitates the conflict.

The good state of U.S.-PRC relations on the Taiwan issue and the belief in Beijing that the United States does not want to see additional conflict in the area should serve to temper, though not eliminate, the negative PRC reactions that would normally accompany some of the improvements in U.S. regional power projection capability mentioned above. In that sense, assuming the adjustments are necessary, it is an auspicious time for the United States to be introducing such changes. It has already been noted by one leading CCP security analyst, Chu Shulong, that the purpose of this realignment, as stated in the U.S. media, is to move some U.S. forces out of their traditional Cold War positions and closer to the arc of instability stretching from Southwest to Southeast Asia. This suggests to Chu that terrorism, not great power rivalry with the PRC, is the major driver of the realignment. This, he believes, will further reduce sensitivities in Beijing. On the other hand, Chu cautions that Chinese analysts could view with concern increased U.S. military activity in areas like Vietnam and the Philippines, especially given the proximity of both to mainland China and Taiwan.[62]

How long this positive environment in U.S.-PRC relations will last is not certain and many in China are greatly concerned about the combination of power and purpose they see the United States asserting in Asia from Iraq to the Korean Peninsula. The state of the PRC's confidence regarding cross-Strait relations and in U.S. restraint on that issue is also not solid. The CCP's sense of confidence could be undermined by events beyond the Party's control, such as economic downturns related to health crises, such as SARS, or financial problems in Japan or the United States, such as a deflationary spiral that many expect in the former and some fear in the latter.

Moreover, although polls in mid-2003 still suggest it is unlikely, President Chen Shui-bian might just find a way to win the Taiwanese national election in March 2004 because of some combination of a breakdown of the pan-Blue opposition and his ability to play on PRC diplomatic mistakes to his advantage. Chen might be able to shake up the political climate by pushing his controversial proposal for national referenda on issues like WHO accession and the construction of nuclear power plants, or by exploiting economic insecurities on the island related to excessive economic dependence on the mainland. Like Americans, Taiwanese certainly enjoy the benefits of trade and overseas investment, but for the most part they also perceive economic interdependence with the mainland as threatening to their security and, therefore, as requiring active government regulation.[63]

If President Chen were to prevail, in his second term he might try to institute policies that could spark new security crises across the Strait and across the Pacific; for example, a referendum on the future political status of the island or a "private" visit to Washington, DC. The policies of the U.S. government toward cross-Strait relations at the time will help determine not only the likelihood of these outcomes, but also just how provocative they will appear in Beijing if they were to occur.

Another area of concern is the future direction of the global war on terror. U.S. assurances to Beijing on Taiwan are credible largely because of international circumstances. Beijing is only reassured because the United States clearly has other areas that are of much greater concern right now than Taiwan, and it needs PRC cooperation or at least acquiescence to deal with these issues effectively. Perhaps there has been a more fundamental change of heart in the Bush administration's suspicion of China and pro-Taiwan leanings, but it has not been noted in Beijing. Therefore, if international events were to change, such as successful handling of the North Korea issue and significant U.S. progress in the global war on terror, U.S. assurances that it does not support Taiwanese independence may become less credible. Such a change would likely allow for renewed PRC suspicions over U.S. intentions regarding Taiwan and the region more generally, and could damage the current cooperative environment. Furthermore, if international events changed and the global war on terror receded into the background, it is possible that the Bush administration's policy toward China and Taiwan would return to the tougher and less conditional policies of early 2001.

Beijing will naturally be concerned about aspects of U.S. regional security policy in India, Pakistan, Central Asia, Southeast Asia, Korea, and Japan, regardless of whether there is an immediate threat of war with the United States. But a war in Korea or increasing tensions in the Taiwan Strait will intensify Chinese concerns about U.S. encirclement greatly, and will increase the chance that the PRC will treat the U.S. presence in the region as a threatening force that must be competed with in zero-sum terms. So, whereas we are not currently seeing an explicit "struggle for the mastery of East Asia," to borrow Aaron Friedberg's phrase, both states are still viewing each other as their most likely great power adversaries in the future and building military capabilities accordingly.[64] The current warm spell in relations between Washington and Beijing provides great opportunities for cooperation on North Korea, proliferation, and anti-terrorism. It could also reduce sensitivity to adoption of any future changes in U.S. force posture along the lines discussed above. Unfortunately, how long the warm spell will last depends on a complex set of factors that are hard to predict in a confident manner beyond the next couple of years. Resolution of the Taiwan question and any fundamental shift in U.S. force posture in East Asia will almost certainly take longer than that.

Endnotes

[1] For a more thorough discussion of the leadership transition, see Joseph Fewsmith, "The 16th Party Congress: Implications for Understanding Chinese Politics," *China Leadership Monitor*, Winter 2003; H. Lyman Miller, "The 10th National People's Congress and China's Leadership Transition," *China Leadership Monitor*, Summer 2003.

[2] For details of Hu becoming chairman of the powerful leading small groups on finance and economics, Taiwan affairs, and foreign affairs, see James Kynge, "Beijing's new leader takes over key post," *Financial Times*, June 18, 2003; Allen T. Cheng, "Hu takes control of strategic Party posts," *South China Morning Post*, June 19, 2003.

[3] See John Pomfret, "Chinese leader solidifies power," *Washington Post*, June 28, 2003; Joseph Kahn, "Analysts see tension in China within the top leadership," *New York Times*, July 1, 2003.

[4] In fact, Chinese interlocutors often warn that political challenges from Taiwan would be particularly dangerous in Hu Jintao's first months of office as president. Hu might feel obliged to react strongly for fear that if he did not he could be accused of being too weak and too liberally minded, with a chilling effect on any hopes of new thinking or political reform on the mainland. Christensen interviews, Shanghai and Beijing, January 2003.

[5] Recent CCP statements present "reunifying the motherland" as one of the three major historical tasks for the new century (advancing modernization and promoting peace and development are the other two). However, especially in the near-term, the less demanding "preserve territorial integrity" is more appropriate. See "Xinhua carries 'full text' of Jiang Zemin report at 16th National Party Congress," Xinhua, November 17, 2002 CPP20021117000087.

[6] See, for example, Huang Shuofeng, *Zonghe Guoli Xin Lun* (A new theory on comprehensive national power), Beijing: Zhongguo Shehui Kexue Chubanshe, September 1999.

[7] For a discussion of these dynamics, see Michael Vatikiotis and David Murphy, "Birth of a trading empire," *Far Eastern Economic Review*, March 20, 2003. See also the chapter on regional economic integration in this volume.

[8] See for example Guo Xuetang, "Zhua zhanlüe jiyu, bi zhanlüe fengxian (Grasp

the strategic opportunity, avoid strategic risks)," *Huanqiu Shibao*, February 21, 2003, p. 1.

9 See "PRC Scholar on Sino-U.S. Ties, Democracy Issues," *Zhanlüe yu Guanli*, March 1, 2003, FBIS CPP20030506000226; see also the original Chinese version of the article, Liu Jianfei, "Zhongguo Minzhu Zhengzhi Jianshe yu ZhongMei Guanxi (The building of democratic politics in China and Sino-U.S. relations)," *Zhanlüe yu Guanli*, March 2003, pp. 76–82.

10 Although reports suggest this year's military budget increase will slow to 9.6 percent, the PLA has had double-digit rate increases for the preceding several years. See Willy Wo-Lap Lam, "Budget surprise for China's army," CNN.com, March 7, 2003.

11 For a thorough detailing of these developments, see U.S. Department of Defense, "Annual Report on the Military Power of the People's Republic of China," July 12, 2002, <www.defenselink.mil>. On the threat of submarines, see Lyle Goldstein and Lt. Cmdr. Bill Murray, "China's Subs Lead the Way," U.S. Naval Institute Proceedings, March 2003; Michael A. Glosny, "Mines Against Taiwan: A Military Analysis of a PRC Blockade," *Breakthroughs*, Spring 2003. On dependence on imports from Russia, see John Pomfret, "China to buy eight more Russian submarines," *Washington Post*, June 25, 2002; John Pomfret, "China signs $2 billion deal to buy Russian fighter jets," *Washington Post*, July 20, 2001.

12 Bonnie S. Glaser, "Sustaining Cooperation: Security Matters Take Center Stage," *Comparative Connections*, January 2003; Jasper Becker, "Side by side against terrorism," *South China Morning Post*, October 20, 2001; and Kenneth Lieberthal, "Has China become an ally?" *New York Times*, October 25, 2002.

13 Thomas J. Christensen, "China," in Richard J. Ellings and Aaron L. Friedberg with Michael Wills, eds., *Strategic Asia 2002–03: Asian Aftershocks*, Seattle: The National Bureau of Asian Research, 2002, pp. 51–94.

14 Song Nianshen, "Meiguo shou ci rending "Dongtu" jiu shi kongbu zuzhi (For the first time the United States maintains that "ETIM" is a terrorist organization)," *Huanqiu Shibao*, August 29, 2002, pp. 1–2.

15 Glosny interviews, Beijing and Shanghai, Summer 2002. For this view, see also Susan Shirk in Leon Hadar, "Powell's Asia trip: success on Iraq, failure on North Korea," *Straits Times*, February 28, 2003.

16 Christensen interviews, Shanghai and Beijing, January 2003.

17 See, for example, Hu Shiqing, "Qianxi Dangqian Taiwan Jingji Xingshi yu Zhanwang (A simple analysis of Taiwan's current economic situation and prospects)," *Taiwan Yanjiu*, no. 4, 2002, pp. 57–66; and Shi Yinhong, "Zu Guo Dalu dui Taiwan: Changqi Youshi dui Duanqi Youshi (The motherland's mainland faces Taiwan: long-term advantages vs. short-term advantages)," *Shijie Jingji yu Zhengzhi*, July 2002, pp. 33–38. Christensen interviews, January 2003 and Glosny interviews, summer 2002, confirmed this confidence.

18 For example, Liu Jianfei, "Hou Lengzhan Shidai de Zhong-Mei Guanxi Yu Taiwan Wenti (Post-Cold War U.S.-China relations and the Taiwan question)," *Zhanlüe yu Guanli*, vol. 6 (2002), p. 108. See also "'Lian-Song zhongyu lianhe, Chen Shui-bian mingnian xiatai?" (Lian-Soong finally unite, will Chen Shui-

bian fall from power next year?), *Nanfang Zhoumo*, February 20, 2003. On the formation of the pan-Blue alliance, see "Joint KMT-PFP presidential ticket announced; hope to improve PRC relations," Agence France-Presse, April 18, 2003. For the fragility of this nascent pan-Blue alliance, see Sandy Huang, "Miscommunication," *Taipei Times*, April 16, 2003, p. 3.

19 On the importance of credible threats and reassurances to deter PRC use of force against Taiwan, see Thomas J. Christensen, "The Contemporary Security Dilemma: Deterring a Taiwan Conflict," *Washington Quarterly*, Autumn 2002.

20 See David E. Sanger, "Bush is offering Taiwan some arms but not the best," *New York Times*, April 24, 2001; David E. Sanger, "U.S. would defend Taiwan, Bush says," *New York Times*, April 26, 2001.

21 See "China, U.S. maintain close contacts following Chen's 'each side a country' remark," *Wen Wei Po*, August 9, 2002, translated in FBIS CPP200208 09000039; and "Taiwan's Chen left friendless after independence remarks," *South China Morning Post*, August 9, 2002.

22 On this issue, see Hei Tai, "From not supporting to opposing Taiwan independence: the United States' stance on Taiwan issue" (in Chinese), *Wen Wei Po*, November 30 and December 4, 2002, FBIS CPP20021204000027. President Bush apparently reiterated his position on Taiwanese independence to Hu Jintao at the G-8 Summit in June 2003. See "Hu, Bush pledge to further develop ties," Xinhua, June 2, 2003.

23 For an example of this thinking, see Liu Jianfei, "Hou Lengzhan Shidai de Zhong-Mei Guanxi." In interviews in January 2003 in Beijing, some analysts expressed doubts about the maintenance of U.S. restraint into the latter part of this decade.

24 Glosny interviews, Beijing and Shanghai, summer 2003, and Christensen interviews, Beijing and Shanghai, January 2003. This is especially true since the pan-Blue alliance is leading the DPP in opinion polls.

25 Interviews with Taiwanese government officials responsible for cross-Strait relations, January 2003.

26 See, for example, "MAC chief apologizes for delay in releasing evaluation report," Taipei Central News Agency, March 17, 2003.

27 "Hu Jintao yu Meiguo Fuzongtong Qieni juxing huitan" (Hu Jintao and U.S. Vice President Cheney hold talks), *Jiefangjun bao*, May, 3, 2002, via Xinhua News Agency.

28 "China FM meets Armitage, comments on terrorism, missile export controls," Xinhua, August 26, 2002, FBIS CPP20020826000147.

29 Frank Ching, "Tough regulations prove Beijing is serious about non-proliferation," *Sunday Morning Post*, October 27, 2002, FBIS CPP20021028 000094.

30 Those analysts were frank in saying that the linkage would stop and that the decision made by Jiang Zemin and Hu Jintao was controversial within the government, thereby basically recognizing that the linkage had been there previously. Glosny interviews, Beijing and Shanghai, August–September 2002; Christensen interviews, Beijing and Shanghai, January 2003. See also John Pomfret, "China embraces more moderate foreign policy," *Washington Post*, October 24, 2002, citing a government official on the de-linking.

[31] This analysis is based on Christensen's interviews in Beijing in January 2003 and, in particular, on a lengthy discussion with a well-connected interlocutor in the Chinese Foreign Ministry.

[32] See Michael Dobbs and Glenn Kessler, "U.S. penalizes Chinese firm over alleged missile aid to Iran," *Washington Post*, May 23, 2003.

[33] Susan Lawrence, "Ties that bind: costly sanctions against a Chinese conglomerate don't seem set to damage Sino-U.S. relations," *Far Eastern Economic Review*, June 5, 2003.

[34] See Lilley quote in Dobbs and Kessler, "U.S. penalizes Chinese firm..."

[35] See John Pomfret and Glenn Kessler, "China's reluctance irks U.S.," *Washington Post*, February 4, 2003; Glenn Kessler, "Bush prods China, Russia on North Korea crisis," *Washington Post*, February 8, 2003; James Dao, "Bush urges Chinese president to press North Korea on arms," *New York Times*, February 8, 2003; and Guy Dinmore, "China urged to put pressure on North Korea over nuclear policy," *Financial Times*, February 8, 2003.

[36] See John Pomfret, "China urges North Korean dialogue," *Washington Post*, April 4, 2003, p. A16; "Kawaguchi, Li to discuss North Korea issues in talks," Kyodo, April 6, 2003, FBIS JPP20030406000025, and "PRC FM Li Zhaoxing holds talks with ROK FM, reiterates stand on DPRK nuclear issue," Xinhua, April 10, 2003, FBIS CPP20030410000202. For an article on the catalytic role played in diplomacy by increasing U.S. threats of force, see Shi Yinhong, "Crisis and hope—North Korean nuclear issue against backdrop of Iraq war," *Ta Kung Pao*, April 15, 2003, FBIS CPP20030421 000045.

[37] For early assessments, see "PRC's Xiong Guangkai urges China to study Iraq war," *Zhongguo Qingnian Bao*, April 17, 2003, CPP20030417000058; "PLA deputy chief of general staff on 'new military changes," *Jiefang Ribao*, May 30, 2003, FBIS CPP20030602000057; Michael Pillsbury, "Initial Assessments of the U.S. War in Iraq," *Chinese Military Update*, June 2003.

[38] See quote in Robert Marquand, "Watching Iraq, China begins to lean on North Korea," *Christian Science Monitor*, April 8, 2003.

[39] On Chinese oil cutoffs, see Howard French, "North Korea's reaction on Iraq is subdued so far," *New York Times*, April 2, 2003; also see Gady A. Epstein, "From Beijing, stern words." Epstein reports that Beijing threatened Pyongyang that it would lift its opposition to international sanctions if the North did not cooperate. On sanctions and PRC defense commitments to North Korea, see Leslie Fung, "China washes hands of N. Korea's antics," *Straits Times*, April 5, 2003. Of course, Beijing may have adopted additional measures not reported or even speculated about in the press.

[40] See Glenn Kessler, "North Korea says it has nuclear arms," *Washington Post*, April 25, 2003; Glenn Kessler and John Pomfret, "North Korea's threats a dilemma for China," *Washington Post*, April 26, 2003; and David E. Sanger, "North Korea says it now possesses nuclear arsenal," *New York Times*, April 25, 2003.

[41] For positive U.S. statements, see "State Department Briefing Transcript," April 25, 2003, available at <http://hongkong.usconsulate.gov/uscn/state/db/2003/0425.htm>; for China's positive spin, see "China upbeat on N. Korea nuclear talks," *Straits Times*, April 25, 2003.

42 Ching Cheong, "China offers DPRK guarantee from U.S. attack, but with some conditions," *Straits Times* (Internet version), May 3, 2003, FBIS SEP 20030503 0000019.

43 See Robin Wright and Barbara Demick, "North Korea's arms are top U.S. concern," *Los Angeles Times*, June 19, 2003; "China cranks up diplomacy over North Korean row," ABC-CBN News, July 6, 2003; "Wary China ups diplomatic pressure," *Taipei Times*, July 7, 2003, p. 5.

44 David Lague, Susan Lawrence, and David Murphy, "The China virus," *Far Eastern Economic Review*, April 10, 2003, pp. 12–15; "China wakes up," *Economist*, April 26, 2003, pp. 18–19; and Laurie Garrett, "China's epidemic discord," *Newsday*, April 27, 2003.

45 "China wakes up," *Economist*; and Joseph Kahn, "When crises strike, China's leaders adapt to survive," *New York Times*, May 4, 2003.

46 In a March 2003 off-the-record meeting, a U.S. scholar who had just visited several ASEAN capitals commented on frustration in those capitals about the PRC's handling of SARS. See also Michael Vatikiotis, "ASEAN and China—united in adversity," *Far Eastern Economic Review*, May 8, 2003.

47 See "In intensive care," *Economist*, April 26, 2003, p. 20.

48 Two token officials, the minister of health and the mayor of Beijing, were sacked. As Bates Gill of the Center for Strategic and International Studies points out, they were likely sacrificial lambs, not actually those responsible for the cover-up. "China wakes up."

49 John Pomfret, "Doctor says Health Ministry lied about disease," *Washington Post*, April 10, 2003, p. A26. For a critical commentary on the CCP's handling of SARS from a Chinese Academy of Social Sciences researcher, see Tang Shiping, "China looks for a SARS silver lining," *Asia Times*, April 22, 2003.

50 Keith Bradsher, "SARS ebbs in East Asia, but financial recovery is slow," *New York Times*, May 31, 2003, p. A8. See also "AFP: China's 2003 GDP Forecast Down to 7.5% from 9.0% Due to SARS," Agence France-Presse, May 22, 2003, FBIS CPP20030522000105; "Xinhua: CSFB forecasts higher GDP growth rate for China," Xinhua, July 4, 2003, FBIS CPP20030704000108; and "PRC State Council says SARS worsening China's already 'grave' employment situation," *China Daily*, May 21, 2003, FBIS CPP20030521000263.

51 Charles Wolf, Jr., et al., *Fault Lines in China's Economic Terrain*, Santa Monica, Calif.: Rand, 2003.

52 For an example of how the Republic of China (ROC) Government Information Office has spun the SARS crisis into discussions of issues such as the military threat from the mainland and Taiwan's diplomatic isolation, see Cecillia Fanchiang, "Measures to control SARS paying off," *Taiwan Journal*, April 18, 2003. Rather than push for "the three links" (direct communications and transportation links between Taiwan and the mainland), Chen was able to reduce the "mini-three links" between the Taiwan-controlled offshore islands and nearby Fujian province. See "Taiwan: MAC announces suspension of 'mini three links'," *China Post*, April 1, 2003, FBIS CPP2003 0331000198. See "AFP: Taiwan suspends 'mini' transport links with China over SARS," Agence France-Presse, May 17, 2003, FBIS CPP20030517000058.

53 See, for example, Lin Fang-yan, "Chen calls SARS a national security issue,"

Taiwan Journal, May 9, 2003, p. 1.

[54] See "Taiwan president, vice president defend 'right' of referendum despite foreign opinion," *Taipei Times*, June 23, 2003, FBIS CPP20030623000201; "Opposition parties push for introduction of referedums," *China Post*, June 29, 2003.

[55] See "Meiguo bing mo fandui Taiwan gongtou (The United States has not opposed a Taiwan referendum," *Hongguan Zhoubao*, June 25, 2003, p. 1.

[56] See "Taiwan: pan-Blue ticket leads poll," *Taiwan News*, February 21, 2003, FBIS CPP20030221000152; "Taiwan: new polls show pan-Blue ticket favored for presidential election," *China Post*, April 20, 2003, FBIS CPP 200304 21000199.

[57] For a few examples of these types of articles, see Kang Xiaoguang, "Weilai Shinian Zhongguo Zhengzhi Fazhan Celüe Tantao (An inquiry into China's political development strategy over the next 10 years)," *Zhanlüe yu Guanli*, January 2003; Lin Zhiyuan, "Zhongyang Jiquan he Difang Fenquan (Centralization and regional decentralization of power)," *Zhanlüe yu Guanli*, January 2003; see the forum "Xin Xingshi Xiade Zhongguo Waijiao (China's diplomacy under new circumstances)," *Xiandai Guoji Guanxi*, April 2003; see also "Qiushi article stresses promoting Party, people's democracy," June 15, 2003, FBIS CPP20030619000003. For a discussion of some of these new trends and new thinking in the realm of foreign policy, see "Evan S. Medeiros and M. Taylor Fravel, "China's New Diplomacy," unpublished manuscript, 2003.

[58] Liu, "The Building of Democratic Politics in China..."

[59] See David Lague, "In the eye of the storm," *Far Eastern Economic Review*, July 31, 2003.

[60] Christensen Interviews, Beijing, January 2003. On this point, see Tang Shiping and Cao Xiaoyang, "Xunqiu Zhong-Mei-Ri Guanxi Xianghu Anquan de Jidian, (In search of the starting points for Sino-U.S.-Japan mutual security)," *Zhanlüe yu Guanli*, 2002, no. 1, p. 107.

[61] See Esther Schrader, "U.S. to realign troops in Asia," *Los Angeles Times*, May 29, 2003; Doug Struck and Akiko Yamamoto, "U.S. Marines on Okinawa under review for relocation," *Washington Post*, May 30, 2003; and Barry Wain, "U.S. considers realigning military presence in Asia," *Wall Street Journal*, June 2, 2003.

[62] Chu Shulong, quoted in Ray Cheung, "U.S. move not seen as threat," *South China Morning Post*, May 30, 2003, FBIS CPP20030530000132.

[63] In MAC polls conducted late last year only 7.8 percent of respondents believed that Taiwan should unconditionally open up direct transportation links with the mainland, while 74.5 percent believed that Taiwan should do so only conditionally. In the past two years a growing majority of Taiwanese respondents called for increased regulations on investment to the mainland with only 20 percent calling for the easing of such restrictions. See "Public Opinion on Cross-Strait Relations in the Republic of China, Mainland Affairs Council, Executive Yuan, Republic of China, December 2002 < www.mac.gov.tw>.

[64] Aaron L. Friedberg, "The Struggle for Mastery in Asia," *Commentary*, November 2000.

Japan – Key Indicators and Forecasts

Economy and Trade	2002^a	2003^b	2004^b
GDP ($tr) / (PPP GDP)	4.0 (PPP GDP in 2002 = $3.3 tr)		
GDP growth (%)	0.3	0.8	1.0
Inflation (%)	-0.9	-0.7	-0.6
Budget balance (% of GDP)	2.8	2.7	3.0
Major export destinations (2001)	U.S. (30%), China (8%), Korea (6%)		

Population and Energy	2002^a	2005^b	2010^b
Population (m)	127.1	127.4	127.2
Population growth (%)	0.1	0.1	-0.1
Oil production (m bbl/d)	<0.1	<0.1	<0.1
Oil consumption (m bbl/d)	5.3	5.4	6.0

Politics	
President	Koizumi Junichiro (LDP, since Apr 2001)
Dominant party	Liberal Democratic Party (since 1986)
Next election	Before June 2004

Military	
Armed forces (2002)	238,000
Defense expenditure (2001)	$39.5 bn (1.0 % of GDP)
Conventional capabilities	Modern capable forces with large navy
	Ongoing modernization of naval forces (incl. possible construction of helicopter carriers)
Weapons of mass destruction	None

Sources: The National Bureau of Asian Research, compiled from International Monetary Fund, *World Economic Outlook*; Central Intelligence Agency, *World Factbook*; U.S. Census Bureau, *International Data Base*; Energy Information Administration, *Country Analysis Brief—Japan*; International Institute of Strategic Studies, *The Military Balance*. Notes: a) Data for 2002 may be estimates; b) Data for 2003, 2004, 2005, and 2010 are projections. Additional data on Japan are available in the Strategic Asia Database at <http://strategicasia.nbr.org>.

TILTING CLOSER
TO WASHINGTON

Michael H. Armacost

ABSTRACT

During the past year, Japan's security policy was shaped decisively by the emergence of a more palpable threat from North Korea. This prompted Tokyo to bolster its alliance with the United States, toughen its stance toward Pyongyang, align its policies more closely with Washington's toward other members of the so-called "axis of evil," and modestly extend the parameters of its evolving international role as a source of offshore, non-combat, logistic services and humanitarian assistance. Japan sought, meanwhile, to enhance its diplomatic maneuverability and diversify its sources of energy by cultivating relations with the major powers—especially China—and other countries of consequence. Tokyo competed with predictable zeal for export opportunities, and encouraged forms of Asian regional cooperation that may offer an eventual counterweight to NAFTA and the European Union. Internal factors influencing Japan's security policies included economic malaise, the complexities of coalition government, and rising nationalist sentiments.

Michael Armacost is a Shorenstein Distinguished Fellow at the Asia/Pacific Research Center at Stanford University. The author would like to express his appreciation to Kenneth Pyle, Daniel Okimoto, Richard Ellings, Michael Wills, and Bill Breer for their helpful comments on earlier drafts of this chapter.

Introduction

In last year's volume of *Strategic Asia*, Richard Samuels and Eric Heginbotham highlighted Japan's pursuit of comprehensive security with a "double hedge."[1] Over the past year, the broad guidelines of this strategy remained intact. But Tokyo devoted more effort to enhancing cooperation with the United States, in particular seeking to align its policies toward Iraq and North Korea more closely with those of Washington. At the same time, it exploited opportunities for independent action in the economic sphere, particularly in its steady encouragement of pan-Asian regional cooperation, while cultivating relations with other powers to advance its commercial and political interest, and to maximize its diplomatic maneuverability.

The reasons for these priorities are not difficult to discern. Above all, Japan faced a more demanding external and domestic environment. As the *Mainichi Shimbun*'s somber January 2003 New Year's editorial pointed out:

> Abroad the nation faces the problem of Iraq and the question of measures to be taken with regard to North Korea, while at home the final disposing of non-performing loans coincides with a slumping economy. The massive government debt continues to increase with no prospect of improvement. This sense of uncertainty is growing, and the world is awash in a series of worries.[2]

North Korea's resumption of nuclear activities and missile testing presented the most ominous and palpable danger. China's buoyant economic growth, accompanied by continuing robust increases in its defense budget and assertive leadership on regional economic issues, reinforced Japanese uneasiness about how Beijing will utilize the power it is rapidly accumulating. South Asia, Central Asia, and Southeast Asia—areas of major economic interest to Japan—remained battlegrounds in the struggle against international terrorism. The Middle East and Persian Gulf region, upon which Japan remains overwhelmingly dependent for its energy supplies, were plagued by turmoil—the U.S. military campaign and its aftermath in Iraq, heightened instability in Iran and Saudi Arabia, and intensified conflict between the Israelis and Palestinians, all complicated the environment. Apprehensions about certain "unilateralist" features of U.S. foreign policy persisted within Japan's policymaking elite, but major geopolitical developments increased America's perceived value as an ally on the part of Japanese leaders and the public alike.[3]

The deterioration of Japan's external security environment occurred against the backdrop of persistent economic sluggishness and generally ineffectual efforts to foster deregulation and overcome deflation. Prime Minister Koizumi Junichiro's strategy for accelerating economic reform was marked by inconsistency and garnered uneven support among colleagues within his own Liberal Democratic Party (LDP). In some respects, Prime Minister Koizumi perfectly embodied Japanese public attitudes toward reform—deep uneasiness about the nation's economic trajectory, yet even deeper apprehensions about the dislocations that reforms inevitably bring. By talking about the need for basic change without implementing far-reaching reform, Koizumi sustained impressive levels of public approval, but economic recovery remained elusive.

Much of Koizumi's popularity appeared attributable to the more muscular stance he adopted on national security issues. He embodied a combination of more assertive nationalism with a practical acknowledgement of the need for U.S. cooperation. North Korea's belligerent brinksmanship underlined the need for the U.S. alliance. On this point the right and left in Japan could agree, though for conflicting reasons. Some regard the alliance as a means of gradually recovering strategic independence; others perceive its value principally as a check on the buildup of Japan's defense forces and the expansion of its international security role. The governing coalition contains politicians of both persuasions—little wonder that establishing a consensus for new policy departures is slow and painstaking.

Under these circumstances, Japan's latitude for pursuing alternative strategic options is limited. Past hopes for carving out a unique role as a "global civilian power," advancing the cause of "human security" while relying essentially on "soft power," confronted the harsh realities of real threats, a sluggish economy, and a tight budget. In the face of heightened danger, Japan naturally accorded priority to relations with the one country with both the motive and means to extend it a strategic guarantee—the United States.

Japan's inclination to rely more heavily on Washington was reinforced by the perceived limits to the support it could expect from others. The Chinese and Russians still loom more as competitors than partners; Moscow's power in Asia has declined, while Beijing's growing economic and military prowess inspires wariness. The Europeans are unable to speak with a single voice, remain preoccupied with their internal arrangements, and have embraced a critical attitude toward the Bush administration that the Japanese neither substantially share nor believe it prudent to express.

Aligning policy with the United States proved in some respects easier than might have been expected. The Bush administration proved to be a less demanding partner than many Japanese feared. The Pentagon did not covet allied participation in military campaigns, and was openly appreciative of Japan's indirect offshore, non-combat support. The White House generally resisted the temptation to offer public criticism and advice on macroeconomic policy. The administration foreswore open attempts to apply "*gaiatsu*" in favor of more subtle forms of pressure. Its decision to pursue a multilateral approach toward North Korea provided Tokyo ample scope for diplomatic maneuver. Meanwhile, Washington's interest in Iran's tacit cooperation vis-à-vis Afghanistan and its hopes for Tehran's restraint toward Iraq allowed Japan running room to pursue its commercial and energy interests with that nation through much of the year.

Still, a year that began with high hopes for a more independent and influential Japanese role vis-à-vis members of the "axis of evil" ended with Tokyo devoting more effort to coordinating its policies toward each of them more closely with Washington. At the same time, Japan shouldered modestly expanded offshore security responsibilities, and challenged, albeit tentatively, long-established shibboleths of its defense policy.

Bolstering the Alliance

Since the mid-1990s Japan's alliance with the United States has functioned relatively smoothly and acquired growing public support. This was facilitated by a number of developments, including the renaissance of U.S. industrial and military power, the steady rise of China, the easing of bilateral trade frictions between Tokyo and Washington, the growing mood of "realism" in Japan on security issues, and periodic reminders that long-standing disputes in Korea and the Taiwan Straits remain fraught with danger. The Bush administration's emphasis on revitalizing the alliance, its discipline in avoiding public criticism of Japanese economic policies, and the evident personal rapport between Prime Minister Koizumi and President George W. Bush helped. So too did the revision of U.S.-Japan Defense Cooperation Guidelines, Japan's dispatch of a peacekeeping contingent to East Timor, and its timely and practical support to the counter-terrorist coalition that ended Taliban rule in Afghanistan.[4]

In remarks to the Council on Foreign Relations in September 2002, Prime Minister Koizumi described the alliance as "closer and deeper than ever in our history."[5] U.S. leaders offered comparable assessments.[6] These reflected U.S. appreciation of the support role Japan played in the military campaign in Afghanistan and Japan's renewed awareness of the value of the U.S. nuclear umbrella. It was apparent in the resumption of cordial "two plus two" meetings in early 2003 between top U.S. and Japanese foreign policy and defense officials after a hiatus of two years,[7] in Deputy Secretary of State Richard Armitage's public pledge to visiting Japanese lawmakers that the United States would retaliate if the North Koreans were so foolish as to attack Japan, in President Bush's affirmative response to Prime Minister Koizumi's request that the United States study joint civilian and military use of the U.S. Air Force base at Yokota, and in the generally amicable manner in which base-related incidents in Japan were managed.

To be sure, Tokyo's policies deviated from Washington's on many security issues. The publication of the administration's U.S. national security strategy in September 2002 evoked scant empathy among the Japanese policy establishment while providing cannon fodder for critics in the weekly magazines. Foreign Minister Kawaguchi Yoriko insisted on meeting with Yasser Arafat during visits to the Middle East, while Washington sought to consign him to the dustbin of history. The Japanese politely but firmly deflected Washington's request to expel Iraqi diplomats prior to the commencement of hostilities. And prospective U.S. force adjustments in South Korea precipitated uneasiness among some Japanese officials who worried that they might be misread both in Seoul and Pyongyang.

Yet the alliance enjoyed solid support from the government, and widespread acceptance within opposition ranks. Since the United States was vulnerable to new security threats and was increasingly "stretched" to meet new commitments in South Asia and the Middle East, it sought more help from its friends, and wanted more from the alliance than unfettered access to bases. For its part, Japan recognized the need to keep the alliance in good working order and continued to refine a new offshore, noncombat international security role that served its interests and found favor in Washington. The tranquil state of Sino-U.S. relations unquestionably facilitated the strengthening of the U.S.-Japan alliance. With Beijing devoting attention to its internal modernization, it sought to avert contentious bilateral problems with Washington, and it toned down the occasionally shrill criticism it had directed against the alliance in the past.

Adjustments in Japan's Defense Strategy

Japanese policy adjustments, as Henry Kissinger has noted, occur through the "accumulation of apparently imperceptible nuances," rather than through public debate and forthright declarations of intent.[8] In the course of the past decade, Japan has in this fashion transformed its role in responding to international security crises. When international conflicts surfaced during the Cold War, the question of Japan's direct involvement was moot. Its security concerns focused on the defense of its own territory and the United States took care of problems over the horizon. Japan shunned direct involvement in military dimensions of the East-West struggle to avoid "entrapment" in Cold War rivalries. To mitigate its parallel fear of "abandonment," Japan found ways of augmenting financial and other support to U.S. forces in Japan when crises appeared, as well as providing economic assistance and political support to parties more directly engaged in conflicts.

In the post-Cold War era, however, more recent conflicts have entailed efforts by like-minded nations to combat threats to an incipient international community from terrorist groups or rogue states. Opting out of participation in such conflicts, as Tokyo learned through bitter experience in the Gulf War of 1990–91, risks inviting international opprobrium. Consequently, Tokyo has been designing a new role for itself as a provider of offshore, rear area, noncombat logistic and other services in support of UN-sponsored peacekeeping operations and, on occasion, the security efforts of ad hoc "coalitions of the willing"—when its interests warrant participation and timely enabling legislation can be secured from the Diet.

Japan's emerging role remains subject to major constraints. It contributed no military units to the International Security Assistance Force (ISAF) on the ground in Afghanistan. Its forces have scrupulously avoided combat zones. Heretofore, its logistic support has excluded the transportation of weapons or ammunition. The rules of engagement under which its forces operate remain uniquely restrictive. While Japan asserts a right to "collective self-defense," it has not sought to exercise that right. In the course of the past year, none of these self-abnegating guidelines were breached.

Yet the range of permissible actions for Japan's Self-Defense Forces (SDF) and their capabilities gradually continues to expand. Aegis-equipped destroyers were deployed for the first time to the naval forces extending refueling support to *Operation Enduring Freedom*, and in the course of 2002 Japanese tankers serviced not only U.S. and British vessels, but an expanding list of European navies, as well as Canadian and New Zealand ships. Through May 31, 2003, Japan provided 80 million barrels of oil to the coalition at a cost to itself of roughly $100 million. With the planned acquisition of aerial refueling tankers, and a sophisticated 13,500 ton helicopter carrier (funds for which are expected to be included in the FY 2004 JDA budget), power projection capabilities will increase. Three emergency national security bills were finally passed after a quarter century of contentious partisan debate.[9] Political support is growing rapidly for ballistic missile defenses.

Of greatest consequence, the Diet on July 25, 2003, authorized the use of the SDF to assist in the reconstruction of Iraq. This legislation breaks new ground by permitting the overseas deployment of ground troops—as well as air force and naval units—to a country in which the identification of combat and non-combat zones is problematic, no local interim government has yet been established, and the UN role is currently marginal.

Other long-standing constraints on the SDF are under active debate. The rules of engagement for Japanese military units are subject to growing domestic criticism for their rigidity, and may be relaxed through reinterpretation or legislative amendment. There are also hints that the government may put forward more comprehensive legislation to institutionalize the government's authority to utilize the SDF in international security operations. Indeed, it may contemplate the establishment of an "international contributions corps" as a permanent unit trained and equipped for overseas peacekeeping and counter-terrorist operations, with or without a UN sanction. Clearly, the atmosphere in which national security issues are discussed is increasingly open, and less inhibited by long-standing taboos.

Needless to add, the evolving offshore, non-combat security role that Japan is assuming still leaves its military units out of the main line of fire[10] and its politicians free of the need to tackle the more politically risky questions involved in amending Article 9 of the Constitution, exercising the right of collective self-defense, altering the line between offensive and defensive systems, or crossing the nuclear threshold—at least for now.

Coping with the "Axis of Evil"

While Japanese policymakers harbored reservations about President Bush's tendency to lump Iraq, North Korea, and Iran together as an "axis of evil," they found ways of narrowing the differences between their approaches to these countries and that of the United States. For Japan, policy toward these rogue nations became less an occasion for "hedging" than a challenge for policy coordination.

North Korea

Some commentators portrayed Koizumi's dramatic meeting with Kim Jong Il in Pyongyang on September 17, 2002 as a gutsy display of diplomatic independence from Washington.[11] Certainly Tokyo was eager to establish its own lines of communication with North Korea at a time when the Bush administration had commenced no substantial dialogue of its own with Pyongyang. Many Japanese were uneasy with the Bush administration's antipathy toward the North and its skepticism toward Kim Dae Jung's "sunshine policy"—toward which Tokyo displayed a strong affinity.

Koizumi's trip to Pyongyang—initially characterized by the Japanese press as an unalloyed diplomatic triumph—produced an admission from Kim Jong Il of North Korea's culpability for abducting Japanese citizens in the 1970s and 1980s, and the prospect of more normal diplomatic relations promised to relieve Japan's "marginalization" in Korean peninsular diplomacy. The Japanese public applauded the prime minister's hard-nosed diplomatic approach, which not only netted the North's unprecedented acknowledgement of past misdeeds but an extension of Pyongyang's moratorium on missile testing and a reaffirmation of its previous nonproliferation commitments. Koizumi's popularity soared, and for a brief moment Tokyo occupied center stage in Korean diplomacy.

The prospects for normalization, of course, quickly soured. The Japanese authorities had misestimated popular reaction to the North's acknowledged responsibility for the abductions. Japanese anger and resentment at Pyongyang's high-handedness intensified when the North stonewalled Tokyo's requests that it allow family members to be reunited with the abductees, clarify the suspicious circumstances in which eight abductees had reportedly died, and initiate investigations into other cases of suspected kidnappings. Growing apprehensions about the North's conduct were reinforced, moreover, by Pyongyang's admission of a clandestine uranium enrichment program, and its subsequent decisions to expel UN inspectors, break the seals on spent fuel rods at Yongbyon, reactivate its plutonium reprocessing facilities, and withdraw from the Nuclear Non-Proliferation Treaty (NPT).

To be sure, these developments did not invariably inspire Japanese policy responses identical to those of Washington. In some respects, Japan's responses to North Korea were more akin to Seoul's. Tokyo was comfortable with the Korean political and territorial status quo. It feared a collapse of the North and/or renewed conflict between Pyongyang and Seoul more than it loathed the provocative brinksmanship or despicable human rights record of Kim Jong Il's regime. It regarded South Korea's magnanimous gestures toward the North, even if unreciprocated, as a plausible means of encouraging a gradual opening of North Korea to the outside world or, at a minimum, as a way of postponing its "implosion." Japan was consequently prepared to contribute to the stabilization of the North if this enhanced chances for a protracted period of peaceful coexistence, not least because it feared the consequences of confrontation (such as active consideration of military options or renewed demands for economic sanctions).

When the United States pushed for a cut-off of further deliveries of heavy fuel oil to the North, following Pyongyang's October 2002 admission of covert violations of the 1994 Agreed Framework, Japan initially resisted, and then only reluctantly acquiesced. It joined Seoul in seeking to keep the Korean Energy Development Organization's (KEDO) light water reactor project alive, despite Washington's objections. It supported the International Atomic Energy Agency's (IAEA) decision to refer North Korea's withdrawal from the NPT to the UN Security Council, but opposed early Security Council action on the report. It consistently urged Washington to pursue a diplomatic solution to the problem while actively discouraging consideration of military options, and characterizing economic sanctions as a "last resort."

Gradually, however, Japan's stance hardened in response to the media frenzy over the abductions, a resumption of Pyongyang's harsh invective against Tokyo, the North's resumption of missile tests, its casual disregard for the non-nuclear pledges contained in the Koizumi-Kim communiqué, Washington's refusal to "reward bad behavior" by reopening bilateral negotiations with the North, and its political will in forcefully disarming Iraq. Indeed, North Korea's provocative brinksmanship produced four major consequences in Japanese policy.

- It heightened the security consciousness of ordinary Japanese and reminded its government that, in confronting North Korean provocations, the U.S. alliance and its nuclear umbrella remained indispensable to Japan's security. Arguably, North Korea's possession of ballistic missiles capable of hitting targets in Japan with weapons of mass destruction (WMD) poses the most significant, immediate, and direct security threat Japan has faced in the past half century.[12]
- It strengthened Japan's readiness to cooperate with the United States on ballistic missile defense (BMD). Previously, cooperation had been confined to "joint research," and official comments on missile defense were laced with caveats about their high cost, questions about their technical efficacy, and worries about their consistency with the government's long-standing commitments to "no military uses of outer space," or its pledge not to exercise its right to collective self-defense. North Korean brinksmanship prompted Japan to order additional PAC-2 Patriot interceptor missiles, to announce plans for a subsequent purchase of PAC-3 Patriots (to be delivered beginning in FY2006), and to hasten requests for budget authorizations needed to begin purchasing long lead-time items required for the "development and deployment" of BMD systems.[13]
- It helped close the gap between Japanese and U.S. diplomatic tactics for dealing with North Korea. This was particularly apparent when Koizumi visited Bush at his ranch in Crawford in late May 2003. Both emphasized that their views on North Korea were nearly "identical," both called for additional "pressure" on Pyongyang to create an environment more conducive to negotiations, and both promised to step up law enforcement efforts to deprive the Democratic People's Republic of Korea (DPRK) of hard currency—Japan by squeezing remittances from North Korean sympathizers in Japan, cutting off illicit sales of drugs in the Japanese market, and tightening implementation of export controls on dual-use items that might find their way into North Korean missile products. Koizumi made it

clear that without a resolution of the nuclear issue, there would be no normalization of relations with Pyongyang. And Japan's forthright stance earned President Bush's public support for Japan's demands on the abduction issue, and its desire to participate in future multilateral talks with the DPRK.

- It enlivened public discussion in Japan of defense options long considered taboo. For example, Defense Agency Director General Ishiba Shigeru noted that "up to now, our defense capability has been formulated on the conviction that it's better not to possess the capability to attack enemy bases." But in an era when North Korean missiles can hit Japan in a matter of minutes, he added, "we need to debate about what would be the best way to defend Japan's independence and peace and protect the lives and property of the people."[14] Heretofore, Japan had provided a shield, the United States the arrows. In response to renewed North Korean missile tests in the Sea of Japan, Ishiba and the Democratic Party's shadow defense minister, Seiji Maehara, agreed in March 2003 that Tokyo might need to consider preemptive attacks on the North.[15] For practical purposes, these represented mere adjustments in Japan's declaratory policy; the SDF, Ishiba subsequently admitted, possessed no capacity to strike back against the North. More importantly, the prime minister dismissed the suggestion that Japan was considering a revision in its long-standing renunciation of offensive military capabilities. "I am aware, he observed, "that there are arguments for obtaining offensive weapons, but the government has no such intention." He added that Japan should "concentrate exclusively on defenses of the minimum necessary scope" and leave the rest to the United States.[16]

Japan did launch, in April 2003, the first of four independent surveillance satellites with which it intended to monitor North Korea's missile developments. The Defense Agency indicated in July 2003 plans to withdraw an Aegis missile destroyer from the Indian Ocean to assure that one of its four vessels was available to keep an eye on North Korea. In June 2003 it commenced strict inspections of all North Korean ships entering Japanese ports. Finally, it placed a North Korean spy vessel sunk by the Maritime SDF (MSDF) in the East China Sea in the Museum of Maritime Science in Tokyo, providing another vivid reminder to its public of Pyongyang's provocative activities against Japan.

There has been much speculation, especially in the United States, as to whether North Korea's nuclear activities may eventually push Japan across the nuclear threshold. Some comments—for example, those of Vice

President Dick Cheney on the NBC Sunday talk show "Meet The Press" in May 2003—may have been designed to persuade the Chinese to step up their pressure on Pyongyang to dismantle its nuclear program lest it inspire Japan's emulation.[17] In Japan, however, there has been little public evidence to date of heightened government interest in a nuclear option. To be sure, discussion of the nuclear option is no longer a sacred taboo. Some, like Nisohachi Hyodo, a former member of the SDF, publicly promote the acquisition of a limited nuclear deterrent like France, which "allows [Paris] to spend far less on defense than Japan while remaining safe from attack."[18] Japanese officials openly dismiss such suggestions, however, and press stories reviewing a 1995 JDA study on the issue suggested by inference that the negative consequences of a decision to go nuclear—a highly divisive domestic debate, the intense suspicions of neighboring countries, high budgetary costs, and the risk of alienating the United States—still heavily outweigh any benefits the option would confer.

Iraq

The U.S. decision to pursue "regime change" in Iraq—a major Japanese oil supplier—posed difficult dilemmas for Tokyo's diplomacy. The United States clearly wanted Japan's forthright political support, the more so as it became clear that several key European allies were determined to oppose rather than endorse U.S. aims, let alone extend practical support.

There was nothing "automatic" about Japan's early, consistent, and forthright public support. The "old guard" in the LDP remained deeply apprehensive about the consequences of military conflict in an area of immense Japanese economic interest. Strategic analysts voiced apprehensions that a war pitting the United States against Iraq might trigger a larger civilizational struggle between the West and Islam. The Japanese public harbored scant enthusiasm for U.S. "preemption" against Iraq, or its ambitious plans to promote the democratization of the Arab world. Many experts favored responding to Iraq's presumed nuclear weapons aspirations through "containment" rather than forceful disarmament. Critics of the government argued that Japanese support should be contingent on a clear and unequivocal UN authorization of the use of force. In short, Prime Minister Koizumi could have found excuses for diplomatic dissembling in the equivocation of key U.S. allies in Europe, the hostility toward U.S. plans from Arab moderates, doubts about Saddam Hussein's links with international terrorists, or widespread domestic criticism of U.S. policies in the Middle East. He chose not to.

When the Bush administration pushed Iraq to the top of its agenda in August 2002, Japan's response was initially cautious. Tokyo was more inclined to avoid or defer a crisis in Iraq rather than to bring matters to a head. It had welcomed the Bush administration's disposition to move toward "smart sanctions." It supported an attempt to reintroduce UN weapons inspectors. Koizumi joined many European leaders in urging Washington to pursue its strategy through the UN Security Council. Japanese government leaders supplied steadfast public support for U.S. efforts to obtain UN legitimization for its policy objectives vis-à-vis Iraq, and, subsequently for its military campaign to disarm Saddam Hussein's regime, despite the failed attempt to obtain a Security Council resolution specifically authorizing the use of force.

What accounts for this? A prime Japanese motivation was its determination to avoid any repetition of its government's hapless performance during the Gulf War.[19] Another was Koizumi's substantive agreement with the U.S. contention that Iraq's repeated defiance of Security Council resolutions undermined the UN's authority and relevance. A third, perhaps, was the conviction that a U.S. invasion of Iraq was more likely to be averted if Saddam Hussein confronted a clear and overwhelming international consensus demanding that he transparently account for and dismantle all WMD. But the decisive consideration, it appears in retrospect, was Japan's clear-eyed recognition that it could not afford to alienate the United States over Iraq at a time when it needed U.S. support in dealing with a reemerging threat in North Korea.

It is a measure of Koizumi's success that he managed to support the United States over Iraq without exposing Japan's military to the risks of direct involvement in combat, and without paying a major diplomatic price in the Middle East or a significant political price at home. In truth, of course, Japan's support for the United States was clearly limited. The United States did not ask Japan to help finance its military campaign against Iraq; nor did Japan volunteer this. The bulk of the support Japan extended was political, economic, and diplomatic. Koizumi publicly endorsed U.S. aims as early as September 2002 in a speech to the Council on Foreign Relations in New York. Although Japan was not a member of the UN Security Council, he publicly championed Security Council Resolution 1441. He subsequently lobbied uncommitted members of the Council to back Washington's attempt to secure a second resolution. At home he criticized demonstrators opposed to U.S. policy (and to his government's support of it) by warning that their activities might be misread in Baghdad. He urged U.S. allies in Europe to support a second resolution lest a misleading signal be conveyed to Saddam Hussein. When that effort proved abortive, Koizumi supported the invasion of Iraq, and argued publicly that the United States possessed ample legal justification for Saddam's forceful disarmament. After the war's end, he defended the outcome by noting, "On Iraq, President Bush made a difficult and brave decision for a just cause. I supported this. Our decision was right."[20]

As war loomed, Japan promptly signaled a readiness to provide economic aid to states surrounding Iraq, to lend a helping hand with humanitarian assistance and refugee relief funds, and to participate in post-war reconstruction efforts. Its logistic support was indirect. The provision of direct rear area support to the United States or other coalition members would have required new enabling legislation. Swift passage of such an authorization bill appeared problematic, and the government was not eager to try. By stepping up its logistic support of allied naval forces in the Arabian Sea, however, Japan was able to help indirectly by allowing U.S. and British naval units to focus their operations on Iraq. Moreover, while Japan sought written assurances from those receiving fuel that its oil would not be utilized in combat operations directed against Iraq, its naval commanders reportedly did not ask too many questions about where individual vessels were heading after refueling operations were accomplished.

Eager to participate in the reconstruction of Iraq, and prepared to accommodate a U.S. desire that this include putting "boots on the ground," Koizumi mobilized the necessary political consensus for the requisite enabling legislation despite evident public misgivings, and it was passed by the Diet on July 25, 2003. Many features of the deployment remain uncertain—where SDF units will operate, whether they will transport weapons and ammunition for U.S. forces, and how they will divide their labors between humanitarian tasks and support of the U.S. occupation. As security conditions have recently deteriorated in Iraq, public support for the mission has fallen sharply. And with Lower House elections looming in the fall, political calculations as well as strategic concerns are likely to determine the timing of SDF deployments and the precise activities in which they participate.

While this prospective assistance reflects Japan's effort to shoulder broader international security responsibilities consistent with its law and prevailing political sensitivities, the government's readiness to participate in Iraq's reconstruction is also designed to enhance Japanese firms' access to lucrative construction contracts in Iraq and position Japan favorably with an important potential oil supplier and commercial partner. And although Japan's stringent budgetary conditions make money difficult to come by, the Ministry of Finance reportedly planned to tap a "technical surplus" in the FY 2002 budget for up to $3 billion to help with Iraq's postwar reconstruction.[21]

Iran

With Washington preoccupied with Iraq and North Korea throughout much of the year, Japan pursued its commercial interests in Iran—a supplier of nearly 15 percent of its oil—with little outside notice or public complaint. A major objective was the conclusion of a contract between INPEX Corporation (controlled by the state-run Japan National Oil Company) to develop Iran's giant Azadegan oil field. But following the U.S. victory over Baghdad, Washington's renewed focus on Iran was reinforced by alleged Iranian interference in Iraq's internal politics and a wave of student demonstrations against Tehran's clerical regime. This served to reinvigorate U.S. efforts—this time in concert with the Europeans—to halt potential Iranian nuclear weapons projects.

Washington's recently reaffirmed resolve to mobilize all available economic leverage behind its nonproliferation objectives in Iran exposed Japan's oil-related deals to increased U.S. scrutiny and criticism. In late June 2003, for example, the United States urged Tokyo to put off signing any new energy contracts with Iran pending the outcome of efforts to persuade Tehran to drop its suspected nuclear weapons program, and agree to more stringent IAEA inspections of all of its nuclear sites. When Tokyo persuaded the consortium to postpone signing the contracts beyond a June 30 Iranian deadline, Tehran promptly invited China and Russia to bid on the deal.[22]

This issue poses delicate trade-offs between Japan's interests in promoting nonproliferation and its stake in diversifying energy sources. In response to pressure from Colin Powell, Condoleezza Rice, and Richard Armitage, Tokyo delayed arrangements to conclude an attractive energy deal and urged the Iranians to clear up suspicions about their nuclear program. It is reluctant to foreswear participation in developing the Azadegan field, however, because it fears it will then go to the French or other Europeans. Its priority has been enhanced in Japanese eyes, moreover, by Russia's reluctance firmly to commit to a pipeline to Nakodka and Japan's loss of a 40-year old drilling concession at Khafji in Saudi Arabia's Neutral Zone. Thus, Iran is destined to provide a more serious test of U.S.-Japan policy coordination in the near future than it has in the past year.

Relations with Other Powers

Consistent with its tradition of "comprehensive security" and "omnidirectional diplomacy," Japan devoted consistent attention to the cultivation of other major powers and key Asian countries in the search for diplomatic maneuverability and the advancement and protection of its commercial and other interests. Happily, from Tokyo's standpoint, the United States could not complain about such efforts; on the contrary, a search for closer ties with all the major powers was a cardinal principle of the Bush administration's new security strategy. In the hierarchy of Japanese interests, after the United States, China held pride of place. A study of foreign policy challenges commissioned by the prime minister's office, chaired by Yukio Okamoto,[23] and completed in the fall of 2002, concluded that China would provide Japan with its most daunting future foreign policy challenge.

China

Japanese attitudes toward China reflect a combination of cool detachment and underlying anxiety; they are marked neither by excessive sentimentality nor cynicism. The PRC's growing manufacturing prowess and military buildup do stimulate apprehension. But many Japanese are also fascinated by the possibilities of Sino-Japanese economic cooperation and exhibit respect for China's rich cultural tradition. Tokyo's relations with Beijing over the past year have been marked by a familiar mix of competition and cooperation. The atmospherics surrounding the relationship appeared more correct than cordial. The robust growth of Sino-Japanese trade and investment fostered the continuing integration of their complementary economies, while political relations were troubled by discordant notes. Both governments seemed determined to avert confrontation, yet they eschewed intimacy.

- Historical memories continued to cast a shadow over the relationship. Prime Minister Koizumi's annual visits to Yasukuni Shrine disrupted the pattern of regular high-level visits, and prevented his participation in Beijing ceremonies commemorating the 30th anniversary of Sino-Japanese normalization agreement, although he was able to meet Hu Jintao on the margins of a multilateral conference in early summer 2003. While Japanese officials are hopeful that the fourth generation of leaders in China will not be as inclined to use the history issue as an element of leverage in the relationship, Koizumi seems unlikely to garner an invitation to visit China so long as his visits to Yasukuni continue.[24]
- Rival Sino-Japanese claims to the Senkaku Islands resurfaced when the Japanese government leased three islets in the chain from private parties, ostensibly to reduce prospects of landings and demonstrations by Japanese rightists. Yet this action served to strengthen its control over the territory while reinforcing its international claim. It set off a brief, though frenzied reaction in Beijing as well as Hong Kong and Taipei, but the fracas was relatively brief.

- Tempers in Japan, meanwhile, flared over Chinese intrusions into the Japanese consulate in Shenyang in pursuit of North Koreans seeking asylum. The incident provoked sustained press commentary in Japan that was critical both of China and Japan's own Ministry of Foreign Affairs. Nonetheless, the incident was settled diplomatically.
- Differences over Taiwan occasionally surfaced, and many younger Japanese Diet members developed closer ties with their Taiwanese counterparts. But the Foreign Ministry also headed off a potential confrontation with Beijing by persuading Keio University to withdraw an invitation to Taiwan's former President Lee Teng-hui.
- Trade disputes continued to accumulate—an almost inevitable result of rapidly expanding bilateral trade and investment flows. In October 2002, the Chinese applied formal safeguards to imports of key Japanese steel products. But Japan registered no formal complaints to the WTO, and each side displayed the restraint that one might expect of trading partners with a growing stake in managing commercial disputes efficiently and more or less amicably.
- Japan also continued to cut official development assistance (ODA) program commitments and disbursements to China. In part this was a natural consequence of a tight budget. There were, however, political overtones as well. The Japanese public, with conservative elements of the LDP in the vanguard, expressed growing frustration with large disbursements of aid to a large neighbor whose economic growth rate far outpaces Japan's, whose military budget has been growing at double digit rates, which has developed its own aid programs, and which only rarely acknowledges, let alone expresses gratitude for, Japan's largesse.

These sources of occasional discord notwithstanding, Tokyo continued to nurture expanded trade and investment flows to China, and bilateral trade topped $90 billion in 2002. Japan's exports to China increased by more than 10 percent during the year, led by semiconductors, electrical equipment, and automobiles. Imports grew even more dramatically, and China replaced the United States as Japan's largest source of imports. Direct Japanese investment commitments in China increased, as Japanese firms continued to relocate Japanese production facilities to the People's Republic of China to capitalize on the availability of cheap labor and strong engineering talent. Many of the intermediate goods produced were exported back into the Japanese market, helping to account for the fact that manufactured goods now constitute 84 percent of Japan's imports from China.[25]

Russia

Tokyo's relations with Moscow evolved quietly this year, yet they revealed little warmth, and were accorded a relatively low priority. Bilateral commercial ties continued to expand at a steady pace, and offer considerable potential given the abundance of undeveloped resources in Siberia and Russia's scientific and technological prowess. Yet the Japanese business community remains wary of major investments in Russia. Moscow gave priority to the construction of a pipeline to supply Siberian energy resources to China, postponing for the time being a decision to build a second pipeline to Nakodka for purposes of distributing oil and natural gas to Japan and others. In June 2003, the Japanese and Russians did sign a $2 billion contract to construct the world's largest liquefied natural gas plant on Sakhalin Island, mostly for export to Japan. Trade in other fields in which Russia possesses a comparative advantage—e.g., defense equipment sales and the provision of nuclear enrichment services—remained modest due to Japanese concerns about national security and commercial reliability.

No progress was achieved on the Northern Territories issue, since neither government possessed the domestic political latitude to contemplate significant concessions. Both sides seem content to let the issue lie; Tokyo because the LDP is still feeling the after-effects of the Muneo Suzuki scandal; Moscow because President Putin is preoccupied with an upcoming presidential election.[26] The North Korean nuclear issue did provide some scope for diplomatic cooperation, but beyond sharing a desire for a nonnuclear Korean peninsula, and seats at the table when the issue comes up for multilateral discussion, the impulse for collaboration is modest.

South Korea

Shared strategic concerns and converging economic interests underpinned Tokyo's strong ties with South Korea. The election of President Roh Moo Hyun introduced a note of uncertainty. He had visited Japan only once, possessed few personal ties with members of the Japanese establishment, and had no track record in the field of foreign policy. Prime Minister Koizumi attended his inauguration, along with a high-powered delegation of government and opposition leaders, and Tokyo accorded Roh extraordinary hospitality during his June 2003 official visit to Japan.

Coordinating policy with Seoul toward Pyongyang proved a challenge. In the past, Tokyo occasionally regarded the Republic of Korea (ROK) as a useful counterweight to Washington's inclination to confront the North. More recently, Tokyo has found itself in the position of joining the United States in encouraging the ROK to toughen its stance toward the DPRK. During their recent summit, Prime Minister Koizumi and President Roh seemed to establish a strong personal rapport. Roh spoke before the Diet, and mentioned the residual problems left by history without histrionics. Both leaders welcomed the continued expansion of bilateral commerce, even as they found common cause on other trade issues, e.g. consideration of a bilateral free trade agreement, protection of agricultural interests in the run up to the Doha Round of multilateral trade negotiations, and representations to China to allow its currency to appreciate.

Association of Southeast Asian Nations (ASEAN)

Because its relations in Southeast Asia are less bedeviled by historical memories, territorial disputes and intractable security problems, Japan has long regarded the area as a theater for foreign policy activism. To the countries of ASEAN, Japan's sizable flows of ODA and private investment are highly coveted and appreciated. Shared security interests—including maritime safety against pirates—have achieved increased salience, and Southeast Asian nations welcome Japan's interest in multilateral security institutions like the ASEAN Regional Forum (ARF).

During the past year Japan continued to seek a broader and more visible political role in the region as a corollary to its major economic presence there. The constraints on its role were also apparent. Japan's sluggish economic performance has undercut its prestige while limiting available ODA resources. China's active economic role presents Japan with a competitive challenge for leadership in Southeast Asia. Tokyo's powerful and protectionist agricultural lobby prevents it from fielding a serious alternative to Beijing's proposal for a China-ASEAN free trade agreement. Yet in pushing ASEAN+3 as its preferred forum for regional cooperation, Tokyo is encouraging the formation of an embryonic counterweight to the EU and NAFTA. This regional forum has clearly gained momentum and relevance vis-à-vis the Asia Pacific Economic Cooperation (APEC) forum—Washington's favored instrument for advancing regional economic initiatives. Tokyo's challenge is to assert its leadership without offending the sensibilities of ASEAN members who fear seeing their identities submerged in a larger regional framework.

Tokyo's preoccupations in Southeast Asia during the year included:

- Encouraging stability in Indonesia in the face of the centrifugal pressures of renewed separatism (in Aceh), and an upsurge in activity by terrorist groups like Jemaah Islamiyah. In practical terms there seemed little Japan could do beyond sustaining a sizable ODA program, preserving a high level of private sector investment, keeping in touch with all the major political forces in the country, maintaining a modest peacekeeping presence in East Timor, and welcoming the proposed reestablishment of official U.S. relationships with the Indonesian military.

- Using its engagement with the ruling junta in Burma to compete politically with China, while differentiating its approach from the United States in a country of modest strategic interest to Washington. More surprisingly, it has recently undertaken concerted efforts with ASEAN countries, Britain, and others to pressure Burmese authorities to release Aung Sang Suu Kyi and to reopen a political dialogue with the opposition.[27]
- Undertaking new financial initiatives to compete effectively for leadership of ASEAN+3 with China. Japan's principal effort was directed at laying the groundwork for a regional bond market. Tokyo's initiative envisages use of the huge foreign exchange reserves held by Asian central banks to create a market in which money can be relent to finance industrial development in the region.

Europe

In recent years Japan's emphasis on cooperation with the European Union (EU) has appeared more a mantra than an action program. On its face this is surprising. There is considerable kinship between Japanese policy reflexes and the aspirations ascribed to Europeans in Robert Kagan's book, *Of Paradise and Power*, to inhabit a world "where military strength and hard power matter less than economic and soft power, an international order where international law and international institutions matter more than the power of individual nations, where unilateral action by powerful states is forbidden, where all nations regardless of their strength have equal rights and are equally protected by commonly agreed-upon international rules of behavior."[28] Many Japanese intuitively embrace such notions, though they would not express their views in such Wilsonian language. Events, however, conspired to limit the sphere for concerted Japanese-EU geopolitical action over the past year. The Japanese government neither shared the intense European reactions to U.S. policy toward Iraq, nor would its spokesmen have considered it prudent to express misgivings so publicly or bluntly. In fact, with respect to U.S. policy toward Iraq, Koizumi chose to position himself closer to Tony Blair than Jacques Chirac.

Tokyo continued to work closely with various European countries in pushing its commercial interests and political agenda. It collaborated closely, for example, with the French in preparing defenses on agricultural issues in the run-up to multilateral trade negotiations. Its preference for "engagement" with Iran closely paralleled the policies of Germany, France, and Russia. However, with Europe unable to speak with a single voice on strategic issues, the United States sensitive to criticism, and Japan confronting more palpable security dangers, Tokyo's disposition to hew closer to U.S. policy than to European criticism of it was clear and understandable.

Domestic Factors and Japanese Strategy

Three domestic developments shaped the evolution of Japanese strategy over the course of the past year—economic weakness, the necessities of coalition government, and rising nationalist sentiments.

For years Japan's diplomacy has relied heavily on its "deep pockets." It could ensure that its interests were taken into account by spreading around lots of cash and credit. Its overwhelming economic strength provided a cushion of sorts, but as Koji Murata, a prominent, young international security specialist, observed, "Generally speaking, Japanese are beginning to feel that this margin is getting smaller and smaller." He added, "We are becoming much more realistic about defense matters, and the reason for this is our economic stagnation."[29]

While paltry growth has exacerbated Japan's budget deficit and imposed financial constraints on its foreign policy, the effects of economic stagnation on foreign policy can be exaggerated. Japan is seeking to reduce its dues to the United Nations, but that reflects frustration with its failure to win a permanent seat on the Security Council as much as budgetary limitations. Tokyo has also cut its ODA program by nearly 30 percent over the past three years. Much of the cut was absorbed by China. Yet by utilizing its aid more strategically, and directing its loans and grants more clearly to the support of critical national interests, Japan may be able to secure a "bigger bang" from its aid program with "fewer bucks."

In any event, the impact of aid cuts on Sino-Japanese relations have been ameliorated by other considerations. China remains the largest recipient of Japan's aid, and a major beneficiary of sizable Japanese private investment flows; Beijing can scarcely gainsay the importance of other high-priority recipients of Japanese aid in South Asia and the Middle East; and current targets of Japanese loans and grants in China—e.g., the development of business infrastructure, the promotion of energy development, the mitigation of environmental degradation, and the expansion of personnel exchanges of all kinds—serve essential objectives for Beijing.

Nor is there much evidence that Japan, despite falling behind the United States as the largest single source of global economic assistance in FY 2002, has been unable for budgetary reasons to make sizable contributions to nascent state-building activities in Afghanistan or Iraq, to sustain its support for the Palestinian Authority, or to maintain robust bilateral aid programs in South, Central, and Southeast Asia. Despite prolonged sluggishness, Japan remains the world's second largest economy and the world's biggest creditor. "Cash register diplomacy" may have fallen into disfavor, but Tokyo retains an impressive capacity to utilize economic leverage in defense of its interests.

The effects of domestic political developments were evident in several features of Japan's foreign policy. A general shift to the right has been perceptible both within the LDP and among its coalition partners.[30] Koizumi paid obeisance to conservatives in honoring his pledge to make an annual visit to Yasukuni Shrine, despite some adverse consequences for Japan's relations with China and Korea. The power of conservative nationalist sentiment has also strengthened the case for cutting aid to China, maintaining a hard line on territorial issues, and resisting concessions to Pyongyang. The LDP's continued reliance on support from the agricultural lobby vitiates government efforts to compete with China's promotion of a free trade agreement with ASEAN.

With respect to defense policy, opposition groups have been moving toward the center, thus facilitating Japan's emerging offshore, non-combat support role in the face of international security challenges. Still, the process of getting coalition partners—like the Komeito Party—on board slows the process of consensus building, and reinforces caution when the government runs up against long-established policy guidelines like the strictures against collective self-defense. As events have demonstrated, it is not impossible to broaden the limits of permissible action. However, rhetoric continues to outpace action, and precedents continue to accumulate at a stately pace.

The policymaking system in Japan has also been undergoing a gradual transformation. On domestic issues it appears particularly ponderous and subject to gridlock. Curiously, it seems to function more efficiently in response to ever-changing security conditions. This is a striking reversal of familiar patterns; in the past, security-related legislation often ran into strong resistance, while even highly contentious economic measures like tax hikes sailed through the Diet.

To some extent this is a consequence of recent political reforms which have strengthened the hand of the prime minister. The electoral reform laws introduced in the mid-1990s empowered local chapters of the governing LDP, and Koizumi utilized these changes to exploit grassroots support within the party to weaken the power of faction leaders, thereby giving him greater control over his cabinet. Government reforms enacted in 1999 bolstered the role of the cabinet against the bureaucracy, and provided the prime minister with a more powerful "bully pulpit" in the Diet where he could make his case to a public increasingly disposed to observe the televised proceedings. The Administrative Reform Act of 2001—passed in the wake of the Kobe earthquake, the Peruvian hostage debacle, and a major oil spill in the Sea of Japan—augmented the prime minister's authority in the field of crisis management, and strengthened the Cabinet Secretariat, enhancing its ability to assist the prime minister in providing integrated policy direction to the cabinet and fostering coordination among the ministries.

On domestic issues, where formidable opposition within the LDP is reinforced by the bureaucracy, the prime minister remains little more than *primus inter pares* within the cabinet. On foreign policy and defense matters, he has begun to display the attributes of a more substantial leader.[31]

In this latter connection, the prime minister has benefited from the continued flowering of nationalist sentiment. To some extent this is a manifestation of frustration with Japan's weak economic performance. It is also inspired by the more self-conscious awareness of security challenges in the neighborhood. It is evident in the popularity of the Tokyo's governor, Shintaro Ishihara, whose nationalism is directed against the United States as well as China, North Korea, and others. Milder expressions of it can be seen in the emphasis placed on "national interests" in the prime minister's task force report on foreign policy, and in the more permissive public attitudes toward national security options that were long considered taboo.

Future Prospects

The trajectory of change in Japanese strategy seems clear. For now, it has chosen to fortify its alliance with the United States, flesh out an offshore, non-combat role in response to international crises, and gradually extend the capabilities of the SDF while incrementally chipping away at traditional post-war limits on its equipment, roles, and missions. At the same time, Japan continues energetically to pursue its commercial and economic interests and leadership in Asian regional ventures in competition with the United States and others, while maximizing its diplomatic maneuverability through the patient cultivation of the great powers and other countries of consequence.

This broad approach—the pursuit of comprehensive security, including continued reliance on the U.S. alliance, while retaining some "anchors to windward"—appears responsive to Japan's external circumstances and enjoys broad support from powerful constituencies at home. What might deflect Japan from this course? Externally, changes in the nature of the security threats confronting Japan and/or growing doubts about the reliability of the U.S. strategic guarantee.

North Korea poses the external challenge most susceptible to change. Pyongyang could conceivably accommodate external pressures, and relinquish its nuclear activities in return for security assurances and economic concessions, thereby attenuating Japan's most immediate and palpable threat. At the other extreme, it might decisively cross the nuclear threshold and accumulate a growing WMD stockpile. Nor can one ignore the continuing risk of North Korea's collapse as a consequence of economic privation and diplomatic isolation. Any of these changes would alter the factor that has most clearly shaped Japan's conduct over the past year, and thereby increase Japan's incentives to explore other policy options.

The United States, the world's preeminent power and Japan's most important partner, has also embarked on the most fundamental adjustments in its foreign policy since the late 1940s. Japan has thus far adjusted to those changes with remarkable equanimity. But if the United States finds itself over-stretched in its struggle against terrorists, bogged down in the task of state-building in Iraq and Afghanistan, or isolated in its policies toward Iran or North Korea, it could either press allies more urgently for expanded support, or, alternatively, reconsider its burgeoning overseas responsibilities or rearrange priorities among them. Depending on the way Washington's emphasis on such new policy concepts as "preemption," "regime change," and "no peer competition" evolves, Japan could either see the underpinnings of its alliance with the United States bolstered, or its inducements to dilute collaboration with Washington strengthened. The Bush administration has already signaled significant future adjustments in its military deployments in South Korea at a time when the U.S.-ROK alliance is subject to evident strains. Such U.S. decisions can, of course, resurrect traditional Japanese fears of "entrapment" or "abandonment" and trigger renewed interest in the full range of policy responses that are usually provoked by them.

On the domestic front, there is also a wide range of alternative possibilities. While Japan has drifted through more than a decade of economic slough, it is not inevitable that stagnation will persist. Tokyo could face a more systemic crisis, particularly in the banking sector; it could bump along for an extended period of time "under-performing" its growth potential while resisting fundamental reforms in its industrial structure; or it could gradually work its way back to impressive levels of self-sustaining growth. The first remains a risk in the short term. The second is a fair bet for several years. But a return to robust growth in the medium-term future should not be excluded.

For all the talk of economic reform, it remains extremely difficult to accomplish. The reasons are not so mysterious. For one thing, the bureaucracy, which stands to lose if market-oriented reforms are implemented, continues to provide formidable resistance. For another, those members of the LDP representing powerful constituencies—e.g. farmers, small businesses, and the construction industry, to mention just a few—tend to oppose those reforms that expose their supporters to serious competition. The opposition parties, meanwhile, have presented few compelling reform proposals of their own. Nor has the general public displayed the sense of urgency about the need for reform that bolsters the courage of timid politicians to support it. In Japan, it appears, social harmony still trumps economic efficiency. And the political system was not arranged to produce heroic leadership. Koizumi, whatever his convictions about the need for change, occupies a relatively weak office. Thus, reform will continue to take place slowly and incrementally. Gradually however, excess capacity will be further reduced in the manufacturing sector, excess loans will continue to be liquidated in the financial sector, and excess regulation will be tempered by the greater interplay of market forces in the service sector. Change is in the air, and its effects will become increasingly visible in the years to come.

It is not, of course, inevitable that the LDP will remain the dominant political force indefinitely, though no major competitors have yet emerged. The most popular current alternative to Prime Minister Koizumi remains Shintaro Ishihara, an independent with strong populist and nationalist credentials. An alternative center of gravity for Japanese politics could be fashioned out of reformist groups with a more internationalist bent. The sharper the discontinuities in the international situation, the more likely a dramatic shift in political sentiment at home, with the accompanying possibility of more dramatic changes in foreign policy and defense strategy. While one cannot exclude such political and policy discontinuities, the odds are that Japan's strategy will continue to evolve in directions and at a pace that are more familiar. And while that may be disconcerting to some, it is a source of reassurance to its neighbors, and should be to the United States as well.

Endnotes

1 Eric Heginbotham and Richard J. Samuels, "Japan," in Richard J. Ellings and Aaron L. Friedberg with Michael Wills, eds., *Strategic Asia 2002–03: Asian Aftershocks*, Seattle: The National Bureau of Asian Research, 2003, pp. 95–130.
2 Hiroshi Fujita, "2003 New Year Editorials: A Deepening Sense of Crisis," *Japan Review of International Affairs*, vol. 17, no. 1 (Spring 2003), p.62.
3 A survey commissioned by the Cabinet Office in early April, 2003 revealed

that 73 percent of those polled regarded the U.S. alliance as making a valuable contribution to Japan's security. See *Japan Digest*, April 7, 2003, p. 10.

[4] In addition to continuing its offshore logistic support for *Operation Enduring Freedom*, Tokyo took the lead in organizing a pledging conference in February 2003 and made the largest contribution—$35 million—to efforts designed to disarm Afghan war lords in order to help consolidate the authority of the government of Hamid Karzai.

[5] Brad Glosserman, "An Oasis of Stability," *Comparative Connections*, July–September 2002, p. 1.

[6] For example, see excerpts from Ambassador Howard Baker's upbeat assessment of the alliance in a speech to the International Friendship Exchange Council in Tokyo on June 30, 2003 in Brad Glosserman, "Still on a Roll," *Comparative Connections*, April–June 2003, pp. 1–2.

[7] The "two plus two" meetings bring the Japanese minister of foreign affairs and Japan defense agency director together periodically with the U.S. secretaries of state and defense.

[8] Henry A. Kissinger, *Diplomacy*, New York: Simon & Schuster, 1994, p. 827.

[9] These included a Bill to Respond to Armed Attacks, a Bill for Revision of the Self Defense Forces Law, and a Bill for Revision of the Security Council of Japan. In the aggregate they provide legislative framework for responding to actual or anticipated attacks on Japan, allow the Self Defense Forces to override local laws and regulations that would impede essential military operations, and revise the Security Council of Japan to transform it into a more effective crisis response mechanism.

[10] In defending the deployment of Japanese troops to Iraq before the Diet in late July, 2003, Koizumi emphasized that they "will not be dispatched to combat zones, they will not participate in combat. They will be there to help reconstruct Iraq." See *Japan Digest*, July 28, 2003, p. 13.

[11] Some thought Koizumi's initiative blind-sided or "wrong-footed" Washington, deepening its isolation in dealing with Pyongyang. But Koizumi informed Bush of his trip in advance, and senior administration officials subsequently stressed the President's support for the trip and the opportunity it provided to raise concerns, such as North Korea's ambitions to develop weapons of mass destruction, that Washington and Tokyo shared. See Brad Glosserman, "An Oasis of Stability," *Comparative Connections*, July–September 2002, p. 2.

[12] For Japan, North Korean actions had several alarming dimensions. It now appeared that Pyongyang's intermediate-range ballistic missiles might, in the relatively near future, be equipped with nuclear weapons. North Korea's aspiration to acquire such weapons, moreover, could inspire emulation from other countries in the region—such as South Korea or Taiwan—thus complicating the security equation in Northeast Asia, and perhaps compelling Japan to tackle the nuclear issue head on at a time when it remains a highly charged source of contention. North Korean obduracy, moreover, could enable China to position itself to play a more central role in managing regional security issues, possibly in closer collaboration with the United States. All these considerations provided Tokyo with incentives to cooperate closely with Washington in the search for a diplomatic resolution to the problem.

[13] *Japan Digest*, June 6, 2003, p. 10.

[14] *Japan Digest*, March 31, 2003, p. 11.

[15] *Japan Digest*, March 31, 2003, p. 12.

[16] *Japan Digest*, March 31, 2003, p. 12.

[17] Karl Schoenberger, "Japan reconsidering the bomb," *San Jose Mercury News*, June 16, 2003.

[18] Howard W. French, "Japan faces burden: its own defense," *New York Times*, July 22, 2003, p. A7.

[19] In 1990–91, in response to Iraq's invasion of Kuwait, Japan possessed neither the legal authority nor a political consensus to support the multilateral coalition's request for "risk –sharing" as well as "cost-sharing." It wound up providing $13 billion in financial assistance to the United States, its coalition partners, and the "front-line" states in the region, but it received little credit for this "cash register" diplomacy. In the aftermath of this conflict the Japanese government went through a good deal of soul-searching, and the Diet passed legislation permitting Japan to participate in future UN authorized peacekeeping ventures.

[20] Brad Glosserman, "Still On a Roll," *Comparative Connections*, April–June 2003, p. 2.

[21] *Japan Digest*, July 14, 2003, p. 16.

[22] Some sources implied that Moscow suggested to the Japanese that they jointly develop the Azadegan field. In return for Japan's capital and technological contributions to this project, Russia, it was rumored, would agree to build an oil pipeline from Angarsk in Siberia to Nakodka either in addition to or as an alternative to China's proposed pipeline from Angarsk to Daqing. See *Financial Times*, July 10, 2003, p. 5.

[23] The "Task Force on Foreign Relations" report was entitled, "A Basic Strategy for Japanese Diplomacy in the 21st Century," See James Przystup, "Congratulations, Concern, Competition, and Cooperation," in *Comparative Connections*, October–December 2002, p. 2.

[24] By contrast, Hu Jintao met frequently with other visiting Japanese leaders in Beijing. These included, among others, Kan Naoto (Democratic Party), Yamasaki Taku (LDP), Fuyushiba Tetsuzo (Komeito), Nikai Toshihiro (New Conservative Party) and Doi Takako (Socialist Party). See James Przystup, "Political Breakthrough and the SARS Outbreak," *Comparative Connections*, April–June 2003, pp. 2–3.

[25] A growing recognition of the role "captive exports" play in Japan's bilateral trade with China also helped to undercut the argument of those critics who argued that China was "exporting deflation" to Japan.

[26] Muneo Suzuki, a prominent LDP Diet member, became identified with Japanese policy toward Russia while serving as Parliamentary Vice Minister of Foreign Affairs in the early 1990's. He was indicted in 2002 for allegedly taking bribes in connection with decisions regarding construction projects in the Northern Territories during his service as Director of the Hokkaido Development Agency.

[27] As of August 1, 2003, Japan's aid to Burma remains suspended pending Suu Kyi's release from jail.

[28] Robert Kagan, *Of Paradise and Power*, New York: Alfred A. Knopf, 2003, p. 37.

[29] Quoted by Howard W. French, "Japan faces burden...."

[30] Even the Communist Party has recently proposed scrapping its demand for the removal of the emperor along with a number of other outdated ideological slogans in response to its evident need to change if it is to preserve its modest electoral base at a time of widespread disaffection with Japan's communist neighbor in North Korea. See David Ibison, "Communists soften their stance as Japan shifts to the right," *Financial Times*, June 26, 2003.

[31] For analysis of these reforms and their consequences, see Tomohite Shinoda, "Koizumi's Top-Down Leadership in the Anti-Terrorism Legislation: The Impact of Political Institutional Changes," *SAIS Review*, vol. 23, no. 1 (Winter–Spring 2003), pp. 19–34.

South Korea – Key Indicators and Forecasts

Economy and Trade	2002[a]	2003[b]	2004[b]
GDP ($tr) / (PPP GDP)	0.5 (PPP GDP in 2002 = $0.8 tr)		
GDP growth (%)	6.1	5.0	5.3
Inflation (%)	2.8	3.5	3.2
Budget balance (% of GDP)	1.3	0.3	0.5
Major export destinations (2001)	U.S. (21%), China (12%), Japan (11%)		

Population and Energy	2002[a]	2005[b]	2010[b]
Population (m)	48.0	48.9	50.2
Population growth (%)	0.7	0.6	0.4
Oil production (m bbl/d)	<0.1	<0.1	<0.1
Oil consumption (m bbl/d)	2.1	2.4	2.8

Politics	
President	Roh Moo Hyun (Dem., since Feb 2003)
Dominant party	Grand National Party (since 1996)
Next election	April 2004 (legislative)

Military	
Armed forces (2002)	686,000
Defense expenditure (2001)	$11.2 bn (2.7% of GDP)
Conventional capabilities	Well-trained military with good equipment Recent addition of F-15s, will soon acquire advanced diesel submarines
Weapons of mass destruction	Has some chemical warfare capabilities

Source: The National Bureau of Asian Research, compiled from International Monetary Fund, *World Economic Outlook*; Central Intelligence Agency, *World Factbook*; U.S. Census Bureau, *International Data Base*; Energy Information Administration, *Country Analysis Brief—South Korea*; International Institute of Strategic Studies, *The Military Balance*. Notes: a) Data for 2002 may be estimates; b) Data for 2003, 204, 2005, and 2010 are projections. Additional data on South Korea are available in the Strategic Asia Database at <http://strategicasia.nbr.org>.

SOUTH KOREA

ANCHORED OR ADRIFT?

Victor D. Cha

ABSTRACT

The past year has seen events in South Korea that present a puzzling, if not incomprehensible picture. At a time of heightened nuclear threats from the Democratic People's Republic of Korea (DPRK), tens of thousands of South Koreans staged demonstrations in Seoul critical of their U.S. ally. Is there fundamental change afoot on the Korean Peninsula in which North Korea is seen as unthreatening, the United States as an impediment to inter-Korean reconciliation, and China as the new patron? This chapter assesses the domestic variables that shape South Korean strategic choice. Although there are factors that point in the direction of such changes, both near-term and longer-term variables work against this trend over the next one to five years. This finding for continuity runs contrary to popular views on Korea, and is undeniably a close call. But with proper attention and management, the United States can shape a positive direction through this undeniable transition period in American relations with Korea.

Victor Cha holds the D. S. Song Chair in Asian Studies and Government in the Edmund Walsh School of Foreign Service, Georgetown University. He thanks Richard Ellings, Michael Wills, Chae Jin Lee, and Aaron Friedberg for comments in earlier drafts.

Introduction

Formed in 1953, the alliance between the United States and the Republic of Korea (ROK or South Korea) stands as one of the most successful political-military relationships forged out of the Cold War era. What started as a pact of mutual convenience between two parties who knew little about one another and had little in common except a common threat has emerged as a prosperous and militarily robust relationship between two market-democracies. From its humble origins, the alliance today represents the model of success for why the Cold War was fought. For 50 years, neither the governments nor their constituents on either side of the Pacific questioned the alliance's rationale, its substance, or its purpose: the United States and the ROK were united to deter and, if necessary, to defend against the threat posed by the regime in the North. The United States stationed forces in Korea for this purpose, and the South Koreans democratized and prospered from the stability provided by the U.S. defense commitment.

Given this history, events in South Korea at the beginning of 2003 presented a puzzling, if not incomprehensible, picture. At a time of heightened nuclear threats from the Democratic People's Republic of Korea (DPRK), with Pyongyang expelling international inspectors from its facilities at Yongbyon, tens of thousands of South Koreans staged demonstrations in Seoul critical of their American ally and ultimately elected a president reputed to oppose the U.S. military footprint in his country.

The proximate causes for these events are generally related to popular South Korean dissatisfaction with the Bush administration's refusal to follow the "sunshine" or engagement policy toward North Korea made famous by the Kim Dae Jung government (1998–2002). Speculation emerged among some Koreans that the United States was pushing for a "hard-landing"/unification of the peninsula for which the South Koreans are not yet prepared. Specifically, the November 2002 acquittal of two U.S. soldiers by a U.S. military court for the accidental vehicular death of two Korean schoolgirls was seen as an unconscionable affront to South Korean sovereignty and fueled the public protests in December 2002 and January 2003.

At a more fundamental level, however, the events of 2002–03 raised the question of whether a new constellation of forces had emerged that could propel Korea in wholly different directions from that which U.S. strategy is accustomed. In analytic shorthand, "anchored Korea" corresponded to a set of geostrategic choices made by Seoul over the past half-century that accorded well with U.S. interests. These included the hosting of a U.S. military presence on the Asian mainland (on favorable terms for the United States); opposition to the North Korean threat; and, along with Japan, act-

Table 1. Notional Paths for South Korean Strategic Choice

"Anchored" Korea	Korea "Adrift"
Allied with the West and the United States	Deteriorating alliance relations
Host U.S. military presence on the Asian mainland (on terms favorable to the United States)	United States pushed off the Peninsula. Loss of Korean toehold, which then raises questions about the rationale for the U.S. military presence in Japan
Oppose the North Korean threat explicitly and China implicitly	Unconditional engagement with North Korea with the objective of peaceful coexistence (implicit acceptance of a nuclear North Korea)
Support liberal democratic and free market principles (not readily accepted by all in Northeast Asia)	Neutrality from the United States and pursuit of China as Korea's new patron
Quasi-alliance with Japan that anchors U.S. influence and power projection in the region	Regional China-Korea alignment, isolating Japan

ing as a free market, democratic anchor of U.S. influence and power projection in the region (see Table 1).

The events of 2002–03 raise the question of whether strategic choices might put "Korea adrift" over the next one to five years, ultimately resulting in outcomes on the peninsula for which U.S. strategy is not prepared. These are summarized in notional terms in Table 1. They include a South Korea that pushes the United States off the peninsula; chooses open-ended engagement with North Korea (even at the cost of nuclear proliferation); seeks a continental accommodation with China (or at least greater equidistance from the United States toward China); or balances (with China) against Japan.

The two notional paths in Table 1 do not cover all the possible strategic options for Korea. A third set of choices—"Korea cut loose"—refers to a more autonomous South Korea that seeks peaceful coexistence (if not unification) with the North and purposefully abstains from alignments with the United States, China, or any other major power, instead playing balance of power politics among the powers. This view, however much romanticized, is not a very realistic option. First, history dictates that success as an off-shore balancer (e.g., Britain) requires power capabilities far beyond what Korea could wield as it balanced between the United States and

China. Second, Korean history shows that every prior attempt by Korea not to ally with a major power and to seek instead a self-contained "hermit" status has been wildly unsuccessful as the major powers competed for dominance on the peninsula. Third, a Korean security self-help strategy would almost certainly include nuclear weapons status, which not only runs contrary to the South's current Nuclear Nonproliferation Treaty (NPT) commitments, but also could render it a pariah nuclear status that could have untold political and economic consequences.

Geostrategic outcomes as described in the second column—"Korea adrift"—are not favorable to the United States. To the extent that the United States has the will to remain an Asia Pacific power, it has no interest in being pushed off the peninsula and losing influence to China. The secondary and tertiary consequences of the outcomes described above, moreover, are not favorable for the region either. An isolated Japan, which for example, does not want to remain the last U.S. military outpost in the region (if the United States leaves Korea) and faces antagonistic relations with China and Korea, may choose a military self-help option that could spark an arms race in the region and potential nuclearization.

To what extent do the events of 2002–03 presage a fundamental change on the Korean Peninsula in which North Korea is seen as unthreatening, the United States as an impediment to inter-Korean reconciliation, or China as the new patron? This chapter will assess the domestic variables that shape Korean strategic choice. Although there are factors that point in the direction of "Korea adrift"-type changes, both near-term and longer-term variables work against this trend over the next one to five years. This finding for continuity runs contrary to popular views on Korea. The call is a close one. In this sense, Korea befits the title "fragility and crisis" for this year's volume of *Strategic Asia*. A critical variable in this regard will be the manner in which the United States rebalances its forces on the peninsula. Although military in nature, this rebalancing plan has potentially major political ramifications that, if managed properly, can work toward outcomes favorable to U.S. interests. However, if implemented without due consideration of the political externalities, the plan could lead to Korean strategic choices antithetical to U.S. interests.

Variables for Change

Generational Change

The most prevalent factor that might indicate fundamentally new directions for Korean strategic choice is the changing South Korean demographic. Often referred to as the "sam-pal-yook" (3-8-6) movement,[1] but generally referring to Koreans in their twenties and thirties, this younger generation has profoundly different opinions of the United States than their elders. Rather than holding the United States in high regard as a savior during the Korean War and a Cold War ally, this group views the United States as a supporter of authoritarian governments in South Korea from the 1960s to 1980s and complicit in the military crackdown at Kwangju in 1980. Whereas the agenda for the older generation was economic sustenance and security survival, the younger, more affluent, and higher-educated generation is more concerned with quality-of-life issues (e.g., labor rights, environmental issues, urban congestion, status-of-forces), of which the externalities of the large U.S. military footprint in Korea is a prominent one.[2]

The election of political maverick and former labor activist lawyer Roh Moo Hyun as the ROK president in December 2002 arguably marked the political arrival of the new generation. Moreover, public anger at the death of the two Korean schoolgirls and criticism of Bush's "axis of evil" designation of North Korea caused many young Koreans, for the first time in South Korean political history, to view the United States as more threatening than the communist regime from across the demilitarized zone (DMZ).[3] Public opinion polls after the election of Roh painted the picture of the changing "post-Korean war" demographic: While 26 percent of middle-aged South Koreans held negative images of the United States, an astounding 76 percent of youth in their 20s and 67 percent of those in their 30s responded in a similar fashion (see Table 2).[4]

Table 2. Negative Attitudes Toward the
United States and North Korea by Age Distribution

Age	United States	North Korea
20–29	76	32
30–39	67	29
40–49	53	39
50+	26	47

Source: Gallup Korea, December 2002.

Moreover, 51 percent of South Koreans polled believed that North Korea's nuclear intransigence at the end of 2002 and beginning of 2003 was the result of the Bush administration's hardline policy. Only 25 percent attributed the problem to North Korean actions and intentions.[5]

These attitudes are reflected at the policymaking level in groups of National Assembly members known as the "reform group" that are in their first or second term as legislators and have connections with the president from his labor activist days.[6] There also is a core group of younger appointees in the Blue House (known as the *undong kwon*), many of whom are former student activists, that allegedly influence Roh on domestic and some foreign policy issues.[7] A critical near-term signpost will be the National Assembly elections in the spring of 2004. The ruling party does not hold a majority in the assembly, and this critical election will determine to what extent the "reform group" can dominate policy for the remaining four years of Roh's presidency.

Sunshine Policy

A permissive condition for the poll numbers and Korea's apparent drifting away from the United States in 2002–03 is the lingering effects of the sunshine policy. This policy of open-ended, unilateral engagement with North Korea, practiced during the Kim Dae Jung government, reached its apex with the June 2000 inter-Korean summit and had a dramatic effect on South Korean perceptions of the U.S. role in North-South relations. The summit meeting between Kim Dae Jung and DPRK leader Kim Jong Il almost overnight dissipated 50 years of zero-sum, adversarial images of the North. According to State Department polls, in 1995 nearly 50 percent of South Koreans were fearful of a North Korean attack to their sovereignty. In the aftermath of the June 2000 summit, this percentage dropped to around 22 percent, despite no major changes in the security situation on the ground. The aftermath of the summit saw unprecedented growth in inter-Korean economic and cultural contacts. Only two years later, the ROK became North Korea's primary trading partner ($642 million in 2002). Whereas only 2,405 South Koreans visited the North between 1989 and 1997, in 2002 alone some 12,825 South Koreans did so. The signature project of inter-Korean cooperation, the Hyundai Kumgangsan tour, hosted over half a million visitors between 1998 and 2003.[8]

Given this backdrop, South Koreans then conflated the waning of inter-Korean reconciliation with the harder line taken by the Bush administration (even though the former preceded the latter), which led to the counterfactual argument among the 3-8-6 generation that North-South reconciliation would have been entirely conceivable if not for the overbearing U.S. preoccupation with proliferation issues on the peninsula. Or as one commentator characterized this position: "There is no task more urgent than the reunification of the Korean nation, and the greatest obstacles to unification are the United States and its politics of strength."[9]

In retrospect, even without the June 2000 summit, one could argue that the sunshine policy would inherently have raised anti-American sentiments in Korea. The policy was open-ended and required no reciprocation by the North, hence there was no barometer for success. More important, the potential was high for the policy's failure being blamed on anyone but the North Koreans. Hence, the United States was in an unenviable catch-22: success of the sunshine policy caused South Koreans to become intolerant of the U.S. military footprint,[10] but on the other hand, the failure of the sunshine policy resulted in the search for scapegoats, of which the U.S. military presence became an easy target.

There are at least two critical indicators for the future in this regard. The first is the extent to which the evolution of South Korean attitudes to U.S. plans for rebalancing its forces on the peninsula (discussed below) affects South Korean views of the sunshine policy and the United States. A great deal of apprehension has emerged even among left-of-center advocates in Korea to the possibility of a reduction in U.S. forces in Korea. If South Koreans feel no need for a "backstop" to unconditional engagement with the North in the face of a changing U.S. presence, then the sunshine policy's legacy will prove to have deeper roots than the administrations that trumpeted the policy. The second indicator relates to public perceptions of the economic "irrationality" of the sunshine policy. Revelations with regard to nearly half a billion dollars in side payments by the Kim Dae Jung government to North Korean leader Kim Jong Il for the June 2000 summit have tarnished the policy significantly. The absence of any serious opposition to similar economically inefficient forms of engagement would be a clear gauge of the sunshine policy's lasting effect on the Korean population.

Unification Jitters

A third variable shaping South Korea's drift away from the United States relates to the issue of unification. After an initial period of overconfidence in the early 1990s about the feasibility of unification (i.e., through South Korean absorption of the North), more sober views have prevailed. This realism grew out of both a better understanding of the difficulties in German unification (which were still comparatively less severe than what would be faced on the Korean Peninsula) and the resource constraints imposed by the 1997–98 Asian financial crisis. The result, however, has been a wholesale rejection of any developments on the peninsula that might precipitate a collapse of the North, with all of its attendant costs.

Such unification jitters have adversely impacted Seoul's ability to form a common front toward North Korea with the United States. Washington maintains that the United States cannot rule out pressure and the use of force to roll back the North's nuclear weapons programs. While maintaining that a nuclear North Korea is intolerable, Seoul also states that the U.S. threat to use force is unthinkable. These two positions might appear consistent, but the South Korean obsession with avoiding a North Korean collapse propels it to strategic choices on the proliferation issue potentially inconsistent with those of the United States. Nowhere was this more apparent than during a visit to Washington by special envoys of the Roh government on February 3–4, 2003. When pressed to enunciate whether a nuclear North Korea was worse than a collapse of the regime, these representatives clearly gave priority to avoiding collapse even at the expense of the proliferation issue.[11]

China School

Another factor that shapes South Korean strategic choice is China's economic pull. What started out in the late 1980s as informal forays by small- and medium-sized Korean firms into China (then still a Cold War adversary) has expanded into a burgeoning diplomatic and economic relationship worth hundreds of billions of dollars per annum.[12]

Table 3. South Korean Trade with the United States and China

	Trade with U.S. ($bn)			Trade with China ($bn)		
	Imports	Exports	Total	Imports	Exports	Total
1995	30.4	24.1	54.5	7.4	9.1	16.5
1996	33.3	21.7	55.0	8.5	11.4	19.9
1997	30.1	21.6	51.7	10.1	13.6	23.7
1998	20.4	22.8	43.2	6.5	11.9	18.4
1999	24.9	29.5	54.4	8.9	13.7	22.6
2000	29.2	37.6	66.9	12.8	18.5	31.3
2001	22.4	31.2	53.6	13.3	18.2	31.5
2002	23.0	32.8	55.8	17.4	23.8	41.2
Total 1998–2002	120.0	153.9	273.8	58.9	86.0	144.9

Source: Korean International Trade Association (KITA), <www.kita.org>.

As Table 3 shows, since 1995 China has grown exponentially in importance for South Korean import and export markets, to the point where the total value of trade is catching up to that between the United States and the ROK (from one-third to one-half of the total value). State Department public opinion polling confirms the significance of these trend lines. Over 50 percent of South Koreans clearly see their closest economic and trade partner over the next five to ten years to be China.[13]

The salient question for South Korean strategic choice relates to the degree to which this economic relationship creates a future political realignment toward China and away from the United States. The growth of China-ROK economic interaction on its own probably does not (indeed there is as much economic competition between China and the ROK as there is complementarity), but the sheer volume of such interaction in conjunction with other common factors might tend toward such realignment.

First, among these complementarities, there is no denying a romanticism among Koreans about China, stemming from a common Confucian heritage. The normalization of diplomatic relations in 1992 was celebrated by Koreans as a return to "normalcy" in Korea's relations with Asia, implying in not-so-subtle fashion that the alignments of the Cold War period were "aberrant." When China offered its good offices to facilitate the secret talks between the two Koreas in preparation for the June 2000 summit, many observed that Beijing was slowly gaining a more influential role on the peninsula than Washington.

Second, South Korean perceptions of U.S. unilateralism and/or entrapment provoke reactionary discussions about China as the alternate partner. Third, the latter argument often gets conflated with South Korean discussions about greater regional security and multilateralism in Asia, moving away from bilateral dependency on the United States. Glimpses of both were evident at the beginning of the Bush administration, when the harder line toward China made many Koreans nervous about being caught between the two powers. Finally, residual historical animosities with Japan, which periodically become inflamed by Yasukuni shrine visits or history textbook controversies, contribute to a natural Sino-Korean alignment against the former colonizer and away from the U.S.-Japan-Korea triangle.

Variables for Continuity

The Evidence on China

The propositions about Sino-Korean alignment are well known and, in theory, are plausible. The evidence to date, however, remains uneven and not irrefutable. China and the ROK have expanded security exchanges and cooperation since the early 1990s, including bilateral defense exchanges and port calls, but these pale in comparison to U.S.-ROK-Japan military cooperation. Much of this activity, moreover, could be seen as standard steps in a renewed political relationship since 1992 (as opposed to a conscious Korean strategic choice to choose China over the United States). According to State Department polls, although 52 percent of Koreans see China as their closest economic partner in ten years, an even larger percentage (60 percent) expect that their closest *security and strategic* partner in five to ten years will still be the United States.[14]

The most direct evidence of China's influence over South Korea is the deference that Seoul shows in policy decisions that run against U.S. interests. Aside from a clear ROK aversion to countenancing visits by the Dalai Lama to Korea (compared with Japanese receptiveness to these visits), the most significant act was Seoul's decision under the Kim Dae Jung government to decline participation in U.S. theater missile defense initiatives for the region. Although Seoul's official explanation rested on strategic rationales (i.e., North Korean artillery threats rather than ballistic missile threats), cost constraints, and the inability to meet technology thresholds, the unofficial reason had to do with a desire not to alienate China with such a decision. Even here, however, the South Korean decision in 2003 to move forward with missile defense systems (that would be linked to U.S. missile defense systems) confounds this piece of evidence.[15]

Furthermore, much of the public and scholarly discussion about China and multilateralism as an alternative to U.S. bilateralism is not well conceived. There appears to be a direct correlation between dissatisfaction with particular U.S. policies and more public discussion of China. (For example, this appeared to be the case early in the Bush administration in the aftermath of the EP-3 incident and prior to September 11). Moreover, serious discussions about multilateral security (as opposed to rhetorical ones) implicitly anchor any notion of greater variety in South Korean external relations to the U.S.-ROK relationship.

Ironically, a critical indicator of how serious the South Koreans consider China and/or multilateralism as alternative security options to the U.S. alliance is not found in their discussions of China per se, but rather in public debate on issues like higher defense spending as a percentage of the national budget, or moving from a conscription-based system to a professional military. This is because the prerequisite for any serious discussion about a "China option" is a discussion about autonomous defense. And such a discussion about self-reliant defense would highlight how much the U.S. alliance has shielded Korea from the ratios of defense spending to GDP that other countries in similarly security-scarce environments have had to bear. These are the points of departure for any true discussion of South Korean security options outside the U.S. alliance and toward China.

Moreover, the North Korean nuclear crisis is a near-term variable that could potentially enhance Sino-South Korean ties to the detriment of the United States. Neither Seoul nor Beijing has a vested interest in rapid changes in the status quo in North Korea. China values the geostrategic buffer on its southern flank against the United States. It also does not want to deal with the massive flood of refugees that would be likely if the regime in Pyongyang lost control. As noted above, South Korea's trepidations about unification scenarios also make it unwilling to contemplate measures that might precipitate regime instability in the North.

These concerns create an innate risk-averseness in how the two deal with the DPRK proliferation problem vis-à-vis the United States. Washington says it wants to resolve the problem peacefully but reserves the right to use pressure if necessary. In this view, the coercive option is not one of first resort but of last resort. As of August 2003, fissures are not as readily apparent among the three countries in large part because both Seoul and Beijing became acutely aware of the seriousness of the North's nuclear weapons ambitions at the April 2003 trilateral (U.S.-China-DPRK) meetings, where the North Korean delegate Li Gun told Assistant Secretary of State James Kelly that North Korea had nuclear weapons and would not dismantle them. Seoul's willingness to tow a harder line in dealing with the North was evident in visits by the South Korean foreign minister and president to Washington in the spring of 2003. Both meetings produced bilateral understandings that South Korea's engagement with the North would be held in check if the nuclear situation got worse. China's harder line was also manifest in the now well-known step of cutting off oil for three days (supposedly for technical reasons) to push the North Koreans to attend the April 2003 meetings in Beijing.[16]

How long Seoul and Beijing are willing to stay in step with U.S. efforts to apply more pressure on North Korea is unclear. As of June 2003, the South Koreans appeared willing to cooperate in terms of applying light interdiction measures against the North, such as cracking down on illegal drug trafficking (as have the Australians and Japanese). And if the North Koreans continue to undertake even more provocative actions (e.g., testing nuclear weapons, reprocessing fuel rods, testing missiles, or exporting fissile material), then Seoul and Beijing may have little choice but to take a harder line, as the immediate negative consequences of DPRK provocations would outweigh the potential consequences of a collapse.

The true test of the U.S.-ROK alliance's strength, however, will be how the South Koreans and Chinese respond not to more bad behavior by North Korea, but to *good behavior*. Washington, Seoul, and Beijing all seek the rolling back of North Korea's nuclear weapons drive, but they disagree on the threshold for an acceptable disarmament concession by Pyongyang that would warrant a lightening of pressure tactics. Indeed, the South Koreans and Chinese, given the risk-aversion to steps that precipitate regime instability, may even set the bar as low as a significant diplomatic signal by the North. For the Bush administration, however, substantive, verifiable, and irreversible disarmament actions are the only acceptable step. If the United States starts to interdict North Korean ships as part of its Proliferation Security Initiative and Pyongyang responds not by escalating but by offering some piecemeal concession, then the capacity of Washington, Seoul, and Beijing to continue cooperating will be tested. Clarity on what and how much the DPRK needs to do to warrant a reduction in pressure and the start of serious negotiations is requisite to avoid splits.

Silent Majority

Although the changing demographic presents a powerful variable for change in South Korean strategic choices, there are countervailing variables for continuity that bode less ominously for U.S. interests and relations with Seoul. There still exists within Korean society a "silent majority" that holds generally right-of-center views on the alliance with the United States and on North Korea. These voices could have been easily missed by the simple snapshots of the domestic scene at the height of public anger over the death of the two Korean schoolgirls and in the heat of a presidential election campaign. They offer evidence that South Korean popular attitudes are far from monolithic and are a critical stabilizing variable in determining Korea's future direction.

In January 2003, for example, amid all the demonstrations sympathetic to the North, a clear 47 percent of South Koreans believed North Korea was seeking nuclear weapons in earnest and not as mere bargaining chips. Thirty-seven percent of South Koreans agreed that military force would be necessary to prevent North Korea from acquiring nuclear weapons if diplomacy failed. And nearly one-third of those polled believed that economic engagement with North Korea should be decreased under the new ROK government. These numbers run contrary (or at least give pause) to the stereotype of South Koreans fearing Bush more than Kim Jong Il.[17] Moreover, evidence of the silent majority in polling figures are made more credible by the fact that they were taken at the height of the demonstrations in 2002–03.[18]

The silent majority was also evident in the "counter-demonstrations" by South Korean non-governmental groups expressing support for the U.S. presence in Korea and calling for continuation of the long-standing alliance. On January 8, 2003, 1,000 Koreans rallied outside the U.S. military base at Osan, burning a North Korean flag and waving pro-U.S. banners. On January 11, a rally of 30,000 Christians gathered near the U.S. embassy in a show of "pro-Americanism." The following week, the largest pro-U.S. rally ever (nearly 100,000 according to organizers) gathered in Seoul supporting the U.S. military presence in Korea, referring to Americans as "blood brothers," and equating support for the alliance with peace in Korea (rather than with war, as anti-American demonstrations had done). And on the weekend after the presidential inauguration in February, civic groups planned a rally of nearly one million in Seoul, including former prime ministers, university presidents, democracy groups and veterans affairs associations, to show support for the United States.[19]

The silent majority shapes Korean strategic choice in two ways. First, their existence highlights how anti-Americanism is a much more contested, and far less one-dimensional, notion than popular perception gives it credit for. And second, their voice highlights how views on the U.S. presence in Korea are far from zero-sum. Nowhere was this more apparent than in April 2003, when civic groups organized another anti-North Korean, pro-U.S. rally in front of Seoul's city hall, while only a few blocks away, another demonstration (near the Kyobo building in Gwanghwamun) protested the South Korean dispatch of troops to the Iraq war.[20] As the "pro-American" demonstrations showed, one can strongly support the United States and its presence in Korea despite disagreeing with its policy toward North Korea. And as the "anti-American" demonstrations showed, one can oppose inequities in the alliance and demand revision of the Status of Forces Agreement, but at the same time support the alliance. Civic group leaders who organized the demonstrations in December 2002 noted exactly this point. Indeed, polls at the height of anti-American sentiment in December still showed a clear majority of respondents (55 percent) still supporting a U.S. troop presence (see Table 4).[21]

Table 4. Attitudes Toward the Withdrawal of U.S. Forces from Korea by Age Distribution

Age	In favor	Opposed	Don't know
20–29	47	42	10
50+	13	68	19
All ages	32	55	13

Source: Gallup Korea, December 2002.

The changing South Korean demographic, hostile to the United States and friendly to the North, has been portrayed publicly by many as the "new reality" among Korea's youth. However, one of the most critical questions over the next one to five years will concern how permanent these attitudes are among the youth. On the one hand, this could truly be a new generation with fundamentally different views of the United States. Indeed, the pragmatic views on the United States that define the silent majority appear not to have been lost on the so-called "anti-American" younger generation of Koreans. Polls in June 2003, on the one year anniversary of the death of two Korean schoolgirls, showed that only 39 percent of 20–30 year-olds held a negative view of the United States, a dramatic drop from the emotional 79 percent that were polled in December 2002.[22] On the other hand, these attitudes may be more malleable, the legacy of a half-decade of education under the sunshine policy (at impressionable ages). A useful signpost in this regard will be North Korean bad behavior. Sustained criticism by this demographic that the United States causes DPRK bad behavior, even in the face of continued North Korean provocations ranging from submarine incursions to ballistic missile tests or even nuclear weapons tests would indicate less malleable and more permanent attitudes.

It's the Economy, Stupid

The brakes that the silent majority place on a pollyannaish view of North Korea among younger South Koreans are augmented by some near-term political and economic realities over the next several years. Even if Roh's reformist-oriented appointees to the Blue House want to engage North Korea and resist the harder line approach of the Bush administration, they are constrained by short-term expediencies. Though the presidential term in Korea is five years, the new government effectively has only one year before the next legislative elections (April 2004). The ruling party lacks a majority in the legislature and the 2004 election will undoubtedly be interpreted as a one-year referendum on the administration's performance. The primary criterion for the South Korean electorate (according to exit polls at the December 2002 presidential elections) will be the economy and, in particular, continuing the slow but steady recovery from the Asian financial crisis. Arguably, the South Korean economy has performed the most admirably among the economies hit by the crisis in terms of somewhat earnest attempts to implement reforms. However, the North Korean nuclear crisis and perceptions of weakness in Seoul's determination to deal with the problem, have had a devastating effect on the South Korean economy. Economic conditions will force Seoul to take a harder line toward the North.

On February 11, 2003, Moody's downgraded South Korea's country outlook for the first time after successive years of positive assessments. The following week, Standard and Poor's (S&P) did not increase Korea's foreign currency and local corporation credit rating reduced expected growth outlooks. This fairly innocuous judgment is significant because S&P upgraded Korea's credit rating the year prior (to A-) and its general country outlook (to stable), leading many experts to bank on further upgrades given improvements in South Korean credit fundamentals in the public and private sectors, as well as progress in corporate restructuring.

The primary reason for these sober assessments? S&P Director Takahira Ogawa could not have been more direct, stating, "There is a risk from the North, which constrains the sovereign rating of South Korea." Those who think that an eternally optimistic South Korean government, committed to the peaceful status quo and engagement with North Korea, will be able to muddle through are sorely mistaken. All it took was one short-range missile test by Pyongyang into the East Sea (or Sea of Japan) for the Korean Composite Stock Market Price Index (KOSPI) to tumble almost 4 percent in one day, despite a litany of parallel confidence-inducing events including Roh Moo Hyun's inauguration, the U.S. announcement of the resumption of food aid to the North, and Secretary Powell's statements in Seoul that the United States would eventually seek dialogue with North Korea.

After North Korea's second short-range missile test in 2003, the Korean stock market dropped to its lowest level in 16 months, the Japanese Nikkei closed at its lowest level in 20 years, and the Korean *won* depreciated to a four-month low. Wall Street investment houses, including JP Morgan, Merrill Lynch, Goldman Sachs, and ABN AMRO, all issued reports in the first quarter of 2003 advising investors to shed Korean shares (despite acknowledging that these shares were undervalued).[23] Investment from the United States tumbled 72 percent during the first quarter of 2003 and the Korean stock market dropped 18.3 percent.[24] South Korean economic growth estimates are predicted to shrink to 1.4 percent in 2003 from 6.2 percent in 2002.

The economics of the North Korean threat therefore suggest that gaps between the United States and South Korea may narrow. Responding to the dips in investor confidence by moving to all-out appeasement with North Korea is not only likely to undercut any international confidence in the new government's competencies, but is also likely to ensure that the North will see success in continuing such threatening behavior. As has been frequently noted, Seoul and Washington may not share identical interests with regard to North Korean proliferation, but this does not rule out the possibility that they might care about the same thing for different reasons.

Unsurprisingly, a key signpost will be how policy progresses after the National Assembly elections in April 2004. If the Roh government wins a majority in the legislature, then we may see ideologues outpacing the pragmatists in gaining more control of the foreign policy toward North Korea and the United States. Many of the younger left-of-center "reformists" appointed in the Blue House have been biting their tongue in the first half of 2003, not only because of economic and short-term electoral exigencies described above, but also because many of these appointees lack any prior government experience. One year of learning the ropes and an electoral victory in 2004 might galvanize this group to press harder for engagement with North Korea and for a tougher line with the United States.

Reality Bites

The Roh government's movement to the center on North Korea and on the United States in the first half of 2003 also reflects a fundamental reality that all previous South Korean leaders have accepted. Korea, whether divided or united, will remain a relatively smaller country in a region of great powers contending for influence on the peninsula. Historically, Korea has contended with this geostrategic environment with one of two grand strategies. One of these has been a policy of isolation or neutrality (hence, the "hermit kingdom"), trying to remove itself from the region's power politics. This proved relatively unsuccessful (and arguably is still practiced in North Korea today). The other strategy has been to ally with one of the great powers. This strategy was fairly successful vis-à-vis China pre-twentieth century, and it was clearly a successful strategy in the postwar era, transforming the South into the most vibrant liberal-democracy in Asia, the third largest economy in the region, and the eleventh largest economy in the world. In the future, it behooves Korea's interests to continue placing their "bets" on a relationship with the region's great power that is the furthest away and shares the same political and market values and regime-type. Detractors might argue for a different strategic choice, but this is largely an idealistic view that does not take account of the powerful, almost indisputable logic of the alliance with the United States. This geostrategic logic inclines President Roh toward a more moderate view of the alliance when compared with his past views.

Just after the December elections, Roh met with anti-American civic groups and called for moderation. Despite campaign statements that he would not meet with Americans purely for photo opportunities, Roh did just that on January 15, 2003, stating that despite his past position supporting a U.S. troop pullout as a human rights lawyer, "U.S. troops are necessary at the present for peace and stability on the Korean peninsula and will be in the future as well."[25] After North Korea's three cruise missile tests in February–March 2003, the ROK president criticized such actions and stated that the prospect of a nuclear North Korea is unacceptable. In terms of critical foreign policy advisors, the president opted for experience over ideology and chose individuals with substantial understanding and interaction with the United States.[26] He publicly supported the U.S. war in Iraq and, in a controversial decision, agreed to dispatch a contingent of non-combatant forces to the country. Despite explicit pledges to maintain a primary role for the South Koreans in "mediating" talks between the North and the United States, Roh not only acceded to being excluded from the U.S.-North Korea-China talks in Beijing (April 23–24, 2003), but also defended the format by saying that substance was more important than form.

In his summit with President Bush, Roh took a harder tack on policy toward North Korea and, in the summit's joint statement, acknowledged that further steps would need to be contemplated in dealing with Pyongyang if there is no improvement in behavior.[27] And in a *New York Times* interview during his first summit trip to the United States, Roh admitted that his signing of a declaration calling for the removal of U.S. forces from the Korean Peninsula in his activist past was a "mistake."[28]

U.S. Rebalancing and Realignment

At the time of this writing, we are still early in the Roh government and things could change rapidly. But there is no denying that since the December 19, 2002 elections, there has been a substantial moderating in the position of the Roh leadership on North Korea and on relations with the United States. When this author wrote an op-ed in the *Washington Post* the day after the South Korean election ("Keep Calm on Korea") foretelling a more conservative turn in the policies of the new ROK government, few believed such a prediction.[29] Nevertheless, as of June 2003, the December 2002 expectations of a train wreck in U.S.-South Korean relations have been replaced by a new, tempered confidence in the relationship.

Whether Korean strategic choices will remain fundamentally "anchored" or cut "adrift" (as notionally depicted in Table 1) is, nevertheless, a close call. A critical variable in this regard will be the ramifications of the U.S. plan to rebalance its forces in Asia. The plan for Korea includes the pullback of the 2nd Infantry Division from forward positions in defense of Seoul to Camp Casey and Camp Red Cloud north of the Han River, and eventually to rear areas south of the Han River. Defense responsibility for forward areas including those in the DMZ would be transferred to the ROK. There will be a major consolidation of U.S. bases—including the closing of Yongsan in Seoul—and the move to air and naval hubs based out of Osan/Pyongtaek and Pusan/Chinhae.[30]

Pundits have raised many questions about how the Koreans will respond to this plan. Will they see this as a precursor to a U.S. preemptive attack against North Korea's nuclear facilities now that U.S. ground troops will no longer be sitting ducks for DPRK artillery? Will they perceive a reduced U.S. commitment to defend the ROK? If so, will the North become emboldened? Will South Korea seek to appease North Korea and draw closer to China?

The wide-ranging nature of these questions stems from the magnitude of the change being posited for the peninsula, by far the most significant since the end of the Korean War. The manner in which South Korea responds to this plan and the degree to which it will make productive rather than unproductive choices, will depend greatly on the U.S. management of the plan and its political implementation. The imperative here is a simple one. Should the United States implement the plan well, it should be capable of shaping Korean responses in a way that mutually reinforces the alliance and U.S. interests in the region. Poor implementation of the plan, however, will cause Seoul to make self-help choices that run contrary to U.S. policy vis-à-vis North Korea and possibly push South Korea into the arms of China.

Historically, the United States has correctly maintained that adjustments of its forward-deployed forces in Korea is a sovereign choice that requires neither approval nor permission from the host nation. For this reason, all past changes to U.S. force levels in Korea (e.g., mid-1950s, 1969 Nixon doctrine, 1975 Carter plan, early 1990s East Asian Strategy Initiative) have been decided by Washington and then communicated to the ally. Nevertheless, if Washington proceeds with the current plan in a manner that conveys unilateralism and a sense of pique (at the anti-American demonstrations), this will almost certainly raise acute fears of abandonment in South Korea. Such fears in the past have indeed propelled Korea in self-help directions that were not productive (e.g., the secret nuclear weapons programs in the 1970s), and they could force strategic choices in Seoul that cut Korea "adrift" amid a rising tide of anti-Americanism.

However, if Washington proceeds with rebalancing in a transparent and consultative fashion with Seoul, and conveys a new formula for forward presence that maintains the U.S. defense commitment with greater capabilities and less intrusive footprints,[31] then the likelihood of Korea making bad choices goes down. U.S. commitments to invest some $11 billion over four years for force enhancement on the peninsula, as well as commitments to continue U.S. military rotational training in forward areas, are useful symbols of the continued defense commitment.[32] Given the size of the changes being contemplated, no amount of consultation and symbols will entirely expunge all South Korean fears of abandonment. But the challenge for the United States over the next one to five years will not be to erase such anxieties, but rather to ensure that they are channeled in the right direction and in productive ways. For example, in 1969–71, when the ROK suffered acute abandonment fears, it channeled these anxieties in unproductive directions (e.g., the covert nuclear weapons program), but it also channeled them in positive directions (e.g., enhanced defense-sharing within the U.S.-ROK alliance and, more important, enhanced defense cooperation with Japan).[33] There is a fine line between U.S. troop reductions that create panic, distrust, and self-help behavior, and those that create *mutual help* solutions. What will move Korea in the latter rather than former direction will rest on the extent to which Washington conveys that troop rebalancing is not the manifestation of ad hoc decisions taken toward a deteriorating and brittle alliance, but is rather an investment in the long-term resiliency of a more equal and mature alliance.

A key signpost in this regard will be how the second phase of the U.S. rebalancing in Asia pans out. If the first phase consists of decisions related to base consolidation and the pulling back of forces, the second phase consists of how forces will be redeployed in the region as the United States looks to deal with other types of threats (particularly of a terrorism-related nature in Southeast Asia). In short, U.S. rebalancing of forces in Korea may not only mean pulling them back from frontline positions, but also their reduction on the peninsula and redeployment elsewhere in the region. U.S. hand-holding efforts to calm abandonment anxieties and channel allied reactions in productive ways could be potentially undermined if South Koreans perceive redeployment of forces to other parts of Asia as a downgrading of the U.S. focus on Korea. Replacing boots-on-the-ground with high-tech weaponry may calm Koreans, but reducing boots-on-the-ground and increasing force numbers elsewhere in Asia may heighten abandonment anxieties again—a situation that may be unavoidable as the United States continues to spearhead the global war on terrorism.

Endnotes

[1] The 3-8-6 generation refers to individuals in their thirties, college-educated in the 1980s, and born in the 1960s.

[2] Examples of these issues include the large U.S. military installation in the center of Seoul that contributes to traffic congestion. In the summer of 2000, there were reports of dumping of toxic chemicals by U.S. forces into the main river artery in Seoul. NGO and civil society agents also organize around issues related to the prostitution networks around U.S. bases, crimes by U.S. servicemen, damage done to South Korean private property as a result of U.S. training exercises, and a host of other civil-military issues.

[3] Nowhere was this view more epitomized than in the *60 Minutes* story that caught a group of young Koreans self-righteously responding to a loaded question that President Bush was more scary to them than Kim Jong Il. *60 Minutes*, aired February 8, 2003.

[4] For example, according to pools in early 2003, 58.7 percent of Koreans in their twenties and thirties viewed the Korean War as a proxy war between the United States and the Soviet Union (versus a national average of 44.5 percent) rather than as the result of an illegitimate armed invasion by the North (24.2 percent versus a national average of 31.2 percent). See Chosun Ilbo-Gallup Korea polls, January 1, 2003, <www.gallup.co.kr/News/2003/release004.html.>

[5] See MBC-Korea Research Center polls, January 1, 2003.

[6] These include individuals such as Chung Dong Young (MDP), Choo Mi Ae (MDP), Song Yong Gil (MDP), Shin Ki Nam, and Chun Jung Bae.

[7] Roh greatly enlarged the Blue House staff in part to accommodate these new imports. They are said to be led by one of the deputy national security advisors, Lee Jong Sok.

[8] Ra Jong-yil, "Engagement with North Korea," *International Herald Tribune*, May 13, 2003.

[9] This radical view (though not the view of the article's author) is cited in Choong Nam Kim, "Changing Korean Perceptions of the Post-Cold War Era and the US-ROK Alliance," *East-West Center Analysis*, no. 67 (April 2003), p. 5.

[10] Indeed, the author witnessed demonstrations in front of Main Post at Yongsan in the immediate aftermath of the June 2000 summit that forced the closing of the main entrance.

[11] Seminar remarks at a private dinner for the special envoy delegation, hosted by the United States Institute of Peace, Washington, DC, February 3, 2003.

[12] Sino-Korean diplomatic normalization occurred in 1992. For an overview, see Victor Cha, "Engaging China: Seoul-Beijing Detente and Korean Security," *Survival*, vol. 41, no. 1 (Spring 1999), pp. 73–98.

[13] Jim Marshall polls, State Department Office of Research, July 2002, <www.strat group.org>.

[14] Jim Marshall polls, State Department Office of Research, July 2002, <www.strat group.org>.

[15] "Missile defense set to take off," *Chosun Ilbo*, June 11, 2003.

[16] See the China chapter in this volume.

[17] Chosun Ilbo-Gallup Korea, January 1, 2003, <www.gallup.co.kr/News/2003/release004.html> and SBS-TN Sofres Poll, aired January 1, 2003, <www.news/sbs.co.kr/vodnews/newssisa_Detail_Index.jhtml?news_id=No311347893&sct=1>.

[18] These figures are more credible, for example, than citing statements against the withdrawal of U.S. forces by ROK non-governmental groups in the aftermath of Defense Secretary Donald Rumsfeld's now-famous March 6, 2003 remarks that "adjustments" in U.S. forces in Korea were coming.

[19] Kyung-Ho Kim, "Conservatives push to keep US troops," *Korea Herald*, February 26, 2003; Jong-Heon Lee, "Anti-US sentiment cooling in South Korea," United Press International, January 20, 2003; Sang-Hun Choe, "Tens of thousands of South Korean Christians rally to support US military, condemn North Korea," Associated Press, January 11, 2003; Jae-Hwan Kim, "Pro-US demonstrators burn North Korean flag outside American air base," Agence France-Presse, January 8, 2003.

[20] "South Korean groups hold rallies against North Korea, US war in Iraq," BBC, April 19, 2003.

[21] "NYT editorial on US troop pullout sparks controversy," *Hankook Ilbo*, December 28, 2002 and "55% of South Koreans want US troops to stay," *Hankook Ilbo*, December 24, 2002.

[22] *Joongang Ilbo*, July 26, 2003.

[23] Na Ji-hong, "Global securities firms pessimistic on Korean shares," *Chosun Ilbo*, March 18, 2003.

[24] "Foreign investment in South Korea falls," Associated Press, April 4, 2003.

[25] Kwanwoo Jun, "South Korean President-Elect Roh softens anti-US image," Agence France-Presse, January 15, 2003.

[26] The appointment of Sung-Joo Han as ambassador to the United States offers a small example of the change in thinking. At the time of then President-Elect Roh's special envoy delegation's trip to Washington, members of the delegation scoffed at the idea that someone identified as a more conservative, establishment-type might be chosen for this post, and yet only a few months later, this was exactly the president's choice.

[27] "Joint Statement Between the United States of America and the Republic of Korea: Common Values, Principles, and Strategy," May 14, 2003, <www.white house.gov/news/releases/2003/05>.

[28] David Sanger, "South Korean leader wants US troops to stay, for now," *New York Times*, May 13, 2003.

[29] Victor D. Cha, "Stay calm on Korea," *Washington Post*, December 20, 2002.

[30] Result of the Second Meeting of "Future of the ROK-US Alliance Policy Initiative," June 6, 2003, <www.usembassy.state.gov/seoulwwwh4104.html>.

[31] For further discussion of this formula, see Victor Cha, "Focus on the Future, Not on the North," *Washington Quarterly*, vol. 26, no. 1 (Winter 2002–03).

[32] Result of the Second Meeting of "Future of the ROK-US Alliance Policy Initiative," June 6, 2003, <www.usembassy.state.gov/seoul/wwwh4104.html>.

[33] For the theoretical and historical argument about how South Korean fears of U.S. abandonment affected the South's policy toward Japan, see Victor Cha, *Alignment Despite Antagonism: The United States-Korea-Japan Security Triangle*, Stanford, Calif.: Stanford University Press, 1999.

North Korea – Key Indicators and Forecasts

Economy and Trade	2002^a	2003^b	2004^b
GDP ($tr) / (PPP GDP)	...	...	...
GDP growth (%)	...	...	...
Inflation (%)	...	...	...
Budget balance (% of GDP)	...	...	...
Major export destinations (2001)	Japan (27%), South Korea (21%), China (20%)		

Population and Energy	2002^a	2005^b	2010^b
Population (m)	22.2	22.9	23.8
Population growth (%)	1.2	0.9	0.6
Oil production (m bbl/d)	0.0	...	...
Oil consumption (m bbl/d)	<0.1	...	...

Politics	
Head of state	Kim Jong Il (KWP, took office Jul 1994)
Dominant party	Korean Workers' Party (since 1948)
Next party congress	2003

Military	
Armed forces (2002)	1,082,000
Defense expenditure (2001)	$2.1 bn est. (11.6% of GDP)
Conventional capabilities	Massive army with large artillery component
	Force degradation due to economic collapse; little prospect of force modernization
Weapons of mass destruction	Has small number of nuclear weapons
	Has limited chemical warfare capabilities

Source: The National Bureau of Asian Research, compiled from Central Intelligence Agency, *World Factbook*; U.S. Census Bureau, *International Data Base*; Energy Information Administration, *Country Analysis Brief—North Korea*; International Institute of Strategic Studies, *The Military Balance*. Data on North Korea's economic performance are unavailable. Notes: a) Data for 2002 may be estimates; b) Data for 2003, 2004, 2005, and 2010 are projections. Additional data on North Korea are available in the Strategic Asia Database at <http://strategicasia.nbr.org>.

THE KOREAN NUCLEAR CRISIS: ON TO THE NEXT LEVEL

Nicholas Eberstadt and Joseph P. Ferguson

ABSTRACT

As the nuclear crisis in North Korea unfolds, it has become clear that there is little agreement about a common approach, either within the U.S. government or among its partners in Northeast Asia. This crisis has been more than a decade in the making, but a round of incidents in the fall of 2002 set off the latest alarm bells. At that time, the North Korean leadership made it clear that the DPRK's nuclear weapons program was alive and well, confirming U.S. intelligence estimates. Whatever the motivations of the DPRK, it is clear that Pyongyang hopes once again to sow discord among U.S. partners in the region. Perhaps the strategy may backfire this time, insofar as all of the nations neighboring North Korea have agreed to a multilateral dialogue to help defuse the situation. The potential outcomes that present themselves, however, do not bode well for an agreement amenable to all sides. The crisis threatens to upset the extremely fragile balance of peace that has existed in Northeast Asia for the past 50 years.

Nicholas Eberstadt holds the Henry Wendt Chair in Political Economy at the American Enterprise Institute in Washington, DC. Joseph Ferguson is Director of Northeast Asia Studies at The National Bureau of Asian Research. The authors wish to express their appreciation to Chuck Downs, Richard Ellings, Michael Wills, and an anonymous reviewer for their comments on earlier drafts of this paper.

Introduction

E. H. Carr's powerful little book *The Twenty Years' Crisis* presciently argued that the events then (1939) ineluctably leading Europe to war were not sudden and new, but rather two decades in the making; that interwar Europe's crisis was rooted in power politics, framed by insatiable ambitions of revisionist states, and intensified by the stubborn unwillingness of some European (and U.S.) leaders to recognize these unpleasant but unyielding realities.[1] Though written in another time and of another place, *The Twenty Years' Crisis* could be offered as briefing material today for those policymakers and students of international affairs struggling to make sense of the rapid escalation in late 2002 and early 2003 of the international drama revolving around the nuclear weapons program of the Democratic People's Republic of Korea (DPRK, or North Korea).

The North Korean nuclear crisis, of course, is not exactly breaking news. If, like Professor Carr, we wish to date the duration of the crisis according to its defining events, we would be obliged to look back many years: in this case, perhaps to Pyongyang's November 1992 refusal to cooperate further with the inspectors from the International Atomic Energy Agency (IAEA) who were attempting to reconstruct the full history of two suspect sites in North Korea's nuclear program;[2] or to the DPRK's initial March 1993 announcement of its intention to withdraw from the Nuclear Nonproliferation Treaty (NPT) that gave IAEA inspectors authority to pursue their inquiry;[3] or even to the attendant March 1993 declaration by DPRK's supreme military commander, Kim Jong Il, of a "semi-state of war,"[4] and the concomitant warning that "a touch-and-go grave situation has been created in which war may break out at any moment."[5]

Indeed, the following depiction of the crisis on the Korean Peninsula, although written in 1993, might just as well have been written yesterday:

> North Korea is in a crisis that threatens its existence...The situation is extraordinarily dangerous because these are the highest stakes possible. The Korean Peninsula, moreover, is heavily militarized and lacking in crisis management capacities. Dealing with nuclear proliferation in this ... setting will be much more difficult than solving proliferation problems in other countries...The absolutist regime in the North has limited maneuvering room and must operate within very shaky military and economic structures. Although there are risks of pressing it too hard, a nuclear-armed North Korea would constitute the long-feared nightmare of the international community: an over-armed state in a desperate position; with unstable decision-makers and poor command and control.[6]

To be sure, the current particulars of the North Korean nuclear crisis differ in some respects from those a decade earlier; but it is the very same crisis, shaped by the very same fundamentals. Just like Carr's *Twenty Years' Crisis*, this Korean crisis may continue to fester for years to come. But eventually, just as in interwar Europe, the perpetuation of an unstable balance will no longer be feasible, and some decisive event could spark dramatic changes that would profoundly reconfigure the region's security equation.

For most of the actors embroiled in the drama—the United States, the Republic of Korea (ROK, or South Korea), Japan, China, and Russia—the preferred outcome to the North Korean nuclear crisis would clearly be a comprehensive resolution through peaceful diplomatic negotiations. In this drama, however, as in that earlier drama in Europe, the most desirable outcome may also be the least likely. Given the character and objectives of the central actor—namely, the DPRK regime—it is difficult to see how the contending interests of Pyongyang and the other concerned parties could be harmonized through a common dialogue on settlement formulae. This is not to suggest that we shall not see international talks convened, or "breakthroughs" claimed; it is instead to suggest that such talks and breakthroughs are exceedingly unlikely to defuse the ongoing crisis itself.

The Crisis Unfolds

How did we reach the current pass? Although the genesis of the Korean crisis goes back many decades, and the nuclear aspect of the crisis is at least a decade old, the most current round began to develop in the late 1990s and rapidly approached boiling point in late 2002 and the first part of 2003.

The earlier North Korean nuclear drama of the early 1990s was seemingly resolved through bilateral negotiations between Pyongyang and Washington, which concluded in October 1994 with an "Agreed Framework." A somewhat curious document (State Department lawyers stressed it was a "framework," not an "agreement") this paper ostensibly arranged for the DPRK to give up its nuclear program and to forswear nuclear weapons development.[7] U.S. officials, however, recognized that Pyongyang might pursue a covert nuclear weapons program despite the Agreed Framework. Indeed, in 1999, U.S. officials were sufficiently concerned about surreptitious DPRK nuclear activities that they provided 500,000 tons of food aid in return for permission to visit suspect underground site at Kumchang-ri.[8]

The Kumchang-ri inspections did not uncover incriminating evidence of a secret North Korean weapons program. But U.S. intelligence about the status of another possible illicit nuclear weapons program in the DPRK began to emerge in the later years of the Clinton administration. Several intelligence findings suggested that the DPRK had embarked upon a covert program to develop highly enriched uranium (HEU)—in evident contravention not only of the 1994 Agreed Framework, but also the NPT and the 1992 North-South Declaration on Denuclearization.

The Bush administration entered office with deep misgivings about the DPRK's purported nuclear freeze. Just weeks after his inauguration, George W. Bush pointedly announced that "We're not certain as to whether or not they're keeping all terms of all agreements."[9] By the spring of 2002, sufficient intelligence had been gathered on surreptitious North Korean nuclear activities to prompt the White House, for the first time, to decline to certify to Congress that North Korea was abiding by the terms of the Agreed Framework.[10] (Congressional funding for the KEDO project was conditional on that annual presidential certification; however, the president also had the authority to waive conditionality in cases of national security, so the funds were allocated under a presidential waiver—a circumstance clearly underscoring the Bush administration's lack of confidence in North Korea.) By the summer of 2002 the CIA had established conclusively that North Korea had indeed embarked on a program to develop HEU, and suggested Pyongyang would be capable of weaponizing this material in the near future (two to three years). As early as the mid-1990s the U.S. intelligence community had surmised that North Korea might already have in its possession one or two crude nuclear weapons that were developed with plutonium from the reprocessing activities which had been halted after the signing of the 1994 Agreed Framework. The more technologically sophisticated HEU program, the United States concluded, would allow North Korea to develop two to three more nuclear weapons each year.[11]

Apprised of this new intelligence, the Bush administration at first played its cards close to its chest. Secretary of State Colin Powell, who was fully aware of the illicit program, met DPRK Foreign Minister Paik Nam Sun at the APEC summit in Brunei in July 2002 and did not raise the issue. Charles Pritchard, then special envoy for negotiations with the DPRK and the U.S. representative to KEDO, traveled to Pyongyang in August 2002 to oversee the groundbreaking for one of the promised light water reactors, but maintained a strictly ceremonial diplomatic schedule.

Eventually the Bush administration moved toward a decision to face the problem directly. A high-level meeting in Pyongyang between U.S. and North Korean officials had been slated for July 2002, but was put off after a DPRK naval attack against two ROK frigates in the Yellow Sea at the end of June. Washington decided to use that postponed meeting as the occasion to present the HEU evidence to the North Korean leadership. Assistant Secretary of State for East Asian and Pacific Affairs James Kelly traveled to Pyongyang on this mission in early October 2002. When confronted with the American brief at an initial meeting with Kelly on October 4, North Korean officials (including Vice Foreign Minister Kim Gye Gwan) denied the existence of such a program, calling the evidence a "fabrication." During meetings the following day, however, DPRK First Vice Foreign Minister Kang Sok Ju reportedly acknowledged the existence of the program—and stated that nuclear weapons were necessary for North Korea as a deterrent against the United States. Moreover, Kang was quoted as declaring that the DPRK government considered the 1994 Agreed Framework to be abrogated due to the policies of the current administration.[12]

It was not until October 16 that the State Department went public with the DPRK revelations, and it apparently did so then only because two American reporters were close to breaking the story.[13] The belated nature of the U.S. announcement was noteworthy, begging the question of why the Bush administration was so slow to react to the brazen DPRK admission.

Possibly Kang Sok Ju's defiant missive was not at all what Washington had expected, or hoped, to hear. This North Korean nuclear challenge demanded immediate attention and action, but the president and his team at that time were deeply preoccupied canvassing congressional and international support for their campaign to disarm the Saddam Hussein regime in Iraq. Silence in the face of Pyongyang's nuclear admission also deferred the task of fashioning a common public response to the provocation with the United States' East Asian allies, Japan and the ROK.[14] Neither of these governments was particularly eager to confront North Korea, least so over new nuclear violations. Differences between the ROK and the U.S. government were particularly pronounced and were thrown into relief as soon as the gist of the October 5 Pyongyang discussions became public knowledge. Immediately after the news of the North Korean HEU violation broke, for example, the ROK Defense Ministry downplayed the report through a release insisting that North Korea lacked the technology to "weaponize" its nuclear materials,[15] and within the week the ROK's Minister of Unification had implied that Kelly may have misrepresented the North Korean statements by "trimming" First Vice Minister Kang's remarks.[16]

When the Bush administration finally decided to speak openly about the DPRK's nuclear violations, it declared that it would refuse to speak with the North Korean government until after Pyongyang had dismantled its nuclear program. Although this strategy was in all likelihood enunciated due to constraints on the U.S. foreign policymaking apparatus at the time, it probably was the most vexing response the United States could have formulated in the opinion of leaders in Pyongyang, short of outright confrontation. The North Korean leadership was undoubtedly seeking a quick U.S. response, most likely a call for immediate negotiations. U.S. officials made it clear that "talks," not "negotiations," would only be feasible if the DPRK came to the table having disassembled its nuclear program.

Throughout the remainder of 2002 and into 2003, the Bush administration tried to play down the North Korean crisis. On December 29, 2002, in a series of televised appearances, Secretary of State Powell repeatedly denied that the North Korean actions of the previous weeks constituted a "crisis."[17] The United States was on the verge of mounting a major military campaign against Iraq, was encountering unexpected difficulties in generating European and UN support for the operation, and was neither disposed nor prepared to deal with an intransigent North Korea. Washington was also hoping that neighboring states in Northeast Asia, particularly China, would be sufficiently moved to try to head off a North Korean nuclear weapons program. To be sure, all the governments of Northeast Asia were alarmed by the DPRK revelations. China and Russia issued a joint statement on the occasion of the Jiang-Putin summit in Beijing in December 2002, saying that any DPRK weapons program would be destabilizing to the region and calling for the DPRK to adhere to IAEA guidelines.[18] The Japanese government denounced the DPRK revelation and declared that normalization efforts with Pyongyang (ongoing since the summer of 2002) would be halted until the nuclear program was stopped and the issue of the abduction of Japanese nationals was resolved. Japan's announcement was undoubtedly something of a blow to Pyongyang, for the DPRK had clearly been hoping that financial aid would come on the heels of normalization of relations with Japan.[19] Yet none of North Korea's nearest neighbors was prepared to take any serious measure to counteract the DPRK's dangerous game of brinkmanship. Although most of the concerned parties mentioned were amenable to multilateral talks, they also called, privately or publicly, for the United States to begin direct negotiations with the North. That common posture was more than a problem-avoidance stratagem, although certainly it was that as well: the call for Washington to fix the North Korean nuclear problem amounted to implicit recognition of their own limited influence with Pyongyang and the United States' predominance in the Northeast Asian security equation.

In November 2002, the Bush administration decided to take a tangible action to penalize North Korea for its infractions. At the monthly KEDO board meeting, Washington successfully pressed for a consensus vote to suspend the oil shipments (500,000 tons annually) that had been promised to North Korea from the Agreed Framework. The measure received willing support from KEDO's European and Japanese members, and more reluctant approval from the ROK. The following month, Pyongyang responded to this relatively modest bid by substantially upping the ante.

On December 12, the DPRK government insisted on its right to restart the reactors that had been shut down as part of the 1994 Agreed Framework because of the new need for energy due to the halting of KEDO oil shipments. (DPRK officials of course did not mention that the Yongbyon facilities were unconnected to their national power grid, and thus incapable of relieving the nation's power shortages under any circumstances.) Later in the month, the DPRK expelled all IAEA monitoring personnel from the country and removed the seals and cameras that had been in place at the major declared nuclear facilities. For good measure, Pyongyang then informed the IAEA that it intended to reactivate its plutonium processing facility within a month or two.[20] The DPRK further announced that the 1994 Agreed Framework now existed "in name only." It declared that the nuclear issue was no longer a multilateral question, but instead should be resolved between the DPRK and the United States, "as it is the product of the latter's hostility in every respect."[21] Pyongyang also warned that the United States faced an "uncontrollable catastrophe" if it did come to a direct settlement with North Korea over their nuclear dispute.[22]

One avenue through which Washington might have made the North Korean nuclear drama into a multilateral security problem was the United Nations and its subsidiary institutions. In late 2002, promising possibilities had crystallized for precisely this sort of "internationalization" of the problem. In October, immediately after the bombshell revelations about the North's HEU program, an IAEA spokesman had reminded the world that the agency had been unable to monitor the DPRK's nuclear program since 1993 due to Pyongyang's continuing intransigence.[23] In November the IAEA issued a resolution calling for the DPRK to open its HEU program to inspectors, and to dismantle its nuclear weapons program immediately.[24] A few days later, Pyongyang rejected the resolution out of hand. When the DPRK went on to expel IAEA inspectors and dismantle IAEA safeguards on its Yongbyon nuclear facilities, its continuing pattern of flagrant and escalating violations of UN nuclear strictures began to look very much like a matter that could be brought before the United Nations Security Council for formal condemnation and sanction. In late December, U.S. officials indicated that Washington intended to press the matter at the Security Council. But on January 6, 2003—the very day the IAEA passed another resolution deploring North Korea's nuclear violations—the Bush administration changed its stance, suggesting instead that it would not bring the North Korean nuclear issue to the Security Council any time soon. "Part of the reason we don't want to get North Korea's problems in front of the Security Council too quickly" an unnamed Bush official explained to the *New York Times*, "is that the Security Council will be overwhelmed by too many problems at once"[25]—a none too veiled reference to the fact that Washington's brief for war against Saddam Hussein was faring poorly. (Another reason may have been North Korea's threat that UN Security Council sanctions "mean a war and the war knows no mercy.")[26]

As soon as it was clear Pyongyang need not fear any UN action, the DPRK raised the stakes on the standoff once again. On January 10, 2003 the DPRK announced that it was withdrawing from the NPT—not because it intended to produce nuclear weapons, but because it wished to establish a separate verification regime directly with the United States.[27] (North Korean officials suggested they would "reconsider" NPT withdrawal, but the NPT withdrawal only, if Washington fully resumed its previous schedule of free KEDO fuel oil shipments.)[28] North Korea steadfastly maintained its insistence on direct negotiations with the United States. The United States conversely broadcast the message that bilateral talks were a non-starter unless the DPRK were prepared to come to the table after dismantling its nuclear program. Both sides at various times hinted at flexibility, but in the end, neither seemed prepared to abandon its original position.

Among the many diplomatic complications facing Washington in responding to the North Korean nuclear challenge, the attitude of its military treaty ally, the ROK, loomed especially large. Seoul's "sunshine policy"— President Kim Dae Jung's variant of *Ostpolitik*—had convinced many ROK policymakers and much of the South Korean public that reconciliation with Pyongyang was well underway. This predisposition toward the Pyongyang regime may help to explain Seoul's excuse-heavy posture over the course of the drama. The ROK government not only publicly doubted the Bush administration's veracity on the October 2002 talks: it lobbied against UN Security Council review of the DPRK nuclear infractions,[29] and even struck the pose that no one could actually prove North Korea possessed nuclear weapons.[30] In a last-gasp gesture to rescue his "sunshine policy," President Kim sent an envoy to Pyongyang in late January to deliver a letter to Kim Jong Il, urging the North Korean government to not withdraw from the NPT; although the North Korean side had approved the trip, Kim Jong Il made a point of neither meeting the envoy nor bothering to pick up the letter.[31]

Despite such mistreatment, South Korea stood ready to inaugurate a government whose disposition toward Pyongyang looked even more forbearing than Kim Dae Jung's. In December, in a bitterly contested plebiscite, human rights lawyer Roh Moo Hyun became the ROK's president-elect. Throughout his campaign Roh had promised that he would not "kowtow" to the United States and consistently criticized Washington for its "hard-line policy" on North Korea.[32] In the month after his election, Roh seemed to rule out any use of military force or economic sanctions to pressure Pyongyang into nuclear compliance, arguing that the DPRK was attempting to "reform" and "open up" to the world.[33] Just weeks before his inauguration, an official Roh delegation in Washington shocked policymakers when one of its members privately suggested that it might be better for the DPRK to acquire nuclear weapons than to collapse.[34] (The delegate in question, who vehemently denied the remarks attributed to him, was subsequently appointed Roh's foreign minister.) As Roh took office, U.S.-South Korean relations seemed to be heading toward a low point. In this context, the burden for dealing with North Korea by default would fall solely on the United States. That burden was all the more onerous given the U.S. preoccupation with the war on terrorism and the upcoming war against Iraq.

During the winter of 2002/03, the Bush administration was increasingly preoccupied with military and diplomatic preparations for the war in Iraq. This did not prevent the Pentagon from deploying B-1 and B-52 bombers to Guam on March 4 as a warning to North Korea that a war in Iraq would not keep the United States so distracted that it could not bring overwhelming force to bear on the regime in Pyongyang. Nevertheless, Washington was eager to enlist the support of partners in Northeast Asia to force the DPRK to abandon its nuclear weapons program. China was a consistent focus of these efforts. President Bush phoned President Jiang Zemin three times in an effort to bring China on board between January and March 2003. Secretary of State Powell visited Beijing in late February with the same goal in mind. Eventually these efforts paid off, and China offered to host multilateral or bilateral talks on the North Korean nuclear issue.

The DPRK leadership maintained an uncompromising position on the issue of direct talks with the United States, and attempted to increase the pressure on Washington in the months before *Operation Iraqi Freedom*. On repeated occasions Pyongyang declared it was prepared to go to war if the United States kept up its political pressure, imposed sanctions, or refused to reach a settlement. A DPRK Foreign Ministry spokesman also pointedly announced that his country could strike U.S. forces anywhere in the world.[35] Moving beyond mere words, Pyongyang reactivated its nuclear reactor at Yongbyon in late February and test fired surface-to-surface missiles into the Sea of Japan (the East Sea in Korean parlance) in February and March. In February, DPRK warplanes violated South Korean airspace; in early March, DPRK fighter jets attempted to force down onto North Korean territory a U.S. reconnaissance plane flying in international airspace 150 miles offshore over the Sea of Japan.

When the war in Iraq broke out on March 20, the DPRK government and its media became uncharacteristically quiet for an extended period—over a month. Kim Jong Il was not seen in public for several weeks. The

North Korean leadership was no doubt absorbing as many lessons as it could from the war, perhaps anticipating a U.S. attack on the DPRK. Months after the swift U.S. military success in Iraq, North Korea's leadership publicly downplayed the results of that operation as the fruit of "psychological warfare," a victory with little bearing on a purportedly high-morale country like their own.[36] Yet on April 12—three days after U.S. troops seized control of Baghdad—the DPRK's leadership reversed itself and hurriedly announced it would now consider the U.S. call for multilateral talks and welcome any form of dialogue, so long as the U.S. leadership agreed to be constructive. Three days later, the White House let it be known that three-party talks—involving the DPRK, the United States, and China—would begin in Beijing in just eight days.

U.S. Assistant Secretary of State Kelly and DPRK negotiator Li Gun, deputy director of the American division of the North Korean Foreign Ministry, met in Beijing on April 23, 2003 with Chinese officials who agreed to mediate the three-way talks. According to press reports, Washington's objective going into the meetings was to discuss how the North Korean nuclear weapons program might be dismantled.[37] But from the U.S. standpoint, the outcome of these talks was as bad as anyone had expected, if not worse. To begin, Pyongyang offered a diplomatic snub to the other participants by sending an official (Li) with a much lower ranking than Kelly— a guarantee, in light of North Korea's decision-making process, that no serious give-and-take could come out of the meetings. Li of course insisted on meeting with Kelly alone, and Kelly of course refused. Later at a cocktail party, Li took Kelly aside. He told Kelly that the DPRK already possessed nuclear weapons and would test them or sell them, as circumstances demanded. Li further stated that Pyongyang had begun reprocessing additional plutonium for weapons, but hinted that it might change course if the United States provided security guarantees and economic aid immediately.

Confronted by what had suddenly become a diplomatic disaster, the Chinese sent in Foreign Minister Li Zhaoxing (who was not scheduled to appear) to salvage what he could, but there was little that could be done to patch up the obviously acrimonious dialogue. As a commentary in the *Wall Street Journal* put it: Li's comments "have made all further dialogue too politically radioactive to contemplate for at least months to come."[38]

As spring turned into summer, the North Korean nuclear crisis superficially seemed to be entering a lull. Pyongyang refrained from martial international actions and the United States affected an air of calm, even dispassion, about Pyongyang's nuclear transgressions. These encouraging atmospherics, however, masked the ominous realities of a situation that was steadily becoming ever more dangerous.

In the months leading up to *Operation Iraqi Freedom*, Washington had affected a stance toward the North Korean nuclear problem that was positively described by the State Department's official spokesperson as "vague."[39] Any hopes that seeming indecision over the North Korean nuclear drama might have been attributable to the total concentration on the Iraq situation were dispelled after the ouster of the Saddam Hussein government. In late May 2003—a month and a half after the fall of Baghdad—a senior Bush administration official confided, "We have consciously made a decision on the part of the U.S. government not to draw red lines"[40] that would trigger a U.S. response in the mounting North Korean crisis.

Washington's dilemma was apparent. Over the previous half-year, it had become obvious that the UN Security Council was averse to taking responsibility for the North Korean nuclear matter, or even to authorizing a resolution that might legitimize U.S. pressure against the DPRK. North Korea's neighbors, for their part, were unwilling to put much pressure on Pyongyang themselves for fear of antagonizing the belligerent state, and while they all urged the United States to solve this problem, none supported any American steps that went much beyond talk. In the aftermath of September 11, U.S. security doctrine had become more open to the prospect of military preemption, and U.S. diplomacy more comfortable with the notion of unilateral international action—but the challenges and risks of military action against North Korea were incomparably greater than they had been in Iraq. The Bush administration described its post-Iraq policy toward Pyongyang as "strategic ambiguity,"[41] but the plain fact was that U.S. policymakers were perplexed, and deeply divided, about how to proceed.

No such indecision characterized North Korean words and deeds. In the spring and summer of 2003, Pyongyang's moves seemed to be following a clear, bold, methodical, and internally consistent plan.

On May 5, just days after the denouement of the Beijing talks, Pyongyang declared that:

> The war in Iraq teaches the lesson that one must only have a powerful physical deterrent to prevent war and safeguard the country's security and national sovereignty. As long as the US hostile policy toward the DPRK continues, we will strengthen our *war deterrent* in all possible ways...[42] [emphasis added]

The following week, North Korea announced that its 1992 joint declaration with Seoul on the de-nuclearization of the Korean Peninsula—the sole remaining accord to which the DPRK was signatory that might seem to constrain it from emerging as a declared nuclear power—was a "dead document."[43] On June 3, Pyongyang again explained it was developing a "war deterrent" to protect the entire Korean people, North and South, against American imperialism, and implied that this deterrent might be instrumental in promoting Pyongyang's longstanding campaign to force U.S. troops to leave South Korea.[44] On June 9, the DPRK finally allowed that the "war deterrent" to which it had coyly referred was in fact nuclear weaponry.[45]

In late June, North Korea again underscored its intention to "not only increase our nuclear deterrent force," but also to "build up something more powerful than that for self defense"[46]—possibly a reference to intercontinental ballistic missile systems. Just days later, U.S. intelligence let it be known that they had detected new weapons-testing facilities in North Korea possibly designed for miniaturizing plutonium warheads so that these could be missile-launched.[47] In early July, North Korean officials reportedly also told the U.S. government that the DPRK "had finished producing enough plutonium to make a half-dozen nuclear bombs, and that [it] intended to move ahead quickly to turn the material into weapons."[48] In mid-July, new U.S. intelligence, described as "worrisome, but still not conclusive," circulated in Washington and allied Asian capitals that suggested the DPRK might have developed a hidden second site for reprocessing plutonium into weapons-grade material.[49]

In July 2003, reflecting on this gradual but seemingly inexorable pattern of North Korean escalation, a U.S. official mused that "There's a body of thought [in the Bush administration] that they are just getting everybody accustomed to the idea…So when they say one day, 'We've gone nuclear,' it's no shock."[50] That same month, North Korea seemed to take a major step toward that very outcome. According to Japanese news reports, Pyongyang indicated that it was now ready to declare itself a nuclear power, and in meetings with then-U.S. envoy Charles Pritchard, a DPRK official had specifically discussed a North Korean nuclear test.[51] As of August 2003, North Korea had not detonated an atomic weapon—but a North Korean nuclear test looked to be a real possibility, perhaps even an imminent one.

Motivations of the DPRK Leadership

The North Korean nuclear crisis of 2002–03 has been treated as a terrible surprise by many observers and practically all of the governments that have become embroiled in it. Before that eruption, it is well to remember, cautious optimism about a newly constructive attitude in Pyongyang had been spreading in international diplomatic circles for several years.[52] The optimists seemed to have facts on their side. In the period between late 1999 and October 2002 relations between Pyongyang and its neighbors—indeed, with the entire international community—were arguably better than at any previous point in the decades since the end of the Korean War.

Recall: Kim Dae Jung's "sunshine policy" had resulted in the first-ever summit meeting between the Korean heads of state in the summer of 2000. In late 2000, U.S. Secretary of State Madeline Albright visited Pyongyang, the highest-level visit by any U.S. official ever to North Korea. In 2000 and 2001, North Korea's international attitude was judged sufficiently propitious that eight European states (including Britain, Germany and Italy) and the European Union (EU) chose to normalize relations with Pyongyang. In September 2002, the Japanese prime minister visited Pyongyang. That was the first visit ever to the DPRK by a Japanese premier—a visit few believed would happen even as late as the spring of 2002. Kim Jong Il conducted two official visits to Russia in 2001 and 2002; these had been preceded by an historic visit to Pyongyang by Russian President Vladimir Putin in the summer of 2000. Chinese President Jiang Zemin also visited Pyongyang in September of 2001. North Korea even seemed to be attempting to emulate China in a brief, failed experiment to liberalize and open up part of its economy in the summer of 2002. As one commentary put it, "Pyongyang seemed to have abandoned its policy of playing Washington, Seoul and Tokyo off one another by addressing the concerns of one while ignoring those of the other two."[53]

Against such a promising backdrop, the sudden radical downward spiral in North Korea's global relations since October 2002 looks all the more dismaying. Central to any appraisal of the unfolding crisis must be an attempt to understand the motivations behind Pyongyang's covert HEU project—and today there are a variety of theories for the DPRK's actions. They run a gamut: from attempts to understand the DPRK regime's strategy in the context of international relations game theory to surmises about the personal psychological condition of Kim Jong Il. More traditional analyses look at international and domestic factors as motivating forces. Some of this work regards the attempt to acquire nuclear weapons as a classic strategy to help assure the DPRK's traditional goal of reuniting the Korean Peninsula militarily.[54] Other analyses emphasize regime survival—a last gasp effort to save the dying regime of Kim Jong Il.[55] Still others see a combination of efforts to assist regime survival, to assure "existential" deterrence against the United States, to prop up regime morale, and to intimidate the DPRK's neighbors in South Korea, and, especially, Japan.[56]

Let us begin, however, by examining some of the hypotheses that *cannot* explain Pyongyang's behavior. In the months since October 2002, much *sotto voce* criticism in diplomatic circles, and not a few comments by editorialists and essayists, have implied or stated that the current nuclear crisis was caused by the United States—more specifically, by the hostile posture of the Bush administration toward the DPRK. In this telling, the

Bush administration's adoption of a doctrine of preemption, its designation of North Korea as a member of an "axis of evil," and the president's own trenchantly expressed "personal loathing" for Kim Jong Il have pressed the North Korean government to abandon a policy of conciliation and instead to grasp for nuclear options.

Renditions of this theme are most commonly heard in Asia and Europe, but some analysts in the United States also subscribe to this view. They argue the North Korean regime is desperate and merely desires recognition, security guarantees, and economic assistance, and suggest that it is ready to give up any program it may already have in a process of international bargaining. These same analysts also question whether Pyongyang is still bent on changing the status quo on the Korean Peninsula. They argue for engagement with the North to divert a potential catastrophe.[57]

Whatever the motivations of the DPRK leadership may be, a quick look at the chronology of the current crisis confutes the contention that the Bush administration is the proximate agent of the current impasse. To put the matter bluntly, the latest turn of the North Korean nuclear crisis did not begin with a change of attitude in Washington: rather, it commenced when the DPRK was caught cheating—and admitted to it.

Moreover, as Western intelligence sources now seem to agree, the DPRK had already embarked on its HEU program by 1997 or 1998[58]— that is to say, years before the Bush administration came to office. That covert program, it is worth noting, barreled forward during the halcyon days of the "sunshine policy." It was underway during the heyday of U.S.-DPRK reciprocal high-level visits; it was going forward as North Korea normalized diplomatic relations with the EU; and it was proceeding even as Prime Minister Koizumi and Kim Jong Il signed a joint declaration pledging to "observe all the international agreements for a comprehensive solution to the nuclear issue on the Korean Peninsula."[59] The tenor of international relations, in other words, seems to have had absolutely no bearing on Pyongyang's disposition to pursue a secret nuclear weapons program. The DPRK leadership was perfectly willing to go along with the illusion of cooperation with South Korea, Japan, the EU, and the United States—even though none of those states would have continued such cooperation had they known that the DPRK had a covert nuclear weapons program.

Another unsatisfactory hypothesis—one canvassed mainly in progressive circles in South Korea—holds that the North devised its HEU program to break out of the existing diplomatic impasse with the United States and reach a more comprehensive settlement of the outstanding disagreements separating Washington and Pyongyang. Noting that North Korea's HEU project looks to be a slow program requiring years to complete, this argument suggests that the DPRK leadership chose this type of program precisely so that they would have time to negotiate and bargain before they actually had a weapon. A modulated version of the same argument is agnostic about the question of whether North Korea opted for an HEU program because of its long lead time, but sees the covert project as an instrument by which the North Korean government intended to gain leverage for a breakthrough in its diplomatic relations with Washington.[60]

Like the previous theory, this one too is empirically challenged. It neglects the fact that North Korea was caught out in a flagrant nuclear violation. Nuclear deceptions and nuclear violations, furthermore, are not exactly ideal lubricants for a diplomatic breakthrough between two mutually mistrustful governments. While it is true that slow progress in accumulating HEU was foreordained by the DPRK's decision to use many small centrifuges for the job, that choice seems to have been dictated by the objective of avoiding detection. And there is absolutely no evidence that the DPRK would have informed its putative negotiating partner about the program if the HEU program had not been detected by U.S. intelligence.

More plausible if nonetheless delimited explanations for the DPRK's rash actions in late 2002 could be couched in terms of the "situational ethics" that informed the regime's responses in the international arena. The DPRK had effectively hidden its program until 2002; in the interim the Bush administration's harsh statements about North Korean leadership, in conjunction with the unfolding U.S. policy of preemption in Iraq, gave the DPRK leadership a perfect justification for defiant nuclear escalation. As Jonathan Pollack writes, "Justifying its behavior by the inattention and misdeeds of its principal adversary was a time-honored North Korean strategy. It is possible that the DPRK might have ultimately decided to reactivate its plutonium program on its own initiative, but the oil cutoff [in December 2002] made it far easier for Pyongyang to justify its actions."[61] This explanation seems sound as far as it goes: but of course it still begs the key question of why North Korea would undertake a covert and contravened nuclear weapons program in the first place.

At the end of the day, there remains a welter of alternative and conflicting theories about the intentions underlying the North Korean decision to pursue a secret nuclear weapons program. Faced with contending possible explanations for less-than-perfectly-understood events, logicians and epistemologists have long favored the simpler explanation over the more complex as the starting point in the pursuit of knowledge. Following this model, we might simply surmise that the North Korean leadership's drive to develop nuclear weapons, of which the covert HEU program was but one component, reflects Pyongyang's deep desire *to possess them.*

There are many subsidiary reasons that the DPRK may wish to possess nuclear weapons. It may want them for deterrence; as a national symbol (or "badge"); for economic benefits; and/or as an instrument for securing the international advance of its agenda. It may want them as an insurance policy for state survival; as a tool in the quest for unconditional reunification with South Korea; and/or as a means of equalizing its highly unequal contest with the United States.

We may not have enough information to permit us to calibrate the importance of the many different factors that contribute to the North Korean leadership's quest for nuclear weapons. We do know, however, that the DPRK has been pursuing its nuclear program for decades—and that it has built, at great expense to a very poor society, a complex and diversified nuclear infrastructure for that very project.[62] As Joseph Bermudez, Jr., noted shortly after the HEU effort was publicly revealed:

> Given what the West knows about North Korea's nuclear programme, it is evident that it has been, and is being, pursued in a manner similar to that of China's. That is, in a parallel manner, exploring multiple paths concurrently rather than in serial form with each development building on the last.[63]

The comparison with China seems particularly instructive. Like Beijing in an earlier era, North Korea has pressed forward with its nuclear project despite popular hardship and even famine and regardless of its impact on relations with other countries. All evidence at our disposal suggests that North Korean leadership has treated the acquisition of a nuclear capability as an enduring and unshakable commitment, a top state priority.

The troubling corollary to the obvious importance Pyongyang accords to its quest for nuclear weaponry is that governments are not easily dissuaded from pursuing their own top priorities. The notion that the Pyongyang regime could be talked out of completing its longstanding nuclear weapons program, in particular, would seem to require from students of international security something like a suspension of belief in the realities of power politics. Paul Bracken incisively parsed the dilemma back in 1993:

> The belief that the Kim regime can accept face-saving offers such as economic concessions or cancellations of U.S. and South Korean military exercises in exchange for nuclear inspections masks a deeper set of impediments that greatly limit the North's power and flexibility. Impediments to change derive from the character of the leadership and institutional characteristics of the North Korean state, both in terms of its internal organization and in terms of its relationship with its subjects...What is taking place is not

just a struggle between a particular regime and the outside world, but a struggle to preserve the basic identity, structure and capacity of the North Korean state.[64]

The dilemma remains unchanged today. Simply put, North Korea's arduous march toward becoming a nuclear power does not look like the sort of "dispute" that is headed off by conventional diplomatic negotiations.

The Reactions of the Other Powers

Over the past year, North Korea's neighbors have all responded to the unfolding nuclear drama in varying ways. The geographical distance from Pyongyang seemed to govern these responses. Paradoxically, the most distant states have expressed the strongest responses, while the states contiguous to the DPRK have reacted rather calmly to the entire situation.

Russia

Considering that Russia (or rather the Soviet Union) probably had more to do with the DPRK's nuclear weapons program than any other government, Moscow has seemed rather nonplussed by the entire situation. Rather than regarding an unstable neighbor's acquisition of nuclear weapons as a ticking time-bomb, it has acted as if the latest crisis were an opportunity. Somewhat curiously, President Putin and his foreign policy apparatus have to date treated North Korea's attempt to develop nuclear weapons not as a threat to international security—or to Russia's own interests—but instead as a device whereby Russia might regain its lost diplomatic foothold in North Korea and re-attain a measure of its former influence in Northeast Asia.

Ironically, Moscow's past actions had much to do with the progress and speed of the North Korean nuclear program. It was the Soviet Union, after all, that agreed in 1985 to help the DPRK with its now-famous Yongbyon reactor. Thanks to that Soviet technology, Pyongyang was able to make enormous strides in its nuclear program. The Soviet Union was also North Korea's major benefactor in the late 1980s, providing the DPRK with up to $1 billion annually in economic assistance[65]—subventions hardly incidental to Pyongyang's nuclear quest, considering the expense of the project. The Soviet hierarchy was hardly unaware of Pyongyang's nuclear ambitions; in 1990, in fact, the KGB issued a report to the Politburo concluding that the DPRK already possessed one or two crude nuclear weapons.[66] In 1990, Moscow's Korea policy suddenly shifted: Russia normalized relations with the ROK, and virtually shut off aid to North Korea. Then the Soviet Union dissolved. Its successor state—Boris Yeltsin's Russian Federation—made a point of freezing Pyongyang out while it cultivated relations with Seoul. It was no coincidence that the North Korean nuclear drama of the early 1990s followed on the heels of this *volte face* by Pyongyang's then-most important patron.[67]

Undaunted, or perhaps driven by, this earlier connection, Putin moved to bring Russia squarely into the middle of the most recent crisis. Moscow has attempted to play a mediating role, thus repositioning Russia on the Korean Peninsula, presumably as part of the greater project of reversing its dramatic economic, political, and strategic decline in Northeast Asia.[68] Putin and Kim Jong Il had met three times since 2000, and he indicated that Russia could work with the DPRK leader.[69] Moscow's call for multilateral dialogue on the Korean Peninsula (to include Russia, of course) dates to the previous nuclear crisis, when Russia felt painfully excluded and was reminded of its political impotence in the region. So it was with some surprise when Putin's special envoy to Pyongyang, Deputy Foreign Minister Alexander Losyukov, emerged from a January 2003 meeting with Kim Jong Il urging the United States to deal directly with the DPRK leadership. In suddenly embracing what was then Pyongyang's fixed position on talks with Washington, Moscow may have been trying to curry favor with North Korea's leadership. Russia's diplomatic gambit went nowhere, however. Undaunted, Moscow kept up its diplomatic offensive and the effort seemingly paid off when Pyongyang agreed, in an announcement in August 2003 by its ambassador in Moscow, that it was prepared to enter into six-party talks that would include Japan and Russia. Moscow has called for the DPRK to abandon any nuclear weapons program it has, but these public calls have usually been in combination with third parties (notably China and Japan)— and qualified by an insistence elsewhere that Russia does not believe the DPRK has nuclear weapons.[70]

By the summer of 2003, there were some signs that Moscow was drawing very slightly closer to Washington on the North Korean nuclear issu. By then, the United States had agreed to include Moscow in multilateral nuclear talks with Pyongyang—and in doing so eliminated a major ostensible Russian objection to the U.S. approach. At least one veteran journalist has speculated that Russia decided to back U.S. non-proliferation policy in Iran and North Korea after the United States officially placed the leader of the Chechen separatist movement on its list of international terrorists.[71] Putin has also been keen on re-establishing a good rapport with the Bush administration after the falling out over the Iraq war. Moscow's North Korea policy could possibly serve as a sacrificial lamb before that altar.

China

It is clear that leaders in the United States view China as the most critical player in persuading or coercing North Korea to give up its nuclear weapons program. Beijing appears to have been perceived in Seoul and Washington as the final link in the chain of shared interests potentially encircling Pyongyang that will ultimately determine whether North Korea will halt its nuclear weapons pursuits and instead pursue policies of engagement with the United States, South Korea, and Japan.

China remained quiet about the North Korean nuclear issue in the months after the HEU revelations. The Chinese leadership was already dealing with a vital domestic political issue—the leadership succession—and was thus more than usually loath to take an active role in a dispute involving North Korea, as Washington had been pleading for it to do.

Chinese leaders have called for North Korea to come clean about their nuclear weapons program and they are no doubt disturbed by the idea of a nuclear crisis on their border leading to a dangerous scenario involving war or the collapse of the North Korean regime. In a joint statement in December 2002, Jiang and Putin said that any DPRK nuclear weapons program would pose great risks for the region. Hu and Putin reiterated the point at their summit meeting in St. Petersburg in May 2003. Yet while they urged the DPRK to submit to IAEA guidelines, they seemed just as concerned about U.S. actions. In a pointed reference to Washington they jointly declared that "scenarios of power pressure or the use of force to resolve the problems [in Korea]…are unacceptable."[72] Chinese leaders reluctantly volunteered their services as mediators in the three-way April talks, but they seem to have felt cornered into this: as one Chinese official put it as the talks commenced, "we don't want another Iraq so near us. We don't want a war on our border."[73]

Beijing seemingly still wishes to limit its involvement in the deliberations with North Korea, and continues to call for the United States to engage the North Korean leadership directly. Even so, recent events have suggested that China is becoming increasingly impatient with the North's brinkmanship. One noted China watcher in Washington argued that China's leadership went from "complacent" to "apoplectic" over North Korea in the space of six months.[74] In his assessment, the change in thinking came in March 2003 when Beijing sent its most senior diplomat, Qian Qichen, to Pyongyang to inform Kim that Beijing was most unhappy with the developing situation. Soon thereafter oil shipments to North Korea were reportedly shut off for several days to reinforce this point. Beijing then agreed to host the three-way talks in April. In early July it was revealed that the CIA believed that the North was developing nuclear warheads small enough to be placed atop its missiles (one of the North's top exports). Not coincidentally, on July 2 diplomats from China, Japan, and South Korea were in Washington to work out a way to induce the DPRK to cease and desist.[75]

There were other signs of Beijing's increasing displeasure with North Korea as well, including some fairly strong signals before March 2003. The week after Pyongyang announced its impending withdrawal from the NPT, for example, China staged a seven-day military exercise near the North Korean border.[76] Chinese trade data suggest that economic subsidies to North Korea were significantly cut between 2001 and 2002, a drop that continued into early 2003. Interestingly enough, though China has apparently used its economic leverage with North Korea now and again, it has to date consistently leaned against the threat of international economic sanctions against the DPRK, perhaps because Beijing fears such measures might actually undermine the North Korean regime, with untold consequences for China, or perhaps because such sanctions would be an application of pressure on the DPRK beyond Beijing's immediate control.

For both China and Russia, the UN Security Council offers a litmus test for their North Korea policies. Will Moscow and Beijing agree to take the DPRK nuclear issue to the Security Council for possible penalties and sanctions? Thus far both have been reluctant to take such action, despite their calls for more multilateral dialogue through the United Nations to address other security problems in the rest of the world. The contradiction is striking—and presumably has been framed by considerations that extend beyond their own often frustrating histories of dealing with Pyongyang.

Japan

Japanese leaders, dealing with the aftermath of their own North Korean crisis involving Japanese abductees, have stood firmly behind the United States on the latest nuclear crisis. When news of the DPRK announcement during Kelly's October Pyongyang trip became public, Tokyo immediately issued a denunciation; Prime Minister Koizumi added that the normalization of relations with Pyongyang could not progress until both the issues of Japanese abductees and the DPRK's nuclear program were resolved.

In the wake of the October revelations, Japan adopted a number of uncharacteristically bold responses; surprisingly, these were met with little domestic opposition, even in the local press. First, in a departure from half a century of Japanese security policy, Japan Defense Agency chief Ishiba Shigeru declared that Tokyo would advocate, and participate in, a preemptive strike against North Korea if Japan were in imminent danger of North Korean missile attack. Foreign Minister Kawaguchi Yoriko publicly supported Ishiba's position, explaining that such a move would be "within the legal framework" of the Japanese constitution, which limits military actions to self-defense.[77] Second, after decades of tolerating such commerce, Japan moved to cut off sources of cash remittances that have been making their way into North Korea from the community of Japanese of Korean descent with ties to Pyongyang (known as *Chosen Soren* in Japanese, *Chochongnyon* in Korean). Japanese authorities also implemented much tighter customs inspections of ferries that run regularly from the west coast of Japan to the DPRK port of Wonsan.[78]

Third, in June 2003, the Japanese Diet passed a series of war contingency bills that allow the government to assume increased powers in times of national emergency.[79] That these bills passed with little controversy attests to the Japanese public's heightened concerns about security threats to their country, especially from North Korea. It should also be noted that Japan's moves were taken with little regard for public opinion across Asia, a consideration that has weighed heavily on its foreign policy in the past.

None of this is to suggest that Tokyo has abandoned its longstanding "hedging" behavior in security policy. Koizumi's September 2002 summit with Kim Jong Il evidently took Washington by surprise—and was executed despite the high likelihood that Tokyo's top policymakers had already been briefed by U.S. counterparts on the new evidence about Pyongyang's HEU violations. Japanese policymakers are well aware that their objectives in North Korea may not mesh perfectly with Washington's. Even so, Japan's stance on the latest North Korean nuclear crisis—and on the latest Iraq war—was almost the polar opposite of its position on the previous one. Still, this shift in posture signified nothing more than that Japan was ready to follow on the North Korean nuclear problem. Tokyo was still unwilling and incapable to lead in a time of regional crisis.

South Korea

The country most directly affected by the North Korean nuclear crisis, of course, is South Korea. Yet initially South Korean leaders seemed to be the least concerned with these ominous events just across the border from Seoul. As the crisis broke in the fall of 2002, Kim Dae Jung was already under siege for irregularities surrounding his "sunshine policy." Evidence had surfaced that his government had made secret and possibly illegal payments to the DPRK, amounting to at least hundreds of millions of dollars, to secure the historic Pyongyang summit of June 2000. President Kim, however, was not prepared to admit that the new North Korean nuclear revelations threatened the very rationale of his beloved "sunshine policy." Instead his administration attempted to conduct business more or less as if the discovery of the HEU program had not occurred. (Just 10 days after the news broke about the covert North Korean HEU program, for example, the ROK government was welcoming to Seoul a North Korean "economic inspection team" that included Chang Song Taek, Kim Jong Il's brother-in-law.)[80]

In late 2002, South Korea was in the midst of a close, heated, and ideologically charged presidential election, upon which the future of the "sunshine policy" hinged. A wave of anti-American sentiment was sweeping the younger generation of South Koreans in the wake of the acquittal of two U.S. soldiers who had accidentally run over two Korean schoolgirls in their military vehicle. It was, needless to say, a less than auspicious time for U.S.-ROK cooperation on the North Korean nuclear issue.

The election of Roh Moo Hyun in December 2002 did nothing to dispel U.S. concerns about the reliability of its partner and ally in these trying times (see the chapter on South Korea in this volume for more detail). In the two months between election and inauguration, the Roh team did almost nothing to suggest to officials in Washington that the new ROK administration would join the United States in facing the North Korean nuclear problem. Doubt was expressed across South Korea that a nuclear weapons program even existed in the North, and at one point Roh himself was quoted as implying that if a war began he would keep South Korea out of the hostilities and act as a mediator between Washington and Pyongyang.[81] Upon taking office, the new president seemed remarkably unperturbed by the aggressive behavior of the state on his northern border. The Roh government paid practically no attention to the North Korean missile launches that greeted his inauguration, and when DPRK fighter jets tried to muscle a U.S. reconnaissance plane, Roh dismissed the incident as "predictable" and warned Washington—not Pyongyang—to exercise restraint.[82] As late as April 2003, Roh would indulgently characterize North Korea's nuclear threats at the Beijing talks as a mere "bargaining chip," averring that it would be "undesirable" to "behave as if something big is happening right now."[83]

If Roh was inclined to equanimity about the mounting North Korean threat, however, others whose opinion he could not ignore were not. In a blow to the confidence of the young Roh administration, the U.S. firm Moody's Investors Services downgraded South Korea's credit rating outlook by two notches, from positive to negative, specifically citing the North Korean nuclear crisis; the ratings cut was accompanied by a significant dip in the South Korean stock market, a drop in foreign direct investment, a spike in borrowing costs, and an economic slowdown, all attributed in part to business jitters about the North Korean situation.[84] At roughly the same time, U.S. Secretary of Defense Donald Rumsfeld broached the idea of drawing back a significant portion of the U.S. troops stationed in South Korea, especially those along the demilitarized zone (DMZ).[85] It soon became clear that this was not a trial balloon, but instead a decision already determined. The prospect of a repositioning of U.S. forces sent an electric shock through the South Korean body politic—and the possibility that the

Pentagon's "rationalization" plan might actually prefigure a U.S. withdrawal was greeted with almost universal dismay, even in circles that had been extremely critical of U.S. policy just weeks beforehand.

Under the exigency of these pressures, the new Roh government and its leading personalities bent and changed course, reassessing and disavowing their most memorable comments from the prior months. Prime Minister Goh Kun called for U.S. forces to remain in Korea for deterrent purposes. Soon thereafter, the ROK government announced that it would deploy engineer and medical support units to assist U.S. forces in Iraq. The South Korean press was quick to take notice of Roh's turn toward the United States. The conservative daily *Chosun Ilbo* approvingly commented that Roh's security policy had gone from "idealistic and liberal to realistic and practical."[86] The ROK military also made pronouncements that added to the credibility of the Roh administration. Army Chief of Staff Nam Jae Joon "clarified" the government's military position by specifically identifying North Korea as the main threat to the security of the ROK. Although this designation might seem unsurprising to most foreign readers, the Kim Dae Jung administration had not been able to bring itself to describe the DPRK in such a manner for most of its time in office. The South Korean news service Yonhap recognized the change. In its words, "experts…said the remarks by top military men are a striking contrast to the 'timid' and often vague approach to this sensitive issue under the last government."[87]

By the time Roh visited Washington in May 2003, it was clear that he wanted to be seen as a partner in a firm alliance with Washington. A healthy and credible U.S.-ROK alliance, Roh had learned, was imperative not only to restore public confidence in his rule in South Korea (a quantity domestic polls already showed to be in near-freefall[88]), but also to reassure the industrial and financial communities at home and abroad that South Korea was still a safe place to do business. Thus the Roh administration found itself in the delicate position of attempting a policy of "dual appeasement"—of simultaneously placating Pyongyang and Washington. It was a tricky business, depending more than a little on vagueness and official indecision. In a June 2003 summit meeting with Japanese Prime Minister Koizumi, for example, Roh concurred in the formulation that a nuclear-armed North Korea would be "intolerable."[89] But he carefully avoided spelling out exactly what measures would be "tolerable" to prevent this eventuality.

United States

The United States has remained the most outspoken advocate of a tough line with Pyongyang—no great surprise, considering President Bush's unconcealed contempt for Kim Jong Il and his administration's doctrinal support for "regime change" as an instrument of international security policy. A harsh attitude toward North Korea and its nuclear violations, however, should not necessarily be mistaken for a coherent and effective policy. (In fact, the Bush team has been accused of lacking a North Korea policy since well before the crisis erupted in the fall of 2002[90]—sometimes even by the administration's own supporters.) At various points during the escalating North Korean crisis, the Bush administration's position has seemed confused, reactive, or vacillating. By the summer of 2003, the administration still seemed to be searching for internal consensus, with major differences of opinion within the government, particularly between the State Department and the Pentagon, by no means completely resolved.[91]

The end of the military campaign in Iraq was expected to free up policy planning time for the North Korean problem, but this does not seem to have happened as of this writing (August 2003). Ironically, in the months after October 2002 the only substantive new U.S. initiative in Korean affairs has involved *South* Korea—this being the envisioned realignment of U.S. forces. While some would argue that the impending realignment was sensible and even long overdue, it seemed difficult to argue that this was the most pressing problem facing the United States in the Korean Peninsula at the time.

By adopting the defiant but nonetheless also largely passive posture of refusing to give in to North Korean blackmail, the Bush administration seems to be looking for other nations to take the lead on Korea. Of course, this stance may pay off sooner or later. The question is: how long can the world wait? Perhaps the White House is privy to reliable intelligence that the North's nuclear weapons program is still far from its objective. One can only hope this is the case, for incipient problems in other regions, including the Middle East, promise to occupy still more of Washington's attention in the none too distant future. (Already another nuclear crisis, this one in Iran, threatens to overshadow the dangerous sequence of events playing out on the Korean Peninsula.) As the summer of 2003 wore on, the Bush administration looked to be playing a waiting game with North Korea— while North Korea seemed to be busily rushing toward the goal of declared nuclear power status. The yawning gap between the problem at hand and the American response to it was palpable: nearly a year into the latest flare-up in the North Korean nuclear crisis, Washington not only lacked a solution for this acute problem, but had not yet begun to fashion a feasible *approach* to such a solution.

Alternative Outcomes

Given this somber analysis, what is the outlook for the current round of crisis? Three major alternative outcomes from the current impasse suggest themselves. The first outcome would be a peaceful negotiated settlement—a diplomatic agreement whereby the North gave up its nuclear weapons program. (This is precisely what many argued the United States had arranged in the 1994 Agreed Framework, with the exchange of the Yongbyon facility for security pledges and economic incentives.) The second possible outcome would be to ignore the DPRK's extortion diplomacy and simply accept the advent of a nuclear-armed North Korea, coping with all the attendant dangers as they arise. A third outcome would be to implement and see through a strategy of regime change in the DPRK.[92]

The peaceful negotiated settlement is clearly the preferable outcome for most of the governments embroiled in the North Korean nuclear crisis. Certainly it would be the least troubling and most immediately advantageous scenario for all of Pyongyang's potential negotiating partners. Carefully crafted proposals have outlined exactly what might be entailed in such a settlement and how the deal might be reached.[93] At this writing (August 2003), six-party talks involving Pyongyang and the five other governments were beginning in Beijing.[94] The very fact that North Korea has assented to this meeting has encouraged speculation that Pyongyang is at last ready to come to terms with the international community.

Unfortunately, the prospect of a negotiated agreement to dismantle Pyongyang's nuclear weapons program permanently and completely is extraordinarily remote. One may appreciate the odds against such an outcome when one considers the many obstacles against it. The first is the problem of North Korean intentions. Over the past dozen years Western diplomacy has devoted no small effort to probing these. In the early 1990s, the ROK's Roh Tae Woo administration probed them for two years, eventually securing a Joint North-South Declaration on the Denuclearization of the Korean Peninsula in 1992. When that agreement collapsed, the Clinton administration and the U.S. government probed Pyongyang's nuclear intentions with the year and a half of diplomacy that culminated in the 1994 Agreed Framework. After 1998, in the wake of the first episode that threatened to topple the Agreed Framework, the Clinton administration probed North Korean nuclear intentions still further through what became known as the "Perry Process." And of course Kim Dae Jung probed North Korean nuclear intentions from 1998 to early 2003 with his now-discredited "sunshine policy." Reviewing this record, one might suggest we actually have a fairly clear idea of North Korea's nuclear intentions—like them or not. From what we can see, those intentions are not conducive to a voluntary deal to denuclearize the DPRK.

A second problem concerns the international precedent that would be established by a negotiated solution to the North Korean nuclear crisis. Thus far, North Korea has violated non-proliferation strictures more explicitly and provocatively than any other contemporary state—yet it has suffered no penalties for its behavior (apart from the cutoff of free KEDO oil supplies). The international community has already purchased an end to the North Korean nuclear program through the now-moribund Agreed Framework. Providing resources to shut down the North Korean nuclear project once again in a new negotiated settlement could only send a destabilizing signal to would-be proliferators in other locales. The lesson of such a deal would likely not be lost on the government of Iran (now in the process of developing weapons, as even Moscow is beginning to admit), or on the people of a reconstructed Iraq (whose former government was punished much more severely for much less threatening nuclear transgressions-perhaps precisely because they were not yet threatening). A negotiated settlement with rewards for Pyongyang would send a very dangerous message to the rest of the world community: namely, swift development of a credible nuclear capability can be a wise and profitable strategy-perhaps especially if a state finds itself in financial trouble.

Apart from all the other obstacles to a diplomatic settlement of the current nuclear crisis, there is also the problem of the practical details that would attend any such negotiation with North Korea. These forbidding particulars should not be forgotten. Apart from the July 1953 armistice ending the Korean conflict-which has been upheld only through continuing U.S. force of arms-it is hard to point to an agreement Pyongyang has abided over its 55 years of state power. For nearly three decades, Pyongyang has been in effective default on hundreds of millions of dollars in loans it contracted in the West, and Soviet bloc archives now reveal that North Korea routinely ignored the terms of its borrowings from socialist creditors. North Korea has regularly and repeatedly flaunted the protocols surrounding the use of diplomatic pouches, using these to transport narcotics and other illegal material to countries in which North Korean officials enjoy diplomatic immunity. The North Korean government has sponsored state terrorism in countries with which it enjoyed diplomatic relations. It has violated the territorial waters of governments who have granted it diplomatic recognition through such state-sponsored shipment of drugs and military contraband. Not least of all, the DPRK has violated the rules of the IAEA (removing cameras, seals, and technicians from nuclear facilities), and has openly stated that it will no longer abide by the 1994 Agreed Framework, the NPT, or the Joint North-South Declaration. Given this history, why should anyone believe that the DPRK would adhere to a new agreement—much less an agreement on nuclear arms?

The second possible outcome of the current crisis ultimately involves living with a nuclear North Korea. The United States has lived with, and outlasted, dangerous nuclear states in the past, as the history of the Cold War attests. Yet the costs and risks posed by a nuclear North Korea would be fearsome. The example of a North Korean nuclear breakout would encourage proliferation in other regions, and a nuclear North Korea could abet that proliferation through export of armaments, technology, or expertise. Within the Northeast Asian region, the impact of North Korean entry into the nuclear club would also be far-reaching. More than any other modern state, Pyongyang makes its living from international military extortion; nuclear weaponry would dramatically improve the returns of that policy. With a hostile nuclear North Korea at its geographic center, the economies of Northeast Asia could not help but suffer: the confidence dip and attendant business downturn that the ROK suffered in early 2003 would presumably represent only a foretaste of what might lie in store for South Korea, Japan, and even China. A nuclear-armed North Korea would necessarily and inescapably undermine the credibility of the U.S.-ROK and the U.S.-Japan alliances: the very security architecture upon which post-war Northeast Asia's economic and political successes have been built. The erosion of deterrence in Northeast Asia could in turn have further unpredictable, possibly cascading, consequences. None of them are likely to be pleasant.

The third possible outcome would be for the international community (or the United States) to aim for, and achieve, regime change in the North. It is more difficult to generalize about this outcome, for it can be envisioned with a great many possible variations, some of them quite divergent. One can be assured that the path to regime change would be fraught with danger, and the result, under even the most optimistic variants, would involve tremendous disruption and uncertainty—at least in the short run. It does not require much imagination, for example, to see how a successful push for regime change in the DPRK could precipitate a mass exodus of starving North Koreans, whether overland into China and Russia, or by boat to Japan and South Korea. There is also a real possibility that the push for regime change in North Korea could result in war, in which case the likelihood of Seoul escaping unscathed—no matter how overwhelming the ultimate victory for the U.S.-ROK alliance—would seem quite small. In any event, however, a push for regime change in Pyongyang does not look to be in the cards over the foreseeable future. Whatever their other differences, the governments of neighboring China, Russia, South Korea, and Japan are today united in their aversion to a policy of promoting regime change in the DPRK. Within the senior reaches of the Bush administration, for its part, the notion of regime change in North Korea has been discussed, but apparently only toyed with. Occasional flirtations notwithstanding, U.S. policy has never to date actually embraced the argument that regime change is either desired or necessary in North Korea. A less drastic form of "regime change" might see Pyongyang give up its nuclear program, become a "normal" nation, and undergo serious economic and social reform under pressure from the international community, led by the five nations surrounding North Korea. But there has never been an indication that the North Korean leadership would even remotely consider such a transformation.

Another Twenty Years' Crisis?

In summation, there has been no coalescence around a strategy for North Korea, either in the United States or among its partners in Northeast Asia. The situation is tilting by the day in an incalculable direction. Like the interwar years in Europe (1919–39) there is an unstable equilibrium and we are faced with an inherently dangerous situation.

One additional factor makes the situation today even more dangerous than is widely appreciated—North Korean leadership's poor recent decision-making record. North Korea's July 2002 "economic reforms" were a patent failure. Pyongyang's attempt to revitalize its economy in September 2002 through a vaunted "special autonomous region" for Sinuiju deteriorated into a fiasco when the project's newly-chosen boss, the controversial Chinese businessman Yang Bin, was detained, tried, and convicted by Chinese authorities. In September 2002, Kim Jong Il's attempted "confession diplomacy" with Japan backfired, setting back prospects for DPRK-Japanese diplomatic normalization even further than they had been before the summit with Prime Minister Koizumi. This series of *faux pas*, of course, was followed by the nuclear tirades of October 2002 and April 2003 at meetings with Assistant Secretary of State Kelly.

The most recent nuclear crisis raises further questions about the ability of the North Korean leadership to manage crises. In past disputes, the North Korean leadership consistently, and often skillfully, attempted to play one nation off against another. Today, by contrast, Kim Jong Il has managed to alienate and alarm most of his neighbors simultaneously—even though they have not yet responded to his mounting threats. To the extent one can detect in Northeast Asia today the nascent components of a coalition to punish North Korea for its nuclear transgressions, it is a prospective coalition being assembled more through the inadvertent actions of Pyongyang than through the conscious design of Washington. To quote once again Paul Bracken's prescient 1993 study:

> This [situation] is dangerous because it indicates that little learning is taking place and that North Korea is a country in which the ruler is all-powerful, but ill-informed and unrestrained by competent advice. The danger ... is heightened by the fact that this deci-

sion-making system has control of an enormous military force and potential nuclear force, however small...What this means is that North Korea is likely to be dangerously bad at crisis management. North Korea's policy is a loose collection of eccentric ideas emanating from the top through an incoherent—yet large and deadly— security structure that is short on caution and coordination.[95]

Bracken's admonition should be kept very much in mind by anyone attempting to envision the eventual outcome of our yet-unfinished ten years' crisis with nuclear North Korea. We may hope that the world community weathers this ten years' crisis in better and wiser fashion than it did the twenty years' crisis some three generations ago; as yet, however, it is not clear that unfolding events can provide support for such a sentiment.

Endnotes

[1] E. H. Carr, *The Twenty Years' Crisis: 1919–1939*, London: Macmillan, 1939.

[2] For general background on the crisis, see Don Oberdorfer, *The Two Koreas: A Contemporary History*, New York: Basic Books, 2001, esp. chapters 11–14.

[3] For the official North Korean announcement, see "KCNA reports statement," Korea Central News Agency (KCNA) radio broadcast, March 12, 1993, Foreign Broadcast Information Service (hereafter FBIS), FBIS-EAS-93-047.

[4] For the official text, see "Kim Chong-il orders army mobilization," Korean Central Broadcast Service, March 8, 1993, FBIS-EAS-93-43. Kim Jong Il has been chairman of the DPRK National Defense Commission since April 1993.

[5] "North Korean heir to power declares a state of 'semi-war'," United Press International, March 8, 1993.

[6] Paul Bracken, "Nuclear Weapons and State Survival in North Korea," *Survival*, vol. 35, no. 3 (Autumn 1993), p. 137.

[7] For its part, the United States was expected to facilitate the financing and construction of two light-water nuclear power reactors (LWRs) in North Korea (with Japanese and South Korean assistance) and to provide free fuel oil for Pyongyang until the LWRs were operational. See Don Oberdorfer, *The Two Koreas*; and Young C. Kim, "North Korea's Strange Quest for Nuclear Weapons," *Problems of Post-Communism*, vol. 50, no. 2 (March/April 2003), p. 4.

[8] For background, see Oberdorfer, *The Two Koreas*. For contemporaneous news accounts, see David E. Sanger, "North Korean site an A-bomb plant, U.S. agencies say," *New York Times*, August 17, 1998. The official DPRK position on the Kumchang-ri inspections was offered by KCNA, "4th DPRK-U.S. underground facility inspection," March 18, 1999.

[9] David E. Sanger, "Bush tells Seoul talks with North won't resume now," *New York Times*, March 8, 2001.

[10] Bush refuses to certify N. Korea abiding by nuclear deal," *Japan Economic Newswire*, April 2, 2002.

[11] Jonathan D. Pollack, "The United States, North Korea, and the End of the

Agreed Framework," *Naval War College Review* (Summer 2003), pp. 11–49.

12 James A. Kelly, "United States to North Korea: we now have a pre-condition," *YaleGlobal Online*, December 12, 2002, as cited in Pollack, "The United States, North Korea..." pp. 35–36.

13 David Jones, "World review," *Washington Times*, October 20, 2002.

14 On his way from Pyongyang back to Washington, Secretary Kelly had stopped in both Seoul and Tokyo, briefing each government on his meetings.

15 "ROK Defense Ministry questions DPRK's technological ability to 'weaponize' plutonium," Yonhap, October 17, 2002, FBIS-EAS-2002-1017.

16 "AFP: rift between South Korea, US widens over P'yongyang nuclear program," Agence France-Presse, October 24, 2002, FBIS-EAS-2002-1024.

17 Jason Hargraves, "Powell insists North Korea 'not yet a crisis'; says war is not imminent," *Washington Times*, December 30, 2002.

18 *Nikkei Shimbun*, December 3, 2002.

19 Young C. Kim, "North Korea's Strange Quest," pp. 4–6.

20 "DPRK informs IAEA of policy to reactivate nuclear facility 'within one or two months'," KBS Radio 1, December 31, 2002, FBIS-EAS-2002-1231.

21 Pollack, "The United States, North Korea," p. 41.

22 Howard W. French, "U.S. gets warning from North Korea," *New York Times*, December 25, 2002.

23 "Spokesman says IAEA unable to monitor N. Korea nuclear program since 1993," Agence France-Presse, October 17, 2002, FBIS-EAS-2002-1017.

24 "International body urges North Korea to accept nuclear inspections," Yonhap, November 29, 2002, BBC Monitoring International Reports.

25 David E. Sanger, "Bush welcomes slower approach to North Korea," *New York Times*, January 7, 2003.

26 Sanger, "Bush welcomes slower approach...," *New York Times*.

27 Most of the chronology is based on timelines developed in the quarterly electronic journal *Comparative Connections* <www.csis.org/pacfor/ccejournal>.

28 "DPRK could 'reconsider NPT withdrawal' if US resumes heavy fuel oil supply," Yonhap, January 10, 2003, FBIS-EAS-2003-0110.

29 "ROKG officials: ROK reluctant to see DPRK nuclear issue go to UNSC," *Korea Times*, December 28, 2002, FBIS-EAS-2002-1227.

30 "ROK's Yonhap: 'no confirmation on North Korea's nuclear weapons: premier," Yonhap, February 12, 2003, FBIS-EAS-2003-0212.

31 "AFP: ROK media call DPRK's envoy snub 'unacceptable insult'," Agence France-Presse, January 30, 2003, FBIS-EAS-2003-0130.

32 "AFP: ROK presidential candidate urges Bush to soften North Korean policy," Agence France-Presse, December 4, 2002, FBIS-EAS-202-1204; Christopher Torchia, "S. Korea new chief vows to work with U.S.," Associated Press, December 19, 2002.

33 James Brooke, "South opposes pressuring North Korea, which hints it will scrap nuclear pact," *New York Times*, January 1, 2003; Howard W. French, "South Korea's president-elect rejects use of force against North Korea," *New York Times*, January 17, 2003; "AFP: ROK's No says DPRK ready to open up; KCNA says US must stop 'hostile policy'," Agence France-Presse, January 17, 2003,FBIS-EAS-2003-0117.

[34] Howard W. French, "Reversals in U.S.-South Korea links, and some jagged fault lines," *New York Times*, February 11, 2003.

[35] "Further on CDPRK FM official tells AFP: N. Korea can hit any US target," Agence France-Presse, February 13, 2003, FBIS-EAS-2003-0213.

[36] "DPRK organ says Iraq fell because of US psychological warfare, not high-tech weapons," *Nodong Sinmun*, May 15, 2003, FBIS-NES-2003-0530; "DPRK says US 'exaggerating' combat power, warns against US' 'psychological operations'," *Nodong Sinmun*, July 11, 2003, FBIS-NES-2003-0731.

[37] "ROK's Yonhap: U.S. to discuss ways of dismantling N.K. nuclear program," Yonhap, April 17, 2003, FBIS-EAS-2003-0417.

[38] Danny Gittings, "Debacle in Beijing," *Wall Street Journal*, April 29, 2003.

[39] Nicholas Kralev, "U.S. vows to continue food aid to N. Korea," *Washington Times*, February 21, 2003.

[40] Bill Sammon, "Bush insists N. Korea give up nukes; vows 'tougher' action against blackmail," *Washington Times*, May 24, 2003.

[41] Sammon, "Bush insists N. Korea give up nukes...," *Washington Times*.

[42] "*Nodong Sinmun* emphasizes DPRK 'magnanimous solution' to nuclear issue, need for 'physical deterrent'," Pyongyang Broadcasting Station, May 5, 2003, FBIS-EAS-203-0505.

[43] "AFP: North Korea nuclear accord with South Korea 'dead document'," Agence France-Presse, May 13, 2003, FBIS-EAS-2003-0513.

[44] "DPRK claims 'war deterrent' for sake of 'entire nation'," *Nodong Sinmun*, June 2, 2003, FBIS-EAS-2003-0626.

[45] David E. Sanger, "North Korea says it seeks to develop nuclear weapons," *New York Times*, June 10, 2003.

[46] "DPRK notes need to 'build up' something 'more powerful' than 'nuclear deterrent'," *Minju Choson*, June 24, 2003, FBIS-EAS-2003-0705.

[47] David E. Sanger, "CIA said to find nuclear advances by North Koreans," *New York Times*, July 1, 2003.

[48] David E. Sanger, "North Korea says it has made fuel for atom bombs," *New York Times*, July 15, 2003.

[49] Thom Shanker with David E. Sanger, "North Korea hides new nuclear site, evidence suggests," *New York Times*, July 20, 2003.

[50] Sanger, "North Korea says it has made fuel for atom bombs," *New York Times*.

[51] "North threatens to have nuke test," *Sunday Territorian*, July 27, 2003.

[52] That cautious optimism was documented, and critiqued, in the 2001–02 and 2002–03 editions of *Strategic Asia*.

[53] James T. Laney and Jason T. Shaplen, "How to Deal With North Korea," *Foreign Affairs*, vol. 82, no. 2 (March/April 2003), p. 17.

[54] See for example, Homer T. Hodge, "North Korea's Military Strategy," *Parameters*, Spring 2003, pp. 68–81.

[55] Young C. Kim, "North Korea's Strange Quest," pp. 3–11.

[56] Victor Cha, "North Korea's Weapons of Mass Destruction: Badges, Shields, or Swords," *Political Science Quarterly*, vol. 117, no. 2 (2002), pp. 209–30.

[57] See Selig Harrison, "Q&A: finding a way out with North Korea," *New York Times*, June 7, 2003; and Leon Sigal, "A bombshell that's actually an olive branch," *Los Angeles Times*, October 18, 2002. See also Leon Sigal, *Disarm-*

ing Strangers: Nuclear Diplomacy with North Korea, Princeton: Princeton University Press, 1998.

58 Laney and Shaplen "How to deal with North Korea," p. 19.

59 "DPRK-Japan Pyongyang declaration", September 17, 2002, <www.korea-np.co.jp/pk/foreign_relations/category01-2.htm>.

60 John Feffer, "Responding to North Korea's Surprise," Nautilus Institute PFO 02-19A, November 1, 2002; Peter Hayes, "North Korea's Negotiating Tactics and Nuclear Strategy," *Nautilus Institute Special Report*, April 18, 2003.

61 Pollack, "The United States, North Korea," p. 42.

62 Joseph Bermudez, Jr., "North Korea's Nuclear Infrastructure," *Jane's Intelligence Review*, vol. 6, no. 2 (February 1, 1994).

63 Joseph Bermudez, Jr., "Lifting the lid on Kim's nuclear workshop," *Jane's Defence Weekly*, November 27, 2002.

64 Bracken, "Nuclear Weapons and State Survival," p. 138.

65 Joseph Ferguson, "Russia's Role on the Korean Peninsula and Great Power Relations in Northeast Asia," *NBR Analysis*, vol. 14, no. 1 (June 2003), p. 35.

66 Vladimir Voronov, "Bomba Zamedlennogo Deistviya," *Novoe Vremya*, no. 3, January 19, 2003.

67 For more on this point, see Herbert J. Ellison, "Russia, Korea and Northeast Asia", in Nicholas Eberstadt and Richard J. Ellings, eds., *Korea's Future and the Great Powers*, Seattle: University of Washington Press, 2001.

68 Economic considerations may have been an aspect of Moscow's calculus. Russia stood to earn huge dividends through rail, oil, and gas projects that would link it with South Korea through North Korean territory. See "Inter-Korean project: preparing for link with North," *Korea Herald*, October 23, 2001; Don Kirk, "Shell chief looks at stake in Korea gas," *New York Times*, June 22, 2002; James Brooke, "North Korea's leader whistle-stops in Siberia," *New York Times*, August 23, 2002; James Brooke, "Russia's latest oil and gas oasis," *New York Times*, May 13, 2003.

69 Putin himself even went so far as to support Kim Jong Il's July 2000 proposal, which offered to resolve international concerns about DPRK ballistic missile development by launching North Korean space satellites from third countries.

70 For example: "Russian atomic energy ninister doubts N. Korea has developed nuclear weapons," Interfax, October 21, 2002, FBIS-SOV-2002-0121; "Diplomat says Russia has no evidence of nuclear program in North Korea," ITAR-TASS, October 26, 2002, FBIS-SOV-2002-1026.

71 Hiroyuki Fuse, "U.S.-Russia deal believed behind North Korean talks," *Daily Yomiuri*, August 21, 2003.

72 See the Kremlin announcement of May 27, 2003, as cited in the chapter of Northeast Asia in this volume, pp. 251-67.

73 John Pomfret, "U.S. envoy opens talks with N. Korea; China included in discussions on crisis; no breakthrough expected," *Washington Post*, April 24, 2003.

74 David Lampton, "China: fed up with North Korea?" *Washington Post*, June 4, 2003.

75 William Safire, "Korea's golden unwedding," *New York Times*, July 3, 2003.

76 "AFP: China stages military exercises in northeast near DPRK," Agence France-Presse, January 23, 2003, FBIS-EAS-2003-0122.

[77] "U.S. attacks possible if North Korea prepares Japan attack," Kyodo News Service, January 24, 2003; James Brooke, "North Koreans demand direct talks with the U.S.," *New York Times*, January 26, 2003.

[78] Bertil Lintner, "Tokyo begins to apply pressure to the North Koreans in Japan," *Wall Street Journal*, March 25, 2003.

[79] Howard French, "Japan adopts laws strengthening military powers," *New York Times*, June 7, 2003.

[80] "DPRK inspection team urged to study South's 'anger' along with economics," *Tong-a Ilbo*, October 28, 2002, FBIS-CHI-2002-1028.

[81] Howard W. French, "Seoul may loosen its ties to the U.S.," *New York Times*, December 20, 2002.

[82] "AFP: ROK urges US not to escalate tensions, not to increase surveillance of DPRK," Agence France-Presse, March 5, 2003, FBIS-EAS-2003-0305.

[83] "AFP: President No Mu-hyon says DPRK's nuclear confession 'a bargaining chip'," Agence France-Presse, April 30, 2003, FBIS-EAS-2003-0430.

[84] Sim Sung-tae, "Moody's poised to cut Korea rating," *Korea Herald*, February 14, 2003; "Seoul asks Moody's and S&P to keep ratings," *Korea Herald*, March 13, 2003; Paivi Munter and Aline van Duyn, "S. Korea in need of benchmark; plans to issue a new sovereign bond may have been delayed by concern over North Korea," *Financial Times*, April 15, 2003.

[85] Sonni Efron and Mark Magnier, "Rumsfeld may reduce forces in S. Korea," *Los Angeles Times*, February 14, 2003; Robert Burns, "Rumsfeld wants U.S. troops in Korea moved further from the Demilitarized Zone or sent home," Associated Press, March 6, 2003.

[86] *Chosun Ilbo*, March 21, 2003.

[87] Yonhap, June 3, 2003.

[88] Between the February 2003 inauguration and August 2003, Roh's domestic approval ratings plunged from 75 to 25 percent. James Brooke, "Ratings Hurt South Korean Leader Before Talks," *New York Times*, August 11, 2003.

[89] Gordon Fairclough, "A surprise in Korean crisis: consensus," *Wall Street Journal*, June 9, 2003.

[90] For one critique, see the Korea chapter in last year's Strategic Asia volume.

[91] Miles A. Pomper, "Foundering Bush Korea Policy Causes Erosion of Confidence," *Congressional Quarterly Weekly*, January 4, 2003, vol. 61, no. 1, p. 40. See also Bill Gertz and Rowan Scarborough, "North Korea split," *Washington Times*, August 5, 2003.

[92] Note that these alternatives are not mutually exclusive. There could be a push for a diplomatic denuclearization agreement after the DPRK attained nuclear power status, or for regime change in Pyongyang alongside DPRK's emergence as a nuclear power. This schema simply attempts to bound the plausible.

[93] See Michael O'Hanlon and Michael Mochizuki, *Crisis on the Korean Peninsula: How to Deal with a Nuclear North Korea*, New York: McGraw-Hill, 2003.

[94] Sim Sung-tae, "N. Korea security to top six-party talks agenda," *Korea Herald*, August 13, 2003.

[95] Bracken, "Nuclear Weapons and State Survival," pp. 141, 145.

Russia – Key Indicators and Forecasts

Economy and Trade	2002[a]	2003[b]	2004[b]
GDP ($tr) / (PPP GDP)	0.3 (PPP GDP in 2002 = $1.1 tr)		
GDP growth (%)	4.3	4.0	3.5
Inflation (%)	16.0	13.4	9.7
Budget balance (% of GDP)	8.8	10.1	6.3
Major export destinations (2001)	Germany (10%), Italy (8%), U.S. (7%)		

Population and Energy	2002[a]	2005[b]	2010[b]
Population (m)	145.0	143.7	142.3
Population growth (%)	-0.3	-0.2	-0.2
Oil production (m bbl/d)	7.6	8.1	9.1
Oil consumption (m bbl/d)	2.4	3.9	4.6

Politics	
President	Vladimir Putin (since May 2000)
Dominant party	Communist Party (since 1995)
Next election	December 2003

Military	
Armed forces (2002)	676,500
Defense expenditure (2001)	$63.7 bn (est.) (4.3% of GDP)
Conventional capabilities	Much diminished military, especially navy
	Professionalization of military continues
	alongside degradation of capabilities
Weapons of mass destruction	Large nuclear arsenal (being reduced)
	Poor safety and security at WMD sites

Sources: The National Bureau of Asian Research, compiled from International Monetary Fund, *World Economic Outlook*; Central Intelligence Agency, *World Factbook*; U.S. Census Bureau, *International Data Base*; Energy Information Administration, *Country Analysis Brief—Russia*; International Institute of Strategic Studies, *The Military Balance*. Notes: a) Data for 2002 may be estimates; b) Data for 2003, 2004, 2005, and 2010 are projections. Additional data on Russia are available in the Strategic Asia database at <http://strategicasia.nbr.org>.

RUSSIA'S SOFT BALANCING ACT

William C. Wohlforth

ABSTRACT

The fallout between the United States and Russia over Moscow's opposition to U.S. policy on Iraq sparked a wave of doubt over the depth and sustainability of Vladimir Putin's turn toward pragmatic cooperation with the West. This chapter presents three assessments that are needed to assess this strategic uncertainty: a reprise of Russia's foreign policy in light of evolving geoeconomic and geopolitical realities; Russia's diplomatic maneuvering on Iraq, an assessment of which requires an understanding of Moscow's view of the coalition dynamics that now shape relations among the major powers; and Russia's strategic interactions with other key actors in Asia. All three assessments yield a single substantive conclusion—the dramatic events of 2003 left Putin's grand strategy intact. The background forces and incentives underlying the basic approach have strengthened over the past year. The implication is that Russia's diplomacy in Asia will continue along pragmatic lines, governed in the near to medium term mainly by the mix of "new security issues," economic incentives, and modernization imperatives that have come to the fore in the last half decade.

William Wohlforth is Associate Professor of Government at Dartmouth College and serves as a Senior Advisor to NBR's Eurasia Studies Program. He is indebted to Richard Ellings, Bruce Parrott, Gael Tarleton, Michael Wills, and Enders Wimbush for their helpful comments on an earlier draft, and to Pavel Teremetsky for research assistance.

Introduction

In 2001, Vladimir Putin engineered a seemingly seminal shift in Russian foreign policy that entailed a more forthright recognition of the country's weakness and the priority that Moscow must place on economic rejuvenation. By the summer of 2002, analysts and policymakers in Washington, Moscow, Beijing, and most other major capitals had concluded that the strategic shift was meaningful and likely to endure. But in the winter and spring of 2003, U.S.-Russian relations appeared to sour as Moscow joined Paris and Berlin in opposition to Washington's Iraq policy. Russian officials once again began to express their preference for a "multipolar world," while Moscow's large contingent of geopolitical pundits relished the prospect that the Russian heartland might serve as the key link between the Russian-Chinese-Indian "Asian strategic triangle" and the Paris-Berlin-Moscow "European axis," thus forging a grand Eurasian alliance against U.S. unipolarity.

Did Russia's maneuvering on Iraq herald a new era in Russia's relations with West and East? Did it show that Putin's celebrated alliance with America's war on terror was illusory or oversold? Answering these questions is critical in assessing Russia's current policy in strategic Asia and its likely options in the years to come. The chief analytical challenge for Russia-watchers is to distinguish the tactical policy shifts that are consistent with the new more pragmatic grand strategy from more substantial moves that might portend a deeper rethinking of strategic priorities in Moscow.

Accordingly, this chapter presents three assessments that are necessary to meet this analytical challenge. The first assessment offers a reprise of Russia's foreign policy in light of the evolving geoeconomic and geopolitical realities on the ground. The second considers Russia's diplomatic maneuvering on Iraq, which requires an understanding of Moscow's view of the coalition dynamics that now shape relations among the major powers. The third assessment concerns Russia's strategic interactions with other key actors in Asia. Individual cases—notably Moscow's nuclear relationship with Iran—suggest dangerously destabilizing Russian behavior. Whether these are portents of more to come or sheer opportunism is a question that can only be answered in light of the larger patterns of strategic interaction.

The Realities Behind Russian Diplomacy

Russia's foreign policy is shaped by the monumental scale of the modernization challenge it faces as well as the powerful external constraint of U.S. unipolarity. Vladimir Putin's approach to both challenges has been marked by pragmatism. He has consistently stressed that Russia's number one task is economic growth, which requires integration into the world economy and domestic institutional rebuilding. The quest to retain great power status that is so dear to the hearts of Russia's military and foreign policy elites, he insists, is inseparable from this modernization imperative.

Putin's oft-repeated goal is "that, in the foreseeable future, Russia will firmly take its place among the truly strong, economically advanced and influential states of the world."[1] He can claim progress in this endeavor, for Russia is in its fifth consecutive year of respectable economic growth, real disposable income has risen at a brisk pace, foreign and domestic investment as well as business confidence are up, capital flight has declined dramatically, and the government's budgetary and foreign exchange positions are strong.[2] Putin has helped to shepherd through major reforms: a revamped tax code; a landmark law allowing private ownership of farmland (including by foreigners); initial legal reforms; the first stages of a crucial restructuring of the judiciary; and many other lesser known regulatory and legislative adjustments. Pending are reforms of pensions, the banking system, subsidized housing and energy, the restructuring of Russia's giant electricity monopoly, and a host of other measures associated with Russia's bid for World Trade Organization (WTO) membership. Reforms on this scale required Putin to spend real political capital, but also reflected a new configuration of interests among major business and interest groups. To signal their assessment of the changes, both the Eurpoean Union (EU) and the United States awarded Russia "market economy" status in 2003. "Extrapolating from recent experience," one economist concludes, "one might begin to entertain seriously the prospect of sustained Russian economic growth and therefore a sustained growth of business profits."[3]

This is a dramatic improvement from the "virtual economy" days of the late 1990s. But the challenges remain formidable, for Russia faces a unique portfolio of geopolitical and geoeconomic challenges. Though it is growing, the Russian economy remains tiny, with GDP in 2003 expected to total $387 billion at market exchange rates—roughly the economic size of New Jersey. While there is no gainsaying the importance of the institutional and legal reforms accomplished during Putin's first term, recent economic performance also owes much to one-off effects of the 1998 ruble devaluation as well as rising world oil and gas prices.[4] Though foreign direct investment (FDI) is on the rise, it remains comparatively tiny (cumulative FDI since 1991 in Russia by April 1, 2002 amounted to $17.2 billion, compared with over $350 billion in China during the same period). Russia's basic industrial and transportation infrastructure is decrepit (on average, more than three times older than the average among the rich countries that belong to the Organization for Economic Cooperation and Development), and updating it will require investments in the trillions of dollars over coming decades—beyond the capacity of domestic sources. Foreign and domestic investment is likely to continue to grow, but most economists expect that it will remain much lower than is needed without extensive reforms in banking, corporate governance, Russia's legal system, and regional institutions.

All of this suggests that in the absence of further institutional reforms, Russian economic growth will remain susceptible to fluctuations in the world prices of oil, gas, metals, and other Russian export commodities. Moreover, Russia will remain geopolitically hamstrung by its inefficient and still unreformed military establishment. Military reform is expensive in economic and political terms, yet without it, increased budgetary outlays for the Ministry of Defense will come to little. The Chechen issue remains a bleeding wound. Meanwhile, other powers—notably China and the United States—are increasing their aggregate economic and military power relative to Russia's. Hence, Putin continues to express deep dissatisfaction with Russia's economic performance, calling for a doubling of the economy over the next decade.[5]

The bottom line is that Russia's chief priorities are and will remain modernization and economic rejuvenation, which create powerful incentives to maintain productive partnerships with the governments of the world's richest and most influential states. Putin is well aware that the fate of Russia's rejuvenation will be determined mainly by the success of domestic institution building. But he and his aides also understand that too much tension in relations with the other major powers may have negative spillover on a range of international economic matters where their support is crucial. A serious polarization in relations with the United States or any other major power could have catastrophic consequences for the state budget and the Russian economy. Moreover, Putin insists that the major near- and medium-term security threats Russia faces do not emanate from other great powers but rather demand their cooperation. As in the case of all the other major powers, new security issues such as terrorism, weapons proliferation, Islamism, organized crime, unregulated migration, and the like, have assumed an increased salience in Russia's hierarchy of strategic interests as opposed to traditional great power security concerns.

Even as it attempts to bargain its way into the world economy on favorable terms, however, Russia still seeks to play a role in the major-power coalition dynamics of unipolarity. Geography dictates Russia's concern with security and economics in most of the world's key regions, and most Russians assume that their bargaining leverage on economic matters is helped rather than hindered by their country's lingering status as a great power. Russian foreign policy reflects the reasonable assumption that the country's interests are better served by more rather than less influence on neighboring regions, as long as the search for diplomatic prestige does not run afoul of the need to maintain good working relationships with each region's major powers.

When participating in bargaining with other major powers, Russia confronts a central feature of today's unipolar international system. America's extraordinary primacy poses problems for other major powers, but the costs of creating a genuine counterpoise to the U.S. giant are too great for them to bear. Scholars of international relations now generally acknowledge that traditional "hard" great power balancing against the United States is not in the cards for the foreseeable future. America's power is too great, too comprehensive, and too far offshore, while the putative balancing states are too weak, too close (and therefore potentially threatening to each other), and too vulnerable to collective action problems for genuine counterbalancing to occur any time soon.[6] As a result, when other states are importuned by U.S. power they are reduced to engaging in "soft balancing," which Robert Pape defines as "the use of international institutions, economic leverage, and diplomatic maneuvering to frustrate American intentions."[7]

While the term "soft balancing" may be somewhat misleading—after all, it has no prospect of affecting the scales of world power—the behavior the term describes is real enough. The challenge for other major powers is that their capability to influence U.S. behavior through international institutions, economic leverage and diplomatic maneuvering is strictly limited. International institutions are a modest tool for checking U.S. power because Washington can act alone or with "coalitions of the willing" on many issues. When U.S. efforts to work within institutions fail because other states block them, Washington may suffer less than the putative soft-balancers themselves, leaving the institutions weakened and even less able to rein in the United States the next time around. Using economic leverage to punish Washington for its unilateral transgressions is also problematic, given that all the other major powers are more dependent on the world economy than is the United States, and so have much to lose if the U.S. economy falters. Finally, diplomatic maneuvering is vulnerable to the collective action problem, in that a "soft balancing" coalition against the United States is vulnerable to defection and free riding.

Russia's experience in its first post-Soviet decade was consistent with this analysis. It lacked the power for "hard balancing," and there is little evidence it seriously tried to exert power in this manner.[8] Throughout the 1990s, Moscow periodically engaged in "soft balancing" under the rubric of its multipolar policy line, but often found its coalition efforts ineffective, damaging to its own economic interests, and subverted by the free riding of other states. One of the precepts of Putin's strategic reassessment was that under Yeltsin and Primakov Russia had overplayed its hand by seeking to lead too many policy coalitions against Washington, setting itself up to be duped by other powers cutting side deals of their own with the Americans. Given Russia's overriding need for economic rejuvenation in order to survive as a major power, the argument was that it was time to scale back claims to leadership in the coalition dynamics of unipolarity.[9]

Diplomatic Scorecard: Putin Plays Coalition Dynamics

An inevitable by-product of Moscow's 2001 strategic reassessment was a reduction in the ambiguity Russia had previously maintained regarding its relationship with the West. Russia's focus on Europe and the United States was now clearer for all to see—both in the West and in Asia. But reducing that ambiguity does not mean eliminating it, for Putin and his foreign policy team believe that eliminating all ambiguity would eliminate Moscow's diplomatic flexibility and hence its bargaining power. Unless the costs become too high, Putin's default strategy is to hedge his bets by nurturing good relationships with all parties—including declared enemies of his new Western friends. At the same time, if the strategic assessments Putin and his aides propounded in the year before September 11 remain operative, then Russia cannot allow such diplomatic maneuvering to risk a genuine deterioration of relations with key economic and strategic partners, including the United States. Does this analysis hold up in light of Russia's falling out with America over Iraq?

In the late 1990s, Russia's policy on Iraq was largely driven by two concerns: constraining the United States via "soft balancing" in the UN Security Council, and extracting economic benefits from Baghdad. Russia reaped rich economic rewards under the UN's oil-for-food program, and Saddam Hussein also offered longer-term inducements, which Russia could realize only if sanctions were withdrawn: a major development contract with Russia's Lukoil (valued at about $12 billion) and the prospect of settling Iraq's state debt to Russia of about $8 billion. As long as there was some possibility that the Iraq issue could be settled with the Baathist regime in power, Russia had incentives to position itself to receive these promised rewards. From this perspective, its Iraqi policy had served Moscow well, especially given that until September 2002, when President Bush challenged the United Nations to confront and disarm Saddam Hussein, the United States did little to pressure the Russians to fall in line with Washington's position.

Until March 2003, Russia attempted to hew to its old policy on Iraq, but adjusted to the tough new U.S. stance by increasing the ambiguity of its position. While Foreign Minister Ivanov made strong statements in opposition to U.S. pronouncements, Putin authorized official contacts with Iraqi opposition figures and chose to support UN Security Council Resolution 1441 in November, warning Iraq of "serious consequences" if it did not meet its disarmament obligations. U.S. officials sought Russian support by offering inducements—honoring Iraqi contracts with Russian oil majors, and a role in post-war stabilization—which they could only deliver after a clear victory. As long as Putin remained uncertain of U.S. resolve and capability to prevail, he would risk more by aligning himself prematurely with the United States than by standing aloof. If American policy had foundered at this stage, Putin would have lost the economic benefits Baghdad provided and gained nothing.

Moreover, Putin probably wanted to gauge the seriousness of the Berlin-Paris opposition. In the past, Europeans had been happy to exploit Russian opposition to Washington, and all the evidence suggests that Putin was wary of getting out in front on this issue. In keeping with the 2001 strategic reassessment, Putin studiously avoided taking a leading role. Putin's policy stance was contingent on Jacques Chirac's, and there was some uncertainty in Moscow—as in London and Washington—over the French president's resolve. Putin's noncommittal posture positioned him to tack toward Washington if the French lost heart. By the time the dynamics of negotiations in the Security Council forced Putin to choose sides, ministerial meetings and presidential consultations with the French and Germans had established the strong resolve of the "Old Europeans." Certain that he would not be left alone against Washington, Putin played the Europe card. On March 5, Russia joined France and Germany in a declaration that "we will not let a proposed resolution pass that would authorize the use of force" against Iraq.

Having revealed his hand, Putin went public with restrained but pointed objections to U.S. policy. The lead-up to the war and the quick fall of Saddam's regime also generated new information on the depth of Russo-Iraqi cooperation. U.S. officials charged that Moscow broke a UN embargo on military sales to Iraq by equipping Baghdad's forces with night-vision goggles and anti-missile defense systems that were later used against U.S. troops. Moreover, Russian generals ostentatiously advertised their own role as "unofficial" advisors to the Iraqis prior to the coalition campaign, and after the war journalists turned up documents attesting to close links between Russia's foreign intelligence agency and Iraq's Mukhabarat. These revelations, coupled with Putin's continued tough stance during and after *Operation Iraqi Freedom*, raised U.S.-Russian tensions to levels not seen since the crisis over Kosovo.

Why did Putin align with Europe? Elite and popular dissatisfaction in Russia with U.S. policy doubtless figured in Putin's calculations, but they simply reinforce the bargaining argument that Washington needed a reminder not to take Russia's deference for granted. In addition, Putin and his foreign policy aides, like their French counterparts, insist that their policy reflected sincere disagreements with Washington's approach to Iraq. And the policy stance on Iraq was consistent with Russia's low-cost "soft balancing" approach of trying to use international institutions to dampen the effects of U.S. hegemony. Given these considerations, there was no good response to U.S. policy on Iraq, only more or less bad ones.

The key, however, was that Putin's move had no effect on Russia's overall Western orientation, for it was a tactical shift between available Western partners. As Putin noted in an interview, "the European Union (EU) accounts for 37 percent of Russia's external trade turnover, and after the expansion of the EU this will increase to 52 percent. Russia is a European country in its geography, history, culture and mentality of the population."[10] On many measures (trade, credit, investment) Germany constitutes Russia's single most important economic relationship. But there is little evidence that the "Paris-Berlin-Moscow axis" that took shape in the Security Council negotiations on Iraq will have much staying power. On the key economic matters, Paris and Berlin act multilaterally through the EU, while on strategic issues, they cannot sustain a consistently anti-U.S. stance. Both governments—especially the Germans—do not want a transatlantic rift, and they lack the capability to offer Moscow major strategic rewards for the costs it might incur with Washington. On economics, border controls, and a broad range of "soft" security issues, the EU—rather than the Germans or French—is Moscow's real interlocutor. And the EU is simultaneously challenging but non-strategic in its dealings with Russia.[11] EU members view Russia as a gas station and a pitifully small (4 percent of overall trade) trading partner. The asymmetry does not work to Russia's advantage in negotiations with Brussels on the issues that are arguably most important.

Hence, Putin and his aides insist that Moscow's tack toward Europe will not come at the expense of a working strategic partnership with the United States. As Putin's foreign policy aide Sergei Prikhodko put it: "Our partnership with the United States is not a hostage of the Iraq crisis. There are far too many common values and common tasks both short term and long term...our co-operation never stopped, even during the Iraq crisis."[12] And this was not just rhetoric; concrete cooperation continued on intelligence sharing, nuclear arms control, NATO expansion, peacekeeping in Afghanistan and the North Korea issue. The policy reflected a bet that the Americans would not allow Iraq to derail the most important parts of the new U.S.-Russian relationship—the anti-terror coalition and managing Russia's further entry into the world economy. As of the summer of 2003, Putin's bet appeared to have paid off. U.S. Secretary of State Powell's visit in mid-May, and Bush's diplomatic tactics at the St. Petersburg summit in June reflected efforts to keep the relationship on track. The Moscow assessment was that Putin had played coalition dynamics like a balalaika. The fallout with Washington was manageable, while Russia's influence vis-à-vis France and Germany was enhanced. Russia's bargaining space was secured as the object of courting by both sides of the transatlantic rift, and the crisis left Putin more popular at home than before—even with congenitally disgruntled sectors of the elite.

Managing Pragmatic Partnerships in Asia

Neither Russia's alignment with Washington after September 11 nor the brief falling out over Iraq had significant repercussions for Moscow's strategic cooperation with neighboring powers in Asia, for the simple reason that the three key drivers of Russian strategy remained firmly in place. The first driver is military and economic weakness. All the manifold challenges of Russia's modernization are manifested in particularly acute form in Asia. Russia's crumbling industrial sector in its Asian regions is largely a legacy of expensive and uneconomic Soviet-era state subsidies, and much of it is unable to survive in market conditions. Demographic, health care, and HIV/AIDS crises are all especially acute in the Russian Far East, exerting downward pressure on productivity and performance.[13] Russia's overall dependence on raw materials exports makes it a candidate for the "resource curse:" the general tendency of countries with a high percentage of natural resources in their exports to under-perform economically.[14] The issue has special salience for Russia's sparsely populated eastern regions. By all appearances, the mechanisms through which resource riches translate into weak institutions, governmental rent seeking, and political corruption operate strongly in precisely those regions, presenting Putin with governance problems he has yet to tackle. Moreover, resource extraction requires a far smaller workforce than the declining manufacturing industry, so the shift toward the region's real comparative advantage will only fuel its ongoing depopulation. As one noted Russian expert summed it up, "Eastern Siberia and the Far East have become the weakest link in Russia's economic security."[15]

The second driving force is the distorted nature of Russia's trade portfolio. Trade is a larger share of Russia's GDP than for all other major Asian powers, and over 55 percent of Russian exports are energy and metals. Hence, Russian officials will remain preoccupied with developing markets for these products in Asia. Moreover, Asia remains the chief market for

Russia's high value added and technology exports, with China and India by far the principal buyers. Military hardware and nuclear and space technology—both declining assets inherited from the Soviet Union—loom large in Russia's small share of such exports. Revenues from arms sales varied between 1.2 to 4 percent of exports from the mid-1990s to the present, and for nuclear materials and technology about half that figure.[16] Despite their small share in Russia's trade portfolio, in both cases, there is virtually no domestic demand for either of these industries. With abundant hydrocarbon-fueled electrical generation capacity and declining demand compared to Soviet times, the domestic market for the Ministry of Atomic Energy (Minatom) has dried up. Similarly, even with recently increased defense spending, the Russian military's procurement needs are miniscule compared to the capacity of the military industry Russia inherited from the Soviet Union. Foreign military sales, therefore, are essential to keeping these two domestic industries alive, and the major markets are in Asia—China and India together accounted for nearly 80 percent of Russia's record arms exports in 2002.

Finally, Russian policy in Asia is driven by a common core of security interests that Moscow shares with the other regional powers, including the United States. While Moscow, Beijing and (much less frequently) Delhi periodically play up the anti-U.S. aspect of their nebulous "strategic triangle," each maintains deeper and wider relations with Washington than with others and none wants to engage in any costly balancing of the United States. All the key powers have defined their near- to medium-term core interests in complementary ways. It follows that Russia's interests require amicable relations with all, including the United States and Japan. Indeed, Moscow's sense of weakness fosters wariness of China's growing economic and diplomatic clout, and a general preference for balancing Russian relationships in the region.

Hence, just as Russia needs at times to balance between the United States and Europe in the West, so too does it seek to spread its bets among the major centers of power in the East. Putin has been careful to ensure that the strategic partnership with China works to his own benefit. For now, that implies a focus on the key near-term security threats that both sides regard as most important—terrorism, North Korea's nuclearization or meltdown, drug trafficking, Muslim extremism, separatism, organized crime, migration, and weapons proliferation—and the avoidance of commitments that would subordinate Russia's larger policies to China's. At their December 2002 summit meeting in Beijing, Putin and Jiang Zemin reiterated their support for a multipolar world order to contain U.S. unilateralism, but the substance of the meeting concerned deepening energy and trade cooperation and the struggle against terrorism within the framework of the Shanghai Cooperation Organization.[17] The reason for the focus on the pragmatic core of their strategic partnership was self-evident: both countries had made major efforts to improve their relations with the United States. While Chinese commentators fretted about Russia's westward drift, Beijing's new leadership proved much more cautious about risking ties with the United States over Iraq than Russia was.

Russia's behavior toward the other key players in the region attested to its underlying interest in hedging its bets among its eastern neighbors. At their summit in January 2003, Putin and Prime Minister Koizumi Junichiro signed a "Japan-Russia Action Plan" that reiterated their commitment to overcome the Kuriles' territorial dispute and broaden energy cooperation beyond the existing projects on Sakhalin. Russia's default hedging strategy was on display in a new "competing pipeline" drama. Japan lobbied insistently for a $5 billion, 2,300-mile project that would link oilfields near the Siberian city of Angarsk to the port city of Nakhodka on the Japan Sea. Beijing championed a smaller and cheaper route to the Chinese city of Daqing. Typically, Moscow played both sides. Russia's Yukos Oil and China National Petroleum signed a preliminary agreement on the Angarsk-Daqing deal on the sidelines of the summit meeting between Putin and Hu Jintao in May. But in subsequent interviews, Putin expressed a clear preference for the Nakhodka plan, stressing its potential to diversify Russia's energy exports in Asia. "The only question is whether it is well-grounded economically," he stressed.[18] Japan took the bait by offering generous subsidies, while Putin and other Russian officials tried to keep everybody happy with the idea of a branch line from Angarsk-Nakhodka to Daqing, provided there is enough oil.

As the chapter on Northeast Asia in this volume attests, Russia's policy on North Korea fits the general pattern of Russian maneuvering for economic advantage and political influence, but within the limits dictated by relative weakness and a basic interest—in this case, in nuclear non-proliferation—that it shares with the other major powers.[19] The question that is likely to dominate the agenda going forward is whether the same analysis applies to Russia's relationship with Iran. In 2001, Moscow and Tehran signed a protocol on mutual relations that featured a commitment to develop cooperation in areas of vital interest to Russia's military-industrial and nuclear complexes: nuclear energy, weapons modernization, air defense, and space programs. Russia's desire for good relations with its Caspian Sea neighbor is understandable. Arms sales to Iran—as in the cases of China, India, and other customers—also present no puzzle. Russia wants to sustain a core defense manufacturing capacity until economic growth affords it the opportunity to modernize its surviving military infrastructure and to transfer excess defense workers and production capacities into more productive sectors. Nuclear cooperation, however, appears to lack a similar strategic rationale. Large sums of money for Minatom are in play—the Bushehr project is worth about $1 billion, more reactor projects are planned, reprocessing fuel is also lucrative, and significant numbers of high-technology jobs are also involved[20]—but the deal is of marginal significance for Russia's larger strategic economic objective of modernization.

In the summer of 2003, Russia's Iran policy was in precisely the same stage of ambiguity as its Iraq policy had been in the fall of 2002. As in the Iraq case, both Putin and his officials stressed commercial concerns—especially the fear that if Russia backed away from its contract with the Iranians to pressure them to comply with U.S. demands, American or European companies might move in to exploit the opening. Still, Putin tacked toward the emerging international consensus that Iran must accept stricter International Atomic Energy Agency oversight. At the June G-8 summit in Evian, Putin seemed to say that Russia's nuclear cooperation with Iran would be contingent on Tehran's acceptance of such a regime—only to be contradicted by Foreign Ministry and Minatom officials the next day. Russian diplomats claimed that getting Iran's agreement is their top priority, but Atomic Energy Minster Rumyantsev insisted that all Moscow required was an Iranian commitment to send all fuel to Russia for reprocessing.[21]

The analysis here suggests that Moscow's policy is opportunistic. Putin's willingness to bring Minatom and its domestic supporters to heel depends on the strength of the international consensus, the sustainability of Moscow's official position that the project is not a proliferation threat, and the degree to which the United States and others can reassure Moscow regarding its commercial concerns. All of this leads to the expectation that if Washington and its other allies remain united and the Iranians continue to resist international pressure to open up their program, Moscow should be amenable to a revision in its relationship with Tehran.

Conclusion

The dramatic events of 2003 left Putin's grand strategy intact. The background forces and incentives underlying the basic approach have strengthened over the past year. The implication is that Russia's diplomacy in Asia will continue along pragmatic lines, governed in the near to medium term mainly by the mix of "new security issues," economic incentives, and modernization imperatives that have come to the fore in the last half decade. However, the strategy is consistent with maintaining some strategic ambiguity on Russia's stance regarding the United States vs. Europe in the

West, and China vs. Japan and the United States in the East. At times, ambiguity also reflects contestation among domestic elites that is magnified by Russia's weak political institutions.

Such ambiguity occasionally feeds the argument that Russia has embarked on a policy aimed at balancing U.S. power. The analysis presented here suggests that such arguments are at best premature. Under Putin, even Russia's propensity to engage in "soft balancing" has moderated. The problem is that balancing the United States risks making Russia less secure, by, for example, subordinating Russia to a rising China or transforming Iran into a nuclear power. Russia's soft balancing is thus often an act—a rhetorical cover for a multilateral strategy that allows a relatively weak Russia to maximize its diplomatic leverage and hedge its bets.

Putin prefers a soft balancing act, as would any likely Russian leader facing the same tough set of internal and external constraints. The question for Moscow is not whether the policy is desirable but whether it is sustainable. The short-term prospects for maintaining it are promising, given the confluence of interests with the other major Asian powers regarding terrorism and North Korea. The most volatile dynamic over the long run is far more likely to concern Chinese rather than U.S. power. The 75 percent of Russian territory that lies in Asia is rich in natural but poor in human resources. Market reforms—a key to Russia's economic recovery—contribute to the region's depopulation by shifting capital away from labor-intensive industry to resource extraction, which requires a much smaller workforce. The proximity of a vibrant Chinese economy with abundant labor resources and an exponentially growing appetite for energy may ultimately feed an expanding sense of China's global and regional role, making Moscow's soft balancing act much harder to sustain in the next decade. Russia may then be presented with a tougher and even more consequential choice than the one Putin made in September 2001.

Endnotes

[1] Transcript of Putin's State of the Nation address: BBC Monitoring, May 16, 2003; *Johnson's Russia List*, no. 7186, May 19, 2003.

[2] Economic Statistics here and below as reported in Keith Bush, "Net Assessment of the Russian Economy, March 2003," Center for Strategic and International Studies <www.csis.org/ruseura/index.htm>; and World Bank, "Russian Economic Report, March 2003," <www.worldbank.org.ru>.

[3] Philip Hanson, "The Russian Economic Recovery: Do Four Years of Growth Tell Us that the Fundamentals have Changed?" *Europe-Asia Studies*, vol. 55, no. 3 (May 2003), p. 379. Hanson's excellent analysis also notes the major challenges to this scenario, along the lines of the paragraph that follows herein.

[4] On the former effect, see World Bank, "Russian Economic Report," and on the latter, Hanson, "The Russian Economic Recovery…"

[5] State of the Nation Address, BBC Monitoring, May 16, 2003; *Johnson's Russia List*, no. 7186, May 19, 2003.

[6] See William C. Wohlforth, "The Stability of a Unipolar World," *International Security*, vol. 21, no. 1 (Summer 1999), pp. 1–36; and G. John Ikenberry, ed., *America Unrivaled: The Future of the Balance of Power*, Ithaca, N.Y.: Cornell University Press, 2002.

[7] Pape, "Welcome to the era of 'soft balancing'," *Boston Globe*, March 23, 2003, p. H1. For more extensive discussions, see T. V. Paul and James J. Wirtz, "The Enduring Axioms of Balance of Power Theory," in Paul and Wirtz, eds., *Balance of Power: Theory and Practice in the 21st Century* (forthcoming); and Stephen M. Walt, "Keeping the World 'Off Balance'," in Ikenberry, *America Unrivaled*.

[8] For a more thorough analysis of this assertion, see William C. Wohlforth, "Revisiting Balance of Power Theory in Central Eurasia," in Wirtz and Paul, *Balance of Power*.

[9] See William C. Wohlforth, "Russia," in Aaron L. Friedberg and Richard J. Ellings, with Michael Wills, eds., *Strategic Asia 2002–03: Asian Aftershocks*, Seattle: The National Bureau of Asian Research, 2003.

[10] Transcript of Putin's interview with the BBC, as reported on *Johnson's Russia List*, no. 7236, June 24, 2003.

[11] Andrei Zagorski, "EU Policies Towards Russia, Ukraine, Moldova and Belarus," in Roland Dannreuther, ed., *The European Union and its Neighbourhood: Towards a Strategy?* (forthcoming).

[12] Quoted in Andrew Jack and Stefan Wagstyl, "Optimism on Russian postwar accord with U.S.," *Financial Times*, May 16, 2003.

[13] See Kennan Institute event summary, "Policy Implications and Consequences of the Demographic and Health Crises in Russia," *Johnson's Russia List*, no. 7184, May 17, 2003.

[14] See the discussion in Hanson "The Russian Economic Recovery," pp. 371–74.

[15] Vilia Gel'bras, "Velikoderzhavnyi i voenno-promyshlennyi kompleksy (The great power complex and the military-industrial complex)," *Expert*, June 11, 2001, p. 29.

[16] Calculated from statistics presented in Celeste A. Wallander, "Russia's Interest in Trading with the 'Axis of Evil'," testimony for "Russia's Policies toward the Axis of Evil: Money and Geopolitics in Iraq and Iran," Hearing before the House Committee on International Relations, February 26, 2003.

[17] For more on this, see the chapter on Central Asia in this volume.

[18] Transcript of Putin's press conference on June 20, 2003.

[19] Russia's official policy—which Putin reiterated emphatically at the G-8 summit in Evian—is that proliferation of weapons of mass destruction "is the main threat of the 21st century." Transcript of Putin's BBC interview on June 22, 2003, reprinted in *Johnson's Russia List*, no. 7236, 24 June 2003.

[20] Minatom claims that the Bushehr contract alone will secure 20,000 jobs and involve work at over 300 Russian companies. Anatoly Andreev, "Mirnyi Atom

dlia Bushera (Peaceful atom for Bushehr)," *Trud*, December 27, 2002, p. 1. For more on Russia's role in proliferation in Asia, see the chapter on proliferation in this volume.

[21] Aleksandr Gol'ts, "Na chistuiu tiazheluiu vodu ([Revealing] clean heavy water)," *Ezhenedel'nyi zhurnal*, June 16, 2003, p. 47.

India – Key Indicators and Forecasts

Economy and Trade	2002^a	2003^b	2004^b
GDP ($tr) / (PPP GDP)	0.5 (PPP GDP in 2002 = $2.7 tr)		
GDP growth (%)	4.9	5.1	5.9
Inflation (%)	4.3	4.1	5.5
Budget balance (% of GDP)	0.9	0.5	0.2
Major export destinations (2001)	U.S. (21%), Britain (6%), Germany (5%)		

Population and Energy	2002^a	2005^b	2010^b
Population (m)	1,034.2	1,080.3	1,155.0
Population growth (%)	1.5	1.4	1.3
Oil production (m bbl/d)	0.7	...	...
Oil consumption (m bbl/d)	2.0	2.3	3.1

Politics	
Prime minister	Atal Bihari Vajpayee (BJP, since Mar 1999)
Dominant party	Bharatiya Janata Party (since 1996)
Next election	March 2004

Military	
Armed forces (2002)	1,298,000
Defense expenditure (2001)	$14.2 bn (2.9% of GDP)
Conventional capabilities	Large army and powerful navy
	Major arms acquisitions from Russia; recent anti-piracy patrols in Southeast Asia
Weapons of mass destruction	Moderate nuclear arsenal

Source: The National Bureau of Asian Research, compiled from International Monetary Fund, *World Economic Outlook*; Central Intelligence Agency, *World Factbook*; U.S. Census Bureau, *International Data Base*; Energy Information Administration, *Country Analysis Brief—India*; International Institute of Strategic Studies, *The Military Balance*. Notes: a) Data for 2002 may be estimates; b) Data for 2003, 2004, 2005, and 2010 are projections. Additional data on India are available in the Strategic Asia database at <http://strategicasia.nbr.org>.

REGIONAL CONCERNS, GLOBAL AMBITIONS

John H. Gill

ABSTRACT

India faces three major challenges in the near term: coping with incipient shifts in domestic politics, sustaining and expanding economic growth, and progressing to a greater role in Asian and world diplomacy. All of these challenges fall under the shadow of India-Pakistan tensions. The two rivals, however, have a rare and fleeting opportunity to move beyond unpredictable and increasingly dangerous crises to build a sustainable process that minimizes the risk of war. The United States, momentarily enjoying good relations with both countries, can assist in this process by careful and consistent attention over the long term. Crucial to stability in South Asia, India will also begin to acquire greater influence on its periphery and across the globe, particularly in Afghanistan, Central Asia, the Persian Gulf, Southeast Asia, and China. India and the United States will have to strike a balance between their mutual interest in cooperation and India's inclinations toward strategic autonomy and a multipolar world order.

John (Jack) Gill is a U.S. Army South Asia Foreign Area Officer on the faculty of the Near East-South Asia Center for Strategic Studies at the National Defense University. He would like to express his appreciation to Stephen Cohen, Richard Ellings, Aaron Friedberg, Neil Joeck, Deepa Ollapally, Marvin Weinbaum, Michael Wills, and an anonymous reader for their insights in reviewing this chapter.

Introduction

South Asia presents the world with two important and immediate security challenges: the prevention of an India-Pakistan conflict under the nuclear shadow, and the construction of a new Afghanistan from the ruins of the Taliban disaster and 23 years of war. Prompted by these crises, the international community since September 11, 2001 has focused unprecedented attention on the region. In the case of India and Pakistan, this was especially true of the United States whose senior envoys made repeated trips to New Delhi and Islamabad between October 2001 and October 2002 to help prevent their tense confrontation from escalating into an open conflict.[1] It is by no means clear that future interventions of this nature would have the same salutary effect. Now, however, as Washington and its allies readjust their policies in the wake of the Iraq war, there remains a rare and fleeting opportunity to move beyond unpredictable crisis response measures to a sustainable process that minimizes the risk of war between the region's nuclear-armed neighbors.

The India-Pakistan conundrum, however, does not exist in isolation, and any process designed to ameliorate this bitter rivalry will necessarily be part of a comprehensive strategy that encompasses broader U.S. interests within the region. Moreover, India-Pakistan tensions intersect with and to some degree dominate the three major challenges India faces as the twenty-first century unfolds: coping with incipient shifts on the domestic political scene, sustaining and expanding economic growth, and progressing to a greater role in Asian and global affairs. This chapter examines these three interconnected challenges, and their likely development over the coming one to five years, to suggest their probable impact on India's international behavior and the character of its domestic politics. Given the salience of the India-Pakistan dynamic over the near term, the chapter concludes with a focused discussion of this rivalry paired with an assessment of U.S.-India relations, especially the potential for a carefully nuanced U.S. role in managing tensions between New Delhi and Islamabad.

The Home Front: Domestic Politics

From globalization to rising literacy rates, significant changes are occurring at every level of Indian society. Three key factors will be especially important in shaping India's international behavior in the coming five years: the new complexion of the domestic political scene, the extent and expression of Hindu-nationalist sentiment, and upcoming leadership changes within the major political parties.

New Political Realities and Coalition Governments

Over the past decade, coalition governments have become the norm in India. This represents a dramatic change from the pattern of domination by what was then the lone truly national political group, the Congress Party, for India's first 40 years of independence. Several factors account for this change. First , there are only two national parties and neither has sufficiently consistent voter support to govern without the active support of numerous smaller partners. The Congress Party, gradually weakened during the 1980s and 1990s, has not recovered its strength and prominence. It remains a crucial player in New Delhi as the leader of the opposition and a political threat to its principal rival, but is unlikely to regain its former status over the coming five years. The other party with national appeal is the Bharatiya Janata Party (Indian People's Party or BJP). Espousing a strong Hindu-nationalist agenda, the BJP made dramatic electoral gains during the 1990s. It now heads the ruling coalition, but it can only do so with the cooperation of more than twenty smaller parties. Moreover, the BJP may be near the limits of its growth, having drawn approximately 25 percent of the popular vote in 1998 and 1999. Absent a major change in the political landscape, it seems unlikely to exceed this figure in the near term.

The second factor behind the shift to coalition governments at the center is the rise of regional parties during the 1990s. Exploiting the decline of the Congress Party and growing mobilization of disadvantaged segments of the population, small political parties have made their way from the state level to the center. Indicative of this shift, the Congress and BJP together only received about half of the votes cast in recent national elections, the rest went to regional parties. Often caste-based and focused on local issues, these parties attract few voters outside their own regional bases and are in no position to aspire to national leadership. However, their strength at the state level ensures representation in the national legislature, a corresponding voice in the formation of ruling coalitions, and a share of ministerial posts commensurate with their political power. Under some circumstances their voice can be powerful, as the need for coalitions means that small parties now "can make or break governments and thereby affect the whole nation."[2] Furthermore, in their home districts they are often in competition with one another or with one of the national parties. The competition at the state level is an especially serious impediment for the Congress Party, hindering its ability to form coalitions and leading it to align itself with the small residual leftist parties. By their presence in New Delhi, therefore, the new regional parties complicate the national political scene by bringing fractious local contests into the formation and maintenance of ruling coalitions for the entire country.

Considering the weaknesses of the Congress Party and the BJP and the expanded influence of regional parties, there is little doubt that coalition governments will continue to lead India for at least the next five to ten years. This situation implies substantial constraints on the national government. Significant alterations in the direction of foreign or economic policy will be difficult to implement without skilled leadership from the center and most likely only after an extended period of consensus building with members of the coalitions and the opposition. The continued pattern of coalition governments also suggests that most prime ministers will have to lead from the center of the political spectrum, with the BJP moderating the more radical aspects of its Hindu-nationalist agenda and the Congress Party curbing its socialist tendencies. In either case, coalition stability and the quality of coalition leadership will be the key variables in assessing how far each government will be willing to proceed with economic reforms or with new foreign policy initiatives. A coalition that expects to remain in office for all or most of its five-year term, for example, will be more inclined to introduce economic reforms and eschew populist measures.[3]

Hindutva Rising?

A second major factor in the evolution of the Indian polity is the accommodation of Hindu-nationalism and the "Hindutva" agenda. "Hindutva" or "Hinduness" is the rubric employed to describe the monoculturalist contention that "Hinduism is not merely a religion but an entire cultural ethos that pervades Indian life and society."[4] Hindu confessional groups argue that India's Hindu majority (83 percent) is under siege from far smaller populations, especially Muslims (12 percent) and Christians (2 percent), whom they argue have been disproportionately advantaged by India's traditional liberal secularism. In its most extreme expression, Hindutva has been interpreted as equating Indian citizenship with acceptance of the principals of Hinduism. Although the proponents of Hindutva engage in routine and completely legal activities such as political mobilization, they have also been involved in attempts to rewrite textbooks with their own historical slant and have been implicated in numerous deadly attacks against minorities.[5] The anti-Muslim rioting in Gujarat in early 2002 that left as many as 2,000 dead is the most spectacular and disturbing recent instance of violence against minorities.[6]

There is no definitive evidence that the Hindutva program has effected any fundamental alteration of India's liberal polity. Indeed, the media and the court system, to name just two important actors on the domestic scene, have served as important counterweights to Hindu extremism. Nonetheless, elements of the Hindutva agenda have been an essential part of the BJP's election campaigns and the party draws heavily on the organizational support of vocal Hindu social and political groups.[7] In power, however, the BJP has moderated its stance to placate its coalition partners. This moderation has come at the price of significant strain between the central government's leading figures and their support base within the BJP apparatus and the wider circle of Hindu-nationalist organizations. Unwilling to move too far from their ideological foundations, the key government leaders must navigate between the often conflicting demands of their voting constituency and the exigencies of maintaining the nation's ruling coalition. As evidenced by some conciliatory moves by the BJP during the spring of 2003, they must also consider the substantial voting population of Muslims. Some observers perceive in this tension a "struggle for India's soul" between the inclusive secular nationalism of the country's founding fathers and the exclusivist majoritarian vision of the Hindu extremists, with the current BJP administration trying to achieve a balance between these two divergent positions.[8]

In addition to contributing to the radicalization of Hindu and Muslim communities within India, the tension between the BJP and its Hindutva backers also has important international repercussions. First, it can hamper efforts at economic reform. Hindutva groups do not necessarily object to domestic reforms, but they have generally opposed more active Indian involvement in the global market place. The current government has proceeded with some steps to open India's economy but has shied away from implementing significant measures in politically sensitive areas such as investment, privatization, and labor law. Second, the rhetoric surrounding the Hindutva movement is frequently vitriolic and often specifically targeted against Muslims. Anti-Muslim statements and violence, even if expressed by a small vocal minority of Indians, have a deleterious effect on India-Pakistan relations.[9] The 2002 violence in Gujarat and the subsequent BJP victory in that state's elections, for example, confirmed for many Pakistanis that the BJP is anti-Muslim. Many Pakistanis also believe that this supposed anti-Muslim sentiment translates into antipathy toward the Pakistani state, underscoring their predisposition to believe that India, specifically the BJP government or a group of loosely defined BJP "hawks," is intent upon "undoing Partition" and "destroying" Pakistan. Such behavior thus reinforces those Pakistanis who advocate continued hostility toward India, or simply waiting indefinitely for a new Indian government to come on to the scene. Furthermore, the appearance of instability and intolerance has a negative impact on the perceptions of other democracies and the readiness of potential investors to commit their capital. The tension between the religious and the secular will remain a fixture of Indian domestic politics for at least the near term and will thus continue to influence Indian foreign policy behavior, especially its relations with Pakistan and its policies on Kashmir.

Leadership Transition: Weaker Coalitions?

The coming change in senior political leadership is a third factor India must consider in the near term as it attempts to cope with complex problems that will put a premium on skilled, visionary leadership both to initiate and sustain policy changes. As Teresita Schaffer points out, the BJP has a "deep bench" of potential leaders, but most of these are older men who, by reputation at least, lack the flexibility and widespread popular appeal of Prime Minister A. B. Vajpayee. They may be able to adapt upon assuming higher office, but their ability to form and perpetuate effective coalitions remains untested.[10] The Congress Party must also cope with important decisions on leadership, balancing the legacy of the Nehru-Gandhi political dynasty—as represented in the Italian-born Sonia Gandhi and her daughter Priyanka, the party's heir-apparent with her own political aspirations—against the option of moving beyond the family for new directions.[11] The regional parties, on the other hand, have not yet been able to advance serious contenders for the prime minister's office since the BJP's electoral success in the late 1990s.[12] Although some leaders at the state level are charismatic and effective, they have not yet developed either the national recognition or the political apparatus to compete successfully for top positions at the center. A smaller party or regional leader could rise to national leadership as a compromise candidate if both the Congress and the BJP suffered severe electoral setbacks. Such a situation, however, seems unlikely over the near term.

The significance of the leadership issue resides in the stability and longevity of the coalitions that elected officials are able to assemble. Skilled politicians who can pull together contending groups and lead them for an extended period will have a greater probability of conceiving, implementing, and, above all, sustaining new initiatives in foreign policy and economic reform. Less capable leadership, on the other hand, will result in less capable coalitions, characterized by repeated shuffling of ministerial portfolios, an inclination toward unsound populist economic measures, and reactive, often inconsistent, behavior on the international stage. An additional change in the next five to ten years will be the rise of the post-independence generation in India's leadership and bureaucracy—a generation perhaps less burdened by reflexive suspicion of Pakistan and the struggle against colonialism. The details of India's domestic politics and the nature of the leaders that emerge from this necessarily messy process will thus demand the close attention of the international community over the next several years.[13]

Economic Progress: Still Slow but Still Steady

The nature of the government will also determine to a large degree the pace and scope of the economic reform process initiated a decade ago. Although the tempo of liberalization slowed after India recovered from the foreign currency crisis in 1990 and 1991, it is unlikely that any prospective coalition in New Delhi would reverse the progress already made and endanger future prospects.[14] Substantial promise is certainly present. With a large, skilled, English-speaking work force, improving telecommunications links, and familiar western laws and institutions, India has truly made its mark in the information technology arena and is "uniquely well positioned to take advantage of the current globalization of the service sector."[15] Foreign trade data for the Indian fiscal year ending in March 2003 are also cause for some "subdued optimism," showing an 18 percent growth over the previous year's figures for an aggregate of more than $50 billion, despite the impact of the terror attacks in the United States and the war in Afghanistan.[16] Looking ahead, economist Joydeep Mukherji argues that the Indian economy can be expected to continue growing at the respectable, if hardly meteoric, rate of between 5 and 6 percent annually through the near term, with the more progressive states achieving growth rates as high as 7 to 9 percent per year.[17] This tremendous economic potential is a key factor in the U.S. government conclusion that India is "poised to become one of the leading nations of the 21st century."[18]

Achieving India's economic potential, however, will require both political will and regional stability. The obstacles are daunting. American officials cite the persistence of an "entrenched bureaucracy, outdated regulations, sticky legal wickets, parochial political prejudices and a worsening fiscal deficit" as major impediments to U.S.-Indian trade.[19] These factors are compounded by tariff barriers, cumbersome taxation and licensing requirements, sluggish progress in privatization, disputes over intellectual property rights, and woefully inadequate infrastructure, particularly in the power sector. On the domestic front, the economic reforms have helped to reduce absolute poverty, but with an estimated 400 million Indians earning less than one dollar a day, the country continues to have the largest concentration of poverty in the world.[20] Indeed, not all of India has benefited from the economic reforms instituted thus far. While some states have reached growth rates of more than 7 percent, others barely register in positive numbers, a disparity that is unlikely to cause serious instability in the near term, but could derail progress in the future if not addressed.[21] Finally, one of the most important hurdles threatening economic progress is regional stability. This situation was vividly demonstrated during the height of the India-Pakistan crisis in early 2002, when uncertainty concerning the security situation led to severe and nearly instant perturbation of the investment climate. Where a more secure and predictable regional environment would help unleash India's potential and promote economic growth, repeated crises and the perception of instability will only continue to retard progress.

India's economic challenges would give any government pause, but they can be managed, even by a coalition, as long as the coalition is relatively stable, well-led, and likely to serve out its five-year term in office. An unstable coalition, or one driven by ideology rather than pragmatic assessments, would almost certainly retain the extant reforms but would probably lack the political will, consensus, and energy to carry these nascent initiatives to the next logical level.

Pakistan Relations: Crisis, Miscalculation, and Hope

With the potential for nuclear use resulting in millions of casualties, another India-Pakistan war would be catastrophic for the region and the world. Given the scale of possible destruction and the rapidity with which crises similar to that of 2002 could erupt in the future, the international community can hardly afford to ignore the danger inherent in persistent South Asian confrontation. Relying on a presumed ability to calibrate brinkmanship leaves too much to chance.[22] The Pakistani assumption that nuclear weapons will always deter New Delhi and the Indian assumption that conventional warfare can be conducted safely under the nuclear threshold exacerbate an already unsatisfactory situation. Moreover, by discouraging investment and perpetuating the image of South Asia as a terminally unstable region, both sides pay a heavy cost even in cases where they are able to pull back from the brink. Repeated military crises with Pakistan also keep India mired in regional affairs, hobbling its efforts to move to a more prominent role in Asia and the world. Barring the implementation of an institutionalized dialogue process, the future seems to be one of continued "ugly stability," with increasingly frequent and increasingly dangerous crises under the nuclear shadow.[23]

The volatility of the India-Pakistan relationship and the danger of war were highlighted by the 2002 crisis. Sparked by a terrorist assault against the Indian parliament complex on December 13, 2001, the crisis led both sides to deploy their armed forces so that by late December, some one million men were massed along the India-Pakistan border. It was the largest deployment in the subcontinent since the 1971 war, and one of the largest anywhere on the globe since World War II. Acidic rhetoric from both sides was punctuated by Indian public statements that referred to air strikes or other "surgical" attacks against suspected terrorist facilities in Pakistan, and Pakistani replies that hinted at using nuclear arms should the confrontation escalate to actual war.[24] Indeed, the two countries came very close to war in early January 2002 and again in the late spring, after a May 14, 2002, terrorist raid on an Indian army camp resulted in the deaths of 33 soldiers and family members. Personal intervention by senior U.S. officials and European and Asian leaders helped to stave off open conflict during the summer, and the proximate crisis was resolved in October 2002, when India used the successful conclusion of state elections in Jammu and Kashmir to announce a phased withdrawal of its troops from the border. Pakistan quickly followed suit. By November, both countries were absorbed in domestic political developments, but there was no diplomatic contact, transportation links were broken, bitter polemics were common, expulsions of diplomats were routine, and an average of eight to ten people continued to die every day in Kashmir.[25] This inflamed situation prevailed through late April 2003, with outrages such as the murder of 24 Kashmiri Hindu villagers in March contributing to the continued state of high tension.[26] Perceiving the limits of military power in addressing the Kashmir problem and relations with Pakistan, Prime Minister Vajpayee has made a bold attempt to break out of the stalemate with his April offer to restore transportation links and reinstate ambassadors. This is a welcome initiative, but it is too soon to tell how far the two sides will be able to sustain the momentum toward dialogue and at least marginal normalization.

What are the near-term prospects for improved relations? Recent efforts to renew official interaction notwithstanding, the road ahead is strewn with significant obstacles. These are not insurmountable but neither are they inconsiderable. In the first place, the 2002 crisis scraped away much of the "insulation" between the "normal" level of India-Pakistan tension and more dangerous confrontations that could escalate into open conflict. "Like porcelain, Indo-Pak relations have to be handled delicately," says Pakistan's Foreign Secretary Riaz Khokar. "If you drop it, it will break."[27] The relationship thus remains unstable and a dramatic flare up in violence in Indian Kashmir or some spectacular terrorist incident could quickly derail the nascent edging toward dialogue and once again push the two rivals toward armed conflict.[28] Furthermore, the "lessons" in brinkmanship and strategic defiance that each side seems to have taken away from the 2002 crisis tend to promote rather than retard future crises. Many in both capitals seem comfortable pursuing risky strategies that stress inflexible maximalist positions and rely on a dangerously weak regional deterrence regime or intervention by outside powers, particularly the United States, to prevent catastrophe.[29] Vajpayee's statesmanlike initiative may temporarily disarm or divert those who urge such risky approaches, but these threatening tendencies will remain part of the context with which he and his Pakistani counterparts must contend. The challenge, then, as India's Minister of External Affairs, Yashwant Sinha, has noted, is not just "starting the dialogue but taking it to a conclusion, it has to be sustained over a period of time."[30]

Second, both sides must include domestic politics in their calculations. Any progress toward normalization will have opponents who will not hesitate to seize on setbacks to demand an end to dialogue and perhaps call for military action across the Line of Control (LOC) in Kashmir or even across the recognized international border. Leaders in New Delhi and Islamabad will have to cope with charges of being "soft" on the other side or "selling out" long-held positions. Elections in several major Indian states during the second half of 2003 and national elections to be held by October 2004 are another complicating domestic factor for New Delhi, as is the presence of a significant voting block of Islamist parties in the new Pakistani national assembly. On the Indian side of the border, the leadership will have to decide how to reconcile pressures to promote especially controversial elements of the Hindutva agenda with appeals to Indian Muslims, particularly Kashmiris. Adjusting the salience of Hindutva in domestic policy offers some opportunities to present a conciliatory face in Kashmir with a tougher line against Pakistan, but this may prove difficult to calibrate and could send unintentionally negative signals to observers in Islamabad or other foreign capitals. Furthermore, in preparing and implementing what could be major shifts in policy, top leaders in both capitals must contend with internal bureaucratic inertia and deep-seated suspicion of the other side.[31]

Beyond these near-term obstacles, several other "environmental" factors hinder normalization and make the current situation unacceptably dangerous. Each country is convinced, for instance, that it understands the other side's perceptions and compulsions, but recent history hardly validates this conclusion. Instead, worst-case intelligence analysis or incorrect assessments of the other party's intentions are the norm. India, for instance, failed to detect the Pakistani incursion at Kargil in 1999, while Pakistan underestimated Indian resolve to evict the intruders. Miscalculation thus remains a serious danger on several critical levels. By attempting to develop a doctrine of a conventional "limited war" for the "strategic space" that some Indian strategists believe exists between low-level conflict and nuclear exchange, India could misjudge Pakistan's nuclear "red lines." Pakistanis, who see the 2002 experience as an example of Indian "cowardice," could underestimate the reaction to provocative actions. Both could misread intense U.S. engagement and the presence of U.S. forces in the region as "insurance against escalation to war."[32] Similarly, many in each country harbor the conviction that the other state poses an unrelenting and even existential threat. Many Pakistanis have no doubt that India is intent on "undoing Partition" and eradicating their nation, while there are more than a few Indians who see Pakistani actions and the virulent speeches of militant leaders as "evidence" of unremitting hostility, especially centered in the Pakistan Army.[33] Statements by hardliners on both sides of the border often reinforce these extreme interpretations, and can find their way into the assumptions upon which the other state's policies are based. Much of this inflammatory rhetoric is intended to influence domestic audiences, but it enters into the international discourse, tainting the atmosphere, alarming external observers, and providing ammunition to those on the other side who have little interest in improved relations.[34]

The presence of militant groups who employ terrorist tactics presents a further complication. In addition to their involvement in the brutal insurgency in Indian Kashmir, now in its 14th year, these unpredictable non-state actors can bring India and Pakistan into confrontation, and possibly into actual conflict as the 2002 crisis demonstrated. The militants' potential to overthrow the policies of sovereign nation-states means that neither New Delhi nor Islamabad can afford an inflexible wait-and-see strategy, persisting in their current approaches with the hope that time will bring some fundamental change in the other country's behavior.[35] Unless the two governments actively seek to manage their tensions, they risk leaving the initiative in the hands of terrorists, many of whom have vague, radically pan-Islamic agendas that are only tangentially relevant to Kashmir or India-Pakistan relations. These groups will almost certainly attempt to destroy the tentative moves toward dialogue through increased violence inside Indian Kashmir and terrorist attacks elsewhere in India.[36]

Nuclear weapons and burgeoning missile arsenals are another source of tension. Both countries will continue to enhance their weapons, delivery systems, command and control procedures, and use doctrine for the foreseeable future. Missile tests have often been used as signals of resolve, and some prominent Indian writers have even advocated additional nuclear tests despite the government's self-imposed moratorium on testing. The United States and others recognize that India has security concerns beyond Pakistan, but view South Asian nuclear and missile programs as detrimental to stability in the India-Pakistan dynamic. Washington, London, Tokyo, and others will likely continue to urge restraint in the development, testing, and deployment of nuclear weapons. Advance notification of missile launches, a confidence-building measure agreed at the 1999 Lahore summit and revived in 2003, is a helpful step toward greater transparency and stability.

These initial steps to normalization, however, highlight some reasons to maintain a certain degree of cautious optimism in this generally gloomy situation. Most important perhaps is the deep reservoir of hope among the populations on both sides of the border. As was evident in early 1999 in the period surrounding the Lahore summit, popular support for bold moves to reduce India-Pakistan tensions can be tapped with the right political leadership. Indeed, the euphoria generated by Lahore proved a problem in itself. The resentment left in India after the 1999 Kargil war and the 2002 crisis is all the more bitter for having followed the exaggerated enthusiasm of Lahore, and the experience has led Indian and Pakistani leaders to adopt a much more measured approach in 2003. Drawing on this potential support can benefit Vajpayee on both domestic and international fronts. At home, it may allow him to reclaim the domestic political agenda. By capitalizing on his unique personal popularity and his image of moderation, he may undercut the opposition Congress Party as well as the hawkish elements in the BJP's support base as the country approaches national elections in 2004.[37]

Internationally, the opening to Pakistan is likely to appeal to outside investors, but it would also help preserve India's traditional foreign policy autonomy by keeping the initiative in New Delhi's hands and restricting the areas in which outside actors can play a useful role.[38] Pakistan too recognizes the benefits to be gained by pursuing the peace effort, particularly the potential enhancement of its international image and improvement of its attractiveness to outside investment. In both countries, businessmen are starting to advocate normalization of relations as a boon for bilateral trade and tourism, long held hostage to bilateral enmity.[39] Continued growth in this pressure from commercial interests will help to establish "constituencies for peace" in the two nations and will give the political leadership additional incentive to persist in their tentative moves toward dialogue.[40] Viewed with all of the requisite cautions, therefore, Vajpayee's 2003 peace initiative represents a crucial opportunity to establish a process for addressing key security concerns and moving toward normalization.

Looking West and East: Foreign Policy on the Larger Stage

Beyond South Asia proper, India will continue its efforts to assume a more prominent role on the global stage. This diplomatic approach constitutes a continuation of previous policies rather than a major new shift, but the Vajpayee government will attempt to accelerate the visible benefits of its international presence for domestic purposes in preparation for the 2004 general elections. Although pragmatic interest in firm and growing relations with the United States will be a central feature of Indian foreign policy, residual skepticism toward U.S. intentions and reliability and an overriding interest in preserving strategic autonomy will determine New Delhi's stance on many international issues.[41] India prefers a multipolar global system of "plurality and consensus" that gives "due weightage" to the "legitimate interests and concerns" of all key actors.[42] It will therefore continue to favor policies that support and reform international institutions, particularly the United Nations, and will continue efforts to build closer ties to China, Japan, and Europe while retaining the remnants of the tattered "special relationship" with Russia.[43] Indeed, non-South Asian governments may occasionally seek to recruit Indian diplomatic assistance on select international issues, increasing New Delhi's value in some multilateral forums. Prime Minister Vajpayee's trip to Europe in early 2003 illustrated not only New Delhi's desire to strengthen its ties to the EU and Russia, but also the willingness of at least some European governments to bolster their positions by calling on Indian support. Significant success in such endeavors is problematic, particularly in the absence of continued economic reform, but such situations will provide India with some increased leverage in dealings with other states in Europe and Asia.

In addition, India will continue to seek improvements in its relations with China. Shortly after returning from his successful European trip, Vajpayee made a major trip to China in June 2003, the first visit by an Indian prime minister in 10 years. The trip provided the occasion for the two governments to reaffirm their commitment to the vital role of the UN in international affairs, and to sign nine bilateral agreements on cooperation in trade, science and technology, justice, and culture. Most significant were the compromises both sides made on major diplomatic issues: India recognized Tibet as part of China and China agreed to initiate commerce through Sikkim, a formerly independent monarchy that Beijing has steadfastly refused to acknowledged as part of India.[44] Additionally, the two parties announced the appointment of special high-level envoys to promote resolution of the disputed 4,500-kilometer border. The two sides have also initiated small-scale military-to-military programs, including Chinese visits to Indian airfields and the first-ever joint naval exercise. These moves are more symbolic than substantive—the special envoys for the border issue are unlikely to achieve much over the next five years—but they signify New Delhi's interest in better relations with Beijing, despite the many differences that divide the two Asian giants. The trip and the agreements also illustrate the ability of both governments to set aside the painful border dispute while advancing their relationship in other mutually beneficial areas. Many Indians argue that this formula could also apply to Kashmir and the other issues that bedevil India-Pakistan relations. Similarly, many observers regard the successful regime of confidence-building measures implemented along the Sino-Indian border in the early 1990s as a basis for steps that could be instituted on the frontier with Pakistan.

Nevertheless, vital interests continue to divide India and China. Above all, these problems include China's strategic ties with Pakistan, the history of Chinese support to Pakistani military programs, and the recent Chinese project to construct a major new port at Gwadar on Pakistan's coast. For many Indians, the Chinese involvement in Pakistan combined with Beijing's friendly relations with Bangladesh and Burma represent an effort to "encircle" and "contain" India. These analysts view Chinese naval modernization as a potential threat to India's primacy in the Indian Ocean.[45] Furthermore, the Sino-Indian border, the cause of a brief war in 1962, remains an unresolved and deeply felt issue despite the fairly comfortable modus vivendi. The two are also likely to find themselves competing for some of the same market and investment opportunities. The relationship is thus rife with its own inherent constraints, and occasional rumors of a China-Russia-India "strategic triangle" are unlikely to be realized. However, while remaining wary of China, in the near term India will politely resist any suggestion that it join any type of strategic alliance directed against China. Instead, it will try to limit Pakistan's ability to rely on China's unquestioned support, while endeavoring to increase its own freedom of action by aligning itself with Beijing on an issue-by-issue basis. Prime Minister Vajpayee summarized this aspect of India's China policy in a speech at Beijing University: "I was struck by the congruence of our positions [at the 2003 G-8 summit in France], if we acted in concert, it would be very difficult for the world to ignore us."[46]

Southeast Asia is one of the arenas where Indian and Chinese interests may clash. Though with limited success thus far, India has attempted to expand its commercial, diplomatic, and military ties with the ASEAN countries over the past decade under a sporadically pursued "Look East" policy. The gradual expansion of India's traditionally good relations with Vietnam, including the provision of military assistance, might be particularly troubling for China. If tangible benefits for India have not been extensive, its membership in the ASEAN Regional Forum has given it a voice in greater Asia, and New Delhi has supplemented its multilateral activities with bilateral initiatives including trade agreements, a program of naval ship visits, and low-level military exchanges. The unrest in Indonesia and the experience of conducting joint patrols in the Strait of Malacca with the U.S. Navy after September 11, 2001, give India further cause to focus greater attention to the east. Moreover, interaction with ASEAN brings Indian officials together with the leaders from the United States and key East Asian states, thus offering New Delhi a gateway to the larger Asia Pacific stage. In this region, India has paid particular attention to Burma, initiating small assistance projects, road construction, and development of natural gas resources in an effort to counter Chinese influence, halt narcotics trafficking, and curtail cross-border support for the pertinacious insurgencies in India's northeastern states.[47] Unlike most Southeast Asian countries, India's attitude toward the U.S. military presence in the region has historically been suspicious rather than welcoming, and New Delhi will watch with great interest as Washington considers new stationing and force projection proposals. Indian interests in Southeast Asia will therefore grow steadily if slowly in the years ahead. Its influence in the region is likely to follow.

To the west, over the near term India's diplomacy will probably succeed in reconciling its burgeoning ties with Israel with its traditionally cordial relations with the Muslim states of the Middle East.[48] India depends on the Persian Gulf for most of its oil and several million expatriate Indian workers reside in the Gulf countries, contributing their remittances to the Indian economy. Many Indians once worked in Iraq and, with a long history of close ties to Baghdad, New Delhi will strive for substantial involvement in the rebuilding of Iraq. If disputes over their command can be resolved, Indian may also contribute troops for stability operations to strengthen its ties with Washington and to expand its official presence in the Gulf. Connections with Iran and the Arab states are thus vital to India's economic and security interests. At the same time, a solid relationship with Israel has considerable value in its own right, especially for the sophisticated military hardware and associated technology that Israel can provide. Moreover, many Indians see this link as an avenue to stronger U.S.-India ties.[49] Under the shadow of September 11, 2001, and its own struggle with Islamic extremists, India has thus stepped carefully to highlight counterterrorism as a bond with Israel and the United States without alienating its Muslim interlocutors.

Despite New Delhi's interests in Israel, closer relations with Iran will also remain a feature of India's foreign policy. With Iran, as with Afghanistan, the war on terrorism and the fall of the Taliban have opened new opportunities for Indian diplomacy and business. Inherent limitations—Tehran's desire to maintain equidistance between New Delhi and Islamabad, and India's close interaction with Israel—will impose constraints on both sides, but cooperative projects such as construction of a major road through Iran to Afghanistan and limited Indo-Iranian military interaction serve India's economic and security interests.[50] India will also work to preserve a significant role for itself in Afghan reconstruction efforts. Involvement in Afghanistan is not only consistent with India's longstanding backing for the former Afghan "Northern Alliance," it also enhances its status as a global player, supports closer U.S.-India ties, and opens access to Central Asia with potential future benefits for India's energy needs.[51] Indian initiatives in Central Asia, on the other hand, will remain subordinate to its investment in Afghanistan and far below the role played by Russia, China, and the United States. Activities such as a small military exercise with Tajikistan, however, may begin to lay the foundation for future development. From New Delhi's perspective, some of these diplomatic and commercial moves will serve the immediate goal of weakening international support for Pakistan and create opportunities to tap new energy sources without relying on transit through Pakistan. The underlying rationale in most cases, however, will aim at the longer-term goal of establishing India as a major international actor with the greatest possible flexibility for independent action.

Implications for the United States

U.S. relations with India have improved steadily since the early 1990s and this trend will likely continue for the foreseeable future as both countries identify increasingly salient mutual interests regionally and across the globe. India's significance for the United States, not only in South Asia, but on the larger Asian and global stages as well, will thus increase. Within the South Asian regional context, as discussed below, India is crucial to removing a vital threat to U.S. interests: the danger of an India-Pakistan conflict. India will also have a vital interest in the stability of its immediate neighbors in the region. Like Washington, therefore, New Delhi will work to promote democracy and an end to the violent insurgencies that threaten the governments of Nepal and Sri Lanka. India will not be able to resolve these vicious conflicts on its own, but its close cooperation will be essential to any lasting improvement in those two troubled countries. Similarly, trade and commerce with India are crucial to the success of any economic recovery and reform effort in Nepal or Bangladesh (such as the development of Nepal's hydropower potential or the exploitation of natural gas deposits in the Bay of Bengal).

India will also have an increasing role to play in neighboring regions: Southeast Asia, Central Asia, the Persian Gulf, and China. Nevertheless, as U.S. scholar Ashley Tellis remarks, New Delhi's ability to influence events in these areas, while growing, will remain limited for the near term.[52] Coordination with the United States, however, will dramatically magnify Indian power in these regions. In addressing its concerns for stability, democracy, and prosperity in Southeast Asia (especially in Burma and Indonesia), for example, close cooperation with the United States will increase India's prospects for success. A similar calculus applies in Afghanistan, Central Asia, and the Persian Gulf, where New Delhi can capitalize on congruence of interests and coordination of policy with Washington to gain an otherwise unattainable level of influence. Differences over Iran will generate some friction and Indian-Pakistani rivalry in Afghanistan will require careful management, but neither of these two challenges is likely to derail greater U.S.-India cooperation in these regions. India will also find the United States useful in developing its relations with China, but, as noted above, New Delhi will try to preserve its strategic independence by avoiding a definitive commitment that alienates either power. On the other hand, Indian interest in and influence over critical East Asian issues such as Taiwan and North Korea will remain minimal for the foreseeable future.

India can also be a key partner in coping with transnational issues. Countering terrorism and proliferation are at the top of the list of mutual interests, but combating the spread of narcotics, promoting democracy, and securing unfettered access to resources are other areas for potential cooperation. India's proven capabilities in international peacekeeping and humanitarian operations remain a useful asset as the United States and the global community seek to restore stability in disrupted areas of the world.

U.S. Policy in South Asia:
From Crisis to Process in India-Pakistan Tensions

U.S. interests in South Asia have become dramatically more prominent since 2001 and the United States will have a helpful and, in some cases, a decisive role to play in the region for the foreseeable future. At the same time, Washington is in the unusual position of having close relations with both New Delhi and Islamabad, perhaps the best relations it has enjoyed with the two rivals simultaneously since they gained independence in 1947.[53] This condition, however, is likely to be as short-lived as it is rare, and the obstructions ahead should not be underestimated. Nonetheless, if seized quickly, the present situation offers unprecedented opportunities for success in the pursuit of U.S. interests, to the ultimate benefit of regional states, the United States, and other powers.

South Asia's increased salience implies readjustment of several fundamental assumptions in U.S. strategy toward the region. In the first place, U.S. interests suggest that the Washington policy community pay more consistent attention to South Asia than has been the case in the past. Instead of episodic involvement in reaction to momentary crises, the United States will gain significant advantages by making South Asia a region of high priority on a regular basis, shaping events to avoid or at least minimize crises. Secondly, Washington's involvement will necessarily be at a higher political level than previously, if the distraction and danger of recurring emergencies are to be precluded. Although U.S. strategy in South Asia must remain "affordable" in terms of the time, effort, and attention required from both the policy bureaucracies and senior decision makers, measured elevation of South Asia to a consistent place on the national policy agenda and on the calendars of more senior officials will help defuse crises and reduce the frequency with which the United States must draw on the power of the cabinet secretaries and the White House to avert disaster.[54]

The key to success for U.S. policy, then, is to shift the policy paradigm vis-à-vis South Asia from *crisis response* to *process support*. The United States will have to encourage and support, as appropriate, the establishment of a bilateral dialogue structure between India and Pakistan to create a durable process that would allow the two sides to manage their tensions, while conducting discussions on all of the issues that divide them, including Kashmir.[55] At the same time, India and Pakistan must recognize that the United States cannot prevent a war if one or the other chooses war as a deliberate policy or if they slip into conflict through some tragic series of misperceptions and miscalculations.[56] However, the United States and other outside powers can help to create a regional environment that is conducive to stability and reduces the likelihood of increasingly dangerous crises arising at increasingly brief intervals.

To build a new foundation for the future, U.S. strategy could consist of three components. The immediate need is to sustain the momentum of the Vajpayee initiatives and discourage a return to acrimony, reflexive accusations, and corrosive rhetoric.[57] A crucial element will be holding President Musharraf and the government in Islamabad to the pledges to halt infiltration across the LOC into Indian Kashmir and to ensure that there are no support facilities for insurgents inside Pakistan (or Azad Kashmir). Cosmetic or minimal measures will only exacerbate tensions. Furthermore, the United States can stress the importance of allowing the tentative political process inside Indian Kashmir to take root and grow. It is critical that both sides nurture this promising development with the aim of reducing violence, improving the lot of the Kashmiri people—Muslim, Hindu, and Buddhist—and wrenching the initiative away from extremists.

The second component of the U.S. approach could be a long-term investment in facilitating an India-Pakistan dialogue process on Kashmir and all other key bilateral issues. This will be a difficult endeavor, requiring sustained involvement over an extended period of years and in the face of serious obstacles. Domestic political conditions in the two countries, particularly the influence of religious extremists in both capitals, will hinder progress, and the history of previous reconciliation efforts is not encouraging. However, the potential for nuclear conflict, irrelevant during earlier efforts to craft Kashmir solutions, lends urgency to international and regional concerns and makes a renewed dialogue imperative. The process must be crafted to accommodate the interests of the various Kashmiri peoples and could include financial incentive packages to promote education and development on both sides of the LOC. With U.S. leadership, cooperation among prospective donor countries could pay high dividends in this area. The United States should also urge India and Pakistan to supplement these measures in the security realm with increased bilateral economic cooperation, perhaps embedded within a larger regional economic framework. These measures will help build "constituencies for peace" on both sides of the border and give the people of the region and their governments a direct stake in the successful continuation of the bilateral process.[58]

The third component of U.S. strategy could be conflict management and confidence-building measures designed to bridge the gap between lowering tensions in the near-term and approaching a resolution of Kashmir over the long haul. Building on the Lahore agreements signed in February 1999, the two countries should develop additional measures such as nuclear risk reduction centers to minimize misperceptions and to limit the potential for crisis.[59] With a robust set of confidence-building measures to create "firebreaks" between incidents of terrorist violence and escalation to open war between sovereign nation-states, New Delhi and Islamabad will create space for their own policy processes to work and reduce the dangers of misunderstanding and worst-case analysis. Over the long term, the two countries may also see some advantages in exploring conventional arms limitation initiatives to enhance regional stability while reducing the military burden on their national economies.[60]

The U.S. approach to the India-Pakistan dynamic presents an opportunity to cooperate with other non-South Asian powers. Britain, the EU, Russia, China, Canada, and Japan have all played useful roles in the past and will continue to be instrumental in initiating and sustaining a durable India-Pakistan dialogue process. Many of these states also have important voices in international financial institutions and could be constructive participants in creating incentive packages.

The United States and India: Advancing and Sustaining a Robust Relationship

Beyond the immediate and enduring interest in promoting reduced tensions between India and Pakistan, the United States will be working to continue the enhancement of bilateral ties with India. Building on shared democratic values and shared strategic interests, Washington has clearly identified India as a key partner for the twenty-first century, and the future promises continued progress in broadening and deepening the relationship. It remains, however, a relatively new relationship after a long, often negative history. Moreover, from the Indian perspective, interaction with the United States is colored by a colonial past and a hard-won independence that is still within the living memory of many senior leaders. Like China, India sees itself as the repository of a rich cultural heritage stretching back thousands of years, but one that suffered centuries of humiliation under occupation by Western powers in recent times. Indians retain a lively awareness of this colonial history and remain apprehensive of any recrudescence of what they perceive as "imperialism."[61]

The U.S.-India relationship will thus require careful nurturing so that it evolves into a robust partnership capable of weathering future disagreements. To avoid disruptive surprises, transparency from both sides must be a central feature of bilateral interaction. At the same time, both New Delhi and Washington will have to avoid overburdening their growing ties with unrealistic expectations that could quickly engender frustration and disappointment. The U.S. administration's efforts to detach U.S.-India relations from the zero-sum notions of the India-Pakistan rivalry and to build close personal and institutional contacts at all levels of government will contribute enormously to strong, enduring bilateral ties. This will be particularly important in diluting the perception held by many Indians that the revived U.S. support for Pakistan in the war on terrorism has retarded U.S.-India relations. The growing maturity of the relationship and a steady eye on its long-term benefits will help both sides weather the inevitable frustrations and disagreements. Military-to-military programs, which have burgeoned since the resumption of Defense Policy Group meetings in late 2001, will remain a major factor in fostering the bilateral agenda. Ironically, ties between the respective defense establishments have grown more rapidly and demonstrated more robustness than the economic links that many observers expected would form the leading edge in the relationship.[62]

Thus, security issues will be high on the U.S. agenda with India, not only ameliorating India-Pakistan confrontations, but also supporting Pakistan's progress toward democracy, discussing developments in China, coordinating policy on Afghanistan, collaborating to counter terrorism, and cooperating on Indian Ocean security. The U.S.-India conversation on Pakistan will be especially important as a weak and unstable Pakistan is in neither Washington's nor New Delhi's interest. As part of the bilateral dialogue, Washington will probably stress the importance of restraint in the development, testing, and deployment of nuclear weapons and missile delivery systems. The United States might also find it useful to caution New Delhi on the dangers inherent in the idea of "limited war" in the South Asian context, that is, the notion that large-scale conventional conflict can be conducted safely below the nuclear threshold.

In addition, expanded trade and commerce will be central to the bilateral relationship. Substantial growth is likely if Indian economic reforms progress and are coupled with significant improvements in infrastructure. Improved economic linkages will give individuals and corporations on both sides a greater stake in closer bilateral ties, adding important "ballast" to the larger U.S.-India relationship.[63] Deeper cooperation in what has come to be called the "trinity" of issues—high technology commerce, civilian nuclear energy exchanges, and collaboration in space—could form the leading edge of this expanding interaction. Movement in these areas has the potential to "take the Indo-U.S. relationship to a qualitatively new level of partnership."[64]

U.S.-India relations will probably continue to improve, but the pace, trajectory, and destination are neither predetermined nor inevitable. The foregoing analysis suggests several key variables of Indian behavior that will help in assessing the development of the relationship over the next several years. In the first place, Indian domestic politics will have to support continued strategic alignment with the United States. A severe setback in bilateral ties, such as an Indian perception that the United States is ignoring Indian security and sovereignty interests, could ignite latent mistrust of the United States and allow domestic political groups to attack U.S.-friendly policies for electoral advantage. The state of relations between majority Hindus and the various Indian minority groups will also have a bearing on foreign policy. An extended period of serious communal violence against Muslims or other minorities in India could absorb India's decision-makers and cast a pall over interactions with Europe and the United States. Likewise, a serious downturn in the Indian economy or a revival of drastic protectionist measures would discourage U.S. investors and have a detrimental effect on the broader bilateral relationship. The state of India-Pakistan relations is the key variable in the foreign policy arena. Repeated military crises will garner all the wrong kinds of attention from the United States and other external actors, damaging commercial ties and crippling efforts to build a robust long-term relationship. New Delhi's behavior toward Beijing and Tehran are the other two critical international links to watch. Although developments in these two relationships are unlikely to disturb progress between the United States and India, a strong Indian shift toward one or both of these countries on issues inimical to U.S. interests could have severe repercussions for ties with Washington.

Pitfalls notwithstanding, the current circumstances in South Asia afford the United States an important opportunity to advance its interests and support regional stability within the context of its larger Asian and global strategy. In the near term, the United States can help underwrite the nascent India-Pakistan rapprochement and assist in establishing a durable process to reduce the dangers inherent in the South Asia rivalry over the years ahead. At the same time, Washington can lay the foundations for significant enhancement of the U.S.-India bilateral relationship, to begin writing a new history of that relationship and realize the transformation envisaged in the U.S. National Security Strategy.[65]

Endnotes

[1] Between October 2001 and October 2002, the U.S. Secretary of State made three trips to New Delhi and Islamabad, the Secretary of Defense went once, and the Deputy Secretary of State twice. These were trips specifically focused on the India-Pakistan crisis and do not include others by the Secretary of Defense and other senior officials to address the war in Afghanistan.

[2] Susanne Hoeber Rudolph and Lloyd I. Rudolph, "New Dimensions of Indian Democracy," *Journal of Democracy*, January 2002.

[3] See also the insightful analyses in Teresita Schaffer, "A Changing India," in Michael R. Chambers, ed., *South Asia in 2020: Future Strategic Balances and Alliances*, Carlisle, Penn.: U.S. Army Strategic Studies Institute, 2002; and Walter Andersen, "Seeking the Middle Ground: Indian Politics in Flux," *Foreign Service Journal*, October 2002.

[4] Sumit Ganguly, "India's Multiple Revolutions," *Journal of Democracy*, January 2002.

[5] Professor K. N. Panikkar highlights the threat posed by tinkering with textbooks for political purposes in "History Retold," *Frontline*, May 24–June 6, 2003. Such rewriting, he says, "tends to weaken the unity of the nation and endanger social harmony."

[6] The tragedy in Gujarat has been described as a pogrom, but it is important to note that violence did not spread to other states. Mohammed Ayoob, remarks at a United States Institute of Peace symposium on "Religious Extremism and Governance in South Asia: Internal and External Pressures," May 15, 2003. A portrayal of a Hindu extremist leader, Bal Thackeray, is in Larissa MacFarquhar, "Letter from India: The Strongman," *New Yorker*, May 26, 2003.

[7] Ashley J. Tellis, "South Asia," in Richard J. Ellings and Aaron L. Friedberg, eds., *Strategic Asia: Power and Purpose 2001–02*, Seattle: The National Bureau of Asian Research, 2001, pp. 235–36.

[8] Partha Ghose, remarks at a United States Institute of Peace symposium on "Religious Extremism and Governance in South Asia: Internal and External Pressures," May 15, 2003.

[9] For a comprehensive summary, see Mandavi Mehta, "The Role of Hindutva in Indian Politics," *South Asia Monitor*, no. 55 (February 1, 2003). On the

radicalization of domestic groups, see Rollie Lal, "The Hindu-Muslim Divide," *Atlantic Monthly*, July/August 2003. Moreover, Fareed Zakaria avers that the rise of Hindu extremism is eroding western good will toward India. Interview with Nona Walia, "Downside of democracy," *Times of India*, June 26, 2003.

[10] Schaffer, "A Changing India," pp. 40–41.

[11] Ms. Gandhi is the widow of former Prime Minister Rajiv Gandhi and the daughter-in-law of former Prime Minister Indira Gandhi.

[12] During the mid-1990s, India had two prime ministers from smaller parties as neither the declining Congress Party nor the rising BJP had the strength to craft ruling coalitions.

[13] Bibek Debroy, "Generation gaps: are policymakers aware of what the post-1970s generation wants?" *Telegraph*, May 23, 2003.

[14] During 1990 and 1991, India experienced a severe foreign currency crisis that led to reforms under the Congress government of Prime Minister Narasimha Rao. See John Adams, "India: Much Achieved, Much to Achieve," in Selig S. Harrison, Paul H. Kreisberg, and Dennis Kux, eds., *India & Pakistan: The First Fifty Years*, Washington, DC: Woodrow Wilson Center Press, 1999.

[15] Joydeep Mukherji, "Economic Reform in India: How Deep? How Fast?" *Foreign Service Journal*, October 2002, p. 26. See also Economist Intelligence Unit, "India Country Report," May 2003, p. 7. The Asian Development Bank's *Asian Development Outlook 2003* projects a growth rate of 6.4 percent for 2004.

[16] As published in "Implications of trade figures," *The Hindu*, May 8, 2003.

[17] Mukherji, "Economic Reform in India: How Deep? How Fast?" p. 28; also Ganguly, "India's Multiple Revolutions," pp. 45–46.

[18] Richard Haass, "The United States and India: A Transformed Relationship," remarks to the Confederation of Indian Industry, Hyderabad, India, January 7, 2003, <www.state.gov>.

[19] Haass, "The United States and India...." See also speeches by U.S. Ambassador Robert D. Blackwill who has famously lamented that U.S.-Indian trade and investment flows are "flat as a chapatti" owing to uncertainty over the continuation of Indian economic reforms. "Transforming the U.S.-India Relationship," speech to the Alumni of the Indian Institute of Technology, San Jose, California, January 18, 2003 <www.newdelhi.usembassy.gov>.

[20] Mukherji, "Economic Reform in India: How Deep? How Fast?" p. 25; Ganguly, "India's Multiple Revolutions," p. 45.

[21] These disparities and associated problems are discussed in a special issue of *India Today*, "India's Best and Worst States," May 19, 2003.

[22] Michael Krepon, *The Stability-Instability Paradox: Misperception and Escalation Control in South Asia*, Washington, DC: The Stimson Center, 2003, p. 10. Satu Limaye, on the other hand, offers the view that the danger has been overstated in "Mediating Kashmir: A Bridge Too Far," *Washington Quarterly*, Winter 2002–03.

[23] Term coined by Ashley J. Tellis, "Stability in South Asia," Santa Monica, Calif.: Rand, 1997.

[24] For example: "Musharraf 'prepared' to use nuclear bomb," BBC News, 7 April 2002.

[25] This number is the author's rough estimate including militants, Indian security

forces, and civilians.

26 Militants attacked a village of Kashmiri Hindus in March 2003, dragged some two dozen of them from their homes, lined them up, and murdered them.

27 Quoted in Raj Chengappa and Indrani Bagchi, "Rocky road to peace," *India Today*, May 12, 2003, p. 21.

28 In congressional testimony, George Tenet, Director of Central Intelligence, has stated that "any dramatic provocation...runs the risk of sparking another major military deployment." Tenet, "The Worldwide Threat in 2003: Evolving Dangers in a Complex World," February 11, 2003 <www.cia.gov>. India's Ministry of External Affairs has highlighted the danger posed by new terrorist attacks. "Kashmir attacks could stop peace moves: India," *Daily Times*, May 16, 2003.

29 Henry L. Stimson Center, *Lessons Learned—The India-Pakistan Crisis of 2002*, July 2002 <www.stimson.org>; and Krepon, *The Stability-Instability Paradox, Misperception, and Escalation Control in South Asia*, p. 13.

30 Quoted in Seema Mustafa, "I hope everyone knows the risks if we fail: Sinha," *Asian Age*, May 14, 2003. Similarly, retired Indian General V. R. Raghavan notes the crucial need for "a continuing and serious mechanism of engagement," in Raghavan, "Do it yourself: there is talk of a road map for Kashmir since the Armitage visit," *Telegraph*, May 22, 2003. Part of this challenge will be rising above day-to-day events to focus on the larger objective, in accordance with remarks by Indian Defense Minister George Fernandes in May 2003: "The issue of peace is much larger than the question of how many people were killed crossing the Line of Control yesterday or today" as quoted in "George in peace push," *Telegraph*, May 22, 2003; and Sandeep Dikshit, "Let infiltration not be the barometer," *The Hindu*, May 22, 2003.

31 Retired Indian Admiral Raja Menon complains about governmental institutions that "have consistently let both countries down" in Menon, "Rigour, not flamboyance," *Outlook*, May 19, 2003. Similar sentiments are expressed in Shekhar Gupta, "A peace of Vajpayee's mind," *Indian Express*, May 10, 2003; and editor Bharat Bhushan opines that "the political and bureaucratic establishment in India could act as a drag on Vajpayee" in Bushan, "Gingerly, Hector, gingerly," *The Telegraph*, May 8, 2003.

32 Polly Nayak, "Reducing Collateral Damage to Indo-Pakistani Relations from the War on Terrorism," *Brookings Institution Policy Brief*, no. 107, September 2002 <www.brookings.org>.

33 Former Vice Chief of the Pakistan Army Staff, General (ret.) Khalid Mahmud Arif, for example, asserts that "the ruling BJP is not reconciled to the creation of Pakistan and dreams of converting South Asia into Akhand Bharat [greater India]." Arif, "Peace prospects in S. Asia," *Dawn*, May 12, 2003. Attacking hardliners on both sides, Husain Haqqani describes "the votaries of Hindutva" for whom "Pakistan is not a neighbor to be engaged but rather an enemy to be defeated or eliminated." See Haqqani, "No room for hardliners," *Indian Express*, May 10, 2003.

34 In a May 2003 interview, Pakistani Foreign Minister Khurshid Mahmud Kasuri commented, "the immediate thing we can do is try to control the rhetoric," Raj Chengappa, *India Today*, May 12, 2003. In a separate interview with another

Indian news magazine, Kasuri draws a careful distinction between comments aimed at international and domestic audiences. Mariana Baabar, "US has played a very useful role," *Outlook*, May 12, 2003. See also BBC News, "Eleven die in Kashmir violence," May 19, 2003 <news.bbc.co.uk>.

35 Some Pakistanis, for example, believe that continued insurgency in Kashmir and troubles elsewhere in India will eventually force India to withdraw from Kashmir entirely (the truly extreme expect India to fragment); others contend that there can be no agreement with a BJP government. In such formulations there is thus no need to consider new policy approaches. Similarly, many Indians see the Pakistani army as the obstacle to normal relations and argue that India has no choice but to wait for a complete change in Pakistan's political arrangements before taking any policy initiative. V. Sudarshan quotes diplomatic sources in New Delhi as saying that "a Pakistan policy which says that you will do nothing cannot be sustained indefinitely." Sudarshan, "Over the boundary at Sher-e-Kashmir," *Outlook*, May 12, 2003.

36 The founder of one such group, Hafiz Mohammed Saeed of the Lashkar-e-Toiba, stated in May 2003: "The solution lies in jihad, not in dialogue." Quoted in "Jamali courts Atal, Pervez hawks," *Telegraph*, May 16, 2003.

37 Shekhar Gupta offers a sophisticated analysis in *Indian Express*, May 10, 2003. See also Saba Naqvi Bhaumik, "Fore and hind sight," *Outlook*, May 19, 2003; Vir Sanghvi, "India's most admired politician," *Hindustan Times*, May 3, 2003; Amy Waldman, "India's leader gambles on peace," *New York Times*, May 3, 2003; and Saeed Naqvi, "Vajpayee, the practical poet," *Indian Express*, May 16, 2003.

38 Commentator M. J. Akbar likens the possibility of American intervention to inviting "an elephant into your drawing room" as "even the friendliest elephant will leave that room in a mess." Akbar, "Hopeful vs. hopeless," *Asian Age*, May 12, 2003. R. Prasannan expresses a similar sentiment in "Keep the Yanks out," *The Week*, May 18, 2003.

39 An important caution is in order: some Pakistanis continue to worry that Indian goods will flood Pakistani markets, while Indian leaders are wary of making India dependent on Pakistan for energy needs by developing pipeline projects from Central Asia or Iran through Pakistan.

40 Kavita Sangani and Teresita Schaffer, "India-Pakistan Trade: Creating Constituencies for Peace," *South Asia Monitor*, no. 56 (March 3, 2003). The secretary of the Federation of Indian Chambers of Commerce is reportedly enthusiastic about improved relations, believing that it "will certainly give a new thrust to India-Pakistan commercial ties," as quoted in "Trade over terror," *Times of India*, May 15, 2003. Likewise, Pakistani Prime Minister Jamali has assured audiences that "prosperity will emanate from this change." Ihtasham ul Haque, "Talks can help prosperity," *Dawn*, May 14, 2003. See also Joanna Slater, "Indian, Pakistani businesses thirst for renewed ties," *Wall Street Journal*, May 15, 2003; "Tourism could boost Indo-Pak ties," *Pioneer*, May 16, 2003; and "The 'Iraq effect' may push India and Pakistan toward peace," *BusinessWeek*, May 19, 2003.

41 Minister of External Affairs Sinha has asked parliament to abjure "compulsive hostility" toward the U.S. Quoted in Indrani Bagchi, "Mending fences," *India*

Today, May 5, 2003, p. 23. For an example of the lingering suspicion, see J. N. Dixit, "Question time, USA," *Indian Express*, May 16, 2003. See also: Ganguly, "The Start of a Beautiful Friendship? The United States and India," *World Policy Journal*, Spring 2003, p. 28; and K. Subrahmanyam, "Cong betrays U.S. allergy," *Telegraph*, July 9, 2003. Juli A. MacDonald offers an insightful overview of military views in *Indo-U.S. Military Relationship: Expectations and Perceptions*, report for the Office of Net Assessment, U.S. Department of Defense, October 2002.

42 Indian National Security Advisor Brajesh Mishra, "India, United States and the New World Order: Prospects for Cooperation," speech to the Council on Foreign Relations, New York, May 7, 2003, <www.meadev.nic.in/speeches>. See also Teresita Schaffer, "Building a New Partnership with India," *Washington Quarterly*, Spring 2002, p. 38.

43 Pramit Pal Chaudhuri, "Why the Indo-Russian relationship is going nowhere in a hurry," *Hindustan Times*, December 16, 2002.

44 India absorbed the tiny independent principality of Sikkim in 1975, but China has never accepted the legality of the Indian action.

45 As an example, see the Rahul Bedi interview with Admiral Madhavendra Singh, Chief of the Indian Naval Staff, in *Jane's Defence Weekly*, May 21, 2003.

46 Speech by Prime Minister Vajpayee, Peking University, June 23, 2003, <www.meadev.nic.in>.

47 Indrani Bagchi, "Wary partners," *India Today*, June 30, 2003; and Rahul Bedi, "Strategic realignments," *Frontline*, June 21, 2003–July 4, 2003.

48 On India's view of Israel, see Brajesh Mishra, address to the American Jewish Committee, May 8, 2003 <www.meadev.nic.in>.

49 National Security Advisor Brajesh Mishra spoke to the American Jewish Committee in May 2003. Deputy Prime Minister Advani downplayed the reference in a June 2003 interview with Sheela Bhatt <www.rediff.com>, but other commentators see a consistent effort to connect the United States and Israel with India. John Cherian, "A pliant policy," *Frontline*, May 24, 2003–June 6, 2003.

50 Indrani Bagchi, "Axis of concern," *India Today*, May 19, 2003; C. Christine Fair, "The Tehran-New Delhi Axis," *Atlantic Monthly*, July/August 2003; and Bedi, "Strategic realignments."

51 Unfortunately, transfer of the India-Pakistan rivalry to Afghanistan has negative implications for Afghan stability as noted by Pakistani scholar Rifaat Hussain as quoted in Khalid Hasan, "U.S. backing a must for Pakistan-India peace," *Daily Times*, May 13, 2003.

52 Tellis, "South Asia," in *Strategic Asia 2001–02*, p. 262. Tellis refers to inner and outer "rings" of Indian influence with New Delhi having dominance in the inner "ring" but less power on its own in the outer "ring."

53 C. Raja Mohan, "A Paradigm Shift toward South Asia?" *Washington Quarterly*, Winter 2002–03.

54 The formulation "affordable" was coined by Stephen P. Cohen.

55 For a promising outline of an India-Pakistan dialogue "process," see Teresita C. Schaffer, "Finding a Kashmir Settlement: The Burden of Leadership," *Strategic Forum*, no. 199, June 2003; and Teresita C. Schaffer and Paul A. Longo, "Can India and Pakistan Seize the Moment?" *South Asia Monitor*, no. 60 (July

1, 2003).

[56] As K. Shankar Bajpai points out, U.S. "encouragement can stimulate bilateral progress" between India and Pakistan, but the "ultimate responsibility" for stability "lies with the two neighbors themselves." Bajpai, "Untangling India and Pakistan," *Foreign Affairs*, May/June 2003, p. 126.

[57] As immediate steps, the United States can encourage the restoration of normal diplomatic contact (permitting full staffing of the respective high commissions, for example), resumption of more cross-border transportation links, easing of visa restrictions, and similar measures. Expanded commercial ties could be a particularly fruitful means of building confidence and generating a stake in success for key community leaders on both sides.

[58] C. Raja Mohan, "U.S. backs trade for peace," *The Hindu*, November 20, 2002.

[59] The United States and others might assist by sharing experiences, technical expertise, and perhaps equipment (such as communications upgrades to bilateral hotlines) to reinforce Indian and Pakistani initiatives.

[60] Some of the treaties and procedures developed for Europe during the Cold War may be helpful in this context once adjusted for the South Asian scenario. Feroz Hassan Khan offers some specific steps to avoid "dangerous military practices" in "Challenges to Nuclear Stability in South Asia," *Nonproliferation Review*, Spring 2003.

[61] Retired Ambassador K. Shankar Bajpai highlights the importance of anti-colonialism in the modern Indian worldview as well as several other key elements that are still relevant today: policy-making autonomy, innate isolationism, the moral aspects of the pre-independence nationalist movement, the imperative of maintaining India's unity, and the influence of British socialism. See Bajpai, "Opportunity and Challenge: Indian Foreign Policy Today," *Foreign Service Journal*, October 2002, pp. 43–45. Minxin Pei argues that U.S. policy-making would benefit from greater sensitivity to history and foreign "nationalism," such as India's, in "The Paradoxes of American Nationalism," *Foreign Policy*, May/June 2003, p. 35.

[62] For a review of the status of military-to-military ties, see Robert D. Blackwill, "U.S.-India defense cooperation," *The Hindu*, May 13, 2003.

[63] Dennis Kux, "A Remarkable Turnaround: U.S.-India Relations," *Foreign Service Journal*, October 2002, p. 23.

[64] Mishra, speech to the Council on Foreign Relations, May 7, 2003 <meadev.nic.in/speeches>.

[65] U.S. President Bush and Prime Minister Vajpayee discussed the "transformation" of U.S.-India relations during Vajpayee's visit to Washington in November 2001. The current U.S. National Security Strategy (p. 27) states that the United States has "undertaken a transformation in its bilateral relationship with India."

Pakistan – Key Indicators and Forecasts

Economy and Trade	2002[a]	2003[b]	2004[b]
GDP ($tr) / (PPP GDP)	<0.1 (PPP GDP in 2002 = $0.3 tr)		
GDP growth (%)	4.6	5.0	5.1
Inflation (%)	3.1	3.9	4.0
Budget balance (% of GDP)	4.0	3.0	0.8
Major export destinations (2001)	U.S. (24%), UAE (8%), Britain (7%)		

Population and Energy	2002[a]	2005[b]	2010[b]
Population (m)	147.7	156.7	171.4
Population growth (%)	2.1	1.9	1.7
Oil production (m bbl/d)	<0.1	...	...
Oil consumption (m bbl/d)	0.4	...	...

Politics	
President	Gen. Pervez Musharraf (since Oct 1999)
Dominant party	Pakistan People's Party (since 2002)
Next election	October 2007

Military	
Armed forces (2002)	619,000
Defense expenditure (2001)	$2.4 bn (17.0% of GDP)
Conventional capabilities	Large army with some modern equipment Military under strain from multiple missions, small improvements in naval capabilities
Weapons of mass destruction	Small nuclear weapons arsenal

Source: The National Bureau of Asian Research, compiled from International Monetary Fund, *World Economic Outlook*; Central Intelligence Agency, *World Factbook*; U.S. Census Bureau, *International Data Base*; Energy Information Administration, *Country Analysis Brief—Pakistan*; International Institute of Strategic Studies, *The Military Balance*. Notes: a) Data for 2002 may be estimates; b) Data for 2003, 2004, 2005, and 2010 are projections. Additional data on Pakistan are available in the Strategic Asia database at <http://strategicasia.nbr.org>.

A STATE UNDER STRESS

John H. Gill

ABSTRACT

Pakistan faces two critical near-term regional security issues: bilateral tensions with India and the reconstruction of Afghanistan. Developing and sustaining Pakistan's progress toward political moderation and economic modernization looms as an equally important security challenge in the medium term. The most direct threats to Pakistan stem from internal problems. Violent Islamists with a variety of domestic, Afghan, Kashmiri, and millenarian agendas undermine the state, endanger its citizens, and threaten its neighbors. Disturbing social indicators compound the growing radicalism and rising anti-American sentiment. Pakistan's future will therefore rest upon its ability to defeat the forces of extremism and to direct its resources toward pressing domestic issues such as education, rule of law, poverty, and population growth. The international community can help by supporting the rebuilding of Pakistan's civil society and governing institutions, but Pakistan's behavior on issues relating to terrorism, proliferation, and democracy will be crucial in determining the level of external assistance that is available.

John (Jack) Gill is a U.S. Army South Asia Foreign Area Officer on the faculty of the Near East-South Asia Center for Strategic Studies at the National Defense University. He would like to express his appreciation to Stephen Cohen, Richard Ellings, Aaron Friedberg, Neil Joeck, Deepa Ollapally, Marvin Weinbaum, Michael Wills, and an anonymous reader for their insights in reviewing this chapter.

Introduction

Pakistan finds itself at the intersection of two immediate and vital South Asian security issues: bilateral tensions with India and the reconstruction of Afghanistan. If these two issues dominate the short term, a third crucial issue for South Asian and indeed global security looms in the medium term: developing and sustaining "Pakistan's progress toward political moderation and economic modernization."[1] While the India-Pakistan question has been discussed in the preceding chapter, this chapter will address internal threats to Pakistan's national stability and coherence in the context of the situation in Afghanistan and its critical ramifications for Pakistan. From the U.S. perspective, Pakistan will also continue to be a crucial pillar in the global war on terrorism through the short term. Additionally, the danger of proliferation will attract high-level attention from Washington and other capitals for the foreseeable future.

Domestic Challenges: The Threat from Within

Pakistan in the early twenty-first century is a country under severe pressure. Although the rivalry with India colors much of Islamabad's worldview and its responses to challenges, the most direct threats to the Pakistani state and society stem from internal problems, especially from militant extremists who seek to promote their causes through violence, often under the cloak of radical Islam. These extremists threaten Pakistan's domestic order and international standing from three directions: continuing terrorism in Afghanistan, domestic sectarian violence, and insurgency in Kashmir.[2] They also endanger the tentative attempts to revive Pakistan's economy. Often loosely termed "jihadis," many of the groups and individuals involved in these causes are closely interlinked and move across the porous inter-group boundaries with ease. Using violence as their means of expression, they foster a culture of radicalism and intolerance, defying government control and fraying the fabric of Pakistan's civil society. In the wake of the October 2002 elections, some of these groups now have a significant voice in Pakistan's national policy-making as well as in the local governments of the two provinces bordering Afghanistan. Moreover, the severe challenges posed by radical groups threaten to undermine progress made across the border in Afghanistan just as they complicate relations with India, the United States, and the rest of the world community.

To some extent, these problems are manifestations of the definitional questions concerning the role of the military and religion in the state that have dogged Pakistan since its inception, problems that have become more acute since September 2001 and will remain key variables in Pakistan's political calculus as the military government attempts to incorporate some democratic reforms without losing ultimate authority over key policy decisions.[3] At its founding in 1947, Pakistan was faced with vital security concerns, but lacked a strong civilian institutional base and quickly lost its key civilian leaders. As a result, the military, specifically the army, played a disproportionate role in setting the country's priorities and has ruled Pakistan directly or indirectly for most of its history. The appropriate role of the uniformed services in governance has never been resolved satisfactorily, but the military's institutional interests have often dominated the government's domestic and foreign agendas. This issue lies at the heart of the current debate between the regime of President and Chief of the Army Staff General Pervez Musharraf and opposition members of the National Assembly. Similarly, the relationship of the state to Islam has been a subject of debate since 1947. Established as the putative homeland for the subcontinent's Muslims, Pakistan still struggles to reconcile competing interpretations of Islam with the demands of domestic governance (most visibly in the legal code and banking practices) and international affairs. The question of how Islam relates to the functions of the state is also linked to the national legislature, which was re-established through elections in October 2002. For the first time, Islamist parties are strongly represented in the legislature, and they have been among the most vocal opponents of President Musharraf's domestic and international policies.

Trouble on the Western Frontier: Continued Support for the Taliban

Pakistan has been central to the success of coalition military operations in Afghanistan (*Operation Enduring Freedom*) and the U.S. war on terrorism. By providing transit, logistical, and basing support to coalition forces and by cooperating in the apprehension of several hundred terrorist suspects, including some very senior Al Qaeda operatives, Islamabad has garnered lavish praise from Washington for its "absolutely magnificent" assistance.[4] Beyond comforting words, Pakistan has gained substantial economic relief since aligning itself with the United States in the war on terrorism, most dramatically in the form of the five-year $3 billion package announced during Musharraf's June 24, 2003 visit to Camp David. Even before the Camp David meeting, Islamabad had benefited from measures such as a $600 million grant that gave critical balance-of-payment and budget support (November 2001), the extension of payment terms for $3 billion in credits (August 2002), the provision of credits through the Export-Import Bank and the Overseas Private Investment Corporation, U.S. support in international lending institutions, and forgiveness of $1 billion in debts. Furthermore, Washington has established a five-year, $100 million education project and a $73 million program to assist in border control. The latter included provision of helicopters, surveillance aircraft, communications equipment, and 1,000 ground vehicles. Of course, in the long run, the greatest benefit to Islamabad is that the 400 to 500 individuals captured thus far are no longer free to foment unrest or perpetrate terrorist acts in Pakistan. As U.S. Deputy Secretary of State Armitage has noted, "Pakistan has very high stakes in the outcome" of the war on terrorism, as success in that war has a direct bearing on the stability of Pakistan itself.[5]

In addition to arresting terrorists inside Pakistan, coordination between U.S. and Pakistani forces along the rugged Afghan-Pakistan border has been, and will remain, an important element of American operations in Afghanistan. The United States continues to "regard the Pakistani government as a partner," but the presence of "some key Taliban figures" in Pakistan and recurring attacks against coalition and Afghan troops by former Taliban, Al Qaeda, and other extremists based in Pakistan could become a serious point of friction between the two capitals.[6] Indeed, the former commander of U.S. forces in Afghanistan, Lieutenant General Dan K. McNeill, has criticized Islamabad for not controlling the movement of terrorists and militants across the border from their havens in Pakistan.[7] Afghan President Hamid Karzai and UN representative Ambassador Lakhdar Brahimi have also complained to Pakistan. Terrorism was a major theme during Karzai's April 2003 visit to Islamabad, and he returned to Kabul with promises of greater cooperation in the arrest and extradition of "criminals of war against the Afghan people," as well as plans for biannual consultations on bilateral security issues and a new trilateral commission with the United States and Pakistan to work on border matters. Border clashes, the attack on the Pakistani embassy in Kabul, and flares in rhetoric, however, show that Pakistan-Afghan relations remain tentative and vulnerable to shocks.[8]

These challenges on its western border illuminate a vital national security interest for Islamabad: the promotion of stability and development in Afghanistan. For some in Pakistan, especially in the border provinces of Balochistan and the Northwest Frontier Province (NWFP), however, the Taliban represented a desirable political order that should be replicated in Pakistan. These groups saw the swift coalition victory as a dire threat. Historically opposed to U.S. global and regional policies, they have responded to events in Afghanistan with intense anti-Americanism and continued support or tolerance for attacks against coalition forces and the Karzai government. Many of these Pakistanis are ethnic Pushtuns, and their links to fellow Pushtuns in Afghanistan reinforce their inclination to counter the U.S. presence on their borders and derail reconstruction efforts under the new Afghan administration. They are particularly angered by what they perceive as the under-representation of Pushtuns in Kabul. The infusion of refugee Taliban and Al Qaeda members since the fall of the Taliban regime has left some border towns looking like scenes "from the old days of the Taliban in Afghanistan," full of unemployed, unattached men with little clear future and no love for the United States.[9] As many Pakistani commentators note, instability in Afghanistan is a direct threat to Pakistan's vital national interests.[10] The activities of Taliban sympathizers not only prompt unrest in Pakistan's two western provinces, hamper bilateral trade, attenuate the federal government's authority, and mar the country's international image, they also cripple Islamabad's efforts to promote a greater Pushtun role in Kabul and to balance Indian influence in the new Afghanistan.[11] Predilections to interfere in Afghanistan, a December 2002 non-interference treaty notwithstanding, could have particularly dangerous repercussions, as any instability across the border is likely to be reflected inside Pakistan itself.

The Home Front: Political Crisis, Intolerance, and Sectarian Violence

In the domestic arena, extremism manifests itself in the broad contours of national politics and in brutal sectarian violence. The October 2002 national and provincial elections, as noted above, brought Islamist parties into unprecedented prominence in the National Assembly and in the two provinces bordering Afghanistan. A precarious alliance of six parties known as the Muttahida Majlis-e-Amal (the United Council for Action or MMA), with a history of supporting the Taliban, denouncing the United States, and questioning Musharraf's limited reform initiatives, now governs the NWFP, wields influence in Balochistan as a partner in the province's ruling coalition, and has an important role in Islamabad. At the federal level, the MMA has joined the parties headed by exiled former prime ministers Nawaz Sharif and Benazir Bhutto in challenging Musharraf over the powers of the president's office, the army's role in policy-making, and Musharraf's continuance as both president and chief of the army staff.[12] This evolving clash of interests poses a serious problem for Pakistan's political structures, but may not result in a complete break between the army and the MMA. Although the Islamist parties that have formed the MMA have attacked Musharraf for his secular intentions and his policy reversal on the Taliban, they have been closely linked to the military for many years, serving the army as a useful ally against the two secular mainstream parties that have traditionally occupied the political center.[13] Indeed, the MMA's present strength owes more to the inability of the two national parties to compete and to the "first-past-the-post" electoral system than it does to the inherent appeal of the MMA parties themselves. As long as these two centrist parties remain a potential threat to the military's institutional interests, the Islamist groups, whether amalgamated as the MMA or not, will continue to have value as political allies, even if only on an issue-by-issue basis.[14] However, if not carefully managed, this complex situation has the potential to spin out of control, extending the political stalemate and possibly leading to the collapse of Prime Minister Mir Zafarullah Khan Jamali's government.[15]

The members of the MMA were expected to moderate their agendas as they ensconced themselves in the nation's capital, but, instead, they have reinforced the negative aspects, especially domestic intolerance, resistance to U.S. demands on nuclear proliferation issues, dangerous meddling in Afghanistan, and maximalist positions vis-à-vis India and Kashmir.[16] Some of these worrisome tendencies are already evident in new ordinances and legislation in the NWFP. Likewise, their lenient and possibly supportive attitude toward Islamist groups is detrimental to Pakistan's domestic stability. Although the Islamist parties do not control the resuscitated national legislature, they have already contributed to a deadlock in parliament, will continue to shape much of the policy debate in Islamabad, and will impose significant political costs should the government attempt to infringe on what they perceive as their parochial interests.

With its new role in the provincial governments of Balochistan and the NWFP (where the federal government's writ is often tenuous at best), the MMA could also hamper efforts to capture fugitive Taliban and Al Qaeda members and could undermine Islamabad's domestic agenda. Many Pakistanis and foreign observers see the MMA as a threat to "civil liberties, freedom of expression, legal reforms, and religious tolerance," especially with respect to the role of women in society.[17] Commenting in early 2003, for example, a Pakistani editorialist wrote "Our survival lies in containing the nuisance value of our extremists who use religion for narrow, selfish political goals."[18] These concerns were reinforced when, in the spring of 2003, the NWFP government made highly publicized steps to enforce strict interpretations of Islam by introducing a "vice and virtue organization" reminiscent of the eponymous Taliban agency. It remains to be seen if measures to curb supposedly lurid advertising, enforce the offering of prayers, ban music, and curtail the consumption of alcohol will remain temporary, symbolic showpieces or whether such moves are the first phase of a program that will extend into more permanent practices that undermine Pakistan's nascent moves toward democracy.[19] In the context of the war on terrorism, however, this action by the NWFP government poses a direct challenge to Musharraf's efforts to restart the Pakistani economy and burnish the country's image as "a tolerant, progressive, and dynamic Islamic state."[20]

Extremism inside Pakistan also manifests itself in brutal sectarian violence between radical Shi'a and Sunni groups. The murder of some 50 Shi'a worshippers at a Quetta mosque in July 2003 is but one example of the bloody gangland-style warfare that takes a heavy physical and psychological toll on both the Sunni majority and the minority Shi'a community (approximately 20 percent of the total population). In addition to its repercussions for law and order, this violence damages Pakistan's international image and contributes to the exodus of educated elites, draining some of the most qualified human resources from the labor force and society at large.

Insurgency in Kashmir: Baleful Impact on Pakistan

The insurgency in Indian Kashmir also has deleterious domestic ramifications for Pakistan. One of the most respected U.S. scholars of South Asia, Stephen P. Cohen, argues, for example, that the benefits of supporting militants on the other side of the line of control (LOC) are questionable: "Most modern westernized Pakistanis are worried about a backlash in Pakistan itself and even some of the military are worried about this."[21] Given the shadowy connections among the various extremist groups in Pakistan, it seems improbable that support for the Kashmir insurgency can be isolated from other dangerous trends, either among Pakistan's domestic sectarian groups or those with international objectives in Afghanistan and elsewhere.[22] Many of the groups engaged in the "jihad" in Kashmir espouse sweepingly radical Islamist causes that contribute to the polarization and radicalization of political thinking inside Pakistan and could easily translate into a serious terrorist threat to the government in Islamabad and to the country's stability overall. In early 2003, for example, the founder of one prominent group stated: "We must fight against the evil trio of America, Israel, and India...the need for jihad against India is paramount," adding that "suicide attack is the best form of jihad."[23] As is often the case with insurgent movements, sympathetic national governments seldom, if ever, have full control over the insurgents' actions and intentions, particularly when the militant agendas are as extreme as those promulgated by some of the groups active in Indian Kashmir.[24] Even if the army itself is not "moving in the direction of radical Islam," the effect on Pakistan's key institutions of governance cannot fail to be negative.[25] There is also a grave danger of radicalizing the Kashmiris—on both sides of the LOC—and thereby destroying the unique culture of the region. As Cohen commented in a different interview, "In regard to tangible support [for militants in Kashmir], there is realization in Pakistan that it is counterproductive to Pakistan's security," at least among some Pakistanis.[26] At present, however, the standard, maximalist policy formulations continue to dominate the general discourse on Kashmir. A more open policy debate of options and alternatives could stimulate creative thinking that would benefit both Pakistan in particular and regional stability in general.

In the larger picture of Pakistan, the growth of destabilizing extremism is compounded by disturbing social indicators that have devastating socio-economic impact. Pakistan, for example, lags in the development of its substantial human capital, particularly with regard to women. The public education system is stagnant, leaving adult literacy at approximately 50 percent for men and only 24 percent for women.[27] The child mortality rate (age zero to five) of 126 per 1,000 is symbolic of the huge gaps in health care, while the 38 percent of the population below the World Bank's poverty line highlights a worrisome situation that is unlikely to improve under the prevailing economic conditions.[28] Law and order problems and the absence of many basic governmental services are other serious impediments to progress.[29] Critical domestic priorities therefore include revitalizing public education, reforming the police and judiciary, expanding the government's ability to collect taxes, building a public health system, and reducing a birth rate that could put Pakistan ahead of Russia in population before the middle of the century. (For more on this, see the chapter on demographic trends in this volume.) Societal indicators such as literacy rates illustrate the long-term erosion of government services and the need for institution building, but reviving the economy and containing extremism are the more immediate and urgent challenges facing the administration in Islamabad. These problems are not new, but they have been exacerbated and made more urgent by the war on terrorism and the conflict in Afghanistan.

The Economy: Improving but Fragile

Pakistan's macroeconomic indicators have shown considerable improvement since the autumn of 2002. Current forecasts project a growth rate of 4.5 percent or slightly better for 2003 (up from 3.6 percent the previous year), and the possibility of reaching 5 percent or better in 2004. These figures represent a significant shift for an economy that recorded a rate of only 2.7 percent growth in 2001. Moreover, foreign exchange reserves are approaching the $10 billion mark, three times the amount available in September 2001, and closing in on the target of a reserve equivalent to eleven month's worth of imports. Partly the fruit of governmental reform policies and International Monetary Fund strictures, these favorable indicators also derive from the coincidence of several fortuitous circumstances: the end of a long drought that crippled the crucial agriculture sector, much higher remittances from overseas Pakistanis, timely debt rescheduling, and the repeated provision of large foreign grants. Exports, led by finished textile products, also grew. Increased quotas, particularly from the EU, were a key factor in the performance of textiles (which grew by 16.4 percent), but primary commodity exports (especially rice, cotton, and wheat) also expanded. Growth in the service sector, on the other hand, is expected to be considerably more modest (approximately 5 percent) over the coming year. Foreign direct investment, expected to reach $600 million in mid-2003, could experience a significant increase over the next two years, particularly if boosted by the planned privatization of large state enterprises such as Pakistan State Oil.[30]

This relatively bright economic outlook, however, is founded on several critical assumptions. In the first place, the domestic political scene must remain stable. Collapse of the civilian portion of the current government or an extended impasse between President Musharraf and the National Assembly will confirm the uncertainty and low investor confidence that prevailed in late 2002 and early 2003. The second basic assumption is stability in foreign relations, particularly in the India-Pakistan dynamic. A return to the confrontational rhetoric and provocative military activity that characterized 2002 will have a disastrous effect on Pakistan's economic prospects.[31] Severe deterioration in Afghanistan's security situation would also have a negative impact for Pakistan's economy, just as it is likely to benefit greatly if conditions improve for its western neighbor. Third, foreign and domestic investors are likely to seek other opportunities if Pakistan appears to be a haven for extremist groups whose radical pronouncements and violent actions threaten the national government and foreign interests. The Taliban-like laws promulgated in the NWFP in May 2003 could make many potential investors reluctant to commit their assets to ventures in that province and in Pakistan as a whole.

Continued economic improvement is thus contingent upon some stability in domestic politics, reduced tensions with India, diminution in the prevailing level of violence, and the extent of extremist influence inside Pakistan. Furthermore, Pakistan must confront a number of other major economic challenges: high poverty indices, low levels of private investment, inadequate basic social services, a dilapidated educational system, weak revenue collection, underutilization of funds, and the drain of large state-owned companies.[32] The investment climate is also tainted by decrepit infrastructure, widespread corruption, complex and outdated regulations, dense thickets of bureaucracy, legal impediments, potential changes in banking practices, and weaknesses in the rule of law.[33] These problems highlight the importance of political and security factors to Pakistan's economy and suggest caution in assessing the durability and longevity of the notable economic achievements of the past year.

Foreign Relations: Continuity and Change

The general outlines of Pakistan's international relations are unlikely to change significantly over the next several years, and Islamabad will continue to evaluate most of its foreign ties in terms of their significance to the India-Pakistan dynamic. In addition to Washington, Beijing and Riyadh will remain Islamabad's principal international partners. China will continue to be Pakistan's most important external source of conventional military hardware and an economic partner, helping with the development of a new port at Gwadar and other projects. At the same time, however, Sino-Indian relations are improving and Beijing will not look favorably on what it perceives as adventuristic or provocative action by Pakistan in its relations with New Delhi. Reflecting its sensitivity to Muslim separatist tendencies in Xinjiang, China will also monitor the presence of extremists in Pakistan. These developments will not alter the Sino-Pakistani relationship fundamentally in the near term, but they suggest the limits inherent in this strategic alliance. The traditionally close ties with Saudi Arabia will remain central to Islamabad's international agenda, although the relationship may acquire a new dimension as the war on terrorism unfolds. Likewise, Pakistan will work hard to maintain its links with other Arab states and its role in the Organization of the Islamic Conference. As in the past, however, it will find only marginal interest and little substantive response to its calls for action on the Kashmir issue.

Little change is likely in relations with Russia given Moscow's close ties to New Delhi and differences over the future of Afghanistan.[34] Terrorism, the unrest in Afghanistan, and Pakistan's domestic stability will continue to overshadow interactions with the European Union states. Musharraf's stops in Europe during his July 2003 foreign trip notwithstanding, these relations will not move beyond limited military transactions and economic assistance.

Mutual suspicion will remain the fundamental theme in Iran-Pakistan interactions. The two countries will cooperate on some specific issues, maintain generally friendly contacts, and avoid active hostility, but contending interests in Afghanistan, worries about growing Iranian-Indian relations, anti-Shi'a violence in Pakistan, and Islamabad's concerns about Tehran's links to Shi'a groups in Pakistan will limit broader cooperation.

Looking northwest, Islamabad will have important choices to make as it charts a course for relations with the new Afghanistan. Setting aside a bitter history (dating from the war against the Soviet Union) will not be easy for either country: Pakistanis see India and other adversaries behind the Northern Alliance elements in Kabul, and many in the Karzai regime are convinced that Pakistan is attempting to destabilize their fledgling government. Cooperation, however, is clearly the most productive path for both countries and the policy that offers Pakistan the best avenue to promote its interests (such as expanded Pushtun representation) across the border. This implies greater Pakistani efforts to eliminate remnant Taliban and Al Qaeda elements in the restive border districts, despite difficult terrain and local opposition to government military operations in traditional tribal areas. The potential for friction inherent in such operations may be offset somewhat by the opportunity for Islamabad to extend its writ into previously inaccessible districts.

The United States and Pakistan: Building Institutions and a Long-Term Relationship

U.S. relations with Pakistan have changed dramatically since September 2001. Facing an ultimatum from Washington in the wake of the terrorist attacks on the United States, Musharraf turned Islamabad's Afghanistan policy around, abandoning the Taliban and accepting U.S. forces on Pakistani soil to conduct the war across the border. In return, Pakistan, a near-pariah before September 11, 2001, has become a key U.S. partner in the fight against terrorism. Washington has conditionally lifted the layers of sanctions that had burdened Pakistan for years, resumed military-to-military contact, provided some limited military hardware, provided $1 billion in debt relief, and supported crucial international loans to keep the Pakistani economy afloat. In many areas, therefore, bilateral relations with the United States have "broadened significantly" since September 2001, and Washington is looking for "the rebirth of a long-term partnership" between the two countries.[35]

It is noteworthy that internal Pakistani opposition to this dramatic policy shift toward the United States was neither as widespread nor as violent as many observers predicted and that the government was able to squelch protest quickly. This experience suggests that the strength of these groups has been overstated and that Islamabad has more flexibility in dealing with restive domestic elements than is generally acknowledged.[36] This governmental success notwithstanding, there is a strong undercurrent of anti-American sentiment across the Pakistani polity. As demonstrated by the attacks on foreigners during 2001 and 2002 and, to a lesser extent, by the October 2002 parliamentary elections, radical elements can tap this undercurrent to challenge the government in Islamabad as well as U.S. interests. The war in Iraq reinvigorated opposition to the United States among many groups, while the passage of time and inadequate enforcement has allowed pro-Taliban elements to regroup inside Pakistan and launch attacks aimed at destabilizing the Kabul government. Thus far, Islamabad's efforts to limit the appeal and expansion of Islamist extremism inside Pakistan have not been notably successful. Indeed, the release of many suspected radicals, including high-profile leaders of several dangerous, U.S.-designated terrorist organizations, could stimulate the growth of these groups.

Interests and Issues:
A Healthy State and a Stable Region

Among the many U.S. interests in Pakistan, four stand out as especially critical over the next three to five years: sustaining cooperation in the global war on terrorism, reducing India-Pakistan tensions, bolstering Pakistan's progress toward democracy, and preventing the proliferation of missiles and weapons of mass destruction. Just as the United States seeks to restore security and stability to Afghanistan so that it does not revert to a terrorist haven, U.S. policy must aim to preserve Pakistan as a partner in the war on terrorism, promote democracy, foster development, and preclude a descent into extremism and lawlessness. Although the scope and depth of the bilateral relationship between Washington and Islamabad has evolved in favorable directions since the opening of the war on terrorism, the time available to provide tangible benefits for the Pakistani people is limited. A recent study concludes that Pakistan is not now a radical state, that its society is not presently dominated by Muslim extremists, and that the danger of a chaotic "deluge" following General Musharraf's administration, while not zero, has been exaggerated. Similarly, an anti-Musharraf coup is improbable, but not impossible, over the near term. Musharraf has stated his intention to serve out his five-year term (through 2007) and his most likely replacement under the current dispensation would be another army officer—albeit one perhaps less inclined to cooperate with Washington—rather than a revolutionary Islamic regime.[37] However, that situation could change for the worse in the medium term. Unless its course can be corrected during the coming five to eight years, Pakistan "could truly become one of the world's most dangerous states."[38] Such a development—an especially grim prospect given Pakistan's nuclear arsenal—would have an immediate and injurious impact on Pakistan's future, India-Pakistan tensions, Afghanistan's stability, and almost every U.S. interest in South Asia. These considerations highlight the vital importance of helping Pakistan avoid a dire domestic future that would have international repercussions. As another U.S. scholar notes "Pakistan's recovery as a healthy state with functioning institutions is a prerequisite for keeping South Asia free of terrorism."[39]

As in Afghanistan, with which it is intimately linked, the most promising strategies in Pakistan are those that strengthen the country's institutions and civil society. While bolstering the economy, the United States can make a crucial contribution through support to education, population control, public health, the police, and the judiciary under a general program of advancing democratic values and structures.[40] To make Pakistan's legislature more effective, for example, the United States might be able to cooperate with allies from the British Commonwealth who have expertise and experience in managing Westminster-style governing bodies. Education is especially critical to weaning young Pakistanis away from the radical and intolerant ideologies propagated in some *madrassahs.* For many lower income families, *madrassahs* (Islamic "seminaries") offer the only semblance of education, but few equip Pakistan's youth for the future and some promote radical ideologies that fuel domestic sectarian violence and international terrorism. Musharraf's modest *madrassah* reforms have stalled and, with so many Islamist members in the new national and provincial assemblies, are unlikely to advance unless outside allies provide substantial incentives. Furthermore, a revived public education system would provide the next generation with the practical modern skills required for a competitive economy and could be a crucial factor in slowing population growth. Measures such as debt relief are, and should remain, a critical component of U.S. policy, but they are invisible to the average Pakistani. Steps to reconstruct institutions, revive civil society, and improve quality of life, on the other hand, will provide clear benefits to ordinary citizens, creating alternatives to radicalism and generating hope for the future.

Bilateral U.S.-Pakistan defense cooperation programs are an important supplement to other policy measures on the state-to-state level, especially as a vehicle to build bridges of understanding and to reduce misperceptions. Military activities should stress professional exchanges, strategic dialogue, peacekeeping, counter-narcotics programs, and cooperation against terrorism rather than hardware. The reinvigoration of the bilateral Defense Consultative Group during 2002 has been an important step in this area. The renewal of bilateral exercises and training opportunities as well as the sale of C-130 transport aircraft and a menu of border security equipment items will help add weight to the relationship. This broad U.S.-Pakistan interaction, especially the strategic dialogue, will provide a venue to revive earlier discussions on export controls for nuclear and missile technology with the goal of countering the proliferation of WMD and missiles.

External variables will also be important in Pakistan's development over the next several years. Events in Afghanistan and India will be especially significant, and U.S. interaction with those two countries can promote stability in Pakistan and greater security for the region as a whole. In Afghanistan, improvements in security and economic conditions that demonstrably enhance the lives of common Afghans will have a reciprocal effect across the border. Just as progress in Pakistan has a salutary effect on Afghanistan's evolution, clear changes for the better in Afghanistan will dilute anti-Americanism, reduce inclinations toward extremism, and open new legitimate economic opportunities, particularly in the two restive provinces on the Afghan frontier. The state of India-Pakistan relations will be equally important. Relative quiet along the LOC and a substantive dialogue with India will address a major grievance expressed by radical Islamists and a cause with which many moderate Pakistanis sympathize. It could also lead to the imposition of effective controls on militant organizations, especially their external activities, and would probably promote greater movement toward democracy inside Pakistan.[41] These external considerations illuminate the crucial significance of an accelerated U.S. and global commitment to the reconstruction of Afghanistan and to the start of a sustainable, institutionalized India-Pakistan dialogue process that covers all key bilateral issues, including Kashmir.

Despite Pakistan's importance to the United States, Washington's efforts to build a robust and lasting relationship could be in danger if Islamabad is perceived to be moving in directions inimical to U.S. interests.[42] Most important will be unflagging pursuit of anti-terrorism goals in Pakistan and around the region. Failure to fulfill the pledges to end support for infiltration across the LOC into India, for instance, would have a severely detrimental effect on bilateral ties. Likewise, continued cooperation with U.S. operations in Afghanistan and support for the stability of the Karzai government will be central to further progress in the relationship. Proliferation is another area of concern.[43] The United States has been apprehensive about Pakistan's connections with North Korea, in particular, and has received firm assurances from Islamabad. Nevertheless, any suggestion regarding proliferation of missiles, WMD, or related technology would likely be viewed as a grave breach of the relationship.[44] Progress toward democracy will also be an important consideration, especially given the menace that Taliban sympathizers and other extremists present to civil society.

These issues pose significant challenges to Pakistan as they involve achieving a balance between vocal domestic interests and commitments to Washington. The U.S. government's annual budget cycle will focus attention on these high-visibility issues at least once a year as Congress reviews and approves federal expenditures. To overcome these challenges and solidify the new relationship, both sides will need to work hard to avoid misunderstanding. At several key junctures in the past, Pakistan has misread U.S. intentions or ignored warnings from Washington, leading to confusion, recrimination, and instability. All too often, the result has been the inadvertent strengthening of those who advocated risky military strategies rather than political or diplomatic resolution of issues.[45] The stakes for both countries are now too high to permit misinterpretation in either capital.

The United States will continue to be concerned with Pakistan's development. Coupled with action in Afghanistan, Washington has a vital interest in supporting political, economic, and social progress in Pakistan to neutralize radical political elements, to maintain Pakistan as a stable, cooperative member of the coalition against terrorism, and to underwrite a moderate, responsible government in Islamabad. Steady movement toward democracy and the construction of effective civil institutions, especially a reliable public education system, will be critical to helping Pakistan cope with the future. Key external variables will continue to be Pakistan's interactions with India and its behavior along the LOC in Kashmir, its relations with Afghanistan, and the status of its missile/WMD activities. Pakistan's domestic political stalemate will complicate efforts to address these difficult issues, distracting the government and creating reasons to eschew or delay tough decisions. However, if disruptions in these critical areas can be avoided, the United States has an opportunity to help Pakistan set itself on a new course toward a progressive, tolerant, dynamic, and modernizing state as part of a comprehensive strategy that embraces accelerated support for stability in Afghanistan and the start of a substantive India-Pakistan dialogue process.

Endnotes

1 Assistant Secretary of State Christina Rocca, "Foreign Assistance Programs in South Asia," testimony before the Senate Committee on Foreign Relations, March 26, 2003 at <www.state.gov>.

2 In his now famous speech of January 12, 2002, Pakistan's President Pervez Musharraf outlined the threat posed by extremism inside Pakistan and his vision of a "progressive and dynamic Islamic welfare state," which is characterized by an "environment of tolerance, maturity, responsibility, patience and understanding" (English text available at <www.pak.gov.pk>).

3 Stephen P. Cohen, "The Nation and the State of Pakistan," *Washington Quarterly*, Summer 2002. Also Mandavi Mehta and Teresita Schaffer, *Islam in Pakistan: Unity and Contradictions*, Center for Strategic and International Studies, October 2002; and Mahnaz Ispahani, "Pakistan: the cauldron," *Friday Times*, June 27, 2003.

4 Deputy Secretary of State Richard Armitage in an interview with GEO TV, May 8, 2003 <www.state.gov>.

5 Armitage interview with GEO TV. For information on U.S. assistance to Pakistan see "Bilateral Multi-Year Assistance: U.S. and Pakistan," *White House Fact Sheet*, June 24, 2003, and transcript of President Bush remarks at Camp

David, June 24, 2003, both at <www.state.gov>.

[6] U.S. envoy Zalmay Khalilzad as quoted in Carlotta Gall, "Terrorists still a threat, U.S. official tells Afghans," *New York Times*, February 11, 2003.

[7] General McNeill quoted in Chris Kaul, "Troops could leave Afghanistan in 2004," *Los Angeles Times*, May 5, 2003. See also his comments in Eric Schmitt, "General urges foreigners to aid Afghans," *New York Times*, July 9, 2003; and George J. Tenet, "The Worldwide Threat in 2003," testimony before the Senate Select Committee on Intelligence, February 11, 2003 <www.cia.gov>.

[8] Karzai quoted in Kathy Gannon, "Afghanistan, Pakistan meet on anti-terror," Associated Press, April 23, 2003; Carlotta Gall, "A pledge to halt Taliban raids from Pakistan," *New York Times*, June 18, 2003; and "Unnecessary tensions with Kabul," *Daily Times*, July 9, 2003.

[9] Carlotta Gall, "In Pakistan border towns, Taliban has a resurgence," *New York Times*, May 6, 2003.

[10] Foreign Minister Kasuri commented in April 2003: "Any situation in Afghanistan is bound to have an effect on Pakistan and we are worried, but there is no cause for alarm yet." Interview cited in B. Muralidhar Reddy, "Cross-border infiltration down: Kasuri," *The Hindu*, April 10, 2003.

[11] Former Foreign Secretary Najmuddin A. Shaikh, "These Afghan spillovers," *Dawn*, May 21, 2003.

[12] These issues are generally bundled together under the rubric LFO (Legal Framework Order), the set of provisions Musharraf promulgated by presidential decree just prior to the October 2002 elections. The LFO measures enhance the power of the president and institutionalize the role of the army in governance. Musharraf and his supporters consider them part of the constitution, but the MMA vehemently objects to this interpretation. Pakistani commentator Ahmed Rashid anticipated the 2003 political crisis in an insightful piece published the day Pakistan went to the polls. Rashid, "Pakistan on the edge," *New York Review of Books*, October 10, 2002.

[13] See detailed analysis in International Crisis Group, "Pakistan: The Mullahs and the Military," *ICG Asia Report*, no. 49, March 20, 2003, pp. 2–9. See also Dilshad Azeem, "MMA likely to give Musharraf till August 14," *The Nation*, May 19, 2003. The army may, however, seek to clip the MMA's political wings by disqualifying some of its members from political office. Rafaqat Ali, "Fate of MMA MPs hangs in balance," *Dawn*, May 19, 2003.

[14] Note that the MMA does not have a majority in Pakistan's 100-seat Senate as some analysts had feared. Prime Minister Jamali's party gained a simple majority in February 2003 senate elections. Paul Anderson "PM's party takes hold in Pakistan," BBC, February 25, 2003.

[15] Najam Sethi, "Ruling the roost," *Friday Times*, May 23, 2003; Husain Haqqani, "The deep rot within," *Indian Express*, May 28, 2003; and Hasan Askari Rizvi, "No gains from confrontation," *Daily Times*, June 9, 2003. The two mainstream parties are the Pakistan People's Party (PPP) and the Pakistan Muslim League (PML). Jamali heads a faction of the Pakistan Muslim League called the PML-Qaid-e-Azam or PML-Q.

[16] The July 2003 trip to India by a key MMA leader, however, indicates at least some flexibility, if only to secure domestic political advantage.

[17] International Crisis Group, "Pakistan: The Mullahs and the Military," p. i; and Judy Barsalou, "Islamic Extremists: How Do They Mobilize Support?" *United States Institute of Peace Special Report*, no. 89, July 2002.

[18] Retired Army officer Ikram Seghal, in "Re-Shaping Maps and Opinions," *Defence Journal*, May 2003.

[19] Iqbal Khattak, "NWFP okays 'vice and virtue' body," *Daily Times*, May 23, 2003.

[20] President Musharraf speech at Pakistan's National Defence College, May 26, 2003 as quoted in Rana Qaisar, "Economic sovereignty restored: Musharraf," *Daily Times*, May 27, 2003; Iqbal Khattak, "Talibanisation, not LFO, the real issue: Musharraf," *Daily Times*, June 11, 2003; and Mohammad Shehzad, "MMA causes U.S. \$200 million losses," *Friday Times*, June 20, 2003.

[21] Interview with Rahul Sagar, "Both India and Pakistan see their relationship with the U.S. as a zero-sum game," October 22, 2001 <www.tehelka.com>. Another prominent American scholar highlights the "awkward contradiction" in Pakistan's policies toward the Taliban and Al Qaeda on the one hand and Kashmir on the other. Robert G. Wirsing, *Kashmir: In the Shadow of War*, Armonk, N.Y.: M. E. Sharpe, 2003, p. 65.

[22] Teresita Schaffer, "U.S. Influence on Pakistan: Can Partners Have Divergent Priorities?" *Washington Quarterly*, Winter 2002–03, p. 175.

[23] Hafiz Mohammed Saeed, founder of the Lashkar-e-Toiba, in an interview with the *Friday Times* of Pakistan as quoted in Ajai Sahni, "Iraq Aftermath: Wishful Thinking," *South Asia Intelligence Review*, April 14, 2003. Another example is Farhan Reza, "Karachi clerics call for jihad against the U.S.," *Daily Times*, March 25, 2003. Pakistan's Foreign Minister Kasuri has played down Saeed's pronouncements: "Pakistan is a free country. Anybody can issue any statements. [But] we don't allow them to carry out any activity." Quoted in "Eleven die in Kashmir violence," BBC, May 19, 2003.

[24] Pakistani Prime Minister Jamali stated in early 2003 in reference to *jihadi* groups: "We can try to rein them in, make them understand. We don't have control over them." Quoted in "Terrorism in J&K outside our purview: Jamali," *Hindustan Times*, May 22, 2003. Foreign Minister Kasuri has made similar comments: "*Jihadis* don't take orders from the Pakistan government," in the guest column of the *Times of India*, May 11, 2003.

[25] Stephen P. Cohen, "Brookings Expert Holds Conference Call Previewing President Musharraf's Visit," February 12, 2002 <www.brook.edu>. Pakistani commentator Zubeida Mustafa writes ("What next in Kashmir?" *Dawn*, May 14, 2003) that Pakistan "must curb the militants who have found sanctuary on our soil," and "violence unleashed by non-state actors cannot be contained in one area." Analyst Ahmed Rashid has commented that "support for the war in Kashmir has not got Pakistan anything so far" and that "to make peace Pakistan has to put an end to any support for extremism." Quoted in Mohammed Shehzad, "Did Musharraf admit to existence of camps in AJK?" *Friday Times*, May 23, 2003. See other op-ed pieces in *The News* (M. B. Naqvi) on May 14 and 21, 2003; *Daily Times*, May 11, 2003; and *Dawn*, April 29, May 11, 12, 13, and 20, 2003. For insightful Indian analyses that cover Pakistani perspectives, see C. Raja Mohan, "Putting Pakistan first," *The Hindu*, May 8, 2003; and B.

Muralidhar Reddy, "Pakistan's albatross," *Frontline*, May 24, 2003.

[26] Comment during a Brookings Institution Press Briefing, "What Role Does the United States Have in the India-Pakistan Crisis?" June 11, 2002 at <www.brook.edu>. Calls for a different approach to the Kashmir issue are appearing in the mass-circulation vernacular press as well as English-language periodicals aimed at Pakistan's elites: John Lancaster, "Pakistanis weigh stance on Kashmir," *Washington Post*, May 28, 2003. See also "Out of Pakistan," *Washington Post* editorial, February 25, 2003.

[27] K. Alan Kronstadt, "Pakistan-U.S. Relations," *Issue Brief for Congress IB94041*, Congressional Research Service, September 24, 2002, p. 12.

[28] Figures from Amin M. Lakhani, "19 Kashmirs Pakistan isn't bothered about," *Indian Express*, September 17, 2002. Similar statistics are in the Pakistani government's 2003 *Human Development Report*. See "Pakistan will have a crisis if poverty persists," *Daily Times*, July 2, 2003.

[29] Tim McGirk, "To have and have not," *Time Asia*, June 16, 2003.

[30] Figures and analysis drawn from the Asian Development Bank's *Asian Development Outlook 2003*, pp. 129–34; Economist Intelligence Unit, *Pakistan Country Report*, April 2003; Saeed Azhar, "Digging itself out of debt," *Far Eastern Economic Review*, February 13, 2003; and Shahid Javed Burki, "Outlook better, brighter," *Dawn*, May 20, 2003. See Nadeem Malik, "Sustainability of growth faces challenges: Shaukat," *The News*, June 6, 2003.

[31] Shahid Javed Burki, "Terrorism's terrible toll," *Dawn*, May 27, 2003; and "Not good enough," editorial in *The Nation*, June 6, 2003.

[32] U.S. Ambassador Nancy Powell, remarks to the American Business Council of Pakistan, Karachi, January 23, 2003 <usembassy.state.gov/islamabad>. See "GDP growth target set at 5.3 percent," *The News*, May 25, 2003.

[33] Sultan Ahmed, "An illusion of prosperity," *Dawn*, May 15, 2003. Ahmed highlights the importance of investor confidence, citing a "credibility gap" he perceives between government projections and actual performance. See also Farhan Bokhari, "Tackling success," *The News*, May 15, 2003; and Masooda Bano, "Who is he fooling?" *The News*, April 11, 2003. Khaled Ahmed discusses some of the problems in possible changes in Pakistan's banking system in an interview with Harry Kreisler, February 19, 2002 <globetrotter.berkeley.edu>.

[34] Kavita Sangani and Terestia Schaffer, "The Changing Face of Russia-South Asia Relations," *South Asia Monitor*, no. 59 (June 1, 2003); and Rouben Azizian and Peter Vasilieff, "Russia and Pakistan: The Difficult Path to Rapprochement," *Asian Affairs*, Spring 2003.

[35] First quote from Assistant Secretary of State Christina Rocca, "United States Relations with South Asia," testimony before the House International Relations Committee Subcommittee on Asia and the Pacific, March 20, 2003 <www.state.gov>. Second quote from Ambassador Powell's remarks to the American Business Council of Pakistan, January 23, 2003 <www.usembassy.state.gov/islamabad>. Deputy Secretary Armitage called for building "a relationship that is deep, enduring, and long-lasting" in his interview with GEO TV, May 8, 2003.

[36] Stephen P. Cohen, "The Jihadist Threat to Pakistan," *Washington Quarterly*, Summer 2003, p. 8. See also an insightful report by the International Crisis

Group, "Pakistan: The Dangers of Conventional Wisdom," March 12, 2002; and Owen Bennett Jones, *Pakistan: The Eye of the Storm*, Cambridge. Mass.: Yale University Press, 2002, p. 25.

[37] Cohen, "Jihadist Threat," pp. 7–21.

[38] Cohen, "Jihadist Threat," p. 8. It should be noted that Musharraf has specifically denied any possibility of an extremist coup in Pakistan: "There is no danger of religious extremism or religious extremists taking over in Pakistan." Rana Qaisar, "Arms imbalance will raise nuke reliance: Musharraf," *Daily Times*, June 20, 2003.

[39] Schaffer, "U.S. Influence on Pakistan," p. 179.

[40] What the National Security Advisor, Condoleeza Rice, calls "important issues of democratization in Pakistan." Quoted in Sridhar Krishnaswami, "U.S. feels 'encouraged' by India, Pakistan moves," *The Hindu*, May 30, 2003.

[41] Cohen, "Jihadist Threat," p. 24.

[42] For U.S. thinking on this aspect of the relationship, see "Commitment Seen to New Relationship between U.S., Pakistan," transcript of a background briefing by a senior administration official, June 24, 2003, U.S. State Department <usinfo.state.gov>. The official stated that the $3 billion assistance program "is predicated on the assumption" that Pakistan is taking steps against terrorism, against proliferation, and toward democracy.

[43] Testimony of the Director of the Defense Intelligence Agency, Vice Admiral Lowell E. Jacoby, to the Senate Select Committee on Intelligence on February 11, 2003 <www.dia.mil>; also reported in Paul Kerr, "Intelligence Chiefs Paint a Grim Picture of Proliferation," *Arms Control Today*, March 2003 <www.armscontrol.org>. Tim Burger and Tim McGirk, "Al Qaeda's nuclear contact?" *Time*, May 19, 2003.

[44] Note that the United States imposed missile-related sanctions on Pakistan and North Korea in March 2003.

[45] Examples include misinterpreting U.S. arms sales during the 1950s and ignoring U.S. warnings about nuclear weapons development during the 1980s as outlined in Schaffer, "U.S. Influence on Pakistan," pp. 169–72. See also Abbas Rashid, "The limits of (super power) friendship," *Daily Times*, December 23, 2002.

Indonesia – Key Indicators and Forecasts

Economy and Trade	2002^a	2003^b	2004^b
GDP ($tr) / (PPP GDP)	0.2 (PPP GDP in 2002 = $0.7 tr)		
GDP growth (%)	3.7	3.5	4.0
Inflation (%)	11.9	9.0	8.4
Budget balance (% of GDP)	4.2	2.2	2.2
Major export destinations (2001)	Japan (21%), U.S. (15%), Singapore (11%)		

Population and Energy	2002^a	2005^b	2010^b
Population (m)	231.3	242.0	258.8
Population growth (%)	1.5	1.4	1.2
Oil production (m bbl/d)	1.3	1.5	1.5
Oil consumption (m bbl/d)	1.0	...	...

Politics	
President	Megawati Sukarnoputri (PDI-P, Jul 2001)
Dominant party	PDI-P (since 1999)
Next legislative election	April 2004

Military	
Armed forces (2002)	297,000
Defense expenditure (2001)	$0.9 bn (0.6% of GDP)
Conventional capabilities	Small military (given Indonesia's size)
	Poor maintenance standards and training,
	Army charged with human rights abuses
Weapons of mass destruction	None

Source: The National Bureau of Asian Research, compiled from International Monetary Fund, *World Economic Outlook*; Central Intelligence Agency, *World Factbook*; U.S. Census Bureau, *International Data Base*; Energy Information Administration, *Country Analysis Brief—Indonesia*; International Institute of Strategic Studies, *The Military Balance*. Notes: a) Data for 2002 may be estimates; b) Data for 2003, 2004, 2005, and 2010 are projections. Additional data on Indonesia are available in the Strategic Asia database at <http://strategicasia.nbr.org>.

TURBULENT TIMES: FROM AUTOCRACY TO DEMOCRACY

John B. Haseman

ABSTRACT

Indonesia's large and predominantly moderate Muslim population, strategic location, and abundant resources make it a regional power of great importance to U.S. interests in Asia. Indonesia is in the fifth year of a transition from autocracy to democracy, and faces simultaneous political, economic, and security challenges. Hard hit by the 1997–98 Asian financial crisis, Indonesia is troubled by secessionist guerrillas, ethnic and religious conflicts, and Muslim extremists. The terrorist bombings of October 2002 in Bali and August 2003 in Jakarta illustrate the presence of terrorist cells lodged deep in Indonesia's social fabric. Indonesia will face important political milestones in 2004, including direct election of the president, continuing devolution of power, and the development of party politics. Although it has undergone many reforms, the military remains the most powerful force in Indonesian society. However, the rise of an inward-looking military leadership lacking international sophistication is worrisome, and may challenge the successful creation of democratic institutions.

Colonel (ret.) John B. Haseman, U.S. Army, was U.S. Defense and Army Attaché at the U.S. Embassy in Jakarta from 1990 to 1994. He currently writes for *Jane's Defence Weekly* and other journals.

Introduction

Indonesia is one of the largest, most populous, and most diverse countries in the world.[1] It is the most populous Muslim country in the world with more than 180 million Muslims, most of whom practice a moderate form of Islam, in contrast to more strident strains common in the Middle East.[2] Indonesia also occupies one of the most strategically important locations in the world. The waterways between its thousands of islands link the Pacific and Indian Oceans, and the country forms a bridge between Asia and Australia. Indonesia's international straits are key strategic lines of communication vital to the movement of commercial and military shipping between the Pacific Basin and Europe, the Middle East, and South Asia. Millions of barrels of oil, huge amounts of cargo, and the warships of many nations pass through Indonesian waterways, although the fact that its waters now experience the largest incidence of piracy anywhere in the world is a matter of both international and regional concern.[3]

Indonesia is a country with deep political and economic problems, social pressures, and internal security challenges. In addition to the difficulties inherent in major political transition, the country must simultaneously cope with a post-financial crisis economic recovery, repair a badly torn social fabric, and manage separatist violence at opposite ends of the archipelago. One of these challenges is difficult enough, yet Indonesia must cope with all of them at the same time.

The political crisis began with the collapse in 1998 of long-time president Suharto's authoritarian New Order government. Suharto was forced from office in large part by the impact of the 1997–98 Asian financial crisis, exacerbated in Indonesia by the high levels of corruption among the political elite as well as Suharto's inability to discern the rising tide of opinion against him.[4] Since Suharto's resignation in May 1998, Indonesia has stumbled through three presidents in its transition from autocracy to democracy. Vice President B. J. Habibie succeeded Suharto but held office for only 18 months, and failed in his bid for re-election. Abdurrahman Wahid was elected president by parliament in October 1999 after skillful political maneuvering, even though his party had not won a plurality. Vice President Megawati Sukarnoputri succeeded to the presidency in July 2001 following Wahid's impeachment for incompetence.

The Asian financial crisis had a devastating impact on Indonesia's economy. GDP contracted for six quarters, the rupiah lost 71 percent of its value, while inflation skyrocketed to 78 percent. Foreign and domestic (largely ethnic Chinese) capital fled from the country, leading to a collapse in business confidence and a sharp increase in unemployment. Indonesia was forced to accept a $5 billion emergency bail-out package from the

International Monetary Fund (IMF) in November 1997. Although considerable progress has been made toward restoring macroeconomic fundamentals, Indonesia has lagged behind the rest of Southeast Asia in its economic recovery, and it remains uncertain whether growth will ever return to the robust rates of the 1990s.

The severity of the crisis-induced economic downturn exacerbated existing socio-economic tensions and led to outbreaks of large-scale ethnic and religious violence in many parts of the country. Thousands were killed in fighting between Muslims and Christians in the Malukus and Sulawesi, while hundreds died in anti-Chinese violence in Java and elsewhere in the immediate aftermath of Suharto's fall.[5] The apparent appeal of more radical Muslim organizations that emerged in the country at this time—such as Laskar Jihad—is a worrisome trend.

The key for Indonesia to solve these multiple challenges is a secure and stable environment within which to implement social, economic, and political reforms. The country's leadership continues to experiment, seeking the right formula to combine a reasonably open political system with the time needed to educate and train a new generation of political and economic leaders. The role of the military, always the most powerful element in Indonesian society, continues to be a matter of internal debate. A strong and professional military is needed to address the country's security challenges—not least maintaining national unity and territorial integrity despite the centrifugal forces that constantly pull on the country— but its role in a newly democratic society has not yet been fully determined.[6] Indonesia's first civilian defense minister in 40 years, Yuwono Sudarsono, noted in 2000 that Indonesia remains one of the least prepared nations for developing the required social and economic institutional underpinnings that facilitate greater democracy.[7]

Against this backdrop, U.S.-Indonesian relations have in recent years been problematic. Previously, the long bilateral relationship has been relatively close, particularly during the Suharto period. The two countries have much in common. Both were forged in war against colonial masters, both have large multi-ethnic, multi-religious populations, and both possess abundant natural resources. Despite a foreign policy driven by the goal of non alignment, for almost four decades Indonesia nevertheless generally carried out policies supportive of U.S. interests in Southeast Asia. Recent events have sent bilateral relations into a period of less robust friendship, however. Human rights violations in East Timor and elsewhere resulted in a break in military-to-military programs.[8] More recently, the murder of two Americans near Timika, Papua, in August 2002 threatens other aspects of the bilateral relationship.[9]

The five years of halting transition from autocracy to democracy have revealed one of Suharto's greatest disservices to his country—his authoritarian rule prevented the development of alternative leaders capable of leading Indonesia in a more democratic era. Indonesia is still largely controlled by the same political elite that was a part of the New Order system and that benefited from decades of authoritarianism and corruption.[10]

Political, Economic, and Security Challenges

Indonesia is a country subject to multiple centrifugal forces, with fragmented geography, ethnic and religious diversity, and glaring imbalances in income distribution. Five years of muddled leadership and policy drift have adversely affected political and economic development within Indonesia, allowed security challenges to worsen, and reduced Jakarta's leadership role in Southeast Asia. Many Indonesians believe that the country needs a strong central government to keep its volatile population at peace. While these people simply long for the relative stability of the Suharto years, some are actively working behind the scenes to reinstall a new form of autocracy. Others are hoping instead that the transition to democracy, as well as decentralization of power to the provinces and regencies, will encourage alternative and competing power centers while maintaining national unity.

The devolution of power from the center began in 2001 and has been fraught with uncertainty while new laws and procedures are implemented. A yearning for local government is partly demonstrated by the rapid formation of new provinces and districts. Four new provinces have been created since 2001, while several more areas have requested provincial status and over 100 new districts have been formed.[11] There is thus a fundamental divergence of opinion on the basic issue of governance for Indonesia—centralized or decentralized.

Such divergence has a negative impact on the security situation. Indonesia faces no external security threats. Its primary security challenges are to overcome internal instability and the difficulties involved with international terrorism and transnational crime.[12] Indonesia's greatest internal security threat is that posed by separatist rebels in Aceh and Papua. (Other security challenges arising from ethnic and sectarian violence and terrorism are described below.) However, there are important differences between secessionist guerrillas whose goal is to secede from the country and gain independence, and less doctrinaire members of popular movements whose grievances center around economic and social exploitation by the central government but who seek greater autonomy rather than formal independence. The record of Indonesia's security forces in dealing with such internal threats indicates that they often do not understand the distinction.

The situation in Aceh is the more serious threat. The Acehnese have historically opposed rule from Jakarta, whether by the Dutch colonial government or that of an independent Indonesia. The most recent period of violence in the province began in the 1970s and escalated dramatically following the fall of Suharto. After several unsuccessful cease fire efforts, the government of Indonesia and the Free Aceh Movement (GAM) signed an agreement to end hostilities in December 2002, facilitated by the Switzerland based Henry Dunant Center.[13] The GAM accepted the provisions of the regional autonomy package provided to Aceh by the central government in 2001 as a basis for negotiations. Indonesia agreed to the presence of international monitors to oversee the separation of forces, the withdrawal of most reinforcing military and police units, and the disarming of the GAM.

Fragile from the start, the agreement at least gave the Acehnese people five months of relative peace. The agreement finally unraveled in May 2003 due to irreconcilable differences over the basic issue of Aceh's future status as either a province of Indonesia or an independent state. The GAM never stopped pursuing a goal of independence in its propaganda and public statements, and used the five months of peace to step up recruiting and acquire new weapons. For its part, Jakarta would not change election laws to give the GAM status as a political party and will never agree to Aceh's separation from Indonesia.

When peace talks broke down, President Megawati declared martial law in Aceh in May 2003, and the military launched its largest operation since the 1975 invasion of East Timor. Taking a cue from *Operation Iraqi Freedom*, the Indonesian version of "shock and awe" included use of British and U.S. made warplanes, airborne operations, and increased artillery bombardments of suspected enemy camps.[14] Military leaders initially predicted a six-month operation to destroy the GAM once and for all, although the head of the armed forces, General Endriartono Sutarto in July acknowledged that the fighting might last years.[15] The military and the president have overwhelming public and political support on this issue, and President Megawati appears to have strengthened her leadership by her firm stand on an issue of territorial integrity and national unity. There are likely to be important political and military ramifications, however, if the military is unable to achieve decisive success within the next few months. A long Vietnam-like war in Aceh will be embarrassing to military leaders who asserted the separatists would be defeated within six months. Inability to fulfill the promise of a six-month conflict might also cause President Megawati to change the senior military leadership lest she also become a political victim of a long and interminable guerrilla war. While much of the population and most political leaders support the current military operation, should the fighting drag on it could become an important factor in the 2004 parliamentary and presidential elections.

At the opposite end of the country, Papua also remains a security concern. Small and uncoordinated separatist groups have conducted anti government operations in the region for years. Those groups have begun to coordinate and communicate among each other since the late 1990s, and have increased political pressure as well. Grievances in Papua include the low return to the province of the fruits of its huge natural resources, concern about a huge government-sponsored influx of non Papuan transmigrants, and resentment of the government's and military's attitude toward the local tribal population.

The situation in Papua is complicated by a presidential decree to split the province into three. Citing the huge size of the province and the remoteness of its towns as justification, President Megawati used a pre-existing decision on the subject to overrule the special regional autonomy provisions granted to Papua by parliament in 2001.[16] Political conflict is likely between those who will benefit from the creation of new provinces, such as civil servants promoted to new positions and well-placed businessmen poised to seek political advantage, on the one hand, and those who view the action as an attack against native Papuan interests, on the other.

Given the huge natural resources in both Aceh and Papua and the importance of national unity and territorial integrity to Indonesia's political and military leaders, Jakarta will never allow either Aceh or Papua to secede. Resolving the security problems in both provinces will require a reduction in tensions between the government and the people, agreement on effective local autonomy, and, on the part of the security apparatus, moderation when carrying out legitimate police and defense operations. Absent these efforts, the outlook is years of sporadic conflict and inflamed relations between Jakarta and these two far-flung provinces.

Indonesia faces these daunting security challenges at the same time that the country prepares for major political change—the first-ever direct election of the president and vice president in mid-2004. For decades, Indonesia's constitution mandated the selection of the president by parliament. Passage of constitutional amendments in 2002, which provide for popular direct election of the president and vice president as a team, is one of the most significant political measures enacted since the fall of Suharto. Direct elections for both houses of parliament, as well as the president and vice president, will provide the most interesting Indonesian political season in many years. Matters of interest include potential candidates for Megawati to choose as her vice president, and specifically whether or not she will choose a member of her own Indonesia Democratic Party of Struggle

(PDI-P) or forge an alliance with another party—as is currently the situation.[17] Political observers in Jakarta predict an informal coalition of the PDI-P with the New Awakening Party (PKB) of former president Abdurrahman Wahid and the long-entrenched Golkar (former president Suharto's instrument of political power). Also of interest will be whether other parties eligible to field presidential candidates can gain strength by picking a charismatic popular dark horse candidate. Further complicating matters, parliament has not yet completed work on all of the required election laws.

The 2004 elections will be key for Indonesia's future. The parliamentary election will usher in new electoral methodology and membership for both legislative houses and will eliminate appointed parliamentary seats (including for the military and police, which now hold a strong bloc of 38 seats). For the first time, the people will vote directly for the president and vice president, enfranchising tens of millions of Indonesians to choose their national leader. This in turn will fundamentally change the political party system throughout the country. Although President Megawati appears to be in the lead for re-election, this is by no means a given outcome. She will have to contend with a record of vacillating leadership, increased charges of cronyism and corruption, and the challenge posed by the potential alliance of Muslim political parties. There are several strong potential opponents including Vice President Hamzah Haz, the boisterous Amien Rais, and Coordinating Minister Jusuf Kalla (who gained great prestige by brokering peace agreements between warring Muslim and Christian armies in Central Sulawesi and the Malukus) in a position to challenge Megawati.

One of the principal issues in the 2004 election campaign is likely to be the state of the economy. Indonesia's economy was more adversely affected by the 1997–98 financial crisis than most other countries in Southeast Asia, and has been the slowest to recover. From 1997 to 1998, GDP growth dropped from 5 to -13 percent, while inflation rose from 7 to 58 percent. The rupiah lost 71 percent of its value, with an enormous impact on Indonesia's debt burden. Inability to repay huge dollar denominated debts forced many of the country's powerful conglomerates into bankruptcy. The economic downturn and the social unrest that accompanied it led to a precipitous decline in foreign investment. So severe was the impact of the financial crisis that Indonesia was forced to turn to the IMF and negotiate terms for a $5 billion emergency bail-out package. The IMF's performance in Indonesia since 1998 has been much criticized. Always politically unpopular, many observers also consider the Fund's rigid conditionalities to have exacerbated the effects of the financial crisis. Jakarta is planning to withdraw from IMF tutelage in 2004, although the IMF will retain a monitoring role via a post-program monitoring (PPM) arrangement.

The combination of crony capitalism, rampant corruption, particularly in the banking sector, and the flight of Indonesia's domestic capital—primarily dominated by Chinese businessmen—continue to lead foreign investors in search of more stable markets elsewhere in the region. Indonesia has nonetheless made considerable progress in recovering from the crisis. GDP growth rose 3.7 percent in 2002, inflation has been brought under control, falling to an annualized 5.7 percent in July 2003, and total trade has increased to $92.8 billion. The real question is whether these developments are taking place fast enough. Indonesia requires an annual growth rate of approximately 6 percent to absorb new entrants into the work force, but GDP growth has not reached that rate since the financial crisis. Growth in 2003 is currently estimated to reach between 3.4 and 3.7 percent. This means that the 40 million strong ranks of the unemployed continue to grow—a particularly volatile element in the ongoing democratic transition, and one easily manipulable for other ends.

Violence, Terrorism, and Political Tools

A country like Indonesia, with so many different ethnic groups, social inequalities, and strong religious sentiments, cannot escape the specter of violence. Even during the late 1980s and early 1990s, when the economy experienced annual growth rates of 7 to 8 percent and Suharto kept a tight lid on social tensions, flare ups of ethnic or social based violence illustrated how close to the surface friction lies across Indonesia.

The continual outbreaks of severe violence among ethnic and religious groups—known in Indonesia as SARA—since the fall of Suharto have deterred foreign investment and are a serious challenge to Indonesia's economic and political recovery.[18] During the Suharto era, SARA conflicts were dealt with quickly, although the harsh response to anti social behavior is a prime reason for the population's dislike of its police and military.

The spontaneous origins of many such clashes made them difficult to predict, while ending such violence is also difficult. The reputation of the Indonesian police and military has been damaged by revelations of prior human rights abuses throughout the country. The police and armed forces are further hampered in their domestic security responsibilities by a lack of training and equipment for non-lethal crowd control. Selected military and police units in some urban areas have received this kind of training and equipment, but when violent incidents occur frequently, in widely scattered areas of the country, trained units and equipment do not stretch nearly far enough, and quick reaction transport is far from adequate.

A more disturbing phenomenon is a legacy of deliberately instigated violence in which the government or powerful individuals incite or inflame

SARA incidents for political purposes. Suharto was a master at using the security and intelligence agencies as *agents provocateurs* to control or eliminate potential rivals and to fragment political opposition. In the years since his downfall, ambitious and powerful groups and individuals have also employed violence as a political tool. Whether the desired goal is to destabilize presidencies, protect business and financial interests, or to assert political power, violence remains an unfortunate element in Indonesia's political equation.

The most notorious recent example of this was the formation and deployment of the radical Muslim group Laskar Jihad. This radical organization was initially the tool of a shadowy cabal of hard-line military and civilian figures opposed to the reform efforts of former president Abdurrahman Wahid. Laskar Jihad was designed as a zealous Islamist militia intended to confront Christian gangs in the Malukus, as well as to embarrass the president. The organization is widely believed to have been formed, financed, trained, and equipped with the assistance of army, police, and civilian government officials. Despite presidential orders to prevent Laskar Jihad from becoming involved in the Maluku violence, thousands of its fighters were transported across Java and moved by ship to the islands, where they were primarily responsible for expanding the sectarian conflict there.

Once involved in the sectarian violence in the Malukus and the Poso region of central Sulawesi, Laskar Jihad expanded in size and power and was soon beyond the control of its sponsors. Radical Muslims from other parts of Indonesia rallied to its cause. Subsequent investigations have tied together individuals from Laskar Jihad, the Sulawesi radical organization Laskar Jundullah, and the regional terrorist organization Jemaah Islamiyah.[19]

Counter-terrorism has now assumed a key priority in strategic planning in Indonesia, although for many months after the September 2001 terrorist attacks Indonesian politicians, particularly those associated with Muslim political parties, denied that Muslim extremist groups were involved in terrorism and refused to admit that terrorism had made inroads in Indonesia. This unwillingness to seriously address the problem of terrorism led to considerable tension between Jakarta and its neighbors in Southeast Asia. Relations with the United States also suffered.

The tragic October 2002 bombing incident in Kuta, Bali, that killed over 200 people, ended Jakarta's prevarication. Indonesia has since gained much credit for moving promptly. With international assistance, the authorities investigated that incident, which has been blamed on Jemaah Islamiyah, and arrested dozens for their involvement. There are still lingering concerns, however, that Indonesia is reluctant to become more assertive in regional and international counter-terrorism efforts because of a misplaced sense that counter-terrorism policies are inherently anti-Muslim. The first trials of terrorists involved in the Bali bombings and prior terrorist attacks in Indonesia began in April 2003, and the first sentences were announced in August. Evidence presented by prosecutors, including confessions of several of the accused and detailed forensic evidence prepared with international assistance, appears convincing.[20] Convictions and heavy sentences will enhance Indonesia's credibility in the international war against terrorism; conversely, failure to convict for political reasons will severely damage Indonesia's standing in the region and beyond.

Indonesia's exposure to terrorism was sadly demonstrated again in August 2003, when terrorists exploded a bomb in front of Jakarta's J. W. Marriott Hotel, the city's newest luxury hotel and a well-known gathering point for both Western and Indonesian elites. Initial investigation tied the bombing to Jemaah Islamiyah, and a week later an Al-Qaeda representative claimed responsibility for the attack. The blast killed 12 and injured more than 150 people. (For more on Jemaah Islamiyah, see the chapter on terrorism in this volume.)

The disclosures emerging from the trials of Bali bombing suspects have political implications for the 2004 elections. Several Muslim political leaders, notably Vice President Hamzah Haz, have in the past publicly praised Abu Bakar Ba'asyir, widely believed to be the head of Jemaah Islamiyah, who is on trial for treason in Jakarta, while other politicians have repeatedly claimed there were no Muslim terrorists in Indonesia. Only after major terrorist incidents took place, and with strong evidence implicating both Indonesian and foreign Islamists, did overt political support cease. The significance of this is that there is apparently a deep well of disaffected extremists in Indonesian society who are willing to engage in terrorism against fellow Indonesian Muslims, as well as a covert support network capable of providing training, shelter, funding, and connections to international terrorist organizations. The Indonesian Mujahideen Council (MMI), a radical but legitimate religious organization, issued statements following the Jakarta bombing accusing Western leaders—including President George W. Bush and Australian Prime Minister John Howard—of being terrorists. Political Islam in Indonesia can claim legitimacy only to the extent it can exercise political power without inflaming the country's extreme Muslim fringe—an objective that remains to be achieved.

The investigation into the Bali and Jakarta bombings revealed the deep involvement of regional and international terrorist organizations in Indonesia.[21] The worrisome reality is that, despite being a tiny minority within Indonesia's large, predominantly moderate Muslim community, violence prone radicals can quickly gain a foothold by exploiting organizations created for other purposes. That terrorists could duplicate the Bali attack in the Marriott bombing in Jakarta—despite the ongoing investigative efforts and trials of the Bali suspects—shows that there are many more trained terrorists and willing recruits in the country than police and intelligence agencies have thus far identified. That important participants in both bombings such as the leading bomb-makers have thus far evaded capture and may have fled abroad is a troublesome indicator of the flexibility of regional terrorist organizations. The implications for the international war on terrorism are many, but certainly two of the most topical for Indonesia are the fertile ground for recruitment of terrorists and their support network, and the ability of terrorists to move, train, and when necessary escape from the country, without attracting official attention.

In addition to indigenous militant groups like Laskar Jihad and regional terrorist organizations like Jemaah Islamiyah, other less structured groups continue to engage in unsavory political activities, serving any individual or group with the funds to pay for the "service" of violence with neither formal structure nor names. Funded by both civilian individuals and security agencies, these groups perform functions that range from organizing political demonstrations to providing protection muscle. Some have been identified for years with various military and police organizations, while others are formed by brokers who distribute funds, food, t-shirts, and weapons, depending on the function to be performed.

Because both police and military employ such groups for their own ends, the security forces have been reluctant to take action against political violence—unless it is to protect their own interests against infringement by others. While Laskar Jihad and other groups announced in the aftermath of the Bali bombings that they had disbanded, it is more likely that these groups have merely moved into the shadows and can quickly be reformed on call. There are disturbing reports, for example, that Laskar Jihad cells have moved into several cities in Papua, where they could become involved in sectarian violence similar to that perpetrated in the Malukus.[22]

The Key Role of the Armed Forces

The military is the single most powerful and influential force in Indonesian society.[23] With its significant role in the struggle for independence from the Dutch, the military has always wielded enormous power in Indonesia. With that power came corruption and arrogance. An army that was once widely respected as the gainer, and then the guarantor, of independence and the glue that held together the scattered islands and peoples of Indonesia, was by the 1990s a force still respected for its strength but increasingly feared and criticized for its abuses of power.

Since 1998, the Tentara Nasional Indonesia (TNI) has implemented some important reforms that have reduced its dominant role in Indonesian politics. The military has withdrawn from day-to-day involvement in politics and does not support any political party. It has accepted the elimination of its dedicated seats in parliament. In addition, military personnel must now retire from active service before they can occupy the thousands of civil government posts once traditionally filled by military appointees.

The military's base of political power emerges from the army's territorial organization.[24] More than half of the army's personnel are assigned to a geographically oriented structure that parallels civil government from the national level down to the tens of thousands of villages at the base of the population pyramid. By its presence at the province, regency, district, and village levels, the military strongly influences every element of society. The territorial system—once targeted for elimination by reformers but now being retained—is a key element of control that continues to guarantee the military significant political and economic powers. Political leverage throughout the civilian governmental structure is assured through posts effectively reserved for recently retired military officers.

The TNI also made it clear that it will not tolerate interference in its business empire. The military business network has its origins in the post colonial era when Dutch enterprises were expropriated by the military to fund its operations. The system was refined during the Suharto era as a tool to control the military leadership as well as a means to allow the government to give higher priority to other funding requirements. Because of this historical legacy of low government funding, the TNI currently receives only about one third of its funding from the national budget. The remainder of its income is derived from outside sources, including funds diverted from other accounts, but mostly from the huge networks of legal and illicit military businesses. The territorial system is the key to the pervasive powers of the military business empire; the two cannot be effectively separated.

The extent of the business empire and the amount of income generated are among the security forces' most closely guarded secrets. Although widely criticized as a tool for the enrichment of senior officers, the military business empire is in fact an important source of administrative and operational funding. Without these revenues, the military could not adequately pay, feed, and house its troops, maintain its equipment, buy spare parts, or train and exercise its personnel.

Since the military business empire cannot be eliminated until the government is able to fully fund the TNI—a prospect that is many years away—reformers have suggested pushing for greater transparency instead. These measures include business training for managers to maximize efficiency and income, regular monitoring to minimize abuses and corruption, elimination of non-productive enterprises, and an end to the illicit aspects of TNI businesses. However, given the ingrained and proprietary interest of the TNI and, as it sees it, the advantages to self-management, even these suggested reforms may be difficult to implement.

Regardless of whether the military's businesses are legal or illicit, and given the power of the territorial system, the Indonesian military establishment is able to fund itself largely apart from national government funding. This creates an unhealthy situation in which the military is less than fully responsive to the government leadership. An intertwined web of intelligence, political power, and money has operated for decades. It will not be easily changed by reformers or a more democratic government.

Indeed, in the post-Suharto period, the extensive network of private arrangements between military commanders and Indonesia's wealthy businessmen continues to function. At its most benign, the relationships provide extra income to the military officers and a degree of personal and business security to the businessmen involved. At its most venal, the system allows threats and intimidation of business competitors, eviction of small holders from their land, and beatings and murder of those who might threaten the arrangement.

The separation of the police from the armed forces, and assignment of internal security responsibilities to the police in 1998 were important steps, but, unfortunately, extremely premature. The poorly trained and equipped police force has been unable to prevent or quell large outbreaks of communal violence—such as those in Kalimantan, the Malukus, and Central Sulawesi—and is inadequate for confronting the separatist guerrilla forces in Aceh and Papua. The TNI has reasserted its claim to responsibility for internal stability, with specific responsibilities in combating insurgents, separatists, guerrillas, and piracy, with back-up responsibility to assist the police in other internal stability problems.

Even so, the TNI is little better off in terms of its ability to deal with even these kinds of threats. Among the military's many shortcomings is the sorry state of its hardware. Indonesia's military equipment is not state-of-the-art, and maintenance has never been strong. Military embargoes imposed by the United States and the European Union (EU) have resulted in a significant degradation of operational readiness. The navy and air force lack sufficient strategic mobility, such that the TNI cannot effectively move multiple quick-reaction army units to assist in natural disasters or internal security emergencies. This was at least one instance of a reason for, and a criticism of, the TNI's failure to react decisively to end violence in Kalimantan, the Malukus, and Central Sulawesi in the early 2000s.

The cut-off of overseas military education in Western countries since the early 1990s has also adversely affected the TNI's software—its personnel and leadership. The dearth of overseas experiences has resulted in an inward-looking military that views the world without the benefit of international experience. Indonesia's armed forces are today led by officers formed and trained by the very system that is so roundly criticized by the country's newly enfranchised population. Rather than address international concerns over human rights abuses, its leadership is increasingly turning to other sources of weaponry and equipment, frustrated by embargos imposed by its traditional suppliers and unwilling to make the political sacrifices needed for resumption of normal military-to-military relations.[25] The chain of command is ineffective in controlling the behavior of its troops in the field; it is there that the abuse of civilians occurs, through lack of supervision or discipline and failure to take corrective action against miscreants.

There will be an ongoing contest for power and influence over domestic and international security policies within the armed forces and between the armed forces and the civilian government. The debate will pit those who support the democratization of the country—a group which includes conservatives who prefer a slow but steady implementation of reforms that will assure the stature of the military—and those who seek a return to the autocratic system of the past, but under a new leader who more fully appreciates the power and support of the armed forces. In either outcome, the military emerges a winner, with its status enhanced.

Near-Term Prospects and Impacts on U.S. Policy

Indonesia is important to U.S. strategic interests in Asia and the world. The country's strategic location, natural resources, investment and market potential, and large, moderate Muslim population make it an important consideration for many U.S. policy objectives. For many years Indonesia has been a welcome, moderate voice in international fora. A long-time leader in the Association of Southeast Asian Nations (ASEAN) and the Asia Pacific Economic Community (APEC) forum, Indonesia has played an important role in regional and global political and economic affairs. However, its recent spate of political and economic troubles has muted that voice and contributed to a sense of drift in regional institutions (for more on this, see the chapter on Southeast Asia in this volume).

Prior to the mid 1990s, the United States enjoyed a successful multifaceted relationship with Indonesia. The tragic shooting of dozens of civilians at the hands of the military in Dili, East Timor in November 1991, however, made human rights issues a determining factor in U.S. policy toward Indonesia, particularly in security matters. While these are an appropriate consideration in U.S. policy decisions, there are other important factors that should be weighed when formulating policy toward such a strategically important country.

Indonesia has not helped itself to improve matters. A series of incidents, including inexcusable violence in East Timor in 1999 and the murder of American teachers in Papua in 2002, continue to tarnish the military's reputation. The TNI has been intractable in declining to punish those responsible for such violence, nor has the civilian leadership been willing to act for fear of alienating the powerful military. As a result, the record of the military remains a key issue in U.S. security relations with Indonesia.

Over the same period, however, U.S. priorities have changed. The events of September 11, 2001 changed American perceptions of threats to U.S. national security and other interests. Indonesia's role in the international fight against terrorism is critical. Revelations of the role of domestic radical Muslim organizations with regional terrorist activities in Indonesia and elsewhere in Southeast Asia, and parallel ties to the worldwide terrorist structure, make it vital that the United States and Indonesia enjoy a cooperative security relationship.

Since the end of U.S. military training to Indonesian military personnel, a generation of Indonesian military officers has been denied the professional education and personal relationships that result from exposure to the role of the U.S. military in American society.[26] There are virtually no senior Indonesian military officers personally familiar with the United States and its culture, society, and policy objectives. The personal friendships that make international relations and policy discussions move more smoothly are no longer present. Indonesia needs the training, and both countries benefit when Indonesia's senior officers have an understanding of the role of the military in a democratic society. A senior U.S. diplomat with many years of experience in Southeast Asia noted that the IMET program is even more important when a country has human rights problems.[27]

There is, however, a strong counterpoint. Many in the United States believe that brutality is ingrained in the Indonesian security forces as part of a decades-long culture of violence and immunity from prosecution. Those who oppose restoring the military-to-military relationship believe that the TNI, which routinely uses soldiers as enforcers for its own businesses (illicit and legal) and those of civilians willing to pay for such service, and which has been complicit in the use of violence as a political tool for decades, cannot be expected to punish soldiers whose violence becomes the focus of international attention.

Nonetheless, given the demands of the war on terrorism and the need for Indonesia to play a fully active and cooperative role in regional counter-terrorism efforts, it is important that relations between Washington and Jakarta be broadened and deepened considerably. Part of this would need to include a resumption of IMET and an increase in U.S. technical assistance and training to the Indonesian national police and to Indonesia's National Intelligence Agency (the Badan Intelijence Nasional—BIN). These two agencies have taken the lead in investigating recent terrorist incidents and have shown laudable results that, with international assistance, could continue to be an effective counter-terrorism partner for the United States.[28]

The United States has a vested interest that Indonesia becomes an economically and politically viable democracy. There are many areas in which U.S. advice and assistance can benefit Indonesia as it continues to struggle with political change and economic recovery. These include increased assistance and training to political, economic, and educational institutions in Indonesia, and provision of support in international fora that can provide economic assistance to Indonesia's still faltering economy. The United States has much that it can provide to nurture a new democratic ethos in Indonesia. Cooperative training and exchanges between the two countries' executive, judicial, and legislative branches could benefit both countries.

In recent years the long-standing cordial relationship between the United States and Indonesia has slowly deteriorated, largely due to reactions to unfortunate incidents perpetrated by the Indonesian military. Indonesia itself has been buffeted by strong political and economic challenges that have weakened its leadership voice in international affairs, which in turn has led to malaise in the previously robust ASEAN. At the same time, the strategic interests of the United States have been changed enormously by the rise of international terrorism. An economically and politically strong Indonesia would play an important role in addressing these strategic concerns. Developments within Indonesia in the coming year will have a substantial influence on determining Indonesia's direction for many years. Two possibilities seem most likely. One is that an increasingly nationalistic Indonesia becomes more and more isolated from Western influences and, beset by seemingly endless domestic problems, withdraws from its long years of helpful international involvement. The other is that Indonesia addresses those issues hindering a broad range of bilateral relations where the dominant national interests of the United States and Indonesia determine policy across the relationship. In this scenario, the two countries could once again work more closely to address the important strategic issues in the region. But in the first case, Indonesia could return to its situation of the 1950s and early 1960s—a nearly-failed state led by nationalists who rally its population against an outside world that is blamed for the nation's problems and held at bay by bellicose rhetoric and obstructionist policies.

It now seems likely that President Megawati will be re-elected with a political mandate from the populace (as opposed to that of a narrow parliamentary selection process). A helpful (not hectoring) military-to-military relationship will be an important aspect of the bilateral relationship because, regardless of the halting progress of Indonesia's move to democratization, the TNI will remain the country's most important element. The greatest challenge in achieving this goal appears to be effectively to communicate the issues and find a cooperative path to success. Given its size, location, and moderate Muslim majority, a democratic Indonesia, fully engaged to meet common strategic objectives, would be a vital partner in addressing strategic challenges facing the United States.

Endnotes

[1] With about 230 million people, Indonesia is the fourth most populous country in the world. The country consists of more than 17,000 islands strung out along the equator. Superimposed on a map of the United States, Indonesia would stretch from San Francisco to Bermuda and from Canada to Mexico.

[2] See, for example, Robert W. Hefner, *Civil Islam: Muslims and Democratization in Indonesia*, Princeton: Princeton University Press, 2000.

[3] The Strait of Malacca is the heaviest traveled waterway in the world. The largest cargo ships and tankers, and major warships such as aircraft carriers, do not use the Strait of Malacca but rather travel a longer route through the wider, deeper, and less congested Makassar Strait (between Sulawesi and Kalimantan) and Ombai Strait (west of the island of Timor). The International Maritime Bureau reported 64 pirate attacks in Indonesian waters in the first six months of 2003—one-quarter of the total attacks reported worldwide. See "Piracy rife in Indonesia archipelago," Associated Press, July 24, 2003.

[4] For a fascinating and detailed account of the tumultuous weeks surrounding Suharto's resignation, see Kevin O'Rourke, *Reformasi: The Struggle for Power in Post Suharto Indonesia*, Sydney: Allen & Unwin, 2002.

[5] For excellent analysis on communal and religious violence in Indonesia, see, inter alia, International Crisis Group, "Indonesia: Overcoming Murder and Chaos in Maluku," *ICG Asia Report*, no. 10, December 19, 2000; International Crisis Group, "Communal Violence in Indonesia: Lessons from Kalimantan," *ICG Asia Report*, no. 19, June 27, 2001; and International Crisis Group, "Indonesia: The Search for Peace in Maluku," *ICG Asia Report*, no. 31, February 8, 2002.

[6] See Angel Rabasa and John B. Haseman, *The Military and Democracy in Indonesia: Challenges, Politics, and Power*, Santa Monica, Calif.: Rand, 2002.

[7] Address to the United States Indonesia Society, Washington, DC, April 11, 2000.

[8] The November 1991 killing of dozens of unarmed civilians in Dili, East Timor, prompted the U.S. Congress to cut the long-standing International Military Education and Training (IMET) program, which pays for foreign military per-

sonnel to receive training and education at U.S. schools and bases. Low-level training programs continued until 1999, when egregious violence by army-backed militia forces in East Timor resulted in the United States cutting military arms sales, as well as all training and education programs for the Indonesian armed forces.

9 The murder of two Americans and one Indonesian (and injuries to many more) in a mountainside ambush near the P. T. Freeport Indonesia gold and copper mine at Tembagapura, Papua, has yet to be resolved. It has become a major block to the restoration of military-to-military ties and, if left unresolved, could also negatively affect wider aspects of the bilateral relationship. There is widespread suspicion that soldiers were involved in the ambush.

10 While Megawati herself could hardly be called a Suharto associate, most of her government and the current members of parliament are holdovers from the Suharto years.

11 The new provinces are Banten (from West Java), Bangka Belitung (from South Sumatra), Gorontalo (from North Sulawesi), and North Maluku (from Maluku). A presidential decree splitting Papua into three provinces will create Central and West Papua provinces. The Luwu and West Sulawesi regions of South Sulawesi province and the island region of Riau province have also requested provincial status.

12 Indonesia's view of its international and domestic security threats are described in its 2003 defense white paper, *Indonesia: Mempertahankan Tanah Air Memasuki Abad 21*, Jakarta, Department of Defense, March 31, 2003.

13 GAM refers to Gerakan Aceh Merdeka, the Indonesian words for Free Aceh Movement.

14 For excellent detailed coverage of Aceh developments, see inter alia, International Crisis Group, "Aceh: Why the Military Option Still Won't Work," *ICG Indonesia Briefing*, May 9, 2003; and International Crisis Group, "Aceh: A Fragile Peace," *ICG Asia Report*, no. 47, February 27, 2003, both authored by Sidney Jones, ICG country director for Indonesia.

15 "Aceh offensive could take years," BBC World Service, July 7, 2003; Jane Perlez, "Indonesia says drive against separatists will not end soon," *New York Times*, July 9, 2003.

16 For details on this issue see International Crisis Group, "Dividing Papua: How Not To Do It," *ICG Indonesia Briefing*, April 9, 2003.

17 Several well-connected political observers in Jakarta reported in late June 2003 that they expect Megawati to choose a retired military officer as her running mate. If not a military man, the vice presidential choice is likely to come from a different political party.

18 SARA stands for "ethnicity, religion, race, and inter group" conflict.

19 Laskar Jundullah members have been convicted of terrorist bombings in Makassar, South Sulawesi. One of its key leaders, who is connected to Jemaah Islamiyah, was tried and convicted of a terrorist bombing in the Philippines. For more on Jemaah Islamiyah, see the chapter on terrorism in this volume; for Indonesia's role in regional counter-terrorism initiatives, see the chapter on Southeast Asia.

20 Evidence made public by Indonesian security and intelligence agencies during

the trials connects Indonesians involved in the Bali and Jakarta bombings to the regional Islamist terrorist organization Jemaah Islamiyah. Other evidence also ties many of those same suspects to a spate of terrorist incidents in several Indonesian cities that took place between 2000 and 2002. Even though the most-wanted terrorist Hambali was captured in August 2003, several important terrorist leaders remain at large. There is also the worrisome likelihood that there are many more Indonesians involved in domestic and regional terrorist planning.

21 For a superb summary of these interlocking connections, see International Crisis Group, "Al Qaeda in Southeast Asia: The Case of The 'Ngruki Network' in Indonesia," *ICG Indonesia Briefing*, August 9, 2002.

22 See, inter alia, International Crisis Group, "Indonesia: Resources and Conflict in Papua," *ICG Asia Report*, no. 39, September 13, 2002.

23 From 1965 until 1998, the Indonesian military was known as Angkatan Bersenjata Republik Indonesia (ABRI)—Armed Forces of the Republic of Indonesia. In 1998, as a symbol of reform, the armed forces renamed itself as the Tentara Nasional Indonesia (TNI—Indonesian National Armed Forces). The change was also meant to reflect the devolvement of the National Police, which had previously been a fourth branch of the military alongside the army, navy, and air force. The Department of Defense and Security (Hankam) was likewise renamed as the Department of Defense (DepHan) to indicate the removal of internal security from the military's mission.

24 For a detailed study of the organization of the Indonesian armed forces, see Robert Lowry, *The Armed Forces of Indonesia*, Sydney: Allen & Unwin, 1996.

25 Among other new equipment and arms purchases, in May 2003 President Megawati announced plans to purchase Russian-made fighter jets and helicopters financed largely through commodity counter-trade.

26 For background, see John B. Haseman, "The United States, IMET, and Indonesia," *USINDO Report*, no. 3, January 1998.

27 Private, off-the-record interview with the author, September 2002.

28 Retired army Lt. Gen. A. M. Hendropriyono, who is close to President Megawati, heads the BIN. He has had extensive U.S. training and education and strongly desires to improve the technical capabilities of the agency. He is the first head of BIN to have been given cabinet rank. Hendropriyono gave early warning of ties between Indonesian Muslim extremists and terrorist organizations in 2001, a time when to do so in Indonesia was politically incorrect. BIN files on terrorists were subsequently of major assistance in apprehending international terrorists, and more than three dozen suspects in the Bali bombings, many of whom have been implicated in earlier terrorist incidents inside Indonesia or have been shown to have ties with international terrorist organizations. For more on this, see the chapter on terrorism in this volume.

STRATEGIC ASIA

REGIONAL STUDIES

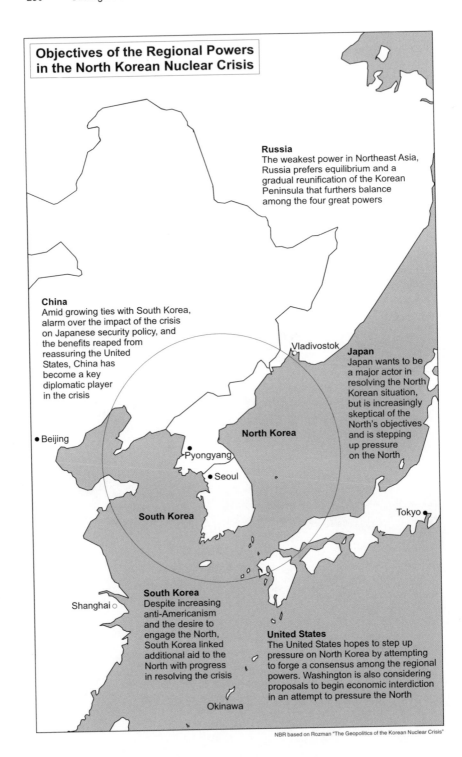

Objectives of the Regional Powers in the North Korean Nuclear Crisis

Russia
The weakest power in Northeast Asia, Russia prefers equilibrium and a gradual reunification of the Korean Peninsula that furthers balance among the four great powers

China
Amid growing ties with South Korea, alarm over the impact of the crisis on Japanese security policy, and the benefits reaped from reassuring the United States, China has become a key diplomatic player in the crisis

Vladivostok

Japan
Japan wants to be a major actor in resolving the North Korean situation, but is increasingly skeptical of the North's objectives and is stepping up pressure on the North

• Beijing

North Korea

Pyongyang

• Seoul

South Korea

Tokyo •

Shanghai ○

South Korea
Despite increasing anti-Americanism and the desire to engage the North, South Korea linked additional aid to the North with progress in resolving the crisis

United States
The United States hopes to step up pressure on North Korea by attempting to forge a consensus among the regional powers. Washington is also considering proposals to begin economic interdiction in an attempt to pressure the North

Okinawa

NBR based on Rozman "The Geopolitics of the Korean Nuclear Crisis"

THE GEOPOLITICS OF THE KOREAN NUCLEAR CRISIS

Gilbert Rozman

ABSTRACT

U.S. unilateralism in rejecting the Sunshine Policy and North Korean unilateralism in seeking regime survival through nuclear weapons have forced Japan, South Korea, China, and Russia to agree to a multilateral approach to reduce threats to their interests. After making clear to the North its own preferred outcome, each has been in close touch with the United States in the hope that a compromise to the current nuclear crisis can be found. After the inconclusive three-way summit in Beijing in April 2003, Washington succeeded in drawing Tokyo and Seoul closer to its approach, and with close inspections of North Korean ships Tokyo grew more assertive. Anxious to avoid a nuclear Japan as well as greater U.S. dominance in Northeast Asia, China seeks a soft landing for North Korea that gives a boost to regionalism, from which it can gain economically and strategically. Pressed by Beijing, Pyongyang agreed at the start of August to six-party talks that will test any regional consensus as well as U.S. willingness to return to multilateralism. Tough negotiations lie ahead if a showdown is averted between North Korea and the United States.

Gilbert Rozman is Musgrave Professor of Sociology at Princeton University. He wishes to thank Ralph Cossa, Richard Ellings, and Michael Wills for helpful comments on earlier drafts.

Introduction

The escalation of the U.S.-North Korean standoff that began in October 2002 constitutes the first 21st century conflict between a failed state relying on the threat of nuclear weapons and their proliferation to ensure regime survival, and a world power intent on preventing such flexing, blackmailing, and transfer of weapons of mass destruction (WMD) to potential terrorists. The U.S.-North Korean crisis parallels the showdown between the United States and Iraq and raises heightened concern about the use of nuclear weapons. In addition, the situation in Northeast Asia poses a threat to South Korea and Japan (and the United States) if WMD-tipped artillery shells and missiles are fired across the North Korean border. The crisis bears close scrutiny as a measure of great power relations, in which the vital interests of four powers and the two Koreas intersect, while the shape of the emergent Northeast Asian region is at stake. Northeast Asia today stands on the brink of economic regionalism, but it lacks a stable balance of power and requisite confidence in security.

The current crisis was precipitated by a series of circumstances, the first of which is the totalitarian nature of the Kim Jong Il regime, which has resisted reform and remains isolated. This position was greatly exacerbated by the loss of support to North Korea from the Soviet Union, and as early as 1990 led to posturing about the use of WMD. The Agreed Framework ended the first nuclear crisis in 1994, but remained a shaky compromise in which both the United States and North Korea were suspicious of the other's commitment to the agreement. The incomplete implementation of the 1994 accord lead to the missile development crisis of 1998, and a second agreement, which boosted the role of multilateral ties resulted from the Perry Process. The fragile progress of 2000, which was dominated by Kim Dae Jung's "sunshine policy," was stymied by uncertain expectations about U.S. cooperation. Thus, the seeds of crisis were present even before the Bush administration showed its disdain for the sunshine policy and South Korea moved from containment based on trust in the United States to appeasement based on emotional bonds with the North and multilateral great power diplomacy. The leadership in the North sought assurances of regime survival as well as massive economic assistance, while Americans found repugnant demands to yield to WMD extortion and willingness to support a state that tramples human rights.

Despite a number of options available to North Korea, its leadership was not satisfied with the limitations that accompanied them. In particular, the North Korean leadership opposed: 1) the South Korean "sunshine" option of family reunions, direct investment, national summits, and gradual reintegration through confederation; 2) the Chinese reform option of special economic zones, market reforms, and gradual global integration with initial reliance on China's support; 3) the Japanese "reparations" option of returning abductees' families, allowing freedom of movement to Japanese spouses of Koreans who had been repatriated to the North, and cooperating on security, which would open the door to large-scale economic assistance in correspondence to what South Korea received in lieu of reparations payments; and 4) the Russian "megaprojects" option to bring in revenue through energy, transportation, and industrial corridors that would allow the state to maintain control without exposing the bulk of the population to the shocks of economic openness. In 2002, Pyongyang made some clumsy attempts at economic change, initiated price reforms, and announced a special economic zone at Shinuiju near China, but all of these options were too risky for a regime clinging to totalitarian methods.

Comprised of many officials who had condemned the Clinton administration's "timid" use of power, the Bush administration was divided on policy toward North Korea. Some who considered it desirable to prevent an unpredictable crisis or to assuage U.S. allies were inclined to stick closely to the framework left by Clinton. After George W. Bush branded North Korea part of the "axis of evil" in his 2002 State of the Union speech, a new approach was set. Diplomatic flexibility was consequently reduced, leaving all four of the other active parties frustrated by the impact on their own strategies toward the North. For a time, Pyongyang explored new options with each of them. Yet with the United States refusing to engage North Korea none were able to advance their preferred solution. The North heard each, in turn, but it treated them as if they were only practice negotiations in preparation for the main event: discussions with the United States.

Debate began on October 3, 2002, when Assistant Secretary of State James Kelly accused the North of cheating on its nuclear promises during a visit to Pyongyang. The Kim Jong Il regime struck back by defiantly admitting to a uranium enrichment program. The crisis then escalated as Pyongyang repeatedly took provocative steps and resorted to bellicose language. Washington mostly soft-pedaled the danger while occasionally inserting a sober reminder about potential military options.

Four Parties Seeking to Shape U.S.-DPRK Relations

North Korea's neighbors have strong interests in the situation on the Peninsula and seek ways to influence developments there. Since 1950, China has linked its security to that of North Korea, in large part because of the country's proximity to Beijing. Once it had reestablished relations with South Korea in 1965, Japan reasserted its claim to have influence on the Korean Peninsula. After the Cold War, the Japanese quest to "reenter Asia" started with a desire to shape the evolution of the Koreas. In the 1990s, Russians were frustrated by their country's loss of international status, pointing to exclusion from 1994 talks on North Korea as a symbol of this fall. It became a matter of urgency to regain influence, not only because of the proximity of North Korea to Vladivostok, but also because of an impression that the future of Russia's status as a power in Asia depends heavily on how the reunification of Korea is resolved. Finally, by the end of the 1990s, South Koreans had decided that they should play the leading role in the transformation of the North. When the Perry Process produced an agreement in September 1999 limiting North Korean missile testing, Pyongyang's neighbors took it as a green light to accelerate their own diplomacy. Once the Clinton administration had signaled its approval, the other four parties planned new approaches to Pyongyang to gain an advantage in shaping the evolution of the peninsula.

Russia as a Marginalized Player

Unexpectedly, Russia has played the most conspicuous role in meetings with Kim Jong Il since 2000. Russia gained visibility as the destination of two summer visits by Kim, a long train trip to Moscow in 2001 and a short summit in the Russian Far East in 2002. No less important, Vladimir Putin, who became identified as the only leader "trusted" by Kim, relayed Kim's message about an extended moratorium on missile testing to the G-7 meeting in Okinawa in 2000, and received the gratitude of Japan's Koizumi for facilitating the September 2002 summit. In January 2003, Putin sent an emissary to Pyongyang amidst expectations that the presence of a special bond could break the deadlock over the nuclear crisis.

If several years earlier Moscow's goals were primarily to regain influence in the region, the Vladivostok summit of late August 2002 focused on securing economic advantages. Putin had decided that the security of the Russian Far East was endangered by illegal Chinese immigration. Contrary to plans under discussion with China, Putin had also calculated that laying an oil pipeline from Angarsk east to Khabarovsk and south to Nakhodka, with possible future extension through the Korean Peninsula, would solidify Russia's hold on the territory. In addition, he focused on the "iron silk road" extension of the Trans-Siberian railway through the Korean Peninsula during talks with Kim Jong Il. Strongly encouraged by the governors of the Russian Far East, Putin linked the long-term security of the eastern third of his country to success in a soft landing for North Korea and economic reintegration of the peninsula in which the South would not be obsessed with absorbing the North.[1] The geography of the Far East puts its main cities and military assets on a line directly north of the Korean Peninsula, giving Putin good reason to link its security with the two Koreas, while boosting ties with Japan and keeping China engaged but at bay.

The second Russian objective follows from the first. Not only does Putin want to prevent China from dominating the Russian Far East, he seeks a path to regionalism in Northeast Asia where Chinese power is contained. This means not only favoring more balance between China and Japan and a continued U.S. presence, but also steering the Korean Peninsula toward an outcome that makes no power stronger than the others. As the weakest power in the region, Russia prefers equilibrium and gradual reunification between North and South Korea that furthers balance among the great powers. Russia therefore treats North Korea as a lever for shaping regionalism. While a crisis is not welcome, neither is a collapse that would bring U.S. power even closer or sow chaos that could spill across the border.[2]

The effort to mediate by sending Deputy Foreign Minister Alexander Losyukov to Pyongyang in January 2003 had economic and geopolitical objectives. With South Korean President Kim Dae Jung's approval, Losyukov discussed joint assistance to replace the KEDO nuclear reactors with hydroelectric plants. Resenting its exclusion from the 1994 reactor construction agreement, Moscow wants to ensure that its economic interests are represented. Yet, as Russia's relations with the United States worsened due to differences over Iraq, a third, more global, goal remained obvious: Putin wants to avoid any outcome by which U.S. power could become impervious to balancing forces. A process that aligned Japan and South Korea more closely with Russia might keep the United States in check.

Support from China was necessary to meet this last objective, and on May 27, 2003, Putin and President Hu Jintao declared that "scenarios of power pressure or the use of force to resolve the problems existing [in Korea] are unacceptable." They added:

> [We] advocate the creation of a nuclear-free status of Korean Peninsula and observance there of the regime of non-proliferation of weapons of mass destruction. Simultaneously, the security of the DPRK must be guaranteed and favorable conditions must be established for its socio-economic development. The parties believe that the key to resolving the problems of Korean Peninsula is the political will of the parties involved to solve the crisis by political and diplomatic methods. The parties will continue a close cooperation in the interests of peace, stability and development on Korean Peninsula.[3]

While leaving no doubt about differences from the U.S. approach, this statement supports the Bush priority of removing nuclear weapons.

During the "white nights" summit of world leaders for St. Petersburg's 300th anniversary, U.S.-Russian relations focused on overcoming differences over Iraq and on U.S. determination to stop Iran's nuclear program, rather than the Korean crisis. It appeared that Russia was once again marginalized over Korea. The idea that Russia will benefit from active diplomacy premised on acceptance by the North has also been criticized. A leading Moscow expert on Korea argued that Russia would do better to give priority to the war against terrorism while pressing for integration with Northeast Asia, rather than seeking a role as friend of Pyongyang.[4] After the war in Iraq strained relations with the United States and left some believing that Russia had overplayed its hand, Russians debated the utility of becoming more cooperative over Korea.[5] Kim Jong Il's extremism undercut Putin's ambition for a mediating role, while Roh Moo Hyun's pragmatic focus on the United States meant no meeting with Putin even when other leaders converged on St. Petersburg. Yet, when Pyongyang agreed to multilateral talks, it not only brought Moscow back into the picture but also had Moscow rather than Beijing make the announcement. If multilateralism is unavoidable, then Pyongyang wants Moscow there.

Japan's Short- and Long-Term Interests

Japan's interest in North Korea in the summer of 2002 is the result of plans that did not fare well after the nuclear crisis began. The Koizumi initiative that led to the summit of September 17, 2002 had a mixture of short-term and long-term calculations. In the short run, Koizumi sought a resolution to the issue of abducted Japanese that could give him a personal boost and raise Japan's profile. Over the long run, he sought to establish Japan as a major actor in the jockeying over North Korea's evolution.[6] Japan also had urgent concern for its security. After North Korea fired a missile over Honshu Island in August 1998, many regarded North Korean missiles as the most serious threat to Japanese territory since World War II. The nuclear crisis intensified this alarm. In the buildup to the Pyongyang summit, some commentators posited that Japan was becoming a driving force on the peninsula while the United States, with its inflexible stance, had lost the initiative.[7] However, Japan's preoccupation with a dangerous North Korea as well as revulsion over the North's admission of abductions of Japanese drove Japan closer to the United States, although it remained more anxious to pursue negotiations than risk the calamitous prospects of a military option.

Japan also regarded the outcome on the Korean Peninsula as vital to its objectives for regionalism. While many Japanese were optimistic about relations with South Korea in the aftermath of the 2002 World Cup, fears soon mounted that the South was drifting closer to China. By making itself indispensable through economic assistance, Japan figured it would become more vital to the South's strategy for economic integration on the peninsula and would gain leverage to balance China. When the nuclear crisis put an end to Koizumi's initiative to Pyongyang, Tokyo had to concentrate on a third objective: balancing its strategic alliance with the United States and its ambitions to "reenter Asia."[8] With talk of a partial withdrawal of U.S. forces from South Korea, Tokyo nervously eyed a breakdown in the regional security system. Under the threat of attack, ties to the United States became the paramount concern for Japan's leaders, even if nationalist voices espousing independent Japanese action were growing stronger.

As the crisis deepened, Japanese commentators of various political orientations took different positions on multilateral possibilities. Funabashi Yoichi of the *Asahi Shimbun* argued that since Chinese relations with the North were filled with tension, China was as likely to apply pressure as the United States. Although he noted that China has been slow to act because of debate raging in its foreign ministry, Funabashi held out hope that Beijing would suspend energy and food shipments to squeeze the North.[9] Vociferous criticism of China, however, did not abate. The May 2002 Shenyang incident, when Chinese police forcibly removed North Korean refugees from Japan's consulate, had damaged China's reputation in Japan, despite reports that the Japanese ambassador had previously asked for Chinese help against refugees seeking diplomatic asylum and that China quickly allowed those who were arrested to leave the country[10]. During the nuclear crisis, some went out of their way to associate China with the North Korean threat, but most coverage credited Beijing with playing a positive role.[11]

Many Japanese feared that the United States would risk military conflagration in order to achieve regime change in the North,[12] or desperately hoped that a breakthrough was within reach because of China's changing diplomacy.[13] But foreign policy experts recognized that this dangerous time required closing ranks with the United States. Seeing the war in Iraq as a precursor to firmness against North Korea, Japan gave more backing to the preemptive U.S. attack than any other ally. In May 2003, Koizumi accepted the opportunity to go to the Crawford Ranch. He prudently refrained from stressing Japanese interest in making Pyongyang a good offer.[14]

The most important change among the other countries in Northeast Asia came after the April 23 three-way summit in Beijing, where Pyongyang flaunted its claim to have nuclear weapons. As the North's statements alarmed many in Japan, Koizumi tilted to the United States in increasing pressure. He decided to cut the flow of money or dual-use items to North Korea, and implemented a plan to inspect the 1,400 North Korean cargo ships that arrive in Japanese ports annually. While the Japanese government was split between those who had embraced the Pyongyang summit and those who had demonized the North over the subsequent months, Koizumi decided that Japan's voice could best be heard inside the tent nudging the North.[15] In June 2003, Japan was at the forefront with warnings and inspections of North Korean ships as the rhetoric from Pyongyang escalated about the retaliation that might be provoked by such actions.

China as a Key Player

China is also attentive to the impact of the nuclear crisis on relations with Japan, but China's leaders have an even more pressing concern. They see North Korea primarily through the lens of Taiwan. This means calculating how any outcome on the Korean Peninsula will affect China's own reunification ambitions, while at the same time fearing that sanctions against the North could be a precedent for sanctions against China in some future confrontation over Taiwan. The cross-Strait model of transition through economic integration also applies.[16] When Pyongyang initiated economic reforms in the summer of 2002 that could have opened the way to a Chinese-style market transition, Beijing may have thought that its repeated encouragement of reform was at last being heard. Yet when the North announced the opening of a "free economic zone" on the border with the Liaodong peninsula, Beijing showed its displeasure by arresting the Chinese businessman managing the effort on charges of corruption.

For years, Chinese assessments had minimized the risk from North Korea's WMD programs, suggesting that patient engagement would work.[17] Beijing insisted that U.S. pressure on the North would only result in more isolation and bluster. In the second half of the 1990s, when Beijing embraced the goal of multipolarity by means of great power triangles or quadrangles, the disquieting impact of the North on security may have served China's purposes.[18] Already in late 1999, however, strategic thinking was changing. China started "smile diplomacy" toward Japan,[19] supported regionalism in Northeast Asia, and even reconciled itself to the reality of greater U.S. power and less benefit from a strategic partnership with Russia. Meanwhile, China's ties with South Korea grew stronger. Fear of isolation after September 11 accelerated this shift in thinking about the North.

The crisis in Iraq solidified this shift in Beijing's thinking. Fearing that the United States would attack North Korea after it had disposed of Iraq's government, China began to consider a new regional strategy. Adding to Chinese disquiet was the impact on Japan of North Korea's nuclear threat, boosting the appeal of cooperation on missile defense with the United States and the potential for subsequent transfer to defend Taiwan. China bided its time as the United States appealed for its help. In March 2003, it joined the UN Security Council coalition in resistance to a U.S. attack on Iraq. While relations with the United States had markedly improved since September 11, Chinese leaders feared that U.S. unilateralism could be turned against China and its claim to Taiwan.

While Beijing generally kept a low profile in the war against Iraq, it could not avoid being embroiled in the North Korean crisis. In addition to becoming the foremost issue in relations with the United States and the testing ground for rival notions of regionalism, policy toward North Korea brought to the fore the fundamental divide in Chinese politics. The Korean crisis worsened just as the leadership transition was under way from Jiang Zemin to Hu Jintao. Despite the transfer of power, Jiang retained the title of chairman of the Central Military Commission, making it hard for Hu to extend his leadership on the Korean crisis. While leading Chinese scholars and business leaders dismissed the North as a burden that threatened to damage relations with the United States, they could not be sure that the leadership would, if forced to choose, abandon the North.

As discussed in the China chapter in this volume, the argument for applying pressure on the North was gaining favor in March and April 2003. It held that China has traditionally been isolated in international relations, and has become more so since Japan and Russia strengthened their ties with the United States from the late 1990s. Since China is heading toward a full market economy and developing a middle-class with increasing democratic aspirations, it goes against its own interest if it allows a Stalinist state, with which it has little in common, to hold its foreign policy hostage.

If quiet pressure on Pyongyang and U.S. willingness to talk with the North in the trilateral setting in Beijing gave the reformers some of what they wanted, a more serious test of China's political divide loomed as the crisis continued.[20] Chinese officials wanted to broker an agreement over the North that drew the countries of Northeast Asia together. Japan became critical to China's plans, as Chinese analysts saw convergence between a hardened U.S. position and Japan's skepticism of the North.[21] After the "axis of evil" reference by Bush and talks between the Japanese and North Koreans, China sensed an opportunity to find a common multilateral language with the Japanese. The 30th anniversary of the reestablishment of relations between Beijing and Tokyo came in late September 2002, just after the Koizumi summit in Pyongyang. Yet the celebratory mood was soon overshadowed by the aftermath of the Kelly visit to Pyongyang and a free-fall in Japanese-North Korean relations. China grew increasingly alarmed over reactions in Japan over North Korea, though "new thinking" favored closer ties with Japan.[22] To salvage regional security, Beijing had to be assertive toward Pyongyang but inviting toward Tokyo. Hu's meetings with Putin and Bush on May 27 and June 1, 2003 offered a balance, chastising the North on nuclear weapons. These brief summits ratcheted up the pressure on the North, while leaving in doubt what China would do if it became North Korea's final lifeline should economic sanctions be imposed.

If the April 23 talks in Beijing won China credit for pressuring the North they also left many Chinese frustrated with Kim Jong Il's saber rattling. Growing trust of South Korea, alarm over the impact of the crisis in Japan, and awareness of benefits from reassuring the United States all led China to push for five-way talks with the North. Reports of Chinese debates on the crisis suggested a new determination to work with the United States.[23] In early August China reaped the gratitude of the other nations for activist diplomacy that brought the North to the table. Once the talks began China would likely be on the spot again in reconciling differences.

South Korea's Role

South Korea stood at the center of the vortex of these great power calculations. Under Kim Dae Jung's leadership from 1998, South Korea had fundamentally reevaluated its relations with each of the powers. In contrast to earlier reasoning that U.S. troops were the "tripwire" to keep the North from attacking, a new belief that Pyongyang's bluster was aimed at winning political and economic concessions to be used in a gradual reintegration process had spread in the South. Despite scant progress in cross-border dialogue, young South Koreans became convinced that their country's foremost goal is to engage their brethren to the North. An unprovoked North Korean naval attack that killed five Southern sailors in June 2002 did not change their minds. At the Pusan Games in September 2002, athletes and cheerleaders from the North were greeted euphorically. Riding high on confidence achieved by bringing democracy to their country and, in the flush of excitement over the successful hosting of the World Cup, young South Koreans eyed the power of engagement with the North idealistically. The first stages of the crisis did not change their thinking, as they voted in Roh Moo Hyun in December 2002.

Despite much that was written in Seoul, the summit of the Koreas on June 15, 2000 no longer appears to have been a decisive turning point. Secretly paying Kim Jung Il a reported $500 million to receive Kim Dae Jung and to secure economic rights for one of the Hyundai companies, the South bought a desired symbol of progress without changing the psychology of the North. Family reunions proved to be a formalistic dud, long on tears, but absent any trust-building. After three years of economic projects, the North had yet to relax its tight controls. Refusing to offend the North's leadership by setting conditions for economic assistance, the South had little leverage. When Roh was elected as prime minister he pledged more of the same, yet he soon was backtracking. Among the reasons were Pyongyang's failure to show restraint, the spillover from anti-Americanism, and a loss of confidence in South Korea by global investors.

Seoul also had a regional objective that was superseding its ties with Washington. This was apparent after September 11, when Kim Dae Jung was slow to support the United States and failed to send support for the war in Afghanistan. This regional goal could be observed in warming ties with the other powers in Northeast Asia, especially China, with which South Korea's bilateral trade reached $40 billion in 2002. Lost in Seoul's obsessional attentiveness to Pyongyang was its simultaneous championing of regionalism. In this pursuit, Japan took second place to China, while Russia achieved political significance that belied its economic weakness. Of course, relations with the United States still had much significance, but demonstrations in favor of reducing or removing U.S. forces reinforced the extent of this thinking.

The voices of both Korean governments shaped the environment for great power maneuvering. On January 1, 2003, North Korea's major newspapers carried a joint editorial entitled "Let Us Fully Demonstrate the Dignity and Might of the DPRK." It called for "perfect unity" of the people, who "absolutely worship and follow their leader," "giving top priority to the army as firm as a rock," and holding high the banner of the June 15 North-South Joint Declaration.[24] It was a defiant assertion that the North needed no external assistance, while appealing to the South to join it against the United States. On February 25, Roh turned his inaugural address into a dual appeal for regionalism and trust-building through peaceful dialogue with the North. He insisted that the "age of Northeast Asia is fast approaching" and the Korean Peninsula is "a big bridge, linking China and Japan, the continent and the ocean."[25] Stating that nuclear development in the North can never be condoned and that the U.S. alliance has significantly contributed to his country's security and economic development, Roh also called for multilateralism through regional partners that recognize the South and the North as "the two main actors in inter-Korean relations."[26]

Suspected of anti-Americanism and unable to win concessions from the North, Roh started his presidency with little credibility in a crisis that had devastating consequences. Foreign investment in South Korea fell precipitously (down to $1.2 billion in the first quarter of 2003 from an average of about $2.5 billion in previous quarters).[27] U.S. defense officials spoke of withdrawing forward-based troops, raising the chances of a U.S. military strike on the North with the South alone left to face the brunt of any military response. It became imperative for Roh to strengthen ties to the

United States, which culminated in a mid-May visit to Washington. Forgoing a joint news conference that would expose differences in their positions, Roh and Bush presented a united front in their appeal for the North to accept a non-nuclear peninsula. Without abandoning Seoul's offer of benefits if the North backed away from brinkmanship, experts in the South gravitated toward a mixed approach. They advocated concentrating on verified removal of nuclear weapons and expressed readiness to support sanctions if the North did not agree to a generous set of incentives.[28]

Fearing that it would be left as an observer after the Iraq war and the disappointing three-way talks in Beijing, Seoul agreed to convey a joint message with the United States and Japan.[29] While reluctant to approve anything beyond "dialogue," even as Japan gave its assent to "pressure," Roh managed to convince Bush and Koizumi that he had shifted direction. Meanwhile, his supporters accused him of "kowtowing" to Bush and being humiliated by Japan's Diet, which on the day of his arrival in Tokyo (Korea's Memorial Day) passed an emergency bill granting the Japanese Self Defense Forces greater powers. Detractors, who control South Korea's main newspapers, insist that nobody trusts Roh because he has no intention of going beyond peaceful coexistence through exchanges with the North.[30]

During the first half of 2003, the cumulative effects of the North's provocations, such as its announcement of withdrawal from the Nuclear Non-Proliferation Treaty (NPT) after expelling international inspectors and removing the seals at the Yongbyon nuclear facilities; its reactivation of the nuclear reactor there; its nullification of the 1992 North-South denuclearization agreement; and its admission that it possessed nuclear weapons, affected South Korea. There was also the economic impact from crisis on the peninsula and growing U.S. concern about the perceived anti-Americanism of the South Koreans and their new leadership. Finally, there was the effect of the quick U.S. success in Iraq allowing Washington to turn more attention to the Korean crisis.

By the time Roh went to Washington on May 14, much had changed (see the chapter on South Korea in this volume). With the North's economic situation further deteriorating, the South proceeded to link additional economic aid to progress in resolving the nuclear issue. When Koizumi met with Bush a week after the Bush-Roh meetings, triangular coordination was restored. Again, the North was warned that its conduct could lead to "further steps," hinting at economic sanctions if not the boarding of ships or even outright military action. After Roh's visit to Tokyo from June 6, meetings began to focus on ways to pressure the North economically. The Japanese were discussing ways to limit the flow of money from Koreans in Japan to the North, and the United States warned of tighter controls on ships from the North. Even while Roh insisted that dialogue would work, intensifying pressure from his allies indicated a lack of confidence in diplomatic routes.

How Far Does Multilateralism Go?

Although it is too early at the time of writing (August 2003) to predict how this crisis will end, it is possible to draw some tentative conclusions about how relations in the region are changing. U.S. and North Korean actions that were not welcomed by the other countries have forced some rethinking. Among China, Japan, Russia, and South Korea, there is some evidence of convergence. All strongly desire a nuclear-free Korean Peninsula, even if they disagree on how much other priorities should be sacrificed for this goal. All welcome a boost in regional security ties, despite different strategies to achieve it. And all resent U.S. unilateralism, although Japan seems more tolerant since it has the least confidence in the diplomatic efforts of the others. Yet Japan and South Korea remain U.S. allies, with U.S. troops stationed on their soil, and the North's threat of targeting their people obliges them to draw closer to the U.S. position in the heat of crisis. This convergence will be tested if the danger from the North recedes. South Koreans are eager for multilateralism with a balancing role, and Japanese continue to seek a way to "reenter Asia" less dependent on the U.S.

Each envisions some sort of regionalism through a division of labor as a desired outcome of the crisis. Japan's offer of billions of dollars for a peace settlement and the South's sustained input of capital would boost economic integration, which would also be attractive to China and Russia because of new transportation routes and border trade. The reconstruction of the North's economy, fueled by market reforms and foreign economic ties, is seen across the region as giving a lift to the whole region. There appears to be a shared longing for regionalism as the outcome of the crisis.

Before that can occur, however, it is first necessary to determine how far the two principals will move toward multilateralism. With little information available on internal debates in Pyongyang, all nations have watched intently for signals from Washington. Messages from the administration after the three-way meeting with the North in Beijing were inconsistent. The United States scorned the North's offer to take only small steps in return for what might be a generous package of benefits. Then Secretary of State Colin Powell, "because of pressure from China, South Korea and Japan," referred to the Beijing session as "quite useful," indicating that continued diplomacy was ahead.[31] Next came an op-ed piece by veterans of the first Bush administration, Brent Scowcroft and Arnold Kanter, calling the session "A Surprising Success on North Korea."[32] Behind the confusion lay two distinct strategies—albeit with some overlap. On the one side are those who praise U.S. patience in the face of provocations and insist that as long as the United States forges a consensus that the North cannot split, Pyongyang will back down.[33] On the other are those who intend to lean on China to make real the threat of economic sanctions (or blame it for abetting the North) amidst the growing likelihood of U.S. military action. The differences remained to be tested, first through coordination with the other parties in Northeast Asia, then through responses from the North. In the meantime, the United States has not given clear indications about how far it would proceed with multilateralism.

Some U.S. experts on Korea criticized "unilateral" policies as provoking and deepening the nuclear crisis while undermining U.S. relations with Northeast Asia. They called for a sequel to the 1994 agreement, leading this time to recognition of the North, promises not to target the North with nuclear weapons, and a package of assistance or even buyouts of missiles.[34] Yet even William Perry's calls for "deep talks" with the North to avoid the military option were barely audible.[35] With Democratic presidential candidates shunning the issue, Bush found little second-guessing of his handling of North Korea at home. A semblance of control, however, did not obscure concern among attentive observers that miscalculations could occur.

To many, Beijing was left as the pivotal third party, needed by Washington in order to avoid a military solution and by Seoul, Tokyo, and Moscow as they anxiously looked for a compromise on the sidelines. The United States, however, sought to play up support from others in Northeast Asia before seeking China's help. As Deputy Defense Secretary Paul Wolfowitz insisted, "On North Korea, the key is confronting them with a unified force from Russia, Japan, South Korea, and to a lesser extent China."[36] The Hu-Bush meeting on the sidelines of the G-8 summit did not yet reveal how far the United States would go to meet China's regional interests, or the degree to which China would address U.S. global interests. If the two could agree on a package, the North would know that economic sanctions would intensify and, failing those, military action could follow.

In times of military tension, the United States continues to have the upper hand over China in Northeast Asia. The South Koreans and the Japanese may want China to press the North hard, but they give preference to ties with the United States, whose power deters North Korea. This may not tell us much about the long-term competition ahead between Washington and Beijing for influence in Northeast Asia. U.S. tactics since 2001 are not popular in Northeast Asia, and, so far, nothing China has done reduces its prospects for renewed centrality in Northeast Asia once the crisis is resolved.

After a series of summit meetings, the United States began economic interdiction with the expectation that the squeeze on the North's economy would intensify. In June and July the United States and Japan acted in consort to begin inspections of the North's ships, South Korea acquiesced despite warnings that such actions could provoke the North and fail to offer it a face-saving outcome,[37] China activated its diplomacy in order to restart talks, and Russia waited until North Korea decided it should be part of multilateral talks. Pyongyang is not likely to suffer the new blows to its economy long before choosing to change its posture by either compromise in six-party talks or drastic action to force a split among those pressuring it.

Offered little opportunity by the North's extreme rhetoric, its four neighbors began to make progress coordinating their approach on the nuclear issue. As long as they held out hope that the United States would return to the negotiating table, they put aside fears that a military confrontation was drawing closer. In the process, efforts toward regionalism were also put on hold. Despite the mismatch between a strident Pyongyang and an unflustered Washington, both of which had reason to obscure the true nature of the situation, the August 27–29 talks in Beijing left only vague hope for finding common ground at the next round of talks, but no lessening of the severity of the conflict.

If North Korea endures as a nuclear weapons state, it may heighten Northeast Asia's dependence on the United States. Japan and South Korea have already demonstrated that their response is to turn to Washington. If through pressure and negotiations the North abandons its nuclear capability, however, there may be a boost to regionalism. South Korea's place at the center of Northeast Asia would be enhanced by both its leading role in the reintegration of the Korean Peninsula and its balancing role between Japan and China. As Washington responds to the North's threat with plans to relocate military bases and establish a regional intelligence headquarters at Misawa in northeast Japan, it envisions a dominant security role for itself. Once this danger passes, however, the countries of Northeast Asia may calculate that the U.S. aim is to solidify its position as a brake to a separate regional arrangement independent of the United States. The enhanced coordination witnessed in the spring of 2003 is but a prelude to the application of economic pressure while seeking a path to negotiations. This next stage could lead in turn to a decisive phase of crisis resolution. Only this will reveal the balance between U.S. predominance and emerging regionalism. Ironically, the multilateralism that the United States professes to manage the nuclear crisis may, in fact, boost regionalism in which U.S. unilateral tendencies leave it with a more peripheral, if still important, role.

Endnotes

[1] Gilbert Rozman, "Russian Foreign Policy in Northeast Asia," in Sam Kim, ed., *The International Relations of Northeast Asia*, Lanham, Md.: Rowman and Littlefield, 2003, pp. 201–24. A "soft landing" signifies gradual transformation of the North, offering it the means to reform without regime change.

[2] A. Vorontsov, "Rossiia i Koreiskii poluostrov: sovremennye realii i perspektivy (Russia and the Korean Peninsula: contemporary realities and perspectives)," *Problemy Dal'nego Vostoka*, no. 3 (2002) pp. 46–58; Iurii Fedorov, "Koreiskaia iadernaia problema (The Korean nuclear problem)," *Analisticheskie zapiski*, no. 1, Moscow: Institut prikladnykh mezhdunarodnykh issledovanii, 2003, pp. 3–20.

[3] "Unofficial translation from Russian: Joint Declaration of the Russian Federation and the People's Republic of China," Kremlin, Moscow, May 27, 2003, FBIS 2003CEP20030528000286.

[4] V. Mikheev, "Koreiskaia problema v svete sobytii 11 Sentiabria (The Korean problem in light of the events of September 11)," *Problemy Dal'nego Vostoka*, no. 3 (2002) pp. 34–45.

[5] "Ekspertnoe soobshchestvo obsuzhdaet posledstviia Irakskoi voiny (Expert association discusses the consequences of the Iraq war)," *Mezhdunarodnaia zhizn'*, no. 4 (2003) pp. 3–36.

[6] Gilbert Rozman, "Japan's North Korean Initiative and U.S.-Japanese Relations," *Orbis*, vol. 47, no. 3 (Summer 2003), pp. 527–39.

[7] *Mainichi Shimbun*, September 15, 2002, p. 3.

[8] Kan Sanjun, Mizuno Naoki, and Lee Jon Won, eds., *Nicho Kosho: Wadai to Tenbo (Japanese-North Korean negotiations: topics and outlook)*, Tokyo: Iwanami Shoten, 2003.

[9] *Asahi Shimbun*, March 6, 2003, p. 14.

[10] *Mainichi Shimbun*, June 2, 2002, p. 3.

[11] See the special issue of *Gaiko forum* devoted to the Korean Peninsula, no. 173 (December 2002).

[12] Toyama Tai, "Beikoku no nerai wa kitachosen no taisei kodai (The U.S. aim is regime change in North Korea)," *Sekai shuho*, April 22, 2003, pp. 42–43; Okonogi Masao, "Kitachosen wa Iraku no 'kyokutoban' ni naru ka? (Will North Korea become the 'Far East version' of Iraq?)," *Sekai shuho*, May 6–13, 2003, pp. 6–9.

[13] Fukubu Kenji, "Kitachosen ni hageshii memukeru Chugoku (China which has its eyes glued on North Korea)," *Sekai shuho*, April 15, 2003, pp. 26–29; Abe Junichi, "Kitachosen mondai ni shuren suru Chugoku gaiko no 'henka' ('Change' in China's foreign policy which is training on the North Korea question)," *Sekai shuho*, April 29, 2003, pp. 50–51.

[14] Tanaka Akihiko, "Sekai kesshite jyanguru ni wa naranai (The world is definitely not becoming a jungle)," *Chuo Koron*, June 2003, pp. 72–80.

[15] *Sankei Shimbun*, May 28, 2003.

[16] An Zhenli, "Chaoxian bandao xingshi bianhua yu Dandong de zhanlüe jueze (Change in the situation on the Korean Peninsula and the strategic choice of Dandong)," *Dongbeiya Luntan*, no. 2 (2002), pp. 66–69.

[17] Cheng Yujie, "Chaoxian bandao de heping jincheng (Peaceful advance on the

Korean Peninsula)," in Zhongguo Xiandai Guoji Guanxi Yanjiusuo, *Yatai Zhanlue Chang* (Asia Pacific strategic arena), Beijing: Shishi Chubanshe, 2002, pp. 385–410.

[18] Gilbert Rozman, "China's Quest for Great Power Identity," *Orbis*, vol. 43, no. 3 (Summer 1999), pp. 383–402.

[19] Gilbert Rozman, "China's Changing Images of Japan 1989–2001: The Struggle to Balance Partnership and Rivalry," *International Relations of the Asia-Pacific*, Winter 2002, pp. 95–129.

[20] David Shambaugh, "China and the Korean Peninsula: Playing for the Long Term," *Washington Quarterly*, Spring 2003, pp. 43–56.

[21] Zhang Yushan, "Chaori guanxi de xianshi yu weilai (The current situation and future of North Korean-Japanese relations)," *Dongbeiya Luntan*, no. 3 (2001), p. 28.

[22] Shi Yinhong, "'Nichu jiejin' wa Chugoku gaiko no shinninmu ('Japanese-Chinese drawing close' is the new task of Chinese diplomacy)," *Sekai Shuho*, May 6–13, 2003, pp. 46–49.

[23] Piao Jianyi, Zhang Liangui, Jin Xide, and Zhang Tuosheng, "Chaoxian he wenti zai yanjiang (Speaking again on the North Korean nuclear question)," *Shijie Zhishi*, June 2003.

[24] "New Year Editorial Democratic People's Republic of Korea, January 1, 2003," in Bush and Dalpino, eds., *Brookings Northeast Asia Survey 2002–2003*, pp. 98–102.

[25] "A New Takeoff Toward an Age of Peace and Prosperity, Inaugural Address of President Roh Moo Hyun," in Bush and Dalpino, eds., *Brookings Northeast Asia Survey 2002–2003*, p. 92.

[26] "A New Takeoff Toward an Age of Peace and Prosperity, Inaugural Address of President Roh Moo Hyun," p. 94.

[27] *Korea Insight*, vol. 5, no. 7, July 2003, p. 4.

[28] Jung-Hoon Lee and Chung-in Moon, "The North Korean Nuclear Crisis Revisited: The Case for a Negotiated Settlement," *Security Dialogue*, vol. 34, no. 2 (June 2003), pp. 131–48.

[29] "Iraku jonjaeng kwa Bukhan haek munje (The Iraq war and the North Korean nuclear question)," *Tongil Hanguk*, May 2003, p. 10.

[30] *Donga Ilbo*, June 11, 2003, p. A2; *Chosun Ilbo*, June 14, 2003, p. A6.

[31] *New York Times*, April 29, 2003, p. A21.

[32] *New York Times*, May 1, 2003.

[33] Dean Nowowiejski, Tamotsu Nakano, and Richard Bush, "Crisis on the Korean Peninsula," in Bush and Dalpino, eds., *Brookings Northeast Asia Survey 2002–2003,* p. 16.

[34] The Task Force on U.S. Korea Policy, "The Nuclear Crisis on the Korean Peninsula: Avoiding the Road to Perdition," and Bruce Cumings, "North Korea: The Sequel," *Current History*, vol. 102, no. 663 (April 2003), pp. 147–51, and 152–69.

[35] *Korea Times*, June 9, 2003, p. 14

[36] *New York Times*, May 31, 2003, A10.

[37] *Korea Herald*, June 9, 2003, p. 1.

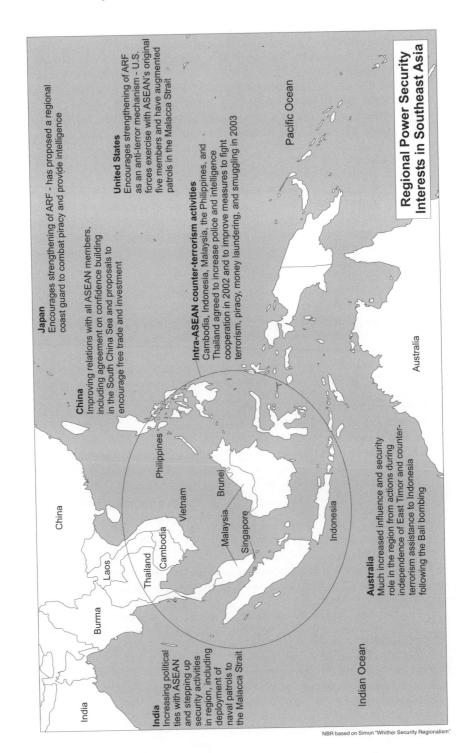

Regional Power Security Interests in Southeast Asia

Japan
Encourages strengthening of ARF - has proposed a regional coast guard to combat piracy and provide intelligence

China
Improving relations with all ASEAN members, including agreement on confidence building in the South China Sea and proposals to encourage free trade and investment

United States
Encourages strengthening of ARF as an anti-terror mechanism - U.S. forces exercise with ASEAN's original five members and have augmented patrols in the Malacca Strait

Intra-ASEAN counter-terrorism activities
Cambodia, Indonesia, Malaysia, the Philippines, and Thailand agreed to increase police and intelligence cooperation in 2002 and to improve measures to fight terrorism, piracy, money laundering, and smuggling in 2003

India
Increasing political ties with ASEAN and stepping up security activities in region, including deployment of naval patrols to the Malacca Strait

Australia
Much increased influence and security role in the region from actions during independence of East Timor and counter-terrorism assistance to Indonesia following the Bali bombing

NBR based on Simon "Whither Security Regionalism"

WHITHER SECURITY REGIONALISM?

Sheldon W. Simon

ABSTRACT

Most Southeast Asians believe that their security is best maintained by engaging the great powers in multilateral endeavors such as the ASEAN post-ministerial conferences, ASEAN+3, and the ASEAN Regional Forum (ARF). While directed toward keeping China and the United States involved in assuring the region's security, ASEAN also welcomes participation by India and Japan in these initiatives. Neither ASEAN nor the ARF, however, have been willing to tackle the core security issues facing the region—be they external support for insurgencies, refugee flows, or disputes over sovereignty. Inclusive memberships in both organizations and the ASEAN consensus principle work against their effectiveness. But although ASEAN cannot solve Southeast Asia's challenges alone, it can still try to control the agenda in its dealings with external powers. Thus, it may be able to enlist the great powers in Southeast Asian concerns, or at least ensure that Northeast Asia not ignore Southeast Asian interests.

Sheldon Simon is Professor of Political Science at Arizona State University and Chairman of the Advisory Board of NBR's Southeast Asia Studies Program. He wishes to express his appreciation to Aaron Friedberg, Richard Ellings, and Michael Wills for their guidance, and to Donald Emmerson, Karl Jackson, and Robert Scher for their helpful comments on an earlier version of this chapter.

Introduction

Until the Asian financial crisis of 1997–98, the Association of Southeast Asian Nations (ASEAN) was generally considered the most successful multinational political organization among developing countries in the world.[1] ASEAN's international reputation was burnished in the 1980s by its ability to keep the United Nations focused on the necessity of repelling Vietnam's invasion and occupation of Cambodia. Hanoi's subsequent withdrawal, though achieved because of other geopolitical changes—a Russo-China rapprochement, the collapse of the Soviet Union, and possibly Hanoi's reconsideration of the costs of occupation—was seen as a major ASEAN victory. ASEAN also arranged annual meetings between the Association and the great powers (the United States, China, Japan, and the European Union) to discuss an agenda of political, economic, and security issues generated by the Southeast Asian states.

This record of Southeast Asian states playing well above their collective weights in global politics came to an end in the late 1990s because of a series of regional challenges to which ASEAN has been unable to respond effectively. These included the region's financial crisis, the Indonesian-generated forest fire haze that periodically blankets Singapore, Malaysia, and the southern Philippines, the upheaval and 1999 referendum in East Timor leading to the latter's independence, the 1997 Cambodian coup which overturned the results of a UN-sponsored and ASEAN-endorsed election, and most recently ASEAN's rebuke of Burma in June and July 2003 for the detention of Nobel Prize winner Aung San Suu Kyi. All of these created what the late Michael Leifer called "a clear failure of regional cooperation" and have led to a crisis of regional identity and credibility within ASEAN.[2]

Nor has ASEAN been of help in resolving persistent sub-regional tensions including: 1) the Thai-Burmese confrontation over the latter's drug trafficking and allegations by Rangoon that Thailand provides sanctuary for Burma's separatist Karen minority; 2) Thai concerns about support from northern Malaysia to separatists in southern Thailand, some of whom seek to unite with their Malay brethren across the border; 3) discord between Kuala Lumpur and Jakarta over hundreds of thousands of illegal Indonesian workers seeking jobs in Malaysia, and a similar problem with illegal Philippine laborers in Sabah; and 4) the ongoing saga over the future of the Spratly Islands where China, Taiwan, Vietnam, Malaysia, the Philippines, and Brunei contest ownership and sometimes seize each other's fishing boats for alleged maritime territory violations.

The primary reason for ASEAN's inability to deal effectively with these issues is its normative attachment to the principle of non-interference. If regionalism is to be more than a process of multilateral policy coordination and negotiation of competing interests, then a sense of collective intersubjective identity is required. ASEAN has not achieved that sense.[3]

From its 1967 inception, ASEAN embedded a non-interference norm that stipulated consultation, consensus, and non-interference with respect to its members' internal affairs as well as any disagreements with other members. The consensus requirement reassured members that sovereignty would remain inviolate, and the domination of the sovereignty principle meant that serious differences among members would be deferred to defuse conflict. Thus, ASEAN approaches to conflict were not geared to external threats to its members, but rather to helping them achieve regime security vis-à-vis their neighbors through confidence building via consultations. This "soft security" approach contrasted sharply with U.S. bilateral security arrangements in Asia geared exclusively to external threats.[4]

Already weakened by the financial crisis and the challenges listed above, Southeast Asia had to cope with the post-September 11 world. Though national responses varied, generally the region has gone through four stages: initial shock and sympathy, then concern and anger over the U.S. war in Afghanistan. This was followed by the third stage, the discovery of a major bomb plot in Singapore in January 2002, and the signing of a U.S.-ASEAN anti-terrorist agreement in August 2002. Finally, the October 2002 and August 2003 Bali and J. W. Marriott bombings—the worst terrorist acts in the region's history, together killing well over 200—heralded unprecedented cooperation among regional and foreign law enforcement agencies in Southeast Asia.[5]

Paradoxically, the terrorist challenge could provide ASEAN with an opportunity to restore cohesion and create a new security agenda comparable to that which emerged in response to Vietnam's occupation of Cambodia in the 1980s. Of course the nature of the threat is different. Instead of a heavily armed state, today the threat is from individuals or relatively small groups operating transnationally that endanger an entire region, requiring governments to cooperate on a priority basis if the threat is to be suppressed. Whether ASEAN is up to this challenge remains to be seen.

Meanwhile, bilateral tensions within Southeast Asia as well as the prospect of domestic implosion in Indonesia continue. Anti-Thai riots in Cambodia in early 2003 that led to the razing of the Thai embassy constitute the most dramatic example of persistent historical animosities lying below the surface of common ASEAN membership. Cambodia's delays in creating a tribunal to deal with former Khmer Rouge leaders and the country's endemic corruption keep foreign loans, grants, and investments at bay, miring the country in poverty. There are rising tensions on Indonesia's land border with Malaysia in Borneo. With the World Court's ruling in December 2002 that the disputed islands of Sipadan and Ligatan belonged to Malaysia, Jakarta is looking for ways to guarantee its sovereignty over other disputed islands and to protect its vast maritime boundaries from smugglers, poachers, and pirates. Given its minimal navy, however, that may be impossible. Indonesia and the Philippines resent Malaysia's expulsion of illegal foreign workers in order to free up more jobs for Malays as the region's economies sputter. Malaysian Prime Minister Mahathir Mohamad has rekindled animosities with Singapore over water usage arrangements, contested islands, and competing port facilities for international maritime commerce.[6]

In light of bilateral tensions within ASEAN, the Association's apparent meager ability to deal with current regional security challenges—separatist movements in Indonesia and the Philippines, transnational arms smuggling, illegal population movements, and drug trafficking, as well as terrorism—the question arises: *whither security regionalism?* The remainder of this chapter is devoted to assessing whether there are significant roles for ASEAN and the ASEAN Regional Forum (ARF) in meeting these challenges and how other regional arrangements are being created to fill the gaps. Although neither ASEAN nor the ARF are leading efforts to resolve the challenges listed above, neither are they irrelevant. The questions for their future effectiveness focus on the structural limits to their capabilities and the norms that might enhance their roles in conflict resolution.

ASEAN: Has Expansion Led to the Peter Principle?

If the five original members of ASEAN remain suspicious of each other and wary of multilateral cooperation despite collaborating since the Association's 1967 inception, how has expansion to all ten Southeast Asian states affected the organization's cohesion? Put another way, has ASEAN's expansion led to the Peter Principle? That is, has the organization expanded to a level of incompetence? Unsurprisingly, the impact has been negative. In economic affairs, a two-tier system has been created whereby progress toward an ASEAN Free Trade Area (AFTA) possesses one set of deadlines for the first six members (2003) and an indefinite delay for the most recent four (Burma, Cambodia, Laos, and Vietnam), though 2010 is a target date. With respect to security, the peaceful settlement of international disputes is a core ASEAN norm. However, ASEAN expansion imposes security burdens arising from additional unsettled maritime boundaries and overlapping maritime exclusive economic zones (EEZs), some of which violate the ASEAN non-use of force, a norm embodied in the 1976 Treaty of Amity and Cooperation. For example, Thai and Burmese forces clash sporadically along their common border over ethnic minority insurgents as well as over Burma-based drug trafficking. Whether ASEAN's new members can be socialized into the interpersonal and informal way in which the Association copes with its differences is still open to question.[7]

Equally problematic is the viability of the norm of non-use of force. No ASEAN member contemplates outright war with its neighbors; nevertheless, regional arms buildups have been (at least until the 1997–98 financial crisis) conducted with an eye toward maintaining a balance with ASEAN partners. Intra-ASEAN military cooperation is tentative, at best. Even Malaysia's suggestion for establishing an ASEAN peacekeeping force, based on the experience of several ASEAN states' armed forces in Cambodia, East Timor, and the Balkans, was shelved partly because it might have been seen as an attempt to turn ASEAN into a military alliance and partly because it would be impolitic to insert such a force into an intra-ASEAN conflict. Practical considerations also stymie ASEAN military cooperation since weapons systems are purchased from so many different national suppliers that interoperability would be problematic.[8]

An important ASEAN principle with respect to the war on terror is that no member will provide sanctuary or support to groups bent on undermining the government of an ASEAN state. While no ASEAN government supports subversion against a neighbor, there are cases of sanctuary in locations which governments have been unwilling or, more probably, unable to suppress such groups. Muslim Thai separatists flee to northern Malaysia; large numbers of Karen are located inside the Thai northern border; Philippine Moros are found in Malaysian Borneo; and Jemaah Islamiyah cells that target several ASEAN states are well entrenched in parts of Indonesia despite Jakarta's efforts at disruption. Jemaah Islamiyah adherents have also been apprehended in the Philippines and southern Thailand. Although law enforcement investigations have revealed that terrorists move readily among several ASEAN states because of visa-free travel, porous borders, and corrupt immigration officials, ASEAN has done little to remedy the situation.[9] Intra-ASEAN differences over the long-standing norm of non-interference are difficult to overcome even when all members face a common threat.

The so-called ASEAN Way emphasizing quiet diplomacy, non-confrontation, and non-interference in domestic affairs, has been supplemented (if not replaced) since September 11 and the Bali and J. W. Marriott bombings by more pro-active measures. Visa-free travel is being reconsidered among ASEAN states. At its November 2001 summit, an ASEAN declaration on joint action to counter terrorism was adopted. Subsequently, in August 2002, a U.S.-ASEAN declaration to counter terror was also endorsed. While these declarations acknowledge the ASEAN-wide challenge, much remains to be done. In May 2002, the ASEAN states agreed on an action plan that provided for enhanced cooperation in intelligence sharing and the coordination of anti-terror laws. Singapore's proposal that each member form a special anti-terrorist team as a contact point was also accepted.[10] Yet, the ASEAN states remain slow to ratify 12 key anti-terrorist conventions, especially the treaty suppressing terrorist finances.

ASEAN members could consider modest steps to harden their borders against the transnational flow of terrorists, including their weapons and funds. Background checks for visas constitute one measure, though it may delay freedom of movement and commerce within ASEAN. Training immigration officials in detecting forged documents is another. Passing legislation requiring closer scrutiny of corporate accounts would bring the ASEAN states in line with the anti-money laundering standards of the Financial Action Task Force, of which currently only Singapore is a member. In the spring of 2003, Thailand and the Philippines passed anti-money laundering legislation. Enforcement, however, will be key to effectiveness.

Maritime policing is another woeful inadequacy among ASEAN states. Favorite routes for illicit arms traffic go from southern Thailand across the northern Strait of Malacca to Aceh, as well as across the South China Sea to Sabah and the southern Philippines.[11] Collaboration among the littoral navies and coast guards, especially in the Strait of Malacca, is difficult. Hot pursuit of pirates has been hampered by the requirement that the pursuing state obtain permission in each instance from the country into whose waters the pirates flee. The annual rate of piracy is on the rise again in Southeast Asia; and, although terrorist groups so far have not hijacked ships, one can imagine the devastation caused if a tanker carrying liquefied natural gas were seized and blown up in the Strait of Malacca. Moreover, maritime insurance rates would skyrocket.[12] In fact, maritime insurance rates did increase after the Bali bombings, and news reports in the past year have speculated that Al Qaeda may be planning to target ships carrying radioactive material through the Straits.

If the littoral states are willing, in addition to augmented U.S. Seventh Fleet patrols in the Malacca Strait, the U.S. and Japanese coast guards could engage selected ASEAN navies in anti-piracy exercises and provide intelligence on suspicious activities in the Malacca Strait and its approaches. During 2002, India also deployed a destroyer to help escort high value vessels through the Strait.[13]

In January 2003, ASEAN police forces meeting in Jakarta proposed an anti-terrorism task force for each country to strengthen collaboration on post-Bali terrorist attacks. The model would be the cooperation between the Indonesian police and the police forces of other countries to arrest the perpetrators of terror and uncover their networks in the region. Malaysia and Indonesia argued that national legislation should be passed in each country making terrorism an extraditable offense. Singapore balked, however, pointing to the different legal systems within ASEAN, although its primary concern is probably the large number of wealthy Indonesian Chinese who fled to Singapore in the wake of anti-Chinese riots in Indonesia in 1998.[14] A blanket extradition treaty among ASEAN states could lead Indonesia to claim that its ethnic Chinese citizens now in Singapore had committed economic crimes by fleeing with their resources.[15]

Other issues on ASEAN's table include the U.S. war in Iraq and the outbreak of Severe Acute Respiratory Syndrome (SARS). The former split the Association, with Singapore, the Philippines, and to a smaller degree Thailand backing Washington, while Malaysia, Indonesia, and other ASEAN states either condemned U.S. actions or remained silent. The Philippines was among 30 countries openly backing the U.S. invasion and hence well positioned, so it believed, to obtain some reconstruction contracts in medical and educational domains. Singapore and Thailand were on a list of 15 countries lending support but preferring to remain anonymous at the time of the U.S. invasion.[16] With respect to postwar reconstruction, Malaysia and Indonesia share the view that the United Nations should be given the major role.

As for SARS, ASEAN held a summit in late April 2003 in Bangkok, to which China was invited. ASEAN health ministers also met in Kuala Lumpur in a special ASEAN+3 setting (with Japan, South Korea, and China) that affirmed the need to bar suspected SARS-infected individuals from leaving their respective countries as the most effective way to prevent the spread of the disease. Additionally, the countries mandated that all travelers from affected countries complete SARS health declaration forms.[17]

The ARF: Is the Tail Wagging the Dog?

Just as ASEAN faces security problems that challenge non-intervention and sovereignty norms, so the ARF now confronts regionwide issues that make consensus difficult to achieve. The ARF emerged from ASEAN in the 1990s. The end of the Cold War left the Asia Pacific searching for a new organizing principle for security. While traditional alliances remained, including bilateral treaties with the United States and the Five Power Defense Arrangement (a multilateral agreement among Great Britain, Australia, New Zealand, Malaysia, and Singapore), these seemed inadequate to deal with security matters of a nonmilitary nature such as transnational crime, environmental hazards, and illegal population movements.[18] Moreover, "traditional" security issues persisted in the form of unresolved territorial disputes, divided states, nuclear weapons proliferation, and conflicting maritime jurisdictions resulting from the 1982 UN Law of the Sea.

Some kind of cooperative security enterprise linking the region to its major partners in Northeast Asia and North America was needed to fill the gap. Through the 1976 Treaty of Amity and Cooperation, ASEAN members had already pledged among themselves to resolve intra-ASEAN disputes peacefully (or postpone their resolution). Underlying the vision of a larger security order was the hope that the treaty's peaceful resolution commitment could be extended to other states. This practice would constitute a kind of minimal diffuse reciprocity. That is, while ASEAN would not expect outsiders to automatically come to members' aid in times of crisis or to their defense if attacked, at least outside countries could be asked to renounce the use of force in settling any conflicts they might have with the Association's members.

The unstated object of these concerns, of course, is China—the only "extra-regional" state with territorial claims in Southeast Asia. This is essentially a realist vision of the ARF. If successful, it would encourage the People's Republic of China (PRC) to explain and clarify its security policy and planning. China's neighbors, through the ARF, could then respond with their concerns about the PRC's policy in hopes of modifying it and thus enhancing regional stability. In exchange for PRC transparency, other ARF members would reciprocate. For Beijing the payoff would not primarily be access to ASEAN defense plans but rather to those of other members such as Japan and the United States.

Fortunately for ASEAN, no exclusive Northeast Asian efforts were made to create a subregional counterpart to ASEAN. China remained wary of security multilateralism as a device to constrain its regional ambitions. Japan was still viewed with suspicion by the rest of Northeast Asia as unrepentant for its World War II brutalities, and the Koreas were understandably focused on their fifty-year military stalemate at the 38th parallel. In effect, ASEAN was able to fill this vacuum by offering to create a new region-wide entity modeled on the Association's process of consultation and dialogue. Because this approach fell well short of collective defense, it was not threatening to any potential adherent. Nor would a new regional forum interfere with individual states' security links to outsiders.

Purposefully imitative of the ASEAN Post-Ministerial Conference (PMC), the ARF's objective was to develop a predictable and constructive pattern of relationships in the Asia Pacific. In sum, the ARF would be a transparency and reassurance mechanism for the Asia Pacific, providing the whole region with opportunities for ASEAN-style dialogue. By themselves, the PMCs were viewed by Northeast Asians as insufficient for broad discussion of their subregion's concerns on such issues as competitive arming, maritime exclusive economic zone rules, and the roles of China and Japan. Although ASEAN understood that these issues needed to be addressed, the Association also desired to create a body that would acknowledge ASEAN's institutional status as *primus inter pares*. The ARF achieved this ASEAN goal by ensuring that ASEAN states would be the venue for the ARF's annual meetings; that ASEAN would dominate the agenda; that intersessional study groups, each composed of two states, would always include an ASEAN member; and that the ASEAN consensus principle would prevail in ARF decisions.

By its second meeting, the ARF agreed on a three-stage progression toward comprehensive security for Asia, which would move from confidence building to preventive diplomacy and finally to the development of mechanisms for conflict resolution. The development of these mechanisms was subsequently renamed "elaboration of approaches to conflict" out of deference to China's concern that conflict resolution could be interpreted as justifying the ARF's interference in members' internal affairs. ASEAN PMCs, senior officers' meetings (SOMs), and ARF workshops have generated a cornucopia of transparency possibilities—that is, the discussion of security intentions. Both ASEAN and the ARF agree that security transparency is a prerequisite for more sophisticated preventive diplomacy and conflict resolution. Confidence-building measures that have been raised in ASEAN-related gatherings include notification of military exercises, hot lines among political and military leaders, extension of the U.S.-Russian incidents-at-sea agreement to the entire Asia Pacific, and a regional maritime, air surveillance, and safety regime. These activities all fall within the ARF's trust and confidence-building category. [19]

The ARF has conducted an extensive security dialogue over the years encompassing human rights in Burma, problems on the Korean Peninsula, the South China Sea islands, weapons of mass destruction (WMD) proliferation, and the implications of ballistic missile defense (BMD) deployments. The Forum has called for support of the Nuclear Nonproliferation Treaty (NPT) and ratification of the Comprehensive Test Ban Treaty. It also addresses transnational security issues, especially piracy and illegal migration as well as narcotics and small arms trafficking. These plenary discussions and intersessional meetings have had some practical results: annual defense policy statements and increased publication of defense white papers, including by China and Vietnam which contribute to transparency; military exchanges at the staff college level; growing involvement and participation of defense officials in ARF deliberations; and the creation of an ARF Register of Experts/Eminent Persons who can be called upon by ARF members in conflict situations.[20] However, the ARF has no secretariat to provide continuity or engage in staff studies between its annual plenary, special meetings, or intersessional group conclaves.

While the ARF has turned from confidence-building measures to preventive diplomacy, the transition is difficult. China's as well as some other members' reluctance reflect a concern that basic national security issues, such as the future of Taiwan, not be subject to ARF deliberations. By contrast, Canada, Australia, Japan, and the United States would like to see ARF strengthened. The United States particularly hopes that the ARF will serve as an anti-terror cooperative mechanism. However, the ARF's consensus rule, adopted from ASEAN, has proven a serious obstacle to managing tensions that arise from the divergent strategic interests of ARF members.[21]

The ASEAN overlay on ARF procedures has provoked resentment among some participants, particularly South Korea, which believes that ASEAN's proprietary attitude has constrained any Northeast Asia dialogue within the Forum. Moreover, even the numerous confidence-building measures implemented by the ARF are mainly declarations of transparency that do not involve constraints on behavior. There may be discussions among defense officials, for example, but no agreement on refraining from adding certain kinds of weapons into national arsenals. Nor can the ARF discuss intra-state conflicts because of Chinese objections.[22] An assessment of preventive diplomacy measures endorsed by the ARF through 2001 reveals that they are peacetime or pre-crisis measures, only marginally applicable to ongoing conflicts where crisis-time responses may be needed.[23]

ARF members vary in their desire for greater institutionalization. In Southeast Asia, the proponents are Singapore, the Philippines, and Thailand. These states are more willing to engage in international peacekeeping and preventive diplomacy than Malaysia, Indonesia, and Vietnam. While Washington did not expect the ARF to be an action-oriented security organization, after September 11, the United States urged the ARF to become more involved in devising ways to actively combat terrorism, by shutting down terrorist finances via ARF transnational crime agreements, for example. Another possibility would be to expand ARF undertakings on search and rescue operations to include simulating a ship hijacking in the Strait of Malacca, requiring cooperation among littoral navies to rescue hostages.[24]

To its credit, the ARF laid out an agenda for its members to block terrorist finances at its July 2002 Brunei summit, urging them to implement UN measures that include blocking terrorists' access to national financial systems, freezing terrorist financial assets, publicizing terrorist organizations whose assets have been seized, and creating national financial intelligence units to share information. These exhortations are exemplary; but they are not mandatory. There is no enforcement mechanism nor any sanctions against ARF members who choose not to comply.[25] Moreover, the ARF consensus principle obstructs joint agreements. This obstacle could be overcome if the ARF adopted an ASEAN procedure used to bypass a similar constraint. Called the "ASEAN minus X" understanding, it permits a "coalition of the willing" whereby those states that agree on a principle may proceed, while those that do not may refrain from participation.

Finally, it is worth noting that the ARF is attempting to play a helpful role in the Korean nuclear standoff. Since the DPRK is an ARF member, Thailand, Singapore, Indonesia, and Australia agreed to urge the ARF to use its good offices to address North Korea's withdrawal from the NPT. Thai Foreign Minister Surakiart Sathirathai stated that the issue should not be viewed as exclusively a bilateral conflict between the United States and the DPRK. At an ARF SOM's preparatory meeting in late April 2003 in Siem Reap, Cambodia, the North Koreans briefed ARF delegates on the talks among themselves, the United States, and China. U.S., South Korean, Japanese, and Chinese senior officials were present. North Korea's willingness to discuss nuclear weapons in the ARF suggests a change in its policy of opposing the internationalization of the crisis.[26] Although the ARF venue did not (and, indeed, was never likely to) resolve the Korean nuclear standoff, it expanded ARF's security agenda to Northeast Asia and illustrated that a nuclear confrontation in Korea affected all of East Asia.

Other Forms of Regional Security Cooperation

While ASEAN and the ARF are the primary Asian regional security institutions, they are not the only means by which Southeast Asian states engage in multilateral security cooperation. The terrorist challenges posed by Al Qaeda, Jemaah Islamiyah, and other groups that transfer personnel, weapons, money, and information across Southeast Asia's borders require a coordinated response among those states most affected. Multinational intelligence sharing is particularly important since captured JI members have provided authorities with useful information leading to further arrests or the discovery of new plots.

Several Southeast Asian states have increased anti-terrorist cooperation with one another. Intelligence organizations in Malaysia, Singapore, and the Philippines are exchanging information about regional terrorist groups as well as with U.S. intelligence agencies and the FBI. Nevertheless, constraints still exist. In February 2003, Indonesian security officials arrested Mas Salamat Kastori, the alleged leader of Jemaah Islamiyah in Singapore, based on information provided by the Singaporean government.

Because the two countries have no extradition treaty, however, Indonesian authorities planned to try Mas Salamat on a false passport charge rather than extradite him to Singapore to face more serious terrorist allegations.[27]

In May 2002, a Southeast Asian anti-terror pact was initialed by the Philippines, Indonesia, and Malaysia, to which Thailand and Cambodia subsequently adhered. The pact was activated in the aftermath of the Davao bombings when Philippine officials claimed that Indonesian nationals were involved in collaboration with elements of the Moro Islamic Liberation Front (MILF), all of whom had trained in terrorist camps in North Cotobato.[28] Similarly, Thai authorities have acknowledged that Jemaah Islamiyah members met in southern Thailand in January 2002 where a decision was made to attack soft targets in the region such as nightclubs and restaurants.[29]

Possible linkages between the Bali and Davao bombings have led to intelligence and police cooperation among Malaysia, Indonesia, and the Philippines. Manila insists that the MILF is responsible for the Davao and other recent attacks on Mindanao, though MILF leaders deny the allegations. Joined by Thailand and Cambodia, the five countries agreed at a January 2003 gathering in Manila that they would establish a communication protocol to fight terror, piracy, money laundering, smuggling, and gunrunning. It is too early to tell whether these plans will facilitate collaboration among law enforcement authorities in the countries most susceptible to terrorism, although Malaysian authorities have stated they are regularly exchanging intelligence with Indonesia and the Philippines.[30]

Asia Pacific defense ministers are also beginning to meet regularly. Singapore hosted the second annual gathering of military and defense officials and analysts, sponsored by the London-based International Institute for Strategic Studies in May–June 2003. Terrorism was high on the agenda as well as non-traditional security concerns, including illegal population movements, drugs, and human trafficking. Whether these meetings will prove to be a springboard for more tangible kinds of defense cooperation, including joint exercises, the exchange of officers for education purposes, or perhaps the discussion of common logistics purchases, remains to be seen. If these annual meetings are to progress beyond "getting to know you" gatherings, that is, confidence building, then an exploration of the possibilities for more tangible cooperation should be expected. However, even if these discussions are confined to explicating national defense doctrines, transparency among national defense establishments will be enhanced.

Unsurprisingly, the most effective form of Southeast Asian security cooperation continues to be bilateral and focused on specific problems. Malaysian armed forces are patrolling waters between Sabah and the southern Philippines to interdict MILF militants fleeing Manila's crackdown.

Australian police have been credited by Indonesia with providing the technical assistance needed to intercept cellular phone conversations that led to the apprehension of many of the Bali bombers.[31]

There have been a significant number of attacks on tankers in the Malacca Strait in 2003, though so far these seem to be piracy rather than terrorism. Piracy is a continuing challenge in Southeast Asia and the possible marriage of piracy with terrorism is worrisome. The deep water channels in the Malacca and a number of Indonesian straits are so narrow that a single burning supertanker and its spreading oil slick could block the route for other tankers. Moreover, in these narrow straits, there may not even be room for naval escorts to screen tankers from attacks by small, fast craft.[32]

While Japan has proposed a regional coast guard to combat piracy, national sensitivities in the littoral states inhibit broader collaboration. Many Southeast Asian countries are unwilling to prosecute pirates apprehended in their territorial waters for acts committed in others' jurisdictions. Most often, pirates are deported rather than prosecuted. Furthermore, since boundaries have not yet been drawn in some parts of the Malacca/Singapore straits, jurisdiction over piracy is unclear.[33] Nevertheless, both Singapore and Malaysia are upgrading their air forces partly to enhance anti-piracy, anti-terrorist, and illegal immigration patrols. Both countries are acquiring air-to-air refueling aircraft, and Singapore has manufactured its own unmanned aerial vehicle (UAV) to extend surveillance over waters surrounding the city-state. Malaysia has also produced its own reconnaissance aircraft, the *Eagle*, which is to be deployed in Sabah for coastal patrols.[34]

Finally, Thailand and the Philippines had deployed peacekeepers to Aceh under the auspices of the December 2002 Cessation of Hostilities Agreement between the Free Aceh Movement (GAM) and the Indonesian government. This involvement in the politics of Indonesian separatism echoed an earlier deployment in the aftermath of East Timor's independence referendum. By May 2003, unfortunately, the ceasefire agreement had unraveled, and Thai and Philippine peacekeepers withdrew as the Indonesian military began a full-scale assault on the rebels. As Philippine and Thai peacekeepers left, Jakarta called upon Malaysia to close its border to any GAM separatists fleeing the war-torn province. Southeast Asian efforts to assist a troubled neighbor seem once again to have failed.[36]

Southeast Asia and a Rising China: An Economic Embrace and Political Caution

China's relations with Southeast Asia continue to burgeon, particularly economic ties. Two-way trade in 2002 of approximately $54 billion has been growing at a rate of over 20 percent annually. Although China now receives 80 percent of foreign direct investment (FDI) going into Asia, it has attempted to reassure the ASEAN states by importing more ASEAN products as well as by negotiating a free trade agreement scheduled to take effect in 2010. Moreover, in diversifying its sources of oil and natural gas, China is concentrating new investments in Southeast Asia and is even considering buying into Indonesian banks. Reflecting the region's optimism toward China's economic engagement, Thai Foreign Minister Surakiart Sathirathai enthused: "China has no intention to take advantage of ASEAN.... A wealthy China creates stability for Southeast Asia."[37]

On the political/security dimension, relations are more complicated. ASEAN hopes to enmesh China in regional organizations such as ASEAN+3 where a Southeast Asian agenda will dominate deliberations. Indeed, China displays a willingness to cooperate in these multilateral venues, demonstrating respect for the ASEAN Way. ASEAN members interpret China's generally accommodating behavior as an indication that its own economic development is both a primary and long-term goal. Thus, maintaining a peaceful environment in the Asia Pacific and the free flow of trade and investment constitute parallel policies for both ASEAN and China. As Philippine President Gloria Macapagal-Arroyo put it: "China is going to become a giant in the twenty-first century. So far, China has been a responsible giant, and we hope it will stay that way."[38]

China is also increasing its security ties with Southeast Asia, holding individual discussions with each ASEAN member (a practice not followed by the United States). ASEAN+3, increasingly dominated by China, has replaced APEC in importance for Southeast Asia. Malaysia's Mahathir Mohamad has particularly promoted ASEAN+3, which leaves the United States on the sidelines.[39] Nevertheless, the United States clearly sustains a dominant security position in the region. U.S. Pacific forces exercise bilaterally with ASEAN's original five members, and U.S. weapons and communications systems are prominent in their inventories. The PRC still has a long way to go if it hopes to equal U.S. security importance in the region.

China has made other conciliatory gestures to ASEAN in 2003, signing the 1976 Treaty of Amity and Cooperation requiring that all disputes be peacefully resolved, and has previously expressed support for, and even signaled its intention to sign, ASEAN's Southeast Asia Nuclear Weapons Free Zone (SEANWFZ) that prohibits the introduction of nuclear weapons into the region. Indeed, in many ways, China appears to be more willing to support multilateral institutions in Southeast Asia than the United States— a remarkable reversal from only a few years ago.

Nevertheless, sovereignty conflicts in the South China Sea continue to bedevil China's relations with ASEAN claimants to the Spratly Islands

(Vietnam, Malaysia, the Philippines, and Brunei). Vietnam and the Philippines are the most confrontational toward the PRC. In the spring of 2003, Manila still held 22 Chinese fishermen arrested the previous year for fishing off Palawan in waters claimed by the Philippines. The Philippine Navy reports that Chinese boats comprise the majority of the hundreds of fishing craft sighted annually in areas claimed by Manila. Vietnam reiterated its claim to the entire Spratly chain when Beijing opted to prohibit fishing in the northern part of the South China Sea that included the Paracel Islands.[40]

In November 2002, China and ASEAN reached a second agreement on restraint and confidence building in the South China Sea at the ASEAN+3 summit in Phnom Penh. While watered down at China's insistence so that no actual Code of Conduct was initialed, nevertheless, the agreement could reduce the chance that territorial disputes over the Spratly Islands will lead to armed conflict. The latest declaration reaffirms freedom of navigation and overflight, and commits the parties to resolve disputes peacefully. However, there is no commitment requiring the claimants to refrain from building new structures on the features they already occupy, as ASEAN proposed, although there is an agreement not to occupy any additional uninhabited islands, reefs, or shoals. Philippine sources subsequently claimed that China is improving facilities on existing military posts but has not occupied new islets.[41]

In the past several years, China has upgraded communications in the three islets it occupies in the Spratlys to coordinate naval patrols in the area and communicate with higher command in the South Sea Fleet. A statement by the PLA's General Political Department averred that China's South China Sea installations possessed "modern weaponry capable of fulfilling the tasks of counter-sneak raids and counter-landing, and adaptable to conducting operations against sea and air attacks."[42]

The Increasing Role of Other Extra-Regional Powers

Most Southeast Asians believe their security is best maintained in the early twenty-first century not by isolating the region from great power activities, as originally envisaged in the 1970s concept of a Zone of Peace Freedom and Neutrality (ZOPFAN), but rather by engaging the powers in multilateral endeavors such as the ASEAN PMCs, ASEAN+3, and the ARF. While initially directed toward keeping China and the United States involved in assuring the region's security, ASEAN also welcomes participation by India and Japan.

India and Japan have exchanged high level visits with virtually every Southeast Asian state. ASEAN members welcome India's efforts to strengthen ties with Burma as a way of balancing China's influence. India is also involved in the ASEAN PMC. Although Delhi has not been able to turn ASEAN+3 into ASEAN+4, India was accepted into the ARF and also managed to prevent an invitation to Pakistan.[43] With Japan, in a 1998 study Southeast Asian public opinion seemed prepared to put Japan's brutal Pacific War occupation of the region in the past. An overwhelming majority of the respondents saw Japan as a trustworthy partner that would not become a military threat.[44]

Australia has also become a significant player in Southeast Asian security. Its key role as midwife to East Timor's independence and its command of peacekeeping forces sent there from Thailand and the Philippines demonstrate Canberra's importance in helping secure regional stability. Australian law enforcement personnel and intelligence have proved crucial for the discovery and apprehension of the Bali bombers. Moreover, Australian police are now deployed at Bangkok's international airport to assist Thai authorities in identifying people traveling under false documents. While Southeast Asian states view Australia with mixed feelings—Malaysia and Indonesia particularly see it as an American surrogate—there is general appreciation for its anti-terrorist expertise and assistance.

For the United States, ASEAN and ARF security deficiencies are not a significant drawback. Washington's security strategy in East Asia continues to rely on bilateral relations, and in Southeast Asia has developed a mix of bi- and multilateral endeavors. In the war against terror, the strongest bilateral tie is with the Philippines, where U.S. military assistance and training, now in their second year, are designed to enhance the Philippine armed forces ability to suppress the Abu Sayyaf group in Mindanao. Although choosing not to become involved in the Philippine army's fight with the Moro Islamic Liberation Front, there is no doubt that U.S. aid to the Philippine military will also be used in its conflict with the MILF.

On the multilateral dimension, little has been accomplished because neither ASEAN nor the ARF have been willing to tackle the core security issues in the region—external support for insurgencies, major refugee flows, or disputes over the sovereignty of islands. Inclusive memberships in both organizations and the ASEAN consensus principle work against their security effectiveness.[45] Thus, Washington's only multilateral security initiative in Southeast Asia is quite modest: the offer to fund a regional anti-terrorism training center in Malaysia which would focus on law enforcement and intelligence exchange but not involve military training. As Stephen Leong of Malaysia's Institute of Strategic and International Studies said, not only would the center show that ASEAN was involved in the anti-terror struggle, but it "will also help to boost the confidence of foreigners who want to invest or travel in the region, especially after the Bali bombing."[46]

Security regionalism in Southeast Asia remains weak. Lack of interoperability among the region's armed forces, embedded suspicions about neighbors' motivations, and an unwillingness or inability to set up effective arrangements to cope with transnational challenges all tend to move security cooperation by default to the bilateral level, where more effective collaboration exists. This principle appears equally true for U.S. security arrangements in Southeast Asia. Bilateral military exercises and bilateral anti-terrorist and law enforcement collaboration predominate. Multilateral exercises, such as *Cobra Gold* in Thailand, while valued, are viewed by Southeast Asians as less useful than bilateral security links to the United States. At present, there is no evidence that this situation will change.[47]

Conclusion

What then does the future portend? Will ASEAN fade away? Has its inability to cope with the financial crisis of the late 1990s, Indonesia's centrifugal tendencies, and the inclusion of hard authoritarian new members—Vietnam, Laos, Cambodia, and Burma—rendered it obsolete? These questions are not the exclusive province of outsiders; ASEAN analysts also raise them. In a June 2003 seminar sponsored by the Indonesian mission to the United Nations, Rizal Sukma of Jakarta's Center for Strategic and International Studies argued that for ASEAN to regain its relevance it must finally become a true security community. As the incoming chair of ASEAN for 2003–04, Indonesia has formally proposed this issue for ASEAN debate. While the details of what an ASEAN security community would entail are vague at this time, Dr. Sukma and his government have raised the appropriate question. The many challenges facing ASEAN, including cross-border terrorism, the future of the South China Sea islands, piracy, illegal population movements, unstable land and maritime boundaries, and regional trade agreements, can only be resolved multilaterally.

In one sense, ASEAN's default position has been to insert Southeast Asia into the deliberations of stronger states via the ARF and ASEAN+3. Even though ASEAN cannot solve Southeast Asia's challenges on its own, it can still try to control the agenda in its dealings with Northeast Asia, India, and the United States. Thus, it may be able to enlist stronger powers in Southeast Asian concerns, such as fighting radical Islamist terrorism, or at least ensure that Northeast Asia not ignore Southeast Asian interests.

However, the default position may no longer be sufficient as Northeast Asia turns its attention to more pressing concerns on the Korean Peninsula and the standoff between China and Taiwan. The question is, therefore, can ASEAN reinvent itself both to be more self-sufficient in dealing with predominantly Southeast Asian issues and in providing a genuine

Southeast Asian contribution to regional security, such as protection of the sea lines of communication (SLOCs)? These concerns can be addressed at a variety of levels, including within ASEAN itself to see if a consensus can be struck, bilaterally with the great powers, and multilaterally across the whole Asian region via the ARF and ASEAN+3.

The United States should encourage Indonesia's nascent call for an ASEAN security community. This would not conflict with U.S. bilateral arrangements and could become a device for greater burden sharing, for example, in anti-piracy patrols through the Southeast Asian straits. Moreover, the reconfiguration of U.S. troop deployments in East Asia that will evolve toward fewer permanent bases and more logistics locations could also fit into a Southeast Asian security arrangement, especially if logistics depots could be used by host country armed forces as well as the United States. An arrangement of this kind is being worked out with the Philippines through a mutual logistics and cross-service agreement that could be a model for other U.S. military depots in the region. A smaller U.S. permanent presence in East Asia combined with frequent visits and exercises could be compatible with an ASEAN security community. This arrangement would continue to reassure Southeast Asians of a U.S. commitment to regional order and at the same time reduce the political volatility of large numbers of U.S. military personnel in host countries. Of course, whether the Indonesian proposal will in fact take ASEAN in a new direction remains to be seen. In the meantime, regional security organizations will remain weak reeds. The Indonesian proposal suggests at least that a new gardener is interested in transplanting them in more fertile soil.

Endnotes

[1] ASEAN members are Brunei, Burma, Cambodia, Indonesia, Laos, the Philippines, Malaysia, Singapore, Thailand, and Vietnam. East Timor, which seceded from Indonesia in 1999, is not yet a member.

[2] Michael Leifer, "The ASEAN Peace Process: A Category Mistake," *Pacific Review*, vol. 12, no. 1 (1999), p. 37.

[3] Lorraine Elliott, "ASEAN and Environmental Cooperation: Norms, Interests, and Identity," *Pacific Review*, vol. 16, no. 1 (2003), pp. 30–31; and Amitav Acharya, *The Quest for Identity: International Relations of Southeast Asia*, Singapore: Oxford University Press, 2000.

[4] Rajshree Jetly, "Conflict Management Strategies in ASEAN: Perspectives for SAARC," *Pacific Review*, vol. 16, no. 1 (2003), p. 55. Also see Amitav Acharya, "Competing and Congruent Approaches to Security Cooperation in the Asia-Pacific Region: A Concept Paper," Singapore: unpublished paper, 2002.

[5] Nayan Chanda, "Southeast Asia After September 11," in Robert Hathaway

and Wilson Lee, eds. *George W. Bush and Asia: A Midterm Assessment*, Washington, DC: Woodrow Wilson Center for Scholars, 2003, pp. 118–19.

[6] A good review of Southeast Asia's bilateral conflicts is found in "Southeast Asia—security," Stratfor.com, February 12, 2003.

[7] Amitav Acharya, *Constructing a Security Community in Southeast Asia: ASEAN and the Problem of Regional Order*, New York: Routledge, 2001, p. 121.

[8] Sheldon W. Simon, "Asian Armed Forces: Internal and External Tasks and Capabilities," in Simon, ed., *The Many Faces of Asian Security*, Lanham, Md.: Rowman and Littlefield, 2001, pp. 49–70; also see Acharya, *Constructing a Security Community in Southeast Asia*, pp. 150–51.

[9] Nayan Chanda, "Southeast Asia After September 11," p. 129.

[10] *Straits Times*, Singapore, May 18, 2002; and Robert Karniol, "A total defence," *Jane's Defence Weekly*, August 28, 2002, p. 25.

[11] Kumar Ramakrishna, "Applying the U.S. National Strategy for Countering Terrorism to Southeast Asia," paper prepared for the Institute for National Strategic Studies-U.S. Institute of Peace Workshop on Terrorism's New Front Lines: Adapting U.S. Counter-Terrorism Strategy to Regions of Concern, Washington, DC, May 8–9, 2003, pp. 7–9.

[12] Author's discussion with a high-ranking U.S. naval officer at the Institute of National Strategic Studies-U.S. Institute of Peace Workshop on Terrorism's New Front Lines, May 8, 2003.

[13] See the discussion in Sheldon W. Simon, "Theater Security Cooperation in the U.S. Pacific Command: An Assessment and Projection," *NBR Analysis*, vol. 14, no. 2 (August 2003).

[14] See "ASEAN police to set up anti-terrorism task force," news release by the ASEAN Secretariat, Jakarta, January 22, 2003.

[15] Andrew Tan, "Terrorism in Singapore: Threat and Implications," *Contemporary Security Policy*, forthcoming.

[16] Agence France-Presse, March 19, 2003 in Foreign Broadcast Information Service, Daily Report: East Asia (hereafter referred to as FBIS-EAS).

[17] Agence France-Presse, April 26, 2003 in FBIS-EAS; and Ellen Nakashima and John Pomfret, "Chinese premier vows to cooperate," *Washington Post*, April 30, 2003.

[18] This new security agenda is explored in Sheldon W. Simon, ed., *The Many Faces of Asian Security*.

[19] Trevor Findlay, "The Regional Security Outlook," in Gary Klintworth, ed., *Asia-Pacific Security: Less Uncertainty, New Opportunities*, New York: St. Martin's Press, 1998, pp. 275–92.

[20] Mely Caballero-Anthony, "Partnership for Peace in Asia: ASEAN, the ARF, and the United Nations," *Contemporary Southeast Asia*, vol. 24, no. 3 (December 2002), pp. 536–37.

[21] See Seng Tan et al., *New Agenda for the ASEAN Regional Forum*, Singapore: Institute for Defense and Strategic Studies, 2002, pp. 14–15.

[22] Tan, *A New Agenda for the ASEAN Regional Forum*, pp. 32 and 35.

[23] Tan, *A New Agenda for the ASEAN Regional Forum*, pp. 37–42.

[24] Tan, *A New Agenda for the ASEAN Regional Forum*, pp. 43, 48, and 66.

25 ARF Statement Against Terrorist Financing, July 30, 2002.

26 Agence France-Presse, April 9 and 30, 2003, in FBIS-EAS. Also see *The Nation*, Bangkok, April 17, 2003 in FBIS-EAS; and Michael Moore, "Neighbours to move on crisis," *Sydney Morning Herald*, 12 March 2003.

27 Mark Manyin et al., *Terrorism in Southeast Asia*, Washington, D.C.: Congressional Research Service Report for Congress, March 26, 2003, pp. 16–17.

28 Agence France-Presse, April 8, 2003 in FBIS-EAS.

29 Agence France-Presse, December 26, 2002 in FBIS-EAS.

30 Agence France-Presse, January 16, April 28, and May 16, 2003 in FBIS-EAS, as well as the *Philippine Daily Inquirer*, April 10, 2003 in FBIS-EAS.

31 Bernama, Kuala Lumpur, March 13, 2003 in FBIS-EAS; and Agence France-Presse, Hong Kong, May 7, 2003 in FBIS-EAS.

32 Neela Banerjee and Keith Bradsher, "A vulnerable time to be moving oil by sea," *New York Times*, October 19, 2002.

33 Mark Valencia, "Southeast Asia piracy runs rampant; coastal states at loggerheads over protection," *Washington Times*, June 4, 2001.

34 "Regional worries speed Singapore-Malaysia arms race," Stratfor.com, August 23, 2002.

36 An excellent summary of the scale of the Aceh conflict and the irreconcilability of the contenders is found in International Crisis Group, "Aceh: Why the Military Option Still Won't Work, Jakarta," *ICG Indonesia Briefing*, May 9, 2003. Also Bernama, Kuala Lumpur, May 21, 2003 in FBIS-EAS.

37 The quote is from Michael Vatikiotis and David Murphy, "Birth of a trading empire," *Far Eastern Economic Review*, March 20, 2003. p. 28. Also see Lyall Breckon, "China-Southeast Asian Relations: Focus is Elsewhere, but Bonds Continue to Grow," *Comparative Connections*, January–March 2003, p. 2, <www.csis.org/pacfor/cc>.

38 Cited in Denny Roy, "China and Southeast Asia: ASEAN Makes the Best of the Inevitable," *Asia-Pacific Security Studies*, vol. 1, no. 4 (November 2002), p. 3.

39 Author's discussion with Professor Donald Weatherbee, who is conducting research on ASEAN+3, Washington, DC, May 7, 2003.

40 Lyall Breckon, "Focus is Elsewhere, but Bonds Continue to Grow," p.3; Agence France-Presse, May 17, 2003 in FBIS-EAS.

41 Lyall Breckon, "Focus is Elsewhere, but Bonds Continue to Grow," and by the same author, "China Caps a Year of Gains," *Comparative Connections*, October–December 2002, pp. 2–3.

42 Cited in David G. Wiencik, "South China Sea Flashpoint Revisited," *China Brief*, vol. 2, no. 24 (December 10, 2002), p. 2.

43 Satu P. Limaye, "India-Southeast Asia Relations: The Weakest Link, but not Goodbye," *Comparative Connections*, October–December 2002.

44 Sueo Sudo, *The International Relations of Japan and South East Asia: Forging a New Regionalism*, New York: Routledge, 2002, p. 54.

45 John Garfano, "Power, Institutions, and the ASEAN Regional Forum: A Security Community for Asia?" *Asian Survey*, vol. 42, no. 3 (May/June 2002), p. 520.

[46] Malaysiakini, Petaling Jaya, October 31, 2002, in FBIS-EAS.
[47] Simon, "Theater Security Cooperation in the U.S. Pacific Command."

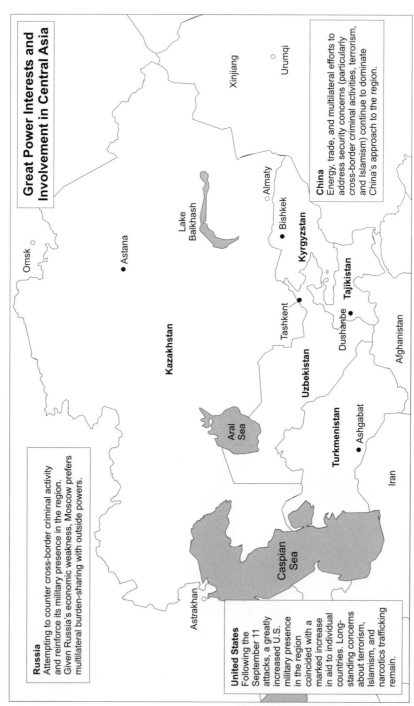

Great Power Interests and Involvement in Central Asia

Russia
Attempting to counter cross-border criminal activity and reinforce its military presence in the region. Given Russia's economic weakness, Moscow prefers multilateral burden-sharing with outside powers.

China
Energy, trade, and multilateral efforts to address security concerns (particularly cross-border criminal activities, terrorism, and Islamism) continue to dominate China's approach to the region.

United States
Following the September 11 attacks, a greatly increased U.S. military presence in the region coincided with a marked increase in aid to individual countries. Long-standing concerns about terrorism, Islamism, and narcotics trafficking remain.

NBR based on Collins & Wohlforth "Defying 'Great Game' Expectations"

DEFYING "GREAT GAME" EXPECTATIONS

Kathleen A. Collins & William C. Wohlforth

ABSTRACT

Although widely expected to spark a new round of competitive rivalry among the major powers, the insertion of U.S. forces into Central Asia after September 11, 2001 had the opposite effect—relations among the United States, Russia, and China both regionally and globally have improved dramatically. This chapter addresses the question of whether this comparatively benign outcome is sustainable. It presents systematic evaluations of the outside powers' chief interests, their actual behavior on the ground, and the Central Asian states' responses. Contrary to the expectations generated by "great game" punditry on the region, we find that there are grounds for continued cooperation among the three large outside powers and that, with continued prudent management, their involvement in the region may foster rather than undermine stability.

Kathleen Collins is Assistant Professor of Political Science at the University of Notre Dame. William Wohlforth is Associate Professor of Government at Dartmouth College and serves as a Senior Advisor to NBR's Eurasia Program. The authors are grateful for the comments of Richard Ellings, Michael Wills, two anonymous reviewers, and, especially, Gael Tarleton on an earlier draft. They would also like to acknowledge the research assistance of Allison Clark and Rajeev Majumdar.

Introduction

Often seen as an arena for a new "great game," Central Asia was widely expected to undergo a new round of geopolitical rivalry after the United States entered the region in force following September 11.[1] Contrary to these expectations, relations among the United States, Russia and China both regionally and globally have improved dramatically. The fundamental question this chapter addresses is whether this state of affairs reflects a potential long-term outcome or just a temporary interlude in the great powers' regional competition. In other words, to what degree does the "great game" lens capture the real dynamics of the major powers' strategic interaction in Central Asia? To address this question, we present three distinct but mutually supporting analyses: a balance sheet of the major powers' competitive versus their mutual interests in the region; an assessment of their behavior in the region after September 11 to determine whether it is consistent with our analysis of their interests; and an analysis of the Central Asian states' response to the great powers' actions, in order to compare their perceptions and behavior to our reading of the great powers' role.

Our conclusion is that a new "great game" is not underway in Central Asia.[2] Although elements of rivalry and competition shadow some relationships, shared strategic interests dominate the concrete actions of the major powers to a remarkable degree. Sustaining this state of affairs is clearly in the United States' interest, but it will require active management.

The Great Powers' Interests in Central Asia

The "great game" narrative features an intense struggle among all the major outside powers for spheres of influence and energy resources in Central Asia. The nature of this struggle is muted among the local great powers (Russia and China) mainly by their shared opposition to the United States' global dominance and its regional presence.[3]

These themes do find reflection in reality. Great powers are always competitive to some extent as their foreign policies generally reflect a basic preference for more influence. Like their counterparts throughout history, officials in Washington, Moscow, and Beijing generally assume that more influence over international affairs is better than less, all other things being equal. To the degree that all players want more influence, their mutual interactions can be seen as a zero-sum game, since more influence for any one player must come at the expense of another. This generalization clearly applies to the major powers' interests in Central Asia. American, Russian, and Chinese decision-makers clearly would prefer to have more say over military and economic developments in the region rather than less. Russian officials seek to stave off the further decline of their influence in the region, and with a growing economy and robust governmental finances, many see opportunities to make up for ground lost to China and the United States over recent years. Chinese policymakers see their state as a rising global and regional power with an expanding menu of interests in Central Asia that demand an enhanced presence. Officials and analysts in both capitals have voiced an interest in limiting or reducing the U.S. role both regionally and globally, advocating a "multipolar" strategy. For their part, U.S. officials have routinely expressed preferences for the region's economic, political and military development that could only be served by a continued or even greatly enhanced role.

In short, the great powers' interests in the region are competitive when viewed in their most expansive terms. Because officials and commentators give voice to these interests and periodically interpret their behavior in the region as an outgrowth of them, there is evidence for the great game narrative. But the game is only truly zero-sum to the degree that these clashing interests are priority rather than optional goals in each power's hierarchy of regional strategic objectives. And the game is only "great" to the degree that these clashing regional interests figure importantly in each power's global strategy. In contrast to the real Great Game between the Russian and British empires in the latter 19th century, neither condition is fulfilled consistently concerning the interests of today's great powers.

For each of the main outside powers, the most pressing security interests in the region are not ones that can be achieved only at another major power's expense. On the contrary, officials at the highest levels of all the governments concerned place the greatest emphasis on security interests that demand cooperation from the other powers.[4] Notwithstanding the defeat of the Taliban regime in Afghanistan, transnational terrorism continues to be the major concern for all. Intricately linked to this issue is religious extremism and, especially, Islamist extremism, which the United States, Russia, and China see not only as a transnational threat from Afghanistan and Pakistan—especially vis-à-vis Kashmir—but also as a potential threat that might emanate from within the Central Asian states—especially Uzbekistan, Tajikistan, and Kyrgyzstan. Russia remains bogged down in an increasingly Islamicized war with Chechnya, which imposes hefty financial costs on the government and drains its military, while hampering reform and generating terror attacks in Moscow and other cities. China is particularly worried about Xinjiang's Uighur separatist movement, which in recent years has taken on Islamic overtones and is reported to have backing from elements within its neighboring states. Russian and Chinese officials claim that the Chechen and Uighur movements belong to a transnational terrorist network with ties to the Taliban and Al Qaeda, and are a principal security threat. The United States has endorsed the thrust of the Russian and Chinese portrayal of their links to wider terror networks.[5]

Proliferation of weapons of mass destruction (WMD) linked to access to chemical, biological, and nuclear materials either in Central Asia or Russia, and made easier by poorly secured facilities and borders, is a second security priority for all concerned, but especially high on the U.S. agenda. For example, in January 2003, masked men raided a Kyrgyz chemical-mechanical plant and stole 460 kilograms of europium oxide power used in nuclear reactors. In remnants of the Soviet nuclear complex in the region, cesium devices are poorly accounted for. The Central Asian states have also been transit routes for WMD materials (e.g. low-enriched uranium, cesium 137, iridium-192 and plutonium), usually moving southward from Russia.[6] Narcotics trafficking—with Russia and the United States as target markets—is another important concern, which has increased dramatically with the Taliban's defeat. Just as importantly, trafficking has been the major source of financing for various regional terrorist groups.[7] Even though the major powers continue to haggle over the best means for addressing this set of issues, it nonetheless creates background incentives for cooperation among them.

Although Central Asia's strategic salience has been on the rise, the major powers' strategic priorities lie elsewhere. For each of the three major outside players, bilateral relationships with the others are far more important than any stake they hold in Central Asia. As the chapters on China and Russia in this volume stress, the most pressing grand strategic objectives of China and Russia remain economic development and modernization. While both are animated by a quest for great power prestige, the current consensus among officials in both capitals is that for the foreseeable future prestige concerns must take a back seat to the drive for modernization whenever the two aims come into conflict. Moreover, for China, Russia, and the United States, more immediate strategic concerns put other regions above Central Asia in their hierarchy of interests. The U.S. war on terrorism has already shifted to the Persian Gulf. Russia's most pressing security concerns remain in Chechnya and the Caucasus, while China remains focused on Taiwan. Developments in Central Asia are, of course, related to the powers' most pressing immediate strategic concerns to a greater (Russia) or lesser (U.S., China) degree, but in no capital can zealous officials or policy advocates make the case that any outcome in the region is pivotal to the country's core security.

This discussion leaves two important aspects of the "great game" narrative intact: the issue of counterbalancing U.S. hegemony, and the scramble for economic resources. There is no doubt the issue of counterbalancing the United States plays a role in the rhetoric emanating from Moscow and Beijing. Both would prefer a multipolar world order. But there is scant evidence that they are willing or able to sacrifice other objectives to obtain it, and consequently the "Asian strategic triangle" has yet to cohere globally.[8] The "multipolar" preference, in practice, reflects both governments' official policies favoring multilateral approaches to common security problems globally and regionally. In addition, anti-U.S. posturing is sometimes useful as a foil for fostering regional cooperation.

Describing the scramble for Central Asian resources and transportation routes as a new great game can be misleading for several reasons. Behind the Anglo-Russian great game was hardheaded thinking about how best to position one's empire for a possible great-power war to the finish. Whatever value one might want to attach to the acquisition of ownership or control over the transportation of natural resources today, they can have minimal bearing on the outcome of a clash between nuclear-armed states. Moreover, there are compelling theoretical reasons, backed up by formidable empirical research, that control over natural resources is irrelevant— or even a hindrance—to the creation of a competitive economy.[9] Chinese, and now Russian, policymakers talk as if they recognize these findings, for they all insist that the road to "great powerdom" lies in the development of a modern competitive economy, not in serving as a resource supplier to others. Finally, governments' ability to play geopolitics with the development of natural resources is far more constrained by market considerations than the more overheated great game rhetoric would suggest. Governments can have decisive influence on certain deals, but firms and markets determine how much they have to pay for that influence. And to assess how much various governments are willing to pay for influence in Central Asia, we must assess their actions even more closely than their words.

Great Power Actions in Central Asia

Some analysts do not agree with this portrayal of the great powers' interests in Central Asia; others contend that even if the powers' objective interests in the region point toward cooperation, then mutual misperceptions, longing for empire or prestige, or "rogue" officials imperfectly controlled by their governments will generate rivalry nonetheless.[10] To assess these arguments, it is necessary to examine what the major powers are actually doing on the ground in Central Asia.

The United States: From Nuclear Security to the War on Terror

After the Soviet collapse, U.S. policy focused on nuclear security—orchestrating the transfer of nuclear weapons from Kazakhstan to Russia and securing the nuclear material remaining on Kazakh territory. Once that pressing issue was addressed, America's broader geo-strategic or security concerns in the region became less clear, and policy drifted towards a focus on energy interests and, consequently, the Caspian states. The lack of active U.S. involvement in negotiating the Tajik or Afghan civil wars in the early to mid 1990s, and the absence of a concrete U.S. response to the Taliban's sweep across Afghanistan revealed Washington's willingness to let Russia deal with instability in the non-energy states of Central Asia.

In the mid-1990s, intense U.S. efforts went into support for American energy interests in Kazakhstan's oil and gas sector. The United States had clear disagreements with Russia over preferred pipelines, which fueled innumerable reports about a new great game. Russia lobbied to expand existing lines going north through its own territory, giving it a near monopoly over oil exports. Although advocating "multiple pipelines" and a "win-win" policy, the United States strongly supported a western route from Azerbaijan through Georgia to Turkey. Tensions heightened, but the "great game" for the region's oil did not lead to conflict or cause a serious decline in U.S.-Russian relations. Ultimately, economic viability issues led to a compromise on two pipelines. In addition to expanding the Russian Novorossisk route, in late 2002 construction of the Baku-Tblisi-Ceyhan (BTC) line began. BTC will become the major east-west energy transport route, but will not necessarily undercut exports north through Russia.

As the 1990s progressed, the United States began to take more action in support of its security goals in the region. The emphasis shifted toward bolstering stronger and more independent states in Central Asia and the Caucasus, which engendered a policy shift toward Uzbekistan and away from Kyrgyzstan. The Kyrgyz government complained bitterly that the United States was giving more aid to its authoritarian neighbor and not seeing Kyrgyzstan through its political transition and economic crisis. Furthermore, U.S. assistance to Kyrgyzstan began to decline as the U.S. Congress became frustrated with backsliding in its democratization. Uzbekistan, meanwhile, became a key participant in the Partnership for Peace program and by 1999 a member of GUUAM, the U.S.-backed security arrangement in Central Asia and the Caucasus that excluded Russia.[11]

The rise of the Taliban, Al Qaeda and the Islamic Movement of Uzbekistan (IMU), a militant and extremist "Islamic" organization, imparted new urgency to the challenge of terrorism between 1998 and 2001, though policy shifts in the region remained subtle. Countering terrorism, preventing Islamist extremism, enhancing border controls, and fighting narcotics trafficking increasingly became elements of U.S. policy and assistance programs—changes that affected the tenor and content of U.S.-Uzbek relations. The United States signed several bilateral defense-related agreements on counter-terrorism and border controls with the Uzbek Ministry of Defense in May 1999. In mid-2000, the State Department put the IMU on its list of terrorist organizations. In June 2001 U.S. Secretary of State Powell and Foreign Minister Komilov of Uzbekistan signed the Cooperative Threat Reduction Agreement, which established a framework to prevent the proliferation of WMD and its technology and scientific expertise. The agreement—similar to the one signed with Kazakhstan in 1993—included a commitment to the dismantling of Soviet military, chemical, and biological weapons facilities remaining on Uzbek territory.

The September 11 attacks transformed U.S. policy into an all-consuming war on terror that drove Washington's greatly expanded involvement in Central Asia. The most striking and visible prong of the new approach was the stationing of U.S. military forces in the region. Shortly after September 11, the U.S. government initiated talks with all five Central Asian states to enlist their cooperation in the war on terror, and specifically in the mission in Afghanistan. The result was the establishment of a U.S. military presence with air bases in Uzbekistan, Kyrgyzstan, and Tajikistan, sending U.S. military advisors to Georgia, and the acquisition of over-flight and refueling rights in Kazakhstan, Turkmenistan, and Azerbaijan.

Uzbekistan was an obvious choice, owing both to its location and track record of military cooperation with the United States. On October 7, 2001, the United States and Uzbekistan signed an agreement following tough negotiations between the Department of Defense and CENTCOM with the Uzbek military and security services. The United States agreed to a "long-term commitment to advance security and regional stability" in Central Asia,[12] and the Uzbek government agreed to ongoing military cooperation with the United States, including allowing 1,500 U.S. troops engaged in the war in Afghanistan to continue to be based in southern Uzbekistan at the Khanabad-Karshi military facility. Although the official rhetoric claimed that the U.S. forces in Uzbekistan could only provide humanitarian assistance, other sources reported that the forces were engaged in military operations. In December 2001, after further difficult negotiations, President Karimov agreed to open the Friendship Bridge linking Uzbekistan and Afghanistan so that coalition forces and UN operations could bring aid and equipment into northern Afghanistan. In January 2002, the operations in Uzbekistan were declared to be part of a long-term, but not permanent, U.S. presence.

Shortly after making the basing agreement with the Uzbeks, the Americans decided to try for a second base in Central Asia. According to one U.S. official, the Uzbek government put up such resistance in the negotiation process that the United States wanted to hedge its bets by using another country as well. Kyrgyzstan and Tajikistan were the most likely choices. Both presidents quickly offered basing rights, despite their countries' membership in the Commonwealth of Independent States (CIS), thus indicating that Russia had not opposed the bases. The United States opted for the Ganchi base at Manas Airport in Kyrgyzstan, mainly due to its good condition. In December 2001, Kyrgyz President Askar Akaev agreed to lease the base to the United States for the positioning of U.S. and coalition forces. These would include up to 3,000 U.S. troops. In sensitivity to both domestic opposition, especially from the more pro-Russian elements of the population and government, as well as Russia, the United States stressed that the base would host a coalition—not just U.S.—presence whose purpose was solely for assisting in humanitarian flights to Afghanistan. Hence, Korean, French, and other coalition forces and support staff were stationed together with the Americans. The Americans and Kyrgyz agreed to a one-year, renewable presence that would be extended as long as necessary to support anti-terror operations.

Meanwhile, the Dushanbe airport in Tajikistan became a temporary base for French Mirage jets, humanitarian missions, and a small number of U.S. troops supporting the war on terror. Tajikistan's border with northeastern Afghanistan became an important entry point for humanitarian aid to Badakhshan. A larger military deployment was not placed in Tajikistan, surprisingly, not out of concern for Russian opposition, but rather due to the poor quality of its bases and general security concerns.

In exchange for the use of the airbases—although not as a direct quid pro quo, according to U.S. government representatives—the U.S. government more than doubled its assistance to the region to $723.51 million in 2002. The total budget in 2001 was $313.47 million, and in 2000 it had been $279.29 million.[13] The largest increases went to Uzbekistan, and then to Kyrgyzstan and Tajikistan. The bulk of assistance goes to security and law enforcement programs (32 percent), which include (non-lethal) military aid and training, enhanced border control, improved security services, and anti-terror and anti-narcotics trafficking programs. Support for economic reforms and humanitarian assistance takes second place. Despite continued rhetoric from State Department representatives about the necessity of reform, far less assistance goes to political or economic reform programs (16 and 9 percent, respectively, in 2002; 16 and 13 percent, respectively in 2001). Pressure on the Central Asian governments for democratization has not been linked to aid, and has met with very limited success.[14]

Despite its poor record of reform, Uzbekistan has emerged as the closest U.S. strategic ally in the region. Indeed, the evolving U.S.-Uzbek rela-

Table 1. U.S. Assistance to Central Asia

	U.S. assistance (FY2002 budgets - $m and %)						
	Total	Kazak.	Kyrgyz.	Tajik.	Turk.	Uzbek.	Region
Democratization	92.4	13.7	22.7	17.4	5.6	30.6	2.5
	(16%)	(16%)	(24%)	(11%)	(29%)	(14%)	(15%)
Market reform	55.3	15.0	18.0	9.4	0.9	11.0	1.0
	(9%)	(17%)	(19%)	(6%)	(5%)	(5%)	(6%)
Security and law	187.2	40.4	37.5	21.6	7.8	79.9	...
	(32%)	(47%)	(40%)	(14%)	(41%)	(37%)	...
Humanitarian aid	142.4	0.7	4.8	87.2	0.6	48.6	0.6
	(24%)	(1%)	(5%)	(57%)	(3%)	(22%)	(4%)
Cross-sectoral	108.2	16.9.	10.7	18.0	4.1	46.5	12.1
	(18%)	(19%)	(15%)	(12%)	(22%)	(21%)	(75%)
Total (FSA/other)[a]	585.6	86.7	93.5	153.5	19.0	216.7	16.2
DoD assistance[b]	137.9	7.2	21.2	29.1	2.2	78.2	...
Total assistance	723.5	93.9	114.7	182.7	21.1	294.9	16.2

Source: Compiled from *Annual Report*, U.S. Department of State, 2002. Note: a) Total for U.S. aid from Freedom Support Act (FSA) funds and other government agency budgets; b) Total for Department of Defense excess and privately donated humanitarian commodities.

tionship has been the most dramatic element of the U.S. expanding influence in Central Asia. The agreement on Khanabad was followed by several others. In January, the United States signed a Memorandum of Understanding with Uzbekistan, which was followed in March by a U.S.-Uzbek "Declaration on the Strategic Partnership and Cooperation Framework." This five-point framework committed both sides to cooperation in political democratization, military-security cooperation, economic reform, humanitarian cooperation, and legal reform. The central element of this agreement, however, was really military-security cooperation. According to the U.S. State Department, "the two countries expect to develop cooperation in combating transnational threats to society, and to continue their dynamic military and military-technical cooperation."[15] The framework specifically notes the need to develop non-proliferation and export controls, border infrastructure, security-military consultations, and to increase Uzbekistan's participation in the Partnership for Peace (PfP). A regular consultative group of U.S. and Uzbek military and security officials was established. The framework may involve U.S. support for the technical modernization and better equipping of the Uzbek military. The agreement further expects the introduction of NATO standards into the armed forces, the training of peacekeeping units, bilateral and multilateral exercises with NATO through the PfP, and the establishment of a NATO PfP Training Center in Uzbekistan.[16]

Perhaps most importantly, the agreement's language suggests enhanced U.S. support for Uzbekistan's security:

> The United States affirms that it would regard with grave concern any external threat to the security and territorial integrity of the Republic of Uzbekistan. Were this to occur, the United States will consult with the Republic of Uzbekistan on an urgent basis to develop and implement an appropriate response in accordance with United States constitutional procedures. For its part, the Republic of Uzbekistan recognizes the critical importance of developing close, cooperative ties with its neighbors and promoting efforts at regional cooperation.[17]

The framework clearly aims to increase bilateral and multilateral strategic cooperation between the United States and Uzbekistan for the chief purpose of increasing Uzbekistan's capacity to be a regional stabilizer and a counter to terrorism of all kinds.

Despite such increased activity in military and security sectors, the United States has not directly expanded its energy interests in the region. Contrary to the expectations of many great game pundits, the U.S. war on terror in Afghanistan has not been followed by U.S. support for oil and gas pipelines from the Caspian and Uzbekistan through Afghan territory to the south. The Asian Development Bank, with the backing of Pakistan, has provided money for a feasibility study,[18] but most U.S. and former Western advocates of this route remain skeptical. As of spring 2003, Unocal, the U.S. oil company avidly exploring the trans-Afghan line in the later 1990s, had not returned to press for this option. In this respect, the United States, Russia, and China are no more at odds about the extraction and transport of oil resources than before the U.S. expansion into Central Asia. The United States has promised increased loans to investors in Central Asia through the Ex-Im Bank in order to relieve the devastating regional economic crisis, but U.S. policy has not been directed at competing with Russian or Chinese economic interests in the region.

The longer-term U.S. position in Central Asia is still unclear. Although the war in Afghanistan ended far more quickly than many had anticipated, the U.S. military presence in the region remains. Except in Uzbekistan, that presence is still declared "short-term" and should depart when the cleanup operation inside Afghanistan winds down. It seems unlikely, however, that the Afghan situation will stabilize in the near future, or that the United States will depart from the region entirely. By most accounts, Afghanistan is dangerously unstable and Taliban supporters remain in hiding, occasionally attacking U.S. troops or assassinating President Hamid Karzai's allies.

Moreover, the threat of Al Qaeda's spread throughout Central Asia—to Iran, Iraq, and Pakistan—has increased as well. Last August, the United States announced a plan to spend $5 million refurbishing the Khanabad base.[19] In spring 2003, the United States appeared to be expanding facilities at the Manas base in Kyrgyzstan as well.[20] According to one U.S. government official, commenting in January 2002, the positioning of U.S. forces in Central Asia, especially Uzbekistan, was already being thought of in the Pentagon as part of a potential backup plan for military action in Iraq should the Gulf countries or Turkey deny the United States access to Iraq via bases in their countries.[21] Ultimately, however, the United States was able to use its long-standing presence in the Middle East to carry out the Iraqi war.

Russia: Coping with New Security Challenges

As Central Asia's former imperial master with a vast web of influence, the greatest security stake, and a large contingent of officials and analysts who view the region through the geopolitical lens, Russia provides the most evidence for the great game narrative. Yet, imperial nostalgia and pugnacious rhetoric notwithstanding, Russia substantially reoriented its strategy in the latter 1990s. It began to take prudent steps to stabilize the region, especially since Putin's rise to power, which ushered in a new economically-driven pragmatism in Moscow's foreign policy.[22]

The question is whether the entry of U.S. military forces in the region has sparked a revision in Russia's basic strategy. One of the main pieces of evidence in support of the argument for a geopolitically resurgent and competitive Russian policy is Moscow's coordinated effort to place its regional military presence on a more secure long-term footing.[23] The problem with this argument is that this effort predated the U.S. entry into the region and was sparked by the threat of transnational terrorism—a security concern Russia shares with the United States, China, and the Central Asian governments themselves.

One example is Russia's policy of reinvigorating the multilateral but Russian-dominated Collective Security Treaty (CST), under whose auspices much of Moscow's military activity in Central Asia takes place.[24] Despite its many declarations and its formal role as the legitimating instrument for Russian deployments in the region, by 1999 the CST was under-funded and poorly organized, had accomplished relatively little, and was dwindling into obscurity.[25] What sparked Moscow's effort to revamp the CST was not the United States, but the summer 1999 incursions of the IMU into the three Central Asian states of Kyrgyzstan, Uzbekistan, and Tajikistan. The escalation of the war in Afghanistan and the Taliban's unexpected ability to seize and maintain power also rekindled Russian fears of Muslim extremism.[26]

The repeat of the IMU's invasion in the summer of 2000 instigated discussions of a joint CST rapid deployment force (CRDF). This force was officially formed in May 2001, but largely remained on paper, chronically short of real military units or capabilities.[27] In spring 2002, Russia and the Central Asian CST members began discussing the upgrading of the CST into a more effective Collective Security Treaty Organization (CSTO). In the spring of 2002, Russia organized formation-level exercises (the "South Anti-terror 2002") with dedicated CRDF battalions from Kazakhstan, Kyrgyzstan, Tajikistan and Russia. In December, presidents Putin and Askar Akaev signed an agreement that writes-off or reschedules portions of Kyrgyzstan's state debt to Moscow in exchange for granting Russia the rights to the former Soviet flight-training airfield at Kant to provide air support for CRDF.[28] By early 2003, three SU-27 fighters, two SU-25 attack planes, and two IL-76 military cargo planes, together with 700 personnel, were reported to constitute the total Russian deployment, as work on the facility—considerably degraded, and rejected by the U.S. military in favor of the international airport at Manas—was still underway in April.[29]

The CSTO experience also highlights the modest nature of the real changes on the ground. In April 2003, member states agreed to strengthen CST institutions, translating the treaty into a full-fledged international organization with permanent governing bodies and a budget.[30] But little has yet been done to create the concrete manifestations of a lasting security institution (budgeting, staffing, headquarters, joint training and operations). Similarly, the CRDF is expected to be operational by 2004. At the same time, CSTO members admit that the organization's plans for such a force may well remain on paper, as in the past.[31] Others suggest that the base is merely a symbol of Russia's presence, but will have too little funding to provide an adequate defense against terrorism or IMU-like incursions.

Also part of Russia's effort to reinforce its regional military presence are negotiations with Tajik President Imomali Rakhmonov for an expanded military profile in Tajikistan. Russian and Tajik officials negotiated an agreement to upgrade Russia's 201st Motorized Division from a "peace-keeping" unit within Dushanbe to a regular military force to be stationed at a full-fledged army base.[32] It is not clear if the numbers of Russian troops will increase, but a formal treaty on the base is expected. Although this would make the Russian presence more permanent, it should not be seen as a departure from previous Russian policy, which had kept the 201st in Tajikistan since 1991, and even long after the signing of the peace accord in 1997. Russia has used the base as a safeguard against both the rise of an Islamist government in Tajikistan and the infiltration of Islamist extremism from Afghanistan.

In addition to the effort to reinforce its military deployments in the region, Russia has also broadened military cooperation with Central Asian governments. Russia remains the chief arms supplier to the region (offering weapons, albeit in the small amounts the states can afford, at favorable terms), maintains important defense-industrial, air-defense, and space facilities in the region, and sustains close military-to-military and intelligence links with local armed forces.[33] Moscow recently signed deals with the Central Asian states that will allow Central Asian citizens to serve in the Russian army, after which they may apply for Russian citizenship. Rather than a ploy to weaken the Central Asian defense systems, this practice would potentially strengthen Central Asian militaries by giving their soldiers training and experience in a poor, but far better off military. If the soldiers return home, they will bring these skills with them.

At the same time, the policy may help resolve a social and demographic problem for Russia.[34] With negative growth in the Russian population—due to a declining birth rate and emigration, especially of youth—Russia's army and labor market in general will likely face severe shortages. Secondly, Russia's army has been plagued by desertions, low morale, and psychological trauma in the 1990s. Soldiers serving in the Chechen wars have left the military, often with shattered lives. Deaths are estimated at over 10,000. Those serving in other districts have left due to low pay and lack of the prestige and respect accorded to the former Soviet military. New recruits from Central Asia would in part address the shortage of Russian soldiers. For Central Asia's states, moreover, the agreement offers job opportunities to young men who would otherwise be unemployed and a potential source of unrest, protest, and crime. In contrast to Russia, population growth in Central Asia (other than Kazakhstan) continued to be high throughout the 1980s and 1990s. The local economies are generally still in decline and cannot absorb the labor surplus. According to Russia's foreign ministry, thousands of Central Asians, especially from Kyrgyzstan and Tajikistan, already travel to Russia illegally as seasonal laborers and create border and visa problems as well as increased criminality and terrorist risks to Russia. The agreement on military service, like the basing agreements, was made on the basis of security interests primarily driven by fears of Islamist extremism and terrorism, not the threat of U.S. expansion.

Another element in Russia's security policy in the region is an effort to increase border controls, decrease narcotics-trafficking, and control the flow of WMD. Since 2001, Russia has accelerated its cooperation with China and the Central Asian members of the Shanghai Cooperation Organization (discussed in the next section). As part of the SCO, Russia has supported the development of the regional Anti-Terror Center, based in

Bishkek since 1999.[35] The center is intended to coordinate and share intelligence information among the member countries. In a recent critical step, Russia is working cooperatively with the United States and International Atomic Energy Agency to import spent fuel from the nuclear research reactor at Uzbekistan's Institute for Nuclear Physics.[36]

The final element in Russia's regional security policy also runs against the great game narrative. Given Russian weakness, the expense of securing the region, and Russia's official preference for multilateralism, Putin has stressed multilateral burden-sharing with outside powers, especially China and the United States. Putin himself, at the May 2002 meeting of the CSTO members, claimed that he approved of a cooperative relationship between the new CSTO and NATO in order to form a new global security system.[37] This is especially noteworthy, given that NATO is slated to take over peacekeeping in Afghanistan at the end of 2003. In addition, Russia has stressed the importance of cooperation with China in the SCO.

Russia's economic policies towards Central Asia, as elsewhere, have been increasingly defined by market forces. Despite long disagreement with the United States over the building of pipelines to the south, east, or west, Russia seems to have accepted that it cannot exclusively control oil extraction and export in the region.[38] Indeed, instead of opposing the U.S.-backed BTC line, major Russian oil and pipeline companies are now buying into the pipeline project. Russia's energy policy (especially in the oil sector) in the region is increasingly driven by profit motivations of private and semi-private Russian firms such as Lukoil.[39] A trans-Afghan line in the near to medium term is far less likely or contentious an issue than Iraq, which has not derailed the U.S.-Russian partnership. More broadly, Russia's strategy in Central Asia has exhibited less an attempt at hegemony than a concern for driving its economic growth through energy exports, investment and trade. Russia's recent deals in Kazakhstan, Kyrgyzstan, and Tajikistan have generally exchanged debt for assets in lucrative energy sectors.[40] Further, Central Asia continues to be a dumping ground for cheap Russian goods. Finally, in a departure from the early 1990s, Russia's latest iteration of the "Eurasian" common economic space was discussed in February 2003 at a summit in Novo-Ogaryovo. Invitations were based on states' potential economic contributions, not on older CIS notions of reconstituting the Russian empire; hence, Kazakhstan was included, whereas Kyrgyzstan, Tajikistan, and Turkmenistan were left out.[41]

China: Responding to Economic and Security Concerns

Hu Jintao's inaugural trip abroad as China's president captured the essentials of Beijing's strategic behavior in Central Asia. At the St. Petersburg summit, Hu and Putin signed an agreement on energy cooperation, and in Moscow's Kremlin they both met with their counterparts in the Shanghai Cooperation Organization (SCO) to initial documents further institutionalizing the grouping. Energy, trade, and multilateral efforts to address common security concerns dominate China's approach to the region.

In the security sphere, China's growing interests in Central Asia have primarily taken the form of bilateral or multilateral actions under the aegis of the SCO. Russian and Chinese leaders have frequently used SCO gatherings to express their preference for a multipolar world, and the grouping is often seen as a coordinating mechanism for counterbalancing U.S. power in the region.[42] Yet a close examination of the organization's real activities belies this interpretation.

In 1996, China initiated the founding of the "Shanghai Five," including China, Russia, Kazakhstan, Kyrgyzstan, and Tajikistan. Its main goal was confidence building among the new states, especially by resolving old Soviet-Chinese border disputes. China further sought to stabilize and secure the borders from Muslim extremism, a factor that threatened not only post-Soviet Central Asia but the restive Xinjiang region of western China. China feared that the Uighur separatists were getting funding, arms and support from Uighurs in its neighboring states, as well as from Afghanistan. Russia shared the common threat of an increasingly Islamicized Chechen separatist movement. Uzbekistan joined the group in 2001 as it sought a common forum for responding to the IMU's transnational guerilla threat.[43] The Shanghai six, now upgraded to the SCO, signed a declaration on June 15, 2001, expanding its mission in the region and focused increasingly on terrorist threats, religious extremism, and to a lesser extent, arms and narcotics trafficking. The organization announced the creation of a counter-terrorism center in Bishkek known as the Regional Anti-Terrorism Structure (RATS), but the project stalled and few assets were invested or resources committed.[44]

Hence, the one key issue that China, Russia and the Central Asians agreed upon that warranted an upgrading of the SCO was counter-terrorism. Having coordinated the grouping around this issue, however, the members were unable to assemble the capabilities required to address it. This shortcoming was made brutally evident after September 11, when U.S.-led *Operation Enduring Freedom* quickly toppled the Taliban and weakened the IMU—the very threats whose rise had just begun to provide the SCO's raison d'être. The U.S. deployment created a clear contradiction between the SCO's rhetorical role as a counterbalancing mechanism and its operational role as a regional security organization. China and Russia resolved the contradiction by bandwagoning with the U.S.-led war on terror. Indeed, on September 14, 2001, the SCO was the first international organization to issue a formal statement condemning the attacks on the United States. An extraordinary meeting of SCO foreign ministers in Beijing in January 2001 pledged the organization's support for the UN Security Council resolutions on Afghanistan and the international war on terror.[45]

In June 2002, SCO leaders announced the organization's charter in St. Petersburg, but they were unable to agree on a final document.[46] Nevertheless, China remained strongly committed to the organization. Under its auspices the first Chinese military exercises abroad were held with the Kyrgyz in October, with the purpose of training the Kyrgyz military in anti-terrorist activities.[47] At the third SCO summit in Moscow in May 2003, Hu Jintao, Putin, and the presidents of Kazakhstan, Kyrgyzstan, Tajikistan, and Uzbekistan signed documents authorizing the organization's budget, official emblem and flag, headquarters, and formal application to the UN for official registration as an inter-governmental organization in 2004. The Chinese were given the headquarters (in Beijing) and the secretary general (the current ambassador to Moscow). The leaders issued a statement confirming the SCO's commitment to the fight against terrorism. They reaffirmed their intention to develop RATS, announcing a joint anti-terror exercise involving the military forces of all member states, to be held in Kazakhstan in August.

Still, a great many practical issues remained unresolved, and the real contributions of the member states remain quite modest, as do the military, intelligence and police assets devoted to RATS. Details on the size of the SCO budget were not forthcoming after the May summit, and given the organization's track record there are grounds for skepticism about whether the member states will be able to commit the resources and decision authority necessary to make RATS an effective counter-terror force. The military and organizational capabilities of all the member states are at a much lower level than NATO norms, and both China and Russia face tight resource constraints. More important, virtually none of the organization's still modest activities could be seen as countering the United States. Indeed, at the May summit, SCO leaders stressed the organization's central concern with terrorism, religious extremism, separatism, and drug trafficking, and portrayed its mission as part of the U.S.-led war on terror.

Economically, China's actions in Central Asia have been relatively limited as well. Although it is often asserted that China is actively competing for Central Asia's resources, China has not been assertive in the Caspian, and is not clearly in competition with Russia or the United States. The Chinese government has long advocated the construction of a pipeline from the Caspian reserves across Kazakhstan and into western China. In fact, in

September 1997, then-Premier Li Peng signed an agreement with Kazakhstan to initiate this route. Neither Moscow nor Washington supports such a route, yet their vocal opposition may not be necessary, since conflict over the issue is unlikely to emerge for two reasons. First, the pure economics of the potential pipeline, estimated at over $8 billion, may well preclude even an aggressive Chinese policy from winning such an energy export route from the Caspian. Second, despite its need for oil resources, most China analysts do not see China as pursuing territorial expansion in order to obtain them.[48] Instead, the Chinese have been actively engaged with Russia in negotiating alternative sources of energy from Russia's Siberian oil and gas deposits.[49] In April 2003, the China National Petroleum Company secured an initial agreement to build an oil pipeline from Russia's Angarsk Siberian fields to Daqing in China.[50] Three other gas and oil lines are under consideration. Eastern routes increase Russian-Chinese cooperation, while decreasing competition in the Caspian.

The Central Asian States' Responses

The Central Asian states have responded to the great powers in varying ways. Most have increasingly hedged their bets between Russia and the United States, while remaining somewhat wary of China. In general, their actions in response to the great powers have been determined more by their need for economic support—whether through military bases or promised aid packages or trade deals—and their fear of regional terrorism, extremism and instability, than by their fear of great power hegemony.

Uzbekistan's Response

The Uzbek response to initial U.S. requests for the use of bases and territory were met with some suspicion, as well as fear of a backlash from the Taliban, from its own Muslim extremist groups, and from Russia. U.S. and UN requests to open the Friendship Bridge became a further serious disagreement. The bridge had been long-closed because of the Taliban's grave security threats to the territorial integrity of Uzbekistan in 1997 and 1998. "The Uzbeks were therefore extremely resistant to the opening of the border. I've never seen such stolid and displeased faces when they made the agreement," said one western diplomat. "They doubted the U.S. commitment to protecting it from an attack. They claimed that it was a better guarded border then the North-South Korean border. In reality, however, a serious push by Taliban forces could have toppled it."[51]

Allowing U.S. forces on the Uzbek-Afghan border represented a significant break from past Uzbek policy, which had rejected Russian offers to station troops on the border to guard against Taliban movements into

Mazar-i-Sharif in 1998. The Uzbek government had also been upset by Russia's threats in 2000 to conduct air strikes against Taliban forces in northern Afghanistan. Uzbekistan had feared both a loss of sovereignty by allowing Russian forces on its territory and a backlash from the Taliban. Although the Russian ambassador to Uzbekistan claimed that Russia was not at all involved in the decision to base U.S. troops on Uzbek soil, and that neither the United States nor Uzbekistan had sought Russia's permission, Russia would not retaliate against Uzbekistan; in fact, trade and investment relations between Russia and Uzbekistan are increasingly strong.[52] Although the Russian Defense Minister Sergei Ivanov was reportedly strongly opposed to the bases, President Putin more importantly was not.

Despite his unease in opening Uzbek territory to outside powers, in a press statement after a meeting with Powell, Karimov indicated that the cooperation with the United States on Afghanistan was part of an increasingly broad relationship, stating: "If you think that we focused our attention mainly on the situation in Afghanistan, you will be mistaken....we have a conflux of questions of mutual interest."[53] Indeed, the subsequent MOU and Strategic Partnership and Cooperation Framework of 2002 reflected much of the expanded relationship with the United States that the Uzbeks had wanted. Although then Deputy Minister of Foreign Affairs Sodyq Safaev forcefully denied that the basing agreement involved a 25-year lease,[54] the Uzbeks nonetheless consistently state that they want a long-term relationship, and that a short-term relationship or quick exit by the United States will increase Uzbekistan's insecurity and regional instability.[55] Most importantly for the Uzbeks, the Strategic Partnership gave Uzbekistan a "security guarantee." The agreement falls far short of a NATO-like guarantee, and is somewhat vague in the implications of the actual commitment demanded of the United States. Still, it strongly suggests that the United States will react to a threat to the territorial integrity of Uzbekistan—from Afghanistan, its Central Asian neighbors, or potentially even Russia. Furthermore, the agreement informally provides the United States some leverage to keep Uzbekistan's territorial ambitions, especially vis-à-vis Kyrgyzstan and Tajikistan, in check—a prospect that bodes well for regional stability. By still holding out from giving Uzbekistan the more comprehensive "security guarantee" it still wants, the United States maintains its most important leverage for influencing this critical Central Asian state to promote the great powers' security interests, and the economic and political reforms that will enhance longer-term domestic and regional stability.

Uzbekistan clearly seeks to become a long-term U.S. strategic partner. In fact, while not openly admitting to the possibility of basing U.S. forces for an attack on Iraq, the Uzbek government was nonetheless the most consistent and open supporter of the U.S.-led action among all the states in the Middle East and Central Asia. In its joint security cooperation consultations in April 2003, the United States continued to declare Uzbekistan its "strategic partner in Central Asia," and reiterated the United States' "willingness to expand its defense and military cooperation."[56] Both sides concluded by stating that "their approaches to the issue of Iraq are in harmony. Uzbekistan supported the U.S. position on the disarmament of Iraq and the postwar reconstruction of that country for the greater stability, freedom, and prosperity of the entire region."[57]

Kyrgyzstan and Tajikistan's Responses

Compared to Uzbekistan, both Kyrgyzstan and Tajikistan have remained to a far larger extent within the sphere of traditional Russian hegemony. Prior to September 11, both were increasingly dependent on Russia economically and militarily. Yet, since September 11, both took the unexpected steps of rapidly offering overflight and then basing rights to the United States. In fact, they were actively competing with each other and Uzbekistan to secure a U.S. base for the military security and economic benefits it was expected to bring. The Kyrgyz in particular expected that a U.S. presence would help to internally stabilize their turbulent country, bring an influx of dollars to the failing economy, intimidate the IMU from undertaking renewed attacks, and further discourage Uzbekistan from making aggressive moves toward its neighbors. Indeed, as seen in Table 1 above, the U.S. assistance package to both has more than doubled in the wake of their agreements to actively participate in the U.S. anti-terror coalition.

In late 2002 and early 2003, both countries agreed to the expansion of the Russian and CSTO military presence on their territory as well (i.e. the CSTO and 201st Division bases discussed above). On the part of Kyrgyzstan, forgiveness of debt was a key factor in closing the deal with Russia. The Kyrgyz also sought a greater security guarantee than had been included in the U.S. MOU of 2002. Although some view their cooperation with China as a sign of their balancing against Russia and the United States, in reality, they are reacting to Chinese pressure to assist in cracking down on the Uighur separatists, whom China views as terrorists with Islamist connections. Kyrgyzstan's joint military exercises with both Russia and China, and the basing agreements with Moscow and Washington, represent a patchwork of efforts to create a security regime for themselves, while not offending their powerful neighbors.

Russia's deal with Tajikistan represents little shift in bilateral relations, since the 201st Division has been in the country for over a decade of independence, rarely serving as a peacekeeping force. Russia was critical in bringing Rakhmonov to power, and Rakhmonov had wanted the 201st Division to remain after the peace deal, since its presence helped to stabilize his regime, which continued to be challenged by lingering armed opposition groups until 2001.[58] Yet, frustrated by lack of major Russian investment in his country, Rakhmonov skillfully used the war on terror to get greater aid from the United States and international financial institutions. With increased leverage, Rakhmonov then successfully sought Russian investment in a key hydroelectric power plant as something of a quid pro quo for the Russian base.[59] The Tajik president, like most of its neighbors, increasingly recognizes that the "Islamic threat" is internal as well, and thus that investment—whether fueled by Russia, the United States, or China— is key to growth, stability, and maintaining his power.[60]

Of the Central Asian states, only in Kyrgyzstan has a large domestic constituency been opposed to the U.S. presence.[61] The irony of this situation is that major elements of the lingering pro-democracy movement have been the leading spokesmen against military cooperation with the United States. They have viewed the U.S.-Kyrgyz deal in a negative light primarily because they believe it has fed government corruption. Despite U.S. State Department efforts to the contrary, the deal is widely perceived as the United States turning a blind eye to Kyrgyzstan's increasingly autocratic regime and escalating human rights abuses in 2002.[62]

Kazakhstan's Response

As the Central Asian state closest to Russia geographically, economically, and politically, Kazakhstan might have been expected to oppose an increased U.S. presence in the region. Certainly, a great game perspective would have anticipated either that the Kazakhs would support Russia in counterbalancing the U.S. presence in Uzbekistan and Kyrgyzstan, or that Moscow would put intense pressure on Astana to resist America's blandishments. Instead, Kazakhstan, presumably with Russia's nod of assent, used September 11 to intensify its ongoing military and economic cooperation with the United States. As noted earlier, the main U.S. (and Russian and Chinese) interest in Kazakhstan had been in the removal of its nuclear weapons facilities. Since then, Kazakhstan had cooperated with the United States militarily within the Partnership for Peace framework. At the same time, it was engaged with Russia in the CST, and with China and Russia in the SCO. Shortly after September 11, Kazakhstan offered the use of airspace, but given the greater strategic salience of Uzbekistan and Kyrgyzstan, Washington did not take advantage of the Kazakh offer.

While some skeptics took the absence of U.S. troops in Kazakhstan as a sign of souring relations, in April 2002 talks between Kazakh President

Nursultan Nazarbaev and U.S. Secretary of Defense Donald Rumsfeld resulted in Kazakhstan offering three southern bases, including Almaty, for coalition use in "emergency situations."[63] Probably observing that U.S. assistance to its more active allies in the war on terror had increased much more dramatically between 2001 and 2002 (the aid budget to Kazakhstan increased only from $93.73 to 93.91 $million[64]), Kazakhstan subsequently indicated that it might be willing to host a larger U.S.-led coalition military presence. At the same time, concern over relations with Russia has probably led Kazakhstan—like its neighbors—to continually state the U.S. presence must be short-term.

U.S. military assistance to Kazakhstan has recently increased. In February 2003, the U.S. delivered the first of a shipment of 39 high-mobility army vehicles to build the Kazakh military's capacity to fight terrorism.[65] Even after tensions between Washington and Moscow had escalated over Iraq, the Kazakh parliament voted in May 2003 to send peacekeepers to Iraq to support the U.S. stabilization force.[66] Nor has China openly opposed U.S.-Kazakh cooperation. In June 2003, Hu Jintao announced the creation of a Chinese-Kazakh energy joint venture, and ongoing discussions for a Kazakh-China oil and gas pipeline.[67] Not unlike its Central Asian neighbors, Kazakhstan's policy has been driven by a desire to maximize its security from terrorism and religious extremism, a desire to get on the U.S. gravy train, and pursuit of foreign investment and energy export markets.

Turkmenistan's Response

Turkmenistan's behavior, driven by its inward-focused, megalomaniacal dictator Saparmurat Niyazov, differs from the more outward-looking hedging among great powers practiced by the other Central Asian states. At the same time, however, it ill fits the great game interpretation. Turkmenistan remained the sole Central Asian state to do little more than offer overflight rights to the United States after September 11. In fact, for most of the 1990s, Turkmenistan did not support CST, SCO, or U.S. initiatives on Afghanistan, since Niyazov did not perceive the Taliban to be a threat. Turkmenistan still does not participate in regional security arrangements. Yet, Turkmenistan's "neutrality" has been driven far less by a fear of Russian retaliation than by the Turkmen president's increasingly erratic behavior. Niyazov has advocated a trans-Afghan pipeline, but he has done little to court U.S. favor. Russia need not worry about U.S. support for the Turkmen initiative, since U.S. government officials and energy executives appear to be avoiding investment in an increasingly precarious "cult-of-personality," which was recently the subject of a failed coup. Meanwhile, relations with Russia have worsened in ongoing disagreements over the Caspian Sea's division and Russian-Turkmen gas deals.[68] Both Moscow and Washington would prefer a change of regime; they may need to cooperate to promote a stable change, since no mechanism of succession currently exists.

In sum, the Central Asian states share significant common security interests with the great powers, and they almost uniformly (with the exception of Turkmenistan) recognize that they cannot address those security concerns without active cooperation with Russia, the United States, and increasingly China as well. The Central Asian states also welcome the economic benefits of increased great power activity in the region, and to a certain extent, they will continue to sell their cooperation to the highest bidders. Finally, a balanced U.S. and Russian military presence throughout the region need not lead to competition or division of the Central Asian states into American versus Russian spheres of influence. To the contrary, stable great power interests may decrease the likelihood of internecine actions among the Central Asian states themselves.

Conclusion

The popular great game lens for analyzing Central Asia fails to capture the declared interests of the great powers as well as the best reading of their objective interests in security and economic growth. Perhaps more importantly, it fails to explain their actual behavior on the ground, as well the specific reactions of the Central Asian states themselves. Naturally, there are competitive elements in great power relations. Each country's policymaking community has slightly different preferences for tackling the challenges presented in the region, and the more influence they have the more able they are to shape events in concordance with those preferences. But these clashing preferences concern the means to serve ends that all the great powers share. To be sure, policy-makers in each capital would prefer that their own national firms or their own government's budget be the beneficiaries of any economic rents that emerge from the exploitation and transshipment of the region's natural resources. But the scale of these rents is marginal even for Russia's oil-fueled budget. And for taxable profits to be created, the projects must make sense economically—something that is determined more by markets and firms than governments.

Does it matter? The great game is an arresting metaphor that serves to draw people's attention to an oft-neglected region. The problem is that the great-game lens can distort realities on the ground, and therefore bias analysis and policy. For when great powers are locked in a competitive fight, the issues at hand matter less than their implication for the relative power of contending states. Power itself becomes the issue—one that tends to be non-negotiable. Viewing an essential positive-sum relationship through zero-sum conceptual lenses will result in missed opportunities for cooperation that leaves all players—not least the people who live in the region—poorer and more insecure.

While cautious realism must remain the watchword concerning an impoverished and potentially unstable region comprised of fragile and authoritarian states, our analysis yields at least conditional and relative optimism. Given the confluence of their chief strategic interests, the major powers are in a better position to serve as a stabilizing force than analogies to the Great Game or the Cold War would suggest. It is important to stress that the region's response to the profoundly destabilizing shock of coordinated terror attacks was increased cooperation between local governments and China and Russia, and—multipolar rhetoric notwithstanding—between both of them and the United States. If this trend is nurtured and if the initial signals about potential SCO-CSTO-NATO cooperation are pursued, another destabilizing shock might generate more rather than less cooperation among the major powers.

Uzbekistan, Kyrgyzstan, Tajikistan, and Kazakhstan are clearly on a trajectory that portends longer-term cooperation with each of the great powers. As military and economic security interests become more entwined, there are sound reasons to conclude that "great game" politics will not shape Central Asia's future in the same competitive and destabilizing way as they have controlled its past. To the contrary, mutual interests in Central Asia may reinforce the broader positive developments in the great powers' relations that have taken place since September 11, as well as reinforce regional and domestic stability in Central Asia.

Endnotes

[1] See, for example, Michael Klare, *Resource Wars: The New Landscape of Global Conflict*, New York: Metropolitan Books, 2002; and Hooman Peimani, "Military buildup ends US-Russian honeymoon," *Asia Times*, August 28, 2002.

[2] We define Central Asia as the region consisting of the five Central Asian states of the former Soviet Union: Kazakhstan, Kyrgyzstan, Tajikistan, Turkmenistan, and Uzbekistan. We distinguish this from the Caucasus region, although we discuss some overlapping security issues.

[3] India, Pakistan, Turkey, Iran, and other outside powers also figure in "great game" interpretations, and have undertaken initiatives in the region over the past several years, but their combined significance pales beside the "big three"—Russia, China and the United States—on which we focus.

[4] See Thomas Christensen, "China," William C. Wohlforth, "Russia," in Richard J. Ellings and Aaron L. Friedberg with Michael Wills, eds., *Strategic Asia 2002–03: Asian Aftershocks*, Seattle: The National Bureau of Asian Research, 2003.

[5] The nature and extent of these links are disputed; the point here is the convergence of official positions. See "Interview with Defense Minister Sergey Ivanov," *Rossiyskaya Gazeta*, January 14, 2003, translated in *CDI Russia Weekly*, no. 240, p. 2; "Text of White Paper on History, Development of Xinjiang," Xinhua, May 26, 2003; and U.S. State Department, "Patterns of Global Terrorism," 2002, <www.state.gov/s/ct/rls/pqtrp/2002>.

[6] Monterey Institute of International Studies, "Summary of Reported Nuclear, Radioisotope, and Dual-Use Materials Trafficking Incidents Involving the NIS," <www.nti.org/db/nistraff/tables/yrcharts/99chart>.

[7] Yekaterina Stepanova, "Illicit drug trafficking in Afghanistan and Central Asia and its relation to the anti-terrorism campaign," *Yadernyy Kontrol*, September 28, 2002; translated in FBIS-CNES-2002-1126.

[8] In addition to the Russia and China Christensen chapters in last year's *Strategic Asia* volume, see Wohlforth, "Revisiting Balance of Power Theory in Central Eurasia," in T. V. Paul and James J. Wirtz, eds., *Balance of Power Theory and Practice in the 21st Century*, Stanford, Calif.: Stanford University Press, forthcoming; and Alastair Iain Johnston, "Is China a Status Quo Power?" *International Security*, vol. 27, no. 3 (Spring 2003), pp. 5–56.

[9] On the economics, see J. D. Sachs and A. Warner, "The Curse of Natural Resources," *European Economic Review*, vol. 24 (2001), pp. 827–38; and on the politics, Adam Przeworski, et. al., *Democracy and Development: Political Institutions and Well-Being in the World, 1950–1990*, Cambridge, Mass.: Cambridge University Press, 2000.

[10] See, for example, Stephen M. Blank, "Central Asia's Strategic Revolution," *NBR Analysis* (forthcoming 2003); Charles Maier, "America Discovers Central Asia," *Foreign Affairs*, vol. 82, no.2 (March/April 2003), pp. 120–32; and Andrew Bacevich, "Bases of Debate: America in Central Asia: Steppes to Empire," *The National Interest*, Summer 2002.

[11] GUUAM members include Azerbaijan, Georgia, Moldova, Ukraine, and Uzbekistan. For an extensive discussion of this period, see Roy Allison, "Structures and Frameworks for Security Policy Cooperation in Central Asia," in Roy Allison and Lena Johnson, eds., *Central Asian Security*, Washington, DC: Brookings Press, 2001, 219–40.

[12] Department of State Press Release, Joint Press Conference with President Islam Karimov, December 8, 2001, <www.state.gov/secretary/rm/2001/dec/6749.htm>.

[13] Figures are from the Department of State, updated as of February 24, 2003.

[14] Kathleen Collins, "U.S. Policy and Political and Economic Reform in Central Asia," manuscript presented to Stanford University, November 15, 2002.

[15] "United States-Uzbekistan Declaration on the Strategic Partnership and Cooperation Framework," State Department Fact Sheet, March 12, 2002, <www.state.gov/r/pa/prs/ps/2002/8736>.

[16] "Declaration on the Strategic Partnership and Cooperation Framework Between the United States of America and the Republic of Uzbekistan," released July 8, 2002, <www.state.gov/p/eur/rls/or/2002/11711>.

[17] "Declaration on the Strategic Partnership and Cooperation Framework…"

[18] Eurasianet.org, 2002.

[19] "U.S. military to finance renovation of Uzbek air base," Eurasianet.org, August 5, 2002.

[20] *Wall Street Journal*, May 27, 2003, p. 1.

[21] Interview with a U.S. government official, Tashkent, January 2002.

[22] From 1996 to 1997, Russia changed course and became actively involved in negotiating a peace accord in Tajikistan. See Kathleen Collins, "Tajikistan: Bad Peace Agreements and Prolonged Civil Conflict," in Chandra Sriram and Karin Wermerster, eds., *From Promise to Practice: Strengthening UN Capacities to Resolve Civil Conflict*, Boulder, Colo.: Lynne Rienner, 2003. On the changes under Putin, see the Russia chapter in last year's *Strategic Asia* volume.

[23] See for example, Stephen Blank, "Scramble for Central Asian bases," *Asia Times*, April 8, 2003.

[24] Signed in 1992 in Tashkent, the CST includes Russia, Belarus, Armenia, Kazakhstan, Kyrgyzstan, and Tajikistan. Uzbekistan withdrew in 1999. Although under pressure by Russia at the time to return, Uzbekistan determined to stay out of the organization.

[25] Stephen Blank, "The Future of Transcaspian Security," Carlisle, Penn.: U.S. Army War College, Strategic Studies Institute, August 2002.

[26] Dmitri Trenin, "Central Asia's Stability and Russia's Security," *PONARS Memo*, no. 168, November 2000.

[27] IISS, *The Military Balance: 2002–2003*, London: International Institute of Strategic Studies, 2003.

[28] IISS, *The Military Balance: 2002–2003*.

[29] The base is expected to open formally in July 2003 (Interfax). William D O'Malley and Roger N. McDermott, "The Russian Air Force in Kyrgyzstan: the military implications," *Central Asia-Caucasus Analyst*, April 23, 2003.

[30] Radio Free Europe, April 28, 2003; Eurasianet.org, April 29, 2003.

[31] Ibragim Alibekov and Sergei Blagov, "New Russian security organization could help expand Russia's influence in Central Asia," April 29, 2003, Eurasianet.org.

[32] Vladimir Mukhin, "Rossiya sozdaet krupnuyu voennuyu bazu v tsentral'noi azii (Russia establishes a major military base in Central Asia)," *Nezavisimaya gazeta*, May 21, 2003.

[33] Arms sales generalization is based on a review of IISS, *The Military Balance*; SIPRI arms transfers database, <www.sipri.org>; and the UN conventional arms register, <disarmament.un.org/un_register.nsf>. A partial exception to the statement about military-to-military ties is Turkmenistan; see Anton Aleekseev, "Vooruzhenye sily Turkmenistana (Turkmenistan's military forces)," *Eksport vooruzhenii*, at Tsentr analiza strategii i tekhnologii, <www.cast.ru/russian/publish/2002/may-june/alexeev.html>. Russian press reports stress that close defense cooperation includes Uzbekistan, despite its non-membership in the CSTO. See Fedor Sukhov, "Islam Karimov meniaet svoiu orientatsiiu (Islam Karimov changes his orientation)," *Obshchaia gazeta*, February 5, 2001, p. 2.

[34] Nicholas Eberstadt, "The Future of AIDS," *Foreign Affairs*, vol. 81, no. 6 (November/December 2002).

[35] O'Malley and McDermott, "The Russian Air Force in Kyrgyzstan: the military implications." The Bishkek Center has yet to be formally opened, though it is routinely referred to as operational.

[36] Radio Free Europe, April 29, 2003; and Sergei Blagov, "All it takes is thugs with clubs," *Asia Times*, January 15, 2003.

[37] Stephen Blank, "Central Asia's Strategic Revolution," p. 125. Blank also notes "talk of having America subsidize the SCO," p. 113.

[38] Adam Stulberg, "Leveraging Preponderance: Russia's Agenda Control and Caspian Pipeline Politics," manuscript presented to the University of Michigan, November 9, 2002.

[39] Catherine Belton, "Putin's delicate balancing game," *Moscow Times*, March 13, 2003, and Stulberg (2002).

[40] See Martha Olcott, "Central Asia," *Strategic Asia 2002–03*, p. 242.

[41] Igor Torbakov, "Russian economic integration effort may leave most of Central Asia behind," Eurasianet.org, March 11, 2003.

[42] See, for example, Sergei Blagov, "Russia seeking to strengthen regional organizations to counterbalance Western influence," *Eurasia Insight*, December 4, 2002, Eurasianet.org.

[43] Interview with senior analyst, Institute of Strategic Studies, Uzbekistan, Tashkent, August 2002.

[44] "Declaration of the Establishment of the Shanghai Cooperation Organization, June 15, 2001," <www.missions.itu.int/~kazaks/eng/sco/sco02>.

[45] "Joint Statement by the Ministers of Foreign Affairs of the Member States of the Shanghai Cooperation Organization," January 7, 2002, Beijing, <www.missions.itu.int/~kazaks/eng/sco/sco06>.

[46] Reports suggested that the delay was partly the result of Russia seeking more binding commitments than the Central Asian members were willing to accept. See Matthew Oresman, "The SCO: A New Hope or to the Graveyard of Acronyms?" *PacNet Newsletter*, no. 21, May 22, 2003, <www.csis.org/pacfor/pac0321.htm>.

[47] BBC Monitoring, October 10, 2002.

[48] Dmitri Trenin, *Limited Partnership: Russia-China Relations in a Changing Asia*, Washington, DC: Carnegie Endowment for International Peace, 1998.

[49] Charles Ziegler, "Russia, China, and Energy in Central and East Asia," manuscript presented at Caspian Security Conference, Seattle, April 29, 2003.

[50] *Economist*, May 24, 2003. See also the analyses in the Northeast Asia and Russia chapters in the volume.

[51] Interview with a UN official, Tashkent, January 8, 2003.

[52] Interview with a high-level Russian official in Uzbekistan, Tashkent, January 2002.

[53] State Department Press Release, Joint Press Conference with President Islam Karimov, December 8, 2001.

[54] Press Conference with Sodyq Safaev, Deputy Minister of Foreign Affairs of Uzbekistan, Tashkent, January 23, 2002.

[55] Interview with a senior advisor to the Ministry of Foreign Affairs of Uzbekistan, Tashkent, August 2002.

[56] United States-Uzbekistan Joint Security Cooperation Consultations, Press Statement, April 15, 2003 <www.state.gov/r/pa/prs/ps/2003/19665>.

[57] United States-Uzbekistan Joint Security Cooperation Consultations, Press Statement.

[58] Interview with a Tajik journalist, Dushanbe, August 2002.

[59] Radio Free Europe, April, 2003.

[60] Viktoriya Panfilova, "Dlya Tsentral'noi azii ne tak strashen Ben Laden, kak defitsit chistoi vody (For Central Asia, Bin Laden is less frightening than the shortage of clean water)," *Nezavisimaya gazeta*, May 20, 2003.

[61] Elizabeth Wishnick, "Growing US Security Interests in Central Asia," Carlisle, Penn.: U.S. Army War College, Strategic Studies Institute, October 2002. Kazakh polling data also shows significant opposition to a long-term presence, though none is there yet.

[62] Interview with Tolekan Ismailova, leader of Coalition of NGOs in Krygyzstan, February 2003.

[63] ITAR-TASS, in *Central Asia–Caucasus Analyst*, April 28, 2002.

[64] Annual Reports, U.S. Department of State, 2000–02.

[65] "United States begins delivery of high mobility army vehicles to Kazakhstan," Associated Press, in *Central Asia–Caucasus Analyst*, January 20, 2003.

[66] Interfax-Kazakhstan, in *Central Asia–Caucasus Analyst*, May 30, 2003.

[67] Ted Weihman, "China making diplomatic push in Central Asia," Eurasianet.org, June 9, 2003.

[68] Stephen Blank, "The Russia-Turkmenistan Gas Deal Gone Awry," *Central Asia–Caucasus Analyst*, July 2, 2003.

STRATEGIC ASIA

SPECIAL STUDIES

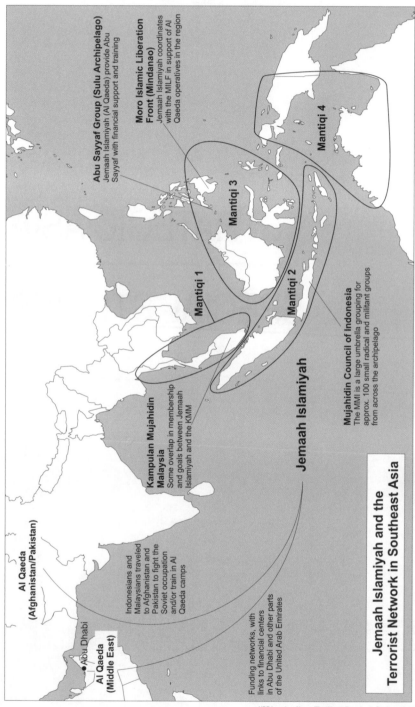

Al Qaeda (Afghanistan/Pakistan)

Indonesians and Malaysians traveled to Afghanistan and Pakistan to fight the Soviet occupation and/or train in Al Qaeda camps

Al Qaeda (Middle East)

Abu Dhabi

Funding networks, with links to financial centers in Abu Dhabi and other parts of the United Arab Emirates

Kampulan Mujahidin Malaysia
Some overlap in membership and goals between Jemaah Islamiyah and the KMM

Abu Sayyaf Group (Sulu Archipelago)
Jemaah Islamiyah (Al Qaeda) provide Abu Sayyaf with financial support and training

Moro Islamic Liberation Front (Mindanao)
Jemaah Islamiyah coordinates with the MILF in support of Al Qaeda operatives in the region

Mujahidin Council of Indonesia
The MMI is a large umbrella grouping for approx. 100 small radical and militant groups from across the archipelago

Mantiqi 1

Mantiqi 2

Mantiqi 3

Mantiqi 4

Jemaah Islamiyah

Jemaah Islamiyah and the Terrorist Network in Southeast Asia

NBR based on Abuza, "The War on Terrorism in Southeast Asia"

THE WAR ON TERRORISM IN SOUTHEAST ASIA

Zachary Abuza

ABSTRACT

Southeast Asia has emerged as a key theater of operations for Al Qaeda through its regional affiliate Jemaah Islamiyah, which has developed a powerful operational capability, culminating in the 2002 Bali bombings in which 202 people were killed. Jemaah Islamiyah, with its established leadership body, regional structure, and a network for recruiting and training, has been affected by the war on terror in Southeast Asia—about 200 Jemaah Islamiyah members had been arrested by August 2003, including some top leaders. Yet most of its senior operatives remain at large. Jemaah Islamiyah is now less able to plan and execute terrorist attacks than in late 2001, but it maintains the capacity to hit soft targets and critical infrastructure. Although every state in Southeast Asia has joined the war on terror, they have done so only to the degree that it benefits them politically and diplomatically. The political will to fight the war has waned as many states in the region entered a year of important elections. Although bilateral cooperation has improved, there are still no effective multilateral tools for fighting terror. There has been little willingness to address terrorist funding in the region.

Zachary Abuza is Assistant Professor of International Politics and the Director of the East Asian Studies Program at Simmons College.

Introduction[1]

Islam in Southeast Asia has traditionally been defined by tolerance, moderation and pluralism. Most of the Muslim inhabitants of Southeast Asia support the secular state, and only a small minority advocates the establishment of Islamic regimes governed by *sharia* (Islamic law). Most eschew the violence and literal interpretations of Islam that have plagued their fellow Muslims in South Asia and the Middle East. There have always been Muslim militants in the region, but the conventional wisdom is they were focused on their own domestic agenda.[2] That analysis, however, underestimates the degree to which radical Islamists in Southeast Asia have linked up with transnational terrorist organizations like Al Qaeda. The devastating attack on the Sari Nightclub in Bali, in which some 202 people were killed, was a wakeup call to governments in denial and skeptics in the region. The October 12, 2002 attack was Al Qaeda's second most deadly after the September 11, 2001 attacks on the United States, and drove home the point that Al Qaeda and its regional arms pose a grave threat to the safety and well-being of states. Though these militants represent a distinct minority of the population, their ability to cause political and economic instability means that we have to understand their motives and capabilities to wage a war of terror. Southeast Asian states, as well as foreign analysts, fundamentally underestimated the degree of penetration in the region by Al Qaeda operatives and their ability to develop local cells. There were two stages of denial—first, the assumption that Southeast Asians were moderate and secular and second, the calculation that although there were Muslim militants in the region, they were home grown and many in fact predated Al Qaeda, and thus had no need for terrorist linkages.

The avowed goal of Jemaah Islamiyah, to establish a pan-Islamic state in Southeast Asia that spreads from southern Thailand through Indonesia and includes the southern Philippines, is unlikely to succeed. Yet Jemaah Islamiyah's determination necessitates greater security cooperation within Southeast Asia. The fact that there were no bilateral or multilateral security mechanisms in place prior to the Bali attacks in October 2002 that could counter terrorist operations further facilitated militant activities. The emergence of Jemaah Islamiyah also necessitates a significant shift in American foreign policy in the region. Since the 1991 closure of two U.S. bases in the Philippines, U.S. foreign policy has been driven by normative rather than strategic interests. The region remains critically important for U.S. national interests and, as terrorism has emerged as the single greatest threat to the region, counter-terrorism must be the centerpiece of U.S. foreign policy toward Southeast Asia.

Al Qaeda Comes to Southeast Asia

Al Qaeda has a number of clearly enunciated goals—to rid the Holy Land of the United States, to defeat Israel, and to establish a pan-Islamic state based on the seventh century caliphate. To that end, it seeks to degrade U.S. capabilities by waging jihad around the world. Al Qaeda was attracted to Southeast Asia for three main reasons: the growth of Islamic grievances within Southeast Asian states since the 1970s for socio-economic and political reasons, the Afghan connection to Middle Eastern extremists, and most importantly, the accessibility of Southeast Asian states as "countries of convenience" for international terrorists. These conditions enabled Al Qaeda to pursue its longer-term strategic goal of spreading jihad globally.

Socio-Economic and Political Grievances

Across the region, there has been an Islamic resurgence in the past few decades. Extremists represent a miniscule proportion of the populations; the potential for any Southeast Asian state to be taken over by a fundamentalist regime is small. The resounding defeat of the inclusion of *sharia* into Indonesia's constitution by the parliament is evidence of this. But Islamism's gradual acceptance into the mainstream of the region's social structures means that many are beginning to at least acknowledge that they share the extremists' grievances, if not methods. And, in some countries, it has become politically incorrect or politically foolhardy to stand up to the extremists, who now comprise a small but vociferous minority with the power to shape the political and social agendas.[3]

Many of the Muslim movements in Southeast Asia have legitimate grievances, whether they have been repressed, clamor for autonomy, or simply seek greater religious freedom. Economically, in all Southeast Asian countries the Muslim communities are less well off. Since the Iranian revolution of 1979, the growth of Islamic extremism around the world has less to do with theology than with the failure of the domestic political economies of their respective countries. Two of the most secular governments in the Muslim world were Malaysia and Indonesia, two of the fastest-growing economies from the mid-1970s to the mid-1990s. Once their economies slowed and became mired in the Asian financial crisis (where the value of their currencies collapsed and public and private debt has soared, causing mass unemployment), Islamism was able to take root among the mainstream populace, whereas before it was on the fringes of society. Clerics were able to veil their political criticisms in Friday prayer sermons. Islam also became more radical because authoritarian secular governments did not give political "space" to religious elites and religious-based political parties, even as the leaders used these groups to buttress their own ascension to power. Religious elites and parties felt that they had been at best ignored or marginalized, and at worst repressed by governments who feared the Islamization of politics.

Yet when it has served their purposes, these governments have turned to religion as a legitimizing force for their rule. In Malaysia, the United Malays National Organization (UMNO) has had to steadily become less secular in order to court Malay defectors to Parti SeIslam (PAS).[4] Islamists have been able to achieve these gains in part because of the spread of democracy in the region. Since the fall of Suharto in Indonesia, radical Muslim parties have been legitimized. Under Suharto, the lack of democratic institutions (political parties, freedom of assembly, and free speech) permitted Islamism to spread within a circumscribed environment—only through the veiled language spoken in the mosques could political dissent be heard. The spread of democracy has opened politics to the extremists, giving them political platforms to express their pent-up grievances. Democratization in Indonesia also has meant a breakdown of central government control and law and order in the archipelago, a phenomenon that has allowed militant groups to step in and pursue their agendas unchecked.

The breakdown of secular institutions, especially the educational and legal systems in the wake of the Asian financial crisis, created a vacuum in which non-secular institutions emerged. Increasingly, parents are turning to *pesantren* and *madrassas* to educate their children as state funding for the educational sector collapses. *Sharia* courts have become more prominent because of the absolute failure of the secular court system in adapting itself to changes in the political economy of a "globalized" world.[5]

Southeast Asian *madrassas* are increasingly beyond state control. Of the 37,362 *madrassas* in Indonesia, only 3,226 (8.6 percent) are run by the state; and 81 percent of the 5.6 million students enrolled in *madrassas* attend privately-funded and privately-run Islamic schools.[6] In the Philippines, only 35 of 1,600 are controlled by the state, with alarming consequences. As one education official put it, the privately-funded *madrassas* "tailor their curricula to the wishes of whoever subsidizes them."[7]

The *madrassas* and *pesantren* in Southeast Asia that have been set up since the late 1980s have advocated a stricter, more intolerant brand of Islam and condemn the secular nation-state. They are the core of a growing and powerful radical Muslim movement and have established networks throughout the region and with the Middle East. There is now a critical mass of students studying in Islamic universities and *madrassas* who are reinforced in their conviction that Malaysia, Indonesia, and Mindanao in the Philippines must become Islamic states in order to overcome the myriad socio-economic and political woes that secularism has wrought. They believe that in Islam, there is no separation between church and state, that Islam is a complete way of life, and that *sharia*, can be the only ordering principle in society. This radical fringe will likely continue to grow as modernization leaves the region's populations more isolated and the political process leaves more people disenfranchised. The Islamists and their supporters will continue to gain political power unless the more secular Muslim community again provides a successful model for a more tolerant and modernist Islam, which it has done fairly successfully for 40 years.

The Afghan Connection

The second reason Al Qaeda migrated to the region was the influence of the Afghan *mujahidin*. Up to 1,000 Southeast Asian Muslims fought with the *mujahidin* in the 1980s. Undeniably, the Afghanistan experience was formative in the lives of Southeast Asian *jihadis*. In Indonesia there was Group 272—returned veterans and key leaders of radical groups in the region who were all veterans of the *mujahidin*. They included Umar Jaffar Thalib, Riduan Isamuddin (Hambali), Nik Aziz Nik Adli, Abdurajak Janjalani, and others. One cannot underestimate the strategic significance of the Afghan connection. It is the basis for today's Al Qaeda network around the world. As one regional intelligence official who had interrogated Jemaah Islamiyah members recounted, they were miserably homesick, spoke poor Arabic, and were unaccustomed to the harshness of their surroundings. Nonetheless, they were driven by the call to jihad.[8] As Peter Bergen wrote:

> Still, in the grand scheme of things the Afghan Arabs were no more than extras in the Afghan holy war. It was the lessons they learned from the jihad, rather than their contribution to it, that proved significant. They rubbed shoulders with militants from dozens of countries and were indoctrinated in the most extreme ideas concerning jihad. They received at least some sort of military training, and in some cases battlefield experiences. Those who had had their tickets punched in the Afghan conflict went back to their countries with the ultimate credential for later holy wars. And they believed their exertions had defeated a superpower.[9]

Southeast Asian militants were also trained in Al Qaeda camps in Afghanistan following the ascension of the Taliban, though the exact numbers are unclear. A Russian intelligence report passed on to the Philippine government asserted that "at least 50 Filipinos [MILF soldiers] were recently trained in one of the 55 camps and bases being maintained in Afghanistan by Osama bin Laden" and are fighting in the Taliban's 8th Division, which includes fighters from across the Muslim world.[10] Many Jemaah Islamiyah members were trained in Afghan camps as well.[11]

These Afghan veterans returned to Southeast Asia and established a network of Wahhabi-inspired *madrassas,* which they used as their bases of operations and recruitment, confident that they could defeat their secular regimes. These schools, which teach a literal interpretation of Islam, are the primary socialization vehicle and recruitment organ for jihad. Tens of thousands of Southeast Asian Muslims have traveled to the Middle East to study in Islamic universities, including those in Egypt, Syria, Yemen and Pakistan. Thousands of Southeast Asians have studied in the Pakistani *madrassas* that gave rise to the Taliban regime. None of the countries in Southeast Asia has an accurate count of how many of their nationals studied in *madrassas* in the past or are currently studying now because their governments do not keep records on privately-funded students studying abroad.[12] In their pursuit of the creation of Islamic states, many Southeast Asian *jihadis* established Islamic schools to indoctrinate, propagate and recruit. The leaders of many militant groups in Southeast Asia, including the Laskar Jihad, Kampulan Mujahidin Malaysia, Jemaah Islamiyah, Wae Kah Rah, and Guragon Mujahidin, returned from Afghanistan and established a network of *madrassas* as the base of their operations, planting the seeds of the goal to establish a pan-Islamic state in the region.

Countries of Convenience

The third reason that made Southeast Asia so appealing to the Al Qaeda leadership was the existing network of Islamic charities, poorly-regulated Islamic banks, business-friendly environments, and economies that already had records of extensive money laundering. If one strips away the terrorist act itself, it becomes clear that terrorists require the same infrastructure as transnational crime networks. Southeast Asia thus becomes an important area because existing criminal infrastructures could be co-opted for terrorist operations. Southeast Asia has long been a center for transnational criminal activity—drug- and gun-running, money laundering, people smuggling, document forging, and the like.[13] Indeed, money laundering has still not been criminalized in every Southeast Asian state. The Financial Action Task Force of the Organization for Economic Cooperation and Development (OECD) still has Indonesia, the Philippines, and Burma on its blacklist of money laundering states. In most cases terrorists differ from transnational criminal organizations only in that the latter are driven by profit motive as opposed to the terrorists' political agenda. One of the quieter counter-terrorism operations in Southeast Asia was the successful breakup of a 13-man document forging team for Al Qaeda in Bangkok.[14]

Malaysia is one of the world's pre-eminent Islamic banking centers, with strong and deep financial ties to Middle Eastern businesses, banks, charities, and other financial institutions.[15] Jamal Ahmed Al-Fadl, a former member of the Al Qaeda network who turned himself in to the Americans and testified against Ramzi Yousef in the 1998 East African U.S. embassy bombings case, claims that Osama bin Laden frequently used Islamic banks in Malaysia.[16] Thailand and Brunei's rush to enter the Islamic banking sector is troubling due to the lack of regulatory oversight.

While some states such as Malaysia and Singapore have strong political institutions and legal infrastructures, most are "weak states." They have weak political institutions and decentralized politics, are resource poor, and are plagued by endemic corruption. Indonesian centralized governmental authority broke down following the collapse of the New Order regime in 1998, with considerable consequences for the outer islands. The effects of failing political institutions are compounded by the decision to abolish the *dwi fungsi* principle of the Indonesian armed forces (TNI), which gave TNI a civil-administrative function in the provinces. Al Qaeda finds the lack of strong central government control attractive. The fact that Jakarta was unaware of some seven terrorist camps in Sulawesi is indicative of the tenuous control the government has over the provinces. Thus, terrorists are able to operate and plan attacks in relative secrecy. Terrorists need to plan attacks meticulously because their acts must have a large impact and cause maximum damage to the political stability and economic well-being of a country. The terrorists frequently have more resources at their disposal than official law enforcement. "We lack the infrastructure," one Philippine police intelligence official complained to me. "We have no computerized immigration or tax data bases. It is easy for foreigners to marry Filipinas and change their names." He said that to break up the Ramzi Yousef cell, which was planning spectacular crimes, he only had two 20-man teams. They simply could not keep up with the terrorists, not to mention all the other domestic insurgent groups.

The importance of tourism on Southeast Asian economies resulted in lax immigration procedures and easy access visas; indeed, Malaysia had no visa requirements for nationals of other Organization of the Islamic Conference (OIC) states until September 11. Southeast Asia's porous borders, especially among the archipelagic states of Indonesia and the Philippines, further exacerbate the immigration control task.

Developing the Network

Jemaah Islamiyah is a separate organization from Al Qaeda. Its members pledge *bayat*—an oath of allegiance—to one of its two leaders, rather than to Osama bin Laden. Yet there are individuals, such as the Jemaah Islamiyah operations chief, Hambali, who are also senior members of Al Qaeda. During the early stages of its development in the 1990s, Jemaah Islamiyah was at the disposal of Al Qaeda. Members established fronts, laundered money, arranged meetings, and procured travel documents. They assisted in operations, providing logistical and intelligence support. Al Qaeda saw the region as a recruiting ground and back office. Only as Jemaah Islamiyah developed its own capabilities did it become a terrorist organization in its own right. It shows the tremendous foresight and planning of Al Qaeda leaders to cultivate and develop a new theater of operations over time.

Al Qaeda's first foray into the region was in the early 1990s, when Osama bin Laden's brother-in-law, Mohammed Jamal Khalifa (a senior member of the Muslim Brotherhood in his native Lebanon), came to the Philippines to support the secessionist efforts of Muslim Moros in the southern Philippines.[17] At the time, he was officially the regional director for the Saudi-based charity, the Islamic International Relief Organization (IIRO), as well as a number of smaller charities.[18] According to one defector, the IIRO was used by bin Laden and Khalifa to distribute funds for the purchase of arms and other logistical requirements of the Abu Sayyaf and MILF. "Only 10 to 30 percent of the foreign funding goes to the legitimate relief and livelihood projects and the rest go to terrorist operations."[19] Khalifa did three things—he established a network of charities and front companies to support the Moro secessionists, he formed liaisons between Al Qaeda and the MILF and the Abu Sayyaf group, and he provided operational support to the Ramzi Yousef cell's Oplan Bojinka.[20]

The MILF is currently the leading Muslim rebel movement fighting the Philippine government and fields roughly 12,000 combatants. Whereas the MILF may have legitimate national liberation aspirations, it has forged linkages with international terrorist groups, notably Al Qaeda, for financial support, especially after funding from Libya waned substantially in the mid-1990s.[21] Ties to Al Qaeda date back to the the Soviet invasion of Afghanistan, when the MILF sent an estimated 600 Filipino Muslims to undergo military training and join the *mujahidin*. "We needed more *mujahidin* who would understand Islam completely," said one veteran who returned after three years of training and then ran the MILF's own military school.[22] Established in the Philippines, Khalifa began to provide covert assistance to the MILF in two ways—financing and training. He provided overt assistance by funding development projects in zones under MILF control, or to areas that constituted core constituencies of MILF supporters.[23]

In a 1998 interview, Al Haj Murad, the MILF vice-chairman for military affairs, acknowledged that bin Laden and Khalifa provided "help and assistance" to MILF cadres who volunteered in the 1980s to help the Taliban struggle against the Soviet-backed Afghanistan government.[24] On February 7, 1999, MILF leader Salamat Hashim in a BBC interview admitted to receiving aid from bin Laden, though again qualifying that this was humanitarian aid for mosque construction and social welfare. In addition to their own statements, the MILF's links to the Al Qaeda network have been revealed by Wali Khan Amin Shah, Mohammed Sadiq Odeh and Wadih El Hage, three Al Qaeda operatives currently under arrest.

The second type of assistance the MILF has received from Al Qaeda has been in the form of training, both in Mindanao and abroad. Beginning in the mid-1990s, a steady flow of Al Qaeda trainers began to arrive in the Philippines to train MILF and Abu Sayyaf guerillas. These trainers included al-Mughira al-Gaza'iri, the commander of an Al Qaeda camp in Afghanistan and a very close associate of Abu Zubaydah, and Omar al-Faruq.[25] Following the Philippine military's capture of the main MILF base, Camp Abu Bakar, in 2001, intelligence personnel discovered a cantonment within the camp specifically for foreign trainers and trainees. Philippine military intelligence believes that the MILF has played host to several hundred trainers from the Middle East.[26] Al Qaeda has placed a large number of instructors in MILF camps since the mid-1990s, not just to assist the MILF, but also for other *jihadis* in the region, such as the Malaysian Kumpulan Mujahidin, Jemaah Islamiyah, and Laskar Jundullah. With their secure base areas, geographic proximity, and porous borders, it has been far easier and more cost-effective for Al Qaeda to bring its trainers to the region than to send hundreds of Southeast Asian militants to Pakistan and Afghanistan.

Of greater public interest than the MILF is the small but very violent Abu Sayyaf. The origins of the Abu Sayyaf can be traced to Afghanistan, where its founder, Ustadz Abdurajak Janjalani, befriended Osama bin Laden in the late 1980s. Janjalani was committed to waging a jihad back in his native Philippines to create an Islamic state in the Moro islands. When bin Laden wanted to expand Al Qaeda he turned to Janjalani to establish a cell in Southeast Asia.[27] Ramzi Yousef, the mastermind of the 1993 World Trade Center bombing, who at the time was teaching at the Khost camp, encouraged the formation of the Abu Sayyaf group and traveled to the Philippines from December 1991 to May 1992 at bin Laden's request. Yousef trained Abu Sayyaf group members in bomb-making in their camp on Basilan. The Abu Sayyaf group quickly made its mark. It began terrorist attacks in 1991 when it killed two American evangelists in a grenade blast in Zamboanga. Between 1991 and 1996, the group was responsible for 67 terrorist attacks, more than half of which were indiscriminate bombings. All together these led to the deaths of 58 people, with another 398 injured.

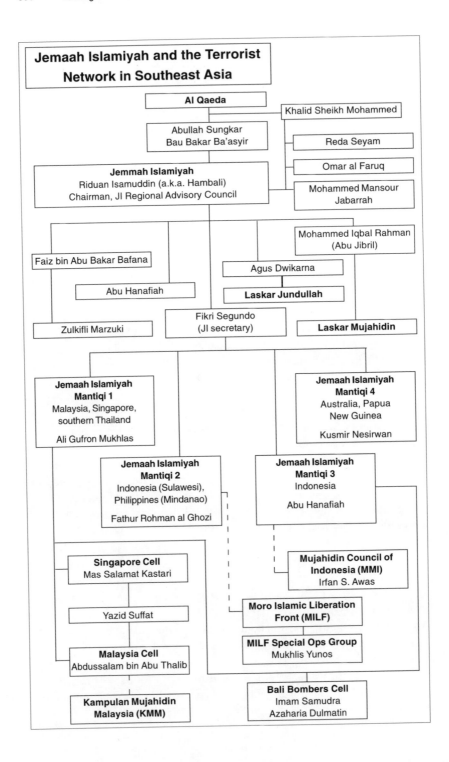

Jemaah Islamiyah and the Terrorist Network in Southeast Asia

Following the World Trade Center bombings, Yousef fled to Pakistan and then traveled to the Philippines where he planned a series of spectacular terrorist plots, known as Oplan Bojinka, including an attempt to bomb 11 U.S. airliners and assassinate the Pope.[28] The planning and scope of the Yousef cell was staggering. Bin Laden proved that he could establish an autonomous cell, evidently impervious to detection, which could plan and execute deadly attacks. The Ramzi Yousef case was always portrayed as a Philippine problem—in 1995, when the Ramzi Yousef cell was broken up and he and his two co-conspirators were arrested, neither U.S. nor Philippine intelligence or law enforcement agencies looked beyond that case.[29] Ramzi Yousef was treated as a lone wolf conducting a single operation and not as part of an international network. There are no indications that officials asked why Al Qaeda came to the Philippines and if they were linking up to regional groups. There were only three arrests and the entire infrastructure was left in place. Al Qaeda suffered a setback, but it simply shifted its area of operations to elsewhere in the region, especially Malaysia.

In the first half of the 1990s, Al Qaeda set out to accomplish several goals in developing its networks. First, it sought to graft on to or co-opt other radical groups, such as the MILF and Kampulan Mujahidin Malaysia. The second goal was then to link these groups into a truly transnational network, the hallmark of Al Qaeda activities. In most instances, the existing radical groups focused primarily on their domestic grievances and tended to have little contact with one another. Networks between once unconnected groups were established, as Al Qaeda understood the benefits in eluding law enforcement when working across borders. The third goal was to establish a regional arm of its own that would become financially independent and technically proficient enough to plan and execute terrorist attacks. The organization became known as Jemaah Islamiyah.

Origins of Jemaah Islamiyah

The origins of the Jemaah Islamiyah network are found in Indonesia, dating back to the 1960s when two radical clerics, Abdullah Sungkar and Abu Bakar Ba'asyir, began demanding the imposition of *sharia*. This issue put them in conflict with the Suharto regime. The two considered themselves the ideological heirs of Sekarmadji Maridjan Kartosuwirjo—the founder of the Darul Islam.[30] In 1972, Sungkar and Ba'asyir established an Islamic boarding school in Solo, Al Mukmin, which taught hardline Wahhabism. One of the masters, Abdul Qadir Baraja, was arrested for writing the jihad guide book for his students that urged jihad against all opponents of *sharia*. The school's alumni read like a *Who's Who* of Southeast Asian terrorists, and includes Fathur Rohman al-Ghozi, Ali Imron, and others. On November 19, 1978, Ba'asyir and Sungkar were arrested and sentenced to nine years for violating a 1963 subversion law. In 1985, they fled to Malaysia where they lived and preached openly for several years, building up a large following of radical Indonesian exiles. They served as a way station for Indonesians and Malaysians who were traveling to Afghanistan and Pakistan to fight the Soviets or train in one of the 40 Al Qaeda camps that were established in the late 1990s.[31]

Sungkar met bin Laden and other senior Al Qaeda members circa 1994 and pledged *bayat*, effectively absorbing his movement into Al Qaeda. Sungkar espoused violent jihad to create a pan-Islamic state in Southeast Asia and instructed two lieutenants, both veterans of the jihad in Afghanistan and members of Al Qaeda, Riduan Isamuddin (Hambali) and Mohammad Iqbal Rahman (Abu Jibril), to develop a regional network of cells. All four of the individuals were itinerant preachers, unaffiliated with any mosque, who preached jihad and recruited in private settings before groups of hard-core followers whom they slowly cultivated throughout Malaysia and Singapore. They began to espouse the doctrine of *Nusantara Raya*, the establishment of a pan-Islamic republic incorporating Malaysia, Indonesia, southern Thailand, and the southern Philippines.[32]

Although Jemaah Islamiyah was founded in 1993–94, the group did not conduct its first terrorist acts until 2000. The leaders spent those first six or seven years patiently building up their network, recruiting, training, and acquiring technical proficiency. In the 1990s, Jemaah Islamiyah operated within Al Qaeda's sphere, establishing front companies and accounts and pursuing recruits. For example, the first time Hambali appeared on any intelligence service's radar screen was when his name appeared on the board of directors of a firm established to facilitate the Oplan Bojinka plot.[33] Jemaah Islamiyah also set up a network of *madrassas* in Indonesia, Malaysia, and southern Thailand as centers for their recruiting efforts. They established a network of cells in each country in the region, each with a particular responsibility or role to pursue the organization's overall mission—the creation of a pan-Islamic state in Southeast Asia.[34] The operational capabilities of Jemaah Islamiyah were still quite limited. Through 2000, Jemaah Islamiyah members were primarily assisting Al Qaeda attacks in the region. For example, in mid-2000, Jemaah Islamiyah members assisted a six-man Yemeni team in planning the truck-bombing of the U.S. Embassy in Jakarta. The attack was thwarted.[35] By 2000, Al Qaeda's leadership was clearly looking to expand their theaters of operation to keep the United States off balance. To do so, they increasingly turned to Jemaah Islamiyah, whose network had grown considerably.

Organizational Structure

Jemaah Islamiyah has a formal structure, with Abdullah Sungkar and Abu Bakar Ba'asyir serving as the group's *amirs*, or spiritual leaders. Hambali became the chairman of the five-member *shura* or "Regional Advisory Council." Other members of the council included Mohammed Iqbal Rahman (Abu Jibril), Agus Dwikarna, Abu Hanafiah and Faiz bin Abu Bakar Bafana. Bafana, a Malaysian businessman, was a key aide to Hambali and served as the Jemaah Islamiyah's treasurer.[36] Beneath the *shura* were the secretaries and different committees, including Missionary Work, Military Committee, Security Committee, Financial Committee, and the heads of the four regional commands, or *mantiqis*.

- Mantiqi 1 – peninsula Malaysia, Singapore and southern Thailand
- Mantiqi 2 – Java and Sumatra
- Mantiqi 3 – the Philippines, Brunei, eastern Malaysia, Kalimantan and Sulawesi
- Mantiqi 4 – being developed to establish cells in Australia and Papua (formerly Irian Jaya) but not Papua New Guinea.

Each *mantiqi* in turn had many sub-cells, or *fiah*. The Jemaah Islamiyah has between 500 and 1,000 members, although the former number is a more likely estimate. These members are spread throughout the region.[37]

With an estimated 200 members, Mantiqi 1 is perhaps the largest Jemaah Islamiyah cell. This cell was led by Abu Hanafiah and Faiz bin Abu Bakar Bafana. It recruited actively among both Indonesian exiles and educated Malays—especially technical students. At least five senior Jemaah Islamiyah members and recruiters were lecturers in the Universiti Tecknologi Malaysia (UTM).[38]

Mantiqi 1 had four discernible functions. First, it worked very closely with the KMM in Malaysia, with whom there is some overlap in membership and goals. Second, it was the primary conduit between Jemaah Islamiyah and Osama bin Laden and Al Qaeda in Afghanistan. The Malaysian cell was the logistical hub for up to 100 Jemaah Islamiyah operatives, who were sent to Afghanistan for training in Al Qaeda camps in addition to running its own camp in southern Malaysia.[39] Third, it was responsible for recruiting and education. Much of the recruiting was done through two *madrassas*, Tarbiyah Luqmanul Hakiem school in Johor Bahru, and the Sekolah Menengah Arab Darul Anuar in Kota Baru. Fourth, Mantiqi 1 was responsible for establishing dozens of front companies that could be used to channel Al Qaeda funds and procure weapons and bomb-making material. These included a firm called Green Laboratory Medicine, which was responsible for procuring 21 tons of ammonium nitrate, and Infocus Technology, an internet firm that sponsored Zaccarias Moussaoui into the United States.[40] Front companies were not the only businesses established by Al Qaeda. There were also many cases in which Jemaah Islamiyah members established businesses, received contracts and business from Jemaah Islamiyah supporters, and then plowed the proceeds back into the organization. According to the Singapore Government's White Paper, "[a]ll Jemaah Islamiyah-run businesses had to contribute 10 percent of their total earnings to the group. This money was to be channeled into the Jemaah Islamiyah's special fund called Infaq Fisbilillah (contributions for the Islamic cause or jihad fund)."[41]

Mantiqi 2 provided the bulk of the membership. In the mid-1990s, there appears to have been little Jemaah Islamiyah activity in Indonesia. Yet following the fall of Suharto in May 1998, there was a surge in Jemaah Islamiyah activity as hundreds of radical Indonesians returned to the archipelago. It was in Indonesia that the Jemaah Islamiyah developed its two paramilitary arms: the Laskar Mujahidin and the Laskar Jundullah from 1999 to 2000. The Indonesia cell is an integral part of Abu Bakar Ba'asyir's overt political organization, the Mujahidin Council of Indonesia (Majelis Mujahidin Indonesia—MMI), a large umbrella grouping for approximately 100 small radical and militant groups from across the archipelago. In addition to recruiting and running a network of radical *madrassas*, the Indonesian cell was responsible for running a network of training camps, including seven in Sulawesi and one in Kalimantan. The Indonesian cell was also very important in liaising with Al Qaeda-linked Islamic charities, especially Al Haramain, and became an important conduit for foreign funding.

Mantiqi 3 was important as a major logistics cell for the network, responsible for acquiring explosives, guns, and other equipment, as well as coordinating with the MILF and supporting Al Qaeda operatives and trainers in the region. They included senior Al Qaeda trainers—Omar al-Faruq, al-Mughira al-Gaza'iri, and Omar al-Hadrani.[42] These trainers also played an important role in establishing the MILF's own terrorist arm, the Special Operations Group, in 1999.[43] The cell leader was an Indonesian, Fathur Rohman al-Ghozi, who had studied at Al Mukmin from 1984 to 1990 before going to a Pakistani *madrassa* where he was recruited into Jemaah Islamiyah. In addition to explosives, al-Ghozi was responsible for the purchase of light arms and assault rifles that were used by the Jemaah Islamiyah's two paramilitary arms engaged in sectarian conflict in Indonesia that started in 1999. These were shipped to Poso for Agus Dwikarna's Laskar Jundullah and for Abu Jibril's Laskar Mujahidin in Ambon.[44]

Mantiqi 4 was the smallest and least developed of the cells. It included Northern Australia, where the Jemaah Islamiyah leaders recruited and sought funding from the large population of Indonesian exiles.[45]

The Fall of Suharto and the Jihad in the Malukus

The fall of President Suharto in May 1998 created a radically changed political environment in Indonesia. The strongman's resignation left a weak democracy in which there was intense political competition between the new president and a parliament with a newfound and intense sense of empowerment. Strong central government control also broke down as the provinces clamored to redress the historical legacy of over-centralization and demanded more autonomy and revenue sharing.

Suharto's fall had another important impact—hundreds of radical Muslim exiles, including Abdullah Sungkar and Abu Bakar Ba'asyir, returned to Indonesia and demanded political space. In mid-2000, Ba'asyir established the Majelis Mujahidin of Indonesia (MMI). The group is ostensibly a civil society organization that tries to implement *sharia* peacefully through the democratic process.[46] Yet, there is substantial evidence that the MMI is also a front for Abu Bakar Ba'asyir's militant and terrorist activities as many MMI leaders are also Jemaah Islamiyah members. For example, the MMI's board included Mohammad Iqbal Rahman (Abu Jibril) and Agus Dwikarna. Both headed Jemaah Islamiyah's two paramilitary arms and both were members of the Jemaah Islamiyah *shura*. The head of the Fatwah council today is Abdul Qadir Baraja. The MMI's director of daily operations is Irfan Suryahardy Awwas, the younger brother of Abu Jibril.

The MMI also serves as an important financial conduit for channeling funding to small radical groups that would otherwise be unable to network abroad. Much of Al Qaeda's funding is thought to come from charities that are either unwitting partners or willing participants in fund diversions. Indonesian intelligence officials estimate that 15–20 percent of Islamic charity funds are diverted to politically-motivated groups and terrorists.

Al Qaeda inserted top operatives into leadership positions in several charities in Southeast Asia in order to secure access to funding.[47] Jemaah Islamiyah and Al Qaeda members often served as regional branch chiefs of or formed alliances with Saudi-backed charities, including MERC, the IIRO, and Al Haramain, as well as an Indonesian charity that served as their counterpart or executing agency, KOMPAK.[48] The leadership of these charities is overlapping. For example, Agus Dwikarna of the MMI was a branch officer in KOMPAK. He also was the local representative of Al Haramain in Makassar in South Sulawesi, which an Al Qaeda official admitted was the largest single source of Al Qaeda funds into Indonesia.[49]

The turning point in Jemaah Islamiyah's operations came in 1999 with the outbreak of sectarian conflict in the Malukus. In the late 1990s, Hambali and Abu Jibril were focused on fundraising and establishing Jemaah Islamiyah's paramilitary arms, the Laskar Mujahidin and the Laskar Jundullah. It was from membership in these organizations that Jemaah Islamiyah identified many of its recruits. It cannot be emphasized enough how important the jihads in the Malukus and Poso were to Jemaah Islamiyah. Although there were local causes, the influx of some *jihadis* escalated the conflicts to a new level. More importantly, the jihads in the Malukus and Poso were a formative experience for the participants—every bit as important as the jihad against the Soviets in Afghanistan in the 1980s. The Maluku conflict gave the members of the Laskar Jundullah, Laskar Mujahidin, and the much larger Laskar Jihad their taste of jihad. It whetted their appetites for more.[50] Al Qaeda also manipulated the conflict to a much greater degree than anyone imagined at the time.

The Laskar Mujahidin was established in 1999 by Abu Jibril, who recruited among Indonesian exiles living in Malaysia and inspired them to return home to fight a holy war. Jibril first traveled to the Malukus in January 2000 leading several hundred *jihadis*. He introduced a centralized command structure and led attacks on Christian communities using high-speed boats. Although there were only some 500 Laskar Mujahidin fighters in the Malukus, they were far better armed and disciplined than the largest group, the Laskar Jihad, which fielded some 3,000 poorly armed and radical students until a raid on a police armory allowed them to arm their fighters. Jibril's forces also liaised closely with Al Qaeda operatives, who were funding and filming the Maluku crisis for propaganda and recruiting purposes.

The second Jemaah Islamiyah paramilitary group, the Laskar Jundullah, was founded by Agus Dwikarna in October 2000. Laskar Jundallah was a small militant organization that conducted "sweeps" of foreigners in Solo and was at the forefront of sectarian conflict in Poso, Sulawesi.[51] It was the armed wing of Dwikarna's civil society organization, the Committee for Upholding Islamic Law in South Sulawesi, that was committed to implementing *sharia*. Al Qaeda funded Laskar Jundullah through Omar al-Faruq, as well as through funds skimmed from the Saudi Al Haramain Foundation, which Dwikarna headed. Laskar Jundullah also received funding from the charity KOMPAK under Dwikarna's leadership.

These holy wars gave Jemaah Islamiyah the network that they needed with a core group of members and supporters. It gave them a taste of jihad and served as a catalyst for radicalizing Jemaah Islamiyah's behavior. The fact that the government did not curtail their activities only emboldened them. The role of Al Qaeda in the conflicts in the Malukus and Sulawesi was significant. For one thing, Al Qaeda provided significant funding for the paramilitaries. According to the Darul Islam's Al Chaidar, Indonesian militant radicals "maintain contact with the international *mujahidin* network, including Osama bin Laden's group." "Wherever a jihad is in force, this network provides money and weapons and all tools needed for the jihad, and they mobilize fighters to go to the jihad area," Chaidar said. "This is exactly what is happening in the Malukus. Osama bin Laden is one of those who have sent money and weapons to jihad fighters in the Malukus." Second, the Maluku conflict served to attract radical Islamists from around the Muslim world. For example, seven Afghans arrived in Ambon on July 7, 2000 and were spirited away by Laskar Mujahidin forces. They joined some 200 other Afghans, Pakistanis, and Malays.[52] Abu Abdul Aziz and one other bin Laden lieutenant were dispatched to Ambon in the height of the crisis, and Mohammed Attef visited the Malukus in June 2000. The Maluku crisis convinced Al Qaeda's leaders that the emphasis of their jihad in Southeast Asia should be shifted to Indonesia. To that end, there was a flow of top Al Qaeda operatives into the region between 1999 and 2001.[53] They trained, funded, and armed Jemaah Islamiyah militants and established the financial infrastructure to make these groups sustainable.

Jemaah Islamiyah Becomes a Terrorist Organization

The Indonesian government's equivocation during and following the Maluku crisis gave new momentum to both Jemaah Islamiyah and Al Qaeda, which by 2000 had decided to escalate their operations. Years of planning and training, as well as the confidence gained in the Malukus and Poso, prepared Jemaah Islamiyah to engage in terrorist attacks around the region. At that time, the Jemaah Islamiyah carried out operations against soft targets with minimal loss of human life, consistent with their limited capabilities.

Beginning in 2000, there was a spate of terrorist attacks around the region; neither regional security services nor journalists and academics at that time recognized that these might be related. The first attack was in July 2000, when a Jakarta shopping mall was bombed by a Malaysian man. In August 2000, the Philippine Ambassador to Indonesia was the target of a bombing. In December 2000, bombs were planted in 30 Indonesian churches in order to "spark a religious civil war in Indonesia."[54] The Jemaah Islamiyah and the MILF engaged in joint operations in December 2000, when the light rail in Metro Manila was bombed. In April 2001, in Yala, Thailand, a train station and hotel were bombed.

For the most part, the terrorist groups did not assess these attacks as successful. In the case of the church bombings in Indonesia, Jemaah Islamiyah operatives set 30 bombs. Only 18 went off, killing 15 people.[55]

This was a far cry from their intended goal of killing thousands. These bombs were small and directed against soft targets. The fact that they tried to launch simultaneous bombings, an Al Qaeda hallmark, indicates a degree of sophistication. Despite their limited effectiveness, these bombings gave Jemaah Islamiyah members additional confidence. As more Jemaah Islamiyah operatives were recruited and trained in Al Qaeda camps in Afghanistan and the southern Philippines, their technical proficiency increased and the network matured. Al Qaeda and Jemaah Islamiyah plotted larger scale operations against harder targets. The Jemaah Islamiyah, like its parent organization Al Qaeda, always placed a very high premium on education and training. Jemaah Islamiyah operatives were very important support personnel in Al Qaeda operations in Southeast Asia.

Following the September 11, 2001 attacks on the United States, Al Qaeda planned a series of attacks against U.S. interests across the region.[56] In August 2001, a young Canadian-Kuwaiti Al Qaeda recruit, Mohammed Mansour Jabarah, was dispatched to the Philippines to prepare an attack on the U.S. embassy, which was later called off because the embassy was sufficiently far from the road that a truck bomb would not damage it. He was then sent to identify targets in Singapore. Video footage was taken and reviewed by Hambali in Kuala Lumpur and then later found in the wreckage of Mohammed Attef's house in Kabul, Afghanistan. In all, seven targets were chosen: the U.S. embassy, the British high commission, the Israeli embassy, and several office towers owned or occupied by U.S. firms.[57]

Malaysian and Singaporean security officials were able to arrest many suspects in late 2001, including several members of Jemaah Islamiyah *shura*. While officials in Singapore and Malaysia were confident that they had eradicated much of the senior Jemaah Islamiyah leadership in their own countries, they expressed tremendous frustration about the lack of cooperation that they received from Indonesian authorities. Most Jemaah Islamiyah fugitives were known to have left for Indonesia, but the Indonesian government offered little assistance. Although Malaysia and Singapore named Abu Bakar Ba'asyir as a prime suspect and leader of the Jemaah Islamiyah network, he continued to live and preach openly until October 2002 following the Bali attacks. Although Ba'asyir was brought in for questioning on January 24, 2002, he was released the next day. He acknowledged teaching 13 of those detained in Malaysia, Singapore and the Philippines. Ba'asyir denied being a member of Al Qaeda. "I am not a member of Al Qaeda, but I really respect the struggle of Osama bin Laden, who has bravely represented the world's Muslims in their fight against the arrogant United States of America and their allies." Following the arrest of a senior Al Qaeda operative in Indonesia in the summer of 2002, Omar al-Faruq, there was further evidence linking Ba'asyir to terrorist operations.[58] The Indonesian government, under pressure from the United States and its neighbors, announced that it would "carry out an investigation" of Ba'asyir, but went on to say that it would "not arrest Abu Bakar just because foreign governments have their suspicions of him."[59] The Indonesians distrusted the CIA report and resented U.S. pressure, and there was considerable popular and political pressure to resist U.S. interference.

Leading Jemaah Islamiyah operatives met in Bangkok in January 2002 where they received orders to attack soft targets such as tourist venues to target westerners.[60] The result of the meeting was played out in October 2002, with the simultaneous bombings of two nightclubs in the tourist district of Bali.[61] It was Al Qaeda's second most deadly attack after the September 11 attacks on the United States. Two hundred and two people were killed, nearly half of them Australians on holiday. The attack provoked an immediate and firm response from the Australian government, which dispatched a large team of Australian Federal Police investigators. In addition, investigators from Japan, Britain, Germany and France as well as from the Federal Bureau of Investigation provided much-needed technical assistance and intense pressure on the Indonesians.

The Bali attack finally galvanized the Indonesian leadership to begin fighting the war on terror. The Indonesian government finally found the conviction to arrest Ba'asyir. He was linked to the 2000 church bombings, but as of summer 2003 he has not been officially linked to the Bali attack, nor has he been tried under a post-September 11 anti-terrorism bill.[62]

The Current State of Jemaah Islamiyah

Regional security services have had measurable success in countering the terrorist threat in the past year. They have arrested several senior Jemaah Islamiyah leaders and thwarted their largest operations. From December 2001 to July 2003, some 80 people in Malaysia, 31 in Singapore, and 12 in the Philippines were arrested. Since the Bali bombings, Indonesian officials have shown the political will to expose and disrupt Al Qaeda and Jemaah Islamiyah. By July 2003, some 60 individuals had been arrested in Indonesia in conjunction with the Bali attacks. Several important operatives were arrested in early 2003, including Mas Salamat Kastari. Indonesia is no longer a relatively safe haven for Jemaah Islamiyah operatives on the run from Singapore and Malaysia. Although the they are less able to plan and execute major terrorist attacks than they were in late 2001, when they came very close to executing major attacks against hard targets in Singapore, Jemaah Islamiyah retains the capability to attack soft targets such as the August 5, 2003 bombing of the J. W. Marriott hotel in Jakarta.

It is nonetheless dangerous to underestimate Jemaah Islamiyah's capabilities or goals. First, although senior organizers and foot soldiers have been arrested (including Zubair, a Malaysian from Negri Sembilan with close links to PAS and the Kampulan Mujahidin Malaysia (KMM), who was apprehended in late July 2003 in Thailand, and Hambali, who was arrested in Thailand in August 2003), there are still at least 12 important "operatives" at large, including Abu Hanafiah from Malaysia; Husain bin Ismail, Mohammed Rashid bin Zainal Abidan, Ushak Mohammed Noohu, and Mohammed Hassan bin Saynudin, Zulkaraenen, and at least six others from Singapore are in Indonesia. Irfan S. Awwas and Fikri Sugundo live openly in Indonesia, while Omar Bandon and Parlindigan Siregar are at large in Indonesia. Philippine authorities believe that one other Indonesian cell member in the country escaped. Malaysian authorities believe that at least five lecturers from the Universiti Tecknologi Malaysia were senior Jemaah Islamiyah members and recruiters who fled to Indonesia including Madya Dr. Azahari bin Husin, Zulkefli bin Marzuki, Noordin Din bin Mohammed Top, Shamsul Bahri bin Hussein, Abdul Razak, Amran, Zulkifli, and Mohammed Rafi bin Udin. In terms of the Bali bombers, Dr. Zahari and Dul Matin remain at large. The five-man Singapore cell led by Mas Salamat Kastari—though he was arrested—remains at large. Syawal, who is Abdullah Sungkar's son-in-law and the head of the Laskar Jundullah, is also at large.

Second, Al Qaeda and Jemaah Islamiyah are working hard to rebuild their network and capabilities. We have seen in the past year no lessening of their will as they make a concerted attempt to rebuild their ranks. Indeed, in late June 2002, a Jemaah Islamiyah suspect in Malaysia was arrested with the same chemicals that comprised the Bali bomb, although in smaller amounts; an early July 2003 arrest in Semerang led to the seizure of an enormous cache of explosives, chemicals, (including 900 kg of potassium chloride, four times the amount used in the Bali bombs), detonators, and small arms. If one independent cell in a highly compartmentalized organization was able to procure such a cache, one must be alarmed by the thought of other cells doing the same thing throughout the region. Inadequately secured embassies in the region, such as the U.S. embassy in Cambodia, remain potential targets. When their capabilities have been reconstituted and they calculate a high likelihood of success, Jemaah Islamiyah and Al Qaeda can be expected to refocus their efforts on larger-scale operations against hard targets and against better defended countries such as Singapore or Australia. Airplane security remains weak, and the proliferation of surface-to-air missiles is troubling.

Third, there is evidence that Jemaah Islamiyah is trying to broaden its network: Omar al-Faruq, one of the senior-most Al Qaeda leaders in Southeast Asia, admitted that the Jemaah Islamiyah had tried to establish links with Muslim militants elsewhere in the region, including Thailand and Burma.[63] In 1999, Abu Bakar Ba'asyir established a coordinating body known as the Rabitatul Mujahidin.[64] The Rabitatul Mujahidin was erroneously described at first as the armed wing of the Jemaah Islamiyah, yet in reality it was simply a group of Jemaah Islamiyah/MMI officials, including Tamsil Linrung, Agus Dwikarna, Al Chaedar, and Omar al-Faruq, along with representatives from MP-GAM in Aceh, the Wae Kah Rah and Guragon Mujahidin in Thailand, and the Rohinga Solidarity Organization from Burma and Bangladesh. The Rabitatul Mujahidin only met three times according to both Faruq and Bafana—the first time in late 1999, the second time in August 2000, and the last time in November 2000.[65] All of the meetings took place in Malaysia. We must also be concerned about growing links between Jemaah Islamiyah leaders and the Harakat ul-Jemaat Islamiya in Bangladesh, which is led by Fazul Rahman, one of the original signers of Osama bin Laden's 1998 *fatwah* against the United States.[66]

Fourth, the most striking failure in counter-terror operations in Southeast Asia has been the inability of all states to shut down the financial pipeline of Al Qaeda and Jemaah Islamiyah.[67] The mechanisms for funding terrorism have continued unabated in Southeast Asia, and to date no terrorist assets or funds have been seized in the region. In early 2003, the U.S. Department of the Treasury's Office of Foreign Asset Control drew up a list of 300 individuals, charities, and corporations in Southeast Asia believed to be Al Qaeda and Jemaah Islamiyah funders. Due to interagency politics and diplomatic considerations, the list was winnowed down to 18 individuals and 10 companies. But as of August 2003, it was still unpublicized due to diplomatic and bureaucratic pressure. As one U.S. official said: "Most of the really sensitive names have been dropped, so it won't have the kind of impact that the full 300 would have, though there'll still be a few surprises."[68] Yet Southeast Asia seems to have gained in importance to Al Qaeda's money men, according to U.S. law enforcement officials. Denis Lormel, the head of the terrorist financing tracking unit at the Federal Bureau of Investigation (FBI), asserts that with the crackdown on Middle Eastern funding mechanisms, especially the financial centers in Abu Dhabi and other parts of the United Arab Emirates, Al Qaeda has increasingly relied on Southeast Asia to move its money and hide its assets.[69]

One of the most unlikely sources of Al Qaeda funding coming into the region was through the Om Al Qura Foundation in Phnom Penh. Always searching for states with poor capacity and regulatory frameworks as well as places to operate without scrutiny, Al Qaeda used the Om Al Qura Foundation for "significant money transfers" for both itself and Jemaah Islamiyah.

The amount that the Om Al Qura Foundation laundered for Al Qaeda is believed to be around several million dollars. On May 28, 2003, three foreign employees of the foundation were arrested, an Egyptian and two Thai Muslims, for plotting to carry out terrorist attacks in Cambodia.[70] The operation, which was conducted with a tip from and support of U.S. intelligence officials, led to the deportation of 28 teachers from the Al Mukara Islamic School and 22 dependents.[71] In addition to their role in money laundering, Cambodian officials said that the three Muslims arrested in May had $50,000 from Al Qaeda to execute an attack in the region.

Fifth, we have to consider that even if Jemaah Islamiyah is eliminated, the political, economic, and social conditions in Southeast Asia will simply give rise to new groups with similar ideological proclivities and goals.

Fighting the War on Terror: Regional Responses

In the immediate aftermath of the September 11 attacks, all governments in the region expressed sympathy for the victims and their concern about terrorism in general. ASEAN issued a brief statement of condolence and a vague call for "strengthening cooperation in combating terrorism around the world." While all the governments condemned terrorism and endorsed UN Security Council Resolution 1368, their individual responses have ranged from robust support for the United States to demands that America refrain from the use of force to an expressed fear that U.S. hegemony and arrogance will only lead to more terrorist attacks. Not surprisingly, the Muslim states of Malaysia and Indonesia were the most overtly critical of the United States' war in Afghanistan and later Iraq.

Southeast Asian governments responded in different ways to the war on terror, each according to their immediate political interests and foreign policy objectives. Indeed, each country's response was clearly aimed more towards their domestic constituencies, though there have been a few regional initiatives. The reactions of the Southeast Asian states have been constrained by the growth of political Islam in their countries. The Islamic resurgence in the region has occurred because of long-standing disputes with secular governments. There are considerable socio-economic inequalities that exist across the region between the different religious communities that have been exacerbated by the Asian financial crisis.

But the fundamental point about the limits to how far governments can go in supporting the U.S.-led war on terror is this: Southeast Asian Muslims, in general, believe that the war on terror is patently anti-Muslim. These sentiments have only grown since the war in Iraq. While political elites tend to be concerned about the growth of militant Islam and support the war on terror, they are mindful of popular political pressure and anti-Americanism. The Pew Global Attitudes Project reported one of the most precipitous drops in support for the United States in the past three years among Indonesians. Whereas 75 and 61 percent of Indonesians had positive images of the United States in 2000 and 2002 respectively, only 15 percent did in 2003. Whereas 31 percent of Indonesians supported the global war on terror in 2002, only 23 percent supported it in 2003, despite the deadly terrorist attacks in Indonesia in October 2002.[72]

Such concerns are exacerbated in a significant political year: Late 2003 will see intense campaigning for the presidential elections in Indonesia and the Philippines, while Malaysia will see the first transition of power in over 20 years, when Prime Minister Mahathir Mohamad steps down.

The fundamental question, however, is have the states done enough in terms of counter-terrorism? Jemaah Islamiyah has not been defeated, nor do any security agencies in the region believe it has been. Its cells throughout the region were dealt a blow, and it is clear that the states have now taken the offensive. Through the interrogation of suspects, they have a much better understanding of how Jemaah Islamiyah operates, how members communicate with one another, and the scope of the organization. Yet governments of the region, as well as the United States, cannot be complacent. Jemaah Islamiyah is seeking to rebuild its network and capabilities, and the range of soft targets available to them is immense. A lesson learned from Bali is that bombs do not have to be as large or lethal to do the same amount of damage to an economy.

Indonesia

Indonesia has the most at stake of any Southeast Asian country. Already politically weak, radical Islamist forces have grown in strength and numbers in its five-year experiment with democracy, and are able to capitalize in the breakdown in law and order and central government control. As the world's largest Muslim country, with a population of over 200 million people, much is at stake for the future of this 17,000-island nation. President Megawati has warned that Indonesia could easily disintegrate into a "Balkans of the Eastern Hemisphere." Secessionist strife rages in Aceh, Papua, and the threat of secessionism in the Malukus prompted the emergence of the Laskar Jihad in 2000.

Much of the problem has been weak leadership. While pledging Indonesia's full support for the war on terror at the White House in September 2001, in the following months Megawati was openly condemning the attacks on Afghanistan in a Jakarta mosque and later attacked the U.S. war in Iraq.[73] She did so for political reasons, her words geared to position her for the 2004 presidential election, in which one of her main competitors will be her Vice President Hamzah Haz of the Islamist United Development Party. Hamzah has reached out to Islamic radicals, including Umar Jafar Thalib of the Laskar Jihad and Abu Bakar Ba'asyir of the MMI/Jemaah Islamiyah. Indeed the MMI all but endorsed Hamzah.[74] Although the attempt to enshrine the Jakarta Charter (*sharia*) into the constitution in the fall of 2002 failed, that it even became an issue at all and garnered as much support as it did was alarming. Haz interceded and had charges against Umar Jaffar Thalib dropped.

Why then did Megawati not play up her secular nationalist credentials and crack down on the militants until Bali? First, she painted herself into a corner by stonewalling the United States and her neighbors for over a year. Second, though secular, the Indonesian population is very nationalist and its current political sensitivity is as fragile as it has ever been. There is a real perceived threat of national disintegration, and many resent the weakened status of the country in the world. Indonesia simply could not give in to the demands of other states. Any leader who does so risks being punished by the electorate. The Laskar Jihad may not have had widespread political support, but they certainly did not have public opprobrium for their militant activities conducted in the name of holding the country together; most of their weaponry came from the army and police. Third, Megawati is vulnerable to attacks from both the Islamists and the nationalists for being a puppet of the Americans. Her own party counseled against cracking down on the militants because the Islamists are their major challenge, and the Independence Party of Indonesia for Struggle (PDI-P) will need to form an alliance with some Muslim groups in the 2004 election. As a senior MMI official said, "If security forces take action against the Muslim community, then I believe what will result will be major turmoil in Indonesia."[75] Fourth, Megawati is facing a considerable challenge from her secular-nationalist rival Golkar, which is fielding strong candidates in the 2004 election. Though Golkar did not field a presidential candidate in 1999, it has a vast field of viable candidates and a very strong and revitalized political network in the provinces. Golkar is no longer perceived as a corrupt machine filled with Suharto-era cronies. The military's support for Megawati is conditional, although it is increasingly alarmed at the threat posed by the Islamists. While there has been a rapid spread in the number of Muslim organizations and parties, there is considerable competition between them and personal rivalries are intense. As Robert Hefner notes, "post-Suharto Indonesia is unlikely to see a single, dominant Islamic grouping any time soon; it is even less likely to see a clear Muslim consensus on the role of Islam in the state."[76] But that is changing, as the groups are beginning to overcome personal rivalries and consolidate their efforts. They were unable to field candidates if they won less than 3 percent of the vote in the 1999 election; and only parties or a coalition of parties that have 20 percent of the parliamentary vote in 2004 will be eligible to field a presidential candidate.

Only after the Bali bombings did the Indonesian government arrest Abu Bakar Ba'asyir, and even then he was not charged with anything connected to Bali but rather under a nebulous treason law. Ba'asyir went on trial in May 2003; the prosecution was abysmal and in late August he was sentenced to four years, a widely criticized judicial decision that was seen as an attempt to satisfy both the Islamists and foreign governments.

Perhaps one of the most constructive actions of the Indonesian government has been its intervention in the sectarian-hit regions of Poso and the Malukus. The government's initial response was lacking and its troops were outnumbered. Bambang Susilo Yudhono, the coordinating minister for political and security affairs, refused to declare either a civil or military emergency, but sent troops to "stop the conflict, conduct raids on firearms and on the presence of a *certain organization* that should not be allowed to stay in Poso."[77] The government has since pledged to "conduct raids on groups in possession of firearms and then to deport all of the outsiders to their place of origin."[78] Government-sponsored peace talks began on 20 December 2001, and a tenuous peace ensued.

The Indonesian police deserve credit for not just their work in the Bali investigations, but also for broadening the scope of and continuing their counter-terrorism efforts. Freed of the political constraints they have done a commendable job, but their resources are limited. Indonesian intelligence officials cooperated with the United States by turning over two foreign nationals believed to be Al Qaeda suspects.[79] Due to a backlash a third suspect, Reda Seyam, was detained in Indonesia on immigration charges.[80]

President Bush provided $400 million in economic aid to stimulate the Indonesian economy in 2001, and asked the U.S. Congress to provide $130 million more in 2002. Bush also lifted bans on non-lethal military sales and direct contact with the Indonesian military, imposed during the East Timor crisis. In addition, the United States pledged to support Indonesia's "territorial integrity," which many saw as a green light for Indonesia to continue coercive policies in Aceh. The United States has also deliberated lifting the ban on International Military Education and Training (IMET) training for TNI forces. Following Bali, the United States extended $35 million in aid for counter-terrorism. But Indonesian leaders in the midst of an election year remain fearful of being labeled as being pro-American and hence are reluctant to overtly support the war on terror.

Although an Indonesian court found the first Bali defendant, Amrozi bin Nurhasyim guilty and sentenced him to death, the August 5 bombing in

Jakarta of the J. W. Marriott hotel drove home the point that terrorist cells remain active in Indonesia and the government must maintain the political will to combat Jemaah Islamiyah.

Malaysia

Malaysian Prime Minister Mahathir Mohamad used the war on terror adroitly to consolidate his position, restore his reputation (tarnished by the Anwar Ibrahim scandal), win back some of the Malay electorate from PAS, laid the ground work for his succession, increase Malaysia's stature in the Organization of the Islamic Conference, and improve ties with the United States. Mahathir used the war on terror to discredit PAS, equating them with the Taliban due to their goals of turning Malaysia into an Islamic state.

Malaysia has been a good partner in the war on terror in the past year. However, this is in large part due to a timely convergence of interests. UMNO, which has steadily lost its core constituency of rural Malay voters to the Islamic PAS, has tried to draw a clear line connecting PAS and the terrorists. Were Mahathir not able to isolate PAS and Islamist radicals and win back support for UMNO, there would have been far less support for the war on terror. It is important to note that the Malaysian government tends to lump Jemaah Islamiyah members into the same category as the KMM. This is intentional as most KMM members are also PAS members, whom the government hopes to discredit.[81]

To understand the Malaysian response, one has to be aware that Malaysia, like its outspoken prime minister, operates at two levels: the rhetorical and the operational. On the one hand Mahathir, who is a bitter foe of non-secular Muslim politics, condemned the September 11 attacks and pledged to fight terrorism within his own borders. At the same time, he was very critical of the unilateral U.S. military responses and has demanded that the United Nations take the lead. Malaysia was one of only a handful of countries among the 56 states that attended the October 2002 Organization of the Islamic Conference to explicitly condemn America's attacks on Afghanistan. He was angry that the United States has done little to address the root causes of terrorism. Mahathir offered mixed support for U.S. investigations. The United States made a direct appeal to Malaysia to hand over suspected terrorists and was rebuffed. Yet the bilateral relationship has improved greatly since September 11. The Malaysian government shut down a web site used by Al Qaeda that was hosted on a Kuala Lumpur "server farm." In another instance, following the breakup of the Portland (Oregon) Al Qaeda cell in October 2002, Malaysia deported a leading member, Ahmed Ibrahim Bilal, who was discovered studying at Malaysia's International Islamic University.

On October 12, 2001, the Malaysian government announced that it was implementing new regulations to make it compulsory for students to register with the Immigration Department if they study abroad, as it acknowledged that it has no information on self-financed students. Prime Minister Mahathir announced on October 15, 2001 that all schools run by PAS, from kindergarten to college, "will come under closer scrutiny." Mahathir expressed considerable alarm as two-thirds of the 2,160 religious schools in Malaysia were linked to PAS. "What is being taught in these schools is not Islam," said Mahathir. "So we need to see what these people are doing."[82]

Malaysia has cracked down on terrorist cells within its borders. The KMM has been effectively routed and there have been significant arrests of Jemaah Islamiyah members. In all, over 80 people are being detained under the Internal Security Act (ISA). The Malaysian government considers the challenge posed by Islamic militants to be its greatest internal security threat and is clearly alarmed at the scope of the KMM and Jemaah Islamiyah networks within its territory. The Malaysian government has dragged its feet, however, in waging the financial war on terror. A large number of Jemaah Islamiyah and Al Qaeda-linked front companies and firms are in Malaysia. Nonetheless, intense Malaysian diplomatic pressure has prevailed and the U.S. government has yet to designate these firms as having terrorist connections and has not frozen their assets.

With the retirement of Prime Minister Mahathir in October 2003, Malaysia will experience its first leadership transition in over 30 years. His heir-apparent Deputy Prime Minister Abdullah Ahmed Badawi is a much less charismatic figure and has a far weaker political base. Although Badawi is a capable man who will continue to maintain the hard line on militants that he has shown as home minister, he will be a weaker leader who will have to bargain more with political rivals. There will be more dissent and factionalism in the ruling Barisan Nasional coalition. Although Badawi has Islamic credentials, as the current Home Minister he ordered the detainment of all Jemaah Islamiyah and KMM suspects. The fall 2003 parliamentary elections will be fiercely contested. PAS is certain to retain control of Terengganu and Kelantan, and could potentially win control of the states of Kedah and Perellis. If PAS makes significant gains in the election, the ability and willingness of the government to maintain its high degree of cooperation in the war on terror will be constrained.

Philippines

If Indonesia has had the most to lose from the war on terrorism, then the Philippines has the most to gain. From the start, the Philippines gave the strongest response to U.S. appeals for assistance in the war on terrorism.

President Gloria Macapagal-Arroyo quickly announced a "14 Pillar of Policy and Action" to combat international terrorism and said that her administration would go "all out" to assist the United States and implement UN Security Council Resolution 1368. The "14 Pillars" included offering Philippine airspace and seaports to U.S. forces, including Subic Bay, the former U.S. naval base, and intelligence sharing and logistical support. Arroyo effectively linked the war on terror to the Muslim insurgencies within the Philippines: "We must never lose sight of our immediate and overriding objective—identify the terrorists within our country, map out their networks, stop them and destroy their cause. In this war, as in any modern enterprise, we must think globally but act locally."[83]

The war on terror gave the Arroyo administration both the domestic and foreign support it needed to confront the ongoing Muslim insurgency in the south. Arroyo's ultimate goal is to defeat Muslim separatists there and to sign a durable autonomy agreement with groups that seek a political solution. Finally, she was greatly rewarded by the United States for her cooperation, when in November 2001, Washington unveiled an aid program worth more than $1 billion. The amount of aid that the Philippines have received since September 11 is approximate to if not more than the bilateral aid it has received since U.S. forces left Subic Bay in 1991. This aid includes $130 million in military assistance, a ten-fold increase in annual military assistance, $1 billion in trade benefits for the Philippines, and nearly $1 billion in other economic and trade benefits.[84] In short, Arroyo saw nothing but opportunity out of the crisis, and she made the most of it. Once the United States began attacks on Afghanistan, her support did not waver and she asked the Philippines to "pay a price" to eliminate terrorism.

President Arroyo was able to solidify her relationship with President Bush in her appeal for U.S. support to fight the Abu Sayyaf group. The fact that the Abu Sayyaf was immediately named by Washington as a "terrorist organization" with "ties to Al Qaeda," certainly bolstered her position. From January to July 2002, the United States put 1,100 troops on the ground in the southern Philippines (including 350 Special Forces) to train Philippine soldiers in counter-insurgency and counter-terrorism against the Abu Sayyaf.[85] A new legal agreement, the Terms of Reference (TOR), supplanted the pre-existing Visiting Forces Agreement. There were some concerns in the Philippines that *Operation Balikatan* and the TOR were the first stage in re-establishing a permanent U.S. base in the Philippines. To that end, the United States was prudent in withdrawing the majority of troops at the end of the exercise (the remaining troops were a military construction brigade that was engaged in development projects in Basilan). However, without U.S. troops on the ground assisting Philippine forces and providing the tactical intelligence, the offensive momentum dissipated and the Abu Sayyaf, which suffered considerable casualties in the first half of 2002, was able to regroup. By May 2003, it had received a consignment of weapons from the MILF and had begun retaking the offensive against Philippine forces.

When a second *Balikatan* exercise was announced in February 2003, Pentagon officials described the mission not as a training exercise, but a combat operation. "This is different. This is an actual combined operation, and it is U.S. forces accompanying and actively participating in Philippine-led offensive operations," a Pentagon spokesman said. This mission was also different in that it had no fixed period: "At this point, we're going into it saying the mission will go on until both sides agree it is finished."[86] The Americans were clearly frustrated with the Philippines and decided that they had to take a proactive role. President Arroyo, who announced in December 2002 that she would not run for re-election in May 2004, felt that she could allow U.S. forces an expanded combat role without any significant potential political backlash. Yet the outcry was immediate and Arroyo back-tracked, insisting that there would be no battlefield role for U.S. troops except in self defense, and that the TOR would be the same as the 2002 *Balikatan* exercise.[87] The United States' public declaration had insulted the Philippines, was clearly in violation of Philippine law, and hurt the gains in the relationship earned during the previous 18 months. U.S. military planners have expressed concern over the impasse and believe that as the Philippines enters into an electoral year, the window of opportunity for U.S. troops to return there is quickly closing.[88]

Manila has been careful to limit U.S. involvement to countering Abu Sayyaf. It is clear that the Philippine government treats each of the Muslim rebel groups differently and has very different strategies for dealing with each. The government has linked the Abu Sayyaf group to Al Qaeda and has vowed to wipe out the rebel group through military force. Although there are far greater and more established ties between the MILF and Al Qaeda than with the Abu Sayyaf, the government understands that the MILF has significant popular legitimacy and a formidable army that the Philippine armed forces are unable to defeat. To that end, the government has convinced the United States to not designate the MILF a terrorist organization and has downplayed the links between the MILF and Al Qaeda, although the cease-fire and peace talks broke down.[89] Unfortunately, the Philippine armed forces do not have the resources to maintain the pace of fighting that has taken place since February 2003. The MILF was linked to the March 2003 bombing of Davao airport; it has become standard practice for the MILF to engage in terrorism when it is suffering battlefield defeats. The June 2003 arrest of Mukhlas Yunos, the head of the MILF's terrorist arm, was a setback in that regard, as were reports that the escaped JI operative Fathur Rohman al-Ghozi was in MILF-controlled territory. As long as the MILF continues to give Jemaah Islamiyah safe haven and a place to train, there will be a terrorism problem in Southeast Asia.

Singapore

Singapore, the ethnic Chinese-dominated island wedged between Malaysia and Indonesia, is clearly alarmed at the spread of Islamism throughout Southeast Asia. Singapore's response has been robust because it considers the single greatest threat to its survival coming from the spread of militant Islamism among its neighbors. Singapore pledged to endorse all UN Security Council resolutions regarding counter-terrorism. Singapore also pledged to give its financial institutions even greater scrutiny, but as Singapore's financial sector is already the most regulated in the region, the chance that any large assets of Al Qaeda are there is slight. Singapore's most robust contribution was in breaking up the Jemaah Islamiyah cell that intended to target the United States, British and Israeli embassies in Singapore, as well as U.S. military personnel and commercial interests.[90] The Singaporean response was swift and thorough. It is difficult to exaggerate the havoc that a single terrorist act could wreak on Singapore's fragile economic recovery, which is so dependent on foreign investment and perceptions of stability. The existence of Jemaah Islamiyah thoroughly shook the Singaporean elite, who are still in shock that a group comprised of lower middle class individuals that had been through state schools and national service, was able to take root in their society. Singapore also has provided the United States military assistance, primarily in authorizing the transit of U.S. ships and planes as well as in intelligence sharing. Singapore has also provided considerable police and intelligence support with the Philippines, Thailand, Malaysia, and Indonesia in support of their counter-terror efforts.

Thailand

Thailand gave a less than vigorous response to the United States, hiding behind the cloak of ASEAN's statement following the September 11 attacks. Prime Minister Thaksin Shinawatra showed hesitancy and contradiction, at first stating that Thailand would be neutral. Thaksin, who is critical of the United States and in particular its role in the Thai economic crisis, came under attack for not living up to his treaty commitments with the United States. Since then, he has become more supportive and stated that "Thailand will cooperate with the United States and the United Nations to eliminate terrorism." The Thai Foreign Ministry announced that as a "longtime friend and treaty ally" Thailand will "render all possible assistance to the United States as Thailand has done consistently in the past."[91] Publicly, Washington did not request access to Thai military facilities as it did during the 1991 Gulf War, yet there were reports that the U-Tapao air field was used by U.S. forces during the bombing of Afghanistan. It was only following the arrest of two Thai Muslim members of Jemaah Islamiyah in Cambodia in May 2003 that the government acknowledged that a cell was operating in Thailand, and subsequently arrested four Thai nationals in June 2003.[92] The arrest of several Jemaah Islamiyah and Al Qaeda operatives in July 2003 led to the August 12 capture of Hambali in Ayuddthya.

The Limits of Regional Cooperation

As terrorism is truly an international threat, states cannot combat terrorism alone and must engage in both bilateral and multilateral cooperation. Despite a common threat, the individual states in Southeast Asia have reacted differently, in particular with respect to their willingness to work closely with the United States. Each state's perception of threat has varied substantially, which has further complicated their efforts to fight terrorism. At this stage, the region must develop common approaches to contain or disrupt the flow of individuals, financial transfers, and explosives and weapons. Here the record on cooperation has been and will continue to be mixed, due to bureaucratic politics and character, historical legacies, and lingering mistrust, as well as the weakness of multilateral institutions in the region. There are a number of problems that make counter-terror operations difficult at the unilateral, bilateral, and multilateral levels. At each level, similar problems tend to multiply in complexity.

At the unilateral level, counter-terrorist operations first require the attention of the security services. It may be surprising to realize that many governments in the region did not consider international terrorism to be on their list of threats facing their countries. Although there are cases in which Malaysia and Thailand knew that foreign terrorist and para-military organizations were operating on their borders, the security services deemed these groups to be of no threat to them or their nationals. They were simply banking, purchasing weapons, transiting, disseminating propaganda, and other back office functions, not threatening the host regime. If a state considers the likelihood that it will be the target of an international terrorist attack to be low, then it will direct its scarce resources elsewhere. Even Singapore's robust and well-funded security apparatus was surprised by the scope of the network of Islamist militants because security officials have always focused their attention on other threats. In some cases, the security services are simply spread too thin with greater and more pressing security threats, even if they know that they are a potential terrorist target. Intelligence services in Southeast Asia are often overly politicized and used for regime maintenance. Too often they are focused on domestic political opponents to the regime, and not to bona fide threats.

The second problem at the unilateral level is that counter-terrorist operations require the cooperation of the security and police forces, first within their own borders. There may be fairly legitimate reasons for a lack of coordination. For example, intelligence gathering is different than building up a police case and using all of the garnered information in a court proceeding with the goal of incarcerating a terrorist for a crime. Yet often the lack of cooperation is often driven by personal rivalries and bureaucratic competition. Such bureaucratic competition and lack of coordination gets exacerbated in conditions of resource scarcity. This is true in most Southeast Asian states where intelligence and security operations are housed in a number of different ministries and competing bureaucracies. Police forces are hampered by center-provincial competition. In the Philippines, there are 11 intelligence and law enforcement agencies, with overlapping jurisdictions and little coordination. Competition in Indonesia between the military's intelligence service (BAIS), the State Intelligence Service (BIN), and the National Police are widespread.

At the bilateral level, coordination and information sharing are even more difficult. The war on terror has led to many states calling for the need for greater police cooperation and intelligence sharing. Yet the nature of intelligence agencies, which tend to be secretive and suspicious, makes information sharing difficult. In some instances states have cooperated well, especially among the police forces. There is a long history, for example, of cooperation among the Malaysian, Singaporean, and Bruneian internal security departments. All three states have shared similar threats, especially from the Malaysian Communist Party, against which they worked together to suppress. All three services were developed on the British model and thus their similar organizational models facilitate cooperation. Singapore and Malaysia worked closely in breaking up the Jemaah Islamiyah network, but there was still some friction.[93] Whereas the Singaporean intelligence service was able to provide operational assistance to Philippine authorities during the arrest of Fathur Rohman al-Ghozi, this has been more the exception than the rule. The Philippines and Singapore have no history of animosity (with the exception of a diplomatic row over Singapore's execution of a Filipina maid for murder). Thailand did not arrest any of the Jemaah Islamiyah suspects who fled from Malaysia in December–January 2002; and it only arrested four citizens in May-June 2003 after incontrovertible evidence arose from the arrests in Thailand, and with significant pressure and assistance from Singapore.

In another instance, throughout 2002, Malaysia and Singapore repeatedly approached the Indonesians to arrest suspected terrorists. Until the Bali bombings they were repeatedly frustrated by Indonesian intransigence and an unwillingness to arrest militants. Indeed, whereas Indonesian officials acknowledged Jemaah Islamiyah's existence in Singapore, Malaysia and the Philippines, they thoroughly denied its existence in Indonesia.[94] Much of Indonesia's intransigence may be attributed to lingering anger toward the two states over past security issues. Indonesian security officials are still unhappy with the Singaporeans after uncovering a huge spy ring targeted on Indonesia in the mid-1990s. Also, for years the primary security threat in Indonesia was that of the Acehnese rebels, yet the Malaysians did little to curtail Free Aceh Movement (GAM's) activities, which included fundraising, gun-running, and transit within Malaysia's borders.[95] Abu Bakar Ba'asyir and Abdullah Sungkar are another case in point. The two were convicted criminals (albeit for political crimes) who fled to Malaysia where they lived openly for 14 years. Although there is no evidence that the Indonesian government sought their extradition, nor is there evidence that the Malaysian government sought to curtail their anti-Indonesian activities.[96] Even Jemaah Islamiyah leader Hambali, who was first indicted in Indonesia, returned to Malaysia but was not arrested.

The investigation into the Bali attack had a profound effect on police officials as they witnessed the benefits of cooperation. It became clear that without international cooperation, especially with the Australian Federal Police, the Bali investigation would not have progressed as quickly or as thoroughly as it did. I Made Mangku Pastika, who led the Balinese investigation, said in his speech before the ASEAN Workshop on Combating Terrorism on January 20, 2003 that the Indonesian national police "[n]eed mutual cooperation" especially in the fields of forensics, computer technology, cellular intercepts, ballistics, money launderings, and chemistry.[97]

There is no doubt that intelligence sharing and police cooperation in Southeast Asia has dramatically improved in the course of the war on terror. It is not overstating it to say that such cooperation has reached new heights, but it also had a relatively low starting point. The successful investigations that led to the breakup of the Jemaah Islamiyah cells around the region, and the uncovering of the Bali attack, are certain to reinforce the understanding that international cooperation is not just beneficial but necessary in combating international terrorism.

There also has to be greater bilateral cooperation with the region's U.S. counterparts. Perhaps the greatest consequence of the war on terror in Southeast Asia has been America's strategic re-engagement. The United States itself has only limited intelligence capabilities in Southeast Asia.

Whereas Washington commands the most advanced technical means, U.S. intelligence and analytical resources have not been focused on the region since the 1980s. The United States, however, does have vast resources at its disposal and can serve as a bridge between different security forces in the region. It can also share signals and other intelligence. Southeast Asian security forces will also have to improve their ties with European, Middle Eastern, South Asian, and Israeli counterparts. Yet the sharing of information is only the first step in improving bilateral coordination. These efforts must be institutionalized as a core feature in civilian-military and military-to-military exchanges and relationships. One way to accomplish this task, which is clearly politically sensitive, is the opening of liaison offices in embassies. There is a push, for example, from Washington and Canberra, to expand the number of liaison offices and police officials of the FBI and Australian police, respectively, in countries throughout the region.

Second, there need to be more bilateral extradition treaties in the region to facilitate law enforcement and counter-terrorism initiatives. A trilateral counter-terrorism treaty was signed by the Philippines, Malaysia and Indonesia in mid-2002 (Thailand later joined), yet it was signed when Indonesia was still in denial about the presence of Al Qaeda and Jemaah Islamiyah on its territory. Another immediate problem is the issue of extradition of suspects. No state in ASEAN has extradition treaties with all other members. Most have only one or two extradition treaties. In the coming years, a series of extradition treaties must be signed. There has been some talk but little movement toward the development of a multilateral extradition treaty in the region. ASEAN officials are currently reviewing a treaty drafted by the Malaysian government to streamline legal issues and processes in counter-terrorism. This draft treaty does include the transfer of witnesses to attend trials and provide testimony, finding and blocking terrorist assets, and facilitating greater police cooperation. It does not, however, address extraditions.[98]

It is essential to further develop a strong foundation for bilateral cooperation. Without such a foundation it will be impossible to develop a multilateral framework for combating terrorism and transnational crime. ASEAN and the United States did hammer out a counter-terrorism declaration in August 2002, but only with considerable U.S. diplomatic arm-twisting.[99] The treaty has few teeth, but the Americans at least got countries, including Indonesia, to acknowledge the importance of counter-terrorism. ASEAN already hosts chiefs of police, military chiefs of staff, and intelligence chiefs' meetings each year. These meetings are an important first step, and if developed they could become important loci of coordination and cooperation. Institutionally, ASEAN does have a role to play, but again, successful multilateralism must be built on the foundation of strong bilateral cooperation. It is telling that no regional mechanism for countering terrorism has yet emerged, nor is there any consensus on the scope of the threat that terrorist groups pose to states in the region. Moreover, regional efforts to confront transnational crime in people and weapons smuggling, money laundering, document forging, and other illegal activities need to be stepped up. Effective counter-terrorism plans and operations should be built from the lessons learned and experience gained through multilateral transnational crime-fighting.

Finally, although the United States encouraged the formation of and offered to fund a regional counter-terrorism center in mid-2002, the implementation has been exceedingly slow. In the spring of 2003, Malaysia announced that the center would be run and funded by the Malaysians themselves without U.S. co-management. By July 2003, the Malaysian government still had not given considerable thought to what the center's mission and scope would be. Although the Americans had originally hoped that it would be an operational center that would share intelligence, the Malaysians are now focusing more on the idea of capacity building for applicable security forces, departments, and ministries from throughout the region. There is no current plan for the center to have any operational role in counter-terrorism, but the center may provide some momentum toward multilateral efforts to fight transnational crime—and this mission may lay the groundwork for a future counter-terrorism role at the center.[100]

Conclusion

The region's states will cooperate with the United States only if it is in their short-term political and diplomatic interests to do so. If there is a convergence of interests, then the United States should expect close cooperation. At the point when U.S. interests diverge, such as with the war in Iraq, then we will likely face the situation that cooperation will be constrained by domestic political concerns. The current political climate in Southeast Asia limits America's ability to influence longer-term regional security developments. We cannot count on sustained cooperation as these countries enter into domestic elections; indeed, the United States must anticipate expressions of xenophobic nationalism.

What if the United States is insensitive to the political constraints of its Southeast Asian partners? The backlash will weaken the political positions of leaders whose cooperation we need to counter terrorism. It will play into the hands of the Islamist opposition, especially in Indonesia and Malaysia. The Islamist opposition in these two states is not large in absolute numbers, but it is vociferous and becoming more entrenched. We should not expect a complete cessation of cooperation with the United States at working levels, even if U.S. officials' pressure to crack down on militants is politically unpopular. Militants do threaten the governments of Southeast Asia. Yet, the security services take their cues from the political leadership. The case of Indonesia has shown that if security services do not have the support of the political leadership they will not act. The average man on the street in central Java still believes that the CIA perpetrated the Bali attack so that the Indonesian government would be forced to crack down on Islamists. Hamzah Haz's statement that the September 11 attacks were a good thing because "they taught the United States a lesson" resonates widely. If politicians believe that widespread public antipathy towards the United States will hurt them politically, or that they will be labeled as "puppets" by their political opponents for their support in the war on terror, then we should expect less cooperation.

The United States and its allies in Southeast Asia have made measurable progress in rounding up suspected terrorists, denying them sanctuary, and in general making it harder for them to conduct operations. But this adversary is determined. Jemaah Islamiyah is patiently reconstituting itself and retains the ability to cause mass harm to the regional economy. The problem, however, is that while the political elites have shared the U.S. perception of the threat, their electorates do not. Indeed, Muslims in Southeast Asia believe that the war on terror is patently anti-Muslim, and antipathy toward the United States over its policies in the Middle East and its invasion of Iraq is growing steadily. Although security services have arrested several fish, the pond is wider and deeper than ever. Terrorism remains the key threat to the political and economic security of states in the region, and to U.S. interests there, for the foreseeable future.

Endnotes

1 A paper that covers such a range of complex issues in so many countries is the result of the time, assistance, and knowledge of many people. Most of the government officials whom I interviewed and spoke with requested anonymity. They hail from the United States, Australia, Canada, Singapore, Malaysia, Indonesia, the Philippines, Brunei, Thailand, India, Switzerland, and Germany. They know who they are and how grateful I am for their assistance. I would also like to thank members of the MILF, the MMI, Jemaah Islamiyah, and their supporters for their insights.

2 Harold Crouch, "Qaeda in Indonesia? The evidence doesn't support worries," *International Herald Tribune*, October 23, 2001.

3 In Indonesia, although the constitutional amendment failed, there are currently 21 bills in parliament that have an Islamic component to them, i.e, the health bill has a provision that all Muslims are entitled to have a Muslim doctor. No

political party is willing to expend the political capital to oppose this Islamization process.

4 Patricia Martinez, "The Islamic State or the State of Islam in Southeast Asia," *Contemporary Southeast Asia*, vol. 23, no. 3 (December 2001), pp. 474–503.

5 Farish Noor, "Negotiating Islamic law," *Far Eastern Economic Review*, September 19, 2002, p. 23.

6 Leonard Sebastian, "Getting to the root of Islamic radicalism in Indonesia," *Straits Times*, August 2002.

7 "Philippine *madrassas* spread north," *Straits Times*, August 5, 2002.

8 Interview no. 25, Singapore, 20 June 2002.

9 Peter Bergen, *Holy War Inc.: Inside the Secret World of Osama Bin Laden*, New York: The Free Press, 2001, p. 56.

10 "Filipino 'terrorist trainees' return," *Straits Times*, November 19, 2001; Lira Lalangin, "Bin Laden seen recruiting ex-MILF," *Philippine Daily Inquirer*, October 24, 2001.

11 Simon Elegant, "Getting radical," *Time Asia*, September 10, 2001. Republic of Singapore, Ministry of Home Affairs, *White Paper: The Jemaah Islamiyah Arrests and the Threat of Terrorism*, Singapore, 2003.

12 In the 1990s the CIA tried to keep track of some 700–1,500 Indonesian students who went to Egypt, Syria and Iran for study. According to a retired CIA officer, "We figured 30–40 percent of them never showed up. We don't know where they went." One Malaysian official recounted how its embassy in Islamabad believed there were 5 to 10 Malaysians studying at a certain *madrassa* in Pakistan; there turned out to be 150. Forty-four Indonesian students were expelled from Yemeni *madrassas* in February 2002 alone. The Indonesian government has no idea how many Indonesians are studying in Egypt, Pakistan or elsewhere. In addition to the Pakistani *madrassas*, many Southeast Asians have attended Egypt's Al Azhar University (where there are some 6,000 Malaysian students) and Yemen's Al Imam University. By December 2001, there were an estimated 200 undocumented Filipinos in Afghanistan and 600 students in Pakistan. Some 200 were "missing" according to the Philippine Embassy in Pakistan, and their whereabouts were unknown. John McBeth, "The danger within," *Far Eastern Economic Review*, September 27, 2001, p. 21; "KL to require students going abroad to register," *Straits Times*, October 13, 2001; Rasheed Abou Alsamh, "Why OFWs are safe in the Middle East," *Philippine Daily Enquirer*, September 28, 2001; Lira Lalangin, "Bin Laden seen recruiting ex-MILF," *Philippine Daily Enquirer*, October 24, 2001.

13 Alan Dupont, *East Asia Imperiled: Transnational Challenges to Security*, New York: Cambridge University Press, 2001.

14 "Thailand a transit point for terror funds," *Straits Times*, March 11, 2002.

15 By June 2001, "total Islamic banking assets stood at RM51.97 billion, or 7.3 percent of overall banking assets." From 1994 to 2000, Islamic banking assets increased by 64 percent. For more see, Baidura Ahmad, "Strong growth seen for Islamic banking and *takaful*," *New Straits Times*, October 2, 2001.

16 Dafna Linzer, "From New York to Kabul and back: star witness at the embassy bombing trial revealed bin Laden's world," Associated Press, October 1, 2001.

[17] Khalifa had close ties to two of bin Laden's top financiers, Wael Jalaidin and Yasin al Qadi, who was the head of the Muwafaq Foundation that was designated by both the Saudi and U.S. governments in 2002 as a terrorist front. Matthew Levitt, "Saudi Financial Counter-Terrorism Measures (Part II): Smokescreen or Substance," *Washington Institute for Near East Policy – Policy Watch*, no. 687, December 10, 2002.

[18] The IIRO was actually established in 1978, but co-opted in 1979 by Saudi Arabian intelligence in order to serve as a financial conduit for Saudi, U.S., and Gulf-state funding to the *mujahidin* in Afghanistan. In the early 1990s, the IIRO decided to have separate directors for each of the countries and Khalifa became the IIRO director for the Philippines. The IIRO claims to have begun charitable work in the Philippines in 1988, but according to documents registered at the Philippine Securities Exchange Commission, the IIRO was legally incorporated in the Philippines on September 20, 1991 with offices in Makati and in several cities in Mindanao, including Cotabato and Zamboanga. Khalifa was listed as the IIRO's president. Dr. Adnan Khalil Basha, "Largest Islamic relief organization maligned," letter to the editor, *Philippine Daily Enquirer*, August 18, 2000. Other Khalifa-linked charities included a branch office of the Saudi charity MERC International and two local NGOs, Islamic Wisdom Worldwide and the Daw'l Immam Al Shafee Center.

[19] Herrera, "Bin Laden funds Abu Sayyaf through Muslim relief group."

[20] Philippine National Police, After Intelligence Operations Report, Camp Crame, Quezon City, Philippines, February 27, 1995.

[21] Al Qaeda assistance was imperative. The MILF's traditional supporter, Libya, had reduced assistance as it was trying to broker a peace agreement between the MILF and the Philippine government in order to have sanctions lifted that had been imposed after the Lockerbie Pan-Am bombing.

[22] Department of the Interior and Local Government, "Country Report of Republic of the Philippines" paper presented to the International Conference on Counter-Terrorism, Baguio City, Philippines, February 18–21, 1996.

[23] Philippine National Police, After Intelligence Operations Report.

[24] Herrera, "Bin Laden funds Abu Sayyaf through Muslim relief group."

[25] Republic of the Philippines, National Intelligence Coordinating Agency, "Summary of Information: Umar Al Faruq," November 2002; Baden Intellijen Negara, "Interrogation Report of Omar al-Faruq," Jakarta, June 2002.

[26] Raymond Burgos, "FBI seeks Philippine help in hunting down terrorists," *Philippine Daily Enquirer*, September 30, 2001; Luz Baguioro, "Jemaah Islamiyah militants may have links with separatist group," *Straits Times*, September 18, 2002.

[27] Marites Danguilan Vitug, and Glenda M. Gloria, *Under the Crescent Moon: Rebellion in Mindanao*, Quezon City: Ateno Center for Social Policy and Public Affairs, 2000.

[28] Simon Reeve, *The New Jackals: Ramzi Yousef, Osama Bin Laden and the Future of Terrorism*, Boston: Northeastern University Press, 1999; Philippine National Police, After Intelligence Operations Report.

[29] Personal correspondence with a senior Philippine intelligence official, March 2002.

[30] Darul Islam was a Muslim-based guerilla force that fought both the Dutch and the secular-nationalist forces of Sukarno, arguing that Sukarno's guerrillas were as much an enemy as the Dutch. "By rejecting Islam as the sole foundation of the state, [the government] had made itself as evil an enemy as the Dutch." This period became known as the "triangular war," after Kartosuniryo established a secessionist Islamic state in West Java on 7 August 1949. Support spread to central Java, Aceh and south Sulawesi. The Darul Islam rebellion lasted until 1962, when its leader was captured and executed and the movement was driven underground. The Darul Islam organization exists to this day, and in many ways it operates much the way the Muslim Brotherhood operated in Anwar Sadat's Egypt. Though it is still an illegal organization, it is more or less tolerated, and members run for political office on the tickets of other parties. See Adam Schwartz, *A Nation in Waiting: Indonesia in the 1990s*, Boulder, Colo.: Westview Press, 1994, p. 169.

[31] Edy Budiyarso, "Indonesia's Afghan-trained *mujahidin*," *Tempo*, October 2–8, 2001.

[32] "Suharto's Detect, Defect and Destroy Policy Towards the Islamic Movement," interview with Abdullah Sungkar, Nida'ul Islam, February-March 1997.

[33] Mark Freeman and Richard C. Paddock, "Response to terror: Indonesia cleric tied to '95 anti-U.S. plot," *Los Angeles Times*, February 7, 2002. This was confirmed in a CIA response to Philippine queries and can be found as an addendum to Philippine National Police, After Intelligence Operations Report.

[34] Indictment of Abu Bakar Ba'asyir, Office of the Attorney General, Republic of Indonesia, April 2003.

[35] The United States came across diagrams and blueprints detailing the U.S. embassy and its security regimen from a terrorist suspect in the Middle East. When U.S. intelligence discovered that the six-member team was dispatched to Surabaya, U.S. Ambassador Robert Gelbard went to the Indonesian intelligence services to arrest the six Yemenis. Indonesian military intelligence, however, brought in local police to do the arrest, because it was a law enforcement issue. Although the United States had already flown in two CIA officials to assist in the arrest and a plane to take the Yemenis to America, the latter were tipped off and fled the country. Interview with a retired U.S. State Department Official, October 27, 2002.

[36] Classified interrogation report of Faiz Bin Abu Bakar Bafana, Singapore, 2002. Also see transcripts of Bafana's video-testimony in the Trial of Abu Bakar Ba'asyir, June 26, 2003; Indictment of Abu Bakar Ba'asyir, Office of the Attorney General, Republic of Indonesia, April 2003.

[37] Indictment of Abu Bakar Ba'asyir, Office of the Attorney General, Republic of Indonesia, April 2003.

[38] "KL arrest prime terror suspect," Associated Press, September 27, 2002.

[39] Singapore Ministry of Home Affairs, *White Paper: The Jemaah Islamiyah Arrests and the Threat of Terrorism*, p. 6.

[40] "Indictment chronicles 'overt acts' that it said led to Sept. 11 attacks," *New York Times*, December 12, 2001, p. B6.

[41] Singapore Ministry of Home Affairs, *White Paper: The Jemaah Islamiyah Arrests and the Threat of Terrorism*, p. 6.

[42] Romesh Ratnesar, "Confessions of an Al Qaeda terrorist," *Time*, September 16, 2002; BIN Interrogation Report of Omar al-Faruq, June 2002.

[43] Republic of the Philippines, National Intelligence Coordinating Agency, "An Update on the Recent Bombings in Mindanao and Metro Manila," Quezon City, November 25, 2002.

[44] Fathur Rohman al-Ghozi, written deposition, July 2002.

[45] For new revelations on the extent of Jemaah Islamiyah's penetration of Australia, see Sally Neighbour, "The Australian connections," Australian Broadcast Corporation, aired on June 9, 2003.

[46] "The MMI is an institution where a lot of people from a lot of Muslim groups including the NU [Nahdlatul Ulama] and Muhammadiyah gather at one table to discuss how to get our vision of *sharia* implemented into national laws.... The long-term strategy is to get Indonesia 100 percent based on *sharia*. As long as Muslims are the majority, the country should be ruled by *sharia*." Interview with Abu Bakar Ba'asyir, Ngruki, Solo, June 11, 2002.

[47] Baden Intellijen Negara, "Interrogation Report of Omar al-Faruq," Jakarta, June 2002.

[48] KOMPAK officials, while acknowledging that they operate in regions struck by sectarian conflict (Aceh, Poso, Malukus, and Bangunan Beton Sumatra), assert they are there to alleviate the crises and provide necessary relief. They denied any links to "jihad activities." Interview with Dr. H. Asep R. Jayanegara, Secretary, Komite Penanggulangan Krisis, Dewan Dakwah Islam Indonesia, Jakarta, January 8, 2003.

[49] BIN Interrogation Report of Omar al-Faruq (June 2002). The office was in Makassar, Sulawesi. Also see Romesh Ratnesar, "Confessions of an Al Qaeda terrorist," *Time*, September 23, 2003, pp. 34–41.

[50] Thousands of people were members of these groups and have now returned home, much the way the members of the G272 returned to Indonesia from Afghanistan in the late 1980s to early 1990s, ready to lead their own jihads to implement *sharia*.

[51] Six foreigners (two Afghans, two Pakistanis, and two Arabs) were detained. The six were thought to be Al Qaeda operatives who conducted training of Laskar Jundullah and other Al Qaeda operatives in the camp in Poso. The police initially refuted the report calling the six men "tourists." A. M. Hendropriyono, the head of intelligence, acknowledged that it was not just a Laskar Jihad or Laskar Jundullah base: "The training site was not used by Indonesians, but by foreigners ... while those who are involved in the conflict in Poso are Indonesians against fellow Indonesians, Muslims against Christians." Hendropriyono stated equivocally that "Poso has been used by international terrorist groups to support activities they plan from outside the country." An Indonesian National Intelligence Body (BIN) report, Al Qaeda Infrastructure in Indonesia, stated clearly that: "The training camp led by Omar Bandon consisted of 8–10 small villages located side by side on the beach, equipped with light weapons, explosives, and firing range. Participants of the training are not only from local people but also from overseas. The instructor of physical training in the camp is Parlindungan Siregar, a member of Al Qaeda's network in Spain." For more information see, Marianne Kearney, "Security forces to disarm Sulawesi fight-

ers," *Straits Times*, December 6, 2001; Fabiola Desy Unidjaja, "International training camp in Poso 'empty'," *Jakarta Post*, December 14, 2001; Fabiola Desy Unidjaja, "Government ready to impose a state of emergency in Poso Town," *Jakarta Post*, December 5, 2001. Fabiola Desy Unidjaja, "State of emergency in Poso on hold: police," *Jakarta Post*, December 8, 2001; BIN, "Al Qaeda's Infrastructure in Indonesia," Jakarta, February 2002.

[52] Interview with a BIN official, Jakarta, January 17, 2003.

[53] BIN, "Al Qaeda's Infrastructure in Indonesia," Jakarta, February 2002.

[54] Romesh Ratnesar, "Confessions of an Al Qaeda terrorist," *Time*, September 23, 2003, pp. 34–41; also see transcripts of Bafana's video-testimony in the Trial of Abu Bakar Ba'asyir, June 26, 2003.

[55] Indictment of Abu Bakar Ba'asyir, office of the Attorney General, Republic of Indonesia, April 2003.

[56] Canadian Secret Intelligence Service, "Interrogation Report of Mohammed Mansour Jabarah," (2002); BIN, "Interrogation Report of Omar al-Faruq," Jakarta, June 2002.

[57] Singapore Ministry of Home Affairs, *White Paper: The Jemaah Islamiyah Arrests and the Threat of Terrorism*, p. 27.

[58] Central Intelligence Agency, "Terrorist Connections of Abubakar Basyir; and Further Details Connection and Activities of Umar Faruq," September 2002.

[59] "Government to investigate Abu Bakar Ba'asyir's alleged involvement in terrorist network," *Tempo*, September 18, 2002.

[60] Canadian Secret Intelligence Service, "Interrogation Report of Mohammed Mansour Jabarah," 2002.

[61] Indictment of Abu Bakar Ba'asyir, Office of the Attorney General, Republic of Indonesia, April 2003; Indictment of Ali Ghufron, alias Mukhlas, Denpassar office of the Counsel of the Prosecution of Justice, Republic of Indonesia, June 2, 2003; Indictment of Abdul Aziz, alias Imam Samudra, Denpassar office of the Counsel of the Prosecution of Justice, Republic of Indonesia, May 20, 2003.

[62] Indictment of Abu Bakar Ba'asyir, Office of the Attorney General, Republic of Indonesia, April 2003.

[63] BIN, "Interrogation Report of Omar al-Faruq," June 2002.

[64] Classified interrogation report of Faiz Bin Abu Bakar Bafana, Singapore 2002. Also see transcripts of Bafana's video-testimony in the Trial of Abu Bakar Ba'asyir, June 26, 2003.

[65] BIN, "Interrogation Report of Omar al-Faruq," June 2002.

[66] Alex Perry, "Deadly cargo," *Time Asia*, October 21, 2002; Bertil Lintner, "A recipe for trouble," *Far Eastern Economic Review*, April 4, 2002, p. 17; Lintner, "A cocoon of terror," *Far Eastern Economic Review*, April 4, 2002, pp. 14–17; Lintner, "Championing Islamist Extremism," *South Asia Intelligence Review*, vol. 1, no. 9 (September 16), 2002.

[67] For more on this issue, see Zachary Abuza, "Funding Terror in Southeast Asia," unpublished paper, July 2003.

[68] Cited in Simon Elegant, "Cash flowing," *Time Asia*, March 24, 2003.

[69] Jane MacCartney and Simon Cameron-Moore, "United States to freeze 'terror' funds in SE Asia," Reuters, March 13, 2003. "FBI watching al-Qaeda funds in Southeast Asia," Agence France-Presse, March 31, 2003.

[70] Already the threat of terrorism in the predominantly Buddhist nation was high. On the basis of Omar Al-Faruq's confession and the confession of Mohammed Mansour Jabarah, both in U.S. custody, U.S. embassies in Malaysia, Indonesia, Cambodia, and Vietnam were shut down for the anniversary of the September 11 attacks. There was also concern that the ASEAN Foreign Ministers' Meeting, to be held in Phnom Penh in June 2003, would be targeted. Later a fourth individual, a Cambodian, was arrested. Ratnesar, "Confessions of an Al Qaeda terrorist"; Raymond Bonner, "Plan to attack embassies in South Asia cited for terror alert," *New York Times*, September 11, 2002.

[71] Ker Munthit, "Three Muslim foreigners arrested in Cambodia," Associated Press, May 28, 2003; Ek Madra, "Cambodia cracks down on foreign Muslims," Reuters, May 28, 2003.

[72] Pew Global Attitudes Project, "Views of a Changing World," Washington, DC: June 2003, pp. 19, 28.

[73] "Terrorism deserves punishment," she said at a Jakarta mosque, but then added, "No individual, group or government has the right to catch terrorist perpetrators by attacking the territory of another country." Derwin Pereira, "Hamzah meets scholars to defuse crisis," *Straits Times*, October 16, 2001; "Megawati hits American air raids on Afghanistan amid protests," Agence France-Presse, October 15, 2001; "Joint Statement Between the United States of America and the Republic of Indonesia," September 19, 2001.

[74] "Government urged to issue stronger statement on Afghanistan," *Jakarta Post*, October 13, 2001; Pereira, "Hamzah meets scholars to defuse crisis," *Straits Times*.

[75] Irfan Awwas, cited in Michael Richardson, "Indonesia divided over extremists," *International Herald Tribune*, January 23, 2002.

[76] Robert W. Hefner, "Islam and the Nation in the Post-Suharto Era," in Adam Schwarz and Jonathan Paris, eds., *The Politics of Post-Suharto Indonesia*, New York: Council on Foreign Relations Press, 1999, pp. 65–66.

[77] Fabiola Desy Unidjaja, "Government ready to impose a state of emergency in Poso town," *Jakarta Post*, December 5, 2001. Fabiola Desy Unidjaja, "State of emergency in Poso on hold: police," *Jakarta Post*, December 8, 2001.

[78] Tiarma Siboro and Badri Djawara, "Troops disarm rivals, expel outsiders from troubled Poso," *Jakarta Post*, December 12, 2001.

[79] Rajiv Chandrasekaran and Peter Finn, "U.S. behind secret transfer of terror suspects," *Washington Post*, March 11, 2002.

[80] Interview with a BIN official, Jakarta, January 17, 2003.

[81] S. Jayasankaran and Lorien Holland, "Profiting from fear," *Far Eastern Economic Review*, October 11, 2001, p. 34; Patrick Sennyah, Ainon Mohd and Hayati Hayatudin, "KMM's opposition link," *New Straits Times*, October 12, 2001.

[82] "KL to require students going abroad to register," *Straits Times*, October 13, 2001; Brendan Pereira, "KL to keep close eye on schools run by PAS," *Straits Times*, October 16, 2001.

[83] Juliet Javellana, "President announces '14-pillar policy' to battle terrorism," *Philippine Daily Enquirer*, September 26, 2001.

[84] James Hookway, "Just say 'no' to U.S. troops," *Far Eastern Economic Re-

view, December 6, 2001, p. 24.

[85] U.S. forces, constitutionally banned from engaging in combat on Philippine territory, nevertheless were with Philippine troops at the front lines, allowed to fight back in self defense, and provide tactical intelligence.

[86] Bradley Graham, "United States bolsters Philippine force," *Washington Post*, February 20, 2003.

[87] "These operations will be led by the Armed Forces of the Philippines with assistance by U.S. forces," said a Pentagon official. The Philippine presidential spokesman Ignacio Bunye said the American troops would only engage in training: "In other words, no combat troops. Everything will be for training and advice." When asked about the Terms of Reference, Secretary of National Defense Angelo Reyes commented, "As I said, we are going to discuss the details.... Nothing is final. The only thing that is final is that anything we will do will be within and in accordance with the Constitution, and we will not violate of any of our laws." Carlito Pablo and Martin P. Marfil, "Palace insists no combat role for U.S. troops," *Philippine Daily Enquirer*, February 22, 2002; "U.S. troops to fight Abu: U.S. defense official," Agence France-Presse, February 22, 2002; Paul Alexander, "Philippines faces fallout on U.S. troops," Associated Press, February 22, 2003.

[88] Conversation with a U.S. military official, Tampa, Fl., June 4, 2004.

[89] In part this was due to the MILF's intransigence at the negotiating table, but it also may be for political reasons. Secretary of Defense Angelo Reyes is running for the presidency and the war against the MILF is politically popular.

[90] Singapore Ministry of Home Affairs, *White Paper: The Jemaah Islamiyah Arrests and the Threat of Terrorism*, p. 27.

[91] "Thailand gives support to war on terrorism," *Bangkok Post*, September 17, 2001.

[92] "Thailand admits presence of militant Muslims," Reuters, May 29, 2003; "Terrorist cell: 3 'Jemaah Islamiyah members' arrested in the south," *The Nation*, June 11, 2003.

[93] Interview, Singapore, June 20, 2002.

[94] Interview with Drs. Prosetyo, MABISPOLRI, Jakarta, June 13, 2002; Interview with Drs. Bagus, Director of Office of Terrorism, Police Intelligence, MABISPOLRI, Jakarta, June 14, 2002.

[95] Interview with a BIN official, Jakarta, January 17, 2003.

[96] Interview with Drs. Prosetyo, MABISPOLRI, Jakarta, June 13, 2002; Interview with Drs. Bagus, Director of Office of Terrorism, Police Intelligence, MABISPOLRI, Jakarta, June 14, 2002.

[97] I Made Mangku Pastika, "The Uncovering of the Bali Blast Case," paper delivered at the ASEAN Workshop on Combating Terrorism, January 20–22, 2003, Jakarta.

[98] "ASEAN plans anti-terror treaty," Agence France-Presse, July 1, 2003.

[99] Slobodan Lekic, "Powell, Asian leaders sign anti-terror pact," Associated Press, August 1, 2002.

[100] Interview with a senior Malaysian Ministry of Foreign Affairs official, Putrajaya, June 9, 2003.

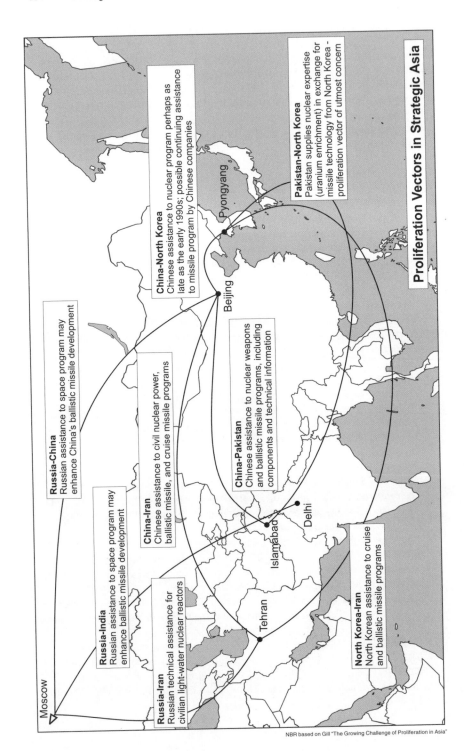

Proliferation Vectors in Strategic Asia

Russia-China
Russian assistance to space program may enhance China's ballistic missile development

Russia-India
Russian assistance to space program may enhance ballistic missile development

Russia-Iran
Russian technical assistance for civilian light-water nuclear reactors

China-Iran
Chinese assistance to civil nuclear power, ballistic missile, and cruise missile programs

China-North Korea
Chinese assistance to nuclear program perhaps as late as the early 1990s; possible continuing assistance to missile program by Chinese companies

China-Pakistan
Chinese assistance to nuclear weapons and ballistic missile programs, including components and technical information

Pakistan-North Korea
Pakistan supplies nuclear expertise (uranium enrichment) in exchange for missile technology from North Korea - proliferation vector of utmost concern

North Korea-Iran
North Korean assistance to cruise and ballistic missile programs

NBR based on Gill "The Growing Challenge of Proliferation in Asia"

THE GROWING CHALLENGE OF PROLIFERATION IN ASIA

Bates Gill

ABSTRACT

The problem of nuclear proliferation in Asia is particularly challenging and is likely to become more so in the years ahead. On the demand side, some Asian states are turning to nuclear weapons in hopes of an ultimate security guarantee in the face of much stronger adversaries. On the supply side, a range of Asian state-to-state proliferation channels have emerged over the past decade. There are also concerns that certain Asian states would purposely or inadvertently assist terrorist organizations in acquiring such weapons. This chapter examines the principal drivers and channels for proliferation in Asia, assesses the prospects for continued proliferation in the region, gauges the efficacy of nonproliferation mechanisms in stemming regional proliferation, and discusses how the proliferation challenge will affect strategic security in Asia. To be effective, nonproliferation efforts will require significant and well-orchestrated multinational commitments of political, diplomatic, military, and economic resources—and still may not work.

Bates Gill holds the Freeman Chair in China Studies at the Center for Strategic and International Studies in Washington, D.C. The author is grateful to Richard Ellings, Aaron Friedberg, Scott Davis, and Michael Wills for their helpful comments and expert insights in the preparation of this chapter.

Introduction

The global challenge of the proliferation of weapons of mass destruction (WMD), particularly nuclear weapons, has increasingly gained center stage as an international security concern. This is particularly true for the United States, which, in the post-September 11, 2001 period, has placed top priority on preventing terrorists from acquiring and using WMD. Beneath the rhetoric of the term "axis of evil" lies the very real threat that states developing nuclear weapons, and which have known terrorist connections, would purposely or inadvertently assist terrorist organizations in acquiring and ultimately using such weapons with devastating consequences. But even nuclear weapons states without readily known terrorist connections—such as Russia or China—are vulnerable to theft of materials from poorly safeguarded WMD-related facilities.

In Asia, the problem of nuclear proliferation is particularly challenging, and is likely to become more so in the years ahead. Asia presents a multi-dimensional set of proliferation channels and drivers, which greatly complicates nonproliferation solutions. On the demand side, some states appear to advance nuclear weapons programs in hopes of developing a security guarantee in the face of much stronger potential adversaries, as in the case of Pakistan, North Korea, and, arguably, China. In some instances, demand-side drivers motivate governments to engage in strategic nuclear competition and arms races, resulting in vertical build-ups of nuclear arsenals, as in the case of the India-Pakistan and India-China dyads. On the supply side, a plethora of state-to-state horizontal proliferation channels have come to light over the past decade, including Chinese transfers to Iran and Pakistan, Russian exports to Iran, and cooperation between Pakistan and North Korea. Straightforward economic and technological benefits serve as both supply and demand side drivers for proliferation in Asia, as Russian, Chinese, North Korean, and Pakistani entities seek remuneration and technical expertise by trading abroad.

The underlying geopolitical foundation in Asia also points to further proliferation challenges in the years ahead. On the one hand, Asia is home to several relatively advanced economies and modern militaries, such as Japan, South Korea, and Taiwan, each of which have the technical capacity to develop nuclear weapons (the latter two have previously initiated and, under U.S. pressure, later halted nuclear weapons programs). On the other hand, Asia encompasses a number of politically and economically fragile or failing states where WMD and related materials could fall into the wrong hands in a time of crisis—such as Pakistan or North Korea—or where terrorists could operate to acquire and develop WMD beyond the reach of the international community, such as in Afghanistan. On top of all of this, recent years have seen a weakening of international nonproliferation regimes and loosening of international nonproliferation norms.

In order to analyze these points more carefully, this chapter examines the principal drivers and channels for proliferation in Asia, assesses the near- to medium-term prospects for continued proliferation in the region, and gauges the efficacy of various nonproliferation mechanisms in stemming proliferation trends. The chapter concludes with an assessment of how the proliferation challenge will affect strategic security in Asia and the role of the United States and other major players in the region.

Two caveats are in order before proceeding. First, the chapter will be largely concerned with the proliferation of nuclear weapons and materials, but will address missile, chemical, and biological proliferation concerns as well. Second, in discussing proliferation channels, the chapter focuses primarily on *intra-Asian* connections. Countries and sub-state actors in Asia have acquired weapons, technologies, and knowledge from suppliers beyond Asia, including from the United States and Europe, both clandestinely and as part of civilian programs. However, the intensification of intra-Asian trade in sensitive technologies, and its implications for Strategic Asia, will receive the greatest attention here.[1]

Supply-side and Demand-side Drivers

The complexities of strategic, political, and economic motivations which drive states and non-state actors to engage in proliferation activities— whether as suppliers, recipients, or both—are multifaceted, and often not readily open to solutions for stemming the spread of WMD. These seem particularly prominent and difficult in Asia, from which many of the most immediate international proliferation concerns emanate: China, India, Iran, North Korea, Pakistan, and Russia. Moreover, a complex web of intra-Asian proliferation relationships—such as between Russia and Iran, Russia and India, China and Iran, North Korea and Iran, China and Pakistan, and North Korea and Pakistan—further complicates the proliferation picture in Asia. To clarify this picture and gain a more nuanced sense of the forces that generate proliferation concerns in Asia, motivations can be roughly divided between demand-side or "pull" factors on the one hand, and supply-side or "push" factors on the other. For greater analytical clarity, each of these drivers can be further divided into sub-categories of strategic, political, and economic factors.[2]

Strategic demand factors are among the strongest reasons for states and sub-state actors to seek WMD. In case after case in Asia, countries pursue WMD and ballistic missiles as a means to achieve fundamental national interests in the face of what are perceived to be dangerous and potentially overwhelming threats. This kind of motivation was clearly at work for China in the 1950s and 1960s, facing as it did nuclear threats first from the United States and later from the Soviet Union. Sensing a strategic threat from China, and with a long-standing, increasingly nuclear-tinged rivalry with Pakistan (which was assisted by China), India tested a "peaceful nuclear device" in 1974 and declared itself a nuclear power in the wake of its 1998 nuclear tests. Pakistan also chose to pursue nuclear weapon and ballistic missile development so as not be blackmailed and overwhelmed by a more powerful India. Iran, as a victim of missile and WMD attacks during the Iran-Iraq war in the 1980s, and perceiving itself under threat from hostile countries armed with WMD, such as Israel and the United States, may likewise be turning to nuclear weapons as a strategic security guarantor. Similarly, North Korea, citing a "grave situation" for its supreme national interests, has apparently chosen the path of nuclear weapons and other WMD as a means of deterring the United States and its allies in the region. For countries such as Iran and North Korea, sensing the prospect of an even more antagonistic relationship with the United States in the future and seeing the experience of a non-nuclear Iraq, a nuclear weapons capability is motivated in part by a strategic hope of deterring and avoiding such outcomes.

Political demand factors seem less tangible and more difficult to pinpoint, but can also be strong motivators to pursue WMD. For countries such as China, India, and Iran, the possession of nuclear weapons is deemed to lend prestige and "great power status"—a particularly strong motivator for countries that believe they have been snubbed or mistreated by the international community, or not been accorded proper deference as "regional powers." States and sub-state actors may also believe that the possession of WMD will allow them to share equal or near-equal political status with larger powers, and hence, place them in a better position to gain political and diplomatic concessions.

Economic demand factors do not appear to be as common as strategic and political demand drivers for WMD. However, North Korea, for example, may pursue the acquisition of WMD (or the threat thereof) in part to leverage economic benefits and concessions from its neighbors.

Examples of *strategic supply* or *"push" factors* also help explain the motivations driving certain proliferation activities in Asia. Some of the Soviet Union's initial interest in supplying weapons to China in the 1950s had to do with drawing China into its orbit in the bipolar Cold War struggle. China has assisted Pakistan in its conventional and unconventional military-technical development as a means to bolster its ally as a strategic counterweight in South Asia vis-à-vis India. Since the mid-1990s, it appears such motivations were partially behind the North Korea-Pakistan nexus: each side provided WMD-related assistance in order to gain the strategic capabilities each sought.

Political supply factors driving proliferation involve interests in extending political and diplomatic influence through military-technical relationships. For example, Russia's hopes of reasserting its influence in South and Southwest Asia are probably at play in supplying weapons and technologies to Iran and India. China too, seeks to establish some greater influence in the Persian Gulf region through its 20-year relationship with Iran.

Finally, *economic supply factors* appear to be very strong in explaining certain proliferation activity in Asia. The cash-strapped Russian military-industrial complex is clearly driven to assist such partners as China, India, and Iran in large measure by economic motivations. Likewise, North Korea's crushing economic problems help explain the country's willingness to sell its missiles and other weapons abroad. A lack of economic resources also helps explain why Pakistan turned to barter trade—providing nuclear expertise to North Korea instead of cash—in return for North Korean missiles and missile technology. But it is not always the case that the country in question is "cash-strapped" or "poor." In some cases—as with certain Chinese transfers to North Korea or Iran—the primary motivator seems to be companies looking for a willing buyer and trying to make a profit, a problem which will persist as long as China's economic dynamism and liberalization outpaces the government's ability to monitor illegal export activities.

Stemming continued proliferation will depend on whether viable alternatives can be presented to either replace the perceived strategic, political, and economic gains driving proliferation activities, or to dissuade actors from pursuing those gains in the first place. This may be possible in the case of some motivating factors, particularly when those motivations are not particularly strong or can be easily met or dissuaded by other means. However, when countries are motivated by strong strategic demand—the cases of China, India, Pakistan, and North Korea come to mind—alternative incentives or dissuasion seem less likely to succeed. Moreover, when more than one of these motivating factors is at work for either a supplier or a recipient, or when these motivations are working strongly in a bilateral military-technical relationship for both the supplier and the recipient, nonproliferation approaches become all the more problematic and difficult.

Proliferation Channels in Asia

Proliferation is certainly not a new phenomenon to Asia. By the mid- to late-1960s, China succeeded in developing and testing an indigenous ballistic missile capability and became the first Asian power to detonate a fission weapon (1964) and a thermonuclear device (1967). China has since steadily built up its nuclear forces to become the world's third largest nuclear power. India began its nuclear weapons program in 1968, and detonated its "peaceful nuclear device" in 1974. China was instrumental in the development of Pakistan's nuclear weapons and ballistic missile programs, and is believed to have assisted in the early stages of the North Korean nuclear and missile programs as well. Taiwan allegedly began a nuclear weapons program in 1964 that was terminated in 1988, and South Korea began a nuclear weapons program in the early 1970s but abandoned the effort by the end of that decade.[3]

However, with the end of the Cold War, the demise of the bipolar international structure and its concomitant set of "patron-client" relations, and the advent of increased regional rivalries and uncertainties, nuclear and other WMD proliferation—both in terms of state-to-state or horizontal proliferation and in terms of national or vertical proliferation—became a far greater concern globally and in Asia in particular.

China-Pakistan

China's most intensive military-technical relationship is with Pakistan. It dates back to the mid-1960s and China's efforts to bolster Pakistan to counterbalance India in South Asia.[4] For 40 years, China has helped maintain Pakistan's military capability through conventional exports of aircraft, armor and artillery, and naval vessels, through the provision of expertise, technical assistance, and development of indigenous weapons production facilities, and through critical support for Pakistan's nuclear weapon and ballistic missile programs.

China is long suspected of assisting Pakistan's development of nuclear weapons, particularly in the 1970s and 1980s. Since China joined the Nuclear Nonproliferation Treaty (NPT) in 1992, the scope and nature of its support to Pakistan's bomb program became less clear. However, according to U.S. intelligence sources, China "provided extensive support in the past to Islamabad's nuclear weapons ... programs."[5] Such assistance may have included acquisition of highly enriched uranium (HEU), assistance in HEU production, and confirmation of Pakistani nuclear weapons designs. For example, it is reported China assisted Pakistan in the construction of a 50- to 70-megawatt plutonium production reactor at Khushab, including the provision of a specialized furnace and advanced diagnostic equipment. In addition, China reportedly also assisted Pakistan in the construction of its reprocessing facility at Chasma, which in combination with the Khushab facility would provide Pakistan with weapons-grade plutonium.

It is widely-known that China has provided extensive assistance to ostensibly civilian nuclear power programs, and the two countries signed a peaceful nuclear cooperation agreement in September 1986 to govern joint design, construction, and operation of uranium enrichment facilities and nuclear reactors. While some of Pakistan's nuclear facilities are under international safeguards, many are not, and analysts express concern that China's civil nuclear cooperation with Pakistan could provide cover for assistance to Pakistan's nuclear weapons program. However, it also should be noted that while China's nuclear-related assistance to Pakistan has been extensive, the Pakistani weapons program benefited enormously from European technology as well: the unsafeguarded Kahuta facility, at the heart of the Pakistani weapons program, includes critical centrifuge technology for uranium enrichment based on Urenco designs stolen from the Netherlands that were instrumental in the development of the Pakistani bomb.[6]

In early 1996, it was reported that Chinese exporters supplied the Kahuta nuclear research laboratory with 5,000 ring magnets—important components for building the high-speed centrifuges necessary to enrich uranium for nuclear weapons use. In response, the United States suspended Export-Import Bank loans to China, and threatened further sanctions. Following intensive negotiations between the United States and China in April 1996, the Chinese publicly pledged in May 1996 they would no longer provide any nuclear assistance to unsafeguarded nuclear facilities, such as those in Pakistan. Moreover, China's September 1997 public regulations on nuclear-related export controls state that exports to unsafeguarded nuclear facilities are prohibited.[7]

Regarding ballistic missile cooperation, Sino-Pakistani relations are likewise intensive and, in some cases, continuing. Beginning in the mid-1980s, China held discussions with a number of countries—including Syria, Libya, Iran, and Pakistan—to sell its new made-for-export M-series ballistic missiles. Pakistan was apparently most interested in the shorter range M-11 variant, a land-mobile, solid-fueled missile with a range of about 300 km. With a potential payload capacity of approximately 500 kg or more, it is believed that the missile is capable of carrying a basic single-warhead nuclear device. By 1991, China had transferred a training missile and launcher, and had shipped 34 M-11 missiles by the end of 1992. However, from the mid-1990s onward, China engaged in extensive cooperation in support of Pakistan's indigenous missile development program. These latter transfers, involving technologies, components, designs, production lines, and the provision of other dual-use assistance—as opposed to the outright transfer of complete missile systems—have helped Pakistan develop its own missile development and production capacity.[8]

Since the early 1990s—in May 1991, August 1993, and September 2001—the United States levied sanctions against China for ballistic missile-related transfers to Pakistan. China has often issued various pledges to curtail such cooperation with Pakistan, including written assurances to the United States in February 1992 that it would abide by the basic guidelines and parameters of the Missile Technology Control Regime (MTCR), and a public statement during the U.S.-China summit of June 1998 that it would "prevent the export of equipment, materials, or technology that could in any way assist programs in India or Pakistan for nuclear weapons or for ballistic missiles capable of delivering such weapons ...."[9] In a November 2000 agreement between the United States and China, Washington agreed to waive economic sanctions against China for "past assistance" to missile programs in Pakistan (and in Iran) in return for halting missile-related transfers and strengthening its export controls.

Nevertheless, in spite of repeated pledges from Beijing about stemming nuclear- and missile-related cooperation with Pakistan, according to U.S. intelligence sources some activities apparently continue. For example, in 2002 and again in 2003, the CIA reported that it "cannot rule out" continued contacts between Chinese entities and elements of Pakistan's nuclear weapons program.[10] In a September 2001 report, the CIA stated:

> With Chinese assistance, Pakistan is moving toward serial production of solid-propellant SRBMs [short-range ballistic missiles], such as the Shaheen-I and Haider-I. Pakistan flight-tested the Shaheen-I in 1999 and plans to flight-test the Haider-I in 2001. Successful development of the two-stage Shaheen-II MRBM [medium-range ballistic missile] will require continued Chinese assistance or assistance from other potential sources.[11]

China's assistance to Pakistan's solid-fuel ballistic missile program was again seen in October 2002 with another flight test of the Shaheen-1 ballistic missile. The CIA's April 2003 report on proliferation further confirmed these findings, and stated that Pakistan would likely require further assistance from Chinese entities to support its solid-fuel medium-range ballistic missile program.[12]

China-Iran

China's military-technical relationship with Iran dates back at least to 1981–82, when, motivated by a mix of strategic, political, and economic aims, China began providing an array of conventional weapons to the newly-established Islamic republic.[13] However, the most controversial Chinese arms transfers to Iran have taken place since the early to mid-1990s, and continue today. They involve more advanced conventional systems—such as anti-ship cruise missiles—and particularly Chinese assistance which can be applied to the development of Iranian WMD and their delivery vehicles, such as ballistic missiles.

Since the beginning of nuclear-related cooperation between the two countries in 1992, China and Iran insist that such assistance is entirely consistent with the provisions of Article 4 of the NPT, which allows for peaceful nuclear cooperation, and that, in any event, Iranian nuclear facilities are under International Atomic Energy Agency (IAEA) safeguards. Until recently, based on its full-scope safeguards agreement with Iran, the IAEA found that Iran was in full compliance with its obligations as a member of the NPT. However, revelations over the past year of clandestine Iranian activities, and Tehran's reluctance to sign on to additional IAEA protocols to allow more intrusive inspections of Iran's nuclear facilities, cast new and troubling doubts on Iran's nonproliferation commitments and raise disturbing concerns about nuclear-related cooperation with the country. The United States since the mid-1990s has strongly pressured China to end its nuclear-related cooperation with Iran, an effort which has yielded some results. Most important was China's pledge in 1997 to halt all new nuclear-related cooperation with Iran. However, prior to this agreement, China allegedly provided Iran with a range of nuclear-related assistance, including cooperation in uranium mining, uranium enrichment and conversion technologies, production facility blueprints, and technical training and assistance.[14]

Chinese entities allegedly provide materials and assistance which can be applied to Iran's ballistic missile and chemical weapons programs as well. The United States has levelled sanctions against China for missile- and chemical-related transfers. In 1997, pursuant to the Chemical and Biological Weapons Control and Warfare Elimination Act, Washington imposed sanctions on five Chinese citizens, two Chinese companies, and a Hong Kong company for exporting commodities—such as dual-use chemical precursors and chemical production equipment and technology—"for knowingly and materially contributing to Iran's chemical weapons program."[15] U.S. sanctions against Chinese entities for chemical weapons related transfers were levied again in June 2001, January 2002, May 2002, and July 2002.[16]

Sino-Iranian missile-related cooperation is even more complex and lengthy, dating back to the mid-1980s and Silkworm anti-ship missile transfers. As part of the 1997 Sino-U.S. summit, Beijing agreed to halt all future anti-ship missile cooperation with Iran, but prior assistance had been considerable, including the transfer of China's C-801 and C-802 anti-ship missiles, which could be fired from ships and from aircraft. With regard to ballistic missile-related transfers, while it appears China has not provided complete systems to Iran, it has provided other, less obvious forms of assistance, including missile-related expertise, technology, and production equipment and facilities. For example, some observers determined that missile-related cooperation was included in the January 1990 Sino-Iranian 10-year memorandum of understanding on military-technical assistance, and in a $4.5 billion arms trade deal between Beijing and Tehran in 1996.[17] A 1995 CIA report leaked to the press found that in 1994–95, China had transferred dozens, and possibly hundreds, of missile guidance systems and computerized machine tools destined for Iran's indigenous missile development programs.[18] Another leaked CIA report stated that the China Precision Machinery Import & Export Corporation, the trading arm of the China Aerospace Corporation, sold Iran missile technology and components, specifically gyroscopes, accelerometers, and test equipment.[19] However, the aforementioned November 2000 agreement between the United States and China agreed to waive economic sanctions against China for "past assistance" to missile programs in Iran in return for halting missile-related transfers and strengthening export controls. Nevertheless, in May and July 2002, and again in May 2003 and July 2003, the U.S. government levied sanctions against Chinese firms, in part over concerns of missile-related transfers from China to Iran.[20]

In spite of official pledges from Beijing, concerns persist that nuclear-, missile-, and chemical-related assistance to Iran continues. In January 2002, the CIA reported that it was "aware of some interactions between Chinese and Iranian entities that have raised questions about [Beijing's] 'no new nuclear cooperation' pledge"[21]; in 2003 it reported concern that "some interactions between Chinese and Iranian entities may run counter to Beijing's expressed bilateral commitments to the United States."[22] China—along with Russia and North Korea—has been cited by U.S. intelligence reports as providing "the largest amount of ballistic missile-related goods, technology and expertise to Iran" and that it "continued to supply crucial ballistic missile-related equipment, technology, and expertise to Iran."[23] In April 2003, the CIA stated that "Chinese firms still provide dual-use chemical weapons-related equipment and technology to Iran."[24]

China-North Korea

China has also provided extensive military-technical assistance to North Korea, though the level and sophistication of that assistance has apparently been curtailed in recent years. China was most active in providing weapons and military assistance to North Korea from the mid-1950s to the mid-1980s, when it sent hundreds of artillery pieces and armored vehicles, hundreds of fighter jets (mostly Soviet MiG-15s and China's version of the

MiG-19, the J-6), and more than 50 coastal patrol and minesweeping ships.[25] Some reporting suggests that low-level provision of conventional weapons and military supplies continued into the late 1990s.[26]

Of greater concern is the China-North Korea connection regarding the latter's development of missiles and nuclear weapons, and subsequent exports of these technologies to third parties. China and North Korea cooperated from the mid-1950s to the mid-1970s on nuclear-related technology programs, including a September 1959 joint cooperation agreement for civil nuclear development, and the exchange of nuclear and missile engineers and scientists through the 1970s. However, it remains unclear whether China made further contributions to North Korea's nuclear program more recently. Current U.S. open source intelligence reporting does not cite Chinese nuclear-related cooperation with North Korea.[27] However, numerous reports suggest that China made an indirect contribution to the North Korean nuclear weapons program through Beijing's assistance to Pakistan's nuclear program in terms of uranium enrichment, which Pakistan in turn helped North Korea develop (see below for more details on the North Korea-Pakistan connection).[28] Since North Korea's revelations of a nuclear weapons program in October 2002 and assertions about the possession of nuclear weapons in May 2003, Chinese leaders have issued highly-public statements insisting that the Korean Peninsula should be free of nuclear weapons.[29]

China was also active in assisting the North Korean missile development program through the late 1970s. According to U.S. intelligence sources, some Chinese entities continue to provide North Korea with dual-use technologies and components that could be applied to Pyongyang's missile program. Some of the most important sets of transfers from China were reportedly the early 1970s shipments of HY-1 anti-ship missiles and HQ-2 missiles (the HQ-2 being Soviet-designed surface-to-air missiles of 1950s vintage) which, with Chinese assistance, North Korea was able to utilize in the development of its ballistic missile programs. China also teamed up with North Korean scientists in the early stages of developing the Chinese DF-61, a liquid-propelled ballistic missile with a range of approximately 600 km; this program was apparently terminated, along with further direct ballistic missile-related cooperation between China and North Korea, in 1978. According to a number of reports, Chinese assistance continued to North Korea through the 1980s, including the provision of design and metallurgical assistance, as well as of propulsion and guidance systems.[30]

In the late 1990s, the involvement of Chinese entities in North Korea's ballistic missile programs apparently continued, though perhaps without the full authorization of the Chinese government. In some cases, according to leaked U.S. intelligence information, China assisted North Korea's satellite launch programs, support which could be applied to ballistic missile development.[31] Other reports have noted Chinese firms providing North Korean counterparts with specialty steels as well as guidance components, such as gyroscopes, for Pyongyang's missile programs.[32] In addition, it is possible that Chinese missile specialists believed to be assisting indigenous missile development in Pakistan and Iran have some professional interactions with North Korean specialists also working in those countries, potentially passing on knowledge which could be applied to North Korean missile development. To date, while the United States has issued démarches and urged Beijing to cut off missile-related trade with North Korea, no sanctions have been imposed against China or Chinese entities by Washington. In 2001, during a U.S. congressional delegation visit, Chinese President Jiang Zemin reportedly told Senate Foreign Relations Committee Chairman Joseph Biden that China would not provide any assistance to North Korea's missile development program.[33] However, according to a 2003 report on global proliferation, the CIA reported that "firms in China have provided dual-use missile-related items, raw materials, and/or assistance to several other countries of proliferation concern such as Iran, Libya, and to a lesser extent, North Korea."[34]

Russian Transfers

Russia is another major supplier of sensitive technologies to recipients across Asia, including Iran, India, China, and possibly North Korea. Russian nuclear-related transfers to Iran have been a particular concern to the United States, and an increasingly contentious issue in Moscow-Washington relations. While Iran is a member in good standing with the IAEA, concerns persist, particularly in the United States, that it is not fully disclosing the extent of nuclear development activities, and may be using its civilian nuclear energy program—including its cooperation with Russia—as a cover to acquire technologies, materials, expertise, and an indigenous infrastructure of use in a weapons program. Russian assistance takes place at a time of other worrying developments inside Iran's nuclear complex. For example, Tehran's announced intention in early 2003 to close its fuel cycle by developing its own capacity to mine uranium and process spent fuel spurred concerns that Iran would use this capability to produce weapons-grade uranium. Under its agreement with Moscow for the Bushehr light water reactor, Russia is to build and supply the fuel for the facility, and Iran was to return the spent fuel to Russia. Becoming self-sufficient in its fuel cycle could allow Iran to ultimately forego foreign assistance, thereby circumventing obligations that such assistance be open to monitoring and verification by the IAEA. In addition, the discovery and subsequent March 2003 inspection by the IAEA of a previously undisclosed uranium enrichment facility at Natanz and a heavy water product plant at Arak, provides further evidence pointing to Iran's intention to build the means to produce weapons-grade material.[35]

Russian assistance to Iran in the form of constructing light water reactors for civilian energy, providing the fuel to run them, and offering technical training and assistance to Iranian nuclear scientists and engineers are at the center of U.S. concerns about Russian-Iranian nuclear-related cooperation. In spite of intense U.S. pressure for Russia to drop the deal, Moscow and Tehran appear likely to complete the Bushehr facility. In addition, owing to Russia's poor economic conditions, concerns persist that Russian entities and individuals, including scientists from Russia's nuclear complex and universities, may be providing clandestine assistance to Iranian nuclear-related programs. However, the 2003 revelations of Iran's secretive nuclear development programs and its reluctance to sign additional IAEA protocols for more intrusive inspections of its nuclear facilities may stop overt cooperation with Russia until these concerns can be resolved.

Russia reportedly also provides various forms of assistance to Iran's ballistic missile program, particularly with regard to Iran's indigenous Shehab-3 and derivative, longer-range systems. In addition, Russia is a major supplier of conventional weapons and technologies to Iran, including tanks, armored vehicles, air-to-air missiles, and ships.[36] According to U.S. intelligence reporting, Russia envisions a potentially lucrative conventional arms market in Iran in the years ahead, especially for the sale of advanced combat aircraft, and expects Iran to become its third-largest recipient of conventional weapons after China and India.[37]

Similarly, Russia is a major supplier of sensitive technologies and conventional weapons to India and China. Russia provides assistance in the development of India's civil nuclear program and is a key supplier of dual-use equipment and technology for Indian ballistic and cruise missile development. Some of Russia's most important contributions to Indian missile-related programs have been in the form of guidance and propulsion. For example, the Indian satellite launch program utilizes some Russian propulsion systems, such as the Russian cyrogenic stage engine used to place India's GSAT-1 in orbit in April 2001.[38] This work in assisting Indian space launch capabilities will have readily applicable spin-on effects for Indian intercontinental ballistic missile (ICBM) development in the future. Russian specialists have also worked closely with Indian counterparts in the joint development and testing of the 280 km-range, supersonic Brahmos cruise missile, capable of being launched from ships, submarines, and aircraft. Russia is India's most important supplier of advanced conventional weapons, having provided a wide range of systems: Su-30 combat aircraft, air-to-air missiles, surface-to-air missiles, Ka-31 attack helicopters, Tu-22 bombers, large-caliber artillery systems, Kilo-class submarines, anti-ship missiles, and frigates. Moscow and New Delhi are also reportedly negotiating the possible transfer of nuclear submarines and an aircraft carrier as well. Through licensed production arrangements—such as for the Su-30 combat aircraft, MiG-21 upgrades, T-72 and T-90 battle tanks, anti-tank missiles, and fast-attack craft—Russia also assists in improving India's indigenous defense production capacity.[39]

Russia also provides assistance to China's civil nuclear development. As with several other countries, including the United States, China has reached a peaceful nuclear cooperation agreement with Russia which envisions the construction of two Russian 1,000-megawatt pressurized water reactors for electricity generation. The two countries finalized a contract in December 1997 to build Lianyungang-1 and -2 nuclear power plants in Jiangsu—they are expected to come on-line in 2004 and 2005—with the possibility that Russia will win follow-on contracts to help build more nuclear reactors. The Soviet Union was instrumental in the early stages of China's nuclear weapons program, including the provision of equipment and technology to produce weapons-grade uranium in the mid-1950s, and an agreement to provide a sample weapon and production data in 1957. However, as the Sino-Soviet rift grew wider, Moscow chose not to provide bombs or bomb designs and refused to provide further assistance to China's bomb program from 1959, precipitating the bitter break-up of the two communist neighbors in 1960.[40]

Similarly, Russia was instrumental in the early development of Chinese ballistic missiles, but the Sino-Soviet split halted further cooperation from about 1960 until the early 1990s. Having received a Soviet R-2 missile in 1958, China nonetheless was able to reverse engineer the missile and move forward in the development of an indigenous ballistic missile production capability.[41] Today, 40 years later, Russian scientists and specialists are reportedly working with Chinese counterparts in the development of China's space-launch and ballistic missile programs. In addition, since the early to mid-1990s, Russia became China's most important supplier of advanced conventional weapons, including transfers of Su-27 and Su-30 combat aircraft, transport aircraft, attack and transport helicopters, air-to-air missiles, surface-to-air missiles, anti-ship missiles, Kilo-class submarines, and Sovremenny class destroyers, and production licenses for China's assembly of Su-27 fighters.[42]

Overall, since the collapse of the Soviet Union and continuing difficult economic conditions in Russia, considerable concerns persist that sensitive materials, technologies, and knowledge have and will continue to leak from Russia. These types of transfers include those undertaken on a state-to-state basis with government knowledge, such as Russia-Iran cooperation, or, most troubling, as a result of clandestine operations or theft at cash-strapped and crumbling Russian nuclear, aerospace, biological, and chemical facilities. Russia is believed to have stockpiles of as much as 1,365 metric tons of weapons-equivalent HEU, 156 metric tons of military-use plutonium, and thousands of tons of chemical weapons agents and biotoxins, not to mention thousands of out-of-work weaponeers.[43] This kind of material and expertise is in high demand globally and across Asia among states and sub-state organizations seeking to procure and deploy WMD.

The North Korea Connection

Over the course of the 1990s and the early 2000s, North Korea has become a far greater proliferation concern, both in terms of providing various forms of nuclear- and missile-related assistance to countries in North Africa, the Middle East, and South Asia, and as a conduit for technologies and systems apparently originating in China. (North Korea's indigenous nuclear and missile development program is discussed below). Of major concern for Asian security are North Korea's programs of military-technical cooperation with Pakistan and Iran.

The case of North Korean-Pakistani cooperation is especially disquieting and complex. By the late 1990s, it became increasingly clear that what may have started as a basic supplier-recipient relationship, with North Korea assisting Pakistan in the development of liquid-fueled missiles, based on the North Korean Nodong missile, became a two-way street, with Pakistan assisting Pyongyang's clandestine bomb program utilizing uranium enrichment technology (the same method Islamabad developed, with Chinese assistance, for its bomb program). The North Korea-Pakistan missile connection began as early as 1991 when Islamabad sought assistance from North Korea (and China) to counter the recent test-firing of the Indian Agni missile. This cooperation included the shipment of North Korean Nodong missiles, with a range of approximately 1,500 km, and eventually led to tests of the Pakistani Ghauri missile in April 1998 and again in April 1999.[44] In June 1999, the North Korea-Pakistan missile connection was openly revealed when Indian vessels detained a North Korean ship bound for Pakistan, that was carrying 148 crates of heavy machinery, guidance systems, blueprints, and other equipment intended for manufacturing and deploying the Hwaesong-5 (Scud-B) and Hwaesong-6 (Scud-C) short-range, liquid-fueled ballistic missiles.[45] According to U.S. intelligence sources, Pyongyang continues to provide significant amounts of ballistic missile-related technologies to Pakistan, including equipment, components, materials, and expertise.[46]

In return for North Korean missile-related assistance, Pakistan began providing nuclear assistance to North Korea, probably around 1997. Pakistan's assistance went toward the North Korean uranium enrichment program, which it undertook clandestinely while at the same time apparently abiding by a freeze of its plutonium-based program in accordance with the 1994 U.S.-North Korea agreed framework. In particular, it is believed Pakistan provided North Korea with equipment and technical assistance—such as frequent visits to North Korea by A. Q. Khan, the "father" of the Pakistan bomb program, as well as other working-level exchanges—and including the provision of high-speed centrifuges for uranium enrichment. It is not known how many centrifuges were transferred. However, U.S. intelligence assessments state that North Korea's uranium enrichment program aims to achieve a fully operational capacity to "produce enough weapons-grade uranium for two or more nuclear weapons per year"[47]. In addition, some analysts note that North Korean scientists were present for the Pakistani nuclear weapons tests in May 1998 and that North Korea has acquired designs of Pakistan's uranium-triggered weapons.[48]

North Korea is also known to have cooperated with Iran in the development of Iran's missile programs. However, it is unclear whether Iran has received assistance from North Korea with an eye to developing nuclear weapons. In the late 1980s, following U.S. pressure on China to halt its HY-2 "Silkworm" anti-ship missile sales to Iran, it appears Tehran may have turned to North Korea as a third-party conduit for the missile transfers, as well as for ballistic missiles such as Scud-Bs and Scud-Cs.[49] Since that time, North Korea has also shipped the 1,300 km-range Nodong missile to Iran, and made other significant contributions to the Iranian missile program, including the provision of equipment, technology, and expertise, allowing Iran to develop an increasingly capable indigenous ballistic missile production capacity: the Iranian missiles Shehab-1, Shehab-2, and Shehab-3 are believed to be based on the North Korean Scud-B, Scud-C, and Nodong missiles, respectively. The United States has repeatedly levied sanctions against a North Korean company, the Changgwang Siyong Company, for missile-related exports to Iran, most recently in July 2003.[50]

By mid-2003, the U.S. intelligence community estimated that Iran now has hundreds of the shorter-range Shehab-1s and -2s, and is in the later stages of deploying some of the medium-range Shehab-3. The Shehab-3 has been tested a number of times in recent years—in July 1998, February 2000, September 2000, and June 2003—but Iran has met with continuing difficulties in perfecting the liquid-fuel engine technology from North Korea.

With the continued assistance of North Korea (as well as China and Russia), Iran will likely develop missiles with longer ranges, including possibly ICBMs, over the next 10 to 15 years.[51]

National Programs: North Korean Pursuit of Nuclear Weapons

In addition to the question of weapons transfers from one state to another, the development of strategic weapons programs *within* states—sometimes referred to as vertical proliferation—also raises concerns in the region. Not only have several such programs in Asia seen significant strides forward in recent years—in India, Pakistan, China, and North Korea—but these national programs may also spur further proliferation, both horizontal and vertical, as neighboring governments react to changes in their security environment.[52]

North Korean nuclear weapons development raises immediate and serious concerns for Asian security. According to U.S. intelligence, North Korea had produced "one, possibly two" nuclear weapons by the mid-1990s.[53] This assessment did not speculate on whether the North had taken steps to mount these weapons on missiles or otherwise have them in active deployment, and presumed the number to stay low as long as the plutonium production activities at the Yongbyon facility remained frozen in accordance with the 1994 U.S.-North Korea Agreed Framework.

However, by mid-2002, the U.S. intelligence community was increasingly certain that North Korea had undertaken a clandestine nuclear weapons development program utilizing a uranium enrichment process with Pakistani assistance, in particular the provision of centrifuges (see above). During his visit to North Korea in October 2002, Assistant Secretary of State James Kelly informed North Korean counterparts of this intelligence, which they initially denied but acknowledged the following day. In response, Washington in November 2002 announced that it would cut off heavy fuel oil shipments to North Korea, one of the United States' principal commitments to the 1994 Agreed Framework in order to secure the freeze on activities at the Yongbyon facility and allow for international inspections and monitoring at North Korean nuclear sites. A month later, in mid-December 2002, Pyongyang announced it would restart the Yongbyon reactor, ostensibly for electricity production in light of the heavy fuel oil cut-off. It then broke the monitoring seals and shut off monitoring cameras at the facility, and by the end of the month ousted remaining IAEA inspectors.

On January 10, 2003, citing a "grave situation where the national sovereignty and supreme interests of the state are most seriously threatened" by a hostile United States, the North Korean government announced its immediate withdrawal from the NPT and its obligations under Article 3 of the treaty to allow inspections of its nuclear facilities.[54] The statement also declared North Korea has "no intention to produce nuclear weapons and our nuclear activities at this stage will be confined only to peaceful purposes such as the production of electricity," and that it would consider arranging a separate verification regime with the United States when Washington stops its "hostile policy" and "nuclear threat."[55] On April 23, 2003, during talks held in Beijing between the United States, China, and North Korea, North Korean Deputy Foreign Minister Li Gun told his U.S. counterparts that North Korea has nuclear weapons and threatened to prove their existence or possibly export them.[56] Up until that point, the North Koreans had never admitted to possessing nuclear weapons. In addition, Li Gun stated that North Korea had completed reprocessing the 8,000 spent fuel rods, which had been stored in cans in a cooling pond awaiting removal from North Korea as envisioned by the Agreed Framework. In a further step to shed what remained of its nonproliferation commitments, in May 2003, North Korea announced that it was also withdrawing from the "Joint Declaration of the Denuclearization of the Korean Peninsula" which it had reached with South Korea in January 1992, and in which the two sides pledged they "shall not test, manufacture, produce, receive, possess, store, deploy or use nuclear weapons."[57] A July 2003 report, citing U.S. intelligence officials, revealed that North Korea has begun developing technologies to permit the operational deployment of a small nuclear warhead atop North Korean missiles.[58]

By mid-2003, the North Koreans were believed to have at least one or two nuclear weapons. It was unclear whether the North had actually reprocessed the 8,000 spent fuel rods into plutonium (such a step presumably would have been detected by U.S. intelligence), but if that process was in train, North Korea could probably produce four to six weapons utilizing this material. A report in July 2003 stated that U.S. intelligence briefings to allies claimed that the North Koreans may have experienced technical difficulties in restarting the reprocessing program, and in a "worst case" assessment, perhaps only a "few hundred" of the 8,000 fuel rods had been reprocessed (some 1,000 to 1,500 rods would be needed to produce a weapon, according to the report).[59]

Less clear was the status of the HEU program. Because this program is more difficult to detect and monitor by intelligence and surveillance technologies, it is unclear whether gas centrifuge separation has begun, and where the program stands in its evolution toward a nuclear weapon. In remarks before the Senate Foreign Relations Committee in March 2003, Assistant Secretary Kelly stated that should North Korea begin reprocessing its spent nuclear fuel rods into plutonium it would have "significant" amounts within six months; he added that North Korea's alternate HEU capability "is not so far behind."[60] U.S. intelligence sources assess that North Korea's intention is to build a uranium enrichment capacity to "produce enough weapons-grade uranium for two or more nuclear weapons per year when fully operational."[61]

These developments strongly suggest that North Korea is doing more than bluffing in an attempt to extract further concessions. Instead, they are strong indicators of the North's serious commitment to become and remain a declared nuclear weapons state no matter what package of incentives and disincentives might be broached by the United States and the international community. Its dogged pursuit of ballistic missiles that can range as far afield as Japan, Alaska, and, over the longer term, could be developed to reach as far as the continental United States, suggests the North Korean intention to mate nuclear weapons with what would otherwise be relatively ineffective weapons.[62]

(In)efficacy of Global, Regional, and National Responses

Given the record of proliferation in Asia and its motivating factors, what measures are in place to stem emergent proliferation challenges? Unfortunately, while the global nonproliferation regime can point to many successes around the world, recent years have dealt it a number of setbacks, especially in Asia.

To begin, Asian participation in and adherence to the major international nonproliferation agreements and regimes is spotty at best. Table 1 provides basic information about Asian participation in nine major international and multilateral nonproliferation agreements and regimes. While participation in the Biological and Toxic Weapons Convention and the Chemical Weapons Convention is widespread in Asia, participation in nuclear-weapons related treaties is less so. Critically, key countries of proliferation concern such as India, Pakistan, and North Korea, are not members of the NPT or the CTBT. China joined the NPT in 1992, but was a staunch and non-adhering critic of the treaty prior to that time. In some cases, the lack of Asian participation in international treaties has repercussions beyond the region itself: in order for the CTBT to come into effect, for example, it must be signed and ratified by 44 specific countries possessing nuclear reactors, including some states which have neither signed nor ratified the treaty and are unlikely to do so in the foreseeable future (including India, North Korea, and Pakistan), or which have not ratified the treaty and will probably not do so in the foreseeable future (such as

Table 1. Participation in Nonproliferation Regimes

	Participation in Nonproliferation Regimes (May 1, 2003)								
	NPT	CTBT	CWC	BTWC	Aust	NSG	Zang	MTCR	Wass[a]
Afghanistan	✓		(✓)	✓					
Australia	✓	✓	✓	✓	✓	✓	✓	✓	✓
Bangladesh	✓	✓	✓	✓					
Bhutan	✓		(✓)	✓					
Brunei	✓	(✓)	✓	✓					
Burma	✓	(✓)	(✓)	(✓)					
Cambodia	✓	✓	(✓)	✓					
Canada	✓	✓	✓	✓	✓	✓	✓	✓	✓
China	✓	(✓)	✓	✓			✓		
India			✓	✓					
Indonesia	✓	(✓)	✓	✓					
Iran	✓	(✓)	✓	✓					
Japan	✓	✓	✓	✓	✓	✓	✓	✓	✓
Kazakhstan	✓	✓	✓						
Kyrgyzstan	✓	(✓)	(✓)						
Laos	✓	✓	✓	✓					
Malaysia	✓	(✓)	✓	✓					
Mongolia	✓	✓	✓	✓					
Nepal	✓	(✓)	✓	(✓)					
New Zealand	✓	✓	✓	✓	✓	✓		✓	✓
North Korea	( )[b]			✓					
Pakistan			✓	✓					
Papua New Guinea	✓	(✓)	✓	✓					
Philippines	✓	✓	✓	✓					
Russia	✓	✓	✓	✓		✓	✓	✓	✓
Singapore	✓	✓	✓	✓					
South Korea	✓	✓	✓	✓	✓	✓	✓	✓	✓
Sri Lanka	✓	(✓)	✓	✓					
Tajikistan	✓	✓	✓						
Thailand	✓	(✓)	✓	✓					
Turkmenistan	✓	✓	✓	✓					
United States	✓	(✓)	✓	✓	✓	✓	✓	✓	✓
Uzbekistan	✓	✓	✓	✓					
Vietnam	✓	(✓)	✓	✓					

Countries in the table are all those in Strategic Asia plus Iran; ✓ denotes that a country has ratified the treaty or is a member of the agreement; (✓) denotes that a country has signed but not ratified the treaty. Sources: United Nations, <http://disarmament.un.org/treatystatus.nsf>; *SIPRI Yearbook 2002: Armaments, Disarmament, and International Security*. Notes: a) NPT = Nuclear Nonproliferation Treaty, CTBT = Comprehensive Test Ban Treaty, CWC = Chemical Weapons Convention, BTWC=Biological and Toxin Weapons Convention, Aust=Australia Group, NSG=Nuclear Suppliers Group, Zang=Zangger Committee, MTCR=Missile Technology Control Regime, Wass=Wassenaar Arrangement; b) North Korea announced its withdrawal from the NPT on January 10, 2003, which, according to the treaty, would become effective April 10, 2003.

China, Iran, and the United States). As countries openly possessing, believed to possess, or believed to be pursuing nuclear weapons, their lack of participation undermines the credibility and long-term viability of the regime. Similarly, without the full participation and compliance of certain Asian states in the NPT, such as India, Iran, Pakistan, and North Korea, the treaty is weakened. The success of both Iraq in the 1980s and North Korea in the 1990s to defer and evade inspection and detection of their nuclear weapons programs, even while members of the NPT and its inspection regime under the IAEA, further undermines the treaty's credibility in preventing the spread of nuclear weapons.

The lack of Asian participation is even more apparent for certain smaller, multilateral, export control regimes such as the Australia Group (concerning biological- and chemical-related exports), the Nuclear Suppliers Group (concerning nuclear-related exports), the Zangger Committee (also nuclear-related), the MTCR (concerning missile-related exports), and the Wassenaar Arrangement (concerned with conventional weapons-related exports) (see Table 1). Membership in these organizations is not open to all countries and is more strictly regulated by the regime members, which are predominantly Western, democratic, and industrialized nations. Some important recent exceptions include China's decision to join the Zangger Committee in 1997 and South Korea's membership in the MTCR effective in 2001. Overall, however, the lack of participation in such export control regimes is a striking indicator of how far active Asian participation in international, multilateral nonproliferation regimes has yet to go.

In addition, Asia does not have effective region-based mechanisms which draw together major regional powers to address intraregional proliferation concerns. The Southeast Asia Nuclear Weapon Free Zone (SEA-NWFZ, established by the Treaty of Bangkok), which includes the 10 states of the Association of Southeast Asian Nations (ASEAN) as full members, obligates the parties, *inter alia,* not to "develop, manufacture, or otherwise acquire, possess or have control over nuclear weapons." However, none of the nuclear weapon states or any other country, have signed the treaty's protocols.[63] The ASEAN Regional Forum (ARF), the most comprehensive and inclusive region-based, security-oriented organization, remains slow to take up sensitive issues such as weapons proliferation in any meaningful way, and is at the earliest stages of helping foster a more stable and confident security environment which might dampen the demand for WMD in Asia (see the chapter on security regionalism in Southeast Asia in this volume). Ad hoc efforts banding together regional "coalitions of the willing," such as the Korean Energy Development Organization (KEDO) to address proliferation concerns in North Korea, while initially promising, fell victim to hostilities between the two principal participants in the process—the United States and North Korea—and Pyongyang's unwillingness to abide by its nonproliferation commitments.

Another nonproliferation approach in the region which has been gaining ground is the introduction and implementation of stricter national export controls and stronger nonproliferation norms within countries of concern. Such moves have often come as a result of intense cajoling and pressures by the United States and others, targeting countries such as Russia and China to improve their ability to regulate and monitor their weapons and technology transfers, while accepting a stronger sense of responsibility to stem the spread of WMD. Recent years have seen some promising progress for Russia and China in this regard. The Russian legislature passed new export control regulations in 1999 and President Vladimir Putin took several steps in 2000 and 2001 to strengthen the export control bureaucracy and see that the new export control laws were implemented, including stricter punishments and new control lists for sensitive exports related to missiles, biological and chemical agents, and dual-use technologies.[64] Since the mid-1990s the Chinese government has issued a number of regulations meant to govern China's exports of militarily-relevant products and technologies. These include new and clarified export control regulations and control lists, closely consistent with the practices and control lists of international regimes and agreements, to govern and monitor nuclear, chemical, biological, missile, conventional weapon, and dual-use-related exports.[65] However, while these Russian and Chinese moves are steps in a positive direction, many questions remain about the effectiveness of their implementation and enforcement, though for different reasons. For Russia, continued economic stagnation and lack of resources will challenge the effectiveness of its export control system. With regard to China, the country's economic dynamism and liberalization is outpacing the government's ability to monitor questionable and illegal export activities.

Stepped-up concern on the part of the United States about the nexus between technology proliferation and terrorism highlights another approach which may gain ground in Asia: unilateral action, or U.S.-led employment of incentives and disincentives to deter proliferation or compel adherence to nonproliferation commitments. The U.S.-led military action against Iraq in 2003, which had as one of stated aims the eradication of that country's WMD, can be seen as an example of this coercive approach. The United States has taken other forceful action, or threatened to do so, putting countries such as North Korea and Iran on notice. For example, in December 2002, the United States, in cooperation with Spain, detained—but eventually released—a North Korean ship bound for Yemen that was carrying 15

Scud missiles. Similar U.S. action, including blockades to prevent WMD shipments, may lie in the future. In addition, the Bush administration, like its predecessor, has further stressed the importance of deterrence and counter-proliferation—including the possible use of conventional strategic strike assets, the deployment of effective missile defenses, and even the use of nuclear weapons to destroy WMD under certain narrow circumstances—to dissuade would-be proliferators.

Future Proliferation Challenges for Strategic Asia

Given the ongoing and emergent proliferation channels in Asia and the mechanisms in place to stem them, future proliferation trends for Strategic Asia are not promising. Over the past five years the region has seen the advent of two new *de facto* nuclear powers—India and Pakistan—and the admission by a third, North Korea, that it possesses nuclear weapons and may take action to "demonstrate" the fact. Nuclear-, chemical-, and missile-related proliferation continues, with entities in China, Russia, and North Korea cited as key suppliers to such recipients as Iran, Pakistan, and others in Asia. The case of Pakistani nuclear-related assistance to North Korea demonstrates that Asian states typically considered as "recipients" of WMD will likely take the path of North Korea to transfer such weapons themselves, particularly when strapped for cash and sensing themselves in a dangerous security environment. Reflective of a greater concern with the possibility of terrorist use of WMD, the CIA noted in early 2003 the likelihood that in today's interdependent world the timelines for developing WMD have been dramatically reduced, even for terrorist organizations. The report added "there are growing numbers of knowledgeable individuals or non-state purveyors of WMD-related materials and technology who are able to act outside the constraints of governments [and] are increasingly capable of providing technology and equipment that previously could only be supplied directly by countries with established capabilities."[66] Moreover, these factors for increased proliferation unfold at a time of weakening international nonproliferation mechanisms, in a region where the technical capacity to produce WMD is widespread, where the demand for WMD is on the rise, where powerful security dilemmas persist, and fragile, insecure regimes and regional instabilities dot the strategic landscape.

Looking ahead at this troubling and complex situation over the next two to three years, strategic analysts will need to consider the principal proliferation concerns in terms of their likelihood, their impact on strategic stability, and their amenability to nonproliferation remedies. To begin, it is highly probable that certain relationships of concern will continue in spite of efforts by the United States or the international community. The demand-side and supply-side drivers for proliferation are strong, and effective non-proliferation solutions are not in place to address those motivations. Both Pakistan and China have strong strategic and political reasons for continuing their longstanding military-technical relationship, especially in the area of ballistic missile cooperation, as well as in ostensibly civilian-related nuclear cooperation. Another key, and likely continuing, supplier-recipient relationship involves an economically-motivated Russia as supplier and a strategically concerned Iran in demand of advanced weapons, possibly including WMD-, and particularly nuclear-related, capabilities. The North Korea-Pakistan connection warrants continued close scrutiny, as both parties have strong strategic and economic motivations, as both suppliers and recipients, to continue their relationship.

Perhaps slightly less likely, but of far more immediate concern for regional strategic stability, is the possibility that North Korea will dramatically move forward with the development, deployment, and proliferation of its nuclear and missile arsenal. Such steps could include reprocessing of its spent fuel rods at Yongbyon, accelerating its clandestine uranium enrichment program, lifting its moratorium to test-launch ballistic missiles of increasing range and accuracy, testing a nuclear device, and transferring knowledge, fissile materials, or crude radiological or nuclear weapons to other states or terrorist organizations. North Korea spoke in the strongest terms of its strategic motivations behind its programs, and clearly has powerful political and economic incentives to build its arsenal further and transfer parts of it abroad. To back up words with action, Pyongyang admitted to its uranium enrichment program, ousted U.N. inspectors, disabled monitoring devices, and restarted activities at Yongbyon, and claimed to have demonstrable nuclear weapons capability. These steps all strongly indicate North Korea's intention to become an open nuclear-weapons state.

Similarly, Iran also presents increased concerns about its nuclear intentions, concerns which gathered pace over 2002 and 2003. Tehran claims to have strong strategic and political motivations to go down the nuclear weapons path, if need be—citing its antagonistic relationship with the nuclear-armed United States and Israel, its traditional role as a major regional power, and having been the target of WMD attack in the past. Moreover, revelations of previously undisclosed nuclear sites (particularly the gas centrifuge uranium enrichment facility at Natanz), indications of interest in closing its nuclear fuel cycle, and an unwillingness to accept additional IAEA protocols for more intrusive inspections of suspect sites, raise further suspicions that Iran may be pursuing nuclear weapons.

Concerns over North Korean and Iranian nuclear weapons programs are often closely associated with another proliferation possibility for the future: terrorist use of radiation dispersal weapons (so-called "dirty bombs") or even nuclear weapons. While the likelihood of such an event is difficult to gauge, the continuing availability and dissemination of technology, fissile materials, expertise, and ever-prevalent strategic, political, and economic motivations means that it is a danger of immediate and increasing concern for the years ahead. In speaking of an "axis of evil" and "outlaw states" President Bush drew attention to the possibility of states such as Iran and North Korea providing WMD to terrorist organizations. It may be true these states possess both the means and the motive to do so. But it is also true that terrorist organizations can acquire such devastating capabilities—and are certainly seeking to do so—from a range of sources, "rogue" or otherwise, by engaging in bribery, theft, smuggling, as well as less-illicit methods. Moreover, while terrorist use of WMD stands out as the most horrific scenario, considerable loss of life and economic havoc can be created by simpler means widely available in Central and South Asia: shoulder-fired missiles.

Another proliferation challenge in Asia for the medium- to longer-term concerns Japan, South Korea, and Taiwan. While it appears highly unlikely these governments would move down the WMD path, this situation could change under certain circumstances. All three possess the technical means to develop and deliver nuclear, chemical, and biological weapons. As noted above, South Korea and Taiwan pursued nuclear weapons programs—Taiwan from 1964 to 1988, and South Korea in the early 1970s—but both dropped these programs under U.S. pressure. South Korea and Taiwan also pursued ballistic missile development programs, which have been actively discouraged by the United States. However, a space launch program continues in South Korea, and Taiwan is conducting ongoing research on ballistic missiles. In joining the Chemical Weapons Convention in 1997, South Korea acknowledged having an offensive chemical weapons program; Taiwan has denied having offensive chemical or biological weapons (CBW) programs, but has revealed a small-scale CBW defense program at the Chungshan Institute for Science and Technology, the island's major weapons research facility.[67] Japan, while one of the world's most vocal proponents of arms control, disarmament, and nonproliferation, has some 30 metric tons of spent fuel kept at reprocessing facilities in France and the United Kingdom, as well as 5 to 6 tons stored domestically that it has the capability to reprocess.[68] Japan has also actively developed an indigenous space launch program, demonstrating a ready capacity to develop and deploy long-range ballistic missiles, if Tokyo chooses.

Moreover, in the face of increasing potential threats posed by the nuclear and missile arsenals in China and North Korea, and with increasing doubts as to the reliability of the U.S. policy of extended deterrence, or "nuclear umbrella," recent years have witnessed more frequent discussion in Taiwan and Japan about developing strategic programs such as ballistic missiles and nuclear weapons. As China conducted missile tests off Taiwan in the summer of 1995, then-Taiwanese president Lee Teng-hui said of possibly possessing nuclear weapons, "We should re-study the question from a long-term point of view," and acknowledged that Taiwan has the ability to develop nuclear weapons.[69] In Japan, this once-taboo subject has become more openly addressed, even prompting Chief Cabinet Secretary Yasuo Fukuda to say that "in legal theory" Japan could have ICBMs and atomic bombs and that the country's longstanding non-nuclear principles—prohibiting the manufacture, possession, and introduction of nuclear weapons—could be changed. In distancing himself from, but not fully repudiating these remarks, Prime Minister Koizumi Junichiro said, "A review of the non-nuclear principles depends on the public's opinion and the international situation, but I have no intentions at all."[70] Depending on the future state of Northeast Asian relations, the advent of a nuclear North Korea, and an even more robust and offensively-oriented Chinese nuclear and conventional missile force posture in the East Asian theater, the possibility of strategic weapon responses in places such as Taiwan and Japan further complicate an already difficult set of nonproliferation challenges in the region. South Korea too could move away from its commitment not to manufacture, possess, store, deploy, or use nuclear weapons should the U.S. security guarantee falter and other countries in the region—such as Japan and North Korea—deploy nuclear weapons.

Taking these trends into account suggests that for the present and foreseeable future, the most pressing proliferation problems are those which emanate from a combination of strategic and political demand motivations on the one hand, and economic supply motivations on the other: insecure states—such as Iran, North Korea, and Pakistan—or fervently committed sub-state actors seek WMD systems, technologies and expertise to achieve their strategic and political goals and find willing suppliers in need of cash and other resources.

Conclusion

For the international community and the United States in particular, certain high priority measures are needed to address the most immediate and threatening of these proliferation challenges. However, approaches that are overly-focused on supply-side denial and deterrence cannot be effective in and of themselves, and have thus far not prevented the continued spread of WMD across Strategic Asia. Indeed, in some cases, the combination of supply-side denial and strong threats of embargos, preemption, and other coercive interventions may drive some states to seek and sell WMD all the more to achieve their perceived strategic, political, and economic objectives. As politically difficult as it may be, countries seeking to slow and rollback proliferation must integrate approaches which address the demand side of the nonproliferation equation—that which leads states and non-state actors to seek WMD in the first place. In addition, different proliferation challenges will need to be dealt with on their own terms, eschewing a "one size fits all" approach to stemming proliferation. Importantly, in a globalized world of increased technology diffusion, effective nonproliferation strategies must be multinational and well-coordinated, especially among the most technologically advanced countries.

In the near term, the highest priority must be given to both North Korea and Iran as proliferators. The most effective approach would be a multilateral mixture of both carrots and sticks, which addresses legitimate security concerns of both as a means to diminish their perceived need for WMD, while offering structured economic and diplomatic incentives in return for verifiable moves away from proliferative activities. Likewise, the United States, China, and like-minded partners should exert considerable pressure on Pakistan to squeeze its ongoing proliferation connection with North Korea, while also working to alleviate the security concerns that drive Islamabad's proliferation pursuits in the first place. A part of this approach to Iran, North Korea, and Pakistan demands the mobilization of strong international support, and especially strong and coordinated support amongst the United States and its allies. In this respect, the strongly-worded warnings in May from the G-8 group of leading industrialized nations to Iran and North Korea, and in support of more robust nonproliferation collaboration more generally, were important and much-needed steps which will need to be further strengthened and sustained.[71]

Strong and close coordination amongst international partners and allies will also be needed in order to clearly articulate the gravity and consequences of WMD falling into the hands of terrorist organizations. Such messages need to be conveyed not only to states such as India, Iran, North Korea, and Pakistan, but also to major suppliers such as Russia and China. These messages need to be backed up by serious penalties such as sanctions and the potential use of military action such as interdiction to prevent the transfer of WMD to terrorist organizations. All the while, as a hedging mechanism and a means to help deter proliferation, the United States, its friends, and allies must coordinate efforts in the development of various counterproliferation measures, including missile defenses, improved intelligence technologies and assets, and conventional strike capabilities.

Finally, given the importance of economic "push" factors in driving proliferation in Strategic Asia today, additional resources should be devoted by the United States and like-minded countries to exercise economic levers—such as economic incentives as well as precisely-targeted economic sanctions—to both persuade and dissuade governments and companies, especially in Russia and China, to get out of the proliferation business.

Looking ahead, hopes for stemming and possibly rolling back the proliferation of WMD will involve greater acknowledgement of and good-faith action on demand-side drivers, the good judgment to treat different challenges in different ways, and energizing like-minded states to engage in a more effective and well-coordinated fight to combat the spread of WMD to emergent state and non-state proliferators. At the end of the day, however, in the face of these substantial regional proliferation challenges, these approaches are extremely complex and will require significant and well-orchestrated multinational commitment of political, diplomatic, military, and economic resources—and still may not work. Unfortunately, the region seems to be headed toward a transition from preventing proliferation to confronting its uncertain and potentially dangerous consequences.

Endnotes

[1] For a fuller elaboration of the various proliferation channels involving Asia—Asian and non-Asian alike—consult the extensive databases and country profiles compiled by the Monterey Institute's Center for Nonproliferation Studies and made available on the Nuclear Threat Initiative website <www.nti.org>. See also the chapter on ballistic missiles in the first Strategic Asia volume, Michael Swaine with Loren Runyon, "Ballistic Missiles," in Richard J. Ellings and Aaron L. Friedberg, eds., *Strategic Asia 2001–02: Power and Purpose*, Seattle: The National Bureau of Asian Research, 2001, pp. 299–360.

[2] These factors do not always separate cleanly; more than one motivation is usually behind the pursuit of WMD, and some motivations will be stronger than others in different cases.

[3] General background information on national WMD development programs drawn from the Center for Nonproliferation Studies databases available at the website of the Nuclear Threat Initiative <www.nti.org/e_research/profiles/index.html>.

[4] For details on Chinese arms transfers to Pakistan from the mid-1960s through the early 1990s, see R. Bates Gill, *Chinese Arms Transfers: Purposes, Patterns, and Prospects in the New World Order*, Greenport, Conn: Praeger Publishers, 1992, especially pp. 141–59.

[5] *Unclassified Report to Congress on the Acquisition of Technology Relating to Weapons of Mass Destruction and Advanced Conventional Munitions, 1 January through 30 June 2000*, Central Intelligence Agency, February 2000, <www.cia.gov/cia/publications/bian/bian_feb_2001.htm>.

[6] Federation of American Scientists <www.fas.org/nuke/guide/pakistan/facility/kahuta.htm>.

[7] An English translation of China's 1997 nuclear export control regulations is available from the Center for Nonproliferation Studies East Asia Nonproliferation Program, and available at the Nuclear Threat Initiative website <www.nti.org/db/china/excon.htm>.

[8] On U.S. concerns about missile-related technology transfers from China to Pakistan, see, Testimony by Robert J. Einhorn, Deputy Assistant Secretary of State for Nonproliferation, before the Subcommittee on International Security, Proliferation, and Federal Services, Senate Committee on Governmental Affairs, 10 April 1997.

[9] Sino-U.S. Presidential Joint Statement on South Asia, Beijing, June 27, 1998, <www.nti.org/db/china/engdocs/sasiasum.htm>.

[10] *Unclassified Report to Congress on the Acquisition of Technology Relating to Weapons of Mass Destruction and Advanced Conventional Munitions, 1 January through 30 June 2001*, Central Intelligence Agency, January 2002, <www.cia.gov/cia/publications/bian/bian_jan_2002.htm>; *Unclassified Report to Congress on the Acquisition of Technology Relating to Weapons of Mass Destruction and Advanced Conventional Munitions, 1 January through 30 June 2002*, Central Intelligence Agency, April 2003, <www.cia.gov/cia/publications/bian/bian_apr_2003.htm#15>.

[11] *Unclassified Report to Congress on the Acquisition of Technology Relating to Weapons of Mass Destruction, 1 July Through 31 December 2000*, Central Intelligence Agency, September 2001, <www.cia.gov/cia/publications/bian/bian_sep_2001.htm#10>.

[12] *Unclassified Report to Congress on the Acquisition of Technology Relating to Weapons of Mass Destruction, 1 January through 30 June 2002*, Central Intelligence Agency.

[13] Greater detail on Sino-Iranian military-technical relations can be found in Bates Gill, "Chinese Arms Exports to Iran," *China Report*, vol. 34 (July–December 1998), pp. 355–379; and Gill, *Chinese Arms Transfers*, pp. 93–104.

[14] For a detailed discussion of Iran's nuclear-related imports, see Andrew Koch and Jeanette Wolf, "Iran's Nuclear Procurement Program: How Close to the Bomb?" *Nonproliferation Review* (Fall 1997), pp. 123–35.

[15] "U.S. Imposes CW Sanctions Against Chinese Entities," Department of State, Office of the Spokesman, May 21, 1997, <secretary.state.gov/www/briefings/statements/970522a.html>.

[16] The June 2001 sanctions, described in Department of State Public Notice 3707, *Federal Register*, vol. 66, no. 123, June 26, 2001; the January 2002 sanctions in Department of State Public Notice 3893, *Federal Register*, vol. 64, no. 16, January 24, 2002; the May 2002 sanctions in Department of State Public Notice 4020, *Federal Register*, vol. 67, no. 95, May 16, 2002; the July 2002 sanctions in Department of State Public Notice 4071, *Federal Register*, vol. 67, no. 143, July 25, 2002.

[17] "Iran, China sign arms technology pact," *Washington Times*, January 22, 1990, p. 2; James Bruce, "Iran and China in $4.5 billion partnership," *Jane's Defence Weekly*, September 11, 1996, p. 3; "Sino-Iranian arms deal," *Jane's*

Defence Weekly, September 18, 1996, p. 13.

[18] Elaine Sciolino, "CIA report says Chinese sent Iran arms components," *New York Times*, June 22, 1995; p. A1; Jeffrey Smith and David Ottaway, "Spy photos suggest China missile trade," *Washington Post*, July 3, 1995, p. 1.

[19] Bill Gertz, "China sold Iran missile technology," *Washington Times*, November 21, 1996.

[20] The May 2002 sanctions are described in United States Department of State Public Notice 4020; the July 2002 sanctions in Department of State Public Notice 4071, *Federal Register*, vol. 67, no. 143, July 25, 2002; the May 2003 sanctions in Department of State Public Notice 4370, *Federal Register*, vol. 68, no. 100, May 23, 2003; the July 2003 sanctions in Department of State Public Notice 4392, *Federal Register*, vol. 68, no. 128, July 3, 2003.

[21] *Unclassified Report to Congress on the Acquisition of Technology...*, Central Intelligence Agency, January 2002.

[22] *Unclassified Report to Congress on the Acquisition of Technology...*, Central Intelligence Agency, April 2003.

[23] See *Unclassified Report to Congress on the Acquisition of Technology...*, Central Intelligence Agency, February 2000; *Unclassified Report to Congress on the Acquisition of Technology...*, Central Intelligence Agency, January 2002.

[24] *Unclassified Report to Congress on the Acquisition of Technology...*, Central Intelligence Agency, April 2003.

[25] Gill, *Chinese Arms Transfers*, especially Appendices 1–4.

[26] "Defense Ministry report on DPRK imports of weapons," *Korea Times*, September 28, 1999.

[27] On past Chinese assistance to North Korean nuclear programs, see the Nuclear Threat Initiative website, <www.nti.org/e_research/profiles/65_681.html>; Joseph S. Bermudez, Jr., "N Korea—set to join the 'nuclear club'?" *Jane's Defence Weekly*, September 23, 1989, p. 594; Joseph S. Bermudez, Jr., "North Korea's Nuclear Programme," *Jane's Intelligence Review* (September 1991) pp. 406, 411; and Joseph S. Bermudez, Jr., "Exposing North Korea's Secret Nuclear Infrastructure—Part One," *Jane's Intelligence Review* (July 1999) pp. 38, 41.

[28] Mohan Malik, "The Proliferation Axis: Beijing-Islamabad-Pyongyang," *Korean Journal of Defense Analysis*, vol. 15, no. 1 (Spring 2003), pp. 57–100.

[29] Jeremy Page, "Putin and Hu find common ground on Korea and Iraq," Reuters, May 27, 2003; "China, Russia issue joint statement," *People's Daily*, December 4, 2002; "Chinese, U.S. presidents talk over phone," *People's Daily*, March 19, 2003.

[30] Information drawn from the Nuclear Threat Initiative website <www.nti.org/e_research/profiles/65_681.html>; John Wilson Lewis and Hua Di, "Beijing's Defense Establishment: Solving the Arms Export Enigma," *International Security*, Fall 1992, pp. 5–40; Gordon Jacobs and Tim McCarthy, "China 's Missile Sales—Few Changes for the Future," *Jane's Intelligence Review*, December 1992, p. 560; Joseph S. Bermudez, Jr., "The North Korean 'Scud B' Program," *Jane's Soviet Intelligence Review*, May 1989, pp. 203–07.

[31] Bill Gertz, "China assists North Korea in space launches," *Washington Times*, February 23, 1999.

[32] Bill Gertz, "China breaks vow, sends N. Korea missile materials," *Washington Times*, January 6, 2000; Bill Gertz and Rowan Scarborough, "China connection," *Washington Times*, November 19, 1999.

[33] "China vows not to help North Korean missile program: senators," Agence France-Presse, August 9, 2001.

[34] *Unclassified Report to Congress on the Acquisition of Technology...*, Central Intelligence Agency, April 2003.

[35] David McGlinchey, "Iran: Uranium Mining, Reprocessing, Could Lead to Nuclear Weapons," Global Security Newswire, February 11, 2003, <www.nti.org/d_newswire/issues/2003/2/11/6s.html>; see also Center for Nonproliferation Studies, "Iran Overview," <www.nti.org/e_research/e1_iran_1. html>.

[36] See data submitted by Russia and Iran to the United Nations Conventional Arms Register, <http://disarmament.un.org/un_register.nsf>.

[37] *Unclassified Report to Congress on the Acquisition of Technology...*, Central Intelligence Agency, April 2003.

[38] Drawn from the Indian Space Research Organization, available on the NTI website, <www.nti.org/e_research/e1_india_mch_00_02.html>.

[39] On Russian conventional arms transfers to India, see United Nations Conventional Arms Register; *SIPRI Yearbook 2002: Armaments, Disarmament, and International Security*, Oxford: Oxford University Press, 2002, Appendix 8C, and previous editions of the *SIPRI Yearbook*.

[40] On the early contributions of the Soviet Union to China's bomb program, see John Wilson Lewis and Xue Litai, *China Builds the Bomb*, Stanford, Calif.: Stanford University Press, 1988.

[41] For an overview of China's ballistic missile programs, see Bates Gill, James Mulvenon, and Mark Stokes, "China's Strategic Rocket Forces: Transition to Credible Deterrence", in James Mulvenon and Richard Yang, eds., *The People's Liberation Army as an Organization*, Santa Monica, Calif.: Rand, 2002.

[42] On Russian conventional arms exports to China, see United Nations Conventional Arms Register; *SIPRI Yearbook 2002*, and previous editions of the *SIPRI Yearbook*. See also Bates Gill and Taeho Kim, *China's Arms Acquisitions from Abroad: A Quest for "Superb and Secret Weapons"*, Oxford: Oxford University Press, 1995, pp. 18–34, 48–70.

[43] See Jon Brook Wolfsthal, et al., eds., *Status Report: Nuclear Weapons, Fissile Materials, and Export Controls in the Former Soviet Union*, Monterey, Calif.: Center for Nonproliferation Studies, 2001; Valentin Tikhonov, *Russia's Nuclear and Missile Complex: The Human Factor in Proliferation*, Washington, DC: Carnegie Endowment for International Peace, 2001; Amy E. Smithson, *Toxic Archipelago: Preventing Proliferation from the Former Soviet Chemical and Biological Weapons Complexes*, Washington, DC: Henry L. Stimson Center, 1999.

[44] The United States imposed sanctions on a North Korean company, the Changgwang Siyong Corporation, the front organization responsible for helping Pakistan develop the Nodong-based missile, at the time of the first Nodong/Ghauri test launch by Pakistan in April 1998. Department of State Public Notice 3708, *Federal Register*, vol. 66, no. 123, 26 June 2001; "U.S. penalizes China, N. Korea cos.," *New York Times*, June 28, 2001.

[45] Manoj Joshi, "India refuses to let N. Korea off the hook," *Times of India*, July 31, 1999; Mohan Malik, "The Proliferation Axis: Beijing-Islamabad-Pyongyang," *Korean Journal of Defense Analysis*.

[46] *Unclassified Report to Congress on the Acquisition of Technology...*, Central Intelligence Agency, April 2003.

[47] *Unclassified Report to Congress on the Acquisition of Technology...*, Central Intelligence Agency, April 2003.

[48] On Pakistan's aid to the North Korean nuclear program, see Seymour M. Hersh, "The cold test," *New Yorker*, January 27, 2003; "Pakistan probably gave nuclear aid recently, officials say," Global Security Newswire, November 13, 2002; David E. Sanger, "In North Korea and Pakistan, deep roots of nuclear barter," *New York Times*, November 24, 2002.

[49] Andres de Lionis, "The Coastal Missile Threat In The Middle East," *Jane's Intelligence Review*, January 1994, pp. 25–28; Gerald B. Boyd, "U.S. says China is arming Iran, despite denial," *New York Times*, June 7, 1987.

[50] The July 2003 sanctions are described in Department of State Public Notice 4392, *Federal Register*, vol. 68, no. 128, July 3, 2003. See also Department of State, Taken Questions, Office of the Spokesman, Washington, DC, July 3, 2003, <www.state.gov/r/pa/prs/ps/2003/22238.htm>.

[51] On North Korean missile-related assistance to Iran, see the Center for Non-proliferation Studies "Iran: Missile Chronology," available at the Nuclear Threat Initiative website, www.nti.org/e_research/e1_iran_mch.html> *Unclassified Report to Congress on the Acquisition of Technology...*, Central Intelligence Agency, April 2003, available at <www.cia.gov/cia/publications/bian/bian_apr_2003.htm#15>; Director of Central Intelligence, *Foreign Missile Developments and the Ballistic Missile Threat Through 2015,* Unclassified Summary of a National Intelligence Estimate (December 2001).

[52] The strategic postures of India, Pakistan, and China, including their nuclear weapons programs, are discussed in their respective country chapters in this and previous Strategic Asia volumes.

[53] *Foreign Missile Developments and the Ballistic Missile Threat through 2015*, Washington, DC: National Intelligence Council, December 2001.

[54] According to the treaty, formal withdrawal comes into effect 90 days after an announcement of intent to withdrawal. However, North Korea did not consider itself bound by this waiting period, arguing that in 1993 it already announced its intent to withdraw from the NPT, and had only "suspended" this intention awaiting the outcome of agreements reached with the United States at that time.

[55] "Statement of DPRK Government on its withdrawal from NPT," Korean Central News Agency (Pyongyang), January 10, 2003, <www.globalsecurity.org/wmd/library/news/dprk/2003/dprk-030110-kcna01.htm>.

[56] Glenn Kessler, "N. Korea says it has nuclear arms," *Washington Post*, April 25, 2003.

[57] "Joint Declaration of the Denuclearization of the Korean Peninsula," January 20, 1992, <www.globalsecurity.org/wmd/library/news/rok/1992/appendix17.htm>.

[58] David E. Sanger, "C.I.A. said to find North Korean nuclear advances," *New*

York Times, July 1, 2003.

[59] Sanger, "C.I.A. said to find North Korean nuclear advances," *New York Times*.

[60] James A. Kelly, "Regional Implications of the Changing Nuclear Equation on the Korean Peninsula,", testimony before the Senate Foreign Relations Committee, March 12, 2003, <www.state.gov/p/eap/rls/rm/2003/18661.htm>.

[61] *Unclassified Report to Congress on the Acquisition of Technology...*, Central Intelligence Agency, April 2003.

[62] According to a 2001 intelligence estimate, North Korea will "most likely" pose an ICBM threat to the United States by 2015; its 10,000 to 15,000 km-range Taepodong-2, believed to be ready for flight testing should North Korea lift its current moratorium on ballistic missile testing, would be able to reach much of the continental United States. Director of Central Intelligence, *Foreign Missile Developments and the Ballistic Missile Threat through 2015*, Unclassified Summary of a National Intelligence Estimate (December 2001).

[63] For more detail and analysis of the Treaty of Bangkok, see *Inventory of International Nonproliferation Organizations and Regimes 2002*, Monterey, Calif.: Center for Nonproliferation Studies, 2002, pp. 169–71.

[64] *Unclassified Report to Congress on the Acquisition of Technology...*, Central Intelligence Agency, April 2003.

[65] On Chinese export controls, see Jing-dong Yuan, Phillip C. Saunders, and Stephanie Lieggi, "Recent Developments in China's Export Controls: New Regulations and New Challenges," *Nonproliferation Review*, vol. 9, no. 3 (Fall–Winter 2002), pp. 153–67; Evan Medeiros and Bates Gill, *Chinese Arms Exports: Policies, Players, Process*, Strategic Studies Institute, Carlisle, Penn.: U.S. Army War College, 2000.

[66] *Unclassified Report to Congress on the Acquisition of Technology...*, Central Intelligence Agency, April 2003.

[67] On the WMD and missile programs of South Korea and Taiwan, see the reporting by the Center for Nonproliferation Studies. On the existence of a defensive CBW program in Taiwan, see Dennis Engbarth, "MND denies it has chemical, biological weapons programs," *Taiwan News*, April 16, 2003, <www.taiwansecurity.org/tn/2003/tn-041603.htm>.

[68] See the country profile on Japan at the Nuclear Threat Initiative website, <www.nti.org/e_research/e1_japan_1.html>.

[69] David Albright and Corey Gray, "Taiwan: Nuclear Nightmare Averted," *Bulletin of the Atomic Scientists*, vol. 54, no. 1 (January/February 1998); "Pro-independence party candidate advocates nuclear weapons," Reuters, August 22, 1999.

[70] "A reckless pro-nuclear comment", *Japan Times*, June 7, 2002 and "Review of nuclear weapons policy on the table," *Mainichi Shimbun*, June 1, 2002; Teruaki Ueno, "Japanese politician defends nuclear remarks," Reuters, April 11, 2002.

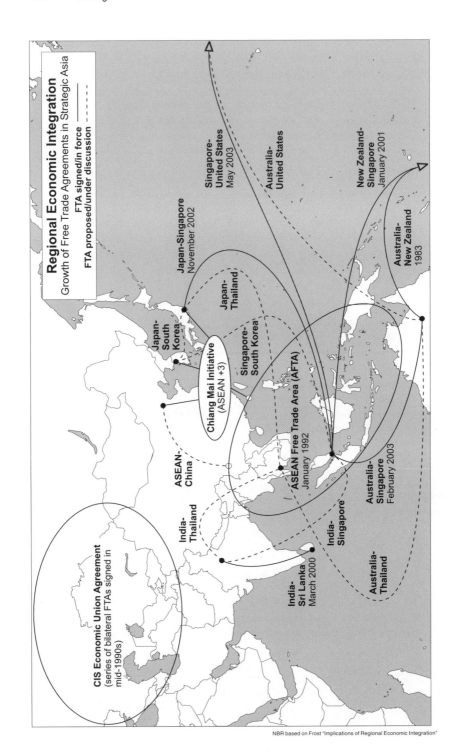

Regional Economic Integration
Growth of Free Trade Agreements in Strategic Asia

FTA signed/in force
FTA proposed/under discussion

Singapore-United States
May 2003

Australia-United States

New Zealand-Singapore
January 2001

Australia-New Zealand
1983

Japan-Singapore
November 2002

Japan-Thailand

Japan-South Korea

Singapore-South Korea

Chiang Mai Initiative (ASEAN +3)

ASEAN-China

ASEAN Free Trade Area (AFTA)
January 1992

Australia-Singapore
February 2003

India-Thailand

India-Singapore

India-Sri Lanka
March 2000

Australia-Thailand

CIS Economic Union Agreement
(series of bilateral FTAs signed in mid-1990s)

NBR based on Frost "Implications of Regional Economic Integration"

IMPLICATIONS OF REGIONAL ECONOMIC INTEGRATION

Ellen L. Frost

ABSTRACT

A network of trade and financial negotiations is creating new linkages among countries in Asia. Free trade agreements are proliferating and a framework for currency swaps is in place. Particularly striking are growing ties between Northeast and Southeast Asia, China's "charm diplomacy," Japan's lagging performance, and the inclusion of India in summit-level discussions with East and Southeast Asia. This drive for intra-Asian economic integration excludes the United States. It will yield few economic benefits compared with trans-Pacific or global integration, but it offers Asian leaders political and security advantages, such as engaging China peacefully in the region, acquiring a stronger collective voice, and, for India, building economic relationships corresponding to its status as an emerging regional power. Over time, market-oriented regional integration works in favor of peace, stability, and democracy and deserves U.S. support.

Ellen Frost is a Visiting Fellow at the Institute for International Economics. She would like to thank Neil Beck for research assistance, Edward Lincoln for sharing his manuscript and research data and for his comments, and Richard Cronin, Richard Ellings, Tommy Koh, Frederick L. Montgomery, Naoko Munakata, John Newhouse, T. J. Pempel, and John Ravenhill for comments on an earlier draft.

Introduction

A network of economic and trade negotiations, real or promised, is creating new linkages among the diverse nation-states of Asia.[1] Economic issues have graduated from "low politics" to "high politics."[2] In a region that lacks formal regional security arrangements, economic agreements—and free trade agreements (FTAs) in particular—are becoming the dominant geopolitical and organizational expression of relations among states.

Economic linkages among neighbors, ranging from the ASEAN Free Trade Area (AFTA) to economic zones among sub-national units, have existed at least since the early 1990s.[3] But FTAs between or among geographically disparate Asian countries are relatively new. Almost a dozen intra-Asian FTAs of this sort have been proposed or are in various stages of negotiation, and one has been signed (Japan-Singapore). They account for a substantial portion of the actual or proposed sub-regional trade agreements in the Asia Pacific Economic Cooperation (APEC) region that have emerged since the end of 1998.[4] (See Table 1 on pages 402–03).

Financial linkages among Asian nations, the underpinning of commercial ties, are an important part of the integration movement. Unlike Europe, where financial integration lagged far behind trade, talks on Asian financial integration were prominent in the late 1990s and appeared to be outpacing trade integration until the recent burst of FTAs. There is now an agreed framework for intra-Asian currency swaps and discussion of new exchange rate regimes, common currencies, and even a yen bloc or a yuan bloc.[5] The ideas behind these trade and financial initiatives are not new, the scope is modest, and there is much room for doubt about what they will actually achieve, but the new diplomatic momentum is unmistakable, and much of it excludes the United States.

The United States has responded by proposing FTAs with individual members of the Association of Southeast Asian Nations (ASEAN). The European Union (EU) is also active, holding Asia-Europe summit meetings and proposing in April 2003 an initiative to strengthen EU-ASEAN trade and investment relations.[6] New Zealand, Mexico, and Chile were also early supporters of FTAs with Asian countries and have succeeded in negotiating a number of them. An exclusive Asian "bloc" is not in the cards, but a substantial number of new trade and financial initiatives now come from, and are limited to, Asians.

At first sight, this pattern looks like too many diplomats chasing too few gains. Economic research consistently shows that global or APEC-wide liberalization reaps more welfare benefits for Asians than narrower, more exclusive arrangements.[7] Developing Asia relies on the West for world-class technology, education and training, and competition as well as for trade, investment, and capital flows. But the geographic scope of many of the new proposals is intra-Asian rather than trans-Pacific or global.

This chapter examines the apparent contradiction between economic realities and political priorities. It focuses on the political and strategic aspects of intra-Asian economic initiatives, that is, on the activities and attitudes of national governments. Adopting this approach bypasses other facets of this complex topic, especially the role of the private sector and the expanding web of non-government organizations.[8] The chapter excludes sub-regional border zones and devotes little space to the integration of Asia with the Asia Pacific economy and the global economy, except by comparison. The scope of the chapter is East and Southeast Asia (minus Australia and New Zealand) plus India because the new linkages among these governments are the ones that raise strategic issues for the United States.

The analysis begins with a brief overview of current trends and recent initiatives in the region. It then looks at the political and economic goals of the major Asian players, weighs the prospects for success, and assesses the strategic implications of the most likely outcome. Finally, it explores to what extent intra-Asian economic integration is compatible with U.S. goals and interests, including the U.S.-China relationship.

Current Trends and Recent Initiatives

Interdependence, Economic Freedom, and Influence

Behind the flurry of intra-Asian economic and trade negotiations is a combination of trends. First, every major country in the region except Japan and Singapore has become significantly more dependent on global trade. Between 1990 and 2001, China's trade, measured as a percentage of GDP, grew from 32 to 49 percent; Indonesia's from 49 to 74 percent; Malaysia's from 147 to 214 percent; Thailand's from 76 to 127 percent; the Philippines' from 61 to 97 percent; South Korea's from 59 to 84 percent; and India's from 17 to 29 percent. (Japan's ratio stayed in the 16–20 percent range, slightly lower than the 21–26 percent level of the United States, while Singapore's has generally remained over 300 percent).[9] For Asians, trade is strategically important.

Second, all major countries in the region, except India, have become more dependent on the economic health of their neighbors. Interdependence is highly skewed because national wealth varies so widely. Despite viewing China as a competitor for foreign investment, all have developed a vested interest in China's continued growth.

Third, economic freedom has gained ground throughout the region. Most of the major Asian governments except Indonesia, India, and China

Table 1. Free Trade Agreements (Implemented and Signed) involving Strategic Asia Countries

Agreement	Countries	Status	Date	Description
AFTA	ASEAN	Implemented	January 1992	ASEAN Free Trade Area - agreement signed 1992; full implementation for original signatories began 2003
ANZCERTA	Australia New Zealand	Implemented	1983	Australian-New Zealand Closer Economic Relations Trade Agreement - elimination of all tariffs
ANZSCEP	New Zealand Singapore	Implemented	January 2001	Agreement between New Zealand and Singapore on Closer Economic Partnership - elimination of all tariffs
EFTA-Singapore FTA	EFTA Singapore	Implemented	January 2003	European Free Trade Association (Iceland, Norway, Liechtenstein, Switzerland)-Singapore FTA
Indo-Lanka FTA	India Sri Lanka	Implemented	March 2000	Indo-Lanka FTA - complete and phased elimination of all tariffs
JSEPA	Japan Singapore	Implemented	November 2002	Japan-Singapore Economic Partnership Agreement - elimination of almost all tariffs (except in agriculture)
CIS EUA	Russia FSU states	Signed	From mid-1990s	Commonwealth of Independent States Economic Union Agreement - variety of bilateral measures to boost trade
Chile-South Korea FTA	Chile South Korea	Signed	February 2003	Chile-South Korea FTA - implementation expected in late 2003 (will eliminate tariffs on most goods)
China-HK CEPA	China Hong Kong	Signed	June 2003	Mainland-Hong Kong Closer Economic Partnership Arrangement - measures to facilitate trade and customs
SAFTA	Australia Singapore	Signed	February 2003	Singapore-Australia FTA - implementation expected in late 2003 (will remove all goods tariffs)
USSFTA	Singapore United States	Signed	May 2003	U.S.-Singapore FTA - implementation expected in 2004 (complete and phased elimination of most tariffs)

Table 1 (cont.). Free Trade Agreements (in Negotiation and Proposed) involving Strategic Asia Countries

Agreement	Status	Date	Description
AUSFTA (Australia-United States)	Negotiation	March 2003	Australia-United States FTA
CECA (India-Singapore)	Negotiation	April 2003	Comprehensive Economic Cooperation Agreement
CERFTA (Australia-Thailand)	Negotiation	August 2002	Closer Economic Relations FTA
Canada-Singapore FTA	Negotiation	October 2001	Four round of negotiations have been completed
GUUAM FTA	Negotiation	September 2000	Georgia-Ukraine-Uzbekistan-Azerbaijan-Moldova FTA
Japan-Mexico FTA	Negotiation	July 2002	Fifth round of negotiations completed in April 2003
Singapore-Mexico FTA	Negotiation	July 2000	Six rounds of negotiations completed
Singapore-South Korea FTA	Negotiation	November 2002	First round of negotiations completed March 2003
ASEAN-China FTA	Proposed	November 2002	Proposal for creation of an FTA within 10 years
India-Thailand FTA	Proposed	November 2002	Proposal to eliminate tariffs by 2006–2010
Japan-South Korea FTA	Proposed	April 2003	Under consideration - preliminary meetings held
Japan-Thailand FTA	Proposed	May 2003	Under consideration - preliminary meetings held
Philippines-Taiwan FTA	Proposed	August 2002	Under consideration
South Korea-United States FTA	Proposed	…	Under consideration per congressional request
Taiwan-United States FTA	Proposed	February 2002	Under consideration per congressional request

Sources: Various government sources, including the Australian Department of Foreign Affairs and Trade, Singapore Ministry of Trade and Industry, Taiwan Board of Foreign Trade, U.S. Chamber of Commerce, U.S. Department of State, U.S. Trade Representative, and USAID; various multilateral organizations, including the Association for Southeast Asian Nations and the South Asian Association for Regional Cooperation; various non-governmental organizations, including the American Chambers of Commerce and the U.S.-ASEAN Business Council; and various media sources, including *Asia Times*, BBC, Reuters, etc. Table does not include a considerable number of bilateral agreements that are designed to lay the groundwork for eventual free trade agreements (such as trade and investment framework agreements). Data compiled by Neil Beck.

score fairly well on the Heritage Foundation's "Index of Economic Freedom," and the three exceptions have improved since the data were first collected.[10] Privatization, deregulation, access to reliable financial information, and fewer barriers to cross-border business work in favor of integration. Governments are losing their monopoly on economic power and influence as private actors acquire a larger stake in open markets and cross-border business. The information revolution has enabled internationally minded government officials to forge coalitions with their counterparts elsewhere in Asia. These coalitions strengthen the position of ministries favoring liberalization in the domestic struggle against protectionism.

This combination of trends is forcing Asian governments to think more strategically about regional economic policy and to consider their own and others' domestic politics to a greater extent than before. Governments with the most influence are those presiding over large, strong economies and offering the most far-reaching trade opportunities to their neighbors. China heads the list, but its financial position is not rock-solid and its ability to offer preferences above and beyond its World Trade Organization (WTO) commitments has not yet been tested.

Is "Natural" Integration Another Trend?

In the absence of a global or APEC-wide breakthrough, economic integration in Asia may make sense. But to be beneficial, sustainable, and conducive to competitiveness, integration must be driven by or at least conform to market forces. Is there a trend toward such "natural" integration?

Evaluating actual economic integration in Asia to date is difficult because much depends on how integration is measured and to what it is compared. First, China's size is so large, and its entry into the regional and global economies so rapid, that its inclusion skews the numbers. Second, Asian economies have become global players. South Korea now trades more with Thailand, for example, but it also trades more with almost every other country in the world.[11] Third, trade is only one measure of integration. Intra-Asian trade is now about half of the region's total trade, but trade rarely entails technology transfer, financial networks, or the movement of skilled personnel, all of which are meaningful signs of integration. Data on this kind of deeper integration in Asia are hard to obtain.

Difficult as it is to measure, Asian economic integration is substantial, but is it outpacing Asia's integration with the rest of the Asia Pacific community or the world? Economist Edward Lincoln, who has analyzed trade and investment linkages in detail, answers in the negative. The region's trade with China has been growing, but not faster than the growth of China's trade with the rest of the world. The rise of intra-Asian integration is moderate and has not come about at the expense of links with the United States or Europe. Malaysia, the Philippines, Thailand, Singapore, and India continue to depend on the U.S. market for 20–30 percent of their exports.[12]

Investment and bank loans tell a similar story, according to Lincoln. Investment links are growing throughout Asia, but, except for Taiwan's heavy investment in China, the pattern is as much trans-Pacific and global as intra-regional. Except for a brief spike in 1997, Japanese aid, investment, and bank loans to the rest of Asia have all been falling since the mid-1990s. European banks account for almost 70 percent of total loans.[13]

ASEAN is not integrating very dramatically either. Thanks in part to the decade-old AFTA, intra-ASEAN exports increased from $44 billion in 1993 to $85 billion in 2001. But by Asian standards these numbers are not remarkable, and the preferential average tariff of 2.7 percent hides many protectionist loopholes. Reporting to Southeast Asian leaders in June 2003, McKinsey management consultants cited ASEAN's many non-tariff barriers, including divergent product standards and customs inefficiencies, to conclude that the region was "at risk" because investors do not see a single ASEAN market.[14] In fact, intra-regional trade as a percentage of total trade has been falling recently. ASEAN's exports to the United States constitute a larger share of ASEAN's exports than do intra-ASEAN exports and generate a large surplus for the region ($40 billion in 2000).

In short, the economic evidence for "natural" regional integration is watery at best. The best one can say is that it is not "unnatural," and the drive to achieve it can be designed to work in the direction of market forces.

Recent Initiatives

The new network of trade, investment, and financial discussions features several interesting alignments. Particularly striking are the emerging links between Northeast and Southeast Asia, China's new "charm diplomacy," and the inclusion of India in the regional dialogue.

Asia's first wave of network-builders were South Korea, Japan, and Singapore. In the wake of the financial crisis of 1997–98 and APEC's failure to bring about meaningful "voluntary" sectoral liberalization, South Korea announced trade initiatives with Chile and Mexico and began preliminary discussions with Japan. (An FTA with Chile was signed in 2003). Meanwhile, Singapore proposed an FTA with Japan. These moves started the bandwagon rolling.

ASEAN, drained by weak leadership and hobbled by numerous barriers to cross-border business, nevertheless is the object of commercial courtship on the part of its northern neighbors. Finding the rest of ASEAN resentful that Singapore had been singled out for an FTA, Japan proposed a "comprehensive economic partnership" with ASEAN in January 2001. Japanese resistance to agricultural liberalization ruled out a standard FTA. In November 2001, China topped Japan's offer by proposing a comprehensive ASEAN-China FTA that would include agriculture. A year later the two sides announced an agreement heralding an ASEAN-China FTA within 10 years and stipulating that talks toward that end proceed "expeditiously." Although a meaningful agreement is years away, both sides hope for an early harvest of "low-hanging fruit," that is, the reduction or elimination of tariffs in areas where political opposition is already low or insignificant.[15]

Even inward-looking India has reached out to ASEAN, adopting a "Look East" policy and, together with Singapore, persuading the remaining ASEAN leaders to hold an unprecedented "ASEAN +1" summit in 2002. In May 2003, India and Singapore began FTA negotiations. In June, Thai Prime Minister Thaksin said that Thailand expects to sign an FTA with India by the end of the year.

The most active regional grouping is ASEAN+3 (ASEAN plus China, Japan, and South Korea), which took shape in 1997. This forum, which links the historically and culturally separate northern and southern regions of Asia, has become the preferred arena for trade and investment negotiations rather than APEC. ASEAN+3 is beginning to take on institutional characteristics, holding regular meetings, establishing working groups, and conducting a study on a possible Asia-wide free trade area.[16] South Korea, a world-class economic power hitherto uninterested in regional leadership beyond the Korean Peninsula, has become an active participant, holding regular meetings with the other "+3" counterparts, China and Japan, as well as with the full group.

The United States, along with other non-Asian APEC members, is excluded from these discussions, but Washington has tabled its own FTA proposals. The Bush administration's Enterprise for ASEAN Initiative offers FTAs to individual ASEAN members committed to economic liberalization, subject only to membership in the World Trade Organization (WTO) and the existence of a "Trade and Investment Framework Agreement" with the United States.[17] President Bush signed America's first-ever Asian bilateral FTA with a member of ASEAN (Singapore) in May 2003, which was approved by Congress in July, and U.S. negotiators are exploring prospects with Thailand. Meanwhile, building on the Clinton administration's FTA with Jordan and backed by a Republican Congress, U.S. Trade Representative Robert Zoellick has managed to strike a politically acceptable balance on the contentious "trade and" issues—trade and worker rights, and trade and environmental protection.[18] This compromise has cooled a long-standing Asian suspicion that Washington was using labor and environmental standards as a smokescreen for protectionism. Washington has also taken a more positive line toward the new Asian currency swap arrangements.

These steps, backed by the vast American market, the presence of U.S. forces, and America's "hyperpower" status, ensure a U.S. seat at the table. At the same time, a pro-"Asia" wind is blowing through the region. This pro-Asia wind is not new, but it has recently gained force. Based on the same logic as regionalism in Europe and the Americas, it promotes openness and is not anti-American as such. In Malaysia and among certain Asian nationalists, however, it attracts a certain kind of thinking that is at least cool toward and subtly resentful of the United States.

By contrast, the last serious drive for Asian economic integration took an inclusive, trans-Pacific form, with global overtones and a strong push from business groups. It began during the late 1980s and early 1990s and peaked at the APEC summits of 1993 and 1994, when Asian and North American leaders proclaimed a goal of "free and open trade and investment" in the Asia Pacific by 2010 (2020 for developing countries). At that time APEC leaders, proclaiming "open regionalism," expressed support for further global trade liberalization through the WTO. Although APEC leaders also endorsed sub-regional agreements that were liberalizing and WTO-consistent in nature,[19] the APEC "vision" was ambitious and inclusive.

After the Osaka summit of 1995, APEC lost its high-level momentum. It lent crucial resources and support for the global liberalization of telecommunication goods and services, but its drive for voluntary liberalization in more traditional sectors never amounted to much. The Asian financial crisis of 1997–98 knocked the wind out of APEC's Asian supporters and toppled several governments in the region. Although APEC still provides a framework for a number of useful improvements in the Asian business environment, it no longer serves as a catalyst for significant Asia Pacific trade liberalization. The goal of "free and open trade and investment" by 2010/2020 now seems beyond reach. A new round of WTO negotiations is underway, with a target date of 2005 and with strong support from the APEC Business Advisory Council. Yet with the exceptions of Singapore and (apart from agriculture) Japan and South Korea, Asian governments' attitude toward far-reaching global liberalization ranges from tepid to cold.

Asian Goals

Why are Asian leaders bent on closer economic integration? A "natural" intra-Asian market is not outpacing integration with the trans-Pacific and global economies. The pegged exchange rates that set the stage for the financial crisis are largely gone. There is no Asian equivalent of the situation in Western Europe in the late 1940s, when the leaders of France and Germany consciously put an end to centuries of war and deliberately bound their markets together. Nonetheless, powerful motivations are at play.

ASEAN: Negotiating from Weakness

In recent years ASEAN has become weaker and more divided. Weak leadership in post-Suharto Indonesia, the geopolitical anchor of ASEAN, has sapped its dynamism. The admission of four smaller and less globalized economies—Cambodia, Laos, Burma, and Vietnam—was meant to strengthen Southeast Asia's identity, but instead it has dragged in new disputes and eroded ASEAN's effectiveness.[20] Brunei is an oil-rich enclave, and Singapore a city-state whose initiatives are global in scope. The following analysis therefore applies mainly (but not exclusively) to the remaining "ASEAN 4"—Thailand, Malaysia, Indonesia, and the Philippines.

The first major goal of ASEAN leaders is reviving their economies and thereby recapturing the political legitimacy that prior governments reaped from strong and steady economic growth. The financial crisis taught them that domestic economic welfare depends crucially on economic success in neighboring countries as well as at home.[21] Seeking to boost the region's competitiveness, these leaders believe that they have no choice but to tie themselves to stronger Asian economies (China, Japan, and South Korea, the "+3") rather than adopt mercantilist policies against them.

The rash of FTAs in Europe and the Americas provided a compelling stimulus because it aroused fears that Asia would be left out. ASEAN officials see regional trade groupings in Asia as a counterweight to these regional blocs. They know that AFTA has bogged down in key areas, but they hope that forging FTAs with their northern neighbors, however unenforceable and riddled with exceptions they may be, will bolster Asian negotiating power vis-à-vis the United States, Europe, and Brazil.[22]

ASEAN leaders are also seeking a stronger voice in the management of the global economy corresponding to the region's potential market of 500 million-plus consumers and a combined GDP of over half a trillion dollars. By enhancing their voice in trade forums, ASEAN leaders believe that intra-Asian economic integration will help them resist, delay, or transform market-opening pressures from the United States and others in politically sensitive sectors or in areas where anticipated job losses would alienate important groups. They see such pressure as politically destabilizing, if not to their individual countries as a whole, then at least to their personal tenures in office. Similarly, they believe that a stronger collective voice will help break down U.S. (and European) barriers to their exports. They also see dangers in relying so heavily on the U.S. market and seek ways of attracting and balancing the various competitors for influence.

More broadly, the effort to knit Asian economies together through trade, investment, and finance lends geopolitical weight and political identity to its participants. Some ASEAN intellectuals have expressed a vision of this identity, hoping that ASEAN will become a true community based on democracy, justice, humanitarianism, openness, and mutual involvement for the good of the region.[23]

Second, ASEAN officials and business leaders are looking for ways to boost productivity, open markets, and stimulate business with each other because they are concerned about the sluggish global economy. Neither the European Union nor Japan has shaken off near-stagnation. Worse still, just as Asia had grown out from under the financial crisis of 1997–98 and the Bali bombing of 2002, the Severe Acute Respiratory Syndrome (SARS) epidemic emptied shops and airplanes in and around the very hub of commercial Asia—the greater China region. Although SARS appears to have abated, the withering of business and travel stemming from fear of contagion may prove to have had a severe commercial impact.

The United States' weak economic performance is also disturbing. The sputtering U.S. economy translates directly into lost trade and investment. The United States no longer appears to be the reliable spearhead of global economic growth. The end of combat operations in Iraq has brought about not the hoped-for spurt of recovery but evidence of economic strain.[24] Like many others, Asians are worried about the ballooning twin deficits—current account and budgetary—that are driving down the dollar and dampening the investment climate. Since most of Asia's international transactions are denominated in dollars, Asian leaders are less worried about the value of the dollar as such than they are about what the fall of the dollar says about the health of their most important customer. Economic integration will not solve this fundamental problem, but it might help at the margin.

Third, the hardship that swept the region during the financial crisis left a lingering sense of disillusionment with the International Monetary Fund (IMF) and the United States, and is driving ASEAN leaders to seek a greater degree of financial self-sufficiency. They were dismayed by Washington's failure to offer assistance to Thailand following the collapse of the baht in July 1997 and contrasted this passivity with U.S. treatment of Mexico after the collapse of the peso in 1994–95. The crisis also taught Asian governments that their economies are linked, if only through vulnerability and contagion. The SARS epidemic reinforced this lesson. Most regional leaders are convinced that they must try to prevent and solve their financial problems themselves, or at least with a greater degree of self-reliance. Their approach is consensual, less formal, less binding, and more respectful of national sovereignty than what they perceive among Westerners.

In some ASEAN countries, notably Malaysia and Indonesia, the role of the IMF is a political issue. The IMF brings relief in crises, discipline to the budgetary process, eligibility for "Paris Club" debt relief, and support for economic reformers.[25] IMF officials argue that their role is to support governments, not to dictate to them. The IMF's primary goals, however, are to manage and stabilize the international financial system, not to support governments. In the public mind the IMF is identified with foreign (essentially U.S.) domination. Its recipes for recovery collide with national pride, the rights and privileges of the middle class, and the short-term needs of the poor. The Asian Monetary Fund (AMF), proposed by Japan in 1997, was seen as an alternative to the IMF. But the rest of the G-7 successfully opposed it, primarily because they believed the AMF would undercut the IMF's ability to bring about needed policy reforms in borrowing countries.

The successor to the AMF, the so-called Chiang Mai Initiative, would not threaten or displace the IMF. Launched at a meeting of ASEAN+3 finance ministers in Thailand in May 2000, the Chang Mai Initiative commits ministers to facilitate the exchange of consistent and timely information and establish a system of economic and financial monitoring and surveillance. Significantly, they also agreed to set up an expanded swap arrangement involving ASEAN as a whole, as well as a network of bilateral swap and repurchase agreement facilities among the ASEAN+3 countries.[26]

Swap arrangements remain a tool of U.S. international financial policy and are widely used in the private sector, but their importance as the centerpiece of the Chiang Mai Initiative is open to debate. On the one hand, such an arrangement is arguably unnecessary. The near-disappearance of fixed or pegged currency rates among the major players (except China) removes the possibility for sudden and massive shocks of the 1997–98 variety, namely, panic-induced selling of currencies that are artificially overvalued. Moreover, the amount of money on the table, $1 billion, is tiny compared to the dimensions of capital flows in Asia. On the other hand, although fixed rates have been abandoned, currency swings are still volatile. Most governments practice "managed floats" and see the need for a modest life preserver. Since the financial crisis, Asian governments have steadily built up their foreign exchange reserves, rendering mutual assistance without the IMF more realistic, and the $1 billion in the pot can always be increased. Whatever one thinks of currency swaps, the Chiang Mai Initiative's emphasis on greater surveillance and transparency, however imperfectly implemented at present, is a positive step.

Fourth, regional economic integration presents a constructive way of dealing with China. As noted in Sheldon Simon's chapter in this volume, ASEAN leaders hope to enmesh China in regional organizations and thereby strengthen the likelihood of maintaining a peaceful environment in Asia. At the same time, ASEAN leaders believe that they are competing with China for investment. This belief is not entirely accurate. For investors, the choice is not either-or. Many of ASEAN's problems in attracting investment are homegrown, such as corruption, erratic regulation, and the weakness of the rule of law. The slow and uneven pace of AFTA liberalization makes the region less attractive than it would be if it had a single market. In Indonesia, investors are concerned by political instability and violence. These disincentives would inhibit investment even in the absence of China. By contrast, in Thailand investment has held up reasonably well.

Nevertheless, government officials and businessmen from India to Indonesia are frightened by China's huge, low-wage, and increasingly productive labor force, whose competitiveness receives an added boost from incoming technology transfer and by China's residual subsidies and undervalued currency. They see this combination—correctly—as a threat to their protected and often inefficient industries. They believe that burgeoning U.S. imports from China have come about largely at the expense of other parts of Asia and that China has siphoned off foreign investment that might otherwise have been destined for ASEAN.[27] In these circumstances, they feel they have no choice but to move in the direction of an integrated market with China in order to expand their own exports to China and develop commercial ties with Chinese firms and entrepreneurs.

At present, trade and investment flows between the two are quite small, but China's membership in the WTO commits Beijing to open the Chinese market to a far greater extent than other major developing countries already in the WTO, such as India.[28] ASEAN leaders hope to gain at least a small piece of China's growing market while avoiding being crushed.[29]

Fifth, some governments in the region see an opportunity to counter what they perceive to be American arrogance, hypocrisy, or bullying. This instinct accounts for the whiff of anti-Americanism that pervades intra-Asian discussions. Americans tend to think that market competition and free trade serve the interest of other countries. And so they do, both in theory and in practice, other things being equal. But things are not equal. Asian governments complain that U.S. negotiators push for competition in areas where U.S. companies are strong (e.g., telecommunications goods and services) and resist it where U.S. companies are vulnerable and/or protectionist (e.g., textiles and steel). Believing that globalization is a smokescreen for American interests, they proclaim that market-opening of the "one size fits all" variety can harm their economies, and they justify retaining a certain degree of protection accordingly.[30]

South Korea: Feeling Vulnerable

South Korea's goals are broadly similar to those of ASEAN, but security concerns weigh more heavily. Seoul gains political prestige by its inclusion in the "+3" with heavyweights China and Japan. A pan-Asia focus makes sense because Korean companies have branches all over Asia.

The need to enhance security cooperation with China is particularly pressing, especially in light of the recent nuclear threats from North Korea and the high level of anti-Americanism in South Korea. Seoul is counting on Beijing to exert a peaceful influence on North Korea, while simultaneously avoiding its sudden collapse. Economic diplomacy has paid off: after years of enmity, China and South Korea are among each other's top customers. China is now South Korea's top export destination and its second largest investment destination.

As democracies, both Singapore and Japan are natural FTA partners for South Korea. Together the two nations encompass 170 million people and a combined GDP of $5 trillion. Like Japan, South Korea exhibits strong agricultural protectionism and thus cannot extend to ASEAN promises of meaningful free trade. In June 2003, the two prime ministers announced that they will strive to start FTA negotiations "at an early date," but both sides are wary and burdened by an unfortunate history. Manufacturing is also a major stumbling block. Predicted benefits of an FTA are limited at best. Nevertheless, if South Korea experiences some kind of shock stemming from developments in North Korea, Japanese support of the kind symbolized by an FTA and the Chiang Mai Initiative will be crucial.[31]

China's Charm Diplomacy

Of the various changes in the Asian strategic and economic landscape, none stands out more forcefully than the rise of China. No other nation has ever expanded its role in international trade as China has.[32] From 1981 to 2000, China's global exports grew by an average of 14.5 percent annually, from $21 billion to $317 billion.[33] By the end of the 1990s, China's total stock of foreign direct investment was almost a third of cumulative foreign direct investment in *all* developing countries.[34]

Chinese leaders now have a huge domestic stake in regional peace and stability in Asia, and they believe that regional integration is likely to foster those conditions. As politicians, they know that the legitimacy of continued one-party rule in China depends almost entirely on satisfying rising economic expectations and hence on economic growth. As nationalists, they have harnessed their drive for prestige to economic engagement in Asia as well as in the global economy. They know that without peace and stability, they will be unable to become an even stronger economic power. As defense strategists, they realize that without national wealth brought about by trade and investment, they will be unable to modernize their military forces. As economic realists, they are well aware that foreign-affiliated firms are responsible for almost half of China's total exports.[35] The recent agreement dismantling most barriers against Hong Kong will further open the economy. As reformers, they are committed to carrying out their ambitious pledges in the WTO without provoking a backlash at home, inciting protection in its major markets, or losing credibility in the world community.

Conscious of Asian fears and concerns, China's leaders have conducted a "charm offensive" that includes commercial diplomacy. Trade is an especially useful diplomatic tool. The offer of an FTA with ASEAN appears generous and symbolizes China's new status as a power in Asia. Forging closer economic ties is also a strand of China's diplomacy toward Central Asia, Russia, and India. Unlike Japan and South Korea, China is willing to liberalize trade in agriculture, which gives Beijing a diplomatic advantage.

Because of pressure from China, Taiwan is officially invisible even though more than 10 percent of China's imports come from Taiwan. Investment across the Taiwan Strait has grown exponentially, especially in the all-important information technology sector. A China-Taiwan investment treaty would make sense. Taiwan is an active and constructive member of APEC. Nevertheless, the Chinese government insists on excluding Taiwan from official discussions of intra-Asian economic integration.

Japan: Lagging Behind

Japan, thwarted by domestic politics, agricultural protectionism, and its near-stagnant economy, has been unable to take much initiative in the trade field. Its characteristic "leadership gap" is still a handicap. Its once-substantial foreign aid has been pruned. It is now China, not Japan, that sets the pace, shape, and direction of regional trade institution-building.[36]

Nevertheless, Japan still retains considerable strategic assets in Asia. The would-be AMF has risen from the dead in more modest garb as the Chiang Mai Initiative. The size of Japan's economy and its extensive corporate and financial networks still wield influence. Moreover, Japan's defense ties with the United States, its strategic awareness, and the emerging reach of its slowly growing military power guarantee a prominent place at the strategic table. The influence game is not zero-sum. On balance, however, China's influence is steadily waxing while Japan's is slowly waning.

Japan's goals with respect to Asian economic integration are both political and economic. Early motivations included the temporary failure of the General Agreement on Tariffs and Trade (GATT) negotiations in 1990, fear that the drive to substantially complete a single European market in

1992 might lead to a Fortress Europe, and the establishment of AFTA and North American Free Trade Agreement (NAFTA).[37] In addition, Japanese leaders want to avoid being left out of the FTA game because they do not want to cede leadership to Beijing. They are watching China's military modernization carefully and prefer to be engaged with China as much as possible. They value their alliance with the United States, but, like all other countries of the region, they do not want to be forced to choose between China and America. ASEAN+3 gives Japan an important intra-Asian forum that excludes the United States, while enabling Tokyo to preserve the U.S.-Japan alliance. With respect to the rest of Asia, offering to expand trade partially offsets recent cutbacks in foreign aid and puts a positive face on Japan's military profile.

On the economic side, FTAs offer Japan greater market access. If there is ever any hope of an export-led recovery in Japan, Asian customers will play a big part in it. Japanese government officials also see FTAs as a policy tool for catalyzing domestic reform and attracting foreign direct investment without having to open up the agricultural sector except in very insignificant ways. Not belonging to a regional FTA network means that Japan would lose negotiating power in multilateral negotiations and miss out on the economic benefits of liberalized trade. Japanese officials may also believe that participation in economic integration initiatives offers Japan better protection of investment and debt positions and more stable access to energy and natural resources.

So far, however, Japan's achievements in Asia have been limited to the Japan-Singapore Economic Partnership Agreement (JSEPA), which excludes agriculture. As mentioned earlier, the commitment to an FTA with South Korea is vague and includes no timetable. FTAs with Thailand and the Philippines are under study by bilateral expert groups, but agriculture is a stumbling block. With the Philippines, the issue will be not only agriculture but also movement of natural persons (i.e., immigration of nurses into Japan).[38] Japan is likely to resist these pressures in the usual ways. Tokyo has indicated that Japan is likely to propose some kind of framework agreement with ASEAN in 2003–04, but its content is likely to be vague. In short, Japan is lagging behind.

India: Playing Catch-Up

India's motives for tapping into regional integration in the rest of Asia are compelling, but its attractiveness as an economic partner is limited.

First, India needs viable economic relationships corresponding to its status as an emerging regional power, but it is surrounded by poor, hostile, strife-torn, or failing states. The South Asian Association for Regional

Cooperation (SAARC) is scarred by tensions between India and Pakistan and has yielded few economic linkages among its members. By contrast, India's trade with Asian countries outside of the SAARC has been growing. By the end of the 1990s about 17 percent of India's exports ($6.1 billion) went to non-SAARC Asia compared with 10 percent ($1.5 billion) in 1988–90. Similarly, India's imports from non-SAARC Asia reached 18.5 percent ($8.1 billion) in 1998–2000, up from 12 percent in 1988–90 ($2.4 billion).[39] The large number of Indian merchants and traders in Southeast Asia should prove helpful in deepening these commercial ties.

Second, Indians have entered the FTA scramble partly because they are unwilling to cede regional economic leadership to Beijing, even though they have little to offer. Despite the thaw in Sino-Indian relations in recent years, Indians remain wary of China's growing power and influence and want to be a full member of the emerging China-India-U.S. triangle.[40] Involvement with ASEAN is a logical next step. It also corresponds to India's more active security posture in the rest of Asia.[41]

Third, India needs the stimulus of FTAs to wrench its polity away from protectionism and toward competition. Despite its 7,000 km of coast, decades of inward-looking and protectionist policies have reduced India's economic role in East and Southeast Asia to a level lower than it enjoyed at the time of independence. By contrast, in prior centuries there was a flourishing trade from the east coast of Africa through India's Coromandel coast to Sumatra and Java.

As an attractive FTA partner, India is a latecomer and has a long way to go. India emerged from the last round of multilateral trade negotiations with tariff levels higher than any developing country, and it opposed a new round. Its infrastructure is woefully inadequate: it takes less time for grain shipments to travel from Australia to southern India than it does from southern to northern India.[42] Efforts to lower sky-high tariffs, relax restrictions on foreign investment, and dismantle the "license Raj" on a nationwide basis face fierce resistance. Many northern and central states remain mired in dated ideology, stifling traditions, maltreatment of women and girls, and corruption. Further military clashes with Pakistan are still possible, fueling high levels of defense spending. There are no near-term signs of an Indian economic "miracle," except perhaps in certain southern and coastal enclaves.

Nevertheless, India has many commercial assets, including an extensive coastline, a huge and literate middle class, a free press with sophisticated economic reporting, trained economists, excellent research institutes, a globally accessible popular culture (films and food in particular), widespread fluency in English, and a vast number of relatively wealthy and well-educated Indians abroad. Even China lacks some of these features.

Reforms of the early 1990s gave individual Indian states more autonomy to enact local economic reforms, opening the door for southern states (and cities) like Karnataka (Bangalore) and Andhra Pradesh (Hyderabad) to compete successfully for investment.

Port cities are taking advantage of new opportunities, and local free trade zones are planned. Allowing foreign and domestic companies to take full advantage of India's assets could lure back the talented Indian diaspora and attract other Asian and Western businessmen in large numbers.

In sum, the dominant "old" Asian goals were to keep United States engaged in Asia through APEC, to expand trans-Pacific and global trade, and to rely on the IMF for advice and assistance in crises. The "new" motivations are: 1) to strengthen Asia's geopolitical identity and increase negotiating leverage vis-à-vis the United States and the European Union; 2) to avoid or minimize the role of the IMF, if possible; 3) to accommodate China; and 4) to strengthen the region's competitiveness and thereby attract trade with and investment from U.S. and other western business interests, without strings and without undue pressure to open markets across the board.

Prospects for Success

Obstacles

A number of daunting obstacles offset the motivations favoring economic integration in Asia. To begin with, colonialism institutionalized the region's diversity. The major imperial powers in the region (the United Kingdom, France, the Netherlands, and later Japan) divided up their colonial markets, fostering trade within them but not encouraging trade among them. Cartels and monopolies were common. The colonialists imposed different regulatory and legal traditions as well as different languages and varieties of education. They promoted some groups over others, nurturing powerful vested interests determined to protect their position. When they left, often after bloody wars of independence, fledgling governments clung to their newly won sovereignty so tightly that the doctrine of "non-interference" became a kind of mantra. Many Asians still believe that colonialism and its neo-colonial aftermath marginalized their industries and that they deserve protection as a result.

Second, political and institutional weakness plagues many countries in the region. There are few political leaders possessed of a regional vision and influential enough to promote it successfully. Likewise, there are few governments with enough power and legitimacy to challenge entrenched protectionist interests. Respect for market principles and entrepreneurial skills are often limited. The institutional framework underpinning a vibrant business environment is uneven at best. In some areas, cross-border criminal activity is flourishing.[43] Except for Singapore, Hong Kong, and Japan (and to some extent Taiwan, Malaysia, and South Korea), legal institutions are weak or overburdened and the peddling of political influence is common. Corruption is widespread, particularly in Indonesia but also in the Philippines, India, China, and Thailand.[44]

Third, economic openness and domestic politics may conflict. Lowering barriers to Chinese exports may be politically disastrous. A national leader may promote prestigious projects in the name of self-sufficiency, carving out exceptions to proposed FTAs. (A prime example is Malaysia's automotive sector). There is often local resistance to foreign ownership.

Fourth, the rush of globalization has greatly accelerated the creation of wealth and raised per capita incomes, but it has also strained the social fabric of individual countries and exposed political strains. In most developing countries that have opened to the global economy, the balance of wealth and power has shifted to those best prepared to take advantage of the new opportunities. These new "winners" tend to live in cities rather than in the countryside and near the coast rather than in the interior. They are often members of an ethnic minority (e.g., Chinese and Indians),[45] and they have access to the Internet. Attracted by the new wealth, large numbers of people have flocked from the countryside to the cities, overburdening urban services such as water and sanitation.

Despite these obstacles, the drive toward economic integration is likely to continue in some form, partly for political reasons, partly because business groups will lobby for it, and partly because in a competitive global economy, leaders believe they have no other choice.

Variables within Asia: Market-Oriented Growth and Stability

Two key determinants of success lie within the region, namely, the containment of threats to stability and the adoption of market-oriented policies and institutions. Stability and security are the underpinnings of sustainable integration, but in Asia they cannot be taken for granted. The nuclear threat from North Korea is jarring, and the regime that gave rise to it shows no signs of imploding. The Bali bombings of 2002 revealed a tangle of terrorist networks. Indonesia has survived the transition to democracy in one piece, but Aceh is once again in flames. Problems in Kashmir are politically searing. The SARS epidemic revealed how quickly business travel, investment, and tourism can shrivel in the face of an unforeseen global plague.

The biggest variable in the stability of the region as a whole is China's evolution.[46] It is not difficult to imagine setbacks to the breathtaking progress achieved thus far. As WTO-related reforms dislodge the privileges long enjoyed by local elites, widespread resistance could erupt. Financial and real estate bubbles could swell and burst. Crackdowns on dissent could silence young people and alienate the West. Chinese leaders are well aware of these threats but are gambling that they can be avoided and that high rates of economic growth can be maintained. Assuming that they are correct, China's entry into the WTO, its investment ties with Taiwan, and its enhanced economic engagement with Asia are likely to enhance regional peace and stability.[47]

Elsewhere in Asia, market-oriented growth supported by wise policies and a sound institutional structure cannot be guaranteed, but to the extent that they exist they will make intra-Asian economic integration easier. Workers displaced by foreign competition will find it easier to find new jobs, and local cross-border trade and investment opportunities will attract new stakeholders with an interest in more open markets. The demand for information will work in favor of transparency and against large-scale corruption. Gradual steps toward joint monitoring and surveillance of financial flows, now in their infancy, will help calm investors' jittery nerves. Except for Burma and North Korea, all of the countries in the region are moving in this direction, although some are taking only baby steps.

India's future is also in question. The spread of communal violence of the sort recently witnessed in Gujarat, while unlikely, could torpedo India's prestige and freeze investment. The growing influence of Hindu supremacists will appeal neither to Asian Muslims, Buddhists, and Christians nor to secular, modernizing Asian governments. In short, unless India maintains a peaceful democratic system and injects itself with a large dose of market-oriented reforms, "ASEAN+1" will not acquire flesh and bones.

On balance, the region remains fragile and subject to many potential crises, but the basic drivers of the pre-crisis "Asian miracle" are still in place throughout most of the region. High rates of savings and investment, respect for education, and openness to learning and competition are prominent. Governance reforms are underway, and institutions are slowly becoming more accountable. Despite the financial crisis, no government has moved away from global engagement.[48]

Variables Outside Asia: Recovery and Global Trade

The other key determinants of the future success of economic integration initiatives in the next 5 to 20 years lie outside of the Asia region. The first is global economic recovery, especially in the United States and Europe. Investors will only consider large scale projects in Asia if they have cash and if potential demand in major global markets justifies those investments.

Such was the pattern throughout much of the 1990s. The economies of the United States and China will likely remain catalysts of growth in the region for the foreseeable future, but growth will not be as robust as it was in the 1990s. Moreover, the possibility of a financial crisis in China cannot be ruled out. U.S. recovery depends on a revival of investor confidence, an intangible factor shaped by developments ranging from peace in the Middle East to the impact of the tax cut on America's huge deficits. In addition, the European market for Asian goods and services is large and growing, but tight anti-inflationary policies and rigidities in the labor market restrain growth. The high value of the euro could further dampen Europe's prospects. Japanese consumer demand could provide a large economic stimulus to the region but is unlikely to materialize as long as the current generation of politicians remains in office.

The second and related variable is the outcome of the Doha Round of WTO trade talks. The main focus of the negotiations has been dubbed the "Doha Development Agenda" because it is widely understood that without significant "concessions" to developing countries, the Round will not succeed. The main field of battle is agriculture. Political resistance to eliminating protectionism and trade-distorting export subsidies remains formidable. Asian motives are mixed: agricultural exporters favor more open markets, but South Korea, Taiwan, and Japan will resist further liberalization. Meanwhile, global quotas on textiles and apparel are scheduled to expire in 2005, but the devil is in the details. Powerful U.S. lobbies have succeeded in capping or requiring U.S. content in textiles and apparel exports in the FTA agreements negotiated thus far and could still devise circuitous forms of protection.

Reaching an acceptable Doha Round agreement will require political support at the highest level. It is possible, but only barely so, that the major developed countries will see the wisdom of agreeing to major market-opening measures. Their incentives include offsetting the threat of terrorism and instability in developing countries, justifying remaining restrictions (notably on immigration) while doing something to alleviate poverty abroad, and providing a stimulus to growth in their own countries. If they do not, some kind of agreement will be cobbled together, perhaps not by the Doha Round deadline (2005) but at least by the time the extended U.S. negotiating authority expires (2007).[49] If the final outcome is disappointing, the case for regional trade liberalization in Asia will become stronger.

Likely Outcomes

In all likelihood the cross-cutting forces described above rule out extreme outcomes. In the next 5 to 20 years the world will see neither an Asian variation of the European Union nor the region-wide "free and open trade and investment" envisioned by APEC leaders in 1994. A closed trading bloc dominated by China or Japan will not arise because Asians benefit substantially from trans-Pacific and global economic ties. There will likely be a new WTO agreement by 2007, and possibly another new round in 2012 or thereabouts, but liberalization will be viscous and lumpy.

The most likely scenario in this time frame is limited intra-Asian economic integration, broadly but not completely compatible with WTO standards, supported by FTAs and growing investment and financial ties. Links between Northeast and Southeast Asia will continue to grow as ASEAN+3 acquires more institutional momentum and as China pursues FTA diplomacy (outpacing Japan). Although intra-Asian rhetoric will stress that Asia or at least ASEAN is a unit, the pattern will be (as Japanese government analyst Naoko Munakata puts it) "talking regional, acting bilateral."[50] Meanwhile, post-Mahathir Malaysia will tone down its rhetoric, and Indonesia will become more stable. But, unless central and local authorities substantially improve Indonesia's investment climate and ASEAN moves closer to open trade, foreign investors will continue to skirt the region even if the U.S. economy improves. Southern India and coastal cities will edge closer to informal integration with the rest of Asia.

Even this moderate scenario will expose and intensify social tensions. The uneven progression of bilateral FTAs will further divide Asia into "haves" and "have-nots," sparking growth and job creation but encouraging rapid migration to urban areas unprepared for the influx. Income gaps between coastal regions and the interior will become wider. Secessionist movements and border disputes will continue to plague the region.

Strategic Implications

The movement toward economic integration in Asia, slow-moving as it is, deserves to be taken seriously. If existing intra-Asian integration is not noteworthy, neither is it shallow or artificial. Geography still matters. Although wider integration would yield far more economic benefits, political leaders in Asia clearly have something to build on. The network that they are slowly building has at least four strategic implications.

The first implication is that economic statecraft has become an integral part of geopolitics and national strategy in Asia. All participating governments in the region find in this activity a path toward collective self-strengthening and an opportunity to promote strategic as well as commercial interests. Everyone can play because no one loses. The obstacles are enormous and the tangible gains are years away, but the process matters almost more than the results.

China is a case in point. Although nimble Singapore has moved farthest and fastest in binding a patchwork of economic ties, China is learning fast. China has edged out Japan in the competition for influence, but China's deepening engagement in the regional economy is in Japan's security interest because it lessens the likelihood of military conflict and encourages cooperative behavior. Watching this competition play out, no one has to hedge their bets because no one has to choose sides.

A second strategic implication is that Asia's nascent economic integration works in favor of peace and stability over time. A peaceful and stable security climate is a prerequisite for successful economic integration (or indeed for sustainable economic activity of any kind). But is the reverse true? In other words, will successful economic integration contribute to a peaceful and stable security climate in Asia? The answer is a qualified "yes."

The answer is qualified because much depends on whether the effort is well grounded in economic fundamentals. Political drivers alone will not work. To succeed, policies promoting economic integration in post-crisis Asia should conform to the same "lessons learned" as those derived from experience with development policy. Broadly speaking, sustainable economic integration must be grounded in open markets, sound macroeconomic policies, a responsible social policy agenda, and enforceable rules.[51] If regional economic integration proceeds along these lines, it will contribute to (but not guarantee) a more peaceful and stable environment in Asia for a number of reasons. Governments that have learned to cooperate on economic issues find it easier to substitute compromise for confrontation. The dialogue associated with integration builds trust and communication and works against the likelihood of war. New groups emerge with a strong stake in peaceful exchange.

But is this rosy scenario actually unfolding in Asia? Again, the answer is a qualified "yes." Parts of Asia remain prone to crisis and are highly flammable, and relationships can deteriorate quickly (e.g., Thailand and Cambodia). But in most of the region closer economic ties are slowly but surely reducing the likelihood of war. Political scientist Ming Wan argues that although economic cooperation in Asia should not be oversold, it has had a "moderate mitigating effect" on conflicts in the South China Sea, the Korean Peninsula, the Taiwan Straits, and Kashmir.[52]

Asian leaders already acknowledge that their large stake in each other's economies strengthens the case for avoiding war. In June 2003, Indonesia urged its fellow ASEAN members to establish a "security community" to ensure that unresolved territorial disputes and other cross-border conflicts would not undermine the region's growing economic ties. The proposal included such measures as a dialogue between defense officials to share information on risks. According to Jakarta, economic prosperity and regional stability are "two sides of the same coin."[53]

Some Asian governments are attempting to turn economic interdependence into strategic advantage by utilizing economic influence to reduce the likelihood of military conflict. Miles Kahler has studied the behavior of South Korea, Singapore, and Taiwan and identified three strategic connections between the management of economic interdependence and reductions in the threat or use of military force: 1) linkage (the use of bargaining power to obtain changes in another country's security policy); 2) a change in the domestic political calculus (of governments facing the rise of new groups with an economic interest in avoiding war); and 3) elite transformation (a learning process or a shift in the composition of ruling elites).[54]

Discussions aimed at fostering closer integration also help Asians tackle a number of non-traditional, cross-border security problems. Like other regions, Asia hosts terrorist cells, criminal networks, drug smugglers, human traffickers, and money launderers. Asians also face health-threatening environmental problems such as air pollution, natural disasters, the depletion of natural resources, and a major new disease (SARS) as well as an older epidemic (HIV/AIDS). These problems debilitate Asia's human resources, discourage investment, spur migration, and fan civil disturbances.[55]

Asian leaders realize that terrorism and other non-traditional security threats make their economic problems worse, and that failure to act cooperatively further damages their prospects. A year before the September 11 attacks, a team from RAND concluded that Asia's economic problems were more likely to impede rather than to encourage multilateral security cooperation in the region.[56] Today the reverse is true. The combination of the Bali bombing, other terrorist incidents, and U.S.-derived intelligence on terrorist cells in the region has forced officials to meet on a regular basis, share sensitive information, and pool resources. Since many of Asia's security problems are financed by criminal networks, Asian officials have also worked together to crack down on illicit transfers of funds.

A third strategic implication, closely related to the second, is that economic cooperation works in favor of (but does not guarantee) democracy. By expanding business opportunities, successful integration stimulates investment, diffuses technology, raises standards of living, and creates jobs, offsetting high and destabilizing levels of unemployment. The need for predictable rules and enforceable contracts encourages the rule of law. Moreover, functioning markets depend on open information, so demand for access to the Internet increases. Journalists expose corruption without getting shot. New stakeholders emerge as political actors, cutting across traditional racial, ethnic, or caste lines. Activists press for accountability and opportunities to be represented. A civil society begins to take shape in an atmosphere of hope. Governments that can successfully nurture this kind of change will acquire more legitimacy in the eyes of the public; the rigid, authoritarian misfits that cannot are headed, sooner or later, for the dustbin.

Japan, South Korea, Taiwan, and democratic ASEAN nations form a peaceful democratic core. China is the holdout, but the ruling party is recruiting businessmen and trying to reform itself from within. China is considerably more democratic today than it was before Deng Xiaoping began steering it in the general direction of a market economy. Since democracies generally do not fight each other, this trend reinforces peace and stability, but the link between economic integration and democracy is by no means automatic. The process is lengthy and subject to derailment.

A fourth strategic implication is that dialogues promoting closer integration enable ASEAN and ASEAN+3 to address cross-border security problems to a greater degree than before. The advantage of these groupings is that they overcome the rigidity of the post-colonial "non-interference" doctrine while preserving sovereignty. ASEAN ministers have been meeting regularly to discuss terrorism, and the ASEAN Regional Forum (ARF, which includes non-regional powers like Russia and the United States) has issued a statement on anti-terrorist measures.[57] In June 2003, ASEAN leaders issued an unprecedented call for fellow ASEAN member Burma to release dissident leader Aung San Suu Kyi from custody.

ASEAN+3 appears to be more effective than ASEAN or the ARF because it brings in the region's three economic powerhouses without the additional complications of U.S. and other non-Asian participation. Of these three, Japan and South Korea are democracies with relatively good records on enforcing contracts, combating economic crime, and fighting corruption. ASEAN+3 has been able to make progress on items long stalled in the ARF. For example, there is a new ASEAN+3 code of conduct with respect to territorial claims in the South China Sea. Although the declarations typically issued are vague and non-binding, and although the absence of the United States limits their implementation, they are a step in the direction of constructive integration based on common security interests.[58]

Implications for the United States: Is Integration Compatible with U.S. Interests?

The National Security Strategy

The National Security Strategy announced by the Bush administration in September 2002 emphasizes the cross-linkages between economics and security to an extent unmatched by any U.S. president since Eisenhower.[59] It specifically includes regional and bilateral trade initiatives on the list of measures designed to promote the forces of freedom. It asserts that free trade, a "moral concept" and a hallmark of freedom, will help expand the "democratic circle" and advance freedom and prosperity worldwide. The NSS envisages regional and bilateral FTAs with a mix of developed and developing countries in all regions of the world.[60]

U.S. Trade Representative Robert Zoellick often reiterates the twin goals of democracy and security. In so doing, he has parted company with the tradition that trade policy should be kept "pure," that is, justified exclusively on the commercial merits and insulated from political and security concerns. Of course, trade policy has never been wholly about trade. But Zoellick, a former aide to Secretary of State James Baker and an acute strategic thinker, has articulated the linkages among trade, democracy, and security more consistently than any of his predecessors. The network of bilateral FTAs envisaged in the Enterprise for ASEAN Initiative is the most tangible—and political—expression of the new policy at work in Asia.

FTAs and U.S. Interests

Granted that FTAs are compatible with America's new strategic outlook, is it wise for the United States to propose new FTAs with Asian countries when global trade liberalization offers so many more benefits? And will intra-Asian FTAs harm U.S. interests?

With some important exceptions noted below, FTAs have many advantages. They can be negotiated more quickly than multilateral agreements in APEC or the WTO. They correspond to changes in the pattern of business.[61] Competition from imports raises standards of quality and customer satisfaction, improves competitiveness, and allocates resources more efficiently. ASEAN economists and reform-minded ministers, many of whom have degrees from the United States or Australia, tend to favor economic integration, provided that it is market-oriented and trade-liberalizing.[62]

Market-opening measures also provide opportunities to tackle long-standing domestic barriers to growth, such as excessive regulation. The commitments associated with FTAs give economic reformers an opportunity to use external pressure to bring about what they want to achieve anyway. Political reformers view FTAs in a similar light. They see market competition and transparency as ways of loosening the economic stranglehold of entrenched elites, nabbing tax evaders, exposing corruption, and promoting accountability. They view large pools of restless and unemployed young people as a threat to their own power and interests and see FTAs as a way of stimulating job creation.

Nevertheless, the exceptions to the liberalizing aspect of FTAs are substantial. As John Ravenhill has observed, they include discrimination against non-members, the bypassing of smaller states or countries that are politically off-limits (Taiwan), the many excluded sectors, windfall earnings or "rents," complex rules of origin preventing transshipment, the diversion of resources, the burden on negotiators, and the creation of export lobbies dedicated to preferential access rather than to global competition.[63] Jagdish Bhagwati has coined the term "spaghetti bowl" to describe the growing tangle of inconsistent agreements. Compared to global free trade, regional or bilateral FTAs are clearly second best.

Political economist Richard Feinberg has analyzed U.S. policy statements justifying support for U.S. FTAs and identified four categories of U.S. interests: 1) opening markets for U.S. traders and investors; 2) establishing precedents or models, or serving as catalysts for wider trade agreements ("competitive liberalization"); 3) rewarding and supporting domestic market-oriented reformers, locking in and legitimizing their reforms, and advancing democratic institutions; and 4) strengthening strategic partnerships and security ties.[64] By these standards, the Enterprise for ASEAN Initiative (EAI) is clearly justified. Eventually, individual EAI agreements could even form the core of a harmonized U.S.-ASEAN FTA. The main caveat is that the EAI should not deflect U.S. attention from pursuing America's primary interest—an open *global* economy.

As for intra-Asian FTAs and U.S. interests, a "Fortress Asia" that would exclude or slap prohibitive tariffs on U.S. goods and services would deprive U.S. companies of a huge market, but such a mentality is nowhere in sight. By contrast, preferential tariffs brought about by intra-Asian FTAs (a far more likely situation) would place U.S. goods and services at a competitive disadvantage in participating countries. This situation is the mirror image of NAFTA. But U.S. companies have coped successfully with situations of this kind for some time, and in any event non-preferential tariffs negotiated in the WTO have been dropping for some time. More important, the United States has a market-opening strategy featuring its own FTAs. That is a major tactical advantage of the EAI.

China versus the United States?

Since China gains from intra-Asian FTAs of which it will be a member, does it follow that such a development works against U.S. interests?

Initially reluctant to participate in any multilateral organization that includes Taiwan (as APEC does), China has become an active and constructive participant in ASEAN+3 and APEC. This is all to the good: the more China evolves into a "normal" trading nation, the better. A growing

Chinese constituency in favor of international trade and investment does not rule out war but is surely good for U.S. security interests.

Nothing in the drive toward intra-Asian economic integration, including a China-ASEAN FTA, threatens the U.S. position in Asia. Such integration does not represent a classic balance-of-power coalition uniting against the United States. Virtually all of the countries in the region need access to the U.S. market and U.S. capital. At the same time, China's new diplomatic activism, combined with lingering doubts in some U.S. circles about its security intentions, underscores the strategic value of the EAI. If successful beyond Singapore, a patchwork of FTAs with the United States will offer a constructive counterweight to and stimulus for China's proposed FTA with ASEAN and other neighbors.

China and India have a history of conflict, but they recently agreed to cooperate more with each other on trade. At the same time, each has a stake in good relations with the United States. Washington is thus in a strong position within a triangular relationship, with China and India each fearing an alignment of the other two against it.[65] There is no reason for Washington to tilt either way; identifying and pursuing common interests is the logical course. For the rest of Asia, India is not that important, but China is. These governments welcome a warmer relationship with Beijing, combined with the opportunity to pursue expanded trade and investment with the United States. They dread a situation in which they would feel forced to choose between Beijing and Washington.

The EAI wisely does not force such a choice. Membership in one FTA does not preclude membership in others. Instead, the EAI adds a new political-economic dimension to the U.S. foreign policy profile in Asia. Although the EAI does not force governments to choose sides and is not a threat to China, it does pose a challenge to Beijing because it "delivers the goods." In the name of "competitive liberalization," it asks, in effect, which Asian power can do more to spur growth in the rest of Asia, China or the United States. The proposed China-ASEAN free trade agreement is probably ten years off, and in any event negotiating with ASEAN as a group faces the usual problem of the least common denominator. By contrast, the United States has already signed a far-reaching FTA with Singapore, and U.S. officials are holding exploratory discussions with Thailand. In short, the United States is in a strong position vis-à-vis China but should welcome growing Chinese engagement in the Asian economy.

Implications for U.S. Policy

U.S. support for intra-Asian economic integration, even as the United States pursues trans-Pacific and global free trade, makes sense. Initiatives promoting such integration and U.S. strategic goals are basically compatible. The more Asians trade with each other, invest in each other's countries, discuss their shared financial interests and concerns, share economic information, and conduct business on the basis of shared norms and rules, the more likely it is that peace, stability, and democracy will flourish in the region. There are reasons to be concerned about the exclusionary aspects of the new intra-Asian tendencies, but Asian motives are understandable. Opposing intra-Asian integration would not only be futile, it would also heap more ill will on the widespread anti-Americanism in the region.[66]

The EAI is commendable because it is positive, mutually beneficial, and conducive to openness, transparency, and cooperation. Beyond Singapore, FTAs not only with Thailand but also with Indonesia, the Philippines, and post-Mahathir Malaysia[67]—and possibly ASEAN as a whole—would all make political sense even though welfare gains to the United States would be relatively small.[68]

Revitalizing and strengthening APEC as a forum for trans-Pacific integration and community-building would also be beneficial. Steps in this direction will bump up against considerable Asian skepticism and disillusionment, but Asians need APEC because trans-Pacific ties are so vital. In addition, APEC members need APEC to keep pace with emerging intra-Asian institutions in areas where such integration initiatives touch on the interests of others. All APEC members need APEC to keep pressing for global liberalization in the Doha Round of WTO negotiations.

APEC has not fulfilled its mission as a framework for regional free trade and investment and lacks credibility in Asia, but it remains a fully representative forum for addressing common concerns. ASEAN+3 could become a kind of revitalizing core, giving Asians a sense that there is a counterweight balancing U.S. predominance. Washington would not always get its way, but, if it devoted the same kind of high-level attention to APEC that marked its participation in the early 1990s, APEC could recapture momentum. Breathing more life into APEC could revive and bring into focus once again APEC's long-standing 2010/2020 deadline for open trade and investment in the Asia Pacific region.

In addition to restoring a liberalizing momentum, APEC could take on a stronger surveillance role with respect to FTAs. APEC trade ministers have declared that any new bilateral or sub-regional trade agreements must be consistent with WTO requirements.[69] Although developing countries have some leeway, the main requirements are that FTAs should cover "substantially all" trade and be trade-creating rather than trade-diverting. Many intra-Asian FTAs, however, are likely to fall short, and the WTO mechanism for ensuring that these requirements are met is weak.

The United States should continue to encourage Asian governments to negotiate agreements that conform to WTO standards and bring about improved surveillance of their provisions in APEC and the WTO, but it should not oppose them if they fail to pass a purity test. No one is completely clean. However patchy and uneven intra-Asian FTAs may be, they nudge forward the progression of free trade, isolate and expose protected sectors, and stimulate those left out to come forward with proposals of their own. To the extent that bilateral FTAs remain a tool of competitive liberalization, they may jumpstart further trade reform within APEC and the WTO, especially if ASEAN+3 chooses to play such a role.[70] All the same, they do require surveillance.

If provided with modest secretarial resources, APEC could be a mechanism for governments participating in FTAs and other modes of economic integration to share what they are doing in a non-threatening political environment. (In that spirit the United States submitted to APEC the text of its FTA with Singapore and invited others to do the same.) APEC could also acquire more power in surveillance of economic trends and financial flows, monitoring of sub-regional trade and investment agreements, trade facilitation, and data gathering in such areas as health and the environment.

An additional task for a revitalized APEC could be to tackle a variety of new cross-border security threats. The arguments against adding traditional security issues to APEC's agenda are compelling,[71] but economic crimes, illicit trafficking, environmental pollution, water shortages, resource constraints, and the rapid spread of disease are hardly traditional. Since these problems are not confined to Asia and are indeed spread by globalization, and since they are at least partly economic in nature, there is a strong case for addressing them under APEC's auspices. APEC ministers are already paying serious attention to a U.S. proposal designed to improve maritime security, including secure containers and tighter procedures governing entry into ports.[72] Where appropriate, there should be low-key communication and cooperation between APEC and the ASEAN Regional Forum to address economic crimes of a violent nature (e.g., piracy at sea, criminal networks, and smuggling).

One factor limiting Asia-Pacific cooperation is domestic protectionism in the United States. Resistance to protectionist forces would be a decisive example of U.S. leadership and would help ensure the success of the Doha Round—still the "first best" option. Doing so requires the president's personal involvement and willingness to spend political capital. Even the extraordinarily capable U.S. Trade Representative can only go so far. A successful outcome of the Doha Round should be put on the list of top strategic priorities.

Finally, economic integration in Asia is a prime example of the need to integrate economic and security perspectives in policymaking. Prosperity and cooperation in Asia are in America's security interest. Too often, decisions are made in "stovepipe" fashion, that is, without integrating other perspectives. Current U.S. trade policy has a strategic core that complements U.S. security policy. What is needed now, building on the National Security Strategy, is corresponding strategic attention to Asia's economic future at the highest levels of the defense and foreign policy community.

Endnotes

1. For purposes of this chapter, "Asia" excludes Australia and New Zealand and includes India.
2. Ming Wan, "Economic Interdependence and Economic Cooperation," in Muthiah Alagappa, ed., *Asian Security Order*, Palo Alto, Calif.: Stanford University Press, 2003, p. 289.
3. See Chia Siow Yue and Lee Tsao Yuan, "Subregional Economic Zones: A New Motive Force in Asia-Pacific Economic Development," in C. Fred Bergsten and Marcus Noland, eds., *Pacific Dynamism and the International Economic System*, Washington, DC: Institute for International Economics, 1993, pp. 225–69.
4. Robert Scollay and John P. Gilbert list 25 such agreements in *New Regional Trading Arrangements in the Asia Pacific?* Washington, DC: Institute for International Economics, 2001, p. 3. A more up-to-date listing appears in John Ravenhill, "The Move to Preferential Trade in the Western Pacific Rim," *Asia Pacific Issues*, no. 69 (June 2003), p. 3.
5. See C. Randall Henning, *East Asian Financial Cooperation*, Washington, DC: Institute for International Economics, 2002; and C. H. Kwan, *Yen Bloc: Toward Economic Integration in Asia*, Washington, DC: Brookings Institution, 2001. Interest in a yen bloc has declined somewhat, but mention of a China-centered "yuan bloc" in the future has appeared occasionally in the *Far Eastern Economic Review*.
6. "EU-ASEAN: laying the foundations for a strengthened trade and economic partnership," *EU Trade News*, April 4, 2003.
7. For some recent modeling results, see Scollay and Gilbert, *New Regional Trading Arrangements in the Asia Pacific?* pp. 57–58 and 149; and Dean DeRosa, "Gravity Model Calculations of the Trade Impacts of U.S. Free Trade Agreements," a paper prepared for the Conference on Free Trade Agreements and U.S. Trade Policy, Institute for International Economics, Washington, DC, May 7–8, 2003, p. 35.
8. For a short but comprehensive description of economic integration, see Jeffrey J. Schott and Ben Goodrich, "Economic Integration in Northeast Asia," pp. 4–5, <www.iie.com>.
9. Source: World Bank, *World Development Indicators*, <www.worldbank.org/data/wdi2003/index.htm>.

[10] See <http://cf.heritage.org/index/indexoffreedom.cfm>.

[11] Jeffrey A. Frankel, for example, calculated that between 1962 and 1964, East Asia's intra-regional trade as a share of total trade grew from 33 to 50 percent. But when Frankel adjusted for the size of national economies and the group's importance in world trade, East Asia's "concentration ratio" declined. *Regional Trading Blocs in the World Economic System*, Washington, DC: Institute for International Economics, 1997, pp. 22–29.

[12] See <www.ita.doc/td/industry/otea/usfth/aggregate/hol+45.html>. The Philippines topped the list, with 29.9 percent of its exports going to the United States in 2000; Indonesia was lowest, at 13.7 percent. The others, including India, were in the 20–22 percent range.

[13] Edward J. Lincoln, "East Asian Economic Regionalism," unpublished manuscript, 2002, p. 67.

[14] Amy Kazmin, "Region 'at risk from lack of integration'," *Financial Times*, June 17, 2003, p. 9.

[15] Whereas China and Thailand agreed in June 2003 to eliminate tariffs on fruits and vegetables, talks between Japan and Thailand are hampered by Japan's reluctance to include Thai farm products.

[16] Scollay and Gilbert, *New Regional Trading Arrangements in the Asia Pacific?* p. 3.

[17] A Trade and Investment Framework Agreement sets up a consultative framework establishing regular meetings on a wide range of bilateral issues of interest to the United States.

[18] The U.S.-Jordan FTA recognizes the right of each country to establish its own labor and environmental standards and commits each side not to reduce them in order to encourage trade. See Howard Rosen, "Free Trade Agreements as Foreign Policy Tools: The U.S.-Israel and U.S.-Jordan Free Trade Agreements," a paper prepared for the Conference on Free Trade Agreements and U.S. Trade Policy, Institute for International Economics, Washington, DC, May 7–8, 2003, p. 17.

[19] See "Toward Open Subregionalism," in *Implementing the APEC Vision: Third Report of the Eminent Persons Group*, Singapore: APEC Secretariat, 1995, pp. 58–59.

[20] Other reasons include ASEAN's failure to respond effectively to the financial crisis of 1997–98, the rise of China as a magnet for investment, and the post-Cold War irrelevance of ASEAN's original anti-communist identity. See Jeannie Henderson, "Reassessing ASEAN," *Adelphi Paper*, no. 328, May 1999, Chapter 2 and pp. 75–79.

[21] Ming Wan, "Economic Interdependence and Economic Cooperation," p. 286.

[22] Japanese government analyst Naoko Munakata calls this "the counter-regionalism factor." See Munakata, "Whither East Asian Economic Integration?" *Brookings Working Paper*, June 2002, p. 2, <www.brook.edu/fp/cnaps/papers/2002_munakata.pdf>. Jeffrey J. Schott of the Institute for International Economics calls it "me, too" regionalism.

[23] Jusuf Wanandi, "The Strategic Implications of the Economic Crisis in Asia," *Indonesian Quarterly*, vol. 26, no. 1, (1998), p. 2–6.

[24] Alan Beattie, "US data to show damage of war on economy," *Financial Times*,

April 22, 2003, p. 4.

[25] The Paris Club is a governmental organization comprised of bilateral creditors, as opposed to the London Club, which consists of private creditors.

[26] Swap arrangements are defined and explained in Henning, *East Asian Financial Cooperation*, p. 16.

[27] Measuring China's investment boom against ASEAN's fundamental competitiveness is difficult because of the 1997–98 financial crisis. From 1996 to 1999, the period covering the crisis, foreign direct investment in China increased from $27 to $45 billion while that into ASEAN dropped from $28 to $11 billion. Without the crisis, both areas might have continued on a strong path.

[28] Daniel H. Rosen, "China and the World Trade Organization: An Economic Balance Sheet," *International Economics Policy Brief*, June 1999.

[29] For a broader discussion of China-ASEAN links, including the notion of an East Asian "community," see the summary of the Fifth China-ASEAN Research Institutes Roundtable in *Asian Studies Newsletter*, vol. 48, no. 2 (Spring 2003), p. 12. A list of papers is at <www.hku.hk/cas/cap/programmes/fr3a5.htm>.

[30] The most articulate spokesman challenging U.S. support for free trade on these grounds is Malaysian Prime Minister Mahathir Mohamad, but distinguished American economists such as Joseph Stiglitz and Dani Rodrik have also raised doubts about the speed and unevenness of the globalization process.

[31] Naoko Munakata, "U.S. Should Bless the Japan-ROK Free Trade Pact," *PacNet Newsletter*, no. 24, June 9, 2003. Economic modeling of various FTA options for Korea demonstrates that either APEC-wide free trade or a comprehensive FTA with the United States would benefit Korea more than a Japan-Korea FTA. See Schott and Goodrich, "Economic Integration in Northeast Asia," Table 7.1, <www.iie.com>. See also John Gilbert, "CGE Simulation of U.S. Bilateral Free Trade Agreements," a paper prepared for the Conference on Free Trade Agreements and U.S. Bilateral Free Trade Agreements, Institute for International Economics, Washington DC, May 7–8, 2003.

[32] Nicholas R. Lardy, *Integrating China into the Global Economy*, Washington, DC: Brookings Institution, 2002, p. 4.

[33] Lincoln, "East Asian Economic Regionalism," p. 90.

[34] Lardy, *Integrating China into the Global Economy*, p. 4.

[35] Lardy, *Integrating China into the Global Economy*, p. 6. Data are from the year 2000.

[36] Eric Heginbotham and Richard J. Samuels, "Japan," in Richard J. Ellings and Aaron L. Friedberg, with Michael Wills, eds., *Strategic Asia 2002–03: Asian Aftershocks*, Seattle: The National Bureau of Asian Research, 2002, p. 109.

[37] Noboru Hatakeyama, "Short History of Japan's Movement to FTAs," *Journal of Japanese Trade and Industry*, November/December 2002, p. 24.

[38] Fukunari Kimura and Mitsuyo Ando, "Strategies for East Asian FTA: A Japanese Perspective," presented to the Annual Convention of the Korea Society of International Economics, Seoul, Korea, December 6, 2002, p. 10.

[39] T. N. Srinivasan and Suresh D. Tendulkar, *Reintegrating India with the World Economy*, Washington, DC: Institute for International Economics, 2003, p. 56.

[40] See John W. Garver, "The China-India-U.S. Triangle: Strategic Relations in the Post-Cold War Era," *NBR Analysis*, vol. 13, no. 5 (October 2002).

[41] For instance, the Indian navy is cooperating with the Indonesian navy to crack down on smuggling in the Andaman Islands.

[42] During a trip to India in November 2002, I encountered this assertion repeatedly but I have been unable to document it.

[43] Factors of this kind undermined the effort to create a subregional economic zone consisting of northeast China, the Russian Far East, South Korea, and the west coast of Japan. See Gilbert Rozman, "Cross-National Integration in Northeast Asia: Geopolitical and Economic Goals in Conflict," *East Asia*, vol. 16, nos. 1/2 (Spring/Summer 1997), p. 28.

[44] Transparency International's 2002 "Corruption Perception Index" ranks the countries discussed in this chapter as follows: Singapore = 5th, (tied with Sweden), Hong Kong = 14th, Taiwan = 29th, Malaysia = 33rd, China = 59th, Thailand = 64th (tied with Turkey), India = 71st (tied with five other countries, including Russia), the Philippines = 77th, and Indonesia = 96th. Data are for 1999–2000 and may be out of date.

[45] Amy Chua argues that the economic privileges enjoyed by minorities are often enhanced by globalization in *World on Fire*, New York: Doubleday, 2003.

[46] See the four "Illustrative Asian Economic Scenarios" in Richard Sokolsky, Angel Rabasa, and C. R. Neu, *The Role of Southeast Asia in U.S. Strategy Toward China*, Santa Monica, Calif.: Rand, 2000, pp. 81–84.

[47] For positive and negative China scenarios and suggestions for U.S. policy, see Howard M. Krawitz, "China's Trade Opening: Implications for Regional Stability," *Strategic Forum*, no. 193, (August 2002).

[48] Stephan Haggard, *The Political Economy of the Asian Financial Crisis*, Washington, DC: Institute for International Economics, 2000, pp. 236–37.

[49] Trade expansion authority expires in 2005, but a possible one-time, two-year extension is built into the legislation.

[50] Munakata, "Whither East Asian Economic Integration?"

[51] See John Williamson, "Did the Washington Consensus Fail?" Outline of remarks at the Center for Strategic and International Affairs, November 6, 2002, <www.iie.com/publications/papers/williamson1102.htm>. Commenting on post-crisis Asia, the IMF called for a "social policy agenda." See Peter S. Heller, "Social Policy Concerns for the New Architecture in Asia," remarks prepared for the Manila Social Forum, November 9, 1999, pp. 2–4, <www.imf.org/external/np/speeches/1999/11099.htm>. Analyzing prospects for the Free Trade Area of the Americas, Jeffrey Schott has developed "Readiness Indicators" that are also relevant to economic integration in Asia. See *Prospects for Free Trade in the Americas*, Washington, DC: Institute for International Economics, 2001.

[52] Ming Wan, "Economic Interdependence and Economic Cooperation," pp. 280–310, especially pp. 293–97.

[53] Amy Kazmin, "ASEAN urged to set up security community," *Financial Times*, June 17, 2003, p. 9.

[54] Miles Kahler, "Strategic Uses of Economic Interdependence," Unpublished manuscript, pp. 3–4.

[55] For examples, see Alan Dupont, "The Environment and Security in Pacific Asia," *Adelphi Paper*, no. 319, London: Institute for International Strategic Studies, 1998; and the various chapters on Asia in Paul B. Stares, ed., *The*

New Security Agenda: A Global Survey, Tokyo and New York: Japan Center for International Exchange, 1998.

[56] Charles Wolf, Jr., Anil Bamezai, K. C. Yeh, and Benjamin Zycher, *Asian Economic Trends and Their Security Implications*, Santa Monica, Calif.: Rand, 2000, p. 75.

[57] Sheldon Simon, "Southeast Asia," in Ellings and Friedberg, eds., *Strategic Asia 2002–03: Asian Aftershocks*, pp. 333–37.

[58] See William H. Lewis and Edward Marks, "Searching for Partners: Regional Organizations and Peace Operations," *McNair Paper*, no. 58, June 1998; and the chapters by Muthiah Alagappa in Alagappa, ed., *Asian Security Order*, Palo Alto, Calif.: Stanford University Press, 2003.

[59] The equivalent document from the Clinton administration, *A National Security Strategy for a New Century*, released in 1999, devotes considerable attention to economic issues but does not spell out the linkages between economics and security quite so clearly or assertively.

[60] The National Security Strategy of the United States, <www.whitehouse.gov/nsc/nssall/html>.

[61] John Ravenhill, "The Regionalization of Production and Competitiveness in East Asia," <http://edie.cprost.sfu.ca/summer/papers/john-ravenhill.html>.

[62] Columbia University professor Jagdish Bhagwati disagrees, arguing that regional and bilateral free trade agreements detract from the goal of global free trade. Bernard K. Gordon, in "A High-Risk Trade Policy," *Foreign Affairs*, vol. 82, no. 3 (July/August 2003), pp. 105–18, argues that U.S. support for regional free trade "promises to severely damage U.S. foreign policy and trade."

[63] John Ravenhill, "The Move to Preferential Trade in the Western Pacific Rim," pp. 3–4.

[64] Richard E. Feinberg, "The Political Economy of United States' Free Trade Agreements," unpublished manuscript, April 2003, pp. 2 and 9.

[65] Garver, "The China-India-U.S. Triangle."

[66] Pew Global Attitudes Project, "What the World Thinks in 2002," pp. 4 and 61.

[67] Malaysia and the United States have not signed a TIFA, a prerequisite for an FTA with the United States, and Mahathir's hostility to U.S. trade policy makes it unlikely that he would agree to an FTA during the rest of his term.

[68] DeRosa has estimated gains to the United States. See "U.S. Free Trade Agreements with ASEAN," paper prepared for presentation at the Conference on Free Trade Agreements and U.S. Trade Policy, Institute for International Economics, Washington, DC, May 7–8, 2003.

[69] These conditions appear in Article XXIV of the General Agreement on Tariffs and Trade (GATT) and Article V of the General Agreement on Trade in Services (GATS).

[70] Inbom Choi and Jeffrey J. Schott, *Free Trade between Korea and the United States?* Washington, DC: Institute for International Economics, 2001.

[71] See Noordin Sopiee, "Should APEC Address Security Issues?" in C. Fred Bergsten, ed., *Whither APEC?* Washington, DC: Institute for International Economics, 1997, pp. 207–09.

[72] The initiative is called Secure Trade in the APEC Region (STAR).

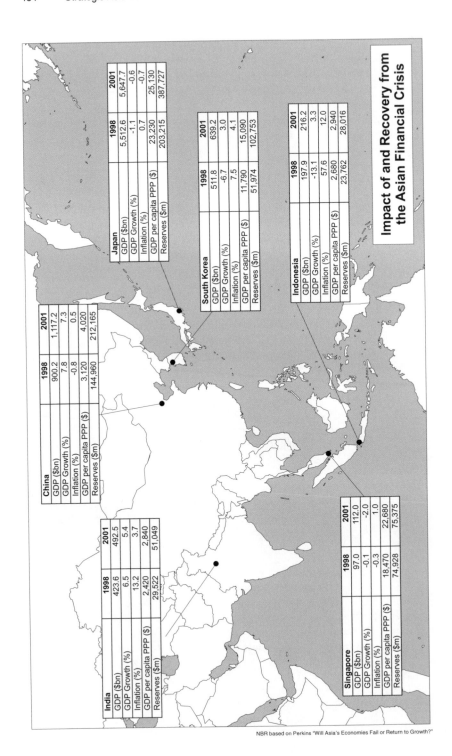

Impact of and Recovery from the Asian Financial Crisis

China

	1998	2001
GDP ($bn)	900.2	1,117.2
GDP Growth (%)	7.8	7.3
Inflation (%)	-0.8	0.5
GDP per capita PPP ($)	3,120	4,020
Reserves ($m)	144,960	212,165

Japan

	1998	2001
GDP ($bn)	5,512.6	5,647.7
GDP Growth (%)	-1.1	-0.6
Inflation (%)	0.7	-0.7
GDP per capita PPP ($)	23,230	25,130
Reserves ($m)	203,215	387,727

South Korea

	1998	2001
GDP ($bn)	511.8	639.2
GDP Growth (%)	-6.7	3.0
Inflation (%)	7.5	4.1
GDP per capita PPP ($)	11,790	15,090
Reserves ($m)	51,974	102,753

Indonesia

	1998	2001
GDP ($bn)	197.9	216.2
GDP Growth (%)	-13.1	3.3
Inflation (%)	57.6	12.0
GDP per capita PPP ($)	2,680	2,940
Reserves ($m)	23,762	28,016

India

	1998	2001
GDP ($bn)	423.6	492.5
GDP Growth (%)	6.5	5.4
Inflation (%)	13.2	3.7
GDP per capita PPP ($)	2,420	2,840
Reserves ($m)	29,522	51,049

Singapore

	1998	2001
GDP ($bn)	97.0	112.0
GDP Growth (%)	-0.1	-2.0
Inflation (%)	-0.3	1.0
GDP per capita PPP ($)	18,470	22,680
Reserves ($m)	74,928	75,375

NBR based on Perkins "Will Asia's Economies Fail or Return to Growth?"

WILL ASIA'S ECONOMIES FAIL OR RETURN TO GROWTH?

Dwight H. Perkins

ABSTRACT

For three decades the economies of East and Southeast Asia grew rapidly despite flaws in the institutions governing them. The Asian financial crisis of 1997–98 revealed the underlying weakness of the industrial policies in the region. Close government-business ties created extreme forms of moral hazard that led to excessively risky investments, which in turn led to weak financial systems overloaded with non-performing assets. Despite these institutional weaknesses, many of the economic fundamentals in East and Southeast Asia remain strong—except in Japan. The rate of investment in most of the region remains high, many countries have large low productivity labor forces that can be shifted to higher productivity jobs, and educational levels in most countries are high. The degree to which these fundamentals will translate into high rates of growth over the next decade will depend on the pace at which these countries reform their economic institutions. In that respect Korea has been a leader; China has also vigorously tackled reform since the late 1990s. Japan and Indonesia, however, albeit for different reasons, have done little to put the necessary reforms in place.

Dwight Perkins is the Harold Hitchings Burbank Professor of Political Economy at Harvard University and Director of the Harvard University Asia Center.

Introduction

East and Southeast Asia in the late 1940s and 1950s were areas racked by war and communist insurgencies. Japan was the exception, an island that regained its independence and began to achieve rates of economic growth never before attained anywhere in the world. By the late 1960s, in contrast, much of the region was in the early stages of three-plus decades of political stability and rapid economic growth, although this change was obscured by the U.S. involvement in the war in Vietnam and China's Cultural Revolution. By the end of these 30 years, East and Southeast Asia were noted not for their instability, but for their achievement of income levels many times higher than at the beginning of the period. China joined this process in 1978 and Vietnam in 1989. Only a few backwaters, such as North Korea and Burma, failed to participate in a transformation that raised per capita incomes four to six times for more than a quarter of the world's population and converted largely poor agricultural societies into urban industrial economies with a rising share of world trade. Then, in 1997–98, this extraordinary transformation seemed to come to an abrupt end, and people around the world began to question whether East and Southeast Asia would return to slower rates of growth (or worse) and periodic political instability.

The Asian financial crisis of 1997–98 was, in part, little more than a financial panic of the kind that periodically sweeps across vulnerable economies around the world. Once the panic subsides, recovery is often quite rapid. That was the case in many countries hard hit by the crisis in Asia, such as Korea and Malaysia and to a lesser extent Thailand. Singapore and Hong Kong also achieved rapid growth within a few years. Only Indonesia continues to wallow deep in a recession, largely because of the country's inability to create a stable political environment for investors.

The crisis was largely the result of macroeconomic mismanagement in Thailand and Korea that precipitated a financial panic. Both countries attempted to maintain overvalued exchange rates after opening their capital markets to foreign investors. When it became apparent that the exchange rates were unsustainable, domestic investors, who had borrowed abroad, and the banks that lent to them tried to get out of the local currencies as fast as possible, precipitating a sharp devaluation of the currency that bankrupted many of the borrowers and severely hurt the profitability of the lenders. Hedge funds have also been accused of initiating the crisis, but there is little evidence to support this claim. Foreign banks calling in their loans accounted for most of the outflow of capital.[1]

The crisis, however, also revealed serious long-term problems that affected not only the crisis-hit countries, but most of the rest of the region as well. Before the crisis, such weaknesses were apparent to anyone who chose to look in depth at these economies, but most observers were caught up in the euphoria of rapid growth and the belief that Asian economies had found the key to sustained economic success. In many respects these economies *had* found the formula for sustained growth, but one did not have to look any further than Japan to realize that fundamental problems were being concealed. The Japanese economy had barely grown since the bursting of the stock market and real estate bubbles at the beginning of the 1990s. Periodic efforts to stimulate the Japanese economy would work for a few months, but then the country would slide back into stagnation. Because these periodic stimulus packages further increased the government's deficit, Japan's debt level rose to 131 percent of GDP in 2001, and plausible forecasts had it rising to 150 percent of GDP by 2007 and to 250 percent by 2015.[2] Only extremely low interest rates keep this level of debt sustainable for the present, but it will likely become unsustainable sometime in the next 10 years.[3] In Asia beyond Japan, notably in Indonesia but also in Thailand, Korea, and elsewhere, the quality of large-scale investments deteriorated markedly as governments backed plans designed to line the pockets of favored individuals and companies.

The problems revealed by the crisis were not temporary aberrations that would disappear on their own. They went to the very heart of how most Asian economies did business. Japan, the lead goose in the "flight pattern of development" that Japanese economists like to discuss, established this business model, and its difficulties in the early 1990s were early an indication of what could happen across the region if steps were not taken to alter this pattern. Some even suggest that the Japanese economy would collapse, and that too would be a harbinger of what the rest of the region could expect in time.

To understand the nature and seriousness of the economic problems facing East and Southeast Asia, it is first necessary to have a picture of how the economies of the region are organized and why they are organized that way. One must understand the nature of the relationship between government and business and why this relationship, which seemed so effective for so long, no longer seems to work. With that understanding as background, one can then analyze the nature of the challenge facing Japan, the current economic slowdown in much of the rest of the region, and whether China will continue to grow rapidly despite seeming to have many of the same problems as the rest of Asia. Put differently, are East and Southeast Asia in for a long period of slow growth or worse, and, in particular, is a fall looming for China's economy? The short answer to these questions is "probably not," but, as the analysis that follows will make clear, the possibility of stagnation or worse in the region cannot be completely ruled out.

Government-Business Relations in Asia

Since the Asian financial crisis, government relations with business in Asia have often been described as "crony capitalism." This pejorative term implies that Asian politicians used their power to line their pockets and found many businessmen willing to collude in this endeavor. The origins of government-led industrialization in the region, however, had little to do with lining the pockets of either politicians or business leaders. The model for government-business relations in Asia began in the 1950s with Japan's Ministry of International Trade and Industry (MITI), and was taken up in the 1960s by Korea and Taiwan and then by a number of Southeast Asian nations. Only Hong Kong, and to a lesser degree Singapore, stuck with something approximating the more market-oriented approaches of the United States and the United Kingdom. When China and then Vietnam decided to abandon Soviet-style central planning, they too began moving toward what they believed to be the Japanese or Korean model.

In its initial form, the industrial policies of Japan, Korea, and Taiwan involved little in the way of politics and not much rent-seeking or corruption. The role of the government was not identical in these three economies, but, in general, government officials promoted certain industries at particular stages of development and then backed up those promotions with tariff protection, easy access to foreign exchange and bank credit, and favorable tax treatment for those businesses willing to carry out the government's industrial plans. Sometimes, as in the 1960s in Korea and Taiwan, this support was available to anyone who met the government's export objectives. At other times, the governments' direction and support was targeted to individual firms.[4]

There was more than a little corruption in Japan, Korea, and Taiwan from the 1950s through the 1970s, but the corruption had little influence on industrial policy decisions. Businessmen in Korea had to ante up to the governing political party in order to be part of the industrial development game, but the decisions about which firm would take on a particular task were largely free of side payments or political considerations. The decisions were made by experts based on technical grounds. In Japan, politics was quite corrupt and sectors such as construction were driven heavily by political and rent-seeking concerns, but MITI officials also made their decisions on technical grounds. MITI was seen as a clean department, although many eventually came to see the *amakudari* system, where officials retired from the ministry and joined the firms they had regulated, as a form of corruption. At the time, however, analysts inside and outside of Japan saw *amakudari* as an important way for government and businesses to maintain a close and well-informed working relationship.

Keeping politics and rent-seeking out of industrial policy decisions is extremely difficult for most countries, however, and it proved to be increasingly challenging for Korea in the 1980s and 1990s. In the 1960s and 1970s, the politicians of Korea and Taiwan did not know whether their country would exist a decade or two hence, and that helped focus their decisions on doing what was right for the economy rather than for their own pocketbooks.[5] By the 1990s, the threat to the very existence of South Korea had subsided, and democratic reforms had produced political leadership no longer preoccupied with industrial policies. The levers of political control over the Korean economy, however, were still in place, and in the 1990s they were explicitly used for political and rent-seeking ends. Where the technocrats of the 1970s produced POSCO, arguably one of the best steel corporations in the world, the politicians of the 1990s created Hanbo Steel, whose bankruptcy in the mid-1990s helped lay the groundwork for the financial crisis that would soon occur.

The application of the Japan-Korea approach to industrial policy fared even less well in Southeast Asia. Malaysia, under Prime Minister Mahathir, also attempted to build a modern heavy industry sector, but this economic goal was intertwined with the national goal of promoting Malay or Bumiputera interests. As a result, by the mid-1990s, foreign firms dominated Malaysia's exports of manufactured goods, Chinese-Malaysian firms produced mainly for the domestic market and received little help from the government, and Bumiputera firms were created by privatizing the former large state enterprises. The Bumiputera businessmen bought these firms with the help of huge government directed loans from the local banks.

The worst problems of political and rent-seeking influences over industrial policy took place in Indonesia. In the 1980s, Indonesia had gradually begun to dismantle many of the government controls over the economy in order to create greater opportunities for foreign investors and local entrepreneurs to start manufacturing businesses that would eventually replace petroleum as the main source of export earnings, and these efforts achieved considerable success. By the 1990s, however, President Suharto had misinterpreted the sources of this success, and he increasingly used government industrial policy to promote the large projects of his family and business associates. At the macro level, this pushed Indonesia closer to having a serious external debt problem. At the micro level, large projects received licenses to operate only if they gave substantial numbers of ownership shares to Suharto's family members.

The main problem with the close ties between government and business throughout East and Southeast Asia, however, was less a matter of corruption than it was the issue of how these ties affected the strength of the local banks and non-bank financial institutions. When the governments used their power to direct lending to industries and firms favored by their industrial policies, they took on an obligation to help out these banks and firms if things went awry and they lost money. The banks and firms in turn, knowing that the government would bail them out if they got into trouble carrying out the governments' wishes, often took bigger risks than they would have if they had shouldered those risks on their own. The economists' term for this phenomenon is "moral hazard," and moral hazard was pervasive throughout Asia in the 1990s and continues to the present.

As a result, Japanese banks readily made loans backed by collateral in the form of highly inflated stock and real estate shares, Korean and foreign banks lent heavily to the *chaebol* to carry out their massive diversification in fields where they had little experience, and Indonesia's state banks lent to whomever the president and his family thought appropriate, however leveraged those investments might be. The result throughout Asia was the perpetuation of very weak banking systems. In Korea, Taiwan, and Indonesia, the state-owned banks dominated the financial markets and were the ones saddled with large non-performing assets. In Japan, Thailand, and Malaysia, private banks held most of the non-performing assets. Private or public, the financial systems throughout the region were very vulnerable to even mild shocks, and what they got in 1997–98 was a major shock. Most of these banks, as a result, were bankrupt or would have been bankrupt if their assets had been properly valued in accordance with international standards. Many non-bank financial institutions were in even worse shape and were, in fact, closed after 1997.

When the governments in the region did begin to clean up the financial mess that the panic and their policies had created, they encountered additional weaknesses in the system. Among other problems, the bankruptcy laws in many of the countries were not up to the task of resolving the mess created by the crisis.[6] Firms with close ties to the government were not supposed to go bankrupt because the government would bail them out when they got into trouble. Bankruptcy laws, therefore, were little used in the days of the economic boom and few worried that the laws were not well-written or, more importantly, that the courts lacked the skills and authority to enforce those bankruptcy rules that did exist. Therefore, South Korea, the one country that did take immediate and determined steps to clean up the mess, relied not on the courts but on the executive branch of the government to force the *chaebol* to restructure and reduce their debt-to-equity ratios to acceptable levels. The main lever for forcing compliance with the restructuring was the executive branch's control over the banks that held most of the *chaebol* debt. Thus, a government that was trying to get away from government-led industrial policies was forced to rely on those policies to achieve its other economic objectives. This contradiction continues to this day. The recently elected Roh Moo Hyun government, for example, continues to rely on interventionist policies to rein in the *chaebol*, and is seen by many as not pushing reform if it does not use such policies. Reform of this kind, however, undermines more fundamental efforts to create a truly level playing field governed by market forces.

Throughout the rest of the region, governments were far less determined to clean up the mess. The extreme case was Indonesia, where the government made only minimal efforts to force local firms to either repay their loans or go out of business when they failed to do so. Some banks were closed and others were restructured, refinanced, and reopened. Many foreign and domestic investors, however, had good reason to fear that little would be done to support their claims against local businesses, even if those claims were unrelated to the financial crisis. The courts were of no help in these efforts because they were widely perceived to be thoroughly corrupt.

But a country did not have to be caught up in the crisis to have trouble in the banking sector. Japan's banks, some have estimated, have at least $1 trillion in non-performing assets, and this situation has persisted since the early 1990s without the government taking major steps to solve the problem.[7] Instead, government regulators have closed down a few banks, but most have continued to operate without major restructuring. According to some analysts, the bank regulators appear to classify bank assets as non-performing based on criteria designed to ensure that these banks stay legally solvent and meet the Bank of International Settlements capital standard of eight percent that is required for operating internationally. The large quantity of bad loans remains on the books as nominally performing and the number of new bad loans continues to rise as the Nikkei stock price index continues to descend from 14,000 in the early 1990s after the collapse (from nearly 40,000 prior to the collapse) to around 8,000–10,000 today. Moreover, the banks keep rolling over loans to firms that are by most standards no longer viable. Japan's banking system, as a result, is severely crippled and unable to provide much support to the parts of the economy that are still dynamic, despite the huge size of the main Japanese banks. Instead, they find it safer to buy government bonds.

Industrial and Financial Policies in China

China sailed through the Asian financial crisis without major problems, although the reported GDP growth rates of over seven percent a year during those two years are very likely inflated. Nevertheless, China has a financial system that is, if anything, in worse shape than most of the others in Asia.

China (and Vietnam) began their economic reforms with a banking system that was inherited from the Soviet-style command economy. Banks in the Soviet-style system mainly enforce centrally planned targets. They have no capacity to judge whether a loan is going for a viable project; that is the purview of the state planning commission. Similarly, these banks have no authority to withhold credit if the purpose for which the credit is being sought is in the central plan. Thus, state enterprises are given whatever credit they ask for subject only to a veto from the planning commission.

In the 1980s, China abolished centrally planned targets and centrally controlled investments and turned many of these decisions over to the state-owned enterprises. The enterprises in turn looked to the banks to provide them with the necessary funds to carry out these decisions. The banks, as they had in the past, simply provided the money without asking many questions. On paper the banking system had gone through a major restructuring with the mono-bank system replaced by a central bank and a number of commercial banks, but the behavior of the bankers did not change with the restructuring—they still kept making loans on request.

None of this was a serious problem as long as the state owned-enterprises made large profits and could pay back their loans. But market reforms ended most of these monopoly profits, as relative prices for industrial products fell. Many state owned-enterprises ended up taking large losses and could no longer repay their loans. The banks, however, kept on lending even when the enterprises were in default. When these practices created serious levels of inflation, the central government would step in and set lending quotas for the banks, only to relax those quotas as soon as the inflation subsided. By the late 1990s, the government finally persuaded the banks to restrict their lending to defaulting enterprises, but these enterprises often simply stopped paying their suppliers, thus, in effect, forcing their suppliers to finance their purchases. It became difficult to tell just which firm was solvent and which was not since so much depended on how one interpreted "accounts receivable," which might never be received.

The result of all of this is a banking system that, from the late 1990s to the present, has had official non-performing loans equivalent to around 25 percent of total bank assets,[8] and many believe that the true figure may be as high as 40 percent.[9] Put differently, all of China's major commercial banks would be bankrupt if their assets were valued in accordance with international standards.

Since the late 1990s, China has taken steps to try to correct this situation. Asset management companies were formed for each of the major state-owned commercial banks and did take over some of the non-performing assets. Banks are becoming more conscious of the need to make judgments about the quality of the projects to which they are lending. The geographic coverage of bank branches has been restructured so that coverage is not identical with the geographic span of local politicians. Most importantly, in the late 1990s, the government began to close many of the loss-making state-owned enterprises, an effort that led to around 30 million layoffs. But despite all of these efforts, politics remains pervasive in much bank lending and the share of non-performing assets does not appear to be declining much.

Some analysts of China's economy are tempted to take the above-described situation and argue that China's economy is on the edge of an abyss and could soon collapse, not unlike what happened elsewhere in Asia in 1997–98. There are key differences between the situation in China today and that in the hard hit economies of Asia in 1997–98, however. One difference is that China has liberalized its currency, the *renminbi*, on the current account but not on the capital account. Thus investors, foreign or domestic, cannot flee quickly from portfolio or other short-term investments in China, however panicked they may be. Far more importantly, China has $346 billion in foreign exchange reserves as of June 2003, an enormous sum by international standards.[10] Those reserves continue to grow because China maintains a current account surplus and $50 billion a year in foreign direct investment, which is considerably larger than the country's outflow of capital, both legal and otherwise. Furthermore, China has very little foreign debt, most of which is long-term. Thus, unlike the situation in Thailand, Indonesia, or Korea in 1997, investors' credits in China are mainly borrowed from domestic sources and, where foreign sources of credit are involved, there is no danger whatsoever that China will be forced to make a major and hurried devaluation of the *renminbi* of the kind likely to set off a panic and a run on the banking system. If there were to be a run on the banking system for some other reason, the central bank could easily finance the commercial banks as long as the run continued, simply printing the money required if necessary.

China, therefore, is not likely to face a financial collapse that would trigger a sharp fall in the real side of the economy. The danger to the Chinese economy lies elsewhere. China's government continues to play a very large role in directing the economy through its control not only of the financial system, but of many of the larger industrial and commercial enterprises as well. Thus, China continues to pursue an industrial policy that has much in common with that in Korea or Japan in the 1960s and 1970s. If anything, the current Chinese government intervenes more often in industrial decisions than did the earlier governments of those two other countries, although this statement requires some qualification. China's agricultural sector and its small- and medium-scale industrial sectors are governed mainly by market forces, and they constitute a larger share of the total economy than was the case in Korea or Japan. There is also far more foreign direct investment in China today than in Korea or Japan in the past, and foreign invested enterprises in China are largely market driven. That said, the Chinese government has more direct control over the large industrial enterprises, a great portion of which remain state-owned, than was the case in Korea or Japan. What is worse, politics and rent seeking play a very large role in the industrial policy and investment decisions of the Chinese government, something that was not the case in Japan and Korea in these earlier years.[11]

Thus China has a banking system that continues to make bad loans and is loaded down with non-performing assets; it has a large scale industrial sector that continues to be state owned to a substantial degree and subject to political and rent-seeking influences; and, since the turn of the century, it has faced a problem of deflation caused in part by insufficient aggregate demand. The government has dealt with the aggregate demand problem by deficit spending on roads, airports, and other infrastructure. The danger is that all of this government-led industrial and infrastructure investment activity, influenced as it is by politics and rent seeking, will lead to inefficient decisions across a wide spectrum of the economy and that could slow growth markedly. Stagnation on the pattern of Japan since 1992 is not very likely because the infrastructure being built in China is, for the most part, needed, unlike the situation in Japan where much of the new government infrastructure has limited or no real value. Like Japan, much of China's industrial output is destined for export and that provides some protection from the really inefficient industrial investments one finds in countries that emphasize import substitution. Nevertheless, China's financial sector is in a worse state than that in Japan. China, however, is still in a stage of development where industry, not services, remain the key to rapid growth. In Japan, by contrast, services should dominate growth, but the efficiency of the Japanese service sector has fallen far short of its American and European counterparts for decades.

The danger for China, therefore, is that inefficient state-led decisions will slow the economy to a pace that will not be sufficient to absorb the 200 to 300 million workers who would move to cities from the countryside if jobs were available. Slow growth, say of four or five percent a year, thus could be accompanied by rising overt unemployment (as contrasted to the disguised unemployment that currently exists in the rural areas), which could undermine political stability.

The challenge for China over the next five to ten years and beyond, therefore, is to move its economy toward one governed by market forces and away from one directed by the government. China's decision to join the World Trade Organization was a major step in the right direction, especially because, to achieve accession, China agreed to open its weak financial sector to what over time will be vigorous foreign competition. But China still has a long way to go before it has the institutions required by a modern market economy to make government intervention unnecessary in many areas. If bankruptcies, mergers and acquisitions, and other such activities are to be driven by market forces rather than by government fiat (as is the case at present), China will need a set of rules to govern those market decisions, and those rules will have to be enforced by either an independent judiciary or and independent regulatory system. At present China has neither, and creating these institutions is likely to take decades, not years.

The Growth Fundamentals

Focusing on the problems of the financial sector and related industrial policies tends to obscure some of the strengths of the East and Southeast Asian economies that are still present. To begin with, most of the countries in the region have enjoyed very high rates of investment as a percentage of GDP, rates that during the boom years were over 30 percent of GDP. In much of the region those rates have fallen to 25–27 percent, which is still a very high figure. Of the countries of concern to this volume, only Indonesia and the Philippines have rates of gross capital formation that are below 20 percent of GDP. Both are at 17 percent, largely because of the uncertain investment environment in both countries. In the Philippines, the army and populist political pressures continue to threaten the stability of the government. In Indonesia, there is the threat of terrorism and internal conflict, but the more serious problem for investors is the government's inability to control widespread corruption within its own ranks. China's gross capital formation rate has averaged an extraordinary 39 percent of GDP.[12] If that level of investment is sustained, China could waste significant amounts of money on poorly chosen investments and still grow rapidly.

These high rates of investment were made possible in part by the high rates of savings in most of these countries, and the high rates of savings were largely the result of the low dependency ratios enjoyed by most Asian nations (the ratio of individuals under 15 or over 64 not in the work force to those between the ages of 15 and 64 that are in the work force). These low dependency ratios reflected the success of Asian fertility regulation, which sharply reduced the percentage of children in the population and occurred before the share of the elderly (64 or older) population began to rise. Most forecasts of the population structure of these countries over the coming decade suggest that these dependency ratios should stay low and hence that savings rates should remain high.[13] Over the longer run, as the essay in this volume by Nicholas Eberstadt points out, China's dependency ratio will rise thanks to the impact of the one-child policy, but this impact will be felt beyond the five to ten year framework that is of concern here.

If the climate for investment stays favorable, as it is in most of the countries discussed here, the high savings rates should translate into high rates of domestic investment. The Philippines is an exception, partly because of its weak investment climate but also because of a higher dependency ratio than the rest of the region. By contrast, Indonesia, despite having a low dependency ratio, has the poorest investment climate, largely because of political instability (as noted above).

Another exception to these low dependency and high savings rates over the next decade is Japan. There the population is aging rapidly and the dependency ratio, comprised increasingly not of children but of people over 64, is rising at the rapid rate of one percent a year. Japan's household savings rate, therefore, continues to fall and the investment rate is falling with it.[14] Despite this gradual decline in the savings rate in Japan, unlike in much of the rest of Asia, the population continues to want to save more than it wants to invest. This behavior in turn forces Japan to either run fiscal deficits or current account surpluses to offset the imbalance.

Japan's future growth, however, as is the case in all countries on the technology frontier, depends less on the rate of investment than on the rate of productivity growth, and productivity growth over the long term is driven by technological innovation through research and development. The other countries in Asia, particularly the poorer countries among them, can continue to generate increases in productivity by adopting technologies developed elsewhere. But Japan, like the United States and Western Europe, must rely on technologies developed in its own laboratories and shop floors.

At the same time, many of the countries of Asia face a favorable demographic situation (at least for achieving relatively rapid growth). Large parts of the work force in China, Vietnam, Indonesia, Thailand, and even Malaysia are still in low productivity occupations in rural areas. The growth of the higher productivity urban labor force, therefore, depends not only on the total number of people in the country entering the work force, a rate largely determined by the population growth rate 15 years earlier. The growth rate of the modern sector labor force depends too on the pace at which people in rural areas can be shifted into higher productivity jobs in the cities. This shift in labor from low to high productivity occupations can alone contribute an extra 1 percent to the GDP growth rate for those countries with a large reservoir of rural labor. No such shift is possible in Japan, of course, nor is it possible in Korea, Taiwan, Singapore, or Hong Kong.

Another major underlying source of strength in East and Southeast Asia is the quality of the labor force. In Japan, Korea, and Taiwan nearly 100 percent of the age group eligible to attend secondary school is in school. In China, the percentage of the eligible population in secondary school is 70 percent, and the percentage for the other successful developers in the region ranges from 48 percent in Thailand to 78 percent in the Philippines. Among the more economically advanced nations in the region, the percentage of population in universities compares favorably with many European nations with higher per capita incomes. In the least developed countries in the world, only 31 percent of the population of secondary school age is enrolled, and the quality of that secondary school education is typically much lower than that in Asia. The health statistics for the labor force of much of East and Southeast Asia also compare favorably with health levels elsewhere in the world at comparable standards of living. In short, East and Southeast Asia have high-quality, disciplined labor forces that adapt easily to the demands of an industrializing economy.

To summarize this brief review of the sources of long-term growth in East and Southeast Asia, the main conclusion is that the key fundamentals for high growth remain strong.

The Future

As Japan has demonstrated since 1990, strong fundamentals do not guarantee continued rapid growth. The missing ingredient is the quality of the institutions that manage the human and physical resources that contribute to economic growth. As has been elaborated above, the institutional framework for managing growth inputs in East and Southeast Asia is far weaker than the quality and quantity of the inputs themselves.

The institutional weaknesses are of several kinds. As explained above, the close ties between government and business created a moral hazard that in turn undermined the potential of the financial systems in all of the economies of the region. These close government-business ties grew out of the perceived strengths of the Japanese and Korean approaches to industrial development, strengths that have not readily been transferred elsewhere in the region and no longer serve Japan or Korea well either.[15]

Relying mainly on market forces to guide the economy, however, is not a viable alternative in the region because certain key institutions necessary to a well-functioning market are also weak. Strong markets require a stable legal system, and the legal system has typically played only a minor role in the economies of the region, even in places such as Japan or Korea where the legal system functions perfectly well in the sphere of civil rights and criminal law. In China, and even more so in Indonesia, the legal system lacks the authority, the integrity, and the competence to take over the critical task of enforcing the rule of law in the commercial sphere.

Fortunately, countries can grow rapidly for some time without correcting all of their institutional shortcomings. If the full range of market-supporting institutions had to be in place before growth could occur, no nation (including the United States and the United Kingdom) would have managed sustained economic growth. A nation can achieve rapid growth for long periods by getting only some of the key ingredients right, and East and Southeast Asia have gotten many of the key ingredients right. But the 1997–98 financial crisis demonstrated how wrong things could go in the short run when key ingredients are missing. Furthermore, Indonesia, at the low per capita income end of the spectrum, and Japan, at the high end, have also demonstrated how wrong things can go over the longer run if steps are not taken to correct the weaknesses once they are exposed. In Indonesia's case, the problem is the difficult one of making a transition to an unfamiliar political system. In Japan's case, it is the inability of the country's democratic system to overcome political resistance to necessary changes in the way the economy is run. Until this situation changes, there is little prospect that Japan will return to per capita income growth of more than one percent a year, if that. If the level of public debt becomes unsustainable, even that forecast will be overly optimistic.

Turning to the rest of the region, Korea has demonstrated how determined action to achieve necessary structural reforms can pay off with renewed rapid growth. And China, despite the enormous magnitude of many of its economic problems, has in recent years demonstrated a willingness to make major structural changes, even when those changes involve large political risks. The other economies and polities of the region fall somewhere in between Japan and Indonesia on the one hand, and Korea and China on the other when it comes to seizing the brass ring of economic reform. The variation in economic performance in the region over the next decade is likely to reflect this variation in the vigor with which economic reform is pursued. Those that pursue reform with vigor and whose per capita income is still quite low should be able to increase their GDP at a rate of six or seven percent a year or even more. Vigorous reformers at higher levels of per capita income will grow more slowly, and the countries that do not continue to make progress with reform will follow the example of Japan. The weakness of financial and other market institutions in so many of the economies of Asia, however, will lead to slower growth over time if those inefficiencies are not gradually corrected, even if nothing else goes wrong. Poor performance because of weak institutions in one or two countries could prove to be contagious. Investors elsewhere in Asia will see what is happening in the poorly performing economies and realize that something similar could happen throughout the region.

What else could go wrong? As the Severe Acute Respiratory Syndrome (SARS) epidemic in 2003 demonstrated, other things could clearly go wrong and there is no ready way of forecasting precisely what kinds of shocks could upset the basically favorable picture of growth prospects in the region. SARS itself has had a devastating impact in the short run on both air travel and tourism in the region. As of this writing (July 2003), SARS appears to be under control, so the long-term impact on the economy is not likely to be great. But what if SARS had raged out of control, affecting millions, and possibly even killing, millions of people? Then the impact on the economies of Asia and much of the rest of the world could have been devastating. This could still happen if SARS makes a comeback during the upcoming flu season, as some fear. Could terrorism impact the regional, or global, economy in a similar way? It seems unlikely, although the October 2002 Bali bombing demonstrated that terrorism can have a major impact on tourism in the region at least for a time. Could there be political upheaval of a more profound kind, as has occurred in Indonesia and has brought rapid growth to a halt? The prospects that this might happen are the subject of other chapters in this volume. All that need be said here is that political upheaval would have obvious negative consequences for growth in the affected country or countries.

A more likely danger for the economies of Asia would be a worldwide slowdown in economic growth and a resulting stagnation in Asia's export markets. If the United States and Europe were to go the way of Japan in the 1990s, a prospect that some analysts think is possible, then the economies of East and Southeast Asia would have to rely mainly on their own domestic markets or on exports to each other for continued rapid growth, a scenario that would not be impossible but would be much less likely. If stagnant export markets were combined with continued weaknesses in the financial systems of these countries and continued government interference that reduced investment efficiency, all of Asia could stagnate. This, however, is a worst case scenario. It is far more likely, given their record of the past several decades, that most of the countries in the region, with the negative example of Japan and the 1997–98 financial crisis in front of them, will respond to the challenge.

Endnotes

1 Martin Baily, Diana Farrell, and Susan Lund, "The Color of Hot Money," *Foreign Affairs*, vol. 79, no.2 (March/April 2000), pp. 99–109.

[2] These government debt figures do not include the social security obligations of the Japanese government. Martin Wolf, "Japan on the brink," *Financial Times*, November 14, 2001.

[3] In fiscal year 2002, national debt service accounted for 20.5 percent of government budget expenditures even with the very low interest rates. JETRO, *Nippon 2002: Business Facts and Figures*, Tokyo: Japan External Trade Organization, 2002, p. 24.

[4] I have considered Taiwan's industrial policies together with those of Korea even though there were important differences between the policies of the two countries. When Taiwan pushed heavy industry, for example, it relied on state-owned enterprises, while Korea implemented its program through the private *chaebol*. Overall, however, there were more similarities than differences. For a more in depth discussion of these differences, see Joseph J. Stern, Ji-hong Kim, Dwight H. Perkins, and Jung-ho Yoo, *Industrialization and the State: The Korean Heavy and Chemical Industry Drive*, Cambridge, Mass.: Harvard University Press, 1995; and Li-min Hsueh, Chen-kuo Hsu, and Dwight H. Perkins, *Industrialization and the State: The Changing Role of the Taiwan Government in the Economy, 1945–98*, Cambridge, Mass.: Harvard University Press, 2001.

[5] Politicians with short time horizons often become more corrupt, but in the case of Korea and Taiwan, these politicians faced not only the possible loss of their offices, but also the loss of their countries. If these countries were taken over by their neighbors, the best these politicians could hope for was refugee status in the United States or elsewhere.

[6] Il Chong Nam and Soogeun Oh, "Asian Insolvency Regimes from a Comparative Perspective: Problems and Issues for Reform," in OECD, *Insolvency Systems in Asia: An Efficiency Perspective*, Paris: Organization for Economic Cooperation and Development, 2001.

[7] William Overholt, "Financial Sector Reform in Japan: The Social Context," Asia Pacific Policy Program, Kennedy School of Government, Harvard University, December 2002, p. 9.

[8] Pieter Bottelier, "Managing China's Transition Debt: A Critical Challenge," Asia Pacific Policy Program, Kennedy School of Government, Harvard University, December 2002, p. 4.

[9] Percentages of this sort depend to a large degree on how one defines a non-performing asset. For a more detailed discussion of the non-performing assets of the Chinese banking system several years earlier, see Nicholas Lardy, *China's Unfinished Economic Revolution*, Washington, DC: Brookings, 1998, pp. 115–24.

[10] National Bureau of Statistics, *China Monthly Economic Indicators*, vol. 38 (May 2003), p. 51.

[11] This discussion is developed further in Dwight H. Perkins, "Industrial and Financial Policy in China and Vietnam: A New Model or a Replay of the East Asian Experience?" in Joseph Stiglitz and Shahid Yusuf, eds., *Rethinking the East Asian Miracle*, Oxford: Oxford University Press, 2001, pp. 247–94.

[12] National Bureau of Statistics, *China Statistical Yearbook, 2002*, Beijing: China Statistics Press, 2002, p. 63.

[13] United Nations Development Program, *Human Development Report, 2000*, New York: United Nations Development Program, 2000, pp. 223–26.

[14] Future projections of the decline of the savings rate portray an even grimmer picture. Robert Dekle, "The Deteriorating Fiscal Situation and an Aging Population," *NBER Working Paper*, no. 9367 (December 2002).

[15] Hong Kong and Singapore are exceptions to this more general pattern largely because government and business were not linked so closely together; this is particularly the case in Hong Kong.

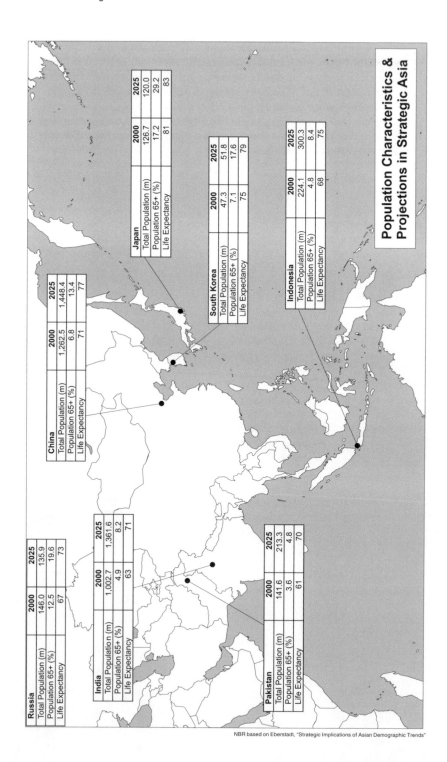

Population Characteristics & Projections in Strategic Asia

Russia

	2000	2025
Total Population (m)	146.0	135.9
Population 65+ (%)	12.5	19.6
Life Expectancy	67	73

India

	2000	2025
Total Population (m)	1,002.7	1,361.6
Population 65+ (%)	4.9	8.2
Life Expectancy	63	71

Pakistan

	2000	2025
Total Population (m)	141.6	213.3
Population 65+ (%)	3.6	4.8
Life Expectancy	61	70

China

	2000	2025
Total Population (m)	1,262.5	1,448.4
Population 65+ (%)	6.8	13.4
Life Expectancy	71	77

Japan

	2000	2025
Total Population (m)	126.7	120.0
Population 65+ (%)	17.2	29.2
Life Expectancy	81	83

South Korea

	2000	2025
Total Population (m)	47.3	51.8
Population 65+ (%)	7.1	17.6
Life Expectancy	75	79

Indonesia

	2000	2025
Total Population (m)	224.1	300.3
Population 65+ (%)	4.8	8.4
Life Expectancy	68	75

NBR based on Eberstadt, "Strategic Implications of Asian Demographic Trends"

STRATEGIC IMPLICATIONS OF ASIAN DEMOGRAPHIC TRENDS

Nicholas Eberstadt

ABSTRACT

In Asia today, three big demographic tendencies are exerting special influence on the region's economic and political calculus. The first is rapid population aging, especially in East Asia. By 2025 China's median age may be approaching 40 years, and Japan's may well exceed 50. Second, adverse mortality trends—in Russia already, but possibly in China and India as well—stand to constrain options for some important actors on the Eurasian stage. Finally, the strange and unnatural phenomenon of rising sex ratios at birth has been extending over much of the Asia terrain. Surplus baby boys today may be unmarriageable bachelors tomorrow. How the problem of rising cohorts of unmarriageable men may affect social cohesion and political relations in the future is as yet uncertain—but the impact may be consequential.

Nicholas Eberstadt holds the Henry Wendt Chair in Political Economy at the American Enterprise Institute in Washington, DC. He wishes to thank Heather Dresser for her help in preparing the tables and figures in this chapter, and also to thank Judith Banister, Richard Ellings, Michael Wills, and Enders Wimbush for their valuable comments and suggestions. The usual caveats obtain.

Introduction

Few would contest the general proposition that the factor population bears directly on the course of the friendly, and sometimes unfriendly, competition between states in the world arena today. Problems arise, however, when we try to move from the general to the specific. *How*, exactly, do human numbers (population size, composition, and trends of change) affect the capability of governments to influence events beyond their borders—or affect the disposition of a country's interactions with outside actors? And no less important for the would-be strategist: how can we use population indicators to anticipate, with some reasonable hope of accuracy, the impact of yet-unfolding demographic forces on the balance of international power?

Auguste Comte, the nineteenth century French mathematician and sociologist, is widely credited with the dictum "Demography is destiny." It is a wonderful aphorism—but it promises too much, and offers too little.[1] A more operational formulation might suggest that demographic forces can alter the realm of the possible, both politically and economically, for regularly established population groupings. Demographic considerations *can* (but are not always required to) alter the complex strategic balance between, and within, countries.

By comparison with other contemporary forms of change—social, economic, political, technological—demographic changes are very slow and very regular. Over the past generation, for example, a 3 percent per annum rate of population growth would have been considered terribly high in Asia, while a 3 percent inflation rate would have been regarded as remarkably low. And demographic change is only sharp and discontinuous in times of utter upheaval and catastrophe.[2] Given the relatively long time horizon over which non-calamitous demographic changes unfold, we are probably well-served to adopt a more extended frame of reference than other chapters in this volume to discuss the effects of population on the strategic environment in Asia. From the standpoint of strategic demography, momentous developments can and do occur from one generation to the next—but rather less of note can be expected over the course of three to five years.

For our purposes in this chapter, we will try to peer as far into the Asian and Eurasian demographic future as the year 2025. To many readers, that may sound like an exercise in science fiction—but such a time horizon is by no means as fantastical as might be supposed.

For one thing, contemporary Asia's population structure invites the "longer view." Apart from a few outposts, most places in East Asia and Eurasia are rather far along on the notional "demographic transition" from high birth and death rates to low ones. In practical terms, this means—barring only horrendous catastrophe—that we can expect relatively little "turnover" within a given population from one year—or even one decade—to the next. Projections by the United Nations Population Division (UNPD) make the point. According to UNPD's most recent medium variant figures, for example, in 2025 roughly four-fifths of the inhabitants of East and Southeast Asia would have been alive in 2000—and 60 to 70 percent of these future East and Southeast Asian inhabitants would be people who were already living in those regions as of the year 2000.[3]

We can also venture to talk with more confidence about Asia/Eurasia's demographic future today than we could in the relatively recent past because a great many blank spots in the region's demographic map have been filled in over the past generation. As recently as the late 1970s, Asia—perennial land of mystery to the western traveler—was also tremendously mysterious to the student of population trends: huge portions of the Asian/Eurasian landmass qualified as a demographic *terra incognita*. China, Vietnam, and North Korea (among other countries in the region) had never conducted a modern national population count, or had not done so for decades, or had not released such internally collected data for decades—and the USSR, well into its "era of stagnation," had taken to suppressing methodically those demographic data that Brezhnev luminaries took to be politically sensitive or ideologically embarrassing. Today, by contrast, practically every Asian or Eurasian country save Afghanistan and Burma has conducted a national census during the past decade—even reclusive North Korea![4] Though most countries in this expanse do not yet maintain comprehensive systems for the annual registration of births and deaths, we nevertheless have a fairly good picture of the demographic contours of the countries in the area—and of the trends which have created, and continue to form, the region's respective population profiles.

The "Population Explosion": Yesterday's News

The Asian/Eurasian territory encompasses an extraordinary crush of humanity. As Table 1 (overleaf) demonstrates, although the population patterns of the countries in question vary markedly, the absolute numbers under discussion are vast: as of mid-2000, over 3.6 billion, roughly three-fifths of the total population of the globe, resided in Asia.[5] Seven of the world's ten most populous countries—China, India, Indonesia, Russia, Pakistan, Bangladesh, and Japan—are located within the Asian/Eurasian perimeter.

Over the past half century, the population of this region has grown on a scale and at a tempo that were without historical precedent. Between 1950 and 2000, by the UNPD's estimates, the population of the collectivity of countries in Table 1 multiplied by a factor of 2.5—rising by almost 2.2 billion in absolute numbers, and at an average annual pace of over 1.8

Table 1. Asian Demographic Statistics, 2000–05

	Total population 2000 (m)	Projected total fertility rate (no. of births)	Projected life expectancy (years)[a]	Population growth rate (%)
East Asia	**1,481.1**	**1.78**	**72.1**	**0.67**
China	1,253.1	1.83[b]	71.0[b]	0.73[b]
Hong Kong	6.8	1.00	79.9	1.07
Macao	0.5	1.10	78.9	0.94
Taiwan	22.2	1.56[c]	76.3[c]	0.69[c]
Japan	127.0	1.32	81.6	0.14
Mongolia	2.5	2.42	63.9	1.29
North Korea	22.3	2.02	63.1	0.54
South Korea	46.8	1.41	75.5	0.57
Southeast Asia	**520.4**	**2.55**	**66.7**	**1.40**
Brunei	0.3	2.48	76.3	2.27
Burma	47.5	2.86	57.3	1.28
Cambodia	13.1	4.77	57.4	2.40
East Timor	0.7	3.85	49.5	4.00
Indonesia	211.6	2.35	66.8	1.26
Laos	5.3	4.78	54.5	2.29
Malaysia	23.0	2.90	73.1	1.93
Philippines	75.7	3.18	70.0	1.79
Singapore	4.0	1.36	78.1	1.69
Thailand	60.9	1.93	69.3	1.01
Vietnam	78.1	2.30	69.2	1.35
South-Central Asia	**1,420.0**	**3.25**	**63.2**	**1.66**
Afghanistan	21.4	6.80	43.1	3.88
Bangladesh	138.0	3.46	61.4	2.02
Bhutan	2.1	5.02	63.2	2.96
India	1,016.9	3.01	63.9	1.51
Kazakhstan	15.6	1.95	66.3	-0.36
Kyrgyzstan	4.9	2.64	68.6	1.40
Nepal	23.5	4.26	59.9	2.23
Pakistan	142.7	5.08	61.0	2.44
Sri Lanka	18.6	2.01	72.6	0.81
Tajikistan	6.1	3.06	68.8	0.86
Turkmenistan	4.6	2.70	67.1	1.54
Uzbekistan	24.9	2.44	69.7	1.51
Russia	**145.6**	**1.14**	**66.8**	**-0.57**

Sources: United Nations Population Division, *World Population Prospects: 2002 Revision*, population database <http://esa.un.org/unpp>; U.S. Census Bureau, International Data Base <www.census.gov/ipc/www/idbacc.html> for data on Taiwan. Notes: a) Male and female life expectancy combined; b) Including Taiwan; c) Data for 2000.

percent per year. Perhaps not so surprisingly, this extraordinary Asian "population explosion" captured the attention and aroused the foreboding of commentators, scholars, and policymakers around the world. (A small library of literature, indeed, was generated over the course of two generations on the purported economic, political, and strategic implications of this vast population shift.) The vision of unrelenting and unprecedented increases in human numbers in Asia continues to inform much popular and policy discussion—thanks in no small part to official alarms regularly sounded by institutions and programs established over the past decades for the express purpose of slowing population growth.

But that vision is by now outdated and increasingly misleading. The great twentieth century demographic boom is over in East Asia. It is winding down rapidly in Southeast Asia, and even in South Asia the situation has changed greatly. (Russia, for its part, has been recording *negative* natural increase—more deaths than births—every year over the past decade.)

The Asian "population explosion" was actually a "health explosion"—it was fueled almost entirely by declining mortality due to dramatic improvements in life expectancy. That same "population explosion" has been defused by ongoing changes in childbearing patterns. Over the past three decades, Asia and Eurasia have witnessed pervasive and typically dramatic declines in local fertility levels. Since the early 1970s, the total fertility rate (or TFR—the synthetic measure of births per woman per lifetime under existing childbearing patterns) is believed to have dropped about three-fifths in East Asia, and by over half in Southeast Asia; even in South Asia fertility rates are thought to have dropped by two-fifths. Thanks to these declines, *sub-replacement* fertility[6] is increasingly the norm in Asia and Eurasia. At this juncture, for example, sub-replacement fertility is thought to characterize every country and locale in East Asia save tiny Mongolia. In Southeast Asia, Singapore and Thailand are already sub-replacement societies, and Indonesia appears to be rapidly closing in on the replacement fertility level. As for South and Central Asia, Sri Lanka and Kazakhstan are outposts of sub-replacement fertility within the region. Elsewhere in that area, fertility change has been more pronounced than is often appreciated. At an estimated TFR of 3.0, for example, India's overall fertility level is still thought to be well above replacement—but it has also plunged by an estimated 45 percent nationwide since the 1950s, and major urban centers like Bombay, New Delhi, and Calcutta are all believed to be sub-replacement now, as are some entire Indian states (e.g., Kerala, Tamil Nadu).[7] Only in Afghanistan are fertility rates probably stuck at pre-modern elevations.

As a consequence of a generation and more of sweeping—and still continuing—fertility decline in Asia and Eurasia, it is no longer accurate to speak of "unprecedented population growth" either for the region as a whole or its major components. For the collectivity of countries in Table 1, the current pace of population growth (projected 1.1 percent per year) is actually distinctly lower than half a century ago (when it is thought to have exceeded 1.8 percent per annum.) Even in Bangladesh, the perennial poster child for the "population explosion," demographic growth, though still rapid (about 2 percent per year), is notably slower than in recent decades—and perhaps ever so slightly slower today than in the early 1950s.[8]

Absolute growth of the region's population also looks to have peaked. For Asia/Eurasia as a whole, the annual increment in population today is estimated at about 43 million persons a year—distinctly less than the estimated 52 million a year of the late 1980s, and indeed lower than the 46 million a year in the late 1960s. According to the UNPD's latest medium variant projections, the absolute annual increase of population peaked in East Asia in the late 1960s and in Southeast Asia in the early 1990s, and, while there is less certainty on this final point, they also suggest that absolute population increments in South and Central Asia may be slightly lower today than they were in the early 1990s.[9]

Is there strategic significance to this fertility decline and the population changes it is relentlessly, but unevenly, enforcing throughout Asia? Arguably so—but probably not in the ways we are most accustomed to hearing about. The "old" literature on the social, economic, and political consequences of rapid population growth in low-income areas often betrayed a hardened Malthusian cast of mind.

In retrospect, it is apparent that such thinking was highly alert to the possible stresses and problems presented by the demographic boom, but exceedingly inattentive to the potential benefits and opportunities it might confer (not the least of these emanating from the health revolution that prompted these population explosions in the first place).

A new literature on the economic implications of population change in Asia is now beginning to emerge, one characterized by a more optimistic assessment of the influence of the region's demographic trends upon prospects for material development. Unfortunately, it is not yet clear that this new tendency, though different in flavor, is free of the stifling *idée fixes* so characteristic of the literature it means to replace.[10]

To get at the actual strategic constraints and opportunities presented by patterns of population change in Asia and Eurasia, we will have to look carefully into specific details.

Do Shifts in Relative Size Matter on the Asian Strategic Stage?

If we consider the two-generation sweep from 1975 to 2025—in which we are currently more or less at midpoint—we will observe that relative population weight is poised to shift appreciably for various dyads—including several pairings of neighboring, and potentially rivalrous, states:[11]

India/China

By the UNPD's "medium variant" projections, between 1975 and 2025, China's population would grow by about half, from about 930 million to over 1.4 billion. India's, on the other hand, would more than double, jumping from around 620 million to over 1.3 billion. A generation ago, there were nearly 50 percent more people in China than in India; a generation hence, the projected differential would be a mere 5 percent.

Thailand/Vietnam

At the end of the Vietnam War, Vietnam's population was about one-sixth greater than Thailand's (48 vs. 41 million). In 2025, due to differential population growth, Vietnam's population is projected to be over 40 percent greater than Thailand's (105 vs. 74 million). In other words: where there were about seven Vietnamese for every six Thais a generation ago, there may be over seven Vietnamese for every five Thais a generation hence.

Japan/Korea

In 1975, the population of the Republic of Korea amounted to less than a third of Japan's (35 vs. 111 million). In 2025, under "medium variant" projections, the ROK's population would be over two fifths of Japan's (50 vs. 123 million). If we imagine a Korean unification under Seoul's aegis sometime before 2025, the population balance would shift all the more sharply: with the united peninsular ROK population equaling three-fifths of Japan's own (75 vs. 123 million).

Pakistan/Russia

The most radical and dramatic shift in the relative population weight of major countries in the region under consideration, however, would involve Pakistan and Russia. In 1975, Russia's population was nearly twice as large as Pakistan's (134 vs. 70 million). By 2025, under "medium variant" projections, the situation will be virtually reversed: Pakistan would be just over twice as populous as Russia (250 vs. 124 million).[12]

These relative demographic shifts are certainly vivid—but are they meaningful? Unfortunately, the answer is not self-evident. In the decades ahead will Pakistan's leadership find its strategic situation *vis-à-vis* Russia transformed, or even significantly altered, by overtaking and decisively surpassing Russia demographically? One can of course write a storyline to that effect—but such a tale would be guided, and indeed dominated, by a host of additional and hardly trivial political and economic assumptions, all introduced precisely to permit us to arrive at our desired outcome.

To be sure, there are historical instances in which the shift of demographic weight between national actors seems to have been invested with real strategic significance. In the "struggle for mastery" in modern Europe, one thinks of the role of population in the ascendance of Germany over France during the nineteenth century.[13] Nearer to home, there is the case of the United States—the current and unrivaled global superpower, with a population larger than all but two contemporary states—where total population is roughly 50 times greater today than it was two centuries earlier.

Is it conceivable that the United States might exert anything like the economic, political, and military influence it enjoys today if its population, instead of surging over 50-fold, had simply doubled over those same two centuries—as actually happened for France?[14] Very clearly, no. But in demographic affairs, as in so many other areas, there may be such a thing as "American exceptionalism." Population, after all, is not the only strength that makes the United States today's sole superpower. And if we consider the race between Germany and France in nineteenth century Europe, it is at once apparent that many other factors beside the demographic were weighing in Berlin's favor.[15] Even if differential population growth did contribute to Germany's primacy over France, it seems safe to say this was neither a sufficient factor—nor even a necessary one.

At first glance, we might assume that changes in raw population totals of potentially contending countries should tell us something meaningful about the strategic options open to their governments—for there is something tribal, even elemental, in the impulse to keep tabs on the changing numbers of "them" and "us." On the modern global stage, however, data on decade-to-decade national shifts in relative population offer distinctly less relevant information than many strategically inclined thinkers would assume—and such limited information as these totals do convey depends critically on context. Until we arrive at a happy political millennium akin to the ones envisioned in Kant's "Perpetual Peace" or Hegel's "End of History," wherein international disputes will be amicably settled on the basis of "one person-one vote" world plebiscites, strategic demography will be better served by focusing on population changes *within* countries, and the constraints or advantages these present to national directorates.

Aging Asia: An Uneven Burden Among Countries

One immediate and obvious example of an internal demographic change fraught with possible economic and political significance is the wave of population aging that is sweeping the Asian/Eurasian region. The current and impending "graying" of Asia and Eurasia is an all but irrevocable force, since it is propelled by the basic arithmetic of longer lives and smaller families—trends, we will recall, that have already been in train within the region for decades if not generations. Only a catastrophe of biblical proportion could forestall the tendency for Asia's populations to age substantially between now and 2025.

Age patterns in Asia/Eurasia vary enormously today. In such places as Afghanistan, Pakistan, Laos, and Cambodia, the "median person" as of the year 2000 was a teenager: over half the population in those countries was probably under 20 years of age. By contrast, Japan's median age in 2000 was over 41 years: by that particular criterion, in fact, Japan is now probably the "grayest" country on earth.[16] Similarly, in 2000 the proportion of total population 65 years of age and older ranged from under 3 percent in Afghanistan to over 17 percent in Japan. Over the coming generation, however, every single population center in Asia/Eurasia is anticipated to age appreciably—some of them at a pace or to an extreme never before witnessed in any ordinary human society (See Figure 1 overleaf.).

Although all of Asia/Eurasia is set to age markedly over the 2000 to 2025 period, most of the region will nonetheless remain relatively youthful. In South and Central Asia, for example, median age is poised to rise by well over six years during this quarter-century (actually a somewhat greater absolute increase than envisioned for the world's "more developed regions" between 2000 and 2025). But even the most "elderly" country in this grouping (Sri Lanka in 2025) is projected to have a somewhat younger profile than did Europe in the year 2000, and in 2025 South and Central Asia together would have a population younger than the Europe of 1950. So, too, in Southeast Asia where, despite a prospective increase in median age from roughly 24 to about 32 between 2000 and 2025, only two countries (Thailand and Singapore) would be as "gray" in 2025 as America today— and the area as a whole would still be younger than the Europe of 1975.

The part of Asia/Eurasia that stands to age most rapidly, and most profoundly, is Eastern Asia—and here we enter uncharted territory. Between 2000 and 2025, East Asia's median age is projected to jump by nine years,

Figure 1. Proportion of Population Age 65+ (1975, 2000, 2025)

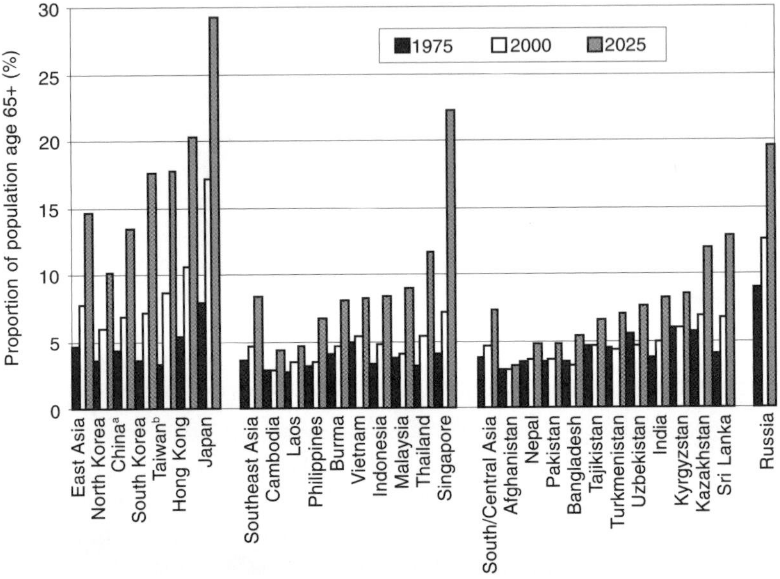

Sources: United Nations Population Division, *World Population Prospects: 2002 Revision*, Population Database <http://esa.un.org/unpp>; U.S. Census Bureau, International Data Base <www.census.gov/ipc/www/idbacc.html>. Notes: a) Includes Taiwan; b) Data from Census Bureau.

to just under 40. By that metric, East Asia in 2025 would be "grayer" than Europe today, where median age in the year 2000 was under 38. Throughout East Asia, many populations will be more elderly than any yet known and some will be aging at velocities not yet recorded in national populations. Between 2000 and 2025, for example, Taiwan is set to experience a leap in median age of almost 11 years, to just under 43.[17] South Korea's median age, in these projections, would soar by 12.5 years to over 44. Absent an unexpected influx of young immigrants, Hong Kong's projected median age in 2025 would be 46—and one in five residents would be 65 or older.

But the most extreme and extraordinary instance of population aging will be witnessed in Japan. By 2025, in UNPD "medium variant" calculations, Japan would have a median age of just over 50. Less than a quarter-century hence, by those same projections, almost 30 percent of Japan's populace would be 65 or older, and *almost every ninth Japanese would be 80 or older.* This future Japan would have very nearly as many octogenarians, nonagenarians, and centenarians as children under 15—and would have barely two persons of traditional "working age" (as the 15–64 cohort is often construed) for every person of notional "retirement age" (65+).

Some of the implications of such extreme and rapid population aging have already been widely discussed and analyzed. To begin, there are the fiscal implications of Japan's version of "graying": under current rules of the budgetary game, these look unambiguously bleak. A 1996 study by OECD researchers, for example, estimated the net present value of the unfunded liabilities in the Japanese national pension system at 70 percent of 1994 GDP. Unless radical changes in that pay-as-you go system were implemented, they warned, Japan's *annual* deficit would approach 7 percent of GDP by 2025, and the total "pure aging effect" on public finances for 2000 to 2030 could be a debt equal to 190 percent of year 2000 GDP.[18]

Given the fact that gross public debt in Japan rose from about 60 percent of GDP to nearly 150 percent of GDP in the decade from 1992 to 2002[19]—in a context of relatively limited population aging—those numbers may sound ominous indeed. But other analysts have offered still darker assessments, with some prophesying that an extended "aging recession" would visit Japan and perhaps never depart.[20]

Without denying the seriousness of the challenges that aging will pose to Japan's society and economy over the decades ahead, it is still possible to suggest that the economic dangers inherent in population aging for Japan (and, by extension, East Asia's smaller prosperous, but graying, tigers) may be exaggerated in some of the contemporary commentary.[21]

Today's writing on the negative effects of population aging in Japan focuses (sometimes to near exclusion of all other factors) on public finances and quite rightly points out the actuarially unviable state of the country's national pension system and the looming liabilities for its public health care sector. There is no concrete commandment, though, that a country must leave parlous budgetary imbalances uncorrected. Painful though such exertions would surely be, it is entirely within the purview of the Japanese policymakers and voters to set the country's pension and health systems on a financially secure course. (Sure enough, OECD calculations suggest that a number of relatively obvious changes could significantly improve the financial health of the national Japanese pension system.)

The budgetary balance, moreover, is only a single component of the overall macro-economy—and the implications of population aging for Japan's consumption, production, savings, investment, and international finance and trade performance are by no means unremittingly negative. The great social and structural shifts occasioned by population aging, recall, will create new economic opportunities in addition to all the new challenges. If gradual economic adjustments are made, if flexibility in factor markets can be achieved, and if relatively productive economic policies could be embraced and maintained, the drag imposed on Japanese economic growth by massive and rapid population aging in the decades immediately ahead need not be major. On balance it would probably remain a negative factor, but not necessarily a critical or even a major one.[22]

The key point here is that Japan's aging process has been stimulated materially by the country's great health revolution. And, thanks to this ongoing revolution, the Japanese are today the world's longest-lived people. It is counter-intuitive, to say the least, to expect a health explosion to lead inexorably to national bankruptcy and economic ruin. Given Japan's patterns of "healthy aging," and the reduced physical rigors of employment in an affluent information-age economy, Japan's older cohorts can now realistically look forward to the real possibility of productive contribution to economic life at ever-later ages. Thus, while the population stagnation and decline that will almost surely attend Japan's particular aging process stand to reduce the overall pace of aggregate economic growth, aging need not thwart the continuing improvement of per capita income—and augmentation of economic capacities—for Japan.[23]

This qualified, perhaps cautiously optimistic, evaluation of the economic implications of rapid and pervasive population aging in Japan (and the smaller East Asian tigers) does not extend to the Chinese mainland. The People's Republic of China will also undergo dramatic aging in the decades immediately ahead, but there are reasons to expect the impact of the process to be more generally adverse—both socially and economically.

Between 2000 and 2025, China's median age is set to rise substantially: from about 30 to around 39. According to UNPD projections, China's median age will be higher than America's in 2025. As Figure 2 indicates, the impending tempo of population aging in China is nearly as rapid as anything history has yet seen. It will be far faster than what was recorded in the more developed regions over the past three decades and is exceeded only by Japan. There is a crucial difference, however, between Japan's recent past and China's prospective future. To put the matter bluntly, Japan became rich before it became old; China will do things the other way around.

Figure 3 highlights this contradistinction. When Japan had the same proportion of population 65 and older as does China today (2000), its level of per capita output was three times higher than China's is now. In 2025, 13.4 percent of China's population is projected to be 65-plus; when Japan crossed the 13.4 percent threshold, its per capita GDP was approaching $20,000 a year (constant 1990 PPP dollars). One need not be a "Sino-pessimist" to suggest China that will be nowhere near that same marker 22 years from now.[24]

Although China's population will hardly be as elderly as Japan's by 2025, its impending aging process promises to generate problems of a sort

Figure 2. Change in Median Age over Three Decades: Japan, Europe, the United States (1970–2000), and China (1995–2025)

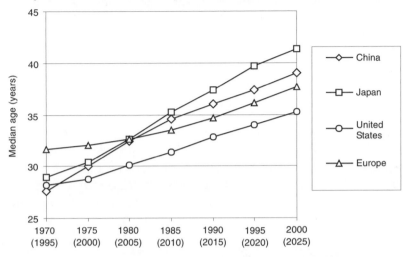

Sources: United Nations Population Division, *World Population Prospects: 2002 Revision*; and United Nations Population Division, *World Urbanization Prospects: 2001 Revision* <http://esa.un.org/unpp>.

Figure 3. Per Capita GDP vs. Population Age 65+: Japan, China, and the United States (1950–2000)

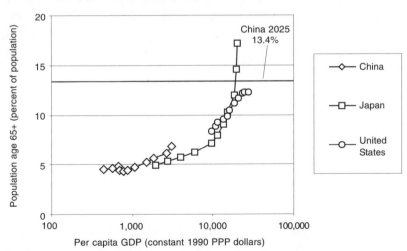

Sources: Angus Maddison, *The World Economy: A Millenial Perspective*, Paris: Organization for Economic Cooperation and Development, 2001; and United Nations Population Division, *World Population Prospects: 2002 Revision* <http://esa.un.org.unpp>.

that Japan does not have to face. The first relates to its national pension system: Japan's may be financially vulnerable, but China's is non-existent. Government or enterprise-based retirement programs cover only about one-sixth of the contemporary Chinese workforce—and nearly all of the pieces in this haphazard patchwork are amazingly unsound in actuarial terms.[25] Although Chinese leadership has been committed since 1997 to establishing a sturdy and universal social security system, to date, actions have lagged far behind words and the system remains only in the planning stage.

For most aging Chinese today, the pension system is the family and even with continuing national economic progress, Chinese families are likely to be placed under mounting pressure by the swelling ranks of seniors. By 2025, there will be nearly 300 million members of China's 60-plus population, but, at the same time, the cohorts rising into that pool will be the same people who accounted for China's sub-replacement fertility patterns in the early 1990s and thereafter. Absent a functioning nationwide pension program, unforgiving arithmetic suggests there may be something approaching a one-to-one ratio emerging between elderly parents and the children obliged to support them. Even worse, from the perspective of a Confucian culture, a sizeable fraction—perhaps nearly one-fourth—of these older Chinese will have no living son to rely upon for sustenance. One need not be a novelist to imagine the intense social tensions such conditions could engender (to say nothing of the personal and humanitarian tragedies).

Second, and no less important, there is no particular reason to expect that older people in China will be able to make the same sort of contributions to economic life as their counterparts in Japan. In low-income economies, the daily demands of ordinary work are more arduous than in rich countries: the employment structure is weighted toward categories more likely to require intense manual labor, and even ostensibly non-manual positions may require considerable physical stamina. According to official Chinese statistics, nearly half of the country's current labor force toils in the fields, and another fifth is employed in mining and quarrying, manufacturing, construction, or transport—occupations generally not favoring the frail.[26] Even with continuing structural transformations, regular work is sure to be much more strenuous in China than in Japan in 2025. Moreover, China's older population may not be as hardy as peers from affluent societies—people likely to have been better fed, housed, and doctored than China's elderly throughout the course of their lives.

Hard data on the health status of older people in China and other countries tend to be spotty and problematic, and comparability of method can never be taken for granted. However, some of the survey data that are available through Réseau Espérance de Vie en Santé (REVES), the international network of "health expectancy" researchers, are thought-provoking. According to a 1989–90 "health expectancy" study for Sichuan province, a person 60 years of age would spend less than half (48 percent) of his or her remaining years in passable health.[27] By contrast, a study in West Germany for 1986 calculated that a 60-year-old woman could expect to spend 70 percent of her remaining time in "good health." For men the fraction was 75 percent.[28] Although one probably should not push those findings too hard, they are certainly consistent with the proposition that China's seniors are more brittle than older populations from more comfortable and prosperous locales.

Thus, China's rapidly graying population appears to face a triple-bind. Without a broad-coverage national pension system, and with only limited filial resources to fall back on, paid work will of necessity loom large as an option for economic security for many older Chinese. But employment in China, today and tomorrow, will be more physically punishing than in OECD countries, and China's older cohorts are simply less likely to be up to the punishment. The aggregation of hundreds of millions of individual experiences with this triple-bind over the coming generation will be a set of economic, social, and political constraints on Chinese development—and power augmentation—that have not as yet been fully appreciated in Beijing, much less overseas.

Unfavorable Mortality Trends

The positive and normative implications of a change in a society's fertility level cannot be described unambiguously in advance. Not so for changes in mortality levels: in any setting or context, people will prefer longer lives to shorter ones. In addition to the incalculable personal benefits of life itself, rising life expectancy and the improvements in health that typically accompany it materially affect economic potential by: increasing the capability of populations to work and learn; extending the period of economically active life; and tilting the calculus of education and training toward increased investment in "human capital."

As already noted, the Asia Pacific has enjoyed a sweeping and completely unprecedented improvement in survival chances over the past half-century. Between the early 1950s and now, life expectancy at birth is estimated to have leapt by about 25 years in both South-Central and Southeast Asia, and to have soared by nearly 30 years in East Asia. Moreover, infant mortality rates in those territories may have fallen by as much as two-thirds, three-fourths, and four-fifths, respectively. That ascent was neither entirely universal nor uninterrupted. In locales across the Asian/Eurasian expanse, it was episodically halted or temporarily reversed by terrible spikes of mortality. On the whole, however, these spasms of death were due to man-made (or more accurately, state-made) disasters—the Great Leap Forward, the Khmer Rouge apocalypse, and the like—and they ceased when the afflicting interventions abated. Given the surge of health that coursed over postwar Asia, the general expectation not unreasonably pervaded that steady improvements in health and mortality were now the natural order of things for humanity and could only be subverted by malign political agency.

At the dawn of the twenty-first century, that happy expectation no longer squares with basic facts about mortality in the Asian/Eurasian region. By the estimates of the U.S. Census Bureau, for example, the five former Soviet Central Asian Republics began the year 2000 with distinctly lower life expectancies than they had enjoyed in 1990—all this in peacetime, and in the absence of any obvious political catastrophe.[29] Other, arguably more politically consequential, mortality setbacks have also struck the Eurasian stage—and still more are poised to unfold.

The most conspicuous—and startling—health and mortality setback in contemporary Eurasia is, of course, the one currently underway in Russia. Modern Russia has given lie to the ameliorative presumption that literate, industrialized societies cannot suffer long-term health declines during times of peace. According to Moscow's official calculations, the country's life expectancy was lower in 2001 than it had been in 1961/62, four decades earlier. For Russia's men, life expectancy had dropped by almost five years over that interim—but female life expectancy was also slightly down over that period. This anomalous circumstance could not be entirely attributed to the deformities of communist rule, for both male and female life expectancy were lower in 2001 than in 1991, the last year of Soviet power.

In absolute terms, this Russian mortality crisis qualifies as a catastrophe of historical dimensions. Over the extended period between 1965 and 2001, age standardized mortality for Russia's men rose by over 40 percent. Perhaps even more surprising, it also increased for Russia's women, by over 15 percent. Against the hardly exemplary health patterns of Gorbachev-era Soviet socialism, Russia has suffered a surfeit of "excess male mortality" since 1991 on the order of three and a half million deaths—the equivalent, for Russia, of twice the deaths in World War I. (Add "excess female mortality" and the post-1991 death toll rises by almost another million.)

Russia's mortality crisis is concentrated on the population traditionally construed as "of working age." (See Figure 4) For Russian men *in every age grouping* within the 20–64 spectrum, age-specific death rates in 2001 were *at least* 40 percent higher than they had been three decades before. In some cases (men 45–54), they were over 60 percent higher. As for women 20–59, their death rates were *at least* 30 percent higher in 2001 than in

Figure 4. Russia: Rise in Mortality (1970/71–2000)

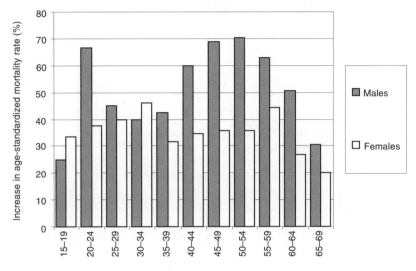

Sources: *Demographic Yearbook of Russia: 2002 Statistical Handbook*, Moscow: State Committee of the Russian Federation on Statistics, 2002, Table 2.6; *Russian Statistical Yearbook*, Moscow: State Committee of the Russian Federation, 1997, Table 2.17.

1970/71. Russia's cause-of-death statistics are far from perfect, but if overall reports can be trusted the proximate explanations for these trends were an explosion of deaths from cardiovascular disease (CVD) and injuries.

Reversing Russia's long-term deterioration in public health will be a more difficult task than might at first be supposed. Throughout low-income Asia after World War II, significant health advances were achieved through new, inexpensive, and relatively easy interventions to control infectious disease (e.g., sulfa drugs, DDT). Russia's burden of illness today, however, is not primarily communicable and infectious, but instead overwhelmingly chronic and/or behavioral—the sorts of problems that are seldom susceptible to quick, cheap medical fixes. Moreover, death from such chronic illnesses as CVD tends to be due to an accumulation of insults against the physiological system over the course of decades—and, to judge by mortality statistics, today's Russian adults have been more assiduous than their parents in accumulating those insults. Indeed, in 2001 Russian men in their late 20s had higher death rates than did men in their early 30s three decades earlier; men in their late 30s suffered nearly the same mortality rates as men in their late forties from that earlier generation; and so on. At any given age, in other words, today's Russians are more likely to succumb to fatal risk than their parents.

Figure 5. Male Life Expectancy: Russia vs. Less Developed World Regions (1950–2025)

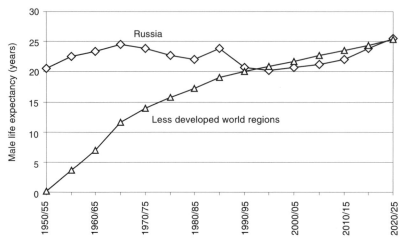

Sources: United Nations Population Division, *World Population Prospects: 2002 Revision*, Population Database <http://esa.un.org/unpp>.

For broad segments of the current Russian population, simply returning to the health patterns of the early 1970s would be a formidable public health challenge. If Russian men in their early 40s were to strive to reattain, by their late 40s, the same survival chances their fathers faced at that stage in their lives, they would have to improve on the mortality rates of today's 45–49 year olds by over 40 percent—and they would have to reduce their own future mortality rates to just five-sixths the level they currently experience! From today's vantage point, that is a pretty imposing task. Success in that quest, moreover, should be evaluated in context: male life expectancy in the Russian Federation in the early 1970s, after all, was just over 63 years—about the same as in India today.

According to UNPD estimates, male life expectancy is lower today for Russia than for the world's less developed regions (see Figure 5). UNPD envisions that Russian male life expectancy will catch up with the less developed world's levels by 2020/25—but for reasons just reviewed, such projections may prove optimistic. It is hard to see how Russia can hope to develop a First World economy on the backs of a work-force with a Third World health profile, and a Third World health profile is almost certainly Russia's lot over the foreseeable demographic future.[30] Consequently, it may not be too much to suggest that unfavorable mortality trends in Russia constitute a tangible factor that will impede Russia's recovery of economic potential, and restoration of international influence in the decades ahead.

Figure 6. Russia: Projected Life Expectancy (2000–2025)

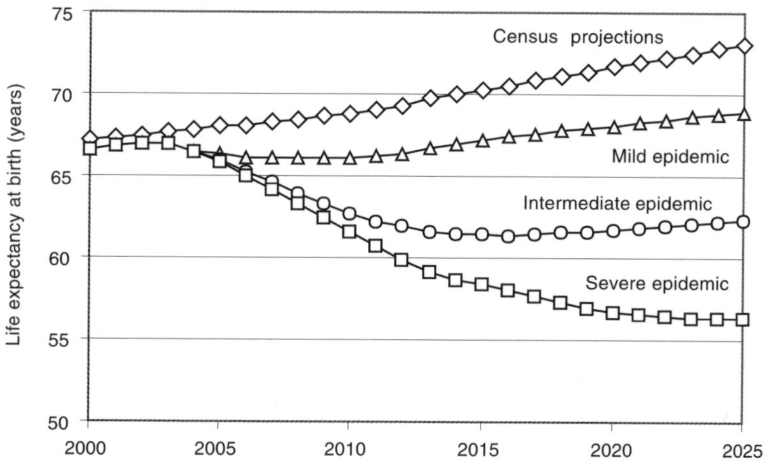

Sources: Nicholas Eberstadt, "Projecting HIV in Eurasia," unpublished paper for American Enterprise Institute <www.aei.org/doclib/20021222_pseber021112s.pdf>.

Furthermore, Russia's health future may look rather worse than we have so far suggested, for our analysis has as yet taken no measure of the possible impact of HIV/AIDS.[31] HIV/AIDS has already made major inroads in Russia and could turn out to be a major cause of death nationwide in the years to come.[32] Reliable estimates for HIV prevalence in Russia today are lacking—but in October 2002 a study by the U.S. National Intelligence Council (NIC) suggested that as many as 1–2 million Russians might be HIV-positive, and, in May 2003, Dr. Vadim Pokrovsky, head of the Russian Federal AIDS Center, indicated that Russia's HIV population might be as large as 1.5 million.[33] By such figures, as many as 2 to 3 percent of Russian adults aged 15–49 could already be infected with HIV. Our limited understanding of HIV/AIDS means that we have no terribly accurate methods for predicting the future trajectories of the pandemic—but, for what it is worth, the NIC study suggested that adult HIV prevalence might reach 6–11 percent by the year 2010. Even presuming a less virulent spread of HIV through Russia, however, the impact of AIDS would be utterly devastating (see Figure 6). A demographic-epidemiological modeling exercise for HIV in Russia undertaken by the author indicated that even with an epidemic stabilized by 2025 at 2 percent adult prevalence—a level possibly lower than Russia's actual existing burden of HIV infection—life expectancy progress in Russia might be cancelled for the next decade. If HIV prevalence ends up closer to 6 percent, Russia's life expectancy in 2025 would be a decade lower than otherwise anticipated—meaning it would be distinctly lower today than at the time of Stalin's death. And a 10 percent HIV prevalence rate would knock 16 years off Russia's prospective 2025 life expectancy, pushing it into essentially sub-Saharan co-ordinates.[34]

Russia, of course, is not the only Eurasian country with a gathering HIV problem. India and China are two others. The aforementioned NIC study ventures to place China's and India's current HIV-positive populations to be 1–2 million and 5–8 million, respectively—and suggests HIV populations in 2010 of 10–15 million for China and 20–25 million for India. Despite the horrific absolute totals, these figures would imply lower levels of adult HIV prevalence than for Russia (1.3–2 percent in China, 3–4 percent in India.)[35] But even these more moderated HIV trajectories would have terrible consequences for national health (see Figures 7 and 8). With 1.5 percent adult HIV prevalence in 2025, projected life expectancy would be depressed by about 4 years for both China and India; with 3.5 percent prevalence in China and 5 percent prevalence in India, life expectancy progress over the coming generation could be cancelled altogether.

Given the fairly tight correspondence between life expectancy and economic productivity across countries or within countries over time, it is reasonable to surmise that major health setbacks imposed by HIV/AIDS would have economic repercussions for Asian and Eurasian countries affected. The notion of a major economic impact from HIV seems all the more plausible when one considers that 1) HIV/AIDS is a lingering and debilitating disease; 2) it tends to hit individuals in the prime of their economically productive life; 3) widespread HIV prevalence could alter individual calculations about investment in training and higher education; and 4) it could equally affect international business confidence in severely affected areas. Thus, although we cannot yet foresee the course that HIV/AIDS may run in Asia/Eurasia, it is not premature to suggest that it could turn out to be a "wild card," impairing the strategic options in coming decades of one or more major actors on the Asian/Eurasian scene.[36]

Imbalances in Sex Ratios at Birth

For ordinary human populations, irrespective of era or locale, there is a pronounced and unyielding biological regularity to the balance at birth between males and females: slightly—but only slightly—more boys than girls can be expected at delivery. Broadly speaking, this observed sex ratio[37] at birth has tended to fall in the range of 103–105 baby boys for every 100 baby girls. This stable, seemingly fixed relationship was among the first facets of human population structure that the earliest students of demography noticed and speculated about.[38] In contemporary Asia, however,

Figure 7. China: Projected Life Expectancy (2000–2025)

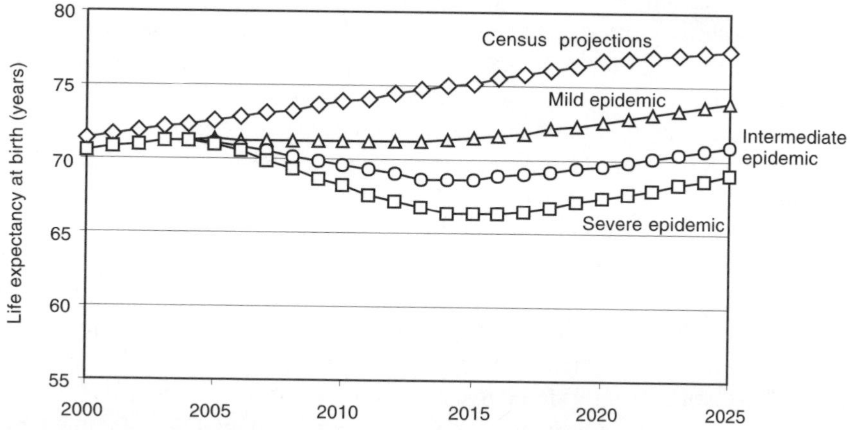

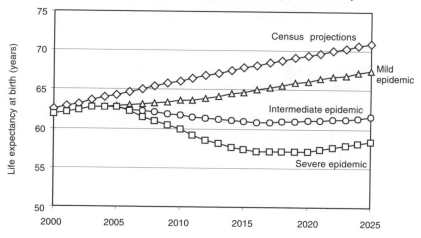

Sources: Nicholas Eberstadt, "Projecting HIV in Eurasia," unpublished paper for American Enterprise Institute <www.aei.org/doclib/20021222_pseber021112s.pdf>.

Figure 8. India: Projected Life Expectancy (2000–2025)

Sources: Nicholas Eberstadt, "Projecting HIV in Eurasia," unpublished paper for American Enterprise Institute <www.aei.org/doclib/20021222_pseber021112s.pdf>.

this age-old balance is today coming undone. In large parts of the expanse, the sex ratio at birth has risen to unnatural and historically unprecedented levels over the past two decades—and in many spots this tendency appears to be continuing unabated, or even intensifying. The growing surfeit, in various Asian locales, of "excess boys" today may have far-reaching implications for social life—and possibly even political affairs—tomorrow.

The most dramatic departure from historic biological norms seems to have occurred in the People's Republic of China.[39] In China's 1953 and 1964 censuses, unexceptional infant sex ratios (i.e. 104–105 for babies under 1 year of age) were reported. In the 1982 census, however, a sex ratio of almost 108 was recorded—and subsequently it became clear that this anomalous sounding was not a temporary aberration. In the subsequent national population counts, China's reported sex ratio at birth rose inexorably—to almost 112 in 1990, then nearly 116 in 1995, and most recently to just under 118 in the November 2000 census.

There are, to be sure, reasons to question the accuracy of these numbers: reported birth totals in the 2000 Chinese census, for example, are implausibly low, leaving open the possibility that baby girls are disproportionately undercounted, while Chinese hospital data record a less extreme (albeit still unnatural) trend in sex ratios at birth for their charges.[40] But the result itself cannot be dismissed as a statistical artifact. For one thing, there is a striking consistency between the results of successive population counts. The same imbalance that is reported in the 1990 census between baby boys and girls shows up for 5-year-olds in the 1995 census, 10-year-olds in the 2000 census, and so too for other birth cohorts. For another, the reported imbalance for the sex ratio of young children is even higher than that reported for infants. Indeed, in China's 2000 population count, the recorded sex ratio for children aged 1–4 was over 120. Only two provinces in the entire country—the non-Han regions of Tibet and Xinjiang—reported sex ratios within the biologically normal human range. At the other end, three provinces (Hubei, Guangdong, and Anhui) tabulated child sex ratios of almost 130—while three others (Hainan, Hunan and Jiangxi) returned with ratios of *over 130* (see Figure 9).

What accounts for China's extraordinary new patterns in sex ratio at birth and in infancy? An immediate suspect might be that age-old abomination, infanticide. Yet perhaps surprisingly, the weight of evidence seems to suggest that, at least over the past decade and a half, infanticide did not play a key role in these unnatural increases in sex ratios for China's infants and children. Instead, this biologically impossible outcome can better be understood as a collision of three modern Chinese tendencies: 1) the strong and enduring cultural preference for sons; 2) low or sub-replacement fertility; and 3) the advent of widespread technology for prenatal sex determination and gender-based abortion. To judge by the data on sex ratio by birth parity, Chinese parents today are typically willing to let nature take its course in the sex of their firstborn child—but have become increasingly disposed to intervene themselves to assure that a second or third child is a boy. In-

Figure 9. China: Sex Ratio Among Children Age 1–4 (2000)

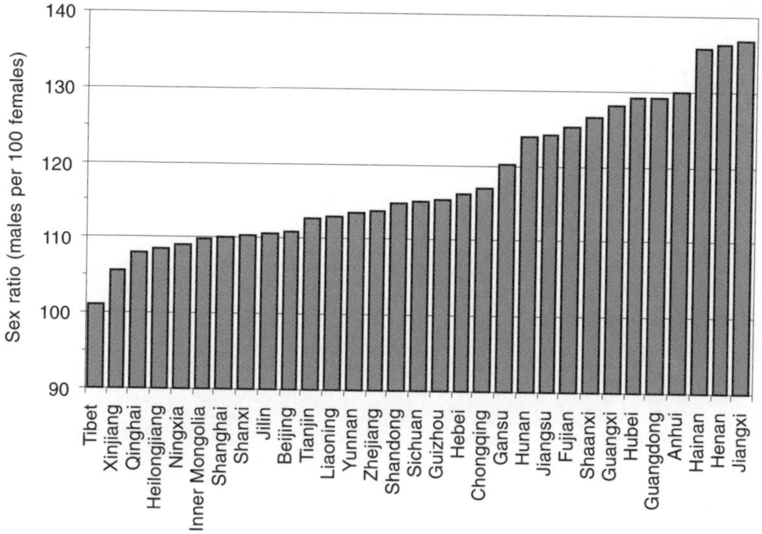

Source: *Tabulation on the 2002 Population Census of the People's Republic of China*, Hong Kong: National Bureau of Statistics—Population Census Office, 2001, volumes I and III.

deed, according to the 2000 China census, *over two-thirds* of all "higher order" infants born in the previous year were male.

China's tilt toward biologically impossible sex ratios at birth seems to have coincided with the inauguration of its coercive antenatal "One Child Policy," which was unveiled in 1979. Is Beijing's population control program responsible for these amazing distortions? A tentative answer would be yes—but not entirely. In other Chinese or Confucian-heritage populations where oppressive population control strictures were not in force—Hong Kong, Taiwan, Singapore, South Korea—unnatural sex ratios at birth also emerged in the 1980s and 1990s. In these other spots, the confluence of son preference, low fertility, and sex-selective abortion likewise have distorted the sex ratio at birth—although none so much as in China today. In most of those other locales, moreover, recent data suggests that sex ratios at birth are lower than they were in the early 1990s (Taiwan, South Korea) or even the 1980s (Singapore), while China's rise as yet shows no signs of reversing.

"Missing girls," to be sure, is not an entirely new feature of the Chinese population profile. Quite the contrary, available demographic data strongly suggests China suffered a surfeit of "excess men" in more traditional, pre-Communist times.[41] That earlier pattern, however, spoke to unfavorable survival prospects for infants, girls, and women—not to gender imbalances at birth. Traditional China, moreover, was characterized by relatively high levels of fertility and over many long stretches experienced sustained population growth. In that dynamic, ever-larger numbers of women were rising through the nation's population pyramid. The situation promises to be very different in the coming decades. Thanks to China's tilt below replacement fertility in the early 1990s, from about 2010 onward each cohort of women in their early 20s will be smaller than the one before. Between 2010 and 2025, this cohort will in fact shrink appreciably—by almost one fourth, according to UNPD projections. (Not much guesswork is involved here, incidentally. Nearly all of the women in question have already been born.)

The prospect of steadily diminishing absolute numbers of women of marriageable age, in conjunction with a steadily increasing surfeit of young men in each new class of prospective bachelors, sets the stage for an historically unprecedented "marriage squeeze" in China in the decades immediately ahead. Simple, back-of-the-envelope arithmetic suggest some very large proportion of tomorrow's young Chinese men—certainly over 10 percent, perhaps 15 percent or more—may find themselves essentially "unmarriageable" on the mainland in the coming decades.

In other places and at other times, significant proportions of the male population completed their lives without ever marrying. In Western Europe in the pre-industrial and early-industrial periods, for example, it was not uncommon for 15 or 20 percent of a male cohort to remain unmarried.[42] But that Western European pattern was built upon a complex and delicate foundation: a mesh of ethical precepts and social arrangements that supported and ratified the institution of honorable bachelorhood.

No similar cultural foundations can be said to exist today in China where until now the expectation of universal male marriage has prevailed, and where Confucian tradition stresses the son's obligation to marry and honor one's ancestors by continuing the family line. A shift to the embrace of honorable bachelorhood would mark a radical departure for Chinese society— and important new cultural traditions, in China or elsewhere, are seldom successfully established on short notice.

The world has never before seen the likes of the bride shortage that will be unfolding in China in the decades ahead, so it is difficult to imagine its many reverberations. Some commentators have warned that this "surplus of males" will make for a "deficit of peace," pushing China toward a more martial international posture.[43] That assessment may rather overstate the actual case for demographically-induced risks of international conflict in Asia (just as a slightly earlier literature's predictions of a pacifistic, ca-

Figure 10. India: Sex Ratio Among Children 0–7 (2001)

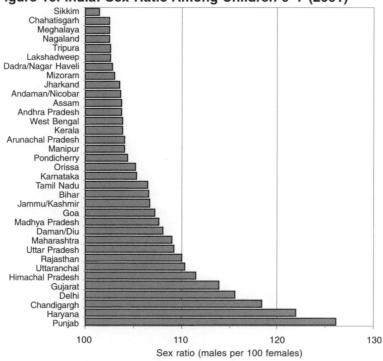

Sex ratio (males per 100 females)

Source: Census of India 2001, <www.censusindia.net/results/provindia2.html>.

sualty-averse turn in the disposition of graying, low-fertility Europe did not anticipate or account for the savage international policy of aging, sub-replacement Serbia in the 1990s).[44]

It does not seem wild, however, to propose that the emergence and rise of the phenomenon of the "unmarriageable male" may occasion an increase in social tensions in China—and perhaps social turbulence as well. Exactly how China's future cohorts of young men are to be socialized with no prospect of settled family life, and no tradition of honorable bachelorhood, is a question that can be asked today, but not answered. (Questions may equally be raised, without any good answers, about the bearing of China's rising and not-necessarily-celibate bachelor class on the risks of HIV transmission in the decades ahead.) And it is hard to see how Beijing will be able to mitigate China's escalating "bride deficit" through any deliberate policy actions for at least a generation.

China will be the first great power in Asia to suffer from a twenty-first century "bride shortage," but it may not be the last. Unsettling trends of a similar nature are already evident in India.[45] Son preference in India remains extremely strong—according to national survey results, women venturing a preference for their next birth voted for boys over girls by a ratio of four to one. With declining fertility and the spread of ultrasound, India's sex ratio is already on the rise. In the 2001 census, India counted almost 108 boys under age 6 for every hundred girls. In Uttar Pradesh, India's most populous state, that ratio was over 110; in Delhi, it was over 115; and in Punjab it was reportedly 126.[46] (See Figure 10.)

It would be cheering to think that the gender imbalances emerging in Asia's major population centers were a vestige of backward ideas and will consequently pass away with increasing modernization. The facts to date, unfortunately, do not support such an interpretation. In both India and China over the past two decades, the nationwide sex ratio at birth has increased along with per capita income, female literacy rates, and urbanization. In China today, the more literate provinces tend in fact to have somewhat *higher*, not lower, sex ratios at birth—and in India it is urban, not rural, areas in which the disproportion between boys and girls is greatest.[47] For the time being, we must live with the disturbing possibility that continuing "development" and "globalization" will heighten rather than reduce nascent gender imbalances in these two enormous countries—and the knowledge that these particular expressions of "Asian values" will have unpredictable but perhaps not inconsequential repercussions on society and politics in these ostensibly rising powers for decades to come.

Concluding Remarks

Barring some intervening earth-shattering catastrophe, we can today offer a relatively clear picture of the Asian/Eurasian population profile in the year 2025.

Over the 2000 to 2025 generation, the expanse's overall population will increase greatly—perhaps by almost one billion persons. As of 2025, the region may have something like 4.5 billion inhabitants. In some of the region's countries—Pakistan and Afghanistan among them—the population will likely still be growing rapidly (i.e., 2 percent a year, or so). In many others—including India, Indonesia, Thailand, and China—numbers may still be increasing, but at a much slower pace than today (i.e., well under 1 percent a year). Still others—Russia and Japan being the most obvious candidates—could be experiencing prolonged population decline.

In this future world, India's aggregate numbers will converge with China's; the Korean peninsula's totals will approach Japan's; and Pakistan could be twice as populous as Russia.

One can of course argue that these absolute, and relative, demographic shifts are rife with strategic consequence. But three demographic trends that are not as commonly considered may prove to have a much greater immediate impact on the economic, political, and strategic environment that unfolds in Asia/Eurasia over the decades immediately ahead. These are: 1) population aging; 2) pronounced health and mortality setbacks; and 3) persistent and unnatural imbalances in the sex ratio of the groups reaching adulthood in an increasing number of societies.

Population aging stands to be most pronounced in the four Asian "tigers" (and in Japan, where median age may exceed 50 by the year 2025); its consequences, however, may be especially severe in China, where by 2025 the median age may be approaching 40 and where most parts of the country will have "grown old before growing rich." Pronounced health and mortality setbacks, for their part, will inexorably constrain options for afflicted countries, undermining economic potential by debilitating human resources. Russia—where life expectancy is currently lower than four decades ago—is already a victim of this unhappy phenomenon, and, even apart from the factor of the AIDS epidemic, prospects for substantial improvements in Russia's health situation over the decades ahead are not encouraging. HIV/AIDS, moreover, could deal a heavy blow to a number of Asian/ Eurasian countries in the years ahead, particularly in Russia, India, and China. Finally, the strange and unnatural phenomenon of rising sex ratios at birth has been extending over much of the Asia terrain. The phenomenon appears to be particularly acute in China, though it is by no means limited to the Chinese mainland. Surplus baby boys today may be unmarriageable bachelors tomorrow. How the problem of rising cohorts of unmarriageable men may affect social cohesion and political relations tomorrow is as yet uncertain—but the impact may be consequential.

Of the countries under consideration in this chapter, the power beset by the most unfavorable trends, by the criteria of strategic demography, would seem to be the Russian Federation. Continuing demographic decline—in the context of high and unyielding adult mortality rates—would appear to have manifestly negative implications for Russia's economic potential, and, without some appreciable economic revival, it is hard to see how Moscow can regain influence on the world stage.

Perhaps more surprisingly, China also stands to be a casualty of unexpected demographic constraints. Rapid population aging and a growing imbalance between the numbers of young men and young women are all-but-inexorable features of China's population profile over the coming generation—and the possibility of a massive HIV/AIDS "breakout" cannot yet be ruled out. Each of these factors could tangibly complicate an ambitious Chinese state to augment its power and extend its influence; arising in conjunction, they might do so appreciably.

If some countries appear to face especially disadvantageous demographic constraints, others perforce enjoy relative strategic advantages from their own population circumstances. Interestingly enough, the Asian Pacific power with the most strategically favorable profile may be one that we have not as yet discussed—the United States.

By the UNPD's medium variant projections, the United States is envisioned to grow from 285 million in 2000 to 358 million in 2025. In absolute terms, this would be by far the greatest increase projected for any industrialized society; in relative terms, this projected 26 percent increment would almost exactly match the proportional growth of the Asia/Eurasia region as a whole. Under these trajectories, the United States would remain the world's third most populous country in 2025. And by the early 2020s, the U.S. population growth rate—a projected 0.7 percent per year—would in this scenario actually be higher than that of Indonesia, Thailand, or virtually any country in East Asia, China included.

In these projections, the U.S. population growth accrues from two by no means implausible assumptions: 1) continued receptivity to newcomers and immigrants and 2) continuing "exceptionalism" in U.S. fertility patterns. (The United States today reports about 2.0 births per woman, as against about 1.5 in Western Europe, roughly 1.4 in Eastern Europe, and about 1.3 in Japan.) Given its sources, such population growth would tend, quite literally, to have a rejuvenating effect on the U.S. population profile: that is to say, it would slow down the process of population aging. Between 2000 and 2025, in these UNPD projections, median age in the United States would rise by just 2 years (from 35.6 to 37.6). By 2025, indeed, the U.S. population would be more youthful, and aging more slowly, than that of China or any of today's "tigers." Further, just to state the obvious, neither a resurgence of HIV/AIDS nor an eruption of imbalanced sex ratios at birth look to be part of the U.S. prospect over the decades immediately ahead. One may of course debate the magnitude of the impact of such relative demographic advantages. For the time being, however, it would appear that demographic trends may, in some limited but tangible measure, contribute to the calculus of U.S. strategic pre-eminence—in the Asia Pacific region, and indeed around the world.

Endnotes

1 John Maynard Keynes's ironic observation that "in the long run, we are all dead" is perhaps an apposite corrective for Comte—especially for those of us who happen to study, in diverse ways, the human events in that brief period between birth and death.

2 Although admittedly, exactly such calamitous circumstances are not entirely unfamiliar to modern Russia, China, Cambodia, and Korea—and a number of

other Asian or Eurasian populations.

3 Calculations derived from United Nations Population Division, *World Population Prospects: 2002 Revision*, population database <http://esa.un.org/unpp>.

4 For a listing of Asia and Eurasia's recent and planned national censuses, see the U.S. Census Bureau, "Census Dates for Countries and Areas of the World: 1995 to 2004" <www.census.gov/ipc/www/cendates>.

5 Note that western Asia—Turkey, the Middle East, and the Saudi Peninsula— is explicitly excluded from discussion in this chapter.

6 That is to say: a pattern of childbearing which, in the absence of migration, would eventually lead to a stabilization of total population numbers and thereafter to an indefinite decrease in population.

7 Christophe Z. Guilmoto and S. Irudaya Rajan, "District Level Estimates of Fertility for India's 2001 Census," *Economic and Political Weekly*, February 16, 2002, pp. 665–72.

8 This discussion relies upon the medium variant projections of the 2002 revisions of UNPD's *World Population Prospects*.

9 The final point turns on whether one prefers the UNPD's "high variant" fertility projections over its "medium" or "low" variants—if so, then one would presume that absolute increments of population in both South-Central Asia and Southeast Asia will continue to increase for another decade.

10 Newly fashionable arguments about the glowing possibilities of "demographic dividends" incumbent in East Asian—or future South and Southeast Asian— trends in domestic "dependency ratios" (the proportion of older and younger citizens in relation to persons "of working age") would seem, on their very face, to exaggerate the contribution of crude demographic structure to actual economic performance. The new "dividendism," for example, proposes to credit much or even most of East Asia's dazzling growth record over the past several decades to its purportedly felicitous "dependency ratios" during the years in question—but neglects to explain why economic performance over that same period should have been so very disappointing for the countries of the Caribbean, even though the two areas exhibited quite similar levels and trends in the evolution of their "dependency ratios" from the mid 1960s to the present.

11 UNPD "medium variant" projections will illustrate possibilities in the 2000– 2025 period. These trends are subject to uncertainty—for there is no reliable and robust method of anticipating long-term fertility trends. Despite the inherent uncertainties, the projections are sturdy enough to support the general points for which they are marshaled in this section.

12 In 1975, of course, Russia was embedded in the larger construct of the Soviet Union. Correspondingly, comparing population totals for Russia and Pakistan for that particular year is an exercise fraught with implicitly ahistorical assumptions. Nevertheless, and in just a quarter of a century, these projections suggest that Russia's population total, which slightly exceeded Pakistan's as recently as 2000, will come to be only half as great as Pakistan's own.

13 The nineteenth century commenced with 11 French for every 10 Germans, and ended with about 15 Germans for every 10 French. Data from W. S. Woytinski and E. S. Woytinksi, *World Population and Production: Trends and Outlook*, New York: Twentieth Century Fund, 1954, p. 44.

14 Around 1800, the population of France (under current boundaries) was about

28 million. In the year 2000, it was roughly 59 million—making for just more than a doubling over the course of the two intervening centuries. Colin McEvedy and Richard Jones, *Atlas of World Population History,* London: Penguin Books, 1978, p. 59; UNPD population database.

15 To name just a few, political unification, technological innovation, industrial modernization, and a revolution in military affairs.

16 Only the 32,000-person retirement community/tax shelter of Monaco appears to have a higher median age, at an estimated 44-plus years. Estimates from the U.S. Census Bureau's International Data Base <www.census.gov/ipc/www/idbagg.html>.

17 These projections are taken from the U.S. Census Bureau's International Data Base. The UNPD does not recognize the sovereignty of the Republic of China on Taiwan, and does not offer estimates or projections for it.

18 Deborah Roseveare, Willi Liebfritz, Douglas Fore, and Eckhard Wurzel, "Ageing Populations, Pension Systems and Government Budgets: Simulations for 20 OECD Countries," *OECD Economics Working Papers*, no. 168 (1996).

19 OECD, *OECD Country Survey: Japan 2002, Supplement 2*, Paris: Organization for Economic Cooperation and Development, 2002, pp. 42, 52. Japan now has the highest ratio of public debt to GDP of any OECD country.

20 See, for example, Robert Stowe England, *The Macroeconomic Impact of Global Aging: A New Era of Economic Frailty?* Washington, DC: Center for Strategic and International Studies, 2002, and Paul S. Hewitt, "The Grey Roots of Japan's Crisis," in *The Demographic Dilemma: Japan's Aging Society,* Washington, DC: Woodrow Wilson Center, January 2003, pp. 4–9.

21 For a parallel argument, see John Creighton Campbell, "Population Aging: Hardly Japan's Biggest Problem," in *The Demographic Dilemma: Japan's Aging Society,* pp. 10–15.

22 Admittedly, however, the policy paralysis exhibited by Tokyo in the face of a full decade of domestic economic woes does not weigh toward optimism on these counts at the moment.

23 Today's fashion of highlighting diverse Japanese weaknesses notwithstanding, we would do well to remember that, on an exchange-rate basis, Japan is still by far Asia's largest economic power (with a GNP, by this measure, over three times larger than China's). World Bank, *World Development Report 2003*, New York: Oxford University Press, 2002, pp. 234–35. Japan's population aging does not threaten to revise that ranking over the foreseeable future.

24 Two alternative scenarios may illustrate the proposition. According to the estimates in Figure 3, China's GDP per capita (in 1990 Gheary-Khamis dollars) in 2000 was just over $3,100. If we assume a steady annual growth rate in per capita GDP of 4 percent between 2000 and 2025, China's calculated per capita GDP would be about $8,300. Even if we assume a long term per capita growth rate of 6 percent per annum—a pace that might be quite difficult to achieve in the decades ahead—China's 2025 per capita GDP would only be about $13,400.

25 According to estimates by the U.S. Census Bureau's International Programs Center, this limited social security network has managed to generate unfounded liabilities with a net present value equal to 125–150 percent of China's current GDP. Personal communication, Dr. Loraine A. West, May 2003.

26 China National Bureau of Statistics, *China Statistical Yearbook 2000*, Beijing:

China Statistics Press, 2000, pp. 120–21. The data are for 1999.

[27] That study, incidentally, seems to have been heavily weighted toward relatively privileged urban groups: in the rural part of the sample, the corresponding figure was barely 40 percent.

[28] Results taken from the REVES database <http://euroreves.ined.fr/reves>.

[29] U.S. Census Bureau's International Data Base.

[30] According to official Russian statistics, Russia ranks 137 in global male life expectancy and 100 in global female life expectancy. Murray Feshbach, *Russia's Health and Demographic Crises: Policy Implications and Consequences*, Washington, DC: The Chemical and Biological Arms Control Institute, 2003, pp. 15–16. And in some ways, Russia's mortality situation looks more unfavorable from the standpoint of economic performance than for other countries with similar age-standardized death rates, due to Russia's concentration of mortality in "working age" cohorts.

[31] As is all too well known, human immunodeficiency virus/acquired immunodeficiency syndrome (HIV/AIDS), a relatively new disease, is a slow-acting virus (lentivirus) transmitted through human fluids, as yet almost invariably fatal and for which there is no known cure. To date perhaps 70 million people worldwide have been infected, and perhaps 25 million or more have died.

[32] The following paragraphs draw upon and update analysis presented in Nicholas Eberstadt, "The Future of AIDS," *Foreign Affairs*, vol. 81, no. 6 (November/December 2002).

[33] U.S. National Intelligence Council, *The Next Wave of HIV/AIDS: Nigeria, Ethiopia, Russia, India and China*, September 2002; "Up to 1.5 million Russians may have HIV: official," Agence France Presse, May 21, 2003.

[34] Note that the projections were derived using U.S. Census Bureau projections of life expectancy as "baseline." Those projections are considerably more "optimistic" for Russia than the UNPD's 2002 revision (in the sense of anticipating more improvement in life expectancy over the coming decades). Using UNPD projections as "baseline," in other words, would have resulted in even more alarming illustrative scenarios for Russia. Note as well that the Census Bureau's life expectancy projections for Russia, China and India do not make any explicit attempt to factor the impact of the prospective local HIV epidemics into the future trajectory for national life expectancy—thus we are not "double counting" in our simulations here.

[35] By accepted convention, HIV prevalence refers to the prevalence rate among the adult population 15–49 years of age—an arbitrary but not entirely unreasonable metric.

[36] The demographic-economic impact of HIV in the decades ahead, of course, could potentially be mitigated by some major "technological fix"—more specifically, by medical breakthroughs that facilitate prevention or transmission of the virus, or perhaps even discovery of some sort of cure for the illness. Without at all discounting these future possibilities, a number of constraints on such prospects must be noted from this 2003 vantage point. First, with respect to current research on possible HIV-vaccines, present expectations within the medical research community are that a viable product of any type is still many years away—and that such a prototype, when developed, is likely to provide protection for only a limited percentage of the population at large.

Second, even if ongoing innovations substantially reduce the cost of anti-retroviral treatment (ART) and simplify the currently complex and exacting medications regimen necessary for people already infected with HIV, ART may still not be affordable for low income populations—in whose ranks vast numbers of China's and India's citizens will certainly remain, even in 2025. Finally, the prospect of a cure for AIDS must be weighed against the simple fact that HIV is a *virus*—and modern medicine is, as yet, incapable of curing *any* virus. (As yet, recall, there is not even a cure for the common cold.)

[37] The number of males per 100 females.

[38] Thus the Prussian Johan Peter Suessmilch (1741): "Graunt, Derham and others have suggested the Creator has reasons for insuring four to five percent more boys than girls lie in the fact that it compensates for the higher males losses due to the recklessness of boys, to exhaustion, to dangerous occupations, to war, to seafaring and immigration, thus maintaining the balance between the two sexes so that everyone can find a spouse at the appropriate age for marriage." Cite by Elisabeth Pisani and Basia Zaba, "Son Preference, Sex Selection and the Marriage Market," paper prepared for the International Union for the Scientific Study of Population (IUSSP) International Conference, Beijing, China, October 1997.

[39] An excellent summary of the Chinese situation can be found in Judith Banister, "Shortage of Girls in China: Causes, Consequence, International Comparisons and Solutions," May 2003 <www.prb.org/preseations/shortageofgirls inchina.ppt>.

[40] This latter point comes from Daniel M. Goodkind, "Recent Trends in the Sex Ratio at Birth in East Asia," U.S. Census Bureau, International Programs Center, unpublished paper, June 2002.

[41] Ansley J. Coale and Judith Banister, "Five Decades of Missing Females in China," *Demography*, vol. 31, no. 3 (July 1994), pp. 459–79.

[42] The classic exposition here is J. Hajnal, "European Marriage Patterns in Perspective," in D. V. Glass and D. E. C. Eversley, *Population in History*, Chicago: Aldine, 1965, pp. 101–43.

[43] Valerie Hudson and Andrea Den Boer, "A Surplus of Men, A Deficit of Peace: Security and Sex Ratios in Asia's Largest States," *International Security*, vol. 25, no. 5 (Spring 2002), pp. 5–38.

[44] Edward N. Luttwak, "Where Are the Great Powers? Home With The Kids," *Foreign Affairs*, vol. 73, no. 4 (July/August 1994), pp. 23–28.

[45] See Fred Arnold, Sunita Kishor, and T. K. Roy, "Sex-Selective Abortions in India," *Population and Development Review*, vol. 28, no. 2 (December 2002), pp. 759–86.

[46] Part of these local, biologically impossible disparities could perhaps be attributed to differential migration or mortality patterns—but the numerical imbalance between boys and girls is too substantial to be explained away altogether.

[47] According to the Indian 2001 census, rural areas counted about 107 boys under 7 for every 100 girls, while in urban areas the corresponding figure was nearly 111. "Sex ratio in the age group 0–6 years," *eCENSUSIndia*, no. 15 (2003) <www.censusindia.net/results/eci15_page1.html>.

STRATEGIC ASIA

INDICATORS

STRATEGIC ASIA
BY THE NUMBERS

The 16 pages that follow contain tables and figures generated from NBR's Strategic Asia database and its sources. This comprehensive database is available online, free of charge, at <http://strategicasia.nbr.org>. The data contained herein provide insights into the economic, demographic, and military trends that are reshaping the strategic environment in the Asia Pacific. This appendix consists of six sections devoted to the following indicators: economic growth, globalization and trade, foreign direct investment, population growth, energy consumption, defense (including defense expenditures), military capabilities, and weapons of mass destruction.

Each section shows data for the top 15 countries in Northeast, Southeast, South, and Central Asia by a relevant measure (e.g., size of the economy, total value of exports, population, etc.), as well as that same data for Australia, Russia, and the United States. Source details for each indicator shown are listed in the endnotes beginning on page 504.

The Strategic Asia database contains additional data for all 37 countries in Strategic Asia. It provides in one place authoritative, up-to-date, and strategically significant data for the years 1990 to 2002. The Strategic Asia database gives users unprecedented access to this information and the tools with which to manipulate, download, and tabulate it. A fuller description of the database is contained in the preface on pages *xii-xiv*.

The information for *Strategic Asia by the Numbers* was compiled by Strategic Asia research assistants Jonathan Acuff, Neil Beck, and Allison Clark.

Strategic Asia—Economies

China's rapid economic growth is singular in its size, continuity, and potential. China's economy, now one-fifth the size of Japan's, will continue its relative growth unless Tokyo undertakes long-needed reforms. Most Southeast Asian states have recovered from the 1997–98 Asian financial crisis. Russia's economy has grown for each of the past four years, but growth in the Central Asian states remains weak.

- Economic power continues to concentrate in Northeast Asia.
- India's economy continues to grow in size, although at a moderate pace that lags behind that of other regional states.
- Southeast Asia's growth is slackening in the current global slowdown.
- Russia's official GDP is still one-third lower than its 1990 level, but its economic outlook is good.

1. Gross Domestic Product

	GDP ($bn constant)				Rank	
	1990	1995	2000	2001	1990	2001
Northeast Asia						
China	396.4	700.2	1,041.2	1,117.2	4	3
Hong Kong	107.3	139.2	164.6	164.8	11	11
Japan	4,936.0	5,291.7	5,680.6	5,647.7	2	2
South Korea	341.6	489.3	617.5	639.2	5	4
Taiwan	160.2	265.0	309.4	...	8	8
Central Asia						
Kazakhstan	32.5	19.9	22.5	25.5	16	18
South Asia						
Bangladesh	30.6	37.9	48.9	51.5	17	16
India	274.4	353.2	467.3	492.5	7	5
Pakistan	48.4	61.2	71.2	73.2	15	15
Southeast Asia						
Indonesia	138.4	202.1	209.2	216.2	9	9
Malaysia	56.5	88.8	111.6	112.1	13	12
Philippines	66.6	74.1	88.2	91.2	12	14
Singapore	53.9	83.4	114.4	112.0	14	13
Thailand	111.1	168.3	171.5	174.6	10	10
Vietnam	13.6	20.2	29.0	31.0	18	17
Other Powers						
Australia	318.1	375.8	451.6	469.2	6	6
Russia	543.7	337.7	359.6	377.6	3	7
United States	6,525.3	7,338.4	8,986.9	9,013.9	1	1

Sources: World Bank, *World Development Indicators*; IMF, *World Economic Outlook*; IMF, *International Financial Statistics*; Central Bank of China (Taipei), *Financial Statistics*.

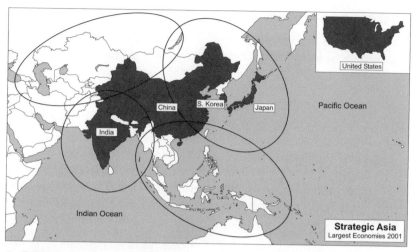

Strategic Asia
Largest Economies 2001

2. GDP Growth and Inflation

	GDP growth (%)			Inflation (%)		
	1990-94	1995-99	2000-02	1990-94	1995-99	2000-02
Northeast Asia						
China	10.7	8.8	7.7	10.4	5.2	0.4
Hong Kong	5.3	2.2	5.3	9.3	4.0	-2.8
Japan	2.2	1.3	0.9	2.0	0.4	-0.8
South Korea	7.5	5.0	6.2	7.0	4.4	3.0
Taiwan	6.8	5.8	1.9	3.9	2.0	0.4
Central Asia						
Kazakhstan	-8.5	-1.0	11.5	...	49.8	9.1
South Asia						
Bangladesh	4.7	5.0	6.2	4.9	6.0	3.3
India	4.9	6.4	4.7	10.2	8.9	4.0
Pakistan	4.5	3.4	3.5	10.5	8.9	3.5
Southeast Asia						
Indonesia	8.0	1.7	4.1	8.6	20.4	9.3
Malaysia	9.3	5.2	4.3	3.8	3.5	1.6
Philippines	1.9	1.9	3.7	11.1	7.9	4.5
Singapore	9.3	6.2	4.1	2.9	1.0	0.7
Thailand	9.0	1.5	3.2	4.8	5.1	1.3
Vietnam	7.3	7.5	6.8	...	5.1	0.6
Other Powers						
Australia	2.4	4.4	2.9	3.0	2.0	4.0
Russia	-8.8	-1.2	7.0	...	74.7	19.3
United States	2.2	3.8	2.2	3.6	2.4	2.6

Sources: World Bank, *World Development Indicators*; IMF, *World Economic Outlook*; IMF, *International Financial Statistics*; Central Bank of China (Taipei), *Financial Statistics*.

Strategic Asia—Globalization and Trade

Globalization is in full swing across Strategic Asia. Almost all the major trading nations increased their dependence on trade during the 1990s, in most cases at considerable rates. This trend began to slow in 2001, in large part due to the global economic slowdown. The United States and Japan continue to be the most preferred markets for Strategic Asia's exporters, although China and Singapore are increasingly important in their region.

- Strategic Asia's most significant exporters (in terms of volume of trade) are located almost exclusively in Northeast Asia.
- Southeast Asia's economies are the most trade-dependent in the region, and thus the most vulnerable to slow world economic growth.
- South Asia's trade performance lags behind the rest of the region.
- Russia's trade is focused predominantly on European markets.

3. Importance of Trade

	Trade as share of GDP (%)				Rank	
	1990	1995	2000	2001	1990	2000
Northeast Asia						
China	31.9	45.7	49.1	49.2	12	12
Hong Kong	260.1	303.2	295.4	282.5	2	2
Japan	19.8	16.8	20.1	20.3	15	18
South Korea	59.4	61.9	86.5	83.5	7	9
Taiwan	...	94.6	106.6	96.1	...	7
Central Asia						
Kazakhstan	...	82.5	108.2	95.0	...	6
South Asia						
Bangladesh	19.9	27.9	37.7	37.7	14	14
India	17.2	25.6	30.5	29.1	16	16
Pakistan	38.9	36.1	34.3	37.4	9	15
Southeast Asia						
Indonesia	49.1	54.0	74.1	73.7	8	10
Malaysia	147.0	192.1	229.6	214.3	3	3
Philippines	60.8	80.5	106.5	96.7	6	8
Singapore	361.2	340.5	339.6	325.4	1	1
Thailand	75.8	90.4	125.4	126.5	5	4
Vietnam	81.3	74.7	112.5	111.5	4	5
Other Powers						
Australia	33.5	39.8	45.6	...	11	13
Russia	36.1	52.2	68.6	61.0	10	11
United States	20.6	23.5	26.2	...	13	17

Sources: World Bank, *World Development Indicators*; Ministry of Economic Affairs (Taipei); IMF, *International Financial Statistics*.

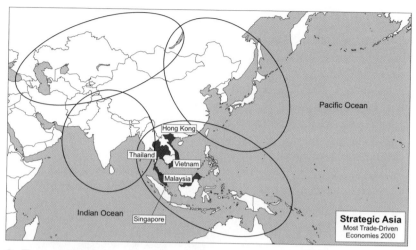

Strategic Asia
Most Trade-Driven
Economies 2000

2. Export Partners

	Exports ($bn) 2001	Export destinations (top three partners in 2001 with percentage share of total exports)
Northeast Asia		
China	266.1	U.S. (20%), Hong Kong (17%), Japan (17%)
Hong Kong	190.9	China (37%), U.S. (22%), Japan (6%)
Japan	383.6	U.S. (30%), China (8%), South Korea (6%)
South Korea	151.3	U.S. (21%), China (12%), Japan (11%)
Taiwan	122.9	U.S. (23%), Hong Kong (22%), Japan (10%)
Central Asia		
Kazakhstan	8.9	Russia (20%), Italy (11%), China (8%)
South Asia		
Bangladesh	6.1	U.S. (30%), Germany (10%), Britain (8%)
India	44.5	U.S. (21%), Britain (6%), Germany (5%)
Pakistan	9.1	U.S. (24%), UAE (8%), Britain (7%)
Southeast Asia		
Indonesia	57.4	Japan (21%), U.S. (15%), Singapore (11%)
Malaysia	88.0	U.S. (20%), Singapore (17%), Japan (13%)
Philippines	31.2	U.S. (28%), Japan (16%), Netherlands (9%)
Singapore	122.5	Malaysia (17%), U.S. (15%), Hong Kong (9%)
Thailand	63.2	U.S. (20%), Japan (15%), Singapore (8%)
Vietnam	15.0	Japan (17%), Australia (8%), U.S. (8%)
Other Powers		
Australia	63.7	Japan (20%), U.S. (10%), South Korea (8%)
Russia	101.9	Germany (10%), Italy (8%), U.S. (7%)
United States	721.8	Canada (22%), Mexico (14%), Japan (8%)

Sources: IMF, *International Financial Statistics*; IMF, *Direction of Trade Statistics*; Central Bank of China (Taipei), *Financial Statistics*; Central Intelligence Agency, *World Factbook*.

Strategic Asia—Investment

With few exceptions, Asian countries were not significantly more dependent on foreign direct investment (FDI) at the end of the 1990s than they were at the beginning of the decade. The high levels of investment growth of the early 1990s slowed—and in some notable cases declined—in the latter half of the decade. The United States, Japan, and Western Europe are generally the largest sources of FDI in Strategic Asia.

- China has emerged as the most favored destination for international capital worldwide and attracts the largest share of FDI in Asia by far.
- For Southeast Asia, the loss of FDI following the Asian financial crisis is compounded by China's increasing attractiveness to investors.
- Indonesia in particular continues to struggle to attract investment, and experienced net outflows of FDI in 2001 and 2002.

5. Importance of Investment

	FDI as share of GDP (%)				Rank	
	1990	1995	2000	2001	1995	2002
Northeast Asia						
China	1.0	5.1	3.6	3.8	3	5
Hong Kong	...	...	38.1	14.1	-	1
Japan	0.1	0.0	0.2	0.1	16	16
South Korea	0.3	0.4	2.0	0.8	14	11
Taiwan	...	...	...	...	...	...
Central Asia						
Kazakhstan	...	4.8	7.0	12.3	4	2
South Asia						
Bangladesh	0.0	0.0	0.6	0.2	15	15
India	0.1	0.6	0.5	0.7	13	12
Pakistan	0.6	1.2	0.5	0.7	10	13
Southeast Asia						
Indonesia	1.0	2.2	-3.0	-2.3	7	17
Malaysia	5.3	4.7	4.2	0.6	5	14
Philippines	1.2	2.0	1.7	2.5	8	7
Singapore	15.2	10.6	5.8	10.1	2	3
Thailand	2.9	1.2	2.8	3.3	9	6
Vietnam	0.2	11.3	4.2	4.0	1	4
Other Powers						
Australia	2.6	3.2	3.0	1.2	6	9
Russia	0.0	0.6	1.0	0.8	12	10
United States	0.8	0.8	3.1	1.3	11	8

Source: World Bank, *World Development Indicators.*

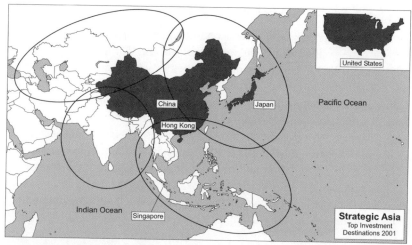

Strategic Asia
Top Investment
Destinations 2001

6. Origins of FDI

	FDI inflows ($bn) 2001	Origins of FDI (leading partners in 2001 with percentage share of total inward investment)
Northeast Asia		
China	44.2	Hong Kong (34%), Virgin Is. (12%), U.S. (10%)
Hong Kong	22.8	China (40%), Netherlands (10%), Britain (10%)
Japan	6.2	U.S. (37%), Netherlands (15%), France (14%)
South Korea	3.2	EU (29%), U.S. (19%), Japan (16%)
Taiwan	4.1	U.S. (17%), EU (13%), Japan (10%)
Central Asia		
Kazakhstan	2.8	U.S. (36%), Britain (17%), Italy (13%)
South Asia		
Bangladesh	0.1	Norway (19%), U.S. (17%), Singapore (14%)
India	3.4	Mauritius (16%), U.S. (7%), Japan (4%)
Pakistan	0.4	Britain (40%), U.S. (40%), Saudi Arabia (7%)
Southeast Asia		
Indonesia	-3.3	Britain (37%), Japan (20%), Netherlands (12%)
Malaysia	0.6	U.S. (38%), Japan (15%), Netherlands (11%)
Philippines	1.8	U.S. (24%), Japan (20%), Netherlands (12%)
Singapore	8.6	U.S. (51%), Japan (21%), France (5%)
Thailand	3.8	U.S. (35%), Japan (24%), Britain (18%)
Vietnam	1.3	Netherlands (32%), Britain (28%), Taiwan (13%)
Other Powers		
Australia	4.4	U.S. (28%), Britain (23%), Japan (8%)
Russia	2.5	U.S. (21%), Cyprus (19%), Netherlands (12%)
United States	130.8	Switz. (42%), Germany (23%), Netherlands (12%)

Source: World Bank, *World Development Indicators*; other sources (Asian Development Bank, UNCTAD; U.S. Bureau of Economic Analysis).

Strategic Asia—Population

Despite lower population growth rates relative to other countries in the region, China—the most populous country in the world—looks set to retain this distinction for the immediate future. South Asia has the highest rates of population growth in Asia, and India's population is closing in on China's. India's population cohort aged 0–14, for example, is growing at a much faster rate than the same cohort in China.

- Japan's slow population growth rate brought it from 6th to 8th place in the region during the 1990s. Aging is also a major concern.
- Russia's population and average life expectancies have shown remarkable declines in the course of the decade.
- Rapid population growth in Pakistan caused the South Asian country's population to surpass that of Russia as of 2000.

7. Population

	Population (m)				Rank	
	1990	1995	2000	2002	1990	2002
Northeast Asia						
China	1,138.9	1,206.0	1,262.5	1,279.2	1	1
Japan	123.5	125.3	126.7	127.1	6	8
South Korea	42.9	45.2	47.3	48.0	12	12
Central Asia						
Uzbekistan	20.6	22.8	24.8	25.6	14	16
South Asia						
Afghanistan	14.7	21.5	25.9	27.8	18	14
Bangladesh	109.9	119.2	130.4	135.7	8	7
India	841.7	922.1	1,002.7	1,034.2	2	2
Nepal	19.3	21.9	24.7	25.9	15	15
Pakistan	114.0	126.6	141.6	147.7	7	5
Southeast Asia						
Burma	38.5	40.2	41.8	42.3	13	13
Indonesia	188.0	205.6	224.1	231.3	4	4
Malaysia	17.5	19.6	21.8	22.7	16	17
Philippines	64.3	71.7	79.7	83.0	10	9
Thailand	55.3	58.9	62.4	63.6	11	11
Vietnam	66.6	73.2	78.5	80.6	9	10
Other Powers						
Australia	17.0	18.1	19.2	19.5	17	18
Russia	148.1	148.1	146.0	145.0	5	6
United States	250.1	266.6	282.3	287.7	3	3

Source: World Bank, *World Development Indicators.*

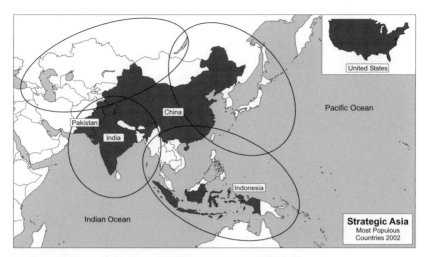

8. Population Growth and Life Expectancy

	Population growth rate (%)			Life expectancy (yrs)		
	1990	2000	2002	1990	2000	2002
Northeast Asia						
China	1.5	0.9	0.9	69	70	71
Japan	0.3	0.2	0.2	79	81	80
South Korea	1.1	0.9	0.9	70	73	74
Central Asia						
Uzbekistan	1.5	1.4	1.6	69	70	63
South Asia						
Afghanistan	2.3	2.6	3.4	43	43	47
Bangladesh	2.0	1.7	1.5	55	61	60
India	2.0	1.8	1.5	60	63	63
Nepal	2.5	2.4	2.2	54	59	58
Pakistan	2.5	2.4	2.1	59	63	61
Southeast Asia						
Burma	1.1	1.2	0.6	57	56	55
Indonesia	1.8	1.6	...	62	66	...
Malaysia	3.0	2.4	...	71	73	...
Philippines	2.2	1.8	...	65	69	...
Thailand	1.8	0.8	...	69	69	...
Vietnam	2.2	1.3	...	67	69	...
Other Powers						
Australia	1.5	1.1	...	77	79	...
Russia	0.4	-0.5	...	69	65	...
United States	1.1	1.2	...	75	77	...

Source: World Bank, *World Development Indicators*.

Strategic Asia—Energy

Throughout Asia, energy consumption levels showed consistent growth throughout the decade. Monumental shifts are now underway in the energy consumption and production patterns, particularly in Northeast Asia and the Russian Far East. Rapid economic growth in China, Taiwan, and South Korea has led to almost doubled consumption levels.

- Oil will remain the primary energy source for most economies because much of the energy demand is driven by the transportation sector.
- China was the world's third largest consumer of petroluem in 2002, and will likely surpass Japan in petroleum consumption in 2003.
- Major extraction projects (oil and natural gas) are underway in the Russian Far East (Sakhalin) and Siberia.
- Japan and South Korea are the world's largest LNG importers.

9. Energy Consumption

	Energy consumption (quadrillion Btu)				Rank	
	1990	1995	2000	2001	1995	2001
Northeast Asia						
China	27.0	35.2	37.0	39.7	2	2
Japan	17.9	20.8	21.8	21.9	4	4
North Korea	2.9	3.0	2.9	2.8	9	11
South Korea	3.8	6.6	7.9	8.1	6	6
Taiwan	2.0	2.9	4.0	4.1	10	9
Central Asia						
Kazakhstan	...	2.0	1.6	1.7	12	15
Uzbekistan	...	1.9	1.9	2.1	13	13
South Asia						
India	7.8	11.1	12.7	12.8	5	5
Pakistan	1.2	1.6	1.9	1.9	14	14
Southeast Asia						
Indonesia	2.3	3.3	4.1	4.6	8	8
Malaysia	1.0	1.5	1.9	2.3	15	12
Philippines	0.7	1.0	1.3	1.3	17	17
Singapore	0.8	1.2	1.6	1.6	16	16
Thailand	1.3	2.2	2.7	2.9	11	10
Vietnam	0.3	0.5	0.7	0.8	18	18
Other Powers						
Australia	3.7	4.1	4.8	5.0	7	7
Russia	...	28.2	27.4	28.2	3	3
United States	84.6	91.5	99.3	97.0	1	1

Source: Department of Energy, *Energy Information Administration.*

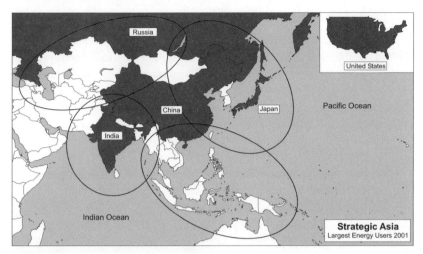

10. Oil Supplies and Reserves

	Oil supply in 2002 (m bbl/d)			Proven oil reserves
	Product.	Consum.	Imports	(bn barrels and main fields)
Northeast Asia				
China	3.4	5.3	1.9	18.3 (Daqing, Shengli)
Japan	<0.1	5.4	5.3	<0.1
North Korea	0.0	<0.1	...	...
South Korea	...	2.1	...	...
Taiwan	0.0	1.0	1.0	<0.1
Central Asia				
Kazakhstan	0.9	0.1	...	9.0 (Tengiz, Karachaganak)
Uzbekistan	<0.2	0.1	0.0	0.6 (Kokdumalak, Shurtan)
South Asia				
India	0.7	2.0	1.2	5.4 (Bombay – offshore)
Pakistan	<0.1	0.4	0.3	0.3 (Dhurnal, Fimkasser)
Southeast Asia				
Burma	1.1	1.2	0.6	<0.1
Indonesia	1.3	1.0	...	5.0 (Duri, Minas, Belida)
Malaysia[a]	0.7	0.4	...	3.0 (Bekok, Bokor)
Philippines	<0.1	0.4	0.3	0.2
Thailand[a]	0.2	0.7	0.5	0.6 (Gulf of Thailand)
Vietnam	0.3	0.1	...	0.6 (Back Ho, Rang Dong)
Other Powers				
Australia[a]	0.6	0.8	0.2	3.5 (Roller, Skate)
Russia[a]	7.4	2.4	...	48.6 (Samotlor, Romashkin)
United States	9.1	19.7	10.4	22.4 (Texas, Alaska)

Source: Department of Energy, Energy Information Administration. Notes: a) Data for Malaysia, Thailand, Australia, and Russia are 2001 estimates.

Strategic Asia—Defense

With few exceptions, defense spending has fallen in Strategic Asia since 1990 as a share of GDP. Russia, the United States, China, and Vietnam have reduced their number of military personnel significantly, but troop levels in South Asia and much of Southeast Asia have risen modestly over the course of the decade. The largest militaries in Strategic Asia remain concentrated in Northeast and South Asia.

- Russia's proportionate military spending continues to decline, mirroring deep manpower reductions and economic restructuring.
- Despite ongoing tensions on the Korean Peninsula, both proportionate military spending and aggregate troop levels have declined.
- Despite a reduction in manpower of nearly one-third over the past 12 years, the Chinese military has become the largest in the region.

11. Manpower

	Armed forces (thousands)				Rank	
	1990	1995	2000	2002	1990	2002
Northeast Asia						
China	3,030	2,930	2,340	2,270	2	1
Japan	219	240	235	238	13	13
North Korea	1,111	1,128	1,082	1,082	5	4
South Korea	750	633	683	651	7	6
Taiwan	400	378	370	370	9	9
Central Asia						
Kazakhstan	...	40	64	60	...	17
South Asia						
Bangladesh	104	116	137	137	15	15
India	1,262	1,145	1,303	1,298	4	3
Pakistan	550	587	612	619	8	7
Sri Lanka	65	125	113	158	17	14
Southeast Asia						
Burma	230	288	344	344	12	10
Indonesia	283	275	297	297	10	12
Philippines	109	107	106	106	14	16
Thailand	283	259	301	306	10	11
Vietnam	952	557	484	484	6	8
Other Powers						
Australia	68	56	51	51	16	18
Russia	3,096	1,339	817	677	1	5
United States	2,118	1,547	1,366	1,414	3	2

Source: International Institute of Strategic Studies, *The Military Balance.*

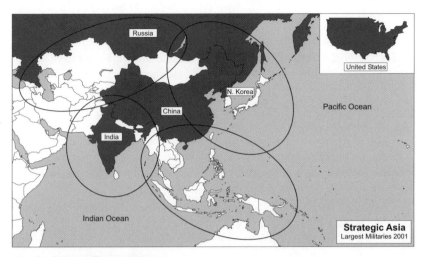

Strategic Asia
Largest Militaries 2001

12. Defense Expenditure

	Def. exp. as share GDP (%)			Def. exp. as share CGE (%)		
	1990-94	1995-99	2000-02	1990-94	1995-99	2000-02[a]
Northeast Asia						
China	5.2	5.7	4.0	31.3	25.3	...
Japan	1.2	1.0	1.0	5.1	6.4	...
North Korea	25.5	17.9	12.2	...	...	...
South Korea	3.8	3.3	2.8	19.7	14.0	...
Taiwan	5.0	4.9	4.7	31.8	27.6	...
Central Asia						
Kazakhstan	...	2.1	1.3	...	6.3	...
South Asia						
Bangladesh	1.8	1.9	1.5	10.4	9.8	...
India	2.8	3.0	3.0	12.8	14.6	...
Pakistan	7.2	6.2	4.2	27.6	26.2	...
Sri Lanka	5.0	5.7	5.2	12.5	18.3	...
Southeast Asia						
Burma	9.7	7.5	2.6	71.7	122.3	...
Indonesia	1.4	2.0	0.5	7.8	7.0	...
Philippines	1.8	2.1	1.7	10.7	8.0	...
Thailand	3.0	2.1	1.9	16.8	10.8	...
Vietnam	7.0	...	7.3	11.0	11.4	...
Other Powers						
Australia	2.2	2.0	1.9	9.5	8.6	...
Russia	8.0	5.8	4.3	29.7	24.0	...
United States	4.6	3.6	3.2	16.8	16.4	...

Sources: International Institute of Strategic Studies, *The Military Balance*; Department of State, *World Military Expenditures and Arms Transfers*. Notes: a) No data available for 2000–02.

Strategic Asia—Conventional Military Forces

Over the past 12 years, Strategic Asia has seen significant arms build-ups. China, India, Pakistan, South Korea, Vietnam, and Japan have enhanced their land warfighting capabilities. Despite the substantial increases in Japanese and, at a more modest level, Thai naval capabilities, the decline of the Russian navy means that the United States is now the only power with both the mission and capabilities to project bluewater naval power.

- The sharp upswing in both Indian and Pakistani land warfare capabilities reflects the ongoing tension in South Asia.
- There has been a massive increase in relative U.S. air power, which has been brought to bear effectively in Afghanistan and Iraq.
- Although Russia has declined in every metric of military power, the sharpest drop has been in its naval and submarine warfare capabilities.

13. Land Warfare Capabilities

	Tanks, APCs/LAVs, Artillery (th)				Rank	
	1990	1995	2000	2002	1990	2002
China	30.9	32.6	31.4	35.4	3	3
North Korea	28.5	23.8	25.6	25.0	4	4
South Korea	13.5	15.3	15.7	15.8	5	5
India	9.1	9.4	11.5	13.5	6	6
Pakistan	4.4	6.5	6.1	7.1	7	7
Vietnam	4.4	6.4	6.5	6.8	8	7
Russia	222.6	80.3	75.2	77.8	1	1
United States	70.4	58.2	41.8	52.6	2	2

Sources: International Institute of Strategic Studies, *The Military Balance*; Federation of American Scientists.

14. Air Warfare Capabilities

	Fixed-wing aircraft[a]				Rank	
	1990	1995	2000	2002	1990	2002
China	5,150	5,100	3,283	2,301	3	3
Japan	457	560	413	536	8	6
North Korea	746	515	582	592	5	5
South Korea	469	433	507	533	7	7
India	1,023	1,182	1,074	1,030	4	4
Taiwan	506	423	570	479	6	8
Russia	6,927	6,592	4,457	2,870	1	2
United States	6,119	4,682	3,962	5,621	2	1

Sources: International Institute of Strategic Studies, *The Military Balance*; Federation of American Scientists. Notes: a) Includes interceptors and ground-attack aircraft.

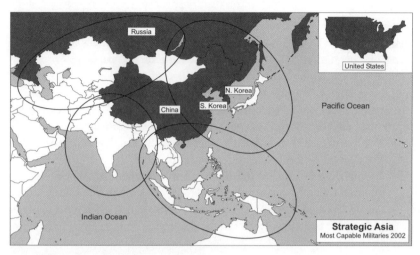

Strategic Asia
Most Capable Militaries 2002

15. Naval Warfare Capabilities

	Principal surface combatants				Rank	
	1990	1995	2000	2002	1990	2002
China	148	139	146	147	3	2
Japan	77	74	121	111	4	3
South Korea	49	55	54	55	6	5
Taiwan	60	59	55	54	5	5
India	47*	44*	45*	34*	7	7
Thailand	15	19	25*	30*	8	8
Russia	364*	198*	66*	56*	2	4
United States	402*	271*	262*	189*	1	1

Source: International Institute of Strategic Studies, *The Military Balance*; Federation of American Scientists. Asterisk (*) denotes possession of aircraft carriers.

16. Submarine Warfare Capabilities

	Submarines				Rank	
	1990	1995	2000	2002	1990	2002
China	92*	50*	64*	68*	3	2
Japan	15	15	16	16	6	6
North Korea	24	25	26	26	4	4
South Korea	3	3	20	20	8	5
India	19	15	16	16	5	6
Pakistan	6	9	10	10	7	8
Russia	242*	138*	43*	40*	1	3
United States	91*	82*	55*	54*	2	1

Source: International Institute of Strategic Studies, *The Military Balance*; Federation of American Scientists. Asterisk (*) denotes possession of strategic submarines.

Strategic Asia—Weapons of Mass Destruction

Although the START treaties slashed overall U.S. and Russian strategic weapons inventories, Strategic Asia has experienced persistent proliferation of nuclear technologies, and has the world's highest concentration of nuclear weapons. During the 1990s, both Pakistan and India openly joined the nuclear club, while North Korea, in violation of the 1994 Agreed Framework, has also developed nuclear weapons and wthdrawn from the NPT.

- North Korea has dramatically increased the number of SRBMs and MRBMs in its possession.
- The increase in Chinese ICBMs has been considerable, although China maintains a no first-use policy and does not keep them on alert status.
- Russia is scheduled to destroy its CBW inventories, but most analysts believe it clandestinely maintains these programs to some extent.

17. Nuclear Weapons

	Nuclear warheads				Rank	
	1990	1995	2000	2002	1990	2002
China	400?	480?	480?	410?	3	3
Japan	0	0	0	0	...	...
North Korea	0	?	?	2?	...	6
South Korea	0	0	0	0	...	...
India	0	0	40-200	40-200	...	4
Pakistan	0	?	40?	40?	...	5
Russia	33,515	15,615	10,544?	10,331?	1	1
United States	20,684	11,226	8,876	8,789	2	2

Sources: Carnegie Endowment for International Peace; International Institute of Strategic Studies, *The Military Balance*; Federation of American Scientists.

18. Chemical and Biological Weapons Programs

	Chemical and/or biological weapons				Rank[a]	
	1990	1995	2000	2002	1990	2001
China	prob	prob	prob	prob	3	4
Japan	✓	✓	[✓]	[✓]	5	6
North Korea	prob	prob	prob	prob	4	3
South Korea	✓	✓	✓	✓	6	7
India	...	...	[✓]	[✓]	...	5
Pakistan	prob	prob	prob	prob	7	8
Russia	✓	✓	✓	✓	1	1
United States	✓	✓	[✓]	[✓]	2	2

Table shows confirmed (✓) and probable (prob) programs; [✓] indicates stocks are being destroyed. Sources: Carnegie Endowment for International Peace; Center for Nonproliferation Studies; Federation of American Scientists. Notes: a) Ranking by number, type, and weapon system.

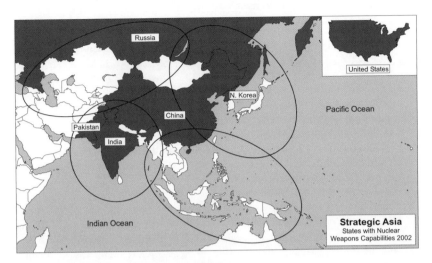

Strategic Asia
States with Nuclear
Weapons Capabilities 2002

19. Short-Range Ballistic Missiles

	SRBMs, MRBMs and IRBMs				Rank	
	1990	1995	2000	2002	1990	2002
China	66?	70	324?	485?	3	2
Japan	0	0	0	0	...	...
North Korea	69	30	320?	566?	4	1
South Korea	12	12	12	12	5	6
India	0	?	44?	86?	...	5
Pakistan	?	18?	122?	144?	6	4
Russia	1,610	600	200	200	1	3
United States	164	0	0	0	2	...

Sources: Carnegie Endowment for International Peace; International Institute of Strategic Studies, *The Military Balance*; Federation of American Scientists.

20. Long-Range Ballistic Missiles

	ICBMs and SLBMs				Rank	
	1990	1995	2000	2002	1990	2002
China	14	19	32?	32	3	3
Japan	0	0	0	0	...	...
North Korea	0	0	?	?	...	...
South Korea	0	0	0	0	...	...
India	0	0	0	0	...	...
Pakistan	0	0	0	0	...	...
Russia	2,514	1,413	1,168	967	1	2
United States	1,624	982	982	982	2	1

Sources: Carnegie Endowment for International Peace, International Institute of Strategic Studies, *The Military Balance*; Federation of American Scientists.

Endnotes

[1] Gross Domestic Product—Table shows GDP in 1995 constant dollars. GDP for Taiwan is shown in 1990 constant dollars. Source: World Bank, *World Development Indicators*, 2003 CD-ROM; CBC, *Financial Statistics*, Taipei: Central Bank of China, various editions.

[2] GDP Growth and Inflation—Table shows annual average rates of GDP growth and inflation. Data for some countries over certain periods is partial. Sources: World Bank, *World Development Indicators*, 2003 CD-ROM; IMF, *World Economic Outlook*, Washington, DC: International Monetary Fund, 2003; IMF, International Financial Statistics, 2003 CD-ROM; CBC, *Financial Statistics*, Taipei: Central Bank of China, various editions.

[3] Importance of Trade—Table shows value of trade as a percentage share of GDP. Data for some countries over certain periods is partial. Sources: World Bank, *World Development Indicators*, 2003 CD-ROM; Ministry of Economic Affairs (Taipei); IMF, *International Financial Statistics*, 2003.

[4] Export Partners—Table shows value of exports and leading export destinations with percentage share of total exports. Sources: IMF, International Financial Statistics, 2003 CD-ROM; IMF, Direction of Trade Statistics, Washington, DC, International Monetary Fund, 2002; CBC, *Financial Statistics*, Taipei: Central Bank of China; CIA, *World Factbook*, Washington, DC: Central Intelligence Agency, 2002.

[5] Importance of Investment—Table shows value of foreign direct investment as a percentage share of GDP. Data for some countries over certain periods is partial. Sources: World Bank, *World Development Indicators*, 2003 CD-ROM.

[6] Origins of FDI—Table shows value of foreign direct investment and leading origins of FDI. Sources: World Bank, *World Development Indicators*, 2003 CD-ROM; other sources (Asian Development Bank, UNCTAD, U.S. Bureau of Economic Analysis).

[7] Population—Table shows size of population. Source: World Bank, *World Development Indicators*, 2003 CD-ROM.

[8] Population Growth and Life Expectancy—Table shows annual population growth rate and average life expectancy at birth (for both males and females). Source: World Bank, *World Development Indicators*, CD-ROM.

[9] Energy Consumption—Table shows primary energy consumption (including petroleum, natural gas, coal, hydroelectric, nuclear, geothermal, solar, wind, and wood and waste power). Source: Department of Energy, Energy Information Administration, *International Energy Annual 2001*.

[10] Oil Supplies and Reserves—Table shows oil production, consumption, and imports (millions of barrels per day), plus proven oil reserves (billions of barrels) and names of major oil fields. Source: Energy Information Administration, *Country Analysis Briefs*, various reports.

[11] Armed Forces—Table shows active duty military personnel only. Source: IISS, *The Military Balance*, International Institute for Strategic Studies, London: Oxford University Press, various editions.

[12] Defense Expenditure—Table shows annual average rate of defense spending as a share of GDP and as a share of central government expenditures. Sources:

IISS, *The Military Balance*, International Institute for Strategic Studies, London: Oxford University Press, various editions; U.S. Department of State, *World Military Expenditures and Arms Transfers*, 2003.

13 Land Warfare Capabilities—Table shows the total of all tanks, light armored vehicles, armored personnel carriers, and artillery with main guns larger then 90 mm. Sources: IISS, *The Military Balance*, International Institute of Strategic Studies, London: Oxford University Press, various editions; Federation of American Scientists <www.fas.org/man/index.html>.

14 Air Warfare Capabilities—Table shows the total of interceptors and ground attack aircraft. Sources: IISS, *The Military Balance*, International Institute of Strategic Studies, London: Oxford University Press, various editions; Federation of American Scientists <www.fas.org/man/index.html>.

15 Naval Warfare Capabilities—Table shows capital ships and other ocean-going combat vessels. Asterisks indicate those countries possessing aircraft carriers. Sources: IISS, *The Military Balance*, International Institute of Strategic Studies, London: Oxford University Press, various editions; Federation of American Scientists <www.fas.org/man/index.html>; Haze Gray and Under Way, *World Navies Today* <www.hazegray.org/worldnav/>.

16 Submarine Warfare Capabilities—Table shows the total number of attack and special operations submarines. Asterisks indicate those countries possessing strategic submarines. Sources: IISS, *The Military Balance*, International Institute of Strategic Studies, London: Oxford University Press, various editions; Federation of American Scientists <www.fas.org/man/index.html>; Haze Gray and Under Way, *World Navies Today* <www.hazegray.org/worldnav/>.

17 Nuclear Weapons—The tables show an amalgam of data drawn from a variety of sources and do not represent a consensus among analysts. There are often wide disparities in estimates of the number of nuclear weapons, even for the United States and Russia (estimates for Russia, for example, range from 8,250 to 10,331). Sources: Bulletin of Atomic Scientists, *Nuclear Notebook* <www.bullatomsci.org/issues/nukenotes/nukenote.html>; Carnegie Endowment for International Peace <http://ceip.org>; Federation of American Scientists <www.fas.org/nuke/index.html>; Center for Nonproliferation Studies <http://cns.miis.edu>; Nuclear Threat Initiative <www.nti.org>; IISS, *The Military Balance*, International Institute of Strategic Studies, London: Oxford University Press, various editions.

18 Chemical and Biological Weapons—Symbols in the table indicate: ✓ = Confirmed existing chemical or biological weapons program and/or weaponized agents; [✓] = Chemical and/or biological weapons stockpile in the process of disposal; and "prob" = Likely chemical and/or biological weapons program, including questionable dual use facilities. Rankings are based on numbers and types of weapons and delivery systems. Sources include: Federation of American Scientists <www. fas.org/nuke/index.html>; Center for Nonproliferation Studies <http://cns.miis.edu>; IISS, *The Military Balance*, International Institute of Strategic Studies, London: Oxford University Press, various editions.

19 Short Range Ballistic Missiles—Table shows numbers of short-range, medium-range, and intermediate-range ballistic missiles. Sources: Carnegie Endowment for International Peace <http://ceip. org>; Federation of American Scientists

<www.fas.org/nuke/index.html>; Center for Nonproliferation Studies <http://cns.miis.edu>; IISS, *The Military Balance*, International Institute of Strategic Studies, London: Oxford University Press, various editions.

[20] Long Range Ballistic Missiles—Table shows numbers of intecontinental and submarine-launched ballistic missiles. While Japan and South Korea have no missiles in their possession or in development, assets from their space programs could be converted to military use. There is considerable debate regarding the maximum range of North Korea's ballistic missiles: some analysts claim that these could reach the continental United States, others argue that their range is much less. Sources: Bulletin of Atomic Scientists, *Nuclear Notebook* <www.bullatomsci.org/issues/nukenotes/nukenote.html>; Carnegie Endowment for International Peace <http://ceip.org>; Federation of American Scientists <www.fas.org/nuke/index.html>; Center for Nonproliferation Studies <http://cns.miis.edu>; Nuclear Threat Initiative <www.nti.org>; IISS, *The Military Balance*, International Institute of Strategic Studies, London: Oxford University Press, various editions.

INDEX

ABOUT THE AUTHORS

Zachary M. Abuza is Assistant Professor of International Politics and the Director of the East Asian Studies Program at Simmons College. He is the author of *Tentacles of Terror: Al Qaeda's Southeast Asian Network* (Lynne Rienner Press, 2003) and *Renovating Politics in Contemporary Vietnam* (Lynne Rienner Press, 2001). He has also written numerous articles on Vietnamese politics and foreign policy and the Khmer Rouge in Cambodia. Professor Abuza was the first American Visiting Research Fellow at the Institute of International Relations in Hanoi, where he completed a manuscript on Vietnamese-Chinese relations. He specializes in terrorism, international relations and security issues in the Asia Pacific, the comparative politics of Southeast Asia, and Vietnamese politics.

Michael H. Armacost is a Shorenstein Distinguished Fellow and Visiting Professor at the Asia/Pacific Research Center at Stanford University and is former President of the Brookings Institution. During his 24 years in government, he served as U.S. Ambassador to Japan, U.S. Ambassador to the Philippines, and Under Secretary of State for Political Affairs at the State Department, and occupied senior policy-making positions at the National Security Council and the Department of Defense. His recent publications include "Japan and the Engagement of China: Challenges for U.S. Policy Coordination," *NBR Analysis* (December 2001, with Kenneth Pyle); "Japan: Policy Paralysis and Economic Stagnation" in *America and the East Asian Crisis* (W. W. Norton, 2000); "Japan and the Unification of Korea: Challenges for U.S. Policy Coordination," *NBR Analysis* (March 1999, with

Kenneth Pyle); *Asian Alliances and American Politics* (Stanford University Press, 1999); and *Friends or Rivals?* (Columbia University Press, 1996).

Victor D. Cha holds the D. S. Song Chair in Asian Studies and Government in the Edmund Walsh School of Foreign Service, Georgetown University. He is the co-author of the forthcoming book *Nuclear North Korea? A Debate on Strategies of Engagement* (Columbia University Press, 2003) and is the author of *Alignment Despite Antagonism: The United States-Korea-Japan Security Triangle* (Stanford University Press, 1999). He has written numerous articles on international relations and East Asia in such journals as *International Security*, *Political Science Quarterly*, *International Studies Quarterly*, *Foreign Affairs*, and *Foreign Policy*. Professor Cha is a former John M. Olin National Security Fellow at Harvard University, two-time Fulbright Scholar, and Hoover National Fellow and CISAC Fellow at Stanford. He serves as a consultant to the U.S. government, Booz Allen Hamilton, SAIC, and CENTRA Technology.

Thomas J. Christensen is Professor of Politics and International Affairs at Princeton University. He is the author of *Useful Adversaries: Grand Strategy, Domestic Mobilization, and Sino-American Conflict, 1947–58* (Princeton University Press, 1996), and numerous articles, including "Posing Problems Without Catching Up," *International Security* (Spring 2001); "China: Getting the Questions Right," with Richard Betts, *The National Interest* (Winter 2000/01); and "Theater Missile Defense and Taiwan's Security," *Orbis* (Winter 2000). He also contributed the China chapters to the 2002–03 and 2001–02 *Strategic Asia* volumes. His research and teaching focus on Chinese foreign policy, East Asian security, and international relations theory. He is currently working on projects relating to China's contemporary military doctrine and U.S. strategy toward East Asia.

Kathleen Collins is Assistant Professor of Political Science at the University of Notre Dame and faculty fellow in Notre Dame's Kellogg Institute for International Studies and Kroc Institute for International Peace Studies. Her recent publications include "The Political Role of Clans," *Comparative Politics* (January 2003), "Clans, Pacts, and Politics," *Journal of Democracy* (July 2002), and "Tajikistan: The Causes of Prolonged Civil Conflict," in Chandra Sriam, ed., *The Prevention of Violent Conflict* (Lynne Rienner Press, 2002). Her forthcoming book is titled *Clans, Politics, and Regime Transformation in Central Asia*. She specializes in the politics of the former Soviet Union, particularly Central Asia and the Caucasus, and her research focuses on regime transition, clan politics, civil conflict, ethnicity, and Islamic politics. She has also done projects for the United Nations, the International Peace Academy, the Commission on Human Security, and the International Crisis Group.

Nicholas N. Eberstadt holds the Henry Wendt Chair in Political Economy at the American Enterprise Institute in Washington, DC, and is Senior Advisor to The National Bureau of Asian Research. He writes extensively on issues in demography, economic development, and international security; advises or consults for various governmental and international organizations; and regularly offers expert testimony before committees of the U.S. Congress. His most recent books are *Prosperous Paupers and Other Population Problems* (Transaction Publishers, 2001), and *Korea's Future and the Great Powers* (The National Bureau of Asian Research and University of Washington Press, 2001, co-editor with Richard Ellings), *Comparing the Soviet and American Economies* (American Enterprise Institute, 2000, co-editor with Jonathan Tombes), and *The End of North Korea* (American Enterprise Institute, 1999). He also contributed the Korea chapters to the 2002–03 and 2001–02 *Strategic Asia* volumes.

Richard J. Ellings is President and Co-founder of The National Bureau of Asian Research. He is the co-editor of *Strategic Asia 2002–03: Asian Aftershocks* (The National Bureau of Asian Research, 2002, with Aaron Friedberg), *Strategic Asia 2001–02: Power and Purpose* (NBR, 2001, with Aaron Friedberg), *Korea's Future and the Great Powers* (NBR and the University of Washington Press, 2001, with Nicholas Eberstadt), and *Southeast Asian Security in the New Millennium* (M. E. Sharpe, 1996, with Sheldon Simon). He is also the founding editor of the *NBR Analysis* series. He has served as a consultant to various governmental agencies and as a legislative assistant in the U.S. Senate. His areas of focus are the international security and political economy of Asia. He is co-authoring a monograph, *Korean Reunification and America's National Interests: A Manual for Policymakers*, (NBR, forthcoming, with Nicholas Eberstadt).

Joseph P. Ferguson is Director of Northeast Asia Studies at The National Bureau of Asian Research, and is a Ph.D. candidate at the Johns Hopkins University Nitze School of Advanced International Studies. He is the author of "Russia's Role on the Korean Peninsula and Great Power Relations in Northeast Asia," *NBR Analysis*, (June 2003). He has also written and published articles on international relations in Northeast Asia, and contributes articles on U.S.-Russian relations for the quarterly electronic journal *Comparative Connections* of the CSIS Pacific Forum. A former visiting

Fulbright Fellow at the Russian Academy of Sciences' Institute for World Economy and International Relations, and a Monbusho Fellow at Aoyama Gakuin University in Tokyo, he worked as an analyst with the Strategic Assessment Center of SAIC from 1995 to 1999. His current areas of research include Japanese politics and foreign policy, Korean security issues, Russian foreign policy in Northeast Asia, and energy security issues.

Aaron L. Friedberg is on leave from Princeton University where he has taught since 1987. He is currently Deputy National Security Advisor and Director of Policy Planning to U.S. Vice President Dick Cheney. He is the co-editor of *Strategic Asia 2002–03: Asian Aftershocks* (The National Bureau of Asian Research, 2002, with Richard Ellings), *Strategic Asia 2001–02: Power and Purpose* (NBR, 2001, with Richard Ellings), and the author of two books. His articles and essays on Asian strategic affairs have appeared in *Commentary*, *Harvard Journal of International Affairs*, *International Security*, *The New York Times*, *Survival*, *The Wall Street Journal*, and *The Weekly Standard*. He was the inaugural Henry A. Kissinger Chair in Foreign Policy and International Relations at the Library of Congress, and has served as a consultant to the National Security Council, the Office of Net Assessment in the Department of Defense, the Central Intelligence Agency, and Los Alamos National Laboratory. He has been a visiting fellow at Harvard University's Center for International Affairs, the Woodrow Wilson International Center for Scholars of the Smithsonian Institution, the Norwegian Nobel Institute in Oslo, and the Australian Strategic Policy Institute in Canberra.

Ellen L. Frost is a Visiting Fellow at the Institute for International Economics and an Adjunct Research Fellow at the Institute for National Strategic Studies at the National Defense University. She is the co-editor of a two-volume study on the impact of globalization on national security, entitled *The Global Century: Globalization and National Security* (National Defense University, 2001, with Richard Kugler) and author of numerous articles and two books, including most recently *Transatlantic Trade: A Strategic Agenda* (Institute for International Economics, 1997). She served as Counselor to the U.S. Trade Representative (1993–95) and Deputy Assistant Secretary of Defense for Economic and Technology Affairs (1977–81). Before that, she held positions in the Treasury Department and the Senate. During the 1980s, she worked in the Washington offices of two major multinational corporations.

Bates Gill holds the Freeman Chair in China Studies at the Center for Strategic and International Studies in Washington, DC. Dr. Gill previously served as a Senior Fellow in Foreign Policy Studies and inaugural Director of the Center for Northeast Asian Policy Studies at the Brookings Institution. He is the author of three books: *Contrasting Visions: U.S., China, and World Order* (Brookings Institution Press, forthcoming); *China's Arms Acquisitions from Abroad: A Quest for "Superb and Secret Weapons"* (Oxford University Press, 1995, with Taeho Kim); and *Chinese Arms Transfers* (Praeger, 1992). A specialist in East Asian foreign policy and politics, his research focuses primarily on Northeast Asian political and security issues, especially with regard to China. His current projects include research on the divergence in strategic outlook between the United States and China, Chinese nuclear weapons modernization, and China's challenging domestic policy agenda, with a special focus on HIV/AIDS.

Colonel John (Jack) H. Gill is a U.S. Army South Asia Foreign Area Officer on the faculty of the Near East-South Asia Center for Strategic Studies (NESA Center) at the National Defense University. Prior to joining the NESA Center, he was assigned to the Defense Intelligence Agency (DIA) as the Assistant Defense Intelligence Officer for South Asia. During 2001 and 2002, he also served as Special Assistant to the Joint Staff Plans and Policy Director for India/Pakistan and as military advisor to Ambassador James Dobbins, the U.S. envoy to the Afghan opposition forces. He has been following South Asia since the mid-1980s in positions with the Joint Staff (J5), the U.S. Pacific Command staff (J5), and a previous tour at the DIA. He planned and participated in the first two U.S.-India Defense Policy Group meetings and various military-to-military events with India, Bangladesh, and Sri Lanka.

Michael A. Glosny is a Ph. D. candidate in political science at the Massachusetts Institute of Technology and a member of MIT's Security Studies Program. He is currently working on a dissertation that examines how states receive and interpret signals sent by opposing states in military crises, with a particular focus on Chinese behavior in historical crises. His research and interests focus on international relations theory, Chinese foreign policy, and security relations in East Asia, especially across the Taiwan Strait.

Colonel (ret.) John B. Haseman served more than 30 years on active duty in the U.S. Army. His career specialties were as a military intelligence officer and Southeast Asia Foreign Area Officer. Colonel Haseman's first Asia assignment in South Korea was followed by two tours of combat duty in Vietnam. Subsequent years saw service in Thailand, Burma, and three assignments in Indonesia, including service as U.S. Defense and Army Attaché in both Burma (1987-90) and Indonesia (1990-94). Since his retirement in

1995, he has written extensively on Southeast Asian political-military affairs. His two most recent books are The Thai Resistance Movement During World War II (Silkworm Books, 2002) and The Military and Democracy in Indonesia: Challenges, Politics and Power (Rand, 2002, with Angel Rabasa). He is the regular Indonesia correspondent for Jane's Defence Weekly and writes for many other journals.

Dwight H. Perkins is the Harold Hitchings Burbank Professor of Political Economy at Harvard University and Director of the Harvard University Asia Center. He joined the Harvard faculty in 1963 and has served in a variety of positions, including Director of the Harvard Institute for International Development (HIID) from 1980 to 1995. He has served as a consultant on economic policy and reform to several Asian governments, the World Bank, the Ford Foundation, various private corporations, and U.S. government agencies. He has also been a visiting professor or scholar at several universities in the United States, China, and Japan and has taught at the Fulbright Economic Training Program in Vietnam. Dr. Perkins has authored or edited 12 books and over 100 articles on economic history and economic development, with special reference to the economies of East and Southeast Asia. His work focuses on the transition from central planning to the market economy, long-term agricultural development, industrial policy, and the sources of economic growth in East Asia.

Gilbert Rozman is Musgrave Professor of Sociology at Princeton University, where he has taught since 1970. Dr. Rozman's work has focused on East Asia and Russia, including 15 monographs and edited books. These include *Stunted Regionalism in Northeast Asia* (Cambridge University Press, forthcoming), *Japan and Russia: The Tortuous Path to Normalization, 1949–1999* (St. Martin's Press, 2000), *Russia and East Asia: The 21st Century Security Environment* (M. E. Sharpe, 1999), *Dismantling Communism: Common Causes and Regional Variations* (Johns Hopkins University Press, 1992), and *Japan's Response to the Gorbachev Era, 1985–1991* (Princeton University Press, 1992). His most recent articles cover Sino-Russian and Sino-Japanese relations as well as questions of national identity and misperceptions in Northeast Asia. Since 2000 he has been studying Korean while examining strategies in neighboring countries for the transformation of the Korean Peninsula. He serves on the editorial committee of *World Politics* and the editorial board of *The China Quarterly*.

Robert A. Scalapino is Robson Research Professor Emeritus of Government at the Institute of East Asian Studies, University of California-Berkeley. He previously served as Director of the Institute of East Asian Studies from 1978 to 1990, as Robson Research Professor of Government at Berkeley from 1977 to 1990, and as founder and first chairman of the National Committee on U.S.-China Relations from 1966 to 1970. Dr. Scalapino has authored more than 30 books and articles, the most recent being "Cross-Strait Relations and the United States," in *American Foreign Policy Interests* (April 2002), "Korea: The Options and Perimeters," in Tsuneo Akaha, ed., *The Future of North Korea* (Routledge, London 2002), and "Japan's Economic Route to Power," in Steven Hook, ed., *Comparative Foreign Policy: Adaptation Strategies of the Great and Emerging Powers* (Kent State University/Prentice Hall, 2002). Dr. Scalapino is also a Fellow at the American Academy of Arts and Sciences, Editor Emeritus of *Asian Survey*, and serves on numerous boards, including the Board of Advisors of The National Bureau of Asian Research. His research focuses on democracy and democratization, ethnic issues, foreign relations and policy, government, modern history, nationalism, and political economy.

Sheldon W. Simon is Professor of Political Science and Faculty Associate of the Center for Asian Studies and Program in Southeast Asian Studies at Arizona State University, where he has been on the faculty since 1975. He has also served as Chairman of Political Science and Director of Asian Studies at ASU. Chairman of the Southeast Asia Studies Program Advisory Board at NBR and a member of the Executive Council of the U.S. Council on Security Cooperation in the Asia Pacific, Professor Simon is author or editor of nine books and over 100 scholarly articles and book chapters. His most recent book is an edited volume, *The Many Faces of Asian Security* (Rowman & Littlefield, 2001). He also contributed the Southeast Asia regional chapter to the 2001–02 and 2002–03 Strategic Asia volumes. He is a consultant to the U.S. Departments of State and Defense and visits Asia annually for research and guest lectures.

Robert G. Sutter is a Visiting Professor in the School of Foreign Service at Georgetown University. He specialized in Asian and Pacific Affairs and U.S. foreign policy in a U.S. government career of 30 years, holding a variety of analytical and supervisory positions with the Library of Congress for over 20 years and has worked with the Central Intelligence Agency, the Department of State, and the Senate Foreign Relations Committee. He has also served as the National Intelligence Officer for East Asia and the Pacific at the National Intelligence Council. He has published 13 books, numerous articles, and several hundred government reports dealing with contemporary East Asian and Pacific countries and their relations with the

United States. His most recent book is *The United States and East Asia: Dynamics and Implications* (Rowman & Littlefield, 2002). Dr. Sutter has held adjunct faculty positions with Georgetown, George Washington, and Johns Hopkins Universities and the University of Virginia.

Michael Wills is Program Manager of the Strategic Asia Program and Director of the Southeast Asia Studies Program at The National Bureau of Asian Research. He is a contributing editor of *Strategic Asia 2002–03: Asian Aftershocks* (The National Bureau of Asian Research, 2002, with Richard Ellings and Aaron Friedberg) and has served as technical editor on numerous books and articles, including most recently *Strategic Asia 2001–02: Power and Purpose* (NBR, 2001) and *The Many Faces of Asian Security* (Rowman & Littlefield, 2001). Before joining NBR, Mr. Wills worked as publications coordinator at the Cambodia Development Resource Institute in Phnom Penh, and prior to that with the international business risk consultancy Control Risks Group in London.

William C. Wohlforth is Associate Professor of Government at Dartmouth College and serves as a Senior Advisor to NBR's Eurasia Program. He previously taught at Princeton and Georgetown Universities, and has held fellowships at International Strategic Studies at Yale, the Center for International Security and Cooperation at Stanford and the Hoover Institution. He is author or editor of *Cold War Endgame* (Pennsylvania State University Press, 2003), *Witnesses to the End of the Cold War* (Johns Hopkins University Press, 1996), and *The Elusive Balance: Power and Perceptions during the Cold War* (Cornell University Press, 1993). He is also author of numerous articles on Soviet and Russian foreign policy, as well as international relations theory, and post-Cold War world politics. He contributed the Russia chapter to the 2002–03 *Strategic Asia* volume. Professor Wohlforth has lived and studied in Russia for extended periods and is currently working on a study of Russia's strategic adaptation to globalization and U.S. unipolarity.